Your Companion Site — Even More Help for Studying!

bedfordstmartins.com/roarkunderstanding

FREE Online Study Guide—
Improve Your Understanding!

Get immediate feedback on your progress with

- Quizzing
- Key terms review
- Map and visual activities
- Timeline activities
- Note-taking outlines
- Chapter study guide steps

FREE History Research and Writing Help

Refine your research skills, evaluate sources, and organize your findings with

- A database of useful images, maps, documents and more at *Make History*
- A guide to online sources for history
- Help with writing history papers
- A tool for building a bibliography
- Tips on avoiding plagiarism

THE CONTEMPORARY WORLD

0	1,500	3,000 miles	
0	1,500	3,000 kilometers	

Greenland
(Den.)

ICELAND

UNITED
KINGDOM

IRELAND

FRANCE

SPAIN

PORTUGAL

Azores
(Port.)

MOROCCO

Canary Is.
(Sp.)

Western Sahara
(Mor.)

Alaska

CANADA

UNITED STATES

ATLANTIC
OCEAN

MAURITANIA

Hawaii

MEXICO

BAHAMAS

DOMINICAN
REPUBLIC

HAITI

CUBA

JAMAICA

BELIZE

GUATEMALA

HONDURAS

EL SALVADOR

NICARAGUA

COSTA RICA

PANAMA

Puerto Rico (U.S.)

ST. KITTS AND NEVIS

ANTIGUA AND BARBUDA

Guadeloupe (Fr.)

DOMINICA

Martinique (Fr.)

ST. VINCENT AND THE GRENADINES

ST. LUCIA

BARBADOS

GRENADA

TRINIDAD AND TOBAGO

GUYANA

VENEZUELA

SURINAME

French Guiana (Fr.)

COLOMBIA

ECUADOR

Galápagos Is.
(Ec.)

CAPE
VERDE

SENEGAL

GAMBIA

GUINEA-BISSAU

MAL

GUINEA

SIERRA LEONE

LIBERIA

CÔTE D'IVOIRE

BURKINA FASO

GHANA

PACIFIC OCEAN

Equator

SAMOA

TONGA

PERU

BRAZIL

BOLIVIA

PARAGUAY

Easter I.
(Chile)

CHILE

URUGUAY

ATLANTIC
OCEAN.

ARGENTINA

Falkland Is.
(U.K.)

80°N

60°N

40°N

20°N

0°

20°S

40°S

60°S

80°S

160°W   140°W   120°W   100°W   80°W   60°W   40°W   20°W

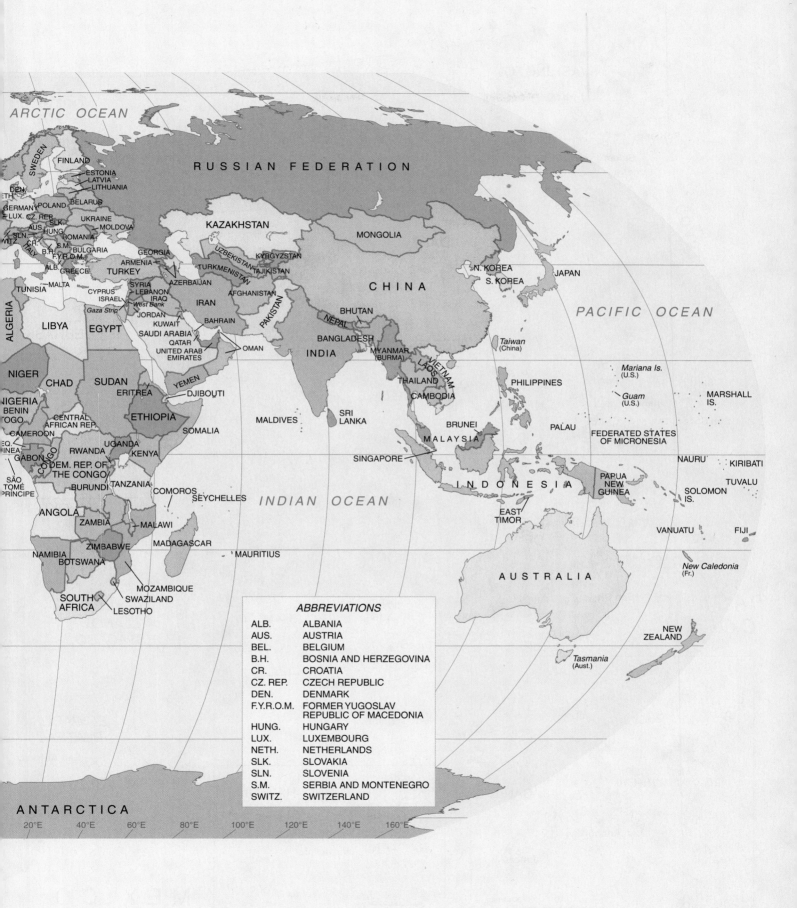

Seattle
Olympia
WASHINGTON
★ Mt. Rainier
(14,410 ft.; 4,392 m)
Mt. St. Helens
(8,366 ft.; 2,550 m)
Portland
Salem
Eugene
CASCADE
OREGON

COAST RANGES

Columbia River

Columbia River

MTS.

Helena
MONTANA
Missouri River
Yellowstone River
Billings

NORTH DAKOTA
Bismarck
BADLANDS

SOUTH DAKOTA
Pierre

Boise
IDAHO
Snake River

ROCKY
WYOMING
GREAT DIVIDE BASIN

BLACK HILLS

GREAT

NEBRASKA
Platte River

Sacramento River
SIERRA
Carson City
San Francisco
Oakland
San Jose
NEVADA
Sacramento
Fresno
Mt. Whitney
(14,494ft.; 4,418 m)
San Joaquin River
CALIFORNIA
Las Vegas
MOJAVE DESERT
Great Salt Lake
Salt Lake City
GREAT BASIN
UTAH

Mt. Elbert
(14,433 ft.; 4,399 m)
Pikes Peak
(14,110 ft.; 4,301 m)
Cheyenne
COLORADO
Denver
Colorado Springs

Colorado River
Arkansas River

PLAINS
KANSAS
Linc
Wich

Los Angeles

San Diego

PACIFIC OCEAN

ARIZONA
Phoenix

Tucson

Santa Fe
Albuquerque
NEW MEXICO

MOUNTAINS

Pecos River
El Paso
Rio Grande

OKLAHOM
Oklahom
C
Red Riv

Lubbock
LLANO ESTACADO

TEXAS
Fort Wc

Colorado River

EDWARDS PLATEAU
Aus
San Antonio

ARCTIC OCEAN
RUSSIA
BROOKS RANGE
ALASKA
Mt. McKinley
(20,320 ft.; 6,194 m)
Yukon River
ALASKA RANGE
CANADA
Anchorage
Bering Sea
Gulf of Alaska
Juneau
ALEUTIAN ISLANDS

0   250   500 miles
0   250   500 kilometers

Kauai
Niihau
Oahu
Honolulu
HAWAII
Molokai
Maui
Lanai
Kahoolawe
PACIFIC OCEAN
Hawaii

0   50   100 miles
0   50   100 kilometers

MEXICO

Understanding
the
American Promise

A BRIEF HISTORY

Understanding
the
American Promise

A BRIEF HISTORY

Volume I
To 1877

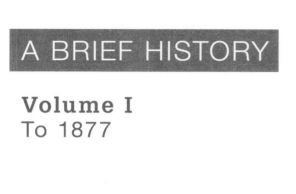

James L. Roark
Emory University

Michael P. Johnson
Johns Hopkins University

Patricia Cline Cohen
*University of California,
Santa Barbara*

Sarah Stage
Arizona State University

Alan Lawson
Boston College

Susan M. Hartmann
The Ohio State University

Bedford/St. Martin's
Boston • New York

For Bedford/St. Martin's

Publisher for History: Mary Dougherty
Executive Editor for History: William J. Lombardo
Director of Development for History: Jane Knetzger
Developmental Editor: Kathryn Abbott
Senior Production Editor: Bridget Leahy
Assistant Production Manager: Joe Ford
Executive Marketing Manager: Jenna Bookin Barry
Editorial Assistant: Robin Soule
Copy Editor: Linda McLatchie
Indexer: Leoni Z. McVey
Photo Researcher: Picture Research Consultants, Inc.
Permissions Manager: Kalina Ingham Hintz
Senior Art Director: Anna Palchik
Text Designer: Jerilyn Bockorick
Cover Designer: Donna Lee Dennison
Cover Photo: Daguerreotype of unidentified woman, probably a member of the Urias McGill family,
   three-quarter length portrait, facing front, holding daguerreotype case. Photographed by Augustus
   Washington, 1820/21–1875. Courtesy of Library of Congress Prints and Photographs Division.
Cartography: Mapping Specialists Limited
Composition: Nesbitt Graphics, Inc.
Printing and Binding: RR Donnelley and Sons

President: Joan E. Feinberg
Editorial Director: Denise B. Wydra
Director of Marketing: Karen R. Soeltz
Director of Production: Susan W. Brown
Associate Director, Editorial Production: Elise S. Kaiser
Managing Editor: Elizabeth M. Schaaf

Library of Congress Control Number: 2010936410

Manufactured in the United States of America.

6   5   4   3   2   1
f   e   d   c   b   a

For information, write: Bedford/St. Martin's, 75 Arlington Street,
Boston, MA 02116
(617-399-4000)

ISBN: 978–0–312–64518–2   (Combined edition)
ISBN: 978–0–312–64519–9   (Vol. I)
ISBN: 978–0–312–64520–5   (Vol. II)

Acknowledgments

PREFACE

In *Understanding the American Promise*, we set out solve a couple of problems that had come to us over the years. First, we knew that, although many students dutifully read their survey texts, they came away confused. They couldn't tell what was most important and they felt overwhelmed. At the same time, their instructors felt that some texts didn't show students what was so exciting and even fun about history. These teachers wanted a way to give their students a grounding in the basics and to show how historians think and work, a text that would show that history is a discipline based upon inquiry, interpretation, and debate. With these issues in mind, we took a hard look at the survey course from all directions. We reflected on our own classes and students and how they've changed. We reviewed state-of-the-art scholarship on effective teaching. We consulted learning experts and instructional designers. We talked to students. And, most importantly, we talked to you— instructors teaching the course—and asked about your needs. *Understanding the American Promise* is the product of these efforts.

With *Understanding the American Promise*, we offer something new—an abridged narrative of U.S. history that concentrates on major developments, combined with an innovative design and pedagogy orchestrated to work together to foster students' comprehension and historical thinking. This brief narrative and distinctive format will help your students grasp important developments and begin to think like historians.

This means that, in *Understanding*, design, pedagogy and narrative work together to help students learn, and then reinforce and retain their knowledge. We started with *The American Promise*, our full-length survey textbook acclaimed for its effective braiding together of political and social history, and reduced the length by over thirty percent. This abridged narrative will better help students discern overarching trends and connect them with the individuals—from Presidents to pipefitters and sharecroppers to suffragettes—that animate the past.

Then, we joined our prose with an innovative pedagogy and a well-crafted design to make a compelling new teaching and learning tool. *Understanding's* chapter architecture supports students' comprehension and helps them to grasp key themes and ideas. To this end, all chapters open with a succinct, single paragraph–length statement about the main themes and events of the chapter, designed to establish clear learning outcomes. At the beginning of each chapter, we also ask students a "Did You Know?" question to invite them to connect what they already know (or think they know) to each chapter's big theme. Chapters are then organized into three to six main sections, with all section titles crafted as big questions to facilitate active reading and to emphasize that history is an inquiry-based discipline. These main sections end with quick review questions that prompt students to check their comprehension and reflect on what they've read. Throughout, chronology boxes show the sequence of events, and marginal definitions highlight key terms, providing on-the-page reinforcement and a handy tool for review. We hope that this structure will help students to grasp meaning as they read and also model how historians think, how they pose questions, and how they answer those questions with evidence and interpretation.

We've also reconsidered the traditional review that comes at the end of the chapter. We've provided a three-step chapter review that will help students with the basic material but also help them go beyond a basic understanding of what happened. In step one, students identify key terms and explain why each matters. In step two, they apply their understanding of basic terms to questions about cause and effect, change over time, and comparison. And in step three, students pull it all together with analytical and synthetic questions that treat the whole chapter. Finally, an active recitation question asks students to consider what is truly important to understand about what they have just read.

As teachers, our guiding principle is to promote intelligent engagement as a catalyst toward historical understanding. This means giving our students an effective textbook that is enjoyable to read and that provides the tools to help them develop their skills of historical analysis and interpretation, and it is our hope that this new approach provides just such a tool. It is our article of faith that when we empower students to engage meaningfully with the past, we encourage habits of thinking essential for a well-rounded general education at any college or university—and beyond. Historical knowledge and the ability to think critically provide a rock-solid foundation for informed and active citizenship, whether that citizen was born in the United States or is a first generation immigrant, as many of our students are.

As always, our use of *American Promise* in our title reflects our emphasis on human agency and our conviction that American history is an unfinished story. For millions, the nation has held out the promise of a better life, unfettered worship, representative government, democratic politics, and other freedoms seldom found elsewhere. But none of these promises has come with guarantees. As we see it, much of American history is a continuing struggle over the definition and realization of the nation's promise. Abraham Lincoln, in the midst of what he termed the "fiery trial" of the Civil War, pronounced the nation "the last best hope of Earth." Kept alive by countless sacrifices, that hope has been marred by compromises, disappointments, and denials, but it lives still. We hope that *Understanding the American Promise* will help students become aware of the legacy of hope bequeathed to them by previous generations of Americans stretching back nearly four centuries, a legacy that is theirs to preserve and build on.

We trust you'll agree that *Understanding the American Promise* achieves its goal of giving students a smart alternative for *understanding* American history. If we help you stir in your students a lifelong passion for history and the habits of critical thinking, the pleasure is ours.

Acknowledgments

We gratefully acknowledge all the helpful suggestions from those who have read and taught from previous editions of *The American Promise: A History of the United States* and *The American Promise: A Compact History*. We would like specifically to acknowledge those scholars and teachers who gave their time and expertise to the draft for this first edition of *Understanding the American Promise*: Cary W. Blankenship, *University of Kentucky;* Roland Frankum Jr., *Millersville*

University; Cecilia Gowdy-Wygant, *Front Range Community College;* Pauline S. Johnson, *Mars Hill College;* Carol A. Keller, *San Antonio College;* Tracy A. Lai, *Seattle Central Community College;* Peggy Lambert, *Lone Star College-Kingwood;* John Mack, *Labette Community College;* Anne Paulet, *Humboldt State University,* Jeffrey Smith, *Lindenwood University;* and Julie Winch, *University of Massachusetts-Boston.*

A project as complex as this requires the talents of many individuals. First, we would like to acknowledge our families for their support, forbearance, and toleration of our textbook responsibilities. Pembroke Herbert and Sandi Rygiel of Picture Research Consultants, Inc., contributed their unparalleled knowledge, soaring imagination, and diligent research to make possible the extraordinary illustration program. Pauline Johnson of Mars Hill College reviewed each chapter's pedagogy with the astute eye of a lifelong teacher.

We would also like to thank the many people at Bedford/St. Martin's who have been crucial to this project. Developmental editor Kathryn Abbott oversaw the development of each chapter and added value at every step. Thanks also go to editorial assistant Robin Soule, who provided unflagging assistance and who coordinated the review program and the turnover of manuscript. We are also grateful to Jane Knetzger, director of development for history, William Lombardo, executive editor, and Mary Dougherty, publisher, for their support and guidance. For their imaginative and tireless efforts to promote the book, we want to thank Jenna Bookin Barry, executive marketing manager, Sally Constable, market development manager, John Hunger, senior history specialist, Sean Blest, eastern history specialist, and Stephen Watson, marketing assistant. With great skill and professionalism, Bridget Leahy, senior production editor, pulled together the many pieces related to copyediting, design, and typesetting, with the able assistance of Lidia MacDonald-Carr and Laura Winstead and the guidance of managing editor Elizabeth Schaaf and assistant managing editor John Amburg. Assistant production manager Joe Ford oversaw the manufacturing of the book. Designer and page makeup artist Jerilyn Bockorick, copyeditor Linda McLatchie, and proofreaders Jan Cocker and Melissa Clark attended to the myriad details that help make the book shine. Leoni McVey provided an outstanding index. The book's covers were designed by Donna Dennison. New media editor Marissa Zanetti, associate editor Jack Cashman, and media producer Nancy Hiney, made sure that *Understanding the American Promise: A Brief History* remains at the forefront of technological support for students and instructors. Editorial director Denise Wydra provided helpful advice throughout the course of the project. Finally, Charles H. Christensen, former president, took a personal interest in *The American Promise* from the start, and Joan E. Feinberg, president, has guided all editions through every stage of development.

James Roark
Michael Johnson
Patricia Cohen
Sarah Stage
Alan Lawson
Susan Hartmann

BRIEF CONTENTS

CONTENTS

1
UNDERSTANDING ANCIENTAMERICA
BEFORE 1492 *3*

2
ENCOUNTERING THE NEW WORLD
1492–1600 *31*

MAPS, FIGURES, AND TABLES

VERSIONS AND SUPPLEMENTS

Understanding the American Promise: A Brief History is supported by loads of resources—study tools for students, instructor materials, and many options for packaging the book with documents readers, trade books, atlases, and other guides—for free or at a substantial discount. Descriptions follow, but for more information, visit the book's catalog site at bedfordstmartins.com/roarkunderstanding/catalog or contact your local Bedford/St. Martin's sales representative.

Available Versions of This Book

To accommodate different course lengths and course budgets, this title is available in several different formats. The e-books are available at a substantial discount.

Combined Volume (Chapters 1–31)—available in paperback and e-book formats
Volume I: To 1877 (Chapters 1–16)—available in paperback and e-book formats
Volume II: From 1865 (Chapters 16–31)—available in paperback and e-book formats

With our innovative e-books your students get the content you want in a convenient format—for about half the cost of a print book. **Bedford/St. Martin's e-Books** have been optimized for reading and studying online. **CourseSmart e-Books** can be downloaded or used online, whichever is more convenient for your students.

Companion site at bedfordstmartins.com/ roarkunderstanding

Our new companion sites gather free and premium resources, giving students a way to extend their Bedford book, online. These book-specific sites provide one destination to practice, read, write, and study—and to find and access quizzes and activities, study aids, and history research and writing help.

▶ **FREE Online Study Guide.** Available at the companion site, this popular resource provides students with self-review quizzes and activities for each chapter, including a multiple-choice self-test that focuses on important concepts; an identification quiz that helps students remember key people, places, and events; a flashcard activity that tests students' knowledge of key terms; and map activities intended to strengthen students' geography skills. It also includes downloadable versions of the textbook chapter study guides. Instructors can monitor students' progress through an online Quiz Gradebook or receive email updates.

▶ **FREE History Research and Writing Help.** Also available on the companion site, this resource includes the textbook authors' *Suggested References* organized by chapter; *History Research and Reference Sources,* with links to history-related databases, indexes, and journals; *More Sources and How to Format a History*

Paper, with clear advice on how to integrate primary and secondary sources into research papers and how to cite and format sources correctly; ***Build a Bibliography,*** a simple Web-based tool that generates bibliographies in four commonly used documentation styles; and ***Tips on Avoiding Plagiarism,*** an online tutorial that reviews the consequences of plagiarism and features exercises to help students practice integrating sources and recognize acceptable summaries.

Instructor Resources

Bedford/St. Martin's has developed a wide range of teaching resources for this book and for this course. They range from lecture and presentation materials to assessment tools and course management options. Most can be downloaded or ordered at bedfordstmartins.com/roarkunderstanding/catalog.

▶ ***HistoryClass for Understanding the American Promise.*** *HistoryClass,* a Bedford/St. Martin's Online Course Space, puts the online resources available with this textbook in one convenient place—an interactive e-book and primary sources reader; maps, images, documents and links; chapter review quizzes; interactive multimedia exercises; and research and writing help. Get into HistoryClass and get all our premium content and tools in one completely customizable course space; then assign, rearrange, and mix our resources with yours. For more information visit yourhistoryclass.com.

▶ **Bedford/St. Martin's Course Cartridges.** Whether you use Blackboard, WebCT, Desire2Learn, Angel, Sakai, or Moodle, we have free content and support available for you to plug our content into your course management system. Registered instructors can download cartridges with no hassle, no strings attached. Content includes our most popular free resources and book-specific content for this title. Visit bedfordstmartins.com/cms to get a demo, find your versions, or download your cartridge.

▶ **NEW PowerPoint Maps, Images, Lecture Outlines, and i>clicker Content.** Look good and save time with *The Bedford Lecture Kit.* These presentation materials are downloadable individually from the Media and Supplements tab at bedfordstmartins.com/roarkunderstanding/catalog, and they are available on *The Bedford Lecture Kit Instructor's Resource CD-ROM.* They include ready-made and fully customizable PowerPoint multimedia presentations built around lecture outlines that are embedded with maps, figures, and selected images from the textbook and are supplemented by more detailed instructor notes on key points. Also available are maps and selected images in JPEG and PowerPoint format; content for i>clicker, a classroom response system, in Microsoft Word and PowerPoint formats; the Instructor's Resource Manual in Microsoft Word format; and outline maps in PDF format for quizzing or handouts. All files are suitable for copying onto transparency acetates.

▶ **Instructor's Resource Manual.** The instructor's manual offers both experienced and first-time instructors tools for presenting textbook material in engaging ways. It includes chapter review material, teaching strategies, and a guide to chapter-specific supplements available for the text.

▶ **Computerized Test Bank.** The test bank includes a mix of fresh, carefully crafted multiple-choice, fill-in-the-blank, short-answer, and essay questions for each chapter. The questions appear in Microsoft Word format and in easy-to-use test bank software that allows instructors to easily add, edit, re-sequence, and print questions and answers. Instructors can also export questions into a variety of formats, including WebCT and Blackboard.

▶ *Make History*—**Free Documents, Maps, Images, and Web Sites.** *Make History* combines the best Web resources with hundreds of maps and images, to make finding the source material you need simple. Browse the collection of thousands of resources by course or by topic, date, and type. Each item has been carefully chosen and helpfully annotated to make it easy to find exactly what you need. Available at bedfordstmartins.com/makehistory.

▶ *Reel Teaching* **Video clips.** This DVD provides a large collection of short video clips for classroom presentation. Designed as engaging "lecture launchers" varying in length from 1 to 15 or more minutes, the 59 documentary clips were carefully chosen for use in both semesters of the U.S. survey course. The clips feature compelling images, archival footage, personal narratives, and commentary by noted historians.

▶ **NEW** *America in Motion: Video clips for U.S. History.* Set history in motion with *America in Motion*, an instructor DVD containing dozens of short digital movie files of twentieth-century American historical events. From the wreckage of the battleship *Maine*, to FDR's Fireside Chats, to Oliver North testifying before Congress, *America in Motion* engages your students with dynamic scenes from key events and challenges them to think critically. All files are classroom-ready, edited for brevity, and easily integrated with PowerPoint or other presentation software for electronic lectures or assignments. An accompanying guide provides each clip's historical context, ideas for use, and suggested questions.

▶ **Videos and Multimedia.** A wide assortment of videos and multimedia CD-ROMs on various topics in U.S. history is available to qualified adopters through your Bedford/St. Martin's sales representative.

Packaging Opportunities

Save your students money and package your favorite text with more! For information on free packages and discounts up to 50%, contact your local Bedford/St. Martin's sales representative.

▶ **e-Book.** The e-book for this title can be packaged with the print text at no additional cost. For a complete list of titles, visit bedfordstmartins.com/ebooks/catalog.

▶ *Reading the American Past: Selected Historical Documents*, **Fourth Edition.** Edited by Michael P. Johnson (Johns Hopkins University), one of the authors of *The American Promise,* and designed to complement the textbook, *Reading the American Past* provides a broad selection of over 150 primary source documents, as well as editorial apparatus to help students analyze the sources. Emphasizing the important social, political, and economic themes of U.S. history courses, these documents provide a wide range of perspectives on environmental, western, ethnic, and gender history. Available free when packaged with the text. For more information, visit bedfordstmartins.com/roarksources/catalog.

▶ *Reading the American Past e-Book.* The reader is available as an e-book. When packaged with the print or electronic version of the textbook, it is available for free. For more information, visit bedfordstmartins.com/ebooks/catalog.

▶ *Rand McNally Atlas of American History.* This collection of more than eighty full-color maps illustrates key events and eras from early exploration, settlement, expansion, and immigration to U.S. involvement in wars abroad an on U.S. soil. Introductory pages for each section include brief overview, timelines, graphs, and photos to quickly establish a historical context. Available for $3.00 when packaged with the text. For a complete list of titles, visit bedfordstmartins.com/americanatlas/catalog.

▶ *Maps in Context: A Workbook for American History.* Written by historical cartography expert Gerald A. Danzer (University of Illinois at Chicago), this skill-building workbook helps students comprehend essential connections between geographic literacy and historical understanding. Organized to correspond to the typical U.S. history survey course, Maps in Context presents a wealth of map-centered projects and convenient pop quizzes that give students hands-on experience working with maps. Available free when packaged with the text. For a complete list of titles, visit bedfordstmartins.com/mapsincontext/catalog.

▶ *The Bedford Glossary for U.S. History.* This handy supplement for the survey course gives students historically contextualized definitions for hundreds of terms—from *abolitionism* to *zoot suit*—that students will encounter in lectures, reading, and exams. Available free when packaged with the text. For a complete list of titles, visit bedfordstmartins.com/usgloss/catalog.

▶ *U.S. History Matters: A Student Guide to World History Online.* This resource, written by Alan Gevinson, Kelly Schrum, and the late Roy Rosenzweig (all of George Mason University), provides an illustrated and annotated guide to 250 of the most useful Web sites for student research in U.S. history as well as advice on evaluating and using Internet sources. This essential guide is based on the acclaimed "History Matters" Web site developed by the American Social History Project and the Center for History and New Media. Available free when packaged with the text. For a complete list of titles, visit bedfordstmartins.com/ushistory matters/catalog.

▶ **The Bedford Series in History and Culture.** More than one hundred titles in this highly praised series combine first-rate scholarship, historical narrative, and important primary documents for undergraduate courses. Each book is brief, inexpensive, and focused on a specific topic or period. For a complete list of titles, visit bedfordstmartins.com/history/series. Package discounts are available.

▶ **Trade Books.** Titles published by sister companies Hill and Wang; Farrar, Strauss and Giroux; Henry Holt and Company; St. Martin's Press; Picador; and Palgrave Macmillan are available at a 50 percent discount when packaged with Bedford/St. Martin's textbooks. For more information, visit bedfordstmartins.com/tradeup.

▶ *Going to the Source: The Bedford Reader in American History.* Developed by Victoria Bissell Brown and Timothy J. Shannon, this reader's strong pedagogical framework helps students learn how to ask fruitful questions in order to evaluate documents effectively and develop critical reading skills. The reader's wide variety of chapter topics that complement the survey course and its rich diversity of sources—from personal letters to political cartoons—provoke students' interest as it teaches them the skills they need to successfully interrogate historical sources. Package discounts are available. For more information, visit bedfordstmartins.com/brownshannon/catalog.

▶ *America Firsthand.* With its distinctive focus on ordinary people, this primary documents reader, by Robert D. Marcus, David Burner, and Anthony Marcus, offers a remarkable range of perspectives on America's history from those who lived it. Popular Points of View sections expose students to different perspectives on a specific event or topic, and Visual Portfolios invite analysis of the visual record. Package discounts are available. For more information, visit bedfordstmartins.com/marcusburner/catalog.

▶ *A Pocket Guide to Writing in History.* This portable and affordable reference tool by Mary Lynn Rampolla provides reading, writing, and research advice useful to students in all history courses. Concise yet comprehensive advice on approaching typical history assignments, developing critical reading skills, writing effective history papers, conducting research, using and documenting sources, and avoiding plagiarism—enhanced with practical tips and examples throughout—have made this slim reference a best-seller. Package discounts are available. For more information, visit bedfordstmartins.com/rampolla/catalog.

▶ *A Student's Guide to History.* This complete guide to success in any history course provides the practical help students need to be effective. In addition to introducing students to the nature of the discipline, author Jules Benjamin teaches a wide range of skills from preparing for exams to approaching common writing assignments, and he explains the research and documentation process with plentiful examples. Package discounts are available. For more information, visit bedfordstmartins.com/benjamin/catalog.

Understanding
the
American Promise

A BRIEF HISTORY

How to use this book to figure out what's **really** important

Memorizing facts and dates for a history class won't get you very far. That's because history isn't just about "facts." It's also about understanding cause-and-effect and the significance of people, places, and events from the past that still have relevance to your world today. This textbook is designed to help you focus on what's truly significant in U.S. history and to give you practice in thinking like a historian.

The opening page gives you a preview of the entire chapter.

> The title tells you the subject of the chapter and identifies the time span that will be covered.

16

RECONSTRUCTING A NATION

1863–1877

> This chapter explores the period known as Reconstruction, in which the nation struggled to define the defeated South's status within the Union and the meaning of freedom for ex-slaves. Despite the end of the Civil War, the nation entered one of its most violent eras, as victorious Northerners, defeated white Southerners, and newly freed African

> The opening paragraph identifies the themes that will be explored, such as the continuing struggle between North and South, the meaning of freedom for ex-slaves, and erupting violence.

> What were Lincoln's plans for wartime reconstruction?

> What vision did Andrew Johnson have for presidential reconstruction?

> How radical was congressional reconstruction?

> Each question opens a new section of the chapter and will be addressed in turn on the following pages.

> How was the battle over reconstruction fought in the South?

> Why did reconstruction collapse?

> Conclusion: What were the achievements and failures of reconstruction?

SAML. DOVE wishes to know of the whereabouts of his mother, Areno, his sisters Maria, Neziah, and Peggy, and his brother Edmond, who were owned by Geo. Dove, of Rockingham county, Shenandoah Valley, Va. Sold in Richmond, after which Saml. and Edmond were taken to Nashville, Tenn., by Joe Mick: Areno was left at the Eagle Tavern, Richmond
Respectfully yours,
SAML. DOVE.
Utica, New York, Aug. 5, 1865.—3m

U. S. CHRISTIAN COMMISSION,
NASHVILLE, TENN., July 20, 1865.

DID YOU KNOW?

The priorities for newly freed African Americans were to locate family members, acquire land, and worship in their own churches.

Voting day, June 5, 1867. Black freedmen line up to vote in Washington, D.C.

427

Each section has tools that help you focus on what's important.

> ## What vision did Andrew Johnson have for presidential reconstruction?

The question in red is the specific topic discussed in this section.

The Black Codes

Titled "Selling a Freeman to Pay His Fine at Monticello, Florida," this 1867 drawing from a northern magazine equates black codes with the reinstitution of slavery. The ascension of Andrew Johnson to the presidency emboldened many southern states to pass laws severely restricting blacks' freedom. Granger Collection.

WITH ABRAHAM LINCOLN'S death on April 15, 1865, Vice President Andrew Johnson of Tennessee became the new president. Congress had adjourned in March and would not reconvene until December. Thus, throughout the summer and fall, Johnson drew up and executed a plan of reconstruction without congressional advice.

Congress reconvened in December to find that, as far as the president and former Confederates were concerned, reconstruction was completed. Most Republicans, however, thought Johnson's puny demands of ex-rebels encouraged the rebirth of the Old South at the expense of black liberty. They proceeded to dismantle Johnson's program and substitute a program of their own.

Marginal key terms give you background on important people, ideas, and events. Use them for reference while you read but also pay attention to which terms are emphasized.

Johnson's Program of Reconciliation

Born in 1808 in Raleigh, North Carolina, **Andrew Johnson** was the son of illiterate parents. Self-educated and ambitious, Johnson moved to Tennessee, where he built a career in politics championing the South's common white people and assailing its "illegitimate, swaggering, bastard, scrub aristocracy." The only senator from a Confederate state to remain loyal to the Union, Johnson held the planter class responsible for secession.

A Democrat all his life, Johnson occupied the White House only because the Republican Party in 1864 had needed a vice presidential candidate who would appeal to loyal, Union-supporting Democrats. Johnson vigorously defended states' rights (but not secession) and opposed Republican efforts to expand the power of the federal government. A steadfast supporter of slavery, Johnson grudgingly accepted emancipation more because he hated planters than because he sympathized with slaves. "Damn the negroes," he said. "I am fighting those traitorous aristocrats, their masters." The new president harbored unshakable racist convictions. Africans, Johnson said, were "inferior to the white man in point of intellect—better calculated in physical structure to undergo drudgery and hardship."

Andrew Johnson
▶ President of the United States from 1865 to 1869, Vice President Johnson became president after the assassination of Abraham Lincoln. Like Lincoln, Johnson sought the quick restoration of civil government in the South and pardoned most ex-Confederates. Johnson battled with Congress over the course of Reconstruction and was the first president in U.S. history to be impeached by the House of Representatives. He barely escaped removal from office by the Senate.

CHAPTER LOCATOR | What were Lincoln's plans for wartime reconstruction?

Like Lincoln, Johnson stressed the rapid restoration of civil government in the South. Like Lincoln, he promised to pardon most, but not all, ex-rebels. Johnson recognized the state governments created by Lincoln but set out his own requirements for restoring the other rebel states to the Union. All that the citizens of a state had to do was to renounce the right of secession, deny that the debts of the Confederacy were legal and binding, and ratify the Thirteenth Amendment, abolishing slavery, which became part of the Constitution in December 1865.

Johnson also returned to pardoned ex-Confederates all confiscated and abandoned land, even if it was in the hands of freedmen. Reformers were shocked. Instead of punishing planters as Republicans expected, his instructions canceled the promising beginnings made by General Sherman and the Freedmen's Bureau to settle blacks on land of their own. As one freedman observed, "Things was hurt by Mr. Lincoln getting killed."

White Southern Resistance and Black Codes

In the summer of 1865, delegates across the South gathered to draw up the new state constitutions required by Johnson's plan of reconstruction. Rather than accept Johnson's plan, delegates balked at even the president's mild requirements to renounce secession, disown their war debts, and ratify the Thirteenth Amendment. Despite this defiance, Johnson did nothing. White Southerners began to think that by standing up for themselves they could define the terms of reconstruction.

State governments across the South adopted a series of laws known as **black codes**, which made a travesty of black freedom. The codes sought to keep ex-slaves subordinate to whites by subjecting them to every sort of discrimination.

Black Codes

Several states made it illegal for blacks to own a gun.

Mississippi made insulting gestures and language by blacks a criminal offense.

The codes barred blacks from jury duty.

Not a single southern state granted any black the right to vote.

At the core of the black codes, however, lay the matter of labor and the desire to force freedmen back to the plantations. South Carolina attempted to limit blacks to either farmwork or domestic service by requiring them to pay annual taxes of $10 to $100 to work in any other occupation. Mississippi declared that blacks who did not possess written evidence of employment could be declared vagrants and be subject to involuntary plantation labor. Under so-called apprenticeship laws, courts bound thousands of black children—orphans and others whose parents they deemed unable to support them—to work for planter "guardians."

CHRONOLOGY

1865
- President Abraham Lincoln is shot; dies on April 15; is succeeded by Andrew Johnson.
- Johnson carries out rapid restoration of civil government in the South.
- Johnson returns confiscated and abandoned land to pardoned ex-Confederates.
- Southern states enact black codes.
- The Thirteenth Amendment, abolishing slavery, becomes part of Constitution.

1866
- Civil Rights Act nullifies black codes and extends civil rights to blacks.

Chronologies for each major section show the sequence of events in this section.

black codes
▶ Laws passed by state governments in the South in 1865 that sought to keep ex-slaves subordinate to whites. At the core of the black codes lay the desire to force freedmen back to the plantations.

The quick review helps you check your recall of the section.

QUICK REVIEW

Why and how did the aims of Congress and the president diverge? What specifically were the issues over which they clashed?

What vision did Andrew Johnson have for presidential reconstruction?	How radical was congressional reconstruction?	How was the battle over reconstruction fought in the South?	Why did reconstruction collapse?	Conclusion: What were the achievements and failures of reconstruction?

433

The chapter locator at the bottom of the page puts this section in the context of the chapter as a whole, so you can see how this section relates to what's coming next.

The Chapter Study Guide provides a 3-step process that will build your understanding and your historical skills.

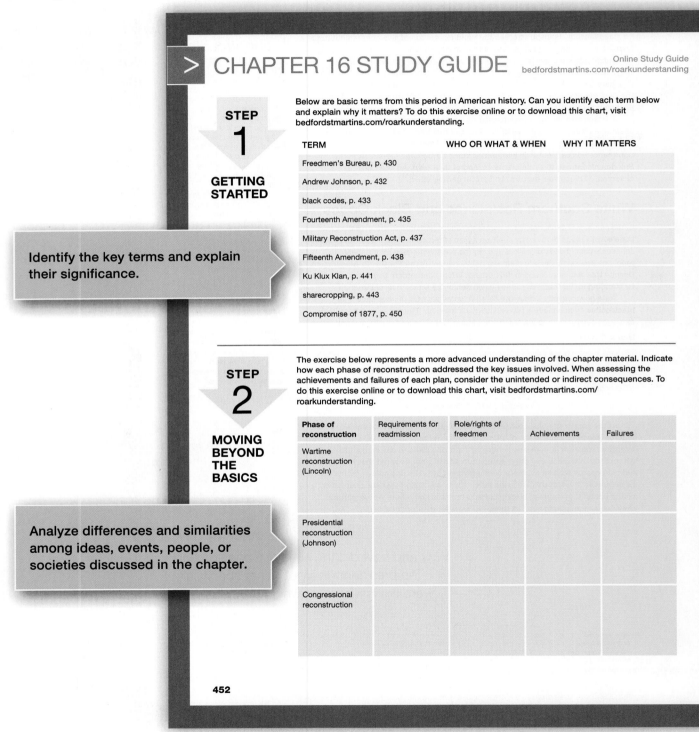

> CHAPTER 16 STUDY GUIDE

Online Study Guide
bedfordstmartins.com/roarkunderstanding

STEP 1

GETTING STARTED

Below are basic terms from this period in American history. Can you identify each term below and explain why it matters? To do this exercise online or to download this chart, visit bedfordstmartins.com/roarkunderstanding.

TERM	WHO OR WHAT & WHEN	WHY IT MATTERS
Freedmen's Bureau, p. 430		
Andrew Johnson, p. 432		
black codes, p. 433		
Fourteenth Amendment, p. 435		
Military Reconstruction Act, p. 437		
Fifteenth Amendment, p. 438		
Ku Klux Klan, p. 441		
sharecropping, p. 443		
Compromise of 1877, p. 450		

> Identify the key terms and explain their significance.

STEP 2

MOVING BEYOND THE BASICS

The exercise below represents a more advanced understanding of the chapter material. Indicate how each phase of reconstruction addressed the key issues involved. When assessing the achievements and failures of each plan, consider the unintended or indirect consequences. To do this exercise online or to download this chart, visit bedfordstmartins.com/roarkunderstanding.

Phase of reconstruction	Requirements for readmission	Role/rights of freedmen	Achievements	Failures
Wartime reconstruction (Lincoln)				
Presidential reconstruction (Johnson)				
Congressional reconstruction				

> Analyze differences and similarities among ideas, events, people, or societies discussed in the chapter.

452

STEP

3

**PUTTING
IT ALL
TOGETHER**

Now that you've reviewed various parts of the chapter, take a step back and try to see the big picture by answering these questions. Remember to use specific examples from the chapter in your answers. To do this exercise online, visit bedfordsmartins.com/roarkunderstanding.

> Answer the big-picture questions using specific examples or evidence from the chapter.

PRESIDENTIAL AND CONGRESSIONAL RECONSTRUCTION

► What role did the black codes play in shaping the course of reconstruction?

► What steps did Congress take between 1865 and 1869 to assist ex-slaves in their lives as freedmen? How effective were these actions?

SOUTHERN RECONSTRUCTION IN ACTION

► How did white Southerners respond during Reconstruction? Consider both Democrats and Republicans in your response.

► How did southern African Americans attempt to shape their own lives during Reconstruction?

LOOKING BACKWARD, LOOKING AHEAD

► How did long-held racial views among whites, in both the South and the North, shape Reconstruction?

► What were the lasting accomplishments of Reconstruction? What were its most important failures?

THE END OF RECONSTRUCTION

► How and why did the decline of northern support for Reconstruction help southern Democrats "redeem" the South?

► Why did white supremacy become the foundation of southern politics in the 1870s?

IN YOUR OWN WORDS

Imagine that you must explain chapter 16 to someone who hasn't read it. What would be the most important points to include and why?

> Explain the important points in your own words to make sure you have a firm grasp of the chapter material.

Visit the FREE Online Study Guide at bedfordstmartins.com/roarkunderstanding
to do these steps on-line and to check how much you've learned.

xxxi

About the Authors

JAMES L. ROARK Born in Eunice, Louisiana, and raised in the West, James L. Roark received his B.A. from the University of California, Davis, and his Ph.D. from Stanford University. His dissertation won the Allan Nevins Prize. Since 1983, he has taught at Emory University, where he is Samuel Candler Dobbs Professor of American History. In 1993, he received the Emory Williams Distinguished Teaching Award, and in 2001–2002 he was Pitt Professor of American Institutions at Cambridge University. He has written *Masters without Slaves: Southern Planters in the Civil War and Reconstruction* (1977). With Michael P. Johnson, he is author of *Black Masters: A Free Family of Color in the Old South* (1984) and editor of *No Chariot Let Down: Charleston's Free People of Color on the Eve of the Civil War* (1984).

MICHAEL P. JOHNSON Born and raised in Ponca City, Oklahoma, Michael P. Johnson studied at Knox College in Galesburg, Illinois, where he received a B.A., and at Stanford University in Palo Alto, California, where he earned his Ph.D. He is currently professor of history at Johns Hopkins University in Baltimore. His publications include *Toward a Patriarchal Republic: The Secession of Georgia* (1977); with James L. Roark, *Black Masters: A Free Family of Color in the Old South* (1984) and *No Chariot Let Down: Charleston's Free People of Color on the Eve of the Civil War* (1984); *Abraham Lincoln, Slavery, and the Civil War: Selected Speeches and Writings* (2001); and *Reading the American Past: Selected Historical Documents*, the documents reader for *The American Promise*.

PATRICIA CLINE COHEN Born in Ann Arbor, Michigan, and raised in Palo Alto, California, Patricia Cline Cohen earned a B.A. at the University of Chicago and a Ph.D. at the University of California, Berkeley. In 1976, she joined the history faculty at the University of California, Santa Barbara. In 2005–2006 she received the university's Distinguished Teaching Award. Cohen has written *A Calculating People: The Spread of Numeracy in Early America* (1982; reissued 1999) and *The Murder of Helen Jewett: The Life and Death of a Prostitute in Nineteenth-Century New York* (1998). She is coauthor of *The Flash Press: Sporting Male Weeklies in 1840s New York* (2008). In 2001–2002 she was the Distinguished Senior Mellon Fellow at the American Antiquarian Society.

SARAH STAGE Sarah Stage was born in Davenport, Iowa, and received a B.A. from the University of Iowa and a Ph.D. in American studies from Yale University. She has taught U.S. history for more than twenty-five years at Williams College and the University of California, Riverside. Currently she is professor of women's studies at Arizona State University at the West campus in Phoenix. Her books include *Female Complaints: Lydia Pinkham and the Business of Women's Medicine* (1979) and *Rethinking Home Economics: Women and the History of a Profession* (1997). She recently returned from China where she had an appointment as visiting scholar at Peking University and Sichuan University.

ALAN LAWSON Born in Providence, Rhode Island, Alan Lawson received his B.A. from Brown University in and his M.A. from the University of Wisconsin. After Army service and experience as a high school teacher, he earned his Ph.D. from the University of Michigan. Since winning the Allan Nevins Prize for his dissertation, Lawson has served on the faculties of the University of California, Irvine, Smith College, and, currently, Boston College. He has written *The Failure of Independent Liberalism* (1971) and coedited *From Revolution to Republic* (1976).

SUSAN M. HARTMANN Susan M. Hartmann received her B.A. from Washington University and her Ph.D. from the University of Missouri. A specialist in modern U.S. history and women's history, she has published many articles and four books: *Truman and the 80th Congress* (1971); *The Home Front and Beyond: American Women in the 1940s* (1982); *From Margin to Mainstream: American Women and Politics since 1960* (1989); and *The Other Feminists: Activists in the Liberal Establishment* (1998). She is currently Arts and Humanities Distinguished Professor of History at The Ohio State University and recently was a fellow at the Woodrow Wilson International Center for Scholars.

Understanding
the
American Promise

A BRIEF HISTORY

1
UNDERSTANDING ANCIENT AMERICA
BEFORE 1492

> This chapter charts the history of ancient Native American peoples from their migration out of Asia to the eve of European contact in 1492. It explores the development of distinct Native American cultures, as well as the common characteristics they shared.

> What is the connection between archaeology and history?

> Who were the first Americans?

> How did Archaic Americans adapt to changing conditions?

> How did agriculture change Native American societies?

> How were native societies organized in the 1490s?

> What were the characteristics of Mexican culture?

> Conclusion: How do we understand the worlds of ancient Americans?

DID YOU KNOW?

In 1492, central Mexico had three times as many people as Spain and Portugal combined.

The Great Tenochtitlan. Detail of the 1945 fresco by Mexican artist Diego Rivera.

What is the connection between archaeology and history?

Mississippian Wooden Mask

Sometime between AD 1200 and 1350, a Native American in what is now central Illinois fashioned this mask from red cedar. Originally, a thin sheet of copper covered the mask, leaving a greenish residue that is still visible today. The mask was used in rituals by Mississippian people connected to Cahokia, a vast ceremonial site located in southern Illinois, just across the Mississippi River from present-day St. Louis. Photograph © 2002 John Bigelow Taylor www.johnbigelowtaylor.com. Illinois State Museum, Springfield, Cat. no. 273.

ARCHAEOLOGISTS AND HISTORIANS share the desire to learn about people who lived in the past, but they usually employ different methods to obtain information. Both archaeologists and historians study artifacts as clues to the activities and ideas of the humans who created them. They concentrate, however, on different kinds of artifacts. Archaeologists tend to focus on physical objects such as bones, spear points, pots, baskets, jewelry, clothing, and buildings. Historians

CHAPTER LOCATOR | What is the connection between archaeology and history? | Who were the first Americans?

4 CHAPTER 1 UNDERSTANDING ANCIENT AMERICA

direct their attention mostly to writings, including personal and private jottings such as letters and diary entries, and an enormous variety of public documents, such as laws, speeches, newspapers, and court cases. Although historians are interested in other artifacts and archaeologists do not neglect written sources if they exist, the concentration of historians on writings and of archaeologists on other physical objects denotes a rough cultural and chronological boundary between the human beings studied by the two groups of scholars, a boundary marked by the use of writing.

Writing is defined as a system of symbols that record spoken language. Writing originated among ancient peoples in China, Egypt, and Central America about eight thousand years ago, within the most recent 2 percent of the four hundred millennia that modern human beings (*Homo sapiens*) have existed. Writing came into use even later in most other places in the world. The ancient Americans who inhabited North America in 1492, for example, possessed many forms of symbolic representation, but not writing.

The people who lived during the millennia before writing were biologically nearly identical to us. Their DNA was the template for ours. But unlike us, they did not use writing to communicate across space and time. They invented hundreds of spoken languages; they moved across the face of the globe, learning to survive in almost every natural environment; they chose and honored leaders; they traded, warred, and worshipped; and, above all, they learned from and taught one another. Much of what we would like to know about their experiences remains unknown because it took place before writing existed.

Archaeologists specialize in learning about people who did not document their history in writing. They study the millions of artifacts these people created. They also scrutinize soil, geological strata, pollen, climate, and other environmental features to reconstruct as much as possible about the world ancient peoples inhabited. Although no documents chronicle the day-to-day lives of ancient Americans, archaeologists have learned to make artifacts, along with their natural and human environment, tell a great deal about the people who used them.

This chapter relies on studies by archaeologists to sketch a brief overview of ancient America, the long first phase of the history of the United States. Ancient Americans and their descendants resided in North America for thousands of years before Europeans arrived. For their own reasons and in their own ways, they created societies and cultures of remarkable diversity and complexity.

KEY FACTORS

Archaeologists
– Focus on physical objects such as bones, spear points, and pottery.

Historians
– Tend to focus more on written records.

QUICK REVIEW <

Why must historians rely on the work of archaeologists to write the history of ancient America?

Who were the first Americans?

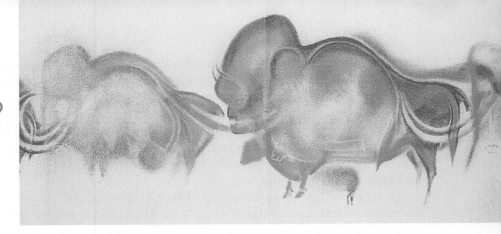

Mammoth Cave Painting Like Clovis peoples in ancient America, human beings elsewhere in the world hunted mammoths. An ancient artist painted this portrait of mammoths on the wall of a cave in southern France about 16,000 BP. North American mammoths stood about fourteen feet tall at the shoulder and weighed eight to ten tons. Hunters armed with stone-tipped wooden spears needed to study such formidable prey to identify their vulnerabilities. Musée de l'Homme.

THE FIRST HUMAN BEINGS to arrive in the Western Hemisphere emigrated from Asia. They brought with them hunting skills, weapon- and tool-making techniques, and a full range of other forms of human knowledge developed millennia earlier in Africa, Europe, and Asia. These first Americans hunted large mammals, such as the mammoths they had learned in Europe and Asia to kill, butcher, and process for food, clothing, building materials, and many other purposes. Most likely, these first Americans wandered into the Western Hemisphere more or less accidentally, hungry and in pursuit of their prey.

African and Asian Origins

Human beings lived elsewhere in the world for hundreds of thousands of years before they reached the Western Hemisphere. They lacked a way to travel to the Western Hemisphere because millions of years before humans existed anywhere on the globe, North and South America became detached from the gigantic common landmass scientists now call Pangaea. About 240 million years ago, powerful forces deep within the earth fractured Pangaea and slowly pushed the continents apart to approximately their present positions (**Map 1.1**). This process of continental drift encircled the land of the Western Hemisphere with large oceans that isolated it from the other continents long before early human beings (*Homo erectus*) first appeared in Africa about two million years ago. (Hereafter in this chapter, the abbreviation *BP*—archaeologists' notation for "years before the present"—is used to indicate dates earlier than two thousand years ago. Dates more recent than two thousand years ago are indicated with the common and familiar notation *AD*—for example, AD 1492.)

More than a million and a half years after *Homo erectus* appeared, or about 400,000 BP, modern humans (*Homo sapiens*) evolved in Africa. All human beings throughout the world today are descendants of these ancient Africans. Slowly, over many millennia, *Homo sapiens* migrated out of Africa and into Europe and

CHAPTER LOCATOR | What is the connection between archaeology and history? | Who were the first Americans?

6 CHAPTER 1 UNDERSTANDING ANCIENT AMERICA

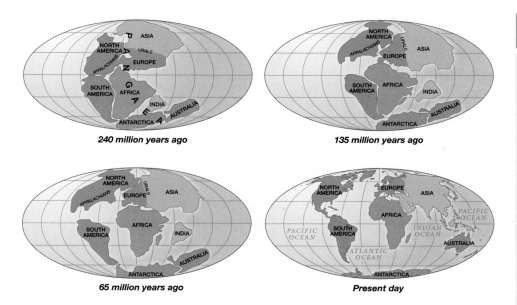

240 million years ago

135 million years ago

65 million years ago

Present day

MAP 1.1 ■ **Continental Drift**
Massive geological forces separated North and South America from other continents eons before human beings evolved in Africa in the past 1.5 million years.

Asia. Unlike North and South America, Europe and Asia retained land connections to Africa, making this migration possible.

Two major developments made it possible for human beings to migrate to the Western Hemisphere. First, humans successfully adapted to the frigid environment near the Arctic Circle. Second, changes in the earth's climate reconnected North America to Asia.

By about 25,000 BP, *Homo sapiens* had spread from Africa throughout Europe and Asia. People, probably women, had learned to use bone needles to sew animal skins into warm clothing that permitted them to become permanent residents of extremely cold regions such as northeastern Siberia. A few of these ancient Siberians walked to North America on land that now lies submerged beneath the sixty miles of water that currently separates easternmost Siberia from westernmost Alaska. During the last global cold spell—the Wisconsin glaciation, which endured from about 25,000 to 14,000 BP—snow piled up in glaciers, causing the sea level to drop as much as 350 feet below its current level. The falling sea level exposed a land bridge between Asian Siberia and American Alaska as well as a long coastline (now underwater). This land bridge and exposed coastline, which scientists call **Beringia**, opened a pathway hundreds of miles wide between the Eastern and Western Hemispheres.

Siberian hunters presumably roamed Beringia for centuries in search of game animals. As the hunters ventured farther and farther east, and probably also along the Alaskan coastline, they eventually became pioneers of human life

Beringia

Beringia
▶ Land bridge that was exposed between Asian Siberia and American Alaska when sea levels fell during the Wisconsin glaciation (25,000–14,000 BP), opening a pathway for the migration of Siberian peoples to the Americas.

How did Archaic Americans adapt to changing conditions?

How did agriculture change Native American societies?

How were native societies organized in the 1490s?

What were the characteristics of Mexican culture?

Conclusion: How do we understand the worlds of ancient Americans?

in the Western Hemisphere. Their migrations probably had very little influence on their own lives, which continued more or less as they had in Siberia. Although they did not know it, their migrations revolutionized the history of the world.

Archaeologists refer to these first migrants and their descendants for the next few millennia as **Paleo-Indians**. They speculate that these Siberian hunters traveled in small bands of no more than twenty-five people. How many such bands arrived in North America before Beringia disappeared beneath the sea will never be known.

When they came is hotly debated by experts. The first migrants probably arrived sometime after 15,000 BP. Scattered and inconclusive evidence suggests that they may have arrived several thousand years earlier. Certainly, humans who originated in Asia inhabited the Western Hemisphere by 13,500 BP.

Paleo-Indians

▶ The first ancient Americans. Paleo-Indians concentrated their hunting activities on big game, such as mammoths and bison.

Paleo-Indian Hunters

When humans first arrived in the Western Hemisphere, massive glaciers covered most of present-day Canada. A narrow corridor not entirely obstructed by ice ran along the eastern side of Canada's Rocky Mountains, and most archaeologists believe that Paleo-Indians probably migrated through the ice-free passageway in pursuit of game. They may also have traveled along the Pacific coast in small boats, hunting marine life and hopscotching from one desirable landing spot to another. At the southern edge of the glaciers, Paleo-Indians entered a hunters' paradise. North, Central, and South America teemed with wildlife. Ample food permitted the Paleo-Indian population to grow. Within a thousand years or so, Paleo-Indians had migrated to the tip of South America and virtually everywhere else in the Western Hemisphere, as proved by discoveries of their spear points.

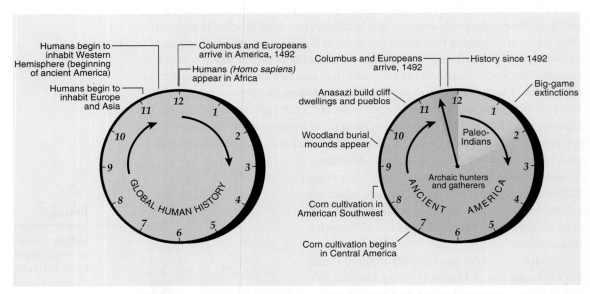

FIGURE 1.1 ■ Human Habitation of the World and the Western Hemisphere
These clock faces illustrate the long global history of modern humans (left) and of human history in the Western Hemisphere since the arrival of the first ancient Americans (right).

CHAPTER LOCATOR | What is the connection between archaeology and history? | Who were the first Americans?

8   CHAPTER 1
UNDERSTANDING ANCIENT AMERICA

Early Paleo-Indians used distinctively shaped spearheads known as **Clovis points**, named for the place in New Mexico where they were first excavated. Archaeologists' discovery of Clovis points throughout North and Central America in sites occupied between 13,500 BP and 13,000 BP provides evidence that these nomadic hunters shared a common ancestry and way of life. Paleo-Indians hunted mammoths and bison—judging from the artifacts and bones that have survived from this era—but they probably also hunted smaller animals. Concentration on large animals, when possible, made sense because just one mammoth kill supplied hunters with meat for weeks or, if dried, for months. In addition to food, mammoth kills provided hides and bones for clothing, shelter, tools, and much more.

About 11,000 BP, Paleo-Indians confronted a major crisis. The mammoths and other large mammals they hunted became extinct. The extinction was gradual, stretching over several hundred years. Scientists are not completely certain why it occurred, although environmental change probably contributed to it. About this time, the earth's climate warmed, glaciers melted, and sea levels rose. Mammoths and other large mammals probably had difficulty adapting to the warmer climate. Many archaeologists also believe, however, that Paleo-Indians probably contributed to the extinctions in the Western Hemisphere by killing large animals more rapidly than they could reproduce. Whatever the causes, within just a few thousand years of their arrival in the Western Hemisphere, Paleo-Indian hunters faced a radical change in the natural environment—namely, the extinction of large mammals.

Paleo-Indians adapted to the drastic environmental change of the big-game extinction by making at least two important changes in their way of life. First, hunters began to prey more intensively on smaller animals. Second, Paleo-Indians devoted more energy to foraging—that is, to collecting wild plant foods such as roots, seeds, nuts, berries, and fruits. When Paleo-Indians made these changes, they replaced the apparent uniformity of the big-game-oriented Clovis culture with great cultural diversity adapted to the many natural environments throughout the hemisphere, ranging from icy tundra to steamy jungles.

These post-Clovis adaptations to local environments resulted in the astounding variety of Native American cultures that existed when Europeans arrived in AD 1492. By then, more than three hundred major tribes and hundreds of lesser groups inhabited North America alone. Hundreds more lived in Central and South America. Hundreds of other ancient American cultures had disappeared or transformed themselves as their people constantly adapted to environmental change and other challenges.

Clovis points

▶ Distinctly shaped spearheads used by Paleo-Indians. The discovery of Clovis points throughout North and Central America is evidence that Paleo-Indian hunters shared a common ancestry and way of life.

Clovis Spear Straightener

Clovis hunters used this bone spear straightener about 11,000 BP at a campsite in Arizona. Presumably Clovis hunters stuck their spear shafts through the opening and then grasped the handle of the straightener and moved it back and forth along the length of the shaft to remove imperfections and make the spear a more effective weapon. Arizona State Museum, University of Arizona.

QUICK REVIEW

Why and how did humans migrate to North America?

How did Archaic Americans adapt to changing conditions?

How did agriculture change Native American societies?

How were native societies organized in the 1490s?

What were the characteristics of Mexican culture?

Conclusion: How do we understand the worlds of ancient Americans?

> How did Archaic Americans adapt to changing conditions?

hunter-gatherer

▶ A nomadic way of life centered on hunting animals and gathering plants for food. For much of their history, ancient Americans were hunter-gatherers.

Archaic Indians

▶ Members of the many different hunting and gathering cultures that descended from Paleo-Indians. The Archaic period lasted roughly from 10,000 BP to somewhere between 4000 BP and 3000 BP.

ARCHAEOLOGISTS use the term *Archaic* to describe the many different hunting and gathering cultures that descended from Paleo-Indians and the long period of time when those cultures dominated the history of ancient America, roughly from 10,000 BP to somewhere between 4000 BP and 3000 BP. The term usefully describes the era in the history of ancient America that followed the Paleo-Indian big-game hunters and preceded the development of agriculture. It denotes a **hunter-gatherer** way of life that persisted in North America long after European colonization.

Like their Paleo-Indian ancestors, **Archaic Indians** hunted with spears, but they also took smaller game with traps, nets, and hooks. Unlike their Paleo-Indian predecessors, most Archaic peoples used a variety of stone tools to prepare food from wild plants. A characteristic Archaic artifact is a grinding stone used to pulverize seeds into edible form. Most Archaic Indians migrated from place to place to harvest plants and hunt animals. They usually did not establish permanent villages, although they often returned to the same river valley or fertile meadow from year to year. In certain regions with especially rich resources—such as present-day California and the Pacific Northwest—they developed permanent settlements. Archaic peoples followed these practices in distinctive ways in the different environmental regions of North America (**Map 1.2**).

CHAPTER LOCATOR | What is the connection between archaeology and history? | Who were the first Americans?

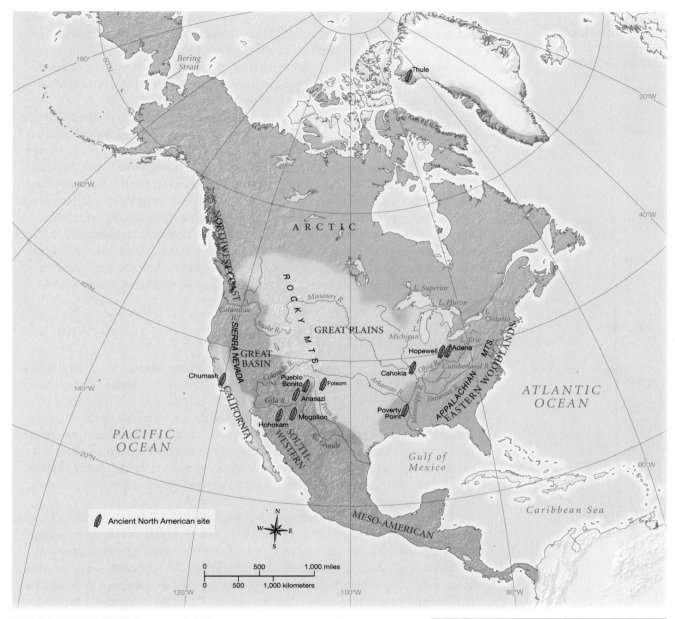

MAP 1.2 ■ Native North American Cultures
Environmental conditions defined the boundaries of the broad zones of cultural similarity among ancient North Americans.

▶ FOR MORE HELP ANALYZING THIS MAP, see the map activity for this chapter in the Online Study Guide at bedfordstmartins.com/roarkunderstanding.

Great Plains Bison Hunters

After the extinction of large game animals, some hunters began to concentrate on bison in the huge herds that grazed the grassy, arid plains stretching for hundreds of miles east of the Rocky Mountains. For almost a thousand years after the big-game extinctions, Archaic Indians hunted bison with spears tipped with flint spear points known as **Folsom points** (named after the site near Folsom, New Mexico, where they were first discovered).

Folsom points
▶ Flint spear points used by some Archaic Indians. Folsom points are named for the site in Folsom, New Mexico, where they were first discovered.

| How did Archaic Americans adapt to changing conditions? | How did agriculture change Native American societies? | How were native societies organized in the 1490s? | What were the characteristics of Mexican culture? | Conclusion: How do we understand the worlds of ancient Americans? |

CHRONOLOGY

c. 10,000–3000 BP
- Archaic hunter-gatherer cultures dominate ancient America.

c. 6000 BP
- Some Eastern Woodland peoples begin to establish permanent settlements.

c. 5500 BP
- Northwest peoples begin to concentrate on whaling and fishing.

c. 5000 BP
- Chumash emerge in the region surrounding present-day Santa Barbara, California.

c. 4000 BP
- Some Eastern Woodland peoples grow gourds and pumpkins and begin making pottery.

c. AD 500
- Bows and arrows appear in North America south of the Arctic.

Like their nomadic predecessors, Folsom hunters moved constantly to maintain contact with their prey. Great Plains hunters developed trapping techniques that made it easy to kill large numbers of animals. At the original Folsom site, careful study of the bones found there suggests that early one winter hunters drove bison into the narrow gulch and speared twenty-three of them. At other sites, Great Plains hunters stampeded bison herds over cliffs.

Bows and arrows reached Great Plains hunters from the north about AD 500. They largely replaced spears, which had been the hunters' weapons of choice for millennia. Bows permitted hunters to wound animals from farther away, arrows made it possible to shoot repeatedly, and arrowheads were easier to make and therefore less costly to lose than the larger, heavier spear points. But these new weapons did not otherwise alter bison hunting on the Great Plains. Although we tend to imagine ancient Great Plains bison hunters on horseback, in fact they hunted on foot, like their Paleo-Indian ancestors. Horses that had existed in North America millions of years earlier had long since become extinct. Horses did not return to the Great Plains until Europeans imported them in the decades after 1492, when Native American bison hunters acquired them and soon became expert riders.

Great Basin Cultures

Archaic peoples in the Great Basin between the Rocky Mountains and the Sierra Nevada inhabited a region of great environmental diversity. Some Great Basin Indians lived along the shores of large marshes and lakes that formed during rainy periods. They ate fish of every available size and type, catching them with bone hooks and nets. Other cultures survived in the foothills of mountains between the blistering heat on the desert floor and the cold, treeless mountain heights. Hunters killed deer, antelope, and sometimes bison, as well as smaller game such as rabbits, rodents, and snakes. These broadly defined zones of habitation changed constantly, depending largely on the amount of rain.

Despite the variety and occasional abundance of animals, Great Basin peoples relied on plants as their most important food source. Unlike meat and fish, plant food could be collected and stored for long periods to protect against shortages caused by the fickle rainfall. Many Great Basin peoples gathered ample supplies of piñon nuts as a dietary staple. By diversifying their food sources and migrating to favorable locations to collect and store them, Great Basin peoples adapted to the severe environmental challenges of the region and maintained their Archaic hunter-gatherer way of life for centuries after Europeans arrived in AD 1492.

Pacific Coast Cultures

The richness of the natural environment made present-day California the most densely settled area in all of ancient North America. The land and ocean offered such ample food that California peoples remained hunters and gatherers for hundreds of years after AD 1492. California's diverse environment also encouraged corresponding diversity among native peoples. Archaic settlements in California included about five hundred separate tribes speaking some ninety languages, each with local dialects. No other region of comparable size in North America exhibited such cultural variety.

CHAPTER LOCATOR | What is the connection between archaeology and history? | Who were the first Americans?

12 CHAPTER 1 UNDERSTANDING ANCIENT AMERICA

Ancient California Peoples

The Chumash, one of the many California cultures, emerged in the region surrounding what is now Santa Barbara about 5000 BP. Comparatively plentiful food resources—especially acorns—permitted Chumash people to establish relatively permanent villages. Conflict, evidently caused by competition for valuable acorn-gathering territory, frequently broke out among the villages, as documented by Chumash skeletons that display signs of violent deaths. Although few other California cultures achieved the population density and village settlements of the Chumash, all shared the hunter-gatherer way of life and reliance on acorns as a major food source.

Another rich natural environment lay along the Pacific Northwest coast. Like the Chumash, Northwest peoples built more or less permanent villages. After about 5500 BP, they concentrated on catching whales and large quantities of salmon, halibut, and other fish, which they dried to last throughout the year. They also traded with people who lived hundreds of miles from the coast. Fishing freed Northwest peoples to develop sophisticated woodworking skills. They fashioned elaborate wood carvings that denoted wealth and status, as well as huge canoes for fishing, hunting, and conducting warfare against neighboring tribes. Much of the warfare among Archaic north-westerners grew out of attempts to defend or gain access to prime fishing sites.

Eastern Woodland Cultures

East of the Mississippi River, Archaic peoples adapted to a forest environment that included many local variants, such as the major river valleys of the Mississippi, Ohio, Tennessee, and Cumberland; the Great Lakes region; and the Atlantic coast (see Map 1.2, page 11). Throughout these diverse locales, Archaic peoples followed similar survival strategies.

Woodland hunters stalked deer as their most important prey. Deer supplied Woodland peoples with food as well as hides and bones that they crafted into clothing, weapons, needles, and many other tools. Like Archaic peoples else-where, Woodland Indians gathered edible plants, seeds, and nuts. About 6000 BP, some Woodland groups established more or less permanent settlements of 25 to 150 people, usually near a river or lake that offered a wide variety of plant and animal resources. The existence of such settlements has permitted archaeologists to locate numerous Archaic burial sites that suggest Woodland people had a life

Chumash Necklace

Long before the arrival of Europeans, ancient Chumash people in southern California made this elegant necklace of abalone shell. Its iridescent splendor demonstrates that Chumash people wore beautiful as well as useful adornments. Natural History Museum of Los Angeles County.

| How did Archaic Americans adapt to changing conditions? | How did agriculture change Native American societies? | How were native societies organized in the 1490s? | What were the characteristics of Mexican culture? | Conclusion: How do we understand the worlds of ancient Americans? |

13

expectancy of about eighteen years, a relatively short time to learn all the skills necessary to survive, reproduce, and adapt to change.

Around 4000 BP, Woodland cultures added two important features to their basic hunter-gatherer lifestyles: agriculture and pottery. Gourds and pumpkins that were first cultivated thousands of years earlier in Mexico spread north to Woodland peoples through trade and migration. Woodland peoples also began to cultivate local species such as sunflowers, as well as small quantities of tobacco, another import from South America. Corn was the most important plant food carried to North America by traders and migrants from Mexico, and it became a significant Woodland food crop around 2500 BP. Most likely, women learned how to plant, grow, and harvest these crops as an outgrowth of their work gathering edible wild plants. Cultivated crops added to the quantity, variety, and predictability of Woodland food sources, but they did not alter Woodland peoples' dependence on gathering wild plants, seeds, and nuts.

Like agriculture, pottery also probably originated in Mexico. Traders and migrants probably brought pots into North America along with Central and South American seeds. Pots were more durable than baskets for cooking and storage of food and water, but they were also much heavier and therefore were shunned by nomadic peoples. The permanent settlements of Woodland peoples made the heavy weight of pots much less important than their advantages compared to leaky and fragile baskets. While pottery and agriculture introduced changes in Woodland cultures, ancient Woodland Americans retained the other basic features of their Archaic hunter-gatherer lifestyle, which persisted in most areas to 1492 and beyond.

> **QUICK REVIEW**

Why did Archaic Indians shift from big-game hunting to foraging and smaller-game hunting?

CHAPTER LOCATOR | What is the connection between archaeology and history? | Who were the first Americans?

14 CHAPTER 1 UNDERSTANDING ANCIENT AMERICA

How did agriculture change Native American societies?

Ancient Agriculture

Dropping seeds into holes punched in cleared ground by a pointed stick, known as a "dibble," this ancient American farmer sows a new crop. Created by a sixteenth-century European artist, the drawing misrepresents who did the agricultural work in many ancient American cultures—namely, women rather than men. However, the three-foot dibble would have been used as shown here. The Pierpont Morgan Library/Art Resource, NY; Jerry Jacka Photography.

▶ FOR MORE HELP ANALYZING THIS IMAGE, see the visual activity for this chapter in the Online Study Guide at bedfordstmartins.com/roarkunderstanding.

AMONG EASTERN WOODLAND PEOPLES and most other Archaic cultures, agriculture supplemented, but did not replace, hunter-gatherer subsistence strategies. Reliance on wild animals and plants required most Archaic groups to remain small and mobile. But beginning about 4000 BP, distinctive southwestern cultures slowly began to depend on agriculture and to build permanent settlements. Later, around 2500 BP, Woodland peoples in the vast Mississippi valley began to construct **burial mounds** and other earthworks that suggest the existence of social and political hierarchies that archaeologists term **chiefdoms**. Although the hunter-gatherer lifestyle never entirely disappeared, the development of agricultural settlements and chiefdoms represented important innovations to the Archaic way of life.

burial mounds
▶ Large earthworks constructed by the Woodland peoples of the Mississippi valley, beginning around 2500 BP. Burial mounds provide evidence of social and political hierarchy among Woodland peoples.

chiefdoms
▶ The term archaeologists use for the social and political hierarchies that emerged among some ancient Americans toward the end of the Archaic period.

| How did Archaic Americans adapt to changing conditions? | **How did agriculture change Native American societies?** | How were native societies organized in the 1490s? | What were the characteristics of Mexican culture? | Conclusion: How do we understand the worlds of ancient Americans? |

CHRONOLOGY

c. 7000 BP
– Corn cultivation begins in Central and South America.

c. 4000 BP
– Distinctive southwestern cultures slowly begin to depend on agriculture and to build permanent settlements.

c. 3500 BP
– Southwestern cultures begin corn cultivation.

c. 2500 BP
– Eastern Woodland cultures start to build burial mounds.
– Some Eastern Woodland peoples begin to cultivate corn.

c. 2500–2100 BP
– Adena culture develops in Ohio.

c. 2100 BP–AD 400
– Hopewell culture emerges in Ohio and Mississippi valleys.

c. AD 200–900
– Mogollon culture develops in New Mexico.

c. AD 500–1400
– Hohokam culture develops in Arizona.

c. AD 800–1500
– Mississippian culture flourishes in Southeast.

c. AD 1000–1200
– Anasazi peoples build cliff dwellings at Mesa Verde and pueblos at Chaco Canyon.

pueblos
▶ Multiunit dwellings that are characteristic of ancient Americans in the Southwest. The ruins of Anasazi pueblos at Mesa Verde, Colorado, and Chaco Canyon, New Mexico, still exist today.

Southwestern Cultures

Southwestern Cultures

Ancient Americans in present-day Arizona, New Mexico, and southern portions of Utah and Colorado developed cultures characterized by agriculture and multiunit dwellings called **pueblos**. All southwestern peoples confronted the challenge of a dry climate and unpredictable fluctuations in rainfall that made the supply of wild plant food very unreliable. These ancient Americans probably adopted agriculture in response to this basic environmental condition.

About 3500 BP, southwestern hunters and gatherers began to cultivate corn. Corn had been grown in Central and South America since about 7000 BP, and it slowly traveled up to North America with migrants and traders. In the centuries after 3500 BP, corn eventually became the most important cultivated crop for ancient Americans throughout North America. In the Southwest, the demands of corn cultivation encouraged hunter-gatherers to restrict their migratory habits in order to tend the crop. A vital consideration was access to water. Southwestern Indians became irrigation experts, conserving water from streams, springs, and rainfall and distributing it to thirsty crops.

About AD 200, small farming settlements began to appear throughout southern New Mexico, marking the emergence of the Mogollon culture. Typically, a Mogollon settlement included a dozen pit houses, each made by digging out a rounded pit about fifteen feet in diameter and a foot or two deep and then erecting poles to support a roof of branches or dirt. Larger villages usually had one or two bigger pit houses that may have been the predecessors of the circular kivas, the ceremonial rooms that became a characteristic of nearly all southwestern settlements. About AD 900, Mogollon culture began to decline, for reasons that remain obscure. Its descendants included the Mimbres people in southwestern New Mexico, who crafted spectacular pottery adorned with human and animal designs. By about AD 1250, the Mimbres culture disappeared, for reasons unknown.

Around AD 500, while the Mogollon culture prevailed in New Mexico, other ancient people migrated from Mexico to southern Arizona and established the distinctive Hohokam culture. Hohokam settlements used sophisticated grids of irrigation canals to plant and harvest crops twice a year. Hohokam settlements reflected the continuing influence of Mexican cultural practices that migrants brought with them as they traveled north. Hohokam people built sizable platform mounds and ball courts characteristic of many Mexican cultures. About AD 1400, Hohokam culture declined for reasons that remain a mystery, although the rising salinity of the soil caused by centuries of irrigation probably caused declining crop yields and growing food shortages.

North of the Hohokam and Mogollon cultures, in a region that encompassed southern Utah and Colorado and northern Arizona and New Mexico, the Anasazi

CHAPTER LOCATOR | What is the connection between archaeology and history? | Who were the first Americans?

16 CHAPTER 1 UNDERSTANDING ANCIENT AMERICA

| Pueblo Bonito, Chaco Canyon, New Mexico | About AD 1000, Pueblo Bonito stood at the center of Chacoan culture, which extended over more than 20,000 square miles in the region at the intersection of present-day Utah, Colorado, Arizona, and New Mexico. The numerous circular kivas show the significance of ceremonies and rituals to the people of Chaco Canyon. Richard Alexander Cooke III. |

▶ FOR MORE HELP ANALYZING THIS IMAGE, see the visual activity for this chapter in the Online Study Guide at bedfordstmartins.com/roarkunderstanding.

culture began to flourish about AD 100. The early Anasazi built pit houses on mesa tops and used irrigation much like their neighbors to the south. Beginning around AD 1000 (again, it is not known why), some Anasazi began to move to large, multistory cliff dwellings whose ruins still exist at Mesa Verde, Colorado, and elsewhere. Other Anasazi communities erected huge stone-walled pueblos with enough rooms to house everyone in the settlement. Pueblo Bonito at Chaco Canyon, New Mexico, for example, contained more than eight hundred rooms. Anasazi pueblos and cliff dwellings typically included one or more kivas used for secret ceremonies, restricted to men, that sought to communicate with the supernatural world.

Drought began to plague the region about AD 1130, and it lasted for more than half a century, triggering the disappearance of Anasazi culture. By AD 1200, the large Anasazi pueblos had been abandoned. The prolonged drought probably intensified conflict among pueblos and made it impossible to depend on the techniques of irrigated agriculture that had worked for centuries. Some Anasazi migrated toward regions with more reliable rainfall and settled in Hopi, Zuñi, and Acoma pueblos that their descendants in Arizona and New Mexico have occupied ever since.

Woodland Burial Mounds and Chiefdoms

No other ancient Americans created dwellings similar to pueblos, but around 2500 BP, Woodland cultures throughout the vast area drained by the Mississippi River began to build burial mounds. The size of the mounds, the labor and organization required to erect them, and differences in the artifacts buried with certain individuals suggest the existence of a social and political hierarchy that

| How did Archaic Americans adapt to changing conditions? | How did agriculture change Native American societies? | How were native societies organized in the 1490s? | What were the characteristics of Mexican culture? | Conclusion: How do we understand the worlds of ancient Americans? |

17

archaeologists term a chiefdom. Experts do not know the name of a single chief, nor do they know the organizational structure a chief headed. But the only way archaeologists can account for the complex and labor-intensive burial mounds and artifacts found in them is to assume that one person—whom scholars term a chief—commanded the labor and obedience of very large numbers of other people, who made up the chief's chiefdom.

Between 2500 BP and 2100 BP, Adena people built hundreds of burial mounds radiating from central Ohio. In the mounds, the Adena usually buried the dead with grave goods that included spear points and stone pipes as well as thin sheets of mica (a glasslike mineral) crafted into the shapes of birds, beasts, and human hands. Over the body and grave goods, Adena people piled dirt into a mound. Sometimes burial mounds were constructed all at once, but often they were built up slowly over many years. About 2100 BP, Adena culture evolved into the more elaborate Hopewell culture, which lasted about five hundred years. Centered in Ohio, Hopewell culture extended throughout the enormous drainage of the Ohio and Mississippi rivers. Hopewell people built larger mounds than their Adena predecessors had and filled them with more magnificent grave goods.

Burial was probably reserved for the most important members of Hopewell groups. Burial rituals appear to have brought many people together to honor the dead person and to help build the mound. Hopewell mounds were often one hundred feet in diameter and thirty feet high. Grave goods at Hopewell sites testify to the high quality of Hopewell crafts and to a thriving trade network that ranged from Wyoming to Florida. Archaeologists believe that Hopewell chiefs probably played an important role in this interregional trade.

Hopewell culture declined about AD 400 for reasons that are obscure. Archaeologists speculate that bows and arrows, along with an increasing reliance on agriculture, made small settlements more self-sufficient and, therefore, less

Ceramic Jar

This handsome jar, crafted about 2000 BP by a Woodland potter (probably a woman), illustrates the usefulness of ceramic pots for storage and cooking and exhibits the human delight in decorative artistry. Gilcrease Museum, Tulsa, Oklahoma.

CHAPTER LOCATOR | What is the connection between archaeology and history? | Who were the first Americans?

dependent on the central authority of the Hopewell chiefs who were responsible for the burial mounds.

Four hundred years later, another mound-building culture flourished. The Mississippian culture emerged in the floodplains of the major southeastern river systems about AD 800 and lasted until about AD 1500. Major Mississippian sites included huge mounds with platforms on top for ceremonies and for the residences of great chiefs. Most likely, the ceremonial mounds and ritual practices derived from Mexican cultural expressions that were carried north by traders and migrants. The largest Mississippian site was **Cahokia**, whose remnants can be seen in Illinois near the confluence of the Mississippi and Missouri rivers.

Major Mississippian Mounds, AD 800–1500

Cahokia

▶ A flourishing urban area that lasted from about AD 800 until about AD 1500. The largest of the Mississippian sites, Cahokia included huge mounds for ceremonies and for the residences of the chiefs. It may have had as many as thirty thousand residents.

Cahokia

Featured one hundred mounds grouped around large open plazas
May have had as many as thirty thousand inhabitants
Residents of Cahokia worshipped a sun god
Evidence of mass human sacrifices demonstrates the coercive power of Cahokia's elites

Cahokia and other Mississippian cultures had dwindled by AD 1500. When Europeans arrived, most of the descendants of Mississippian cultures lived in small, dispersed villages supported by hunting and gathering supplemented by agriculture. Clearly, the conditions that caused large chiefdoms to emerge—whatever they were—had changed, and chiefs no longer commanded the powers they had once enjoyed.

QUICK REVIEW

How and why did the societies of the Southwest differ from eastern societies?

How did Archaic Americans adapt to changing conditions?

How did agriculture change Native American societies?

How were native societies organized in the 1490s?

What were the characteristics of Mexican culture?

Conclusion: How do we understand the worlds of ancient Americans?

How were native societies organized in the 1490s?

ABOUT THIRTEEN MILLENNIA after Paleo-Indians first migrated to the Western Hemisphere, a new migration—this time from Europe—began in 1492 with the journey of Christopher Columbus. In the decades before 1492, Native Americans continued to employ their ancestors' time-tested survival strategies of hunting, gathering, and agriculture. Those strategies succeeded in both populating and shaping the new world Europeans encountered.

By the 1490s, Native Americans lived throughout North America, but their total population is a subject of spirited debate among scholars. Some experts claim Native Americans numbered 18 million to 20 million, while others place the population at no more than a million. A prudent estimate is about 4 million. On the eve of European colonization, the small island nation of England had about the same number of people as all of North America. The vastness of North America meant that the population density was low, just 60 people per hundred square miles, compared to more than 8,000 in England. Compared to England and elsewhere in Europe, Native Americans were spread thin across the land because of their survival strategies of hunting, gathering, and agriculture.

CHAPTER LOCATOR | What is the connection between archaeology and history? | Who were the first Americans?

Regions in North America with abundant resources had relatively high populations. About one-fifth of Native Americans lived along the West Coast in food-rich California and the Pacific Northwest, where the population density was, respectively, six times greater and four times greater than the average for the whole continent (**Figure 1.2**). The food-scarce Great Plains, Great Basin, and Arctic regions held about one-quarter of Native Americans, but the population density was extremely low, roughly one-tenth the continental average. About a quarter of Native Americans resided in the arid Southwest, where irrigation and intensive agriculture permitted a population density about twice the continental average. But even in California, the most densely inhabited region of North America, population density was just one-twentieth of England's.

The enormous Woodland region east of the Mississippi River was home to about one-third of Native Americans, whose population density approximated the continental average. Eastern Woodland peoples clustered into three broad linguistic and cultural groups: Algonquian, Iroquoian, and Muskogean.

Algonquian tribes inhabited the Atlantic seaboard, the Great Lakes region, and much of the upper Midwest (**Map 1.3**). The relatively mild climate along the Atlantic permitted the coastal Algonquians to grow corn and other crops as well as to hunt and fish. Around the Great Lakes and in northern New England, however, cool summers and severe winters made agriculture impractical.

KEY FACTORS

In 1492, Native Americans populated all of North America:
- One-fifth lived along the Pacific coast.
- One-fourth lived in the Southwest.
- One-third lived east of the Mississippi.
- One-fourth lived in the regions of the Great Plains, the Great Basin, and the Arctic.

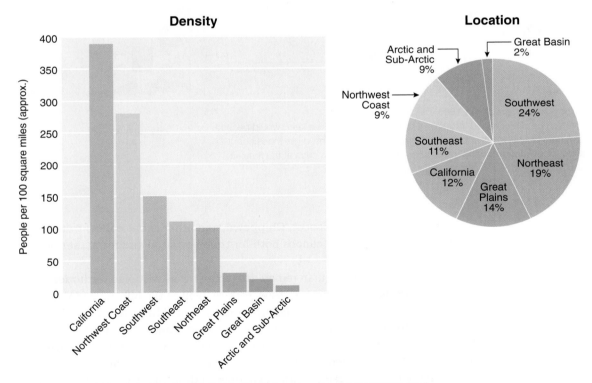

FIGURE 1.2 ■ Native American Population in North America about 1492 (Estimated)
The population density on the enormous expanses of the Great Plains, Great Basin, and Arctic regions was very low, although in total about a quarter of all native North Americans resided in these areas. Overall, the population density in North America was less than 1 percent of the population density of England, a fact that helps explain why European colonists tended to view North America as a comparatively empty wilderness.

| How did Archaic Americans adapt to changing conditions? | How did agriculture change Native American societies? | **How were native societies organized in the 1490s?** | What were the characteristics of Mexican culture? | Conclusion: How do we understand the worlds of ancient Americans? |

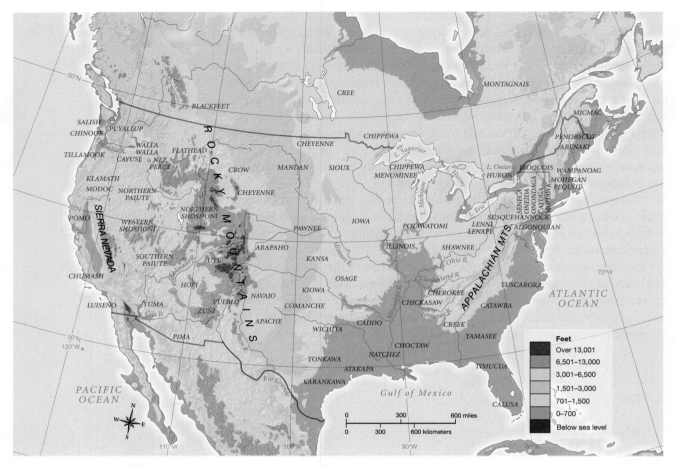

MAP 1.3 ■ **Native North Americans about 1500**
Distinctive Native American peoples resided throughout the area that, centuries later, would become the United States. This map indicates the approximate location of some of the larger tribes about 1500. In the interest of legibility, many other peoples who inhabited North America at the time are omitted from the map.

Instead, the Abenaki, Penobscot, Chippewa, and other tribes concentrated on hunting and fishing, using canoes both for transportation and for gathering wild rice.

Inland from the Algonquian region, Iroquoian tribes occupied territories centered in Pennsylvania and upstate New York, as well as the hilly upland regions of the Carolinas and Georgia. Three features distinguished Iroquoian tribes from their neighbors. First, their success in cultivating corn and other crops allowed them to build permanent settlements, usually consisting of several bark-covered longhouses up to one hundred feet long and housing five to ten families. Second, Iroquoian societies adhered to matrilineal rules of descent. Property of all sorts belonged to women. Women headed family clans and even selected the chiefs (normally men) who governed the tribes. Third, for purposes of war and diplomacy, an Iroquoian confederation—including the Seneca, Onondaga, Mohawk, Oneida, and Cayuga tribes—formed the League of Five Nations, which remained powerful well into the eighteenth century.

CHAPTER LOCATOR | What is the connection between archaeology and history? | Who were the first Americans?

22   CHAPTER 1
UNDERSTANDING ANCIENT AMERICA

Muskogean peoples spread throughout the woodlands of the Southeast, south of the Ohio River and east of the Mississippi. Including the Creek, Choctaw, Chickasaw, and Natchez tribes, Muskogeans inhabited a region that provided abundant food from hunting, gathering, and agriculture. Remnants of the earlier Mississippian culture still existed in Muskogean religion.

Great Plains peoples accounted for about one out of seven Native Americans. Inhabiting the huge region west of the Eastern Woodlands and east of the Rocky Mountains, many tribes had migrated to the Great Plains within the past two hundred years, forced westward by Iroquoian and Algonquian tribes. Some Great Plains tribes—especially the Mandan and Pawnee—farmed successfully, growing both corn and sunflowers. But the Teton Sioux, Blackfeet, Comanche, Cheyenne, and Crow on the northern plains and the Apache and other nomadic tribes on the southern plains depended on buffalo (American bison) for their subsistence.

Southwestern cultures included about a quarter of all native North Americans. These descendants of the Mogollon, Hohokam, and Anasazi cultures lived in settled agricultural communities, many of them pueblos. They continued to grow corn, beans, and squash using methods they had refined for centuries. However, their communities came under attack by a large number of warlike Athabascan tribes who invaded the Southwest beginning around AD 1300. The Athabascans—principally Apache and Navajo—were skillful warriors who preyed on the sedentary pueblo Indians.

About a fifth of all native North Americans resided along the Pacific coast. In California, abundant acorns and nutritious marine life continued to support high population densities, but they retarded the development of agriculture. Similar dependence on hunting and gathering persisted along the Northwest coast. Salmon was so abundant that at The Dalles, a prime fishing site on the Columbia River on the border of present-day Oregon and Washington, Northwest peoples caught millions of pounds of salmon every summer and traded it as far away as California and the Great Plains. Although important trading centers existed throughout North America, particularly in the Southwest, it is likely that The Dalles was the largest Native American trading center in North America.

While trading was common, all native North Americans in the 1490s still depended on hunting and gathering for a major portion of their food. Most of them also practiced agriculture. Some used agriculture to supplement hunting and gathering; for others, the balance was reversed. People throughout North America used bows, arrows, and other weapons for hunting and warfare. None of them employed writing, expressing themselves instead in many other ways: drawings sketched on stones, wood, and animal skins; patterns woven in baskets and textiles; designs painted on pottery, crafted into beadwork, or carved into effigies; and songs, dances, religious ceremonies, and burial rites.

These rich and varied cultural resources of Native Americans did not include features of life common in Europe during the 1490s. Native Americans did not use wheels; sailing ships were unknown to them; they had no large domesticated animals such as horses, cows, or oxen; their use of metals was restricted to copper. However, the absence of these European conveniences mattered less to native North Americans than their own cultural adaptations to the natural environment local to each tribe and their adaptations to the social environment among neighboring peoples. That great similarity—adaptation to natural and social environments—underlay all the cultural diversity among native North Americans.

| How did Archaic Americans adapt to changing conditions? | How did agriculture change Native American societies? | **How were native societies organized in the 1490s?** | What were the characteristics of Mexican culture? | Conclusion: How do we understand the worlds of ancient Americans? |

23

It would be a mistake, however, to conclude that native North Americans lived in blissful harmony with nature and one another. Archaeological sites provide ample evidence of violent conflict among Native Americans. Skeletons bear the marks of wounds as well as of ritualistic human sacrifice and even cannibalism. Religious, ethnic, economic, and familial conflicts must have occurred, but they remain in obscurity because they left few archaeological traces.

Native Americans not only adapted to the natural environment; they also changed it in many ways. They built thousands of structures, from small dwellings to massive pueblos and enormous mounds, permanently altering the landscape. Their gathering techniques selected productive and nutritious varieties of plants, thereby shifting the balance of local plants toward useful varieties. The first stages of North American agriculture, for example, probably resulted from Native Americans gathering wild seeds and then sowing them in a meadow for later harvest. It is almost certain that fertile and hardy varieties of corn were developed this way, first in Mexico and later in North America. To clear land for planting corn, Native Americans set fires that burned off thousands of acres of forest.

Native Americans also used fires for hunting. Great Plains hunters often started fires to force buffalo together and make them easy to slaughter. Eastern Woodland, Southwest, and Pacific coast Indians also set fires to hunt deer and other valuable prey. Throughout North America, Indians started fires along the edges of woods to burn off shrubby undergrowth and encroaching tree seedlings. These burns encouraged the growth of tender young plants that attracted deer and other game animals, bringing them within convenient range of hunters' weapons. The burns also encouraged the growth of food plants that Indians relished, such as blackberries, strawberries, and raspberries.

Because fires set by Native Americans usually burned until they ran out of fuel or were extinguished by rain or wind, enormous regions of North America were burned over. In the long run, fires created and maintained meadows for hunting and agriculture, cleared underbrush from forests, and promoted a diverse and productive natural environment. Fires, like other activities of Native Americans, shaped the landscape of North America long before Europeans arrived in 1492.

> QUICK REVIEW

What common characteristics underlay Native American diversity in the 1490s?

CHAPTER LOCATOR | What is the connection between archaeology and history? | Who were the first Americans?

24 CHAPTER 1 UNDERSTANDING ANCIENT AMERICA

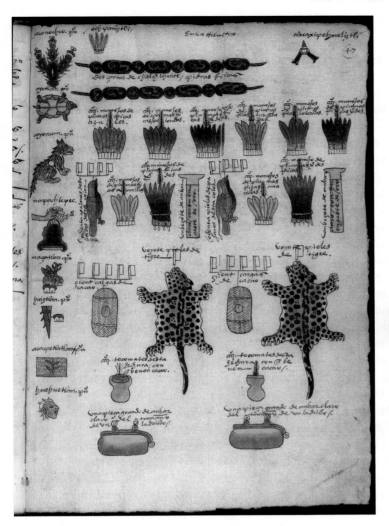

Mexican Tribute Account

This page from the *Codex Mendoza* records the tribute paid to the Mexican capital by the Xoconochco province, a tropical region near present-day Chiapas near the Guatemalan border. In this case, the tribute includes, among many other things, two large strings of green stones, fourteen hundred bundles of rich feathers, and eighty complete bird skins. The tribute exacted by the Mexicans from their empire made them wealthy and created resentment among conquered peoples. Bodleian Library, Oxford, U.K., MS Arch.Self.A1.Fol.47r.

THE INDIGENOUS POPULATION of the New World (the Western Hemisphere) numbered roughly 80 million in the 1490s, about the same as the population of Europe. Almost all these people lived in Mexico and Central and South America. Like their much less numerous North American counterparts, they too lived in a natural environment of tremendous diversity. They too developed hundreds of cultures. But among all these cultures, the Mexica stood out. (Europeans often called these people Aztecs, a name the Mexica did not use.) Their empire stretched from coast to coast across central Mexico, encompassing between 8 million and 25 million people (experts disagree about the total population). We know more about the Mexica than about any other Native American society of the time, principally because of their massive monuments and their Spanish conquerors' well-documented interest in subduing them.

The Mexica began their rise to prominence about 1325, when small bands settled on a marshy island in Lake Texcoco, the site of the future city of Tenochtitlán, the capital of the Mexican empire. Resourceful, courageous, and cold-blooded warriors, the Mexica often hired out as mercenaries for richer, more settled tribes.

Mexica

▶ Native peoples who, by 1490, had built an empire in central Mexico. Also known as Aztecs, the Mexica were a warrior people whose society was built around conquest and the extraction of tribute from conquered peoples.

How did Archaic Americans adapt to changing conditions?

How did agriculture change Native American societies?

How were native societies organized in the 1490s?

What were the characteristics of Mexican culture?

Conclusion: How do we understand the worlds of ancient Americans?

25

c. AD 1325
- Small bands of Mexica settle on a marshy island in Lake Texcoco.

c. AD 1430
- Mexica succeed in asserting their dominance over their former allies and leading their own military campaigns.

c. 1490
- Mexican empire stretches from coast to coast in central Mexico and encompasses between 8 and 25 million people.

AD 1492
- Christopher Columbus arrives in New World, beginning European colonization.

By 1430, the Mexica succeeded in asserting their dominance over their former allies and leading their own military campaigns in an ever-widening arc of empire building. By the 1490s, the Mexica ruled an empire that covered more land than Spain and Portugal combined and contained almost three times as many people.

The empire exemplified the central values of Mexican society. The Mexica worshipped the war god Huitzilopochtli. Warriors held the most exalted positions in the social hierarchy, even above the priests who performed the sacred ceremonies that won Huitzilopochtli's favor. In the almost constant battles necessary to defend and to extend the empire, young Mexican men exhibited the courage and daring that would allow them to rise in the carefully graduated ranks of warriors. The Mexica considered capturing prisoners the ultimate act of bravery. Warriors usually turned over the captives to Mexican priests, who sacrificed them to Huitzilopochtli by cutting out their hearts. The Mexica believed that human sacrifice fed the sun's craving for blood, preventing a fatal descent into everlasting darkness and chaos.

The empire contributed far more to Mexican society than victims for sacrifice. At the most basic level, the empire functioned as a military and political system that collected tribute from subject peoples. The Mexica forced conquered tribes to pay tribute in goods, not money. Tribute redistributed to the Mexica as much as one-third of the goods produced by conquered tribes and included everything from textiles to basic food products such as corn and beans, as well as exotic luxury items such as gold, turquoise, and rare bird feathers.

Tribute reflected the fundamental relations of power and wealth that pervaded the Mexican empire. The relatively small nobility of Mexican warriors, supported by a still smaller priesthood, possessed the military and religious power to command the obedience of thousands of non-noble Mexicans and of millions of other non-Mexicans in subjugated provinces. The Mexican elite exercised their power to obtain tribute and thereby to redistribute wealth from the conquered to the conquerors, from the commoners to the nobility, from the poor to the rich. This redistribution of wealth made possible the achievements of Mexican society that eventually amazed the Spaniards: the huge cities, fabulous temples, teeming markets, and luxuriant gardens, not to mention the storehouses stuffed with gold and other treasures.

On the whole, the Mexica did not interfere much with the internal government of conquered regions. Instead, they usually permitted the traditional ruling elite to stay in power—so long as they paid tribute. The conquered provinces received very little in return from the Mexica, except immunity from punitive raids. Subjugated communities felt exploited by the constant payment of tribute to the Mexica. By depending on military conquest and the constant collection of tribute, the Mexica failed to create among their subjects a belief that Mexican domination was, at some level, legitimate and equitable. After 1492, Spanish intruders would exploit this high level of discontent to conquer the Mexica.

> ## QUICK REVIEW

How did the conquest and creation of an empire exemplify the central values of Mexican society?

CHAPTER LOCATOR | What is the connection between archaeology and history? | Who were the first Americans?

26   CHAPTER 1
UNDERSTANDING ANCIENT AMERICA

© Charles and Josette Lenars/Corbis.

Conclusion: How do we understand the worlds of ancient Americans?

ANCIENT AMERICANS SHAPED the history of human beings in the New World for more than twelve thousand years. They established continuous human habitation in the Western Hemisphere from the time the first big-game hunters crossed Beringia until 1492 and beyond. Ancient Americans achieved their success through resourceful adaptation to the hemisphere's ever-changing natural environments. Their creativity and artistry are unmistakably documented in the artifacts they left at kill sites, camps, and burial mounds.

In the five centuries after 1492—just 4 percent of the time human beings have inhabited the Western Hemisphere—Europeans and their descendants began to shape and eventually to dominate American history. Native American peoples continued to influence major developments of American history for centuries after 1492. But the new wave of strangers that at first trickled and then flooded into the New World from Europe and Africa forever transformed the peoples and places of ancient America.

SO NOW YOU KNOW

At the beginning of the chapter, you were asked if you knew that central Mexico had three times as many people in 1492 as did Spain and Portugal combined. Now you know that the Americas were rich, diverse, and fully populated, some areas very densely, others much less so. Ancient Americans had their own cultures, values, religious beliefs, and ways of understanding the world that were sometimes as varied from one another as they would be from those of the Europeans and Africans whom they would soon encounter.

How did Archaic Americans adapt to changing conditions?

How did agriculture change Native American societies?

How were native societies organized in the 1490s?

What were the characteristics of Mexican culture?

Conclusion: How do we understand the worlds of ancient Americans?

STEP 1

GETTING STARTED

Below are basic terms from this period in American history. Can you identify each term below and explain why it matters? To do this exercise online or to download this chart, visit bedfordstmartins.com/roarkunderstanding.

TERM	WHO OR WHAT & WHEN	WHY IT MATTERS
Beringia, p. 7		
Paleo-Indians, p. 8		
Clovis points, p. 9		
hunter-gatherer, p. 10		
Archaic Indians, p. 10		
Folsom points, p. 11		
burial mounds, p. 15		
chiefdoms, p. 15		
pueblos, p. 16		
Cahokia, p. 19		
Mexica, p. 25		

STEP 2

MOVING BEYOND THE BASICS

The exercise below represents a more advanced understanding of the chapter material. Consider the differences between the major Indian cultural groups in 1490. As you fill in the chart, consider the relationship between the information you include under the three column headings for each cultural group. How, for instance, did geography and climate shape the group's economy and lifestyle? How did economy and lifestyle shape the group's social and political organization? To do this exercise online or to download this chart, visit bedfordstmartins.com/roarkunderstanding.

Indian peoples in 1490	Geography and climate	Economy and lifestyle (sources of food and material goods, economic organization, trade)	Social/political organization (religion, family structures, social hierarchy)
Southwestern cultures			
Eastern Woodland cultures			
Pacific coast cultures			
Great Basin cultures			
Great Plains cultures			

STEP

3

PUTTING IT ALL TOGETHER

Now that you have reviewed key elements of the chapter, take a step back and try to explain the big picture. Remember to use specific examples from the chapter in your answers. To do this exercise online, visit bedfordstmartins.com/roarkunderstanding.

THE FIRST AMERICANS

▶ When and how did humans first arrive in the Americas?

▶ Describe the lifestyle of the Paleo-Indians. How did they adapt to the extinction of mammoths and other large mammals around 11,000 BP?

AGRICULTURE AND ADAPTATION

▶ How did Archaic Indians differ from their Paleo-Indian ancestors?

▶ How did the advent of agriculture change the settlement patterns and social organization of some Indian groups?

NATIVE AMERICAN CULTURES IN 1490

▶ What factors shaped population density across North America?

▶ What set the Mexica apart from the other Indian cultures of North America?

LOOKING BACKWARD, LOOKING AHEAD

▶ What accounts for the diversity of Indian peoples on the eve of European contact?

IN YOUR OWN WORDS

Imagine that you must explain chapter 1 to someone who hasn't read it. What would be the most important points to include and why?

2
ENCOUNTERING THE NEW WORLD

1492–1600

> This chapter examines the causes, course, and impact of Europeans' exploration of parts of the world previously unknown to them, from early Portuguese efforts to chart the coast of Africa to the establishment of a Spanish colonial empire in the New World. It explores the many changes in both the New World and the Old World caused by Europeans' encounters with Native Americans during the sixteenth century.

> What factors led to European exploration in the fifteenth century?

> What did Spanish explorers discover in the western Atlantic?

> How did Spaniards explore, conquer, and colonize New Spain?

> How did New Spain influence sixteenth-century Europe?

> Conclusion: What promise did the New World offer Europeans?

DID YOU KNOW?

The conquest of the Americas made Spain the most powerful European country in the sixteenth century.

"Europeans Encountering Indians," unknown artist, ca. 1700.

What factors led to European exploration in the fifteenth century?

Portuguese Caravel

Portuguese exploration in the fifteenth century was helped immensely by technological advances in navigation. By the mid-1400s, the sturdy caravel could withstand the dangers of sailing in rough open seas.
© National Maritime Museum, London.

HISTORICALLY, the East—not the West—attracted Europeans. Around the year 1000, Norsemen crossed the North Atlantic and founded a small fishing village at L'Anse aux Meadows on the tip of Newfoundland that lasted only a decade or so. Viking sagas memorialized the Norse "discovery," but it had virtually no other impact in the New World or in Europe. Instead, wealthy Europeans developed a taste for luxury goods from Asia and Africa, and merchants competed to satisfy that taste. As Europeans traded with the East and with one another, they acquired new information about the world they inhabited. A few people—sailors, merchants, and aristocrats—took the risks of exploring beyond the limits of the world known to Europeans.

Mediterranean Trade and European Expansion

From the twelfth through the fifteenth centuries, spices, silk, carpets, ivory, gold, and other exotic goods traveled overland from Persia, Asia Minor, India, and Africa and then funneled into continental Europe through Mediterranean trade routes (**Map 2.1**). Dominated primarily by the Italian cities of Venice, Genoa, and Pisa, this trade enriched Italian merchants and bankers, who fiercely defended their near monopoly of access to Eastern goods. The vitality of the Mediterranean trade offered participants few incentives to look for alternatives.

In the mid-fourteenth century, Europeans suffered a catastrophic epidemic of bubonic plague. The Black Death, as it was called, killed about a third of the European population. The plague had major long-term consequences. By drastically reducing the population, it made Europe's limited supply of food more plentiful for survivors. Many survivors inherited property from plague victims, giving them new chances for advancement.

Understandably, most Europeans perceived the world as a place of alarming risks where the delicate balance of health, harvests, and peace could quickly be tipped toward disaster by epidemics, famine, and violence. Most people protected themselves from the constant threat of calamity by worshipping the supernatural, by living amid kinfolk and friends, and by maintaining good relations with the rich and powerful. But the insecurity and uncertainty of fifteenth-century European life also encouraged a few people to take greater risks, such as embarking on dangerous sea voyages through uncharted waters to points unknown.

In European societies, exploration promised fame and fortune to those who succeeded. Monarchs such as Isabella of Spain who hoped to enlarge their realms

CHAPTER LOCATOR | What factors led to European exploration in the fifteenth century?

32 CHAPTER 2
ENCOUNTERING THE NEW WORLD

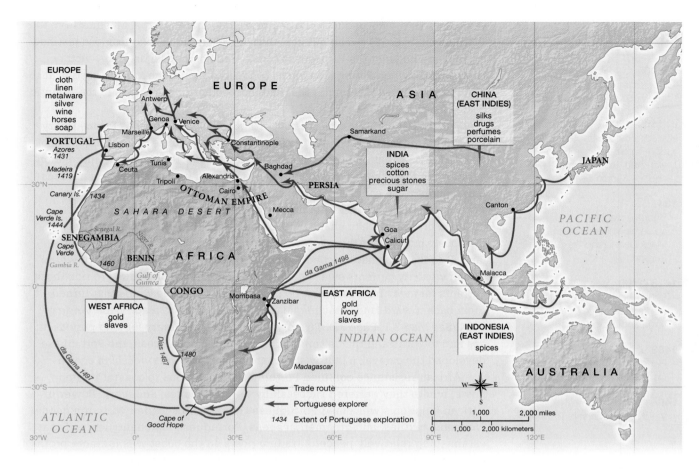

The map contains the following labels:

EUROPE
cloth
linen
metalware
silver
wine
horses
soap

PORTUGAL
Azores
1431
Madeira
1419

Canary Is. 1434

Cape Verde Is. 1444

SENEGAMBIA
Cape Verde

BENIN 1460

Gambia R.

Senegal R.

Niger R.

Gulf of Guinea

WEST AFRICA
gold
slaves

CONGO

Dias 1487

1480

da Gama 1497

ATLANTIC OCEAN

Cape of Good Hope

Antwerp
Genoa
Venice
Marseille
Lisbon
Ceuta
Tunis
Tripoli
Alexandria
Cairo
Constantinople
Baghdad
Mecca

OTTOMAN EMPIRE

SAHARA DESERT

AFRICA

EUROPE

ASIA

CHINA (EAST INDIES)
silks
drugs
perfumes
porcelain

Samarkand

INDIA
spices
cotton
precious stones
sugar

PERSIA

Canton

JAPAN

PACIFIC OCEAN

Goa
Calicut

da Gama 1498

Mombasa
Zanzibar

EAST AFRICA
gold
ivory
slaves

Malacca

INDIAN OCEAN

INDONESIA (EAST INDIES)
spices

Madagascar

AUSTRALIA

→ Trade route
→ Portuguese explorer
1434 Extent of Portuguese exploration

0 1,000 2,000 miles
0 1,000 2,000 kilometers

and enrich their dynasties also had reasons to sponsor journeys of exploration. More territory meant more subjects who could pay more taxes, provide more soldiers, and participate in more commerce, magnifying a monarch's power and prestige. Voyages of exploration also could stabilize a monarch's regime by diverting unruly noblemen toward distant lands. Some explorers, such as Columbus, were commoners who hoped to be elevated to the aristocracy as a reward for their daring achievements.

Scientific and technological advances also helped set the stage for exploration. The invention of movable type by Johannes Gutenberg around 1450 in Germany made printing easier and cheaper, stimulating the diffusion of information, including news of discoveries, among literate Europeans. By 1400, crucial navigational aids employed by maritime explorers were already available: compasses; hourglasses, useful in estimating speed; and the astrolabe and quadrant, devices for determining latitude. While many people knew about these and other advances, the Portuguese were the first to use them in a campaign to sail beyond the limits of the world known to Europeans.

A Century of Portuguese Exploration

Portugal devoted far more energy and wealth to the geographic exploration of the world between 1415 and 1460 than all the other countries of Europe combined. Facing the Atlantic on the Iberian Peninsula, the Portuguese lived on the fringes of the thriving Mediterranean trade. As a Christian kingdom, Portugal cooperated

MAP 2.1 ■ European Trade Routes and Portuguese Exploration in the Fifteenth Century
The strategic geographic position of Italian cities as a conduit for overland trade from Asia was slowly undermined during the fifteenth century by Portuguese explorers who hopscotched along the coast of Africa and eventually found a sea route that opened the rich trade of the East to Portuguese merchants.

c. 1000
– Norsemen found small village on the tip of Newfoundland.

c. 1100–1500
– Mediterranean trade routes dominate European trade with Asia, India, Africa, and the Middle East.

1347
– Bubonic plague epidemic known as the Black Death reaches Europe.

1415–1460
– Prince Henry the Navigator works to advance Portuguese trade and exploration.

1488
– Bartolomeu Dias rounds Cape of Good Hope.

1498
– Vasco da Gama sails to India.

Prince Henry the Navigator
▶ Portuguese prince who, between 1415 and 1460, collected information about sailing techniques and geography, sought new sources of trade for Portugal, and financed voyages of exploration. His efforts contributed to Portugal's creation of a commercial empire in Africa, India, Indonesia, and China in the early sixteenth century.

with Spain in the Reconquest, the centuries-long drive to expel Muslims from the Iberian Peninsula. The religious zeal that propelled the Reconquest also justified expansion into what the Portuguese considered heathen lands. A key victory came in 1415 when Portuguese forces conquered Ceuta, the Muslim bastion at the mouth of the Strait of Gibraltar that had blocked Portugal's access to the Atlantic coast of Africa.

The most influential advocate of Portuguese exploration was **Prince Henry the Navigator**, son of the Portuguese king (and great-uncle of Queen Isabella of Spain). From 1415 until his death in 1460, Henry collected the latest information about sailing techniques and geography, supported new crusades against Muslims, sought fresh sources of trade, and pushed explorers to go farther still.

Neither the Portuguese nor anybody else in Europe knew the immensity of Africa or the length or shape of its coastline. At first, Portuguese mariners cautiously hugged the west coast of Africa, seldom venturing beyond sight of land. By 1434, they had reached the northern edge of the Sahara Desert, where strong westerly currents swept them out to sea. They soon learned to ride those currents far away from the coast before catching favorable winds that turned them back toward land, a technique that allowed them to reach Cape Verde by 1444 (See Map 2.1, Page 33). To stow the supplies necessary for long periods at sea and to withstand the battering of waves in the open ocean, the Portuguese developed the caravel, a sturdy ship that became explorers' vessel of choice.

African resistance confined Portuguese expeditions to coastal trading posts, where they bartered successfully for gold, slaves, and ivory. Powerful African kingdoms welcomed Portuguese trading ships loaded with iron goods, weapons, textiles, and ornamental shells. Portuguese merchants learned that establishing relatively peaceful trading posts on the coast was far more profitable than attempting the violent conquest and colonization of inland regions. In the 1460s, the Portuguese used African slaves to develop sugar plantations on the Cape Verde Islands, inaugurating an association between enslaved Africans and plantation labor that would be transplanted to the New World.

About 1480, Portuguese explorers began a conscious search for a sea route to Asia. In 1488, Bartolomeu Dias sailed around the Cape of Good Hope at the southern tip of Africa and hurried back to Lisbon with the exciting news that it appeared to be possible to sail on to India and China. In 1498, after ten years of careful preparation, Vasco da Gama commanded the first Portuguese fleet to sail to India. Portugal quickly capitalized on the commercial potential of da Gama's new sea route. By the early sixteenth century, the Portuguese controlled a far-flung commercial empire in India, Indonesia, and China (collectively referred to as the East Indies). Their new sea route to the East eliminated overland travel and allowed Portuguese merchants to charge much lower prices for the Eastern goods they imported and still make handsome profits.

> **QUICK REVIEW**

Why did European exploration expand dramatically in the fifteenth century?

What did Spanish explorers discover in the western Atlantic?

IN RETROSPECT, the explorations of the African coast and the East Indies during the fifteenth century seemed to make the Portuguese ideally qualified to venture across the Atlantic. However, Portuguese and most other experts believed that sailing west across the Atlantic to Asia was literally impossible. The European discovery of America required someone bold enough to believe that the experts were wrong and that the risks could be overcome. That person was **Christopher Columbus**. His explorations inaugurated a geographic revolution that forever altered Europeans' understanding of the world and its peoples, including themselves. Columbus's landfall in the Caribbean originated a thriving exchange between the people, ideas, cultures, and institutions of the Old and New Worlds that continues to this day.

The Explorations of Columbus

Columbus went to sea when he was about fourteen, and he eventually made his way to Lisbon, where he married Felipa Moniz, whose father had been raised in the household of Prince Henry the Navigator. Through Felipa, Columbus gained access to explorers' maps and information about the tricky currents and winds encountered in sailing the Atlantic. Columbus himself ventured into the Atlantic frequently and sailed at least twice to the central coast of Africa.

Christopher Columbus

▶ Genoese sailor who, under Spanish auspices beginning in 1492, made a series of voyages across the Atlantic Ocean in search of a western route to Asia. His discovery of the Americas began the process of European expansion in the New World.

| What did Spanish explorers discover in the western Atlantic? | How did Spaniards explore, conquer, and colonize New Spain? | How did New Spain influence sixteenth-century Europe? | Conclusion: What promise did the New World offer Europeans? |

1492
- Christopher Columbus lands on Caribbean island that he names San Salvador.

1493
- Columbus makes second voyage to New World.

1494
- Portugal and Spain negotiate Treaty of Tordesillas.

1497
- John Cabot searches for Northwest Passage.

1513
- Vasco Núñez de Balboa crosses Isthmus of Panama.

1519
- Ferdinand Magellan sets out to sail around the world.

Like other educated Europeans, Columbus believed that the earth was a sphere and that theoretically it was possible to reach the East Indies by sailing west. With flawed calculations, he estimated that Asia was only about 2,500 miles away, a shorter distance than Portuguese ships routinely sailed between Lisbon and the Congo. In fact, the shortest distance to Japan from Europe's jumping-off point was nearly 11,000 miles. Convinced by his erroneous calculations, Columbus set out to prove he was right.

In 1492, after years of unsuccessful lobbying in Portugal and Spain, plus overtures to England and France, Columbus finally won financing for his journey from the Spanish monarchs, Isabella and Ferdinand. They saw Columbus's venture as an inexpensive gamble: The potential loss was small, but the potential gain was huge.

After scarcely three months of preparation, Columbus and his small fleet—the *Niña*, the *Pinta*, and the *Santa María*—headed west. Six weeks after leaving the Canary Islands, where he stopped for supplies, Columbus landed on a tiny Caribbean island about three hundred miles north of the eastern tip of Cuba.

Columbus claimed possession of the island for Isabella and Ferdinand and named it San Salvador, in honor of the Savior, Jesus Christ. He called the islanders "Indians," assuming that they inhabited the East Indies somewhere near Japan or China. The islanders called themselves Tainos, which in their language meant "good" or "noble." The Tainos inhabited most of the Caribbean islands Columbus visited on his first voyage. An agricultural people, the Tainos grew cassava, corn, cotton, tobacco, and other crops. Instead of dressing in the finery Columbus had expected to find in the East Indies, the Tainos "all . . . go around as naked as their mothers bore them," Columbus wrote. Although Columbus concluded that the Tainos "had no religion," in reality they worshipped gods they called *zemis*, ancestral spirits who inhabited natural objects such as trees and stones. The Tainos mined a little gold, but they had no riches. "It seemed to me that they were a people very poor in everything," Columbus wrote.

At first, Columbus got the impression that the Tainos believed the Spaniards came from heaven. But after six weeks of encounters, Columbus decided that "the people of these lands do not understand me nor do I, nor anyone else that I have with me, [understand] them. And many times I understand one thing said by these Indians . . . for another, its contrary." The confused communication between the Spaniards and the Tainos suggests how strange each group seemed to the other. Columbus's perceptions of the Tainos were shaped by European attitudes, ideas, and expectations, just as the Tainos' perceptions of the Europeans were no doubt colored by their own culture.

Columbus's First Voyage to the New World, 1492–1493

Taino Zemi Basket

Crafted sometime between 1492 and about 1520, this basket is an example of the effigies Tainos made to represent *zemis*, or deities. The basket maker used African ivory and European mirrors as well as Native American fibers, dyes, and designs. *Archivio Fotografico del Museo Preistorico Etnografico L. Pigorini, Roma.*

CHAPTER LOCATOR | What factors led to European exploration in the fifteenth century?

Columbus and his men understood that they had made a momentous discovery, but they found it frustrating. Although the Tainos proved friendly, they did not have the riches Columbus expected to find in the East. In mid-January 1493, he started back to Spain, where Queen Isabella and King Ferdinand were overjoyed by his news. With one voyage, Columbus appeared to have made Spain a serious challenger to Portugal in the race for a sea route to Asia. The Spanish monarchs elevated Columbus to the nobility and awarded him the title "Admiral of the Ocean Sea."

Soon after Columbus returned to Spain, the Spanish monarchs rushed to obtain the pope's support for their claim to the new lands in the West. When the pope, a Spaniard, complied, the Portuguese feared their own claims to recently discovered territories were in jeopardy. To protect their claims, the Portuguese and Spanish monarchs negotiated the Treaty of Tordesillas in 1494. The treaty drew an imaginary line eleven hundred miles west of the Canary Islands (**Map 2.2**). Land discovered

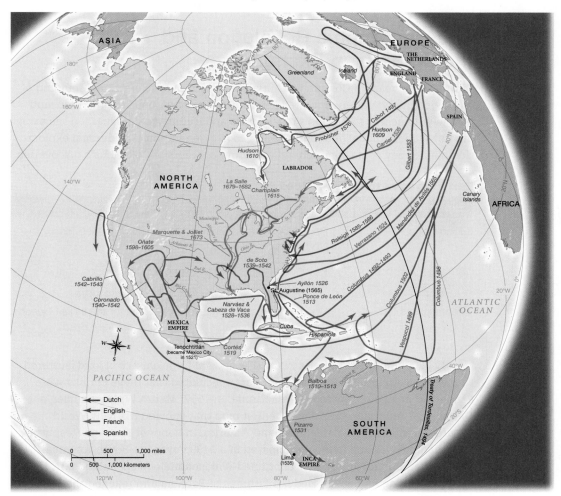

MAP 2.2 ■ European Exploration in Sixteenth-Century America
This map illustrates the approximate routes of early European explorations of the New World.

▶ FOR MORE HELP ANALYZING THIS MAP, see the map activity for this chapter in the Online Study Guide at bedfordstmartins.com/roarkunderstanding.

What did Spanish explorers discover in the western Atlantic?	How did Spaniards explore, conquer, and colonize New Spain?	How did New Spain influence sixteenth-century Europe?	Conclusion: What promise did the New World offer Europeans?

west of the line (namely, the islands that Columbus discovered and any additional land that might be located) belonged to Spain; Portugal claimed land to the east (namely, its African and East Indian trading empire).

Isabella and Ferdinand moved quickly to realize the promise of their new claims. In the fall of 1493, they dispatched Columbus once again, this time with a fleet of seventeen ships and more than a thousand men who planned to locate the Asian mainland, find gold, and get rich. Before Columbus died in 1506, he returned to the New World two more times (in 1498 and 1502) without relinquishing his belief that the East Indies were there, someplace. Other explorers continued to search for a passage to the East or some other source of profit without success. Nonetheless, Columbus's discoveries forced sixteenth-century Europeans to think about the world in new ways: It really was possible to sail from Europe to the western rim of the Atlantic and return to Europe. And, most important, across the Atlantic lay lands and peoples entirely unknown to Europeans.

The Geographic Revolution and the Columbian Exchange

Within thirty years of Columbus's initial discovery, Europeans' understanding of world geography underwent a revolution. An elite of perhaps twenty thousand people with access to Europe's royal courts and trading centers learned the exciting news about global geography. But it took a generation of additional exploration before they could comprehend the larger contours of Columbus's discoveries.

Early Voyages to the Americas

Explorer	Voyage
John Cabot	Reached Newfoundland in 1497 while searching for a Northwest Passage to Asia.
Amerigo Vespucci	Participated in a Spanish expedition that landed on the northern coast of South America in 1499.
Pedro Álvars Cabral	Commanded a Portuguese fleet bound for the Indian Ocean that accidentally made landfall on the coast of Brazil.

By 1500, European experts knew that several large chunks of land cluttered the western Atlantic. A few cartographers speculated that these chunks were connected in a landmass that was not Asia. In 1507, Martin Waldseemüller, a German cartographer, published the first map that showed the New World separate from Asia. He named the land America, in honor of Amerigo Vespucci, an Italian businessman who participated in a 1499 voyage to South America.

Two additional discoveries confirmed Waldseemüller's speculation. In 1513, Vasco Núñez de Balboa crossed the Isthmus of Panama and reached the Pacific Ocean. Clearly, more water lay between the New World and Asia. Ferdinand Magellan discovered how much water there was when he led an expedition to circumnavigate the globe in 1519. Sponsored by King Charles I of Spain, Magellan's voyage took him first to the New World, around the southern tip of South America, and into the Pacific late in November 1520. Crossing the Pacific took

CHAPTER LOCATOR | What factors led to European exploration in the fifteenth century?

38 CHAPTER 2
ENCOUNTERING THE NEW WORLD

almost four months, decimating his crew with hunger and thirst. Magellan himself was killed by Philippine tribesmen. A remnant of his expedition continued on to the Indian Ocean and managed to transport a cargo of spices back to Spain in 1522.

In most ways, Magellan's voyage was a disaster. One ship and 18 men crawled back from an expedition that had begun with five ships and more than 250 men. But the geographic information it provided left no doubt that America was a continent separated from Asia by the enormous Pacific Ocean. Magellan's voyage made clear that it was possible to sail west to reach the East Indies, but that route was a terrible way to go. After Magellan, most Europeans who sailed west set their sights on the New World, not on Asia.

Columbus's arrival in the Caribbean anchored the western end of what might be imagined as a sea bridge that spanned the Atlantic, connecting the Western Hemisphere to Europe. This new sea bridge launched the **Columbian exchange**, a transatlantic trade of goods, people, and ideas that has continued ever since.

Spaniards brought novelties to the New World that were commonplace in Europe, including Christianity, iron technology, sailing ships, firearms, wheeled vehicles, horses and other domesticated animals, and much else. Unknowingly, they also brought many Old World diseases that caused devastating epidemics of smallpox, measles, and other maladies that killed the vast majority of Indians during the sixteenth century and continued to decimate survivors in later centuries. European diseases made the Columbian exchange catastrophic for Native Americans. In the long term, these diseases were decisive in transforming the dominant peoples of the New World from descendants of Asians, who had inhabited the hemisphere for millennia, to descendants of Europeans and Africans, the recent arrivals from the Old World by way of the newly formed sea bridge.

Ancient American goods, people, and ideas made the return trip across the Atlantic. Europeans were introduced to New World foods such as corn and potatoes that became important staples in European diets, especially for poor people. Columbus's sailors became infected with syphilis in sexual encounters with New World women and unwittingly carried the deadly disease back to Europe. New World tobacco created a European fashion for smoking. But for almost a generation after 1492, this Columbian exchange did not reward the Spaniards with the riches they yearned to find.

Columbian exchange
▶ The transatlantic trade of goods, people, ideas, and diseases initiated by Columbus's arrival in the Caribbean. The Columbian exchange transformed both the Americas and Europe.

QUICK REVIEW

How did Columbus's landfall in the Caribbean help revolutionize Europeans' understanding of world geography?

What did Spanish explorers discover in the western Atlantic?

How did Spaniards explore, conquer, and colonize New Spain?

How did New Spain influence sixteenth-century Europe?

Conclusion: What promise did the New World offer Europeans?

How did Spaniards explore, conquer, and colonize New Spain?

Cortés Arrives in Tenochtitlán This portrayal of the arrival of Cortés and his army in the Mexican capital illustrates the Spaniards' military advantages of horses, armor, and Indian supporters. Bibliothèque Nationale de France.

Hernán Cortés

▶ Spanish conquistador who, along with his followers, conquered the Mexica in 1521. The conquest of the Mexican empire brought enormous wealth to Spain and prompted other would-be conquerors to explore the Americas.

Malinali

▶ Fourteen-year-old girl from the Yucatán peninsula who served as Cortés's interpreter during his 1519 march through Mexico. Malinali, whom the Spaniards called Marina, was given to Cortés by a local chief. Her fluency in a number of the region's languages proved indispensable to Cortés and his men.

DURING THE SIXTEENTH CENTURY, the New World helped Spain become the most powerful monarchy in both Europe and the Americas. Initially, Spanish expeditions reconnoitered the Caribbean, scouted stretches of the Atlantic coast, and established settlements on the large islands of Hispaniola, Puerto Rico, Jamaica, and Cuba. Spaniards enslaved Caribbean tribes and put them to work growing crops and mining gold. But the profits from these early ventures barely covered the costs of maintaining the settlers. After almost thirty years of exploration, the promise of Columbus's discovery seemed illusory.

In 1519, however, that promise was fulfilled, spectacularly, by Hernán Cortés's march into Mexico. By about 1545, Spanish conquests extended from northern Mexico to southern Chile, and New World riches filled Spanish treasure chests. Cortés's expedition served as the model for Spaniards' and other Europeans' expectations that the New World could yield bonanza profits for its conquerors.

The Conquest of Mexico

Hernán Cortés, an obscure nineteen-year-old Spaniard, arrived in the New World in 1504. He fought in the conquest of Cuba and elsewhere in the Caribbean. In 1519, the governor of Cuba authorized Cortés to organize an expedition of about six hundred men and eleven ships to investigate rumors of a wealthy kingdom somewhere in the interior of the mainland.

Landing first on the Yucatán peninsula, Cortés had the good fortune to receive from a local chief the gift of a fourteen-year-old girl named **Malinali**, who spoke several native languages, including Mayan and Nahuatl, the language of the

Cortés's Invasion of Tenochtitlán, 1519–1521

0 25 50 mi.
0 25 50 km.

Gulf of Mexico

Texcoco • Otumba • Zautla • Jalapa
• Veracruz
Tlaxcala • Cholula
Tenochtitlán

⟶ Cortés's original route, 1519
⟶ Cortés's retreat, 1520
⟶ Cortés's return route, 1520–1521

Mexica, the most powerful people in what is now Mexico and Central America (see chapter 1). Malinali, whom the Spaniards called Marina, soon learned Spanish and became Cortés's interpreter. "Without her help," wrote one of the Spaniards who accompanied Cortés, "we would not have understood the language of New Spain and Mexico." With her help, Cortés talked and fought with Indians along the Gulf coast of Mexico, trying to discover the location of the fabled kingdom.

In Tenochtitlán, the capital of the **Mexican empire**, the emperor **Montezuma** heard about some strange creatures sighted along the coast. (Montezuma and his people are often called Aztecs, but they called themselves Mexica.) Montezuma sent representatives to bring the strangers large quantities of food and perhaps postpone their dreaded arrival in the capital. Before the Mexican messengers served food to the Spaniards, they sacrificed several hostages and soaked the food in their blood. This fare disgusted the Spaniards and might have been enough to turn them back to Cuba. But along with the food, the Mexica also brought the Spaniards another gift, a "disk in the shape of a sun, as big as a cartwheel and made of very fine gold," as one of the Mexica recalled.

In August 1519, Cortés marched inland to find Montezuma. Leading about 350 men armed with swords, lances, and muskets and supported by ten cannons, four smaller guns, and sixteen horses, Cortés had to live off the land, establishing peaceful relations with indigenous tribes when he could and killing them when he thought necessary. On November 8, 1519, Cortés reached Tenochtitlán. Montezuma came out to welcome the Spaniards. After presenting Cortés with gifts, Montezuma ushered the Spaniards to the royal palace. Quickly, Cortés took Montezuma hostage and held him under house arrest, hoping to make him a puppet through whom the Spaniards could rule the Mexican empire. This uneasy peace existed for several months until one of Cortés's men led a massacre of many Mexican nobles, causing the people of Tenochtitlán to revolt. They murdered Montezuma, who seemed to them a Spanish puppet, and they mounted a ferocious assault on the Spaniards. On June 30, 1520, Cortés and about a hundred other Spaniards fought their way out of Tenochtitlán and retreated about one hundred miles to Tlaxcala, a stronghold of bitter enemies of the Mexica. The Tlaxcalans allowed Cortés to regroup, obtain reinforcements, and plan a strategy to conquer Tenochtitlán.

In the spring of 1521, Cortés and tens of thousands of Indian allies laid siege to the Mexican capital. With a relentless, scorched-earth strategy, Cortés finally defeated the last Mexican defenders on August 13, 1521. The great capital of the Mexican empire "looked as if it had been ploughed up," one of Cortés's soldiers remembered.

The Search for Other Mexicos

Conquistadors quickly fanned out from Tenochtitlán in search of other sources of treasure. The most spectacular prize fell to Francisco Pizarro, who conquered the **Incan empire** in Peru. The Incas controlled a vast, complex region that contained more than nine million people and stretched along the western coast of South America for more than two thousand miles. In 1532, Pizarro and his army of

Mexican empire
▶ An empire, ruled by the Mexica, stretching from coast to coast in what is now Mexico and Central America. Often called Aztecs, the Mexica were the most powerful people in that area. With the help of Tlaxcala Indian allies, the Spanish, led by conquistador Hernán Cortés, conquered the Mexican empire in 1521.

Montezuma
▶ Emperor of the Mexican empire at the time of Cortés's 1519 expedition. Montezuma saw the Europeans as a potential threat, but in November 1519, he allowed Cortés and his men to enter Tenochtitlán and invited them into his palace. Presented with this opportunity, Cortés took Montezuma hostage, beginning a chain of events that ended with Spanish conquest of the Mexican empire.

conquistadors
▶ Soldiers who led Spain's initial efforts to conquer and control the wealth of the Americas. In addition to defeating native peoples in battle, conquistadors played a key role in extracting labor from indigenous populations.

Incan empire
▶ Vast empire of more than nine million people that stretched along the western coast of South America. Along with the Mexican empire, the Inca empire provided the gold and silver that contributed to Spain's preeminence in the sixteenth century.

| What did Spanish explorers discover in the western Atlantic? | **How did Spaniards explore, conquer, and colonize New Spain?** | How did New Spain influence sixteenth-century Europe? | Conclusion: What promise did the New World offer Europeans? |

1519
- Hernán Cortés leads expedition to find wealth in Mexico.

1520
- Mexica in Tenochtitlán revolt against Spaniards.

1521
- Cortés conquers Mexica at Tenochtitlán.

1532
- Francisco Pizarro begins conquest of Peru.

1539
- Hernando de Soto begins exploring southeastern North America.

1540
- Francisco Vásquez de Coronado starts to explore Southwest and Great Plains.

1542
- Juan Rodríguez Cabrillo explores California coast.

1549
- Repartimiento reforms begin to replace encomienda.

c. 1560
- Major centers of Indian civilization are conquered and colonized by the Spaniards.

1565
- St. Augustine, Florida, is settled.

1598
- Juan de Oñate explores New Mexico.

1599
- Pueblos revolt against Oñate.

fewer than two hundred men captured the Incan emperor Atahualpa and held him hostage. As ransom, the Incas gave Pizarro gold and silver equivalent to half a century's worth of precious-metal production in Europe. With the ransom safely in their hands, the Spaniards executed Atahualpa.

Other would-be conquistadors came up empty-handed. Juan Ponce de León had sailed along the Florida coast in 1513. Encouraged by Cortés's success, he went back to Florida in 1521 to find riches, only to be killed in a battle with Calusa Indians. A few years later, Lucas Vázquez de Ayllón explored the Atlantic coast north of Florida to present-day South Carolina. In 1526, he established a small settlement on the Georgia coast that he named San Miguel de Gualdape, the first Spanish attempt to establish a foothold in what is now the United States. This settlement was soon swept away by sickness and hostile Indians. Pánfilo de Narváez surveyed the Gulf coast from Florida to Texas in 1528. The Narváez expedition ended disastrously with a shipwreck on the Texas coast near present-day Galveston.

In 1539, Hernando de Soto, who had taken part in the conquest of Peru, set out with nine ships and more than six hundred men to find another Peru in North America. Landing in Florida, de Soto spent three years searching for the rich civilizations he believed were there. After the brutal slaughter of many Native Americans and much hardship, de Soto died in 1542, and his men turned back to Mexico, disappointed.

Tales of the fabulous wealth of the mythical Seven Cities of Cíbola lured Francisco Vásquez de Coronado to search the Southwest and Great Plains of North America. In 1540, Coronado left northern Mexico with more than three hundred Spaniards, a thousand Indians, and a priest who claimed to know the way to what he called "the greatest and best of the discoveries." Cíbola turned out to be a small Zuñi pueblo of about a hundred families. When the Zuñi shot arrows at the Spaniards, Coronado attacked the pueblo and routed the defenders after a hard battle. Convinced that the rich cities must lie somewhere over the horizon, Coronado kept moving all the way to central Kansas before deciding in 1542 to abandon his search.

Juan Rodríguez Cabrillo led a maritime expedition in 1542 that sailed along the coast of California. Cabrillo died on Santa Catalina Island, offshore from present-day Los Angeles, but his men sailed on to Oregon, where a ferocious storm forced them to turn back toward Mexico.

These probes into North America by de Soto, Coronado, and Cabrillo persuaded other Spaniards that although enormous territories stretched northward, their inhabitants had little to loot or exploit. After a generation of vigorous exploration, the Spaniards concluded that there was only one Mexico and one Peru.

New Spain in the Sixteenth Century

For all practical purposes, Spain was the dominant European power in the Western Hemisphere during the sixteenth century (**Map 2.3**). Portugal claimed the giant territory of Brazil under the Tordesillas treaty but was far more concerned with exploiting its hard-won trade with the East Indies than in colonizing the New World. England and France were absorbed by domestic and diplomatic concerns in Europe and largely lost interest in America until late in the century. In the decades after 1519, the Spaniards created the distinctive colonial society of New Spain, which showed other Europeans how the New World could be made to serve the purposes of the Old.

CHAPTER LOCATOR | What factors led to European exploration in the fifteenth century?

42 CHAPTER 2 ENCOUNTERING THE NEW WORLD

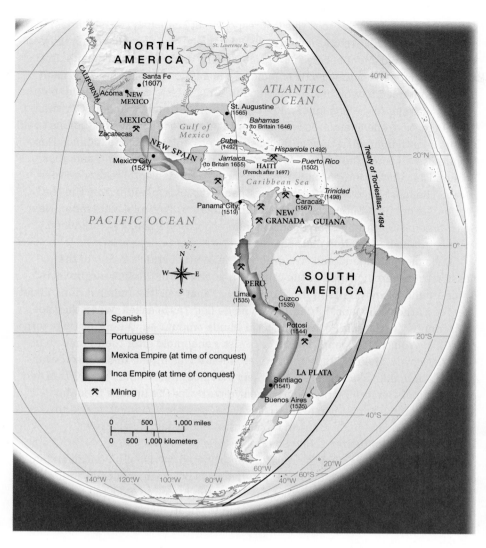

MAP 2.3 ■ Sixteenth-Century European Colonies in the New World
Spanish control spread throughout Central and South America during the sixteenth century, with the important exception of Portuguese Brazil. North America, though claimed by Spain under the Treaty of Tordesillas, remained peripheral to Spain's New World empire.

The Spanish monarchy claimed ownership of most of the land in the Western Hemisphere and gave the conquistadors permission to explore and plunder. The crown took one-fifth of any loot confiscated and allowed the conquistadors to divide the rest. In the end, most conquistadors received very little after the plunder was divided among leaders such as Cortés and his favorite officers. To compensate his disappointed soldiers, Cortés gave them towns the Spaniards had subdued.

The distribution of conquered towns institutionalized the system of *encomienda*, which empowered the conquistadors to rule the Indians and the lands in and around their towns. Encomienda transferred to the Spanish *encomendero* (the man who "owned" the town) the tribute that the town had previously paid to the Mexican empire. In theory, encomienda involved a reciprocal relationship between the encomendero and "his" Indians. In return for the tribute and labor of the Indians, the encomendero was supposed to be responsible for their material well-being, to guarantee order and justice in the town, and to encourage the Indians to convert to Christianity.

encomienda

▶ The system in which conquered towns were distributed to conquistadors who were empowered to rule the Indians and surrounding lands. *Encomenderos*, conquistadors who had been granted towns, subjected the Indians under their control to chronic overwork, mistreatment, and abuse.

What did Spanish explorers discover in the western Atlantic?

How did Spaniards explore, conquer, and colonize New Spain?

How did New Spain influence sixteenth-century Europe?

Conclusion: What promise did the New World offer Europeans?

Catholic missionaries took this last responsibility seriously. Missionaries believed that God expected them to save the Indians' souls by convincing them to abandon their old sinful beliefs and to embrace the one true Christian faith. But after baptizing tens of thousands of Indians, the missionaries learned that many Indians continued to worship their own gods. Most priests came to believe that the Indians were lesser beings inherently incapable of fully understanding Christianity.

In practice, encomenderos were far more interested in what the Indians could do for them than in what they or the missionaries could do for the Indians. Encomenderos subjected the Indians to chronic overwork, mistreatment, and abuse. Economically, however, encomienda recognized a fundamental reality of New Spain: The most important treasure the Spaniards could plunder from the New World was not gold but uncompensated Indian labor. To exploit that labor, New Spain's richest natural resource, encomenderos forced Indians to work when, where, and how Spaniards pleased.

Encomienda engendered two groups of influential critics. A few of the missionaries were horrified at the brutal mistreatment of the Indians, believing it undermined their efforts to make converts. "What will [the Indians] think about the God of the Christians," Friar Bartolomé de Las Casas asked, when they see their friends "with their heads split, their hands amputated, their intestines torn open? . . . Would they want to come to Christ's sheepfold after their homes had been destroyed, their children imprisoned, their wives raped, their cities devastated, their maidens deflowered, and their provinces laid waste?" Las Casas and other outspoken missionaries won some sympathy for the Indians from the Spanish monarchy and royal bureaucracy. The Spanish monarchy moved to abolish encomienda in an effort to replace the conquistadors with royal bureaucrats as the rulers of New Spain.

In 1549, a reform called the *repartimiento* limited the labor an encomendero could command from his Indians to forty-five days per year from each adult male. The repartimiento, however, did not challenge the principle of forced labor, nor did it prevent encomenderos from continuing to cheat, mistreat, and overwork their Indians. Slowly, repartimiento replaced encomienda as the basic system of exploiting Indian labor.

The practice of coerced labor in New Spain grew directly out of the Spaniards' assumption that they were superior to the Indians. As one missionary put it, the Indians "are incapable of learning. . . . [They] are more stupid than asses and refuse to improve in anything." Therefore, most Spaniards assumed, Indians' labor should be organized by and for their conquerors. Spaniards seldom hesitated to use violence to punish and intimidate recalcitrant Indians.

From the viewpoint of Spain, the single most important economic activity in New Spain after 1540 was silver mining. Spain imported more New World gold than silver in the early decades of the century, but that changed with the discovery of major silver deposits at Potosí, Bolivia, in 1545 and at Zacatecas, Mexico, in 1546 (**Figure 2.1**). The mines required large capital investments and many miners. Typically, a few Spaniards supervised large groups of Indian miners, who were supplemented by African slaves later in the sixteenth century.

For Spaniards, life in New Spain after the conquests was relatively easy. Encomienda gave them a comfortable, leisurely life that was the envy of many Spaniards back in Europe. As one colonist wrote to his brother in Spain, "Don't hesitate [to come]. . . . This land [New Spain] is as good as ours [in Spain], for God has given us more here than there, and we shall be better off."

CHAPTER LOCATOR | What factors led to European exploration in the fifteenth century?

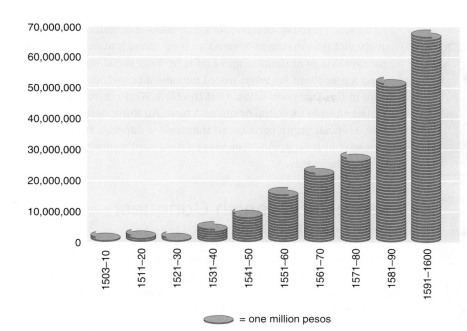

FIGURE 2.1 ■ **New World Gold and Silver Imported into Spain during the Sixteenth Century, in Pesos**
Spain imported more gold than silver during the first three decades of the sixteenth century, but the total value of this treasure was quickly eclipsed during the 1530s and 1540s, when rich silver mines were developed. Silver accounted for most of Spain's precious-metal imports from the New World.

= one million pesos

During the century after 1492, about 225,000 Spaniards settled in the colonies. Virtually all of them were poor young men who came directly from Spain. Laborers and artisans made up the largest proportion, but soldiers and sailors were also numerous. Throughout the sixteenth century, men vastly outnumbered women, although the proportion of women grew from about one in twenty before 1519 to nearly one in three by the 1580s.

The gender and number of Spanish settlers shaped two fundamental features of the society of New Spain. First, Europeans never made up more than 1 or 2 percent of the total population. Although Spaniards ruled New Spain, the population was almost wholly Indian. Second, the shortage of Spanish women meant that Spanish men frequently married Indian women or used them as concubines. For the most part, the relatively few women from Spain married Spanish men, contributing to a tiny elite defined by European origins.

Social and Racial Hierarchy in New Spain

Peninsulares	People born on the Iberian Peninsula. Peninsulares enjoyed the highest social status in New Spain.
Creoles	The children born in the New World to Spanish men and women. Creoles were below peninsulares but still considered part of the white elite. Together, peninsulares and creoles made up between 1 and 2 percent of the population of New Spain.
Mestizos	The offspring of Spanish men and Indian women, who accounted for 4 or 5 percent of the population. A few mestizos rose into the ranks of the elite, especially if their Indian ancestry was not obvious from their skin color.
Indians	The largest group in New Spain, who made up the bottom of the social pyramid. Indians comprised more than 90 percent of the population of New Spain.

Español con India,
Mestizo.

Mestizo con Española
Castizo.

Castizo con Española
Español.

Español con Mora
Mulato.

5

6

Mulato con Española
Morisco.

Morisco con Española
Chino.

7

Chino con India
Salta atras.

Salta atras con Mulata
Lobo.

Mixed Races

These eighteenth-century paintings illustrate forms of racial mixture common in sixteenth-century New Spain. In the first painting, a Spanish man and an Indian woman have a mestizo son; in the fourth, a Spanish man and a woman of African descent have a mulatto son; in the fifth, a Spanish woman and a mulatto man have a *morisco* daughter. Bob Schalkwijk/INAH.

▶ FOR MORE HELP ANALYZING THIS IMAGE, see the visual activity for this chapter in the Online Study Guide at bedfordstmartins.com/roarkunderstanding.

The small number of Spaniards, the masses of Indians, and the frequency of intermarriage created a steep social hierarchy defined by perceptions of national origin and race. This social arrangement created a precedent for what would become a pronounced pattern in the European colonies of the New World: a society stratified sharply by social origin and race. All Europeans of whatever social origin considered themselves superior to Native Americans; in New Spain, they were a dominant minority in both power and status.

The Toll of Spanish Conquest and Colonization

By 1560, the major centers of Indian civilization had been conquered, their leaders overthrown, their religion held in contempt, and their people forced to work for the Spaniards. Profound demoralization pervaded Indian society. As a Mexican poet wrote:

> Nothing but flowers and songs of sorrow are left in Mexico . . . where once we saw warriors and wise men. . . .
> We are crushed to the ground; we lie in ruins.
> There is nothing but grief and suffering in Mexico.

Adding to the culture shock of conquest and colonization was the deadly toll of European diseases. As conquest spread, Indians succumbed to epidemics of measles, smallpox, and respiratory illnesses. They had no immunity to these diseases because they had not been exposed to them before the arrival of Europeans. The isolation of the Western Hemisphere before 1492 had protected ancient Americans from the contagious diseases that had raged throughout Eurasia for millennia. The new post-1492 sea bridge eliminated that isolation, and by 1570, the Indian population of New Spain had fallen about 90 percent from what it was when Columbus arrived. The destruction of the Indians was a catastrophe unequaled in human history. A Mayan Indian recalled that when sickness struck his village, "great was the stench of the dead. . . . The dogs and vultures devoured the bodies. The mortality was terrible." For most Indians, New Spain was a graveyard.

For Spaniards, Indian deaths meant that the most valuable resource of New Spain—Indian labor—dwindled rapidly. By the last quarter of the sixteenth century, Spanish colonists felt the pinch of a labor shortage. To help supply laborers, the colonists began to import African slaves. In the years before 1550, while Indian labor was still adequate, only 15,000 slaves were imported from Africa. Even after Indian labor began to decline, the relatively high cost of African slaves kept imports low, totaling approximately 36,000 from 1550 to the end of the century. During the sixteenth century, New Spain continued to rely primarily on a shrinking number of Indians.

Spanish Outposts in Florida and New Mexico

After the explorations of de Soto, Coronado, and Cabrillo, officials in New Spain lost interest in North America. The monarchy claimed that Spain owned North America and insisted that a few North American settlements be established to give some tangible reality to its claims. Settlements in Florida also served to protect Spanish ships from pirates and privateers who hoped to prey on the Spanish treasure fleet sailing toward Spain.

In 1565, the Spanish king sent Pedro Menéndez de Avilés to create settlements along the Atlantic coast of North America. In early September, Menéndez founded St. Augustine in Florida, the first permanent European settlement within what became the United States. By 1600, St. Augustine had a population of about five hundred, the only remaining Spanish beachhead on the vast Atlantic shoreline of North America.

More than sixteen hundred miles west of St. Augustine, the Spaniards founded another outpost in 1598. Juan de Oñate led an expedition of about five hundred people to settle northern Mexico, now called New Mexico, and to claim the booty rumored to exist there. After a two-month journey from Mexico, Oñate and his companions reached pueblos near present-day Albuquerque and Santa Fe. From there, Oñate sent out scouting parties to find the legendary treasures of the region and to locate the ocean, which he believed must be nearby. Meanwhile, many of his soldiers planned to mutiny, and relations with the Indians deteriorated. When Indians in the Acoma pueblo revolted against the Spaniards, Oñate ruthlessly suppressed the uprising, killing eight hundred men, women, and children. Although Oñate's response to the Acoma pueblo revolt reconfirmed the Spaniards' military superiority, he did not bring peace or stability to the region. After another pueblo revolt occurred in 1599, many of Oñate's settlers returned to Mexico, leaving New Mexico as a small, dusty assertion of Spanish claims to the North American Southwest.

QUICK REVIEW <

Why did New Spain develop a society
highly stratified by race and national origin?

| What did Spanish explorers discover in the western Atlantic? | **How did Spaniards explore, conquer, and colonize New Spain?** | How did New Spain influence sixteenth-century Europe? | Conclusion: What promise did the New World offer Europeans? |

47

How did New Spain influence sixteenth-century Europe?

► FOR MORE HELP ANALYZING THIS IMAGE, see the visual activity for this chapter in the Online Study Guide at bedfordstmartins.com/roarkunderstanding.

Algonquian Ceremonial Dance

When the English artist John White visited the coast of present-day North Carolina in 1585 as part of Raleigh's expedition, he painted this watercolor portrait of an Algonquian ceremonial dance. This and White's other portraits are the only surviving likenesses of sixteenth-century North American Indians that were drawn from direct observation in the New World. The British Museum, London, UK/The Bridgeman Art Library.

THE RICHES OF NEW SPAIN helped make the sixteenth century the Golden Age of Spain. After the deaths of Queen Isabella and King Ferdinand, their sixteen-year-old grandson became King Charles I of Spain in 1516. Three years later, just as Cortés ventured into Mexico, Charles I was selected as Holy Roman Emperor Charles V. His empire encompassed more territory than that of any other European monarch. He used the wealth of New Spain to protect this empire and to promote his interests in the fierce dynastic battles of sixteenth-century Europe. He also sought to defend orthodox Christianity from the insurgent heresy of the Protestant Reformation. In short, the Spanish monarchy used New World wealth to bankroll Old World ambitions.

The Protestant Reformation and the European Order

In 1517, Martin Luther, an obscure Catholic priest in central Germany, initiated the **Protestant Reformation** by publicizing his criticisms of the Catholic Church. Luther's ideas won the sympathy of many Catholics, but they were considered

Protestant Reformation
► Multifaceted religious movement launched by the Catholic priest Martin Luther that divided Europe in the sixteenth century. The end of the Catholic Church's monopoly on European religious authority had long-lasting religious, cultural, and political consequences.

CHAPTER LOCATOR | What factors led to European exploration in the fifteenth century?

extremely dangerous by church officials and monarchs such as Charles V who believed that, just as the church spoke for God, they ruled for God.

Luther preached a doctrine known as "justification by faith": Individual Christians could obtain salvation and life everlasting only by having faith that God would save them. Giving offerings to the church, following the orders of priests, or participating in church rituals would not put believers one step closer to heaven. Also, the only true source of information about God's will was the Bible, not the church. By reading the Bible, any Christian could learn as much about God's commandments as any priest. Indeed, Luther called for a "priesthood of all believers."

In effect, Luther charged that the Catholic Church was in many respects fraudulent. He insisted that priests were unnecessary for salvation and that they encouraged Christians to violate God's will by promoting religious practices not specifically commanded by the Bible. The church, Luther declared, had neglected its true purpose of helping individual Christians understand the spiritual realm revealed in the Bible and had wasted its resources in worldly conflicts of politics and wars. Luther hoped his ideas would reform the Catholic Church, but instead they ruptured forever the unity of Christianity in western Europe.

Charles V pledged to exterminate Luther's Protestant heresies. The wealth pouring into Spain from the New World fueled his efforts to defend orthodox Catholic faith against Protestants, as well as against Muslims in eastern Europe and against any nation that contested Spain's supremacy. As the wealthiest and most powerful monarch in Europe, Charles V, followed by his son and successor Philip II, assumed responsibility for upholding the existing order of sixteenth-century Europe.

New World Treasure and Spanish Ambitions

Both Charles V and Philip II fought wars throughout the world during the sixteenth century. Mexican silver funneled through the royal treasury and was dissipated in military adventures that served the goals of the monarchy but did little to benefit most Spaniards. Moreover, Charles V's and Philip II's expenses for constant warfare far outstripped the revenues arriving from New Spain. To help meet military expenditures, both kings raised taxes in Spain more than fivefold during the sixteenth century. When taxes failed to produce enough revenue to fight its wars, the monarchy borrowed heavily from European bankers. By the end of the sixteenth century, interest payments on royal debts swallowed two-thirds of the crown's annual revenues. In retrospect, the riches from New Spain proved a short-term blessing but a long-term curse.

Sixteenth-century Spaniards did not see it that way. As they looked at their accomplishments in the New World, they saw unmistakable signs of progress. They had added enormously to their knowledge and wealth. They had built mines, cities, Catholic churches, and even universities on the other side of the Atlantic. Their military, religious, and economic achievements gave them great pride and confidence.

Europe and the Spanish Example

The lessons of sixteenth-century Spain were not lost on Spain's European rivals. Spain proudly displayed the fruits of its New World conquests. In 1520, for example, the German artist Albrecht Dürer wrote in his diary that he "marveled over the

| What did Spanish explorers discover in the western Atlantic? | How did Spaniards explore, conquer, and colonize New Spain? | **How did New Spain influence sixteenth-century Europe?** | Conclusion: What promise did the New World offer Europeans? |

49

subtle ingenuity of the men in these distant lands" who created such "things . . . [as] a sun entirely of gold, a whole fathom [six feet] broad." But the most exciting news about "the men in these distant lands" was that they could serve the interests of Europeans, as Spain had shown. With a few notable exceptions, Europeans saw the New World as a place for the expansion of European influence, a place where, as one Spaniard wrote, Europeans could "give to those strange lands the form of our own."

France and England tried to follow Spain's example. Both nations warred with Spain in Europe, preyed on Spanish treasure fleets, and ventured to the New World, where they too hoped to find an undiscovered passageway to the East Indies or another Mexico or Peru.

In 1524, France sent Giovanni da Verrazano to scout the Atlantic coast of North America from North Carolina to Canada, looking for a Northwest Passage (see Map 2.2, page 37). Eleven years later, France probed farther north with Jacques Cartier's voyage up the St. Lawrence River. Encouraged, Cartier returned to the region with a group of settlers in 1541, but the colony they established— like the search for a Northwest Passage—came to nothing.

English attempts to follow Spain's lead were slower but equally ill-fated. Not until 1576, almost eighty years after John Cabot's voyages, did the English try again to find a Northwest Passage. This time Martin Frobisher sailed into the waters of northern Canada (see Map 2.2, page 37). His sponsor was the Cathay Company, which hoped to open trade with China. Like many other explorers, Frobisher was mesmerized by the Spanish example and was sure he had found gold. But the tons of "ore" he hauled back to England proved worthless, the Cathay Company collapsed, and English interests shifted southward to the giant region on the northern margins of New Spain.

English explorers' attempts to establish North American settlements were no more fruitful than was their search for a northern route to China. Sir Humphrey Gilbert led expeditions in 1578 and 1583 that made feeble efforts to found colonies in Newfoundland until Gilbert vanished at sea. Sir Walter Raleigh organized an expedition in 1585 to settle Roanoke Island off the coast of present-day North Carolina. The first group of explorers left no colonists on the island, but two years later, Raleigh sent a contingent of more than one hundred settlers to Roanoke under John White's leadership. White went back to England for supplies, and when he returned to Roanoke in 1590, the colonists had disappeared, leaving only the word *Croatoan* (whose meaning is unknown) carved in a tree. The Roanoke colonists most likely died from a combination of natural causes and unfriendly Indians. By the end of the century, England had failed to secure a New World beachhead.

Roanoke Settlement, 1585–1590

How did Spain's conquests in the New World
shape Spain's position in Europe?

CHAPTER LOCATOR | What factors led to European
exploration in the fifteenth
century?

Private Collection/Picture Research Consultants & Archives.

Conclusion: What promise did the New World offer Europeans?

THE SIXTEENTH CENTURY in the New World belonged to the Spaniards who employed Columbus and to the Indians who greeted him as he stepped ashore. Isabella of Spain helped initiate the Columbian exchange between the New World and the Old that massively benefited first Spain and later other Europeans and that continues to this day. The exchange also subjected Native Americans to the ravages of European diseases and Spanish conquest. The exchange illustrated one of the most important lessons of the sixteenth century: After millions of years, the Atlantic no longer was an impassable barrier separating the Eastern and Western Hemispheres.

Spain remained a New World power for almost four centuries, and its language, religion, culture, and institutions left a permanent imprint. By the end of the sixteenth century, however, other European monarchies began to contest Spain's dominion in Europe and to make forays into the northern fringes of Spain's New World preserve. To reap the benefits the Spaniards enjoyed from their New World domain, the others had to learn a difficult lesson: how to deviate from Spain's example. That discovery lay ahead.

SO NOW YOU KNOW

The conquest and colonization of the New World made Spain the most powerful nation in sixteenth-century Europe. Columbus's voyages and Spanish efforts of exploration and aggressive colonization funneled the vast wealth of the Mexican and Incan empires to Spain, making it *the* nation that other Europeans competed with and sought somehow to emulate.

What did Spanish explorers discover in the western Atlantic?

How did Spaniards explore, conquer, and colonize New Spain?

How did New Spain influence sixteenth-century Europe?

Conclusion: What promise did the New World offer Europeans?

STEP 1

GETTING STARTED

Below are basic terms from this period in American history. Can you identify each term below and explain why it matters? To do this exercise online or to download this chart, visit bedfordstmartins.com/roarkunderstanding.

TERM	WHO OR WHAT & WHEN	WHY IT MATTERS
Prince Henry the Navigator, p. 34		
Christopher Columbus, p. 35		
Columbian exchange, p. 39		
Hernán Cortés, p. 40		
Malinali, p. 40		
Mexican empire, p. 41		
Montezuma, p. 41		
conquistadors, p. 41		
Incan empire, p. 41		
encomienda, p. 43		
Protestant Reformation, p. 48		

STEP 2

MOVING BEYOND THE BASICS

The exercise below represents a more advanced understanding of the chapter material. In this exercise, you will reflect on the nature and impact of exploration and conquest in the Age of Exploration. What were the motives behind expansion across the Atlantic? Why did monarchs support overseas expeditions? Why did men like Columbus undertake such dangerous journeys? Identify key conquests and discoveries for each nation. Finally, describe the impact of exploration and colonization in the Americas both in the New World and in Europe. To do this exercise online or to download this chart, visit bedfordstmartins.com/roarkunderstanding.

EXPLORATION, 1492–1600	Motives for exploration and settlement	Conquests and discoveries	Impact in New World	Impact in Europe
Portugal				
Spain				
France				
England				

STEP

3

PUTTING IT ALL TOGETHER

Now that you have reviewed key elements of the chapter, take a step back and try to explain the big picture. Remember to use specific examples from the chapter in your answers. To do this exercise online, visit bedfordstmartins.com/roarkunderstanding.

EXPANSION AND EXPLORATION

▶ Why was Portuguese maritime exploration focused on the west coast of Africa? What did Portugal hope to gain from such journeys?

▶ What was the Columbian exchange, and what were its consequences for both the peoples of the Americas and those from the Old World?

CONQUEST AND COLONIZATION

▶ Describe the government and society of New Spain. How did New Spain reflect the values, beliefs, and goals of the Spanish conquerors?

▶ How did Spanish conquest and colonization affect the peoples of the Americas?

THE IMPACT OF DISCOVERY IN EUROPE

▶ What role did New World wealth play in the clash between Protestants and Catholics in sixteenth-century Europe?

▶ What lessons did other European powers draw from Spain's experience in the New World?

LOOKING BACKWARD, LOOKING AHEAD

▶ How did the isolation of the peoples of the Americas before 1492 affect the course and consequences of European expansion in the New World?

▶ How did Spanish success in the New World influence European competition for control of the Americas?

IN YOUR OWN WORDS

Imagine that you must explain chapter 2 to someone who hasn't read it. What would be the most important points to include and why?

King Powhatan commands C. Smith to be slain
daughter Pokahontas beggs his life his thankful
d by Iames Rever   and how he subiected 30 of their kings. reade t

3

FOUNDING THE SOUTHERN COLONIES

1601–1700

> This chapter examines the growth of England's southern mainland colonies in the seventeenth century, as well as the small Spanish borderland outposts in Florida and New Mexico. It explores the early years of the Virginia colony, the rise of tobacco culture in the Chesapeake, its impact on the region's social and political environment, tensions in the Spanish borderland, and the transition to African slaves as a major labor force.

DID YOU KNOW?

Tobacco made Virginia a successful colony.

> What challenges faced early Chesapeake colonists?

> How did a tobacco society take shape?

> How and why did Chesapeake society change in the late seventeenth century?

> What caused tensions in the Spanish borderland?

> When and why did the southern colonies move toward a slave labor system?

> Conclusion: Why were export crops and slave labor important in the growth of the southern colonies?

**Scene from Captain John Smith, *A General Historie of Virginia,* in which Pocohontas "saves" Smith's life, 1624.

What challenges faced early Chesapeake colonists?

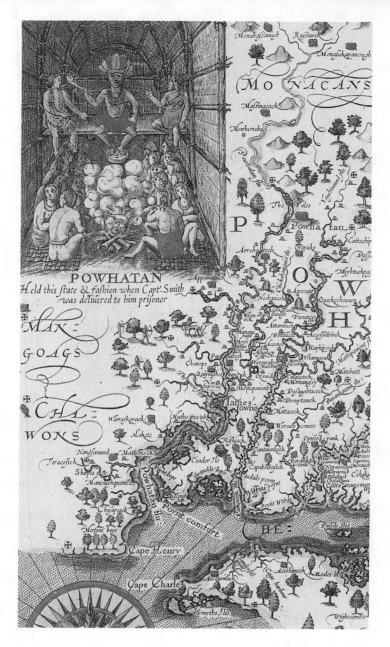

In 1612, John Smith published a detailed map that showed not only geographic features of early Virginia but also the limits of exploration (indicated by small crosses), the locations of the houses of the Indian "kings" (indicated by red boxes), and "ordinary houses" of indigenous people (indicated by dots). The map shows the early settlers' intense interest in knowing where the Indians were—and were not. Notice the location of Jamestown (upriver from Point Comfort) and of Powhatan's residence at the falls (just to the right of the large P outside the hut on the upper left side). Princeton University Libraries, Department of Rare Books and Special Collections.

WHEN JAMES I became king of England in 1603, he eyed North America as a possible location for English colonies that could be as profitable as the Spanish colonies. Although Spain claimed all of North America under the 1494 Treaty of Tordesillas (see chapter 2), King James believed that England could encroach on the outskirts of Spain's New World empire.

In 1606, London investors organized the Virginia Company, a joint-stock company. English merchants had pooled their capital and shared risks for many years by using joint-stock companies for trading voyages to Europe, Asia, and Africa. The Virginia Company, however, had larger ambitions: to establish a colony in North America that might somehow benefit England as Spain's New World empire had

CHAPTER LOCATOR | What challenges faced
early Chesapeake
colonists?

rewarded Spain. King James granted the company more than six million acres in North America. In effect, the king's land grant was a royal license to poach on both Spanish claims and Native Americans' possessions.

The Virginia Company investors hoped to found an empire that would strengthen England both overseas and at home. Richard Hakluyt, a strong proponent of colonization, claimed that a colony would provide work for poor "valiant youths rusting and hurtfull by lack of employment" in England. Colonists could buy English goods and supply products that England now had to import from other nations. Of course, the primary reason the Virginia Company investors risked their capital was that they hoped to reap quick profits from the new colony.

Enthusiastic reports from the Roanoke voyages twenty years earlier (see chapter 2) claimed that in Virginia, "the earth bringeth foorth all things in aboundance . . . without toile or labour." Even if these reports were exaggerated, investors hoped that some ready source of large profits would be found in North America. Such hopes failed to address the difficulties of adapting European desires and expectations to the New World already inhabited by Native Americans. The Jamestown settlement struggled to survive for nearly two decades, until the royal government replaced the private Virginia Company, which never earned a penny for its investors.

The Fragile Jamestown Settlement

On April 26, 1607, 144 Englishmen aboard the ships *Susan Constant, Discovery,* and *Godspeed* arrived at the mouth of the Chesapeake Bay. That night, while the colonists rested on shore, a band of Indians attacked and dangerously wounded two men. The attackers were followers of **Powhatan**, the Algonquian chief who dominated the region. The attack gave the colonists an early warning that the North American wilderness was not quite the paradise described by the Virginia Company's publications in England. A few weeks later, they went ashore on a small peninsula in the midst of Powhatan's chiefdom. There, they quickly built a fort, the first building in the settlement they named **Jamestown**.

The Jamestown fort showed the settlers' awareness that they needed to protect themselves from Indians and Spaniards. Spain planned to wipe out Jamestown when the time was ripe, but that time never came. Powhatan's people defended Virginia as their own. For weeks, the settlers and Powhatan's warriors skirmished repeatedly. English muskets and cannons repelled Indian attacks on Jamestown, but the Indians' superior numbers and knowledge of the Virginia wilderness made it risky for the settlers to venture far beyond the peninsula. Late in June 1607, Powhatan sensed a stalemate and made peace overtures.

The settlers soon confronted dangerous, invisible threats: disease and starvation. During the summer, many of the Englishmen lay "night and day groaning in every corner of the Fort most pittiful to heare," wrote George Percy, one of the settlers. By September, fifty colonists had died. The colonists increased their misery by bickering among themselves, leaving crops unplanted and food supplies shrinking. "For the most part [the settlers] died of meere famine," Percy wrote.

Powhatan's people came to the rescue of the weakened and demoralized Englishmen. Early in September 1607, they began to bring corn to the colony for barter. Accustomed to eating food derived from wheat, English people considered

CHRONOLOGY

1606
– Virginia Company receives royal charter.

1607
– English colonists found Jamestown settlement.

1607–1610
– Starvation plagues Jamestown.

1618
– Powhatan dies; Opechancanough becomes chief of the Algonquians.

1619
– House of Burgesses begins to meet in Virginia.

1622
– Opechancanough leads first Indian uprising against Virginia colonists.

1624
– Virginia becomes royal colony.
– Population of Virginia reaches 1,200.

Powhatan
▶ The supreme chief of about fourteen thousand Algonquian Indians who inhabited the coastal plain of present-day Virginia, near the Chesapeake Bay. Without the help of Powhatan, the Jamestown colony would not have survived.

Jamestown
▶ The colony established by the joint-stock company called the Virginia Company in 1607. Mortality rates in the early years of the colony were high, as disease, famine, and Indian attacks took their toll.

How did a tobacco society take shape?	How and why did Chesapeake society change in the late seventeenth century?	What caused tensions in the Spanish borderland?	When and why did the southern colonies move toward a slave labor system?	Conclusion: Why were export crops and slave labor important in the growth of the southern colonies?

corn the food "of the barbarous Indians which know no better . . . a more convenient food for swine than for man." The famished Jamestown colonists soon overcame their prejudice against corn. Indians' corn acquired by both trade and plunder managed to keep 38 of the original settlers alive until a fresh supply of food and 120 more colonists arrived from England in January 1608.

It is difficult to exaggerate the fragility of the early Jamestown settlement. Although the Virginia Company sent hundreds of new settlers to Jamestown each year, few survived. When a new group of colonists arrived in 1610, they found only 60 of the 500 previous settlers still alive. The Virginia Company continued to pour people into the colony, promising in a 1609 pamphlet that "the place will make them rich." But most settlers went instead to early graves.

Cooperation and Conflict between Natives and Newcomers

Powhatan's people stayed in contact with the English settlers but maintained their distance. Few Indians converted to Christianity, and the English devoted scant effort to proselytizing. Marriage between Indian women and English men also was rare, despite the acute shortage of English women in Virginia in the early years. Few settlers other than John Smith bothered to learn the Indians' language.

The miscommunication and misunderstandings between the settlers and Powhatan's people are illustrated by the story of the capture and release of **Captain John Smith**. In December 1607, Smith was captured by warriors of Powhatan. According to Smith, Powhatan "feasted him after their best barbarous manner." Then, Smith recalled, "two great stones were brought before Powhatan: then as many [Indians] as could layd hands on [Smith], dragged him to [the stones], and thereon laid his head, and being ready with their clubs, to beate out his braines." At that moment, **Pocahontas**, Powhatan's eleven-year-old daughter, rushed forward and "got [Smith's] head in her armes, and laid her owne upon his to save him from death." Pocahontas, Smith wrote, "hazarded the beating out of her owne braines to save mine, and . . . so prevailed with her father, that I was safely conducted [back] to James towne."

Historians believe that this episode happened more or less as Smith described it. But Smith did not understand why Pocahontas acted as she did. Most likely, when Pocahontas intervened to save Smith, she was a knowing participant in an Algonquian ceremony that expressed Powhatan's supremacy and his ritualistic adoption of Smith as a subordinate chief, or *werowance*. What Smith interpreted as Pocahontas's saving him from certain death was instead a ceremonial enactment of Powhatan's willingness to incorporate Smith and the white strangers at Jamestown into Powhatan's empire.

In 1613, after relations between Powhatan and the English colonists had deteriorated into bloody raids by both parties, the colonists captured Pocahontas and held her hostage at Jamestown. Within a year, she converted to Christianity and married one of the colonists, a widower named John Rolfe. After giving birth to a son named Thomas, Pocahontas, her husband, and the new baby sailed for England in the spring of 1616. Pocahontas died in England in 1617. Her son, Thomas, however, ultimately returned to Virginia.

Captain John Smith
▶ Leader of the Jamestown colony. Smith learned the Algonquian language of his Indian neighbors; however, this did not prevent him from misunderstanding the meaning behind his capture and redemption by Powhatan and his daughter Pocahontas in 1607.

Pocahontas
▶ The daughter of Powhatan. Pocahontas played a key role in a ceremonial enactment of incorporating Captain John Smith into Powhatan's society. Later captured and held hostage at Jamestown, Pocahontas converted to Christianity and married John Rolfe, the man who helped develop the tobacco crop that resulted in Virginia's success.

CHAPTER LOCATOR | What challenges faced early Chesapeake colonists?

Events like the capture of Pocahontas gave Powhatan's people good reason to regard the English with suspicion. Although the settlers often made friendly overtures to the Indians, they did not hesitate to use their guns and swords to enforce English notions of proper Indian behavior. More than once, the Indians refused to trade their corn to the settlers, evidently hoping to starve them out. Each time, the English broke the boycott by attacking the uncooperative Indians, pillaging their villages, and confiscating their corn.

The Indians retaliated against English violence, but for fifteen years they did not organize an all-out assault on the European intruders, probably for several reasons. Although Christianity held few attractions for the Indians, the power of the settlers' God impressed them. One chief told John Smith that "he did believe that our [English] God as much exceeded theirs as our guns did their bows and arrows." Powhatan probably concluded that these powerful strangers would make better allies than enemies. As allies, the English strengthened Powhatan's dominance over the tribes in the region. They also traded with his people, usually exchanging European goods for corn. Native Virginians had some copper weapons and tools before the English arrived, but they quickly recognized the superiority of the intruders' iron and steel knives, axes, and pots. The trade that supplied the Indians with European conveniences provided the English settlers with a necessity: food.

But why were the settlers unable to feed themselves for more than a decade? First, as the staggering death rate suggests, many settlers were too sick to be productive members of the colony. Second, very few farmers came to Virginia in the early years. Instead, most of the newcomers were gentlemen and their servants. The proportion of gentlemen in Virginia in the early years was six times greater than in England, a reflection of the Virginia Company's urgent need for investors and settlers. John Smith declared repeatedly that in Virginia "there is no country to pillage [as in New Spain]. . . . All you can expect from [Virginia] must be by labor." For years, however, colonists clung to English notions that gentlemen should not work with their hands and that tradesmen should work only in trades for which they had been trained. These ideas made more sense in labor-rich England than in labor-poor Virginia. In the meantime, the colonists depended on the Indians' corn for food.

The persistence of the Virginia colony created difficulties for Powhatan's chiefdom. Steady contact between natives and newcomers spread European diseases among the Indians, who suffered deadly epidemics in 1608 and between 1617 and 1619. The settlers' need for corn introduced other tensions within Powhatan's villages. To produce enough corn for their own survival and for trade

Ætatis suæ 21. A°.1616.

Matoaks als Rebecka daughter to the mighty Prince Powhatan Emperour of Attanoughkomouck als Virginia converted and baptized in the Christian faith, and Wife to the wor.ll M.r Tho: Rolff.

Pocahontas in England

Shortly after Pocahontas and her husband, John Rolfe, arrived in England in 1616, she posed for this portrait dressed in English clothing suitable for a princess. The portrait captures the dual novelty of England for Pocahontas and of Pocahontas for the English. The mutability of Pocahontas's identity is displayed in the identification of her as "Matoaks" or "Rebecka." National Portrait Gallery, Smithsonian Institution/Art Resource, NY.

| How did a tobacco society take shape? | How and why did Chesapeake society change in the late seventeenth century? | What caused tensions in the Spanish borderland? | When and why did the southern colonies move toward a slave labor system? | Conclusion: Why were export crops and slave labor important in the growth of the southern colonies? |

with the English required the Indians to spend more time and effort growing crops. Since Native American women did most of the agricultural work, their burden increased along with the cultural significance of their chief crop. The corn surplus grown by Indian women was bartered for desirable English goods such as iron pots, which replaced the baskets and ceramic jugs that Native Americans had used for millennia. But from the Indians' viewpoint, the most important fact about the English colonists was that they were not going away.

Powhatan died in 1618, and his brother Opechanca-nough replaced him as supreme chief. In 1622, Opechan-canough organized an all-out assault on the English settlers. As an English colonist observed, "When the day appointed for the massacre arrived [March 22], a number of savages visited many of our people in their dwellings, and while partaking with them of their meal[,] the savages, at a given signal, drew their weapons and fell upon us murdering and killing everybody they could reach[,] sparing neither women nor children, as well inside as outside the dwellings." In all, the Indians killed 347 colonists, nearly a third of the English population. But the attack failed to dislodge the colonists. In the aftermath, the settlers unleashed a murderous campaign of Indian extermination that in a few years pushed the Indians beyond the small circumference of white settle-ment. Before 1622, the settlers knew that the Indians, though dangerous, were necessary to keep the colony alive. After 1622, most colonists considered the Indians their perpetual enemies.

From Private Company to Royal Government

The 1622 uprising prompted a royal investigation of affairs in Virginia. The investigators discovered that the appalling mortality among the colonists was caused more by disease and mismanagement than by Indian

Advertisement for Jamestown Settlers

Virginia imported thousands of indentured servants to labor in the tobacco fields, but the colony also advertised in 1631 for settlers like those pictured here. The notice features men and women equally, although men heavily outnumbered women in the Chesapeake region. Harvard Map Collection, Pusey Library, Harvard University.

CHAPTER LOCATOR | What challenges faced early Chesapeake colonists?

raids. In 1624, King James revoked the charter of the Virginia Company and made Virginia a royal colony, subject to the direction of the royal government rather than to the company's private investors, an arrangement that lasted until 1776.

The king now appointed the governor of Virginia and his council, but most other features of local government established under the Virginia Company remained intact. In 1619, for example, the company had inaugurated the **House of Burgesses**, an assembly of representatives (called burgesses) elected by the colony's inhabitants. (Historians do not know exactly which settlers were considered inhabitants and were thus qualified to vote.) Under the new royal government, laws passed by the burgesses had to be approved by the king's bureaucrats in England rather than by the company. Otherwise, the House of Burgesses continued as before, acquiring distinction as the oldest representative legislative assembly in the English colonies. Under the new royal government, all free adult men in Virginia could vote for the House of Burgesses, giving it a far broader and more representative constituency than the English House of Commons.

The demise of the Virginia Company marked the end of the first phase of colonization of the Chesapeake region. From the first 105 adventurers in 1607, the population had grown to about 1,200 by 1624. Despite mortality rates higher than during the worst epidemics in London, new settlers still came. Their arrival and King James's willingness to take over the struggling colony reflected a fundamental change in Virginia. After years of fruitless experimentation, it was becoming clear that English settlers could make a fortune in Virginia by growing tobacco.

House of Burgesses
▶ An assembly of representatives (called burgesses) established by the Virginia Company in 1619. After 1624 and until 1670, all free adult men in Virginia could vote for the House of Burgesses, regardless of landownership.

QUICK REVIEW

Why was the Jamestown settlement so dependent on Powhatan's people for survival during its first decade?

How did a tobacco society take shape?	How and why did Chesapeake society change in the late seventeenth century?	What caused tensions in the Spanish borderland?	When and why did the southern colonies move toward a slave labor system?	Conclusion: Why were export crops and slave labor important in the growth of the southern colonies?

How did a tobacco society take shape?

European Smoking Club

In Europe, tobacco smokers congregated in clubs to enjoy the intoxicating weed. In this seventeenth-century satirical print, a dog cleans up after those who cannot hold their smoke. Koninklijke Bibliotheek, The Hague.

TOBACCO GREW WILD in the New World, and Native Americans used it for thousands of years before Europeans arrived. During the sixteenth century, Spanish colonists in the New World sent tobacco to Europe, where it was an expensive luxury used sparingly by a few. During the next century, English colonists in North America sent so much tobacco to European markets that it became an affordable indulgence used often by many people.

Initially, the Virginia Company had no plans to grow and sell tobacco. John Rolfe—the husband-to-be of Pocahontas—planted West Indian tobacco seeds in 1612 and learned that they flourished in Virginia. By 1617, the colonists had grown enough tobacco to send the first commercial shipment to England, where it sold for a high price. After that, Virginia changed from a colony of rather aimless adventurers who had difficulty growing enough corn to feed themselves into a society of dedicated planters who grew as much tobacco as possible.

By 1700, nearly 100,000 colonists lived in the Chesapeake region, encompassing Virginia, Maryland, and northern North Carolina (**Map 3.1**). They exported more than 35 million pounds of tobacco, a fivefold increase in per capita production since 1620. Clearly, Chesapeake colonists mastered the demands of tobacco agriculture, and the "Stinkinge Weede" (a seventeenth-century Marylander's term for tobacco) also mastered the colonists. Settlers lived by the rhythms of tobacco agriculture, and their endless need for labor attracted droves of English indentured servants to work in the tobacco fields.

Tobacco Agriculture

A demanding crop, tobacco required close attention and a great deal of hand labor year-round. Like the Indians, the colonists "cleared" fields by cutting a ring of bark from each tree (a procedure known as "girdling"), thereby killing the tree.

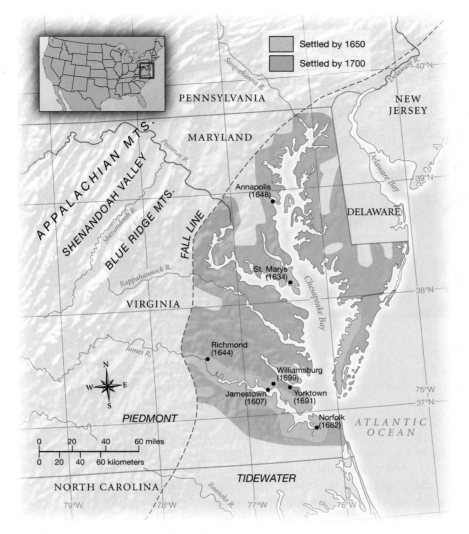

CHRONOLOGY

1612
– John Rolfe begins to plant tobacco in Virginia.

1617
– First commercial tobacco shipment leaves Virginia for England.

1619
– First Africans arrive in Virginia.

1632
– King Charles I grants Lord Baltimore land for colony of Maryland.

1634
– Colonists begin to arrive in Maryland.

1700
– Population of the Chesapeake region reaches 100,000.
– Chesapeake region exports 35 million pounds of tobacco to England.

MAP 3.1 ■ Chesapeake Colonies in the Seventeenth Century
The intimate association between land and water in the settlement of the Chesapeake in the seventeenth century is illustrated by this map. Although Delaware had excellent access to navigable water, it was claimed and defended by the Dutch colony at New Amsterdam (see chapter 4) rather than by the English settlements in Virginia and Maryland shown on this map.

▶ FOR MORE HELP ANALYZING THIS MAP, see the map activity for this chapter in the Online Study Guide at bedfordstmartins.com/roarkunderstanding.

Girdling brought sunlight to clearings but left fields studded with tree stumps, making the use of plows impractical. Instead, colonists used heavy hoes to till their tobacco fields. To plant, a visitor observed, they "just make holes [with a stick] into which they drop the seeds," much as the Indians did. Growing tobacco with such methods left little time for idleness, but the colonists enjoyed the fruits of their labor. "Everyone smokes while working or idling," one traveler reported, including "men, women, girls, and boys, from the age of seven years."

The English settlers worked hard because their labor promised greater rewards in the Chesapeake region than in England. One colonist proclaimed that

How did a tobacco society take shape?	How and why did Chesapeake society change in the late seventeenth century?	What caused tensions in the Spanish borderland?	When and why did the southern colonies move toward a slave labor system?	Conclusion: Why were export crops and slave labor important in the growth of the southern colonies?

This print illustrates the processing of tobacco on a seventeenth-century plantation. Workers cut the mature plants and put the leaves in piles to wilt (left foreground and center background). After the leaves dried somewhat, they were suspended from poles in a drying barn (right foreground), where they were seasoned before being packed in casks for shipping. Sometimes, tobacco leaves were left to dry in the fields (center background). From "About Tobacco," Lehman Brothers.

"the dirt of this Province affords as great a profit to the general Inhabitant, as the Gold of Peru doth to . . . the Spaniard." Although he exaggerated, it was true that a hired man could expect to earn two or three times more in Virginia's tobacco fields than in England. Better still, in Virginia land was so abundant that it was extremely cheap compared to land in England.

By the mid-seventeenth century, common laborers could buy a hundred acres for less than their annual wages—an impossibility in England. New settlers who paid their own transportation to the Chesapeake received a grant of fifty acres of free land (termed a **headright**). The Virginia Company initiated headrights to encourage settlement, and the royal government continued them for the same reason.

A Servant Labor System

Headrights, cheap land, and high wages gave poor English folk powerful incentives to immigrate to the New World. Yet many potential immigrants could not afford to pay for a trip across the Atlantic. Their poverty and the colonists' crying need for labor formed the basic context for the creation of a servant labor system.

About 80 percent of the immigrants to the Chesapeake during the seventeenth century were **indentured servants**. Twenty Africans arrived in Virginia in 1619, but scanty records make it impossible to know their fate. Until the 1670s, however, only a small number of slaves labored in Chesapeake tobacco fields. (Large numbers of slaves came in the eighteenth century, as chapter 5 explains.) A few indentured servants of African descent served out their terms of servitude and became free. A few slaves purchased their way out of bondage and lived as free people, even owning land and using the local courts to resolve disputes, much as freed white servants did. A small number of Native Americans also became servants. But the overwhelming majority of indentured servants were white immigrants from England. Instead of a slave society, the seventeenth-century Chesapeake region was fundamentally a society of white servants and ex-servants.

headright
▶ A grant of fifty acres of free land to new English settlers who could pay their own passage to Virginia. Most new Virginians, however, could not afford passage and arrived as indentured servants.

indentured servants
▶ English immigrants who agreed to work for four to seven years as servants in exchange for passage to America. Indentured servitude was the primary source of labor in seventeenth-century Virginia.

CHAPTER LOCATOR | What challenges faced early Chesapeake colonists?

To buy passage aboard a ship bound for the Chesapeake, an English immigrant had to come up with about £5, roughly a year's wages for an English servant or laborer. Unable to pay for their trip across the Atlantic, poor immigrants agreed to a contract called an indenture, which functioned as a form of credit. By signing an indenture, an immigrant borrowed the cost of transportation to the Chesapeake from a merchant or ship captain in England. To repay this loan, the indentured person agreed to work as a servant for four to seven years in North America.

Once the indentured person arrived in the colonies, the merchant or ship captain sold his right to the immigrant's labor to a local tobacco planter. To obtain the servant's labor, the planter paid about twice the cost of transportation and agreed to provide the servant with food and shelter during the term of the indenture. When the indenture expired, the planter owed the former servant "freedom dues," usually a few barrels of corn and a suit of clothes.

Ideally, indentures allowed poor immigrants to trade their most valuable assets—their freedom and their ability to work—for a trip to the New World and a period of servitude followed by freedom in a land of opportunity. Planters reaped more immediate benefits. A planter expected a servant to grow enough tobacco in one year to cover the price the planter paid for the indenture. Servants' labor during the remaining three to six years of the indenture promised a handsome profit for the planter. No wonder one Virginian declared, "Our principall wealth . . . consisteth in servants." But roughly half of all servants became sick and died before serving out their indentures, reducing planters' gains and destroying the servants' hopes. Planters still profited, however, since they received a headright of fifty acres of land from the colonial government for every newly purchased servant.

About three out of four servants were men between the ages of fifteen and twenty-five when they arrived in the Chesapeake. Typically unemployed and often homeless, most servants had no special training or skills, although the majority had some experience with agricultural work. "Hunger and fear of prisons bring to us onely such servants as have been brought up to no Art or Trade," one Virginia planter complained. A skilled craftsman could obtain a shorter indenture, but few risked coming to the colonies since their prospects were better in England.

Women were almost as rare as skilled craftsmen in the Chesapeake and more ardently desired. In the early days of the tobacco boom, the Virginia Company shipped young single women servants to the colony as prospective wives for male settlers willing to pay "120 weight [pounds] of the best leaf tobacco for each of them," in effect getting both a wife and a servant. The company reasoned that, as one official wrote in 1622, "the plantation can never flourish till families be planted, and the respect of wives and children fix the people on the soil." The company's efforts as a marriage broker proved no more successful than its other ventures. Women remained a small minority of the Chesapeake population until late in the seventeenth century.

The servant labor system perpetuated the gender imbalance. Although female servants cost about the same as males and generally served for the same length of time, only about one servant in four was a woman. Planters preferred male servants for field work, although many servant women hoed and harvested tobacco fields. Most women servants also did household chores such as cooking, washing, cleaning, gardening, and milking.

| **How did a tobacco society take shape?** | How and why did Chesapeake society change in the late seventeenth century? | What caused tensions in the Spanish borderland? | When and why did the southern colonies move toward a slave labor system? | Conclusion: Why were export crops and slave labor important in the growth of the southern colonies? |

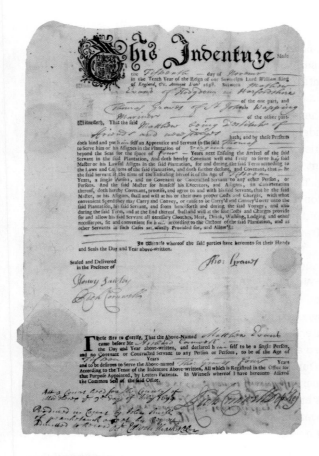

Indenture Contract

Indenture contracts were so common that forms were printed with blank spaces for details to be written in. In this 1698 contract, fifteen-year-old Matthew Evans agreed to serve mariner Thomas Graves, or anybody to whom Graves sold his rights, for four years in Virginia. The Library of Virginia.

Servants—whether men or women, whites or blacks, English or African—tended to work together and socialize together. During the first half century of settlement, racial intermingling occurred, although the small number of blacks made it infrequent. Courts punished sexual relations between blacks and whites, but the number of court cases shows that sexual desire readily crossed the color line. In general, the commonalities of servitude caused servants—regardless of their race and gender—to consider themselves apart from free people, whose ranks they longed to join eventually.

Servant life was harsh by the standards of seventeenth-century England and even by the frontier standards of the Chesapeake. Unlike servants in England, Chesapeake servants had no control over who purchased their labor for the period of their indenture. Many servants were bought and sold several times before their indenture expired. A Virginia servant protested in 1623 that his master "hath sold me for £150 sterling like a damnd slave."

For servants, the dreams of a new life that prompted them to leave England withered when they confronted the rigors of labor in the tobacco fields. James Revel, an eighteen-year-old thief punished by being indentured to a Virginia tobacco planter, declared he was a "slave" sent to hoe "tobacco plants all day" from dawn to dark. Severe laws aimed to keep servants in their place. Punishments for petty crimes stretched servitude far beyond the original terms of indenture. After midcentury, the Virginia legislature added three or more years to the indentures of most servants by requiring them to serve until they were twenty-four years old.

Women servants were subject to special restrictions and risks. They were prohibited from marrying until their servitude had expired. A servant woman, the law assumed, could not serve two masters at the same time: one who owned her indentured labor and another who was her husband. However, the predominance of men in the Chesapeake population inevitably pressured women to engage in sexual relations. About a third of immigrant women were pregnant when they married. As a rule, if a woman servant gave birth to a child, she had to serve two extra years and pay a fine. However, for some servant women, premarital pregnancy was a path out of servitude: The father of an unborn child sometimes purchased the indenture of the servant mother-to-be, then freed and married her.

Harsh punishments reflected four fundamental realities of the servant labor system. First, planters' hunger for labor caused them to demand as much labor as they could get from their servants, including devising legal ways to extend the period of servitude. Second, servants hoped to survive their servitude and use their freedom to obtain land and start a family. Third, servants' hopes frequently conflicted with planters' demands. Since servants saw themselves as free people in a temporary status of servitude, they often made grudging, halfhearted workers. Finally, planters put up with this contentious arrangement because the alternatives were less desirable.

Planters could not easily hire free men and women because land was readily available and free people preferred to work for themselves on their own land. Nor could planters depend on much labor from family members. The preponderance of

CHAPTER LOCATOR | What challenges faced early Chesapeake colonists?

men in the population meant that families were few, were started late, and thus had few children. And, until the 1680s and 1690s, slaves were expensive and hard to come by. Before then, masters who wanted to expand their labor force and grow more tobacco had few alternatives to buying indentured servants.

Cultivating Land and Faith

Villages and small towns dotted the rural landscape of seventeenth-century England, but in the Chesapeake, acres of wilderness were interrupted here and there by tobacco farms. Tobacco was such a labor-intensive crop that one field worker could tend only about two acres of the plants in a year (an acre is slightly smaller than a football field), plus a few more acres for food crops. A successful farmer needed a great deal more land, however, because tobacco quickly exhausted the fertility of the soil. Since each farmer cultivated only 5 or 10 percent of his land at any one time, a "settled" area comprised swatches of cultivated land surrounded by forest. Arrangements for marketing tobacco also contributed to the dispersion of settlements. Tobacco planters sought land that fronted a navigable river in order to minimize the work of transporting the heavy barrels of tobacco onto ships. A settled region thus resembled a lacework of farms stitched around waterways.

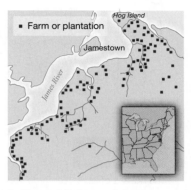

Settlement Patterns along the James River

Most Chesapeake colonists were nominally Protestants. Attendance at Sunday services and conformity to the doctrines of the Church of England were required of all English men and women. Few clergymen migrated to the Chesapeake, however, and too few of those who did were models of righteousness and piety. Certainly, some colonists took their religion seriously. Church courts punished fornicators, censured blasphemers, and served notice on parishioners who spent Sundays "goeing a fishing." But on the whole, religion did not awaken the zeal of Chesapeake settlers, certainly not as it did the zeal of New England settlers in these same years (see chapter 4).

The situation was similar in the Catholic colony of Maryland. In 1632, England's King Charles I granted his Catholic friend Lord Baltimore about six and a half million acres in the northern Chesapeake region. Lord Baltimore intended to create a refuge for Catholics, who suffered severe discrimination in England. He fitted out two ships; gathered about 150 settlers; and sent them to the new colony, where they arrived on March 25, 1634. However, Maryland failed to live up to Baltimore's hopes. The colony's population grew very slowly for twenty years, and most settlers were Protestants rather than Catholics. The religious turmoil of the Puritan Revolution in England (discussed in chapter 4) spilled across the Atlantic, creating conflict between Maryland's few Catholics—most of them wealthy and prominent—and the Protestant majority, most of them neither wealthy nor prominent. During the 1660s, Maryland began to attract settlers, mostly Protestants, as readily as Virginia. Although Catholics and the Catholic faith continued to exert influence in Maryland, the colony's society, economy, politics, and culture became nearly indistinguishable from Virginia's. Both colonies shared a devotion to tobacco, the true faith of the Chesapeake.

QUICK REVIEW <

Why did so many English men and women agree to come to the Chesapeake as indentured servants?

| How did a tobacco society take shape? | How and why did Chesapeake society change in the late seventeenth century? | What caused tensions in the Spanish borderland? | When and why did the southern colonies move toward a slave labor system? | Conclusion: Why were export crops and slave labor important in the growth of the southern colonies? |

How and why did Chesapeake society change in the late seventeenth century?

Inside a Poor Planter's House

The houses of seventeenth-century Chesapeake settlers were typically "earth-fast": The structural timbers that framed the house were simply placed in holes in the ground, and the floor was packed dirt. No seventeenth-century house was substantial enough to survive until today. This photo shows a carefully documented reconstruction of the interior of a poor planter's house at Historic St. Mary's City, Maryland. Image courtesy of Historic St. Mary's City.

THE SYSTEM OF INDENTURED SERVITUDE sharpened inequality in Chesapeake society by the mid-seventeenth century, propelling social and political polarization that culminated in 1676 with Bacon's Rebellion. The rebellion prompted reforms that stabilized relations between elite planters and their lesser neighbors and paved the way for a social hierarchy that muted differences of landholding and wealth and amplified racial differences. Amid this social and political evolution, one thing did not change: Chesapeake colonists' dedication to growing tobacco.

Social and Economic Polarization

The first half of the seventeenth century in the Chesapeake was the era of the **yeoman**—a farmer who owned a small plot of land sufficient to support a family and tilled largely by servants and a few family members. A small number of elite planters had larger estates and commanded ten or more servants. But for the first several decades, few men lived long enough to accumulate fortunes sufficient to set them much apart from their neighbors.

Until midcentury, the principal division in Chesapeake society was less between rich and poor planters than between free farmers and unfree servants. Although these two groups contrasted sharply in their legal and economic status, their daily lives had many similarities. Servants looked forward to the time when their indentures would expire and they would become free and eventually own land.

yeoman

▶ A farmer who owned a small plot of land sufficient to support a family and tilled largely by servants and a few family members. During the first half of the seventeenth century in the Chesapeake, nearly all farmers were yeomen.

CHAPTER LOCATOR | What challenges faced early Chesapeake colonists?

During the third quarter of the century, three major developments splintered the equality. First, as planters grew more and more tobacco, the ample supply depressed tobacco prices in European markets. Cheap tobacco reduced planters' profits and made saving enough to become landowners more difficult for freed servants. Second, because the mortality rate in the Chesapeake colonies declined, more and more servants survived their indentures, and landless freemen became more numerous and grew more discontented. Third, declining mortality also encouraged the formation of a planter elite. By living longer, the most successful planters compounded their success. The wealthiest planters also began to serve as merchants, marketing crops for their less successful neighbors, importing English goods for sale, and extending credit to hard-pressed customers.

By the 1670s, the society of the Chesapeake had become polarized. Landowners—the planter elite and the more numerous yeoman planters—clustered around one pole. Landless colonists, mainly freed servants, gathered at the other. Each group eyed the other with suspicion and mistrust. For the most part, planters saw landless freemen as a dangerous rabble rather than as fellow colonists with legitimate grievances. Governor William Berkeley feared the political threat to the governing elite posed by "six parts in seven [of Virginia colonists who] . . . are poor, indebted, discontented, and armed."

Government Policies and Political Conflict

In general, government and politics strengthened the distinctions in Chesapeake society. The most vital distinction separated servants and landowners, and the colonial government enforced it with an iron fist. As discontent mounted among the poor during the 1660s and 1670s, colonial officials tried to keep political power in safe hands. Beginning in 1661, for example, Governor William Berkeley did not call an election for the House of Burgesses for fifteen years. In 1670, the House of Burgesses outlawed voting by poor men, permitting only men who headed households and owned land to vote.

The king also began to tighten the royal government's control of trade and to collect substantial revenue from the Chesapeake. A series of navigation acts funneled the colonial trade exclusively into the hands of English merchants and shippers. The **Navigation Acts of 1650 and 1651** specified that colonial goods had to be transported in English ships with predominantly English crews. A 1660 act required colonial products to be sent only to English ports, and a 1663 law stipulated further that all goods sent to the colonies must pass through English ports and be carried in English ships manned by English sailors. Taken together, these navigation acts reflected the English government's mercantilist assumptions about the colonies: What was good for England should determine colonial policy.

Governor William Berkeley

This portrait illustrates the distance that separated Governor Berkeley and other Chesapeake grandees from poor planters, landless freemen, servants, and slaves.
Courtesy of Berkeley Castle Charitable Trust, Gloucestershire.

CHRONOLOGY

c. 1600–1650
- Yeoman farmers predominate in the Chesapeake region.

1644
- Opechancanough leads second Indian uprising against Virginia colonists.

1660
- Navigation Act imposes an import tax on colonial tobacco brought into England.

1661–1676
- No elections called in the House of Burgesses.

1670
- House of Burgesses outlaws voting by poor men.

1676
- Bacon's Rebellion.

Navigation Acts of 1650 and 1651
▶ Acts of Parliament that specified that colonial goods had to be transported in English ships with predominantly English crews. The acts reflected the English government's belief that the interests of England should determine colonial policy.

How did a tobacco society take shape?	**How and why did Chesapeake society change in the late seventeenth century?**	What caused tensions in the Spanish borderland?	When and why did the southern colonies move toward a slave labor system?	Conclusion: Why were export crops and slave labor important in the growth of the southern colonies?

mercantilism

▶ Economic policies that regulated colonial commerce for the enrichment of the mother country. Seventeenth-century English colonial policy was based on mercantilist assumptions.

Assumptions about **mercantilism** also underlay the import duty on tobacco inaugurated by the Navigation Act of 1660. The law assessed an import tax of two pence on every pound of colonial tobacco brought into England, about the price a Chesapeake tobacco farmer received. The tax gave the king a major financial interest in the size of the tobacco crop. During the 1660s, these tobacco import taxes yielded about a quarter of all English customs revenues, an impressive sign of the growing importance of the Chesapeake colonies in England's Atlantic empire.

Bacon's Rebellion

Bacon's Rebellion

▶ A colonial uprising in 1676 sparked by Virginia's Indian policy. Although Indian attacks triggered the rebellion, it was also the result of underlying social and political tensions in the colony.

Colonists, like residents of European monarchies, accepted social hierarchy and inequality as long as they believed that government officials ruled for the general good. When rulers violated that precept, ordinary people felt justified in rebelling. In 1676, **Bacon's Rebellion** erupted as a dispute over Virginia's Indian policy. Before it was over, the rebellion convulsed Chesapeake politics and society, leaving in its wake death, destruction, and a legacy of hostility between the great planters and their poorer neighbors.

Opechancanough, the Algonquian chief who had led the Indian uprising of 1622 in Virginia, mounted another surprise attack in 1644 and killed about five hundred Virginia colonists in two days. During the next two years of bitter fighting, the colonists eventually gained the upper hand, capturing and murdering the old chief. The treaty that concluded the war established policies toward the Indians that the government tried to maintain for the next thirty years. The Indians relinquished all claims to land already settled by the English. Wilderness land beyond the fringe of English settlement was supposed to be reserved exclusively for Indian use. The colonial government hoped to minimize contact between settlers and Indians and thereby maintain the peace.

If the Chesapeake population had not grown, the policy might have worked. But the number of land-hungry colonists, especially poor, recently freed servants, continued to multiply. In their quest for land, they pushed beyond the treaty limits of English settlement and steadily encroached on Indian land. During the 1660s and 1670s, violence between colonists and Indians repeatedly flared along the advancing frontier. The government, headquartered in the tidewater region near the coast, far from the danger of Indian raids, took steps to calm the disputes and reestablish the peace. Frontier settlers thirsted for revenge against what their leader, Nathaniel Bacon, termed "the protected and Darling Indians." Bacon proclaimed his "Design not only to ruine and extirpate all Indians in Generall but all Manner of Trade and Commerce with them." Indians were not the only enemies Bacon and his men singled out. Bacon also urged the colonists to "see what spounges have suckt up the Publique Treasure." He charged that grandees, or elite planters, operated the government for their private gain, a charge that made sense to many colonists. Bacon crystallized the grievances of the small planters and poor farmers against both the Indians and the colonial rulers in Jamestown.

Hoping to maintain the fragile peace on the frontier in 1676, Governor Berkeley pronounced Bacon a rebel, threatened to punish him for treason, and called for new elections of burgesses who, Berkeley believed, would endorse his get-tough policy. To Berkeley's surprise, the elections backfired. Almost all the old burgesses were voted out of office, and they were replaced by local leaders, including Bacon. The legislature was now in the hands of minor grandees who, like Bacon, chafed at the rule of the elite planters.

CHAPTER LOCATOR | What challenges faced early Chesapeake colonists?

In June 1676, the new legislature passed a series of reform measures known as Bacon's Laws. Among other changes, the laws gave local settlers a voice in setting tax levies, forbade officeholders from demanding bribes or other extra fees for carrying out their duties, placed limits on holding multiple offices, and restored the vote to all freemen. Under pressure, Berkeley pardoned Bacon and authorized his campaign of Indian warfare. But elite planters soon convinced Berkeley that Bacon and his men were a greater threat than the Indians.

When Bacon learned that Berkeley had once again branded him a traitor, he declared war against Berkeley and the other grandees. For three months, Bacon's forces fought the Indians, sacked the grandees' plantations, and attacked Jamestown. Berkeley's loyalists retaliated by plundering the homes of Bacon's supporters. The fighting continued until late October, when Bacon unexpectedly died, most likely from dysentery, and several English ships arrived to bolster Berkeley's strength. With the rebellion crushed, Berkeley hanged several of Bacon's allies and destroyed farms that belonged to Bacon's supporters.

The rebellion did nothing to dislodge the grandees from their positions of power. If anything, it strengthened them. When the king learned of the turmoil in the Chesapeake and its devastating effect on tobacco exports and customs duties, he ordered an investigation. Royal officials replaced Berkeley with a governor more attentive to the king's interests, nullified Bacon's Laws, and instituted an export tax on every hogshead of tobacco as a way of paying the expenses of government without having to obtain the consent of the House of Burgesses.

In the aftermath of Bacon's Rebellion, tensions between great planters and small farmers gradually lessened. Bacon's Rebellion showed, a governor of Virginia said, that it was necessary "to steer between . . . either an Indian or a civil war." The ruling elite concluded that it was safer for the colonists to fight the Indians than to fight each other, and the government made little effort to restrict settlers' encroachment on Indian land. Tax cuts also were welcomed by all freemen. The export duty on tobacco imposed by the king allowed the colonial government to reduce taxes by 75 percent between 1660 and 1700. In the long run, however, the most important contribution to political stability was the declining importance of the servant labor system. During the 1680s and 1690s, fewer servants arrived in the Chesapeake, partly because of improving economic conditions in England. Accordingly, the number of poor, newly freed servants also declined, reducing the size of the lowest stratum of free society. In 1700, as many as one-third of the free colonists still worked as tenants on land owned by others, but the social and political distance between them and the great planters did not seem as important as it had been in 1660. The main reason was that by 1700, the Chesapeake was in the midst of transition to a slave labor system that minimized the differences between poor farmers and rich planters and magnified the differences between whites and blacks.

QUICK REVIEW

Why did Chesapeake colonial society become increasingly polarized between 1650 and 1670?

How did a tobacco society take shape?

How and why did Chesapeake society change in the late seventeenth century?

What caused tensions in the Spanish borderland?

When and why did the southern colonies move toward a slave labor system?

Conclusion: Why were export crops and slave labor important in the growth of the southern colonies?

What caused tensions in the Spanish borderland?

Spanish Stirrup This seventeenth-century stirrup used by Spaniards on the northern frontier of New Spain illustrates the use of elaborate ornamentation and display to convey a sense of Spanish power. It is no accident that the stirrup is in the shape of a Christian cross, a vivid symbol of the Spaniards' belief in the divine source of their authority. © George H. H. Huey.

WHILE ENGLISH COLONIES in the Chesapeake grew and prospered with the tobacco trade, the northern outposts of the Spanish empire in New Mexico and Florida stagnated. Instead of attracting settlers and growing crops for export, New Mexico and Florida appealed to Spanish missionaries seeking to harvest Indian souls. The missionaries baptized thousands of Indians in Spanish North America during the seventeenth century, but they also planted the seeds of Indian uprisings against Spanish rule.

The Spanish Borderlands

Only about 4,500 Spanish colonists lived in the borderlands: 1,500 in Florida and 3,000 in New Mexico.

Indians outnumbered Spanish colonists ten or twenty to one.

Royal officials considered eliminating both colonies because their costs greatly exceeded their benefits.

Missionaries persuaded the Spanish government to continue to support the colonies.

Royal officials hoped that the missionaries' efforts would pacify the Indians and preserve Spanish footholds in North America.

CHAPTER LOCATOR | What challenges faced early Chesapeake colonists?

Dozens of missionaries came to Florida and New Mexico, as one announced, to free the Indians "from the miserable slavery of the demon and from the obscure darkness of their idolatry." The missionaries believed that the Indians' religious beliefs and rituals were idolatrous devil worship and that their way of life was barbaric. The missionaries followed royal instructions that Indians should be taught "to live in a civilized manner, clothed and wearing shoes . . . [and] given the use of . . . bread, linen, horses, cattle, tools, and weapons, and all the rest that Spain has had." In effect, the missionaries sought to convert the Indians not just into Christians but also into imitation Spaniards.

The missionaries supervised the building of scores of Catholic churches across Florida and New Mexico. Typically, they conscripted Indian women and men to do the construction. Adopting practices common elsewhere in New Spain, they forced the Indians both to work and to pay tribute in the form of food, blankets, and other goods. Although the missionaries congratulated themselves on the many Indians they converted, their coercive methods subverted their goals. A missionary reported that an Indian in New Mexico asked him, "If we [missionaries] who are Christians caused so much harm and violence [to Indians], why should they become Christians?"

The Indians retaliated repeatedly against Spanish exploitation, but the Spaniards suppressed the violent uprisings by taking advantage of the disunity among the Indians, much as Cortés did in the conquest of Mexico (see chapter 2). In 1680, however, Pueblo Indians organized a unified revolt under the leadership of Popé, who ordered his followers, as one recounted, to "break up and burn the images of the holy Christ, the Virgin Mary, and the other saints, the crosses, and everything pertaining to Christianity." During the **Pueblo Revolt**, the Indians desecrated churches, killed two-thirds of the Spanish missionaries, and drove the Spaniards out of New Mexico to present-day El Paso, Texas. The Spaniards managed to return to New Mexico by the end of the seventeenth century, but only by restraining the missionaries and reducing labor exploitation. Florida Indians never mounted a unified attack on Spanish rule, but they too organized sporadic uprisings and resisted conversion, causing a Spanish official to report by the end of the seventeenth century that "the law of God and the preaching of the Holy Gospel have now ceased."

Pueblo Revolt

▶ A 1680 Indian uprising in colonial New Mexico led by Popé. The rebels killed two-thirds of the Spanish missionaries and drove Spaniards out of New Mexico for several years until they returned at the end of the seventeenth century.

QUICK REVIEW ◀

Why did the Pueblo Indians revolt against Spanish missionaries in 1680?

How did a tobacco society take shape?

How and why did Chesapeake society change in the late seventeenth century?

What caused tensions in the Spanish borderland?

When and why did the southern colonies move toward a slave labor system?

Conclusion: Why were export crops and slave labor important in the growth of the southern colonies?

When and why did the southern colonies move toward a slave labor system?

Sugar Plantation

This portrait of a Brazilian sugar plantation shows the house of the Brazilian owners, attended by numerous slaves. Courtesy of the John Carter Brown Library at Brown University.

DURING THE SIXTEENTH CENTURY, Spaniards and Portuguese in the New World supplemented Indian laborers with enslaved Africans. On this foundation, European colonizers built African slavery into the most important form of coerced labor in the New World. During the seventeenth century, English colonies in the West Indies followed the Spanish and Portuguese examples and developed sugar plantations with slave labor. In the English North American colonies, however, a slave labor system did not emerge until the last quarter of the seventeenth century. During the 1670s, settlers from Barbados brought slavery to the new English mainland colony of Carolina, where the imprint of the West Indies remained strong for decades. In Chesapeake tobacco fields at about the same time, slave labor began to replace servant labor, marking the transition toward a society of freedom for whites and slavery for Africans.

The West Indies: Sugar and Slavery

The most profitable part of the English New World empire in the seventeenth century lay in the Caribbean (**Map 3.2**). Barbados, colonized in the 1630s, was the

CHAPTER LOCATOR | What challenges faced early Chesapeake colonists?

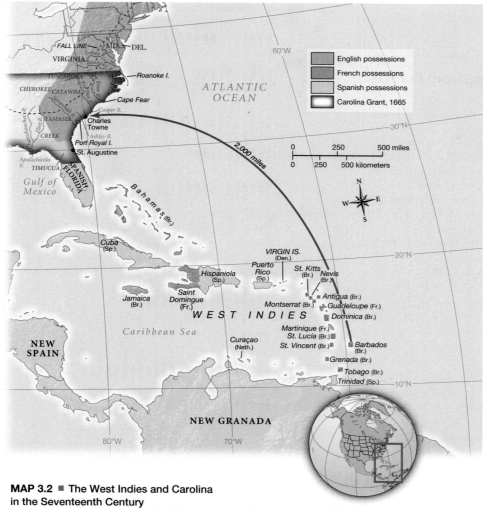

MAP 3.2 ■ The West Indies and Carolina
in the Seventeenth Century

Although Carolina was geographically near the Chesapeake colonies, it was culturally closer to the West Indies in the seventeenth century because its early settlers—both blacks and whites—came from Barbados. South Carolina maintained strong ties to the West Indies for more than a century, long after the arrival of many later settlers from England, Ireland, France, and elsewhere.

jewel of the English West Indies. During the 1640s, Barbadian planters began to grow sugarcane with such success that a colonial official proclaimed Barbados "the most flourishing Island in all those American parts, and I verily believe in all the world for the production of sugar."

Sugar commanded high prices in England, and planters rushed to grow as much as they could. By midcentury, annual sugar exports from the English Caribbean totaled about 150,000 pounds; by 1700, exports reached nearly 50 million pounds.

Sugar transformed Barbados and other West Indian islands. Poor farmers could not afford the expensive machinery that extracted and refined sugarcane juice. Planters with the necessary capital to grow and process sugarcane got rich. By 1680, the wealthiest Barbadian sugar planters were, on average, four times richer than tobacco grandees in the Chesapeake. The sugar grandees differed

| How did a tobacco society take shape? | How and why did Chesapeake society change in the late seventeenth century? | What caused tensions in the Spanish borderland? | **When and why did the southern colonies move toward a slave labor system?** | Conclusion: Why were export crops and slave labor important in the growth of the southern colonies? |

Migration to the New World from Europe and Africa, 1492–1700

Before 1640, Spain and Portugal reaped the rewards of their sixteenth-century voyages of discovery by sending four out of five European migrants to the New World, virtually all of them bound for New Spain or Brazil. But from 1640 to 1700, more migrants came from England than from any other European nation and nearly as many as from all other European nations combined, a measure of the growing significance of England's colonies in both the Caribbean and North America during the seventeenth century.

While few enslaved Africans were carried across the Atlantic before 1580, from the voyages of Columbus to 1700, more Africans than Europeans crossed the Atlantic to the New World, and virtually all of them were slaves. What might explain the shifting destinations of enslaved Africans?

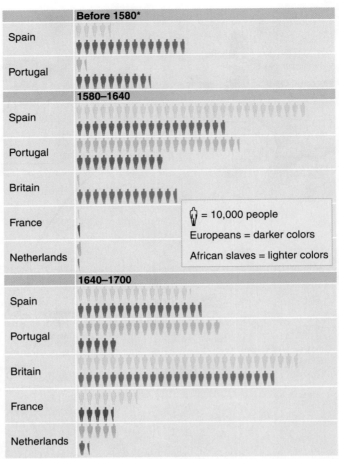

$\bigwedge$ = 10,000 people

Europeans = darker colors

African slaves = lighter colors

*Note: Before 1580, migration from Britain, France, and the Netherlands was negligible.

from their Chesapeake counterparts in another crucial way: The average sugar baron in Barbados owned 115 slaves in 1680.

African slaves planted, cultivated, and harvested the sugarcane that made West Indian planters wealthy. Beginning in the 1640s, Barbadian planters purchased thousands of slaves to work their plantations, and the African population on the island mushroomed. For slaves, work on a sugar plantation was a life sentence to brutal, unremitting labor. Slaves suffered high death rates. Since slave men outnumbered slave women two to one, few slaves could form families and have children. These grim realities meant that in Barbados and elsewhere in the West Indies, the slave population did not grow by natural reproduction. Instead, planters continually purchased enslaved Africans. Although sugar plantations did not gain a foothold in North America in the seventeenth century, the West Indies nonetheless exerted a powerful influence on the development of slavery in the mainland colonies.

Carolina: A West Indian Frontier

The early settlers of what became South Carolina were immigrants from Barbados. In 1663, a Barbadian planter named John Colleton and a group of seven

CHAPTER LOCATOR | What challenges faced early Chesapeake colonists?

other men obtained a charter from England's King Charles II to establish a colony south of the Chesapeake and north of the Spanish territories in Florida. The men, known as "proprietors," hoped to siphon settlers from Barbados and other colonies and encourage them to develop a profitable export crop comparable to West Indian sugar and Chesapeake tobacco. Following the Chesapeake example, the proprietors offered headrights of up to 150 acres of land for each settler. In 1670, they established the colony's first permanent English settlement, Charles Towne (later spelled Charleston) (see Map 3.2, page 75).

As the proprietors had planned, most of the early settlers were from Barbados. In fact, Carolina was the only seventeenth-century English colony to be settled principally by colonists from other colonies rather than directly from England. The Barbadian immigrants brought their slaves with them. More than a fourth of the early settlers were slaves, and as the colony continued to attract settlers from Barbados, the black population multiplied. By 1700, slaves made up about half the population of Carolina.

The Carolinians experimented unsuccessfully to match their semitropical climate with profitable export crops of tobacco, cotton, indigo, and olives. In the mid-1690s, colonists identified a hardy strain of rice and took advantage of the knowledge of rice cultivation among their many African slaves to build rice plantations. Settlers also sold livestock and timber to the West Indies, as well as another "natural resource": They captured and enslaved several thousand local Indians and sold them to Caribbean planters. Both economically and socially, seventeenth-century Carolina was a frontier outpost of the West Indian sugar economy.

Slave Labor Emerges in the Chesapeake

By 1700, more than eight out of ten people in the southern colonies of English North America lived in the Chesapeake. Until the 1670s, almost all Chesapeake colonists were white people from England. By 1700, however, one out of eight people in the region was a black person from Africa. A few black people had lived in the Chesapeake since the 1620s, but the black population grew fivefold between 1670 and 1700 as hundreds of tobacco planters made the transition from servant to slave labor.

For planters, slaves had several obvious advantages over servants. Although slaves cost three to five times more than servants, slaves never became free. Since the mortality rate had declined by the 1680s, planters could reasonably expect a slave to live longer than a servant's period of indenture. Slaves also promised to be a perpetual labor force, since children of slave mothers inherited the status of slavery.

Slaves had another important advantage over servants: They could be controlled politically. Bacon's Rebellion had demonstrated how disruptive former servants could be when their expectations were not met. A slave labor system promised to avoid the political problems caused by the servant labor system.

The slave labor system polarized Chesapeake society along lines of race and status: All slaves were black, and nearly all blacks were slaves; almost all free people were white, and all whites were free or only temporarily bound in indentured servitude. Unlike Barbados, where slaves constituted more than three-fourths of the population by the end of the seventeenth century, the Chesapeake

| How did a tobacco society take shape? | How and why did Chesapeake society change in the late seventeenth century? | What caused tensions in the Spanish borderland? | When and why did the southern colonies move toward a slave labor system? | Conclusion: Why were export crops and slave labor important in the growth of the southern colonies? |

77

retained a vast white majority. Among whites, huge differences of wealth and status still existed. By 1700, more than three-quarters of white families had neither servants nor slaves. Nonetheless, poor white farmers enjoyed the privileges of free status. They could own property, get married, have families, and bequeath their property and their freedom to their descendants; they could move when and where they wanted; they could associate freely with other people; they could serve on juries, vote, and hold political office; and they could work, loaf, and sleep as they chose. These privileges of freedom—none of them possessed by slaves—made lesser white folk feel they had a genuine stake in the existence of slavery, even if they did not own a single slave. By emphasizing the privileges of freedom shared by all white people, the slave labor system reduced the tensions between poor folk and grandees that had plagued the Chesapeake region in the 1670s.

In contrast to slaves in Barbados, most slaves in the seventeenth-century Chesapeake colonies had frequent and close contact with white people. Slaves and white servants performed the same tasks on tobacco plantations, often working side by side in the fields. Slaves took advantage of every opportunity to slip away from white supervision and seek out the company of other slaves. Planters often feared that slaves would turn such seemingly innocent social pleasures to political ends, either to run away or to conspire to strike against their masters. Slaves often did run away, but they were usually captured or returned after a brief absence. Despite planters' nightmares, slave insurrections did not occur.

Although slavery resolved the political unrest caused by the servant labor system, it created new political problems. By 1700, the bedrock political issue in the southern colonies was keeping slaves in their place, at the end of a hoe. The slave labor system in the southern colonies stood roughly midway between the sugar plantations and black majority of Barbados to the south and the small farms and homogeneous villages that developed in seventeenth-century New England to the north (see chapter 4).

> **QUICK REVIEW**

Why had slave labor largely displaced indentured servant labor by 1700 in Chesapeake tobacco production?

HIP/Art Resource, NY.

Conclusion: Why were export crops and slave labor important in the growth of the southern colonies?

BY 1700, the colonies of Virginia, Maryland, and Carolina were firmly established. Their societies differed markedly from English society in most respects, yet the colonists considered themselves English people who happened to live in North America. They claimed the same rights and privileges as English men and women, while they denied those rights and privileges to Native Americans and African slaves.

The English colonies also differed from the example of New Spain. Settlers and servants flocked to English colonies, in contrast to the small number of Spaniards who trickled into New Spain. Few English missionaries sought to convert Indians to Protestant Christianity, unlike the numerous Catholic missionaries in the Spanish settlements in New Mexico and Florida. Large quantities of gold and silver never materialized in English North America. English colonists never adopted the Spanish system of forced labor known as encomienda (see chapter 2). Yet some forms of coerced labor and racial distinction that developed in New Spain had North American counterparts, as English colonists employed servants and slaves and defined themselves as superior to Indians and Africans.

By 1700, the remnants of Powhatan's people still survived. As English settlement pushed north, west, and south of the Chesapeake Bay, the Indians faced the new colonial world that Powhatan and Pocahontas had encountered when John Smith and the first colonists had arrived at Jamestown. By 1700, the many descendants of Pocahontas's son, Thomas, as well as other colonists and Native Americans, understood that the English had come to stay.

The Virginia Planters Best TOBACCO.

SO NOW YOU KNOW

Tobacco made the Virginia colony a success. It transformed life in Virginia and the rest of the Chesapeake region. Large plantations producing rice developed in Carolina while even larger plantations grew sugarcane in Barbados. By the end of the seventeenth century, all these plantation societies relied heavily on African slaves for their success.

How did a tobacco society take shape?	How and why did Chesapeake society change in the late seventeenth century?	What caused tensions in the Spanish borderland?	When and why did the southern colonies move toward a slave labor system?	Conclusion: Why were export crops and slave labor important in the growth of the southern colonies?

STEP 1

GETTING STARTED

Below are basic terms from this period in American history. Can you identify each term below and explain why it matters? To do this exercise online or to download this chart, visit bedfordstmartins.com/roarkunderstanding.

TERM	WHO OR WHAT & WHEN	WHY IT MATTERS
Powhatan, p. 57		
Jamestown, p. 57		
Captain John Smith, p. 58		
Pocahontas, p. 58		
House of Burgesses, p. 61		
headright, p. 64		
indentured servants, p. 64		
yeoman, p. 68		
Navigation Acts of 1650 and 1651, p. 69		
mercantilism, p. 70		
Bacon's Rebellion, p. 70		
Pueblo Revolt, p. 73		

STEP 2

MOVING BEYOND THE BASICS

The exercise below represents a more advanced understanding of the chapter material. In this exercise, you will reflect on the social and economic development of the English colonies and the Spanish borderland. Begin by identifying the important economic activities of each region. What was involved in making each colony a financial success? What resources (both material and human) were necessary? How did each settlement develop socially? What were the challenges and successes, both political and social, that occurred as each colony developed? To do this exercise online or to download this chart, visit bedfordstmartins.com/roarkunderstanding.

Colony	Economy (including labor, land use and distribution, resources, crops)	Population and social hierarchy	Challenges	Successes
Chesapeake				
New Mexico				
Barbados				
Carolina				

STEP

3

PUTTING IT ALL TOGETHER

Now that you've reviewed various parts of the chapter, take a step back and try to see the big picture by answering these questions. Remember to use specific examples from the chapter in your answers. To do this exercise online, visit bedfordsmartins.com/roarkunderstanding.

JAMESTOWN AND THE CHESAPEAKE

▶ How did interactions with the Algonquians shape the Jamestown colony's early history?

▶ How did the development of tobacco cultivation transform the Chesapeake?

INDENTURED SERVITUDE AND BACON'S REBELLION

▶ What role did indentured servants play in the transformation of the Chesapeake in the early seventeenth century?

▶ What events led to Bacon's Rebellion, and why did Virginia erupt into violence in 1676?

SLAVERY

▶ What role did sugar play in the development of African slavery in the New World?

▶ How did the introduction of African slaves affect the development of Chesapeake society?

LOOKING BACKWARD, LOOKING AHEAD

▶ How did the seventeenth-century English colonies differ from their sixteenth-century Spanish counterparts?

▶ How did the introduction of African slaves contribute to the emergence of a distinct southern colonial society?

IN YOUR OWN WORDS

Imagine that you must explain chapter 3 to someone who hasn't read it. What would be the most important points to include and why?

Why why Lord of Early Finny [illegible] minding
[illegible] a World of [illegible] Work. Fames [illegible] Years
Then [illegible] Work [illegible] thy Wars
[illegible] Joins thy [illegible]: I am yet forye
The [illegible] Drums to him my head
Faith (which can) my Fort Subvert)
[illegible] after grace) with Glory.

4
CREATING THE NORTHERN COLONIES

1601–1700

> This chapter explores the development of the northern colonies in the seventeenth century, examining the factors that gave each colony its unique character. It gives particular emphasis to the importance of religion in the evolution of New England and to England's attempts to control colonial trade.

> How did the English Reformation influence Puritans?

> What was distinctive about the settlement of New England?

> How did New England society change during the seventeenth century?

> What was distinctive about the middle colonies?

> What was the role of the North American colonies in the English empire?

> Conclusion: What made the English colonization of North America distinctive?

> **DID YOU KNOW?**

New England Puritans did not celebrate Christmas or Easter.

Thomas Smith, a New England mariner, created colonial America's oldest known self-portrait around 1680.

83

How did the English Reformation influence Puritans?

Queen Elizabeth's Funeral Procession

The death of Elizabeth I in 1603 created uncertainty about the balance of Protestantism and Catholicism in England. Since Elizabeth had no children, James, Elizabeth's nephew and the son of the staunch Catholic Queen Mary (Elizabeth's sister), assumed the throne and soon cracked down on Protestants, especially Puritans. Courtesy of the Trustees of the British Library.

Puritans
▶ Dissenting members of the Church of England who sought to purify the Church of England of remnants of Catholicism. Puritanism was less an organized movement than a set of ideas and religious principles.

English Reformation
▶ The break between the English church and the Catholic Church. The English Reformation began in 1534 when Henry VIII outlawed the Catholic Church and made himself head of the Church of England.

THE RELIGIOUS ROOTS of the **Puritans** who founded New England reached back to the Protestant Reformation, which arose in Germany in 1517 (see chapter 2). The Reformation spread quickly to other countries, but the English church initially remained within the Catholic fold and continued its allegiance to the pope in Rome. King Henry VIII, who reigned from 1509 to 1547, understood that the Reformation offered him an opportunity to break with Rome and take control of the church in England. In 1534, Henry formally initiated the **English Reformation**. At his insistence, Parliament passed the Act of Supremacy, which outlawed the Catholic Church and proclaimed the king "the only supreme head on earth of the Church of England." Henry seized the vast properties of the Catholic Church in England as well as the privilege of appointing bishops and others in the church hierarchy.

In the short run, the English Reformation allowed Henry VIII to achieve his political goal of controlling the church. In the long run, however, the Reformation brought to England the political and religious turmoil that Henry had hoped to avoid. Henry himself sought no more than a halfway Reformation, one that preserved Catholic religious beliefs and practices while giving control of the church

CHAPTER LOCATOR | How did the English Reformation influence Puritans?

to the English crown. Many English Catholics wanted to revoke the English Reformation. But many other English people insisted on a genuine, thoroughgoing Reformation; these people came to be called Puritans.

During the sixteenth century, Puritanism was less an organized movement than a set of ideas and religious principles that appealed strongly to many dissenting members of the Church of England. They sought to purify the Church of England by eliminating what they considered the offensive features of Catholicism. For example, they demanded that the church hierarchy be abolished and that ordinary Christians be given greater control over religious life. They wanted to do away with the rituals of Catholic worship and instead emphasize an individual's relationship with God developed through Bible study, prayer, and introspection. Although there were many varieties and degrees of Puritanism, all Puritans shared a desire to make the English church thoroughly Protestant.

The fate of Protestantism waxed and waned under the monarchs who succeeded Henry VIII. When he died in 1547, the advisers of the new king, Edward VI—the nine-year-old son of Henry and his third wife, Jane Seymour—initiated religious reforms that moved in a Protestant direction. The tide of reform reversed in 1553 when Edward died and was succeeded by Mary I, the daughter of Henry and Catherine of Aragon, his first wife. Mary was a steadfast Catholic, and shortly after becoming queen, she married Philip II of Spain, Europe's most powerful guardian of Catholicism. Mary attempted to restore the pre-Reformation Catholic Church. She outlawed Protestantism in England and persecuted those who refused to conform, sentencing almost three hundred to burn at the stake.

The tide turned again in 1558 when Mary died and was succeeded by Elizabeth I, the daughter of Henry and his second wife, Anne Boleyn. During her long reign, Elizabeth reaffirmed the English Reformation and tried to position the English church between the extremes of Catholicism and Puritanism. Above all, she desired a church that would strengthen the monarchy and the nation. By the time Elizabeth died in 1603, many people in England looked on Protestantism as a defining feature of national identity.

When Elizabeth's successor, James I, became king, English Puritans petitioned for further reform of the Church of England. James authorized a new translation of the Bible, known ever since as the King James version. However, neither James I nor his son Charles I, who became king in 1625, was receptive to the ideas of Puritan reformers. In 1629, Charles I dissolved Parliament—where Puritans were well represented—and initiated aggressive anti-Puritan policies. Many Puritans despaired about continuing to defend their faith in England and began to make plans to emigrate. Some left for Europe, others for the West Indies. The largest number set out for America.

CHRONOLOGY

1534
– King Henry VIII breaks with Roman Catholic Church; English Reformation begins.

1547
– Edward VI becomes king of England; Church of England moves in the direction of Protestantism.

1553
– Mary I becomes queen of England and attempts to restore Catholicism.

1558
– Elizabeth I becomes queen of England and establishes moderate Protestantism as the state religion.

QUICK REVIEW <

How did Henry VIII seek to benefit from the English Reformation?

| What was distinctive about the settlement of New England? | How did New England society change during the seventeenth century? | What was distinctive about the middle colonies? | What was the role of the North American colonies in the English empire? | Conclusion: What made the English colonization of North America distinctive? |

What was distinctive about the settlement of New England?

Seal of Massachusetts Bay Colony

In 1629, the Massachusetts Bay Company designed this seal depicting an Indian man inviting English settlers to "come over and help us." The seal was an attempt to lend an aura of altruism to the Massachusetts Bay Company's colonization efforts. In reality, colonists in Massachusetts and elsewhere were far less interested in helping Indians than in helping themselves. For the most part, that suited the Indians, who wanted no "help" from the colonists. Courtesy of Massachusetts Archives.

▶ FOR MORE HELP ANALYZING THIS IMAGE, see the visual activity for this chapter in the Online Study Guide at bedfordstmartins.com/roarkunderstanding.

PURITANS WHO IMMIGRATED to New England aspired to escape the turmoil and persecution of England and to build a new, orderly, Puritan version of English society. Puritans established the first small settlement in New England in 1620, followed a few years later by additional settlements by the Massachusetts Bay Company. Allowed self-government through royal charter, these Puritans were in a unique position to direct the new colonies according to their faith. Their faith shaped the colonies they established in almost every way.

CHAPTER LOCATOR | How did the English Reformation influence Puritans?

The Pilgrims and Plymouth Colony

One of the first Protestant groups to emigrate, later known as **Pilgrims,** espoused an unorthodox view known as separatism. These Separatists sought to withdraw— or separate—from the Church of England, which they considered hopelessly corrupt. In 1608, they moved to Holland; by 1620, they realized that they could not live and worship there as they had hoped. William Bradford, a leader of the Separatists, believed that America promised to better protect their children's piety and preserve their community. Separatists obtained permission to settle in the extensive territory granted to the Virginia Company (see chapter 3). To finance their journey, they formed a joint-stock company with English investors. In August 1620, 102 Pilgrim immigrants boarded the *Mayflower*, arriving eleven weeks later at the outermost tip of Cape Cod, in present-day Massachusetts.

The Pilgrims realized immediately that they had landed far north of the Virginia grants and had no legal authority to settle in the area. To provide order and security as well as a claim to legitimacy, they drew up the Mayflower Compact on the day they arrived. They pledged to "covenant and combine ourselves together into a civil Body Politick, for our better Ordering and Preservation." The signers (all men) agreed to enact and obey necessary and just laws.

The Pilgrims settled at Plymouth in 1620 and elected William Bradford their governor. That first winter "was most sad and lamentable," Bradford wrote later. "In two or three months' time half of [our] company died . . . being the depth of winter, and wanting houses and other comforts [and] being infected with scurvy and other diseases." In the spring, Wampanoag Indians rescued the floundering Plymouth settlement. First Samoset and then Squanto befriended the settlers. Samoset arranged for the Pilgrims to meet and establish good relations with Massasoit, the Wampanoag chief whose territory included Plymouth. Squanto, Bradford recalled, "was a special instrument sent of God for their [the Pilgrims'] good. . . . He directed them how to set their corn, where to take fish, and to procure other commodities, and was also their pilot to bring them to unknown places." With the Indians' guidance, the Pilgrims managed to harvest enough food to guarantee their survival through the coming winter, an occasion they celebrated in the fall of 1621 with a feast of thanksgiving attended by Massasoit and other Wampanoags.

Still, the Plymouth colony remained precarious. The colonists quarreled with their London investors, who became frustrated when Plymouth failed to produce the expected profits. These struggles to survive constantly frustrated the London investors, but the Pilgrims persisted, living simply and coexisting in relative peace with the Indians. They paid the Wampanoags when settlers gradually encroached on Indian land. By 1630, Plymouth had become a small permanent settlement, but it failed to attract many other English Puritans.

The Founding of Massachusetts Bay Colony

In 1629, shortly before Charles I dissolved Parliament, a group of Puritan merchants and country gentlemen obtained a royal charter for the **Massachusetts Bay Company**. In addition to the usual privileges granted to joint-stock companies, the charter included a unique provision that permitted the government of the Massachusetts Bay Company to be located in the colony rather than in England.

CHRONOLOGY

1620
– Plymouth colony is founded.

1621
– Thanksgiving feast is attended by Pilgrims and Wampanoags.

1629
– Massachusetts Bay Company receives royal charter.

1630
– John Winthrop leads Puritan settlers to Massachusetts Bay.

Pilgrims
▶ Puritan Separatists who founded the Plymouth colony in Massachusetts in 1620. The Pilgrims believed that the Church of England could not be reformed and hoped to create their own religious community outside of England.

Massachusetts Bay Company
▶ Joint-stock company that established settlements around present-day Boston in 1630. The company's charter included a unique provision that permitted its government to be located in the colony rather than in England.

What was distinctive about the settlement of New England?	How did New England society change during the seventeenth century?	What was distinctive about the middle colonies?	What was the role of the North American colonies in the English empire?	Conclusion: What made the English colonization of North America distinctive?

John Winthrop

► Puritan lawyer and landowner who served as the first governor of New England. Winthrop hoped to reform the Church of England by setting an example of godliness in the New World.

To lead the emigrants, the stockholders of the Massachusetts Bay Company elected **John Winthrop**, a prosperous lawyer and landowner, to serve as governor. In March 1630, eleven ships crammed with seven hundred passengers sailed for Massachusetts; six more ships and another five hundred emigrants followed a few months later. Winthrop's fleet arrived in Massachusetts Bay in early June. Unlike the Separatists, Winthrop's Puritans aspired to reform the corrupt Church of England (rather than separate from it) by setting an example of godliness in the New World. Winthrop and a small group chose to settle on the peninsula that became Boston, and other settlers clustered at promising locations nearby (**Map 4.1**).

In a sermon to his companions aboard the *Arbella* while they were still at sea, Winthrop proclaimed the cosmic significance of their journey. The Puritans had "entered into a covenant" with God to "work out our salvation under the power and purity of his holy ordinances," Winthrop declared. This sanctified agreement with God meant that the Puritans had to make "extraordinary" efforts to "bring into familiar and constant practice" religious principles that most people in England merely preached. To achieve their pious goals, the Puritans had to subordinate their individual interests to the common good. "We must be knit together in this work as one man," Winthrop preached. "We must delight in each other, make others' conditions our own, rejoice together, mourn together, labor and suffer together." The stakes could not be higher, Winthrop told his listeners: "We must consider that we shall be as a city upon a hill. The eyes of all people are upon us."

That belief shaped seventeenth-century New England as profoundly as tobacco shaped the Chesapeake. Winthrop's vision of a city on a hill fired the Puritans' fierce determination to keep their covenant and live according to God's laws.

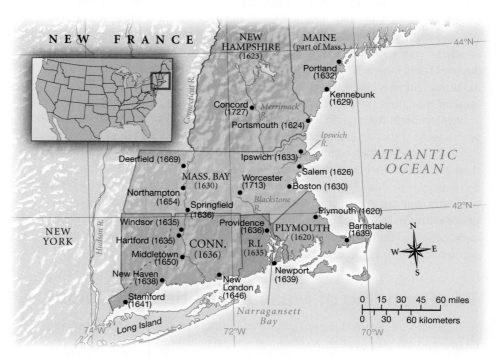

MAP 4.1 ■ New England Colonies in the Seventeenth Century
New Englanders spread across the landscape town by town during the seventeenth century. (For the sake of legibility, only a few of the more important towns are shown on the map.)

CHAPTER LOCATOR | How did the English Reformation influence Puritans?

And each year from 1630 to 1640, ship after ship followed in the wake of Winthrop's fleet. In all, more than twenty thousand new settlers came, their eyes focused on the Puritans' city on a hill.

Often, when the Church of England cracked down on a Puritan minister in England, he and many of his followers moved together to New England. Smaller groups of English Puritans moved to the Chesapeake, Barbados, and elsewhere in the New World, including New Amsterdam (present-day New York). A few ministers sought to carry the message of Christianity to the Indians, accompanied by instructions replacing what missionary John Eliot termed the Indians' "unfixed, confused, and ungoverned . . . life, uncivilized and unsubdued to labor and order." For the most part, however, the colonists focused less on saving Indians' souls than on saving their own.

On the whole, the immigrants came from the middle ranks of English society. The vast majority were either farmers or tradesmen, including carpenters, tailors, and textile workers. Indentured servants, whose numbers dominated the Chesapeake settlers, accounted for only about a fifth of those headed for New England. Most New England immigrants paid their way to Massachusetts, even though the journey often took their life savings. They were encouraged by the promise of bounty in New England reported in Winthrop's letter to his son: "Here is as good land as I have seen there [in England]. . . . Here can be no want of anything to those who bring means to raise [it] out of the earth and sea."

In contrast to Chesapeake newcomers, New England immigrants usually arrived as families, with women and children making up a solid majority of the region's population. Each family was considered a "little commonwealth" that mirrored the hierarchy among all God's creatures. Just as humankind was subordinate to God, so young people were subordinate to their elders, children to their parents, and wives to their husbands. The immigrants' family ties reinforced their religious beliefs with universally understood notions of hierarchy and mutual dependence. While immigrants to the Chesapeake were disciplined mostly by the coercions of servitude and the caprices of the tobacco market, immigrants to New England entered a social order defined by the interlocking institutions of family, church, and community.

QUICK REVIEW

What was a "little commonwealth," and why was it so important to Puritan settlement in New England?

What was distinctive about the settlement of New England?	How did New England society change during the seventeenth century?	What was distinctive about the middle colonies?	What was the role of the North American colonies in the English empire?	Conclusion: What made the English colonization of North America distinctive?

> How did New England society change during the seventeenth century?

This 1670 painting depicts the children of Joanna and Anthony Mason, a wealthy Boston baker. The artist lavished attention on the children's elaborate clothing. The portrait is unified not by signs of warm affection, innocent smiles, or familial solidarity, but by the trappings of wealth and sober self-importance. The painting expresses the growing respect for wealth and its worldly rewards in seventeenth-century New England. Fine Arts Museums of San Francisco. Gift of Mr. and Mrs. John D. Rockefeller III.

THE NEW ENGLAND COLONISTS, unlike their counterparts in the Chesapeake, settled in small towns, usually located on the coast or by a river (see Map 4.1, page 88). Massachusetts Bay colonists founded 133 towns during the seventeenth century, each with one or more churches. Church members' fervent piety, buttressed by the institutions of local government, enforced remarkable religious and social conformity in the small settlements. During the century, tensions within the Puritan faith and changes in New England communities splintered religious orthodoxy and weakened Puritan zeal. By 1700, however, Puritanism still maintained a distinctive influence in New England.

Church, Covenant, and Conformity

Puritans believed that the church consisted of men and women who had entered a solemn covenant with one another and with God. Each new member of the covenant had to persuade existing members that she or he had fully experienced conversion.

CHAPTER LOCATOR | How did the English Reformation influence Puritans?

Puritans embraced a distinctive version of Protestantism derived from Calvinism, the doctrines of John Calvin, a sixteenth-century Swiss Protestant theologian. Calvin insisted that Christians strictly discipline their behavior to conform to God's commandments announced in the Bible. Like Calvin, Puritans believed in predestination—the idea that the all-powerful God, before the creation of the world, decided which few human souls would receive eternal life. Only God knows the identity of these fortunate predestined individuals—the "elect" or "saints." Nothing a person did in his or her lifetime could alter God's choice or provide assurance that the person was predestined for salvation or damnation.

Despite the ultimate unknowability of God's choice of the elect, Puritans believed that if a person lived a rigorously godly life, his or her behavior was likely to be a hint, a visible sign, that he or she was one of God's chosen few. Puritans thought that "sainthood" would become visible in individuals' behavior, especially if they were privileged to know God's Word as revealed in the Bible.

The connection between sainthood and saintly behavior, however, was far from certain. The slippery relationship between saintly behavior—observable by anybody—and God's predestined election—invisible and unknowable to anyone—caused Puritans to worry constantly that individuals who acted like saints were fooling themselves and others. Nevertheless, Puritans thought that visible saints—people who passed their demanding tests of conversion and church membership—probably, though not certainly, were among God's elect.

Members of Puritan churches ardently hoped that God had chosen them to receive eternal life and tried to demonstrate saintly behavior. Their covenant bound them to help one another attain salvation and to discipline the entire community by saintly standards. Church members kept an eye on the behavior of everybody in town. Infractions of morality, order, or propriety were reported to Puritan elders, who summoned the wayward to a church inquiry. By overseeing every aspect of life, the visible saints enforced a remarkable degree of righteous conformity in Puritan communities. Total conformity, however, was never achieved. Puritans differed among themselves; non-Puritans shirked orthodox rules. Despite the central importance of religion, churches played no direct role in the civil government of New England communities. Puritans were determined to insulate New England churches from the contaminating influence of the civil state and its merely human laws. Although ministers were the most highly respected figures in New England towns, they were prohibited from holding government office.

Puritans had no qualms, however, about their religious beliefs influencing New England governments. As much as possible, the Puritans tried to bring public life into conformity with their view of God's law. For example, fines were issued for Sabbath-breaking activities such as working, smoking a pipe, and visiting neighbors. Puritans mandated other purifications of what they considered corrupt English practices. They refused to celebrate Christmas or Easter because the Bible did not mention either one. They outlawed religious wedding ceremonies; couples were married by a magistrate in a civil ceremony (the first wedding in Massachusetts performed by a minister occurred in 1686). They prohibited elaborate clothing and finery such as lace trim and short sleeves—"whereby the nakedness of the arm may be discovered." They banned cards, dice, shuffleboard, and

CHRONOLOGY

1636
- Roger Williams is banished from Massachusetts Bay.
- Rhode Island colony is established.

1638
- Anne Hutchinson is excommunicated for heresy.

1642
- Puritan Revolution inflames England.

1649
- English Puritans win civil war and execute Charles I.

1656
- Quakers arrive in Massachusetts and are persecuted there.

1660
- Monarchy is restored in England; Charles II becomes king.

1662
- Many Puritan congregations adopt Halfway Covenant.

1692
- Salem witch trials.

THE

World turn'd upfide down:
OR,

A briefe defcription of the ridiculous Fafhions
of thefe diftracted Times.

By T.J. a well-willer to King, Parliament and Kingdom.

London : Printed for *John Smith*. 1 6 4 7.

**The Puritan Challenge
to the Status Quo**

The World Turn'd Upside Down, a pamphlet printed in London in 1647,
satirizes the Puritan notion that the contemporary world was deeply flawed.
The pamphlet refers to the "distracted Times" of the Puritan Revolution in
England. The drawing on the title page ridicules criticisms of English society
that also were common among New England Puritans. By permission of The
British Library.

▶ FOR MORE HELP ANALYZING THIS IMAGE, see the visual activity for this
chapter in the Online Study Guide at bedfordstmartins.com/roarkunderstanding.

other games of chance, as well as music and dancing. The distinguished minister
Increase Mather insisted that "Mixt or Promiscuous Dancing . . . of Men and
Women" could not be tolerated since "the unchaste Touches and Gesticulations
used by Dancers have a palpable tendency to that which is evil." On special occa-
sions, Puritans proclaimed days of fasting and humiliation, which, as one preacher
boasted, amounted to "so many Sabbaths more."

Government by Puritans for Puritanism

It is only a slight exaggeration to say that seventeenth-century New England was
governed by Puritans for Puritanism. The charter of the Massachusetts Bay Company
empowered the company's stockholders, known as freemen, to meet as a body
known as the General Court and make the laws needed to govern the company's
affairs. The colonists transformed this arrangement for running a joint-stock company
into a structure for governing the colony. Hoping to ensure that godly men would
decide government policies, the General Court expanded the number of freemen in
1631 to include all male church members. Only freemen had the right to vote for governor, deputy governor, and other colonial officials. As new settlers were recognized
as freemen, the size of the General Court grew too large to meet conveniently. So in
1634, the freemen in each town agreed to send two deputies to the General Court to
act as the colony's legislative assembly. All other men were classified as "inhabitants," and they had the right to vote, hold office, and participate fully in town government. A "town meeting," composed of a town's inhabitants and freemen, chose the
selectmen and other officials who administered local affairs. Almost every adult man
could speak out in town meetings and fortify his voice with a vote. However, all
women—even church members—were prohibited from voting, and towns did not
permit "contrary-minded" men to become or remain inhabitants. Although town
meeting participants wrangled from time to time, widespread political participation
tended to reinforce conformity to Puritan ideals.

CHAPTER LOCATOR | How did the English
Reformation influence
Puritans?

92 CHAPTER 4
CREATING THE NORTHERN COLONIES

One of the most important functions of New England government was land distribution. Settlers who desired to establish a new town entered a covenant and petitioned the General Court for a grant of land. The court granted town sites to suitably pious petitioners but did not allow settlement until the Indians who inhabited a grant agreed to relinquish their claim to the land, usually in exchange for manufactured goods. For instance, William Pynchon purchased the site of Springfield, Massachusetts, from the Agawam Indians for "eighteen fathams [arm's lengths] of Wampum, eighteen coates, 18 hatchets, 18 hoes, [and] 18 knives."

Having obtained their grant, town founders apportioned land among themselves and any newcomers they permitted to join them. Normally, each family received a house lot large enough for an adjacent garden as well as one or more strips of agricultural land on the perimeter of the town. Although there was a considerable difference between the largest and smallest family plots, most clustered in the middle range—roughly fifty to one hundred acres—resulting in a more nearly equal distribution of land in New England than in the Chesapeake.

The Splintering of Puritanism

Almost from the beginning, John Winthrop and other leaders had difficulty enforcing their views of Puritan orthodoxy. In England, persecution as a dissenting minority had unified Puritan voices in opposition to the Church of England. In New England, the promise of a godly society and the Puritans' emphasis on individual Bible study led New Englanders toward different visions of godliness. Puritan leaders, however, interpreted dissent as an error caused either by a misguided believer or by the malevolent power of Satan. Whatever the cause, errors could not be tolerated.

The case of **Roger Williams** provides an example of division and its consequences. In 1633, Williams became the minister of the church in Salem, Massachusetts. Most New England Puritans believed that churches and governments should enforce both godly belief and behavior according to biblical rules. They claimed that "the Word of God is . . . clear." In contrast, Williams believed that the Bible shrouded the Word of God in "mist and fog." Williams pointed out that devout and pious Christians could and did differ about what the Bible said and what God expected. That observation led him to denounce the emerging New England order as impure, ungodly, and tyrannical.

Williams also disagreed with the New England government's requirement that everyone attend church services. He argued that forcing people who were not Christians to attend church was wrong in four major ways. First, Williams preached, it was akin to requiring "a dead child to suck the breast, or a dead man [to] feast." The only way for any person to become a true Christian was by God's gift of faith revealed to the person's conscience. Second, churches should be reserved exclusively for those already converted, separating "holy from unholy . . . [and] godly from ungodly." He said requiring everybody to attend church was "False Worshipping" that promoted "spiritual drunkenness and whoredom, a soul sleep and a soul sickness." Third, the government had no business ruling on spiritual matters. Williams termed New England's regulation of religious behavior "spiritual rape" that inevitably would lead governments to use coercion and violence to enforce their misguided ways. Finally, Williams believed that governments should tolerate all religious beliefs because only God knows the Truth; no

Roger Williams
▶ Puritan minister who criticized the political and religious order in New England and advocated religious toleration. After his banishment from New England in 1636, Williams went on to found Rhode Island.

| What was distinctive about the settlement of New England? | How did New England society change during the seventeenth century? | What was distinctive about the middle colonies? | What was the role of the North American colonies in the English empire? | Conclusion: What made the English colonization of North America distinctive? |

93

person and no religion can understand God with absolute certainty. "I commend that man," Williams wrote, "whether Jew, or Turk, or Papist, or whoever, that steers no otherwise than his conscience dares." In Williams's view, toleration of religious belief and liberty of conscience were the only paths to religious purity and political harmony.

New England's leaders denounced Williams's arguments and banished Williams for his "extreme and dangerous" opinions. He escaped from an attempt to ship him back to England and in 1636 spent fourteen weeks walking south to Narragansett Bay, "exposed to the mercy of an howling Wilderness in Frost and Snow." There he founded the colony of Rhode Island, which enshrined "Liberty of Conscience" as a fundamental ideal and became a refuge for other dissenters.

Shortly after banishing Williams, the Puritan leadership confronted another dissenter, this time a devout Puritan woman steeped in Scripture and absorbed by religious questions: **Anne Hutchinson**. The mother of fourteen children, Hutchinson settled into her new home in Boston in 1634, and neighbors—women and men—gathered there to hear her weekly lectures on recent sermons. As one listener observed, she was a "Woman that Preaches better Gospell then any of your blackcoates [male preachers] . . . [from] the Ninneversity."

Hutchinson expounded on the sermons of John Cotton, her favorite minister. Cotton stressed what he termed the covenant of grace—the idea that individuals could be saved only by God's grace in choosing them to be members of the elect. Cotton contrasted this familiar Puritan doctrine with the covenant of works, the erroneous belief that a person's behavior—one's works—could win God's favor and ultimately earn a person salvation. Belief in the covenant of works and in the possibility of salvation for all was known as Arminianism. Hutchinson's lectures emphasized her opinion that many of the colony's leaders affirmed the Arminian position that a person's behavior could influence their chances for salvation.

Anne Hutchinson

▶ Puritan woman who challenged the Massachusetts Bay colony's position on religious issues, specifically whether a person's works could help earn salvation. Hutchinson began holding mixed-sex discussions at her house, leading the governor of the colony, John Winthrop, to become concerned. She was formally charged with and convicted of heresy in 1638 and banished from the colony.

Old Ship Meeting House

Built in Hingham, Massachusetts, in 1681, this meetinghouse is one of the oldest surviving buildings used for church services in English North America. The unadorned walls and windows reflect the austere religious aesthetic of New England Puritanism. The family pews mark boundaries of kinship and piety visible to all. The elevated pulpit bathed in light signals the illumination of God's Word as preached by the minister. Old Ship Church, Hingham, MA, photo by Bruce Benedict.

CHAPTER LOCATOR | How did the English Reformation influence Puritans?

The meetings at Hutchinson's house alarmed her nearest neighbor, John Winthrop, who believed that she was subverting the good order of the colony. In 1637, Winthrop had formal charges brought against Hutchinson and denounced her lectures as "not tolerable nor comely in the sight of God nor fitting for your sex." He told her, "You have stept out of your place, you have rather bine a Husband than a Wife and a preacher than a Hearer; and a Magistrate than a Subject."

In court, Winthrop interrogated Hutchinson, fishing for a heresy he could pin on her. Winthrop and other Puritan elders referred to Hutchinson and her followers as antinomians, people who believed that Christians could be saved by faith alone and did not need to act in accordance with God's law as set forth in the Bible and as interpreted by the colony's leaders. Hutchinson nimbly defended herself against the accusation of antinomianism. Yes, she acknowledged, she believed that men and women were saved by faith alone; but no, she did not deny the need to obey God's law. "The Lord hath let me see which was the clear ministry and which the wrong," she said. Finally, Winthrop had cornered her. How could she tell which ministry was which? "By an immediate revelation," she replied, "by the voice of [God's] own spirit to my soul." Winthrop spotted in this statement the heresy of prophecy, the view that God revealed his will directly to a believer instead of exclusively through the Bible, as every right-minded Puritan knew.

In 1638, the Boston church formally excommunicated Hutchinson. The minister decreed, "I doe cast you out and . . . deliver you up to Satan that you may learne no more to blaspheme[,] to seduce and to lye. . . . I command you . . . as a Leper to withdraw your selfe out of the Congregation." Banished, Hutchinson and her family moved first to Roger Williams's Rhode Island and then to present-day New York, where she and most of her family were killed by Indians.

The strains within Puritanism exemplified by Anne Hutchinson and Roger Williams caused communities to splinter repeatedly during the seventeenth century. Puritan churches divided and subdivided as acrimony developed over doctrine and church government. Sometimes churches split over the appointment of a controversial minister. Sometimes families who had a long walk to the meetinghouse simply decided to form their own church nearer their houses. These schisms arose from ambiguities and tensions within Puritan belief. As the colonies matured, other tensions developed as well.

Religious Controversies and Economic Changes

A revolutionary transformation in the fortunes of Puritans in England had profound consequences in New England. Disputes between King Charles I and Parliament, dominated by Puritans, escalated in 1642 to civil war in England, a conflict known as the Puritan Revolution. Parliamentary forces led by Oliver Cromwell were victorious, executing Charles I in 1649 and proclaiming England a Puritan republic. From 1649 to 1660, England's rulers were not monarchs who suppressed Puritanism but believers who championed it. In a half century, English Puritans had risen from a harassed group of religious dissenters to a dominant power in English government.

When the Puritan Revolution began, the stream of immigrants to New England dwindled to a trickle, creating hard times for the colonists. When

| What was distinctive about the settlement of New England? | How did New England society change during the seventeenth century? | What was distinctive about the middle colonies? | What was the role of the North American colonies in the English empire? | Conclusion: What made the English colonization of North America distinctive? |

immigrant ships became rare, the colonists faced sky-high prices for scarce English goods and few customers for their own colonial products. As they searched to find new products and markets, they established the enduring patterns of New England's economy.

New England's rocky soil and short growing season ruled out cultivating the southern colonies' crops of tobacco and rice that found ready markets in Atlantic ports. Exports that New Englanders could not get from the soil they took instead from the forest and the sea. During the first decade of settlement, colonists traded with the Indians for animal pelts, which were in demand in Europe. By the 1640s, furbearing animals had become scarce unless traders ventured far beyond the frontiers of English settlement. Trees from the seemingly limitless forests of New England proved a longer-lasting resource. Masts for ships and staves for barrels of Spanish wine and West Indian sugar were crafted from New England timber.

The most important New England export was fish. During the turmoil of the Puritan Revolution, English ships withdrew from the rich North Atlantic fishing grounds, and New England fishermen quickly took their place. Dried, salted codfish found markets in southern Europe and the West Indies. The fish trade also stimulated colonial shipbuilding and trained generations of fishermen, sailors, and merchants, creating a commercial network that endured for more than a century. But this export economy remained peripheral to most New England colonists. Their lives revolved around their farms, their churches, and their families.

Although immigration came to a standstill in the 1640s, the population continued to boom, doubling every twenty years. In New England, almost everyone married, and women often had eight or nine children. Long, cold winters minimized the warm-weather ailments of the southern colonies and reduced New England mortality. The descendants of the immigrants of the 1630s multiplied, boosting the New England population to roughly equal that of the southern colonies (**Figure 4.1**).

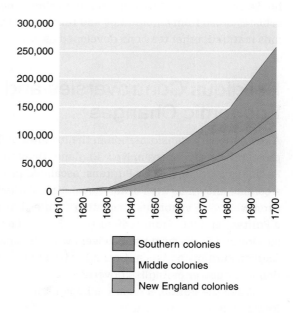

FIGURE 4.1 ■ Population of the English North American Colonies in the Seventeenth Century
The colonial population grew at a steadily accelerating rate during the seventeenth century. New England and the southern colonies each accounted for about half the total colonial population until after 1680, when growth in Pennsylvania and New York contributed to a surge in the population of the middle colonies.

Southern colonies

Middle colonies

New England colonies

CHAPTER LOCATOR | How did the English Reformation influence Puritans?

During the second half of the seventeenth century, under the pressures of steady population growth and integration into the Atlantic economy, the red-hot piety of the founders cooled. After 1640, the population grew faster than church membership. In some towns, only 15 percent of the adult men were members. A growing fraction of New Englanders, especially men, embraced what one historian has termed "horse-shed Christianity": They attended sermons but loitered outside near the horse shed, gossiping about the weather, fishing, their crops, or the scandalous behavior of neighbors. Most alarming to Puritan leaders, many of the children of the visible saints of Winthrop's generation failed to experience conversion and attain full church membership. Puritans tended to assume that sainthood was inherited—that the children of visible saints were probably also among the elect. Acting on this premise, churches permitted saints to baptize their infant sons and daughters, symbolically cleansing them of their contamination with original sin. As these children grew up during the 1640s and 1650s, however, they seldom experienced the inward transformation that signaled conversion and qualification for church membership. The problem of declining church membership and the watering-down of Puritan orthodoxy became urgent during the 1650s when the children of saints, who had grown to adulthood in New England but had not experienced conversion, began to have children themselves. Their sons and daughters—the grandchildren of the founders of the colony—could not receive the protection that baptism afforded against the terrors of death because their parents had not experienced conversion.

Puritan churches debated what to do. To allow anyone, even the child of a saint, to become a church member without conversion was an unthinkable retreat from fundamental Puritan doctrine. In 1662, a synod of Massachusetts ministers reached a compromise known as the Halfway Covenant. Unconverted children of saints would be permitted to become "halfway" church members. Like regular church members, they could baptize their infants. But unlike full church members, they could not participate in communion or have the voting privileges of church membership. The Halfway Covenant generated a controversy that sputtered through Puritan churches for the remainder of the century. With the Halfway Covenant, Puritan churches came to terms with the lukewarm piety that had replaced the founders' burning zeal.

Nonetheless, New England communities continued to enforce piety with holy rigor. Beginning in 1656, small bands of **Quakers**—members of the Society of Friends, as they called themselves—began to arrive in Massachusetts. Many of their beliefs were at odds with orthodox Puritanism. Quakers believed that God spoke directly to each individual through an "inner light" and that individuals needed neither a preacher nor the Bible to discover God's Word. Maintaining that all human beings were equal in God's eyes, Quakers refused to conform to mere temporal powers such as laws and governments unless God requested otherwise. Women often took a leading role in Quaker meetings, in contrast to Puritan congregations, where women usually outnumbered men but remained subordinate.

New England communities treated Quakers with ruthless severity. Some Quakers were branded on the face "with a red-hot iron with [an] H. for heresie." When Quakers refused to leave Massachusetts, Boston officials hanged four of them between 1659 and 1661.

Quakers
▶ Religious dissenters who believed that God spoke directly to each individual. Quaker beliefs clashed with those of Puritans and Anglicans, and they were persecuted in both England and Massachusetts.

What was distinctive about the settlement of New England?

How did New England society change during the seventeenth century?

What was distinctive about the middle colonies?

What was the role of the North American colonies in the English empire?

Conclusion: What made the English colonization of North America distinctive?

Witches Show Their Love for Satan

This seventeenth-century print portrays Satan with clawlike hands and feet, the tail of a rodent, the wings of a bat, and the head of a lustful ram attached to the torso of a man. Notice that women predominate among the witches eager to express their devotion to Satan and to do his bidding.
UCSF Library/Center for Knowledge Management.

New Englanders' partial success in realizing the promise of a godly society ultimately undermined the intense appeal of Puritanism. In the pious Puritan communities of New England, leaders tried to eliminate sin. In the process, they diminished the sense of utter human depravity that was the wellspring of Puritanism. By 1700, New Englanders did not doubt that human beings sinned, but they were more concerned with the sins of others than with their own.

Witch trials held in Salem, Massachusetts, signaled the erosion of religious confidence and assurance. In 1692, the frenzied Salem proceedings accused more than one hundred people of witchcraft, a capital crime. The Salem court executed nineteen accused witches, signaling enduring belief in the supernatural origins of evil and gnawing doubt about the strength of Puritan New Englanders' faith.

> **QUICK REVIEW**

Why did Massachusetts Puritans adopt the Halfway Covenant?

CHAPTER LOCATOR | How did the English Reformation influence Puritans?

What was distinctive about the middle colonies?

N. AMSTERDAM ou N. IORK in Ameriq.

New Amsterdam

The settlement on Manhattan Island—complete with a windmill—appears in the background of this 1673 Dutch portrait of New Amsterdam. Wharves connect Manhattan residents to the seaborne commerce of the Atlantic world. In the foreground, the Dutch artist placed native inhabitants of the mainland, drawing them in such a way that they resemble Africans rather than Lenni Lenape (Delaware) Indians. The portrait contrasts orderly, efficient, businesslike New Amsterdam with the exotic natural environment of America. © Collection of the New-York Historical Society.

SOUTH OF NEW ENGLAND and north of the Chesapeake, a group of middle colonies were founded in the last third of the seventeenth century. Before the 1670s, few Europeans settled in the region. For the first two-thirds of the seventeenth century, the most important European outpost in the area was the relatively small Dutch colony of **New Netherland**. By 1700, however, the English monarchy had seized New Netherland, renamed it New York, and encouraged the creation of a Quaker colony in Pennsylvania led by William Penn. Unlike the New England colonies, the middle colonies of New York, New Jersey, and Pennsylvania originated as land grants by the English monarch to one or more proprietors, who then possessed both the land and the extensive, almost monarchical, powers of government (**Map 4.2**). These middle colonies attracted settlers of more diverse European origins and religious faiths than were found in New England.

New Netherland
► Dutch colony north of the Chesapeake and south of New England established in the early seventeenth century. Although relatively small, it was an important European outpost. In 1664, England seized the colony and renamed it New York.

From New Netherland to New York

In 1609, the Dutch East India Company dispatched Henry Hudson to search for a Northwest Passage to the Orient. Hudson sailed along the Atlantic coast and ventured up the large river that now bears his name until it dwindled to a stream that obviously did not lead to China. A decade later, the Dutch government granted the West India Company—a group of Dutch merchants and shippers—exclusive rights to trade with the Western Hemisphere. In 1626, Peter Minuit, the resident director of the company, purchased Manhattan Island from the Manhate Indians for trade

What was distinctive about the settlement of New England? | How did New England society change during the seventeenth century? | **What was distinctive about the middle colonies?** | What was the role of the North American colonies in the English empire? | Conclusion: What made the English colonization of North America distinctive?

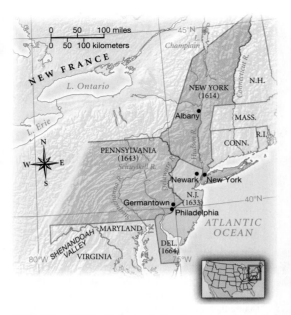

MAP 4.2 ■ Middle Colonies in the Seventeenth Century
For the most part, the middle colonies in the seventeenth century were inhabited by settlers who clustered along the Hudson and Delaware rivers. The vast geographic extent of the colonies shown in this map reflects land grants authorized in England. Most of this area was inhabited by Native Americans rather than settled by colonists.

goods worth the equivalent of a dozen beaver pelts. New Amsterdam, the small settlement established at the southern tip of Manhattan Island, became the principal trading center in New Netherland and the colony's headquarters.

New Netherland did not attract many European immigrants and never realized its sponsors' dreams of great profits. Though few in number, New Netherlanders were remarkably diverse, especially compared with the homogeneous English settlers to the north and south. Religious dissenters and immigrants from Holland, Sweden, France, Germany, and elsewhere made their way to the colony. A minister of the Dutch Reformed Church complained to his superiors in Holland that several groups of Jews had recently arrived, adding to the religious mixture of "Papists, Mennonites and Lutherans among the Dutch [and] many Puritans . . . and many other atheists . . . who conceal themselves under the name of Christians." The West India Company struggled to govern the motley colonists. Peter Stuyvesant, governor from 1647 to 1664, tried to enforce conformity to the Dutch Reformed Church, but the company declared that "the consciences of men should be free and unshackled," making a virtue of New Netherland necessity. The company never permitted the colony's settlers to form a representative government. Instead, the company appointed government officials who established policies, including taxes, that many colonists deeply resented.

CHRONOLOGY

1609
– Henry Hudson searches for Northwest Passage.

1626
– Manhattan Island is purchased; New Amsterdam is founded.

1664
– English seize Dutch colony and rename it New York.
– Colony of New Jersey is created.

1681
– William Penn receives charter for colony of Pennsylvania.

Dutch Patroonships

Allotments of eighteen miles of land along the Hudson River
Given to wealthy stockholders who would bring fifty families to the colony
Only one patroonship succeeded; the others failed to attract permanent settlers

In 1664, New Netherland became New York. Charles II, who became king of England in 1660 when Parliament restored the monarchy, gave his brother James, the Duke of York, an enormous grant of land that included New Netherland. Of course, the Dutch colony did not belong to the king of England, but that did not deter the king or his brother. The duke quickly organized a small fleet of warships, which appeared off Manhattan Island in late summer 1664, and demanded that Stuyvesant surrender. With little choice, he did.

As the new proprietor of the colony, the Duke of York exercised almost the same unlimited authority over the colony as had the West India Company. The duke never set foot in New York, but his governors struggled to impose order on the unruly colonists. Like the Dutch, the duke permitted "all persons of what Religion soever, quietly to inhabit . . . provided they give no disturbance to the publique peace, nor doe molest or disquiet others in the free exercise of their religion." This policy of religious toleration was less an affirmation of liberty of conscience than a recognition of the reality of the most heterogeneous colony in seventeenth-century North America.

CHAPTER LOCATOR | How did the English Reformation influence Puritans?

New Jersey and Pennsylvania

The creation of New York led indirectly to the founding of two other middle colonies, New Jersey and Pennsylvania (see Map 4.2, page 100). In 1664, the Duke of York subdivided his grant and gave the portion between the Hudson and Delaware rivers to two of his friends. The proprietors of this new colony, New Jersey, quarreled and called in a prominent English Quaker, **William Penn**, to arbitrate their dispute. In the process of working out a settlement, Penn became intensely interested in what he termed a "holy experiment" of establishing a genuinely Quaker colony in America.

Unlike most Quakers, William Penn came from an eminent family. His father had served both Cromwell and Charles II and had been knighted. Born in 1644, the younger Penn trained for a military career, but the ideas of dissenters from the reestablished Church of England appealed to him, and eventually he became a devout Quaker. By 1680, he had published fifty books and pamphlets and spoken at countless public meetings, although he had not won official toleration for Quakers in England.

The Quakers' concept of an open, generous God who made his love equally available to all people manifested itself in behavior that continually brought them into conflict with the English government. Quaker leaders were ordinary men and women, not specially trained preachers. Quakers allowed women to assume positions of religious leadership. "In souls there is no sex," they said. Since all people were equal in the spiritual realm, Quakers considered social hierarchy false and evil. They called everyone "friend" and shook hands instead of curtsying or removing their hats—even when meeting the king. These customs enraged many non-Quakers and provoked innumerable beatings and worse. Penn was jailed four times for such offenses, once for nine months.

Despite his many run-ins with the government, Penn remained on good terms with Charles II. Partly to rid England of the troublesome Quakers, in 1681 Charles made Penn the proprietor of a new colony of some 45,000 square miles called Pennsylvania.

Toleration and Diversity in Pennsylvania

English Quakers flocked to Pennsylvania in numbers exceeded only by the great Puritan migration to New England fifty years earlier. Quaker missionaries also encouraged immigrants from the European continent, and many came, giving Pennsylvania greater ethnic diversity than any other English colony except New York. The Quaker colony prospered, and the capital city, Philadelphia, soon rivaled New York as a center of commerce. By 1700, the city's five thousand inhabitants participated in a thriving trade exporting flour and other food products to the West Indies and importing English textiles and manufactured goods.

Quaker Immigration to Pennsylvania

1682–1685: Nearly eight thousand Quaker immigrants arrive in Pennsylvania.

Most are from England, Ireland, and Wales.

Artisans, farmers, and laborers predominate.

William Penn

▶ Prominent Quaker who was made the proprietor of the new royal colony of Pennsylvania in 1681. Penn established freedom of religion in the colony and was determined to make peace with the colony's Indians.

William Penn

This portrait was drawn about a decade after the founding of Pennsylvania. At a time when extravagant clothing and a fancy wig proclaimed that the wearer was an important person, Penn is portrayed informally, lacking even a coat, his natural hair neat but undressed—all a reflection of his Quaker faith. Historical Society of Pennsylvania.

| What was distinctive about the settlement of New England? | How did New England society change during the seventeenth century? | What was distinctive about the middle colonies? | What was the role of the North American colonies in the English empire? | Conclusion: What made the English colonization of North America distinctive? |

Penn was determined to live in peace with the Indians who inhabited the region. His Indian policy expressed his Quaker ideals and contrasted sharply with the hostile policies of the other English colonies. As he explained to the chief of the Lenni Lenape (Delaware) Indians, "God has written his law in our hearts, by which we are taught and commanded to love and help and do good to one another . . . [and] I desire to enjoy [Pennsylvania lands] with your love and consent." Penn instructed his agents to obtain the Indians' consent by purchasing their land, respecting their claims, and dealing with them fairly.

Penn declared that the first principle of government was that every settler would "enjoy the free possession of his or her faith and exercise of worship towards God." Accordingly, Pennsylvania tolerated Protestant sects of all kinds as well as Roman Catholicism. All voters and officeholders had to be Christians, but the government did not compel settlers to attend religious services, as in Massachusetts, or to pay taxes to maintain a state-supported church, as in Virginia.

Despite its toleration and diversity, Pennsylvania was as much a Quaker colony as New England was a stronghold of Puritanism. Penn had no hesitation about using civil government to enforce religious morality. One of the colony's first laws provided severe punishment for "all such offenses against God, as swearing, cursing, lying, profane talking, drunkenness, drinking of healths, [and] obscene words . . . which excite the people to rudeness, cruelty, looseness, and irreligion."

As proprietor, Penn had extensive powers subject to review only by the king. He appointed a governor, who maintained the proprietor's power to veto any laws passed by the colonial council, which was elected by property owners who possessed at least one hundred acres of land or who paid taxes. The council had the power to originate laws and administer all the affairs of government. A popularly elected assembly served as a check on the council; its members had the authority to reject or approve laws framed by the council.

Penn stressed that the exact form of government mattered less than the men who served in it. In Penn's eyes, "good men" staffed Pennsylvania's government because Quakers dominated elective and appointive offices. Quakers, of course, differed among themselves. Members of the assembly struggled to win the right to debate and amend laws, especially tax laws. They finally won the battle in 1701 when a new Charter of Privileges gave the proprietor the power to appoint the council and in turn stripped the council of all its former powers and gave them to the assembly, which became the only single-house legislature in all the English colonies.

> QUICK REVIEW

How did the middle colonies differ from the New England and Chesapeake colonies?

CHAPTER LOCATOR | How did the English Reformation influence Puritans?

What was the role of the North American colonies in the English empire?

Pine Tree Shilling In violation of English rules that forbade colonies from issuing their own currency, John Hull, a wealthy Boston merchant and shipowner, began to mint coins in 1652. Shown here is one of his pine tree shillings, both sides boldly announcing its origins. Courtesy of the Museum of the American Numismatic Association.

PROPRIETARY GRANTS to faraway lands were a cheap way for the king to reward friends. As the colonies grew, however, the grants became more valuable. After 1660, the king took initiatives to channel colonial trade through English hands and to consolidate royal authority over colonial governments. Occasioned by such economic and political considerations and triggered by **King Philip's War** between colonists and Native Americans, these initiatives defined the basic relationship between the colonies and England that endured until the American Revolution (**Map 4.3**).

Royal Regulation of Colonial Trade

English economic policies toward the colonies were designed to yield customs revenues for the monarchy and profitable business for English merchants and shippers. Also, the policies were intended to divert the colonies' trade from England's enemies, especially the Dutch and the French.

The Navigation Acts of 1650, 1651, 1660, and 1663 (see chapter 3) set forth two fundamental rules governing colonial trade. First, goods shipped to and from the colonies had to be transported in English ships using primarily English crews. Second, the Navigation Acts listed colonial products that could be shipped only to England or to other English colonies. While these regulations prevented Chesapeake planters from shipping their tobacco directly to the European continent, they interfered less with the commerce of New England and the middle colonies, whose principal exports—fish, lumber, and flour—were not listed in the regulations and could legally be sent directly to their most important markets in the West Indies.

By the end of the seventeenth century, colonial commerce was defined by regulations that subjected merchants and shippers to royal supervision and gave them access to markets throughout the English empire. In addition, colonial commerce received protection from the English navy. By 1700, colonial goods (including those from the West Indies) accounted for one-fifth of all English imports and for

King Philip's War
▶ Brief but brutal war between New England colonists and Wampanoag, Nipmuck, and Narragansett Indians between 1675 and 1676. Led by the Indian leader Metacomet—known to the English as King Philip—and fighting against encroachment on their lands, the Indians destroyed thirteen English settlements before being defeated.

| What was distinctive about the settlement of New England? | How did New England society change during the seventeenth century? | What was distinctive about the middle colonies? | **What was the role of the North American colonies in the English empire?** | Conclusion: What made the English colonization of North America distinctive? |

1660
- English crown begins to intensify efforts to take political and economic control of the colonies.

1675–1676
- King Philip's War.

1686
- Dominion of New England is created.

1688
- England's Glorious Revolution; William III and Mary II become new rulers.

1691
- Massachusetts becomes a royal colony.

1700
- Colonial goods account for one-fifth of all English imports and for two-thirds of all goods reexported from England to the European continent.

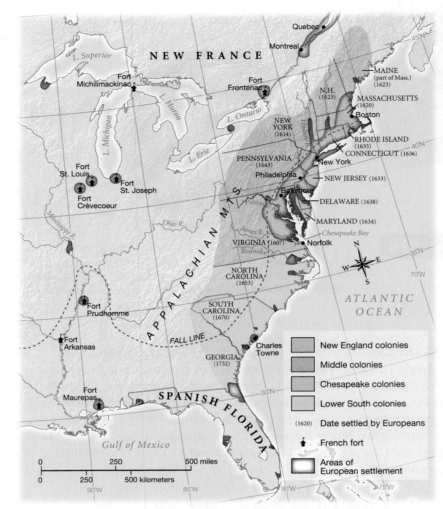

MAP 4.3 ■ American Colonies at the End of the Seventeenth Century

By the end of the seventeenth century, settlers inhabited a narrow band of land that stretched more or less continuously from Boston to Norfolk, with pockets of settlement farther south. The colonies' claims to enormous tracts of land to the west were contested by Native Americans as well as by France and Spain.

▶ FOR MORE HELP ANALYZING THIS MAP, see the map activity for this chapter in the Online Study Guide at bedfordstmartins.com/roarkunderstanding.

two-thirds of all goods reexported from England to the European continent. In turn, the colonies absorbed more than one-tenth of English exports. The commercial regulations gave economic value to England's proprietorship of the American colonies.

King Philip's War and the Consolidation of Royal Authority

The monarchy also took steps to exercise greater control over colonial governments. Virginia had been a royal colony since 1624; Maryland, South Carolina, and the middle colonies were proprietary colonies with close ties to the crown.

CHAPTER LOCATOR | How did the English Reformation influence Puritans?

King Philip's War, 1675–1676

• Indian settlement
◉ English settlement attacked

The New England colonies possessed royal charters, but they had developed their own distinctively Puritan governments. Charles II, whose father, Charles I, had been executed by Puritans in England, took a particular interest in gaining greater royal control of the New England colonies. The occasion was a royal investigation following King Philip's War.

In 1675, warfare between Indians and colonists erupted in the Chesapeake and New England. Massachusetts settlers had massacred hundreds of Pequot Indians in 1637, but they had established relatively peaceful relations with the more powerful Wampanoags. In the decades that followed, New Englanders steadily encroached on Indian land, and in 1675 the Wampanoags struck back with attacks on settlements in western Massachusetts. Metacomet—the chief of the Wampanoags (and son of Massasoit), whom the colonists called King Philip—probably neither planned the attacks nor masterminded a conspiracy with the Nipmucks and the Narragansetts, as the colonists feared. But when militias from Massachusetts and other New England colonies counterattacked all three tribes, a deadly sequence of battles killed more than a thousand colonists and thousands more Indians. The Indians destroyed thirteen English settlements and partially burned another half dozen. By the spring of 1676, Indian warriors ranged freely within seventeen miles of Boston. The colonists finally defeated the Indians, principally with a scorched-earth policy of burning their food supplies. King Philip's War left the New England colonists with an enduring hatred of Indians, a large war debt, and a devastated frontier. And in 1676, an agent of the king arrived to investigate whether New England was abiding by English laws.

Not surprisingly, the king's agent found many deviations from English rules, and the monarchy decided to govern New England more directly. In 1684, an English court revoked the Massachusetts charter. Two years later, royal officials incorporated Massachusetts and the other colonies north of Maryland into the **Dominion of New England**. To govern the dominion, the English sent Sir Edmund Andros to Boston. Some New England merchants cooperated with Andros, but

Dominion of New England

▶ Administrative union established in 1686 of the English colonies north of Maryland. Designed to strengthen royal control over the northern colonies, the Dominion was dissolved in 1689 in the aftermath of the Glorious Revolution.

Wampanoag War Club
This seventeenth-century war club was used to kill King Philip, according to the Anglican missionary who obtained it from Indians early in the eighteenth century. Although the missionary's tale is probably a legend, the club is certainly a seventeenth-century Wampanoag weapon that might well have been used in King Philip's War. Courtesy of the Fruitlands Museums, Harvard, Massachusetts.

| What was distinctive about the settlement of New England? | How did New England society change during the seventeenth century? | What was distinctive about the middle colonies? | **What was the role of the North American colonies in the English empire?** | Conclusion: What made the English colonization of North America distinctive? |

most colonists were offended by his open disregard of Puritan traditions. Worst of all, the Dominion of New England invalidated all land titles, confronting every landowner in New England with the prospect of losing his or her land.

Events in England, however, permitted Massachusetts colonists to overthrow Andros and retain title to their property. When Charles II died in 1685, he was succeeded by his brother James II, a zealous Catholic. James's aggressive campaign to appoint Catholics to government posts engendered such unrest that in 1688, a group of Protestant noblemen in Parliament invited the Dutch ruler William III of Orange, James's son-in-law, to claim the English throne.

When William III landed in England at the head of a large army, James fled to France, and William III and his wife, Mary II (James's daughter), became co-rulers in the relatively bloodless "Glorious Revolution," reasserting Protestant influence in England and its empire. Rumors of the revolution raced across the Atlantic and emboldened colonial uprisings against royal authority in Massachusetts, New York, and Maryland.

In Boston in 1689, rebels tossed Andros and other English officials in jail, destroyed the Dominion of New England, and reestablished the former charter government. New Yorkers followed the Massachusetts example. Under the leadership of Jacob Leisler, rebels seized the royal governor in 1689 and ruled the colony for more than a year. That same year in Maryland, the Protestant Association, led by John Coode, overthrew the colony's pro-Catholic government, fearing it would not recognize the new Protestant king.

But these rebel governments did not last. When King William III's governor of New York arrived in 1691, he executed Leisler for treason. Coode's men ruled Maryland until the new royal governor arrived in 1692 and ended both Coode's rebellion and Lord Baltimore's proprietary government. In Massachusetts, John Winthrop's city on a hill became another royal colony in 1691. The new charter said that the governor of the colony would be appointed by the king rather than elected by the colonists' representatives. But perhaps the most unsettling change was the new qualification for voting. Possession of property replaced church membership as a prerequisite for voting in colony-wide elections.

Even though colonists chafed under increasing royal control, they still valued English protection from hostile neighbors. While the northern colonies were distracted by the Glorious Revolution, French forces from the fur-trading regions along the Great Lakes and in Canada attacked villages in New England and New York. Known as King William's War, the conflict with the French was a colonial outgrowth of William's war against France in Europe. The war dragged on until 1697 and ended inconclusively in both Europe and the colonies. But it made clear to many colonists that along with English royal government came a welcome measure of military security.

> **QUICK REVIEW**

Why did England try to establish greater control of its American colonies in the 1690s?

Worcester Art Museum.

Conclusion: What made the English colonization of North America distinctive?

BY 1700, the diverse English colonies in North America had developed along lines quite different from the example New Spain had set in 1600. In the North American colonies, English immigrants and their descendants created societies of settlers unlike the largely Indian societies in New Spain ruled by a tiny group of Spaniards. Although many settlers came to North America from other parts of Europe and a growing number of Africans arrived in bondage, English laws, habits, ideas, and language dominated all the colonies.

Economically, the English colonies thrived on agriculture and trade instead of mining silver and exploiting Indian labor as in New Spain. Although servants and slaves could be found throughout the North American colonies, many settlers depended principally on the labor of family members. Relations between settlers and Native Americans often exploded in warfare, but Indians seldom served as an important source of labor for settlers, as they did in New Spain.

Protestantism prevailed in the North American settlements, relaxed in some colonies and straitlaced in others. Catholics, Quakers, Anglicans (members of the Church of England), Jews, and others settled in the middle and southern colonies, creating considerable religious toleration, especially in Pennsylvania and New York.

Politics and government differed from colony to colony, although English institutions and practices existed everywhere. Local settlers who were free adult white men had an extraordinary degree of political influence, far beyond that of colonists in New Spain or ordinary citizens in England. During the next half century, that English colonial world would undergo surprising new developments built on the achievements of the seventeenth century.

SO NOW YOU KNOW

The Puritans did not celebrate Christmas or Easter because the Bible did not mention either one. Puritans tried to live according to a strict and literal interpretation of the Bible. Puritans' zeal to turn New England into a shining example of Christian piety, into a city on a hill, shaped every feature of New England life.

What was distinctive about the settlement of New England?

How did New England society change during the seventeenth century?

What was distinctive about the middle colonies?

What was the role of the North American colonies in the English empire?

Conclusion: What made the English colonization of North America distinctive?

STEP 1

GETTING STARTED

Below are basic terms from this period in American history. Can you identify each term below and explain why it matters? To do this exercise online or to download this chart, visit bedfordstmartins.com/roarkunderstanding.

TERM	WHO OR WHAT & WHEN	WHY IT MATTERS
Puritans, p. 84		
English Reformation, p. 84		
Pilgrims, p. 87		
Massachusetts Bay Company, p. 87		
John Winthrop, p. 88		
Roger Williams, p. 93		
Anne Hutchinson, p. 94		
Quakers, p. 97		
New Netherland, p. 99		
William Penn, p. 101		
King Philip's War, p. 103		
Dominion of New England, p. 105		

STEP 2

MOVING BEYOND THE BASICS

The exercise below represents a more advanced understanding of the chapter material. Compare and contrast the northern colonies: Why was each settled, what kind of political and social structures defined the colony, and what were the bases of its economic organization? To do this exercise online or to download this chart, visit bedfordstmartins.com/roarkunderstanding.

Colony	Reasons for settlement	Social/political structures (religion, family, legal system)	Economics (land use and distribution, industry, income, labor)
Plymouth			
Massachusetts Bay			
Rhode Island			
New Netherland/ New York			
Pennsylvania			

STEP

3

PUTTING
IT ALL
TOGETHER

Now that you have reviewed key elements of the chapter, take a step back and try to explain the big picture. Remember to use specific examples from the chapter in your answers. To do this exercise online, visit bedfordsmartins.com/roarkunderstanding.

NEW ENGLAND

▶ What kind of society did the early settlers of New England hope to create?

▶ What forces challenged Puritan domination of New England?

THE MIDDLE COLONIES

▶ How did the settlement of the middle colonies differ from that of New England?

▶ What explains the religious and ethnic diversity of the middle colonies?

THE EMPIRE

▶ How did the English crown seek to regulate colonial trade?

▶ How did the colonists respond to the English crown's efforts to assert political authority?

LOOKING BACKWARD, LOOKING AHEAD

▶ How did European colonization of the Americas in the seventeenth century differ from Spanish colonization in the previous century?

▶ How did the growth and development of English colonies in the seventeenth century set the stage for conflict between England and its colonies in the eighteenth century?

IN YOUR OWN WORDS

Imagine that you must explain chapter 4 to someone who hasn't read it. What would be the most important points to include and why?

5
THE CHANGING WORLD OF COLONIAL AMERICA

1700–1770

> This chapter explores the development of New England, the middle colonies, and the southern colonies between 1700 and 1770. It examines the factors that resulted in regional differences, as well as the common experiences, assumptions, and attitudes that contributed to a growing sense of unity among the colonists. These unifying trends helped prepare the foundation for what would become the United States of America in 1776.

DID YOU KNOW?

In 1776, Philadelphia was the largest city in the British empire except London.

> How and why did British North America change in the eighteenth century?

> What changed in New England life and culture?

> How were the middle colonies distinctive?

> How did slavery become the defining feature of the southern colonies?

> What were the unifying experiences for British American colonists?

> Conclusion: What was the dual identity of British North American colonists?

Chandler Wedding Tapestry. New England, artist unknown, 1756.

How and why did British North America change in the eighteenth century?

New York City Street This painting depicts John Street, a residential neighborhood of New York City, in 1768, as recalled by the artist Joseph B. Smith in the early nineteenth century. Notice that fences separate house yards from the street, rather than houses from one another, hinting of friendly relations among neighbors. Old John Street United Methodist Church.

THE MOST IMPORTANT FACT about eighteenth-century British America is its phenomenal population growth: In 1700, colonists numbered about 250,000; by 1770, they tallied well over 2 million. An index of the emerging significance of colonial North America is that in 1700, there were nineteen people in England for every American colonist; by 1770, there were only three. The eightfold growth of the colonial population signaled the maturation of a distinctive colonial society. That society was by no means homogeneous. Colonists of different ethnic groups, races, and religions lived in varied environments under thirteen different colonial governments, all of them part of the British empire.

In general, the growth and diversity of the eighteenth-century colonial population derived from two sources: immigration and natural increase (growth through reproduction). Natural increase contributed about three-fourths of the population growth, immigration about one-fourth. Immigration shifted the ethnic and racial balance among the colonists, making them by 1770 less English and less white than ever before. In 1670, more than 9 out of 10 colonists were of English ancestry, and only 1 out of 25 was of African ancestry. By 1770, only about half of the colonists were of English descent, while more than 20 percent descended from Africans. Thus, by 1770, the people of the colonies had a distinctive colonial—rather than English—profile (**Map 5.1**).

The booming population of the colonies hints at a second major feature of eighteenth-century colonial society: an expanding economy. In 1700, after almost a century of settlement, nearly all the colonists lived within fifty miles of the Atlantic coast. The almost limitless wilderness stretching westward made land relatively

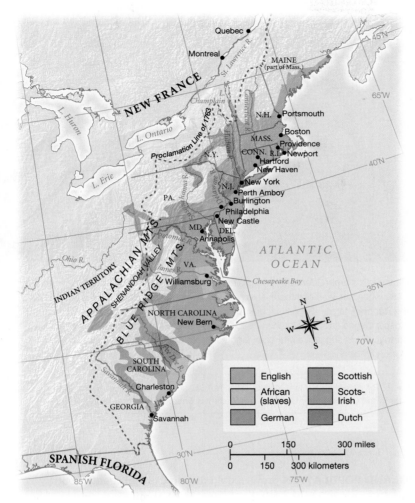

In 1770

- Colonial population had grown to more than 2 million, compared with 250,000 in 1700.
- England's population was three times greater than that of colonial America, compared with nineteen times in 1700.
- About half of American colonists were of English descent, while 20 percent were of African descent.

MAP 5.1 ■ Europeans and Africans in the Eighteenth Century

This map illustrates regions where Africans and certain immigrant groups clustered. It is important to avoid misreading the map. Predominantly English and German regions, for example, also contained colonists from other places. Likewise, regions where African slaves resided in large numbers also included many whites, slave masters among them. The map suggests the diversity of eighteenth-century colonial society.

cheap. Land in the colonies commonly sold for a fraction of its price in the Old World. The abundance of land in the colonies made labor precious, and the colonists always needed more. The insatiable demand for labor was the fundamental economic environment that sustained the mushrooming population. Economic historians estimate that free colonists (those who were not indentured servants or slaves) had a higher standard of living than the majority of people elsewhere in the Atlantic world. The unique achievement of the eighteenth-century colonial economy was this modest economic welfare of the vast bulk of the free population.

QUICK REVIEW

How did the North American colonies achieve the remarkable population growth of the eighteenth century?

What changed in New England life and culture?	How were the middle colonies distinctive?	How did slavery become the defining feature of the southern colonies?	What were the unifying experiences for British American colonists?	Conclusion: What was the dual identity of British North American colonists?

What changed in New England life and culture?

Boston Common in Needlework

Hannah Otis embroidered this exquisite needlework portrait of Boston Common in 1750 when she was eighteen years old. The large house (center right) belonged to the Hancock family. John Hancock, who later signed the Declaration of Independence, is shown on horseback in the foreground. What features of this portrait would suggest a city to an eighteenth-century viewer? Photograph © 2008 Museum of Fine Arts, Boston.

▶ FOR MORE HELP ANALYZING THIS IMAGE, see the visual activity for this chapter in the Online Study Guide at bedfordstmartins.com/roarkunderstanding.

THE NEW ENGLAND POPULATION grew sixfold during the eighteenth century but lagged behind the growth in the other colonies. Most immigrants chose other destinations because of New England's relatively densely settled land and because Puritan orthodoxy made these colonies comparatively inhospitable to religious dissenters and those indifferent to religion. As the population grew, many settlers in search of farmland dispersed from towns, and Puritan communities lost much of their cohesion. Nonetheless, networks of economic exchange linked New Englanders to their neighbors, to Boston merchants, and to the broad currents of Atlantic commerce.

Natural Increase and Land Distribution

The New England population grew mostly by natural increase, much as it had during the seventeenth century. Nearly every adult woman married. Most married women had children—often many children, thanks to the relatively low mortality rate in New England. The perils of childbirth gave wives a shorter life expectancy than husbands, but wives often lived to have six, seven, or eight babies.

The growing New England population pressed against a limited amount of land. Compared to colonies farther south, New England had less land for the expansion of settlement (see Map 5.1, page 113). Moreover, as the northernmost group of British colonies, New England had contested northern and western frontiers.

CHAPTER LOCATOR | How and why did British North America change in the eighteenth century?

Powerful Native Americans, especially the Iroquois and Mahican tribes, jealously guarded their territory. The French (and Catholic) colony of New France also menaced the British (and mostly Protestant) New England colonies when provoked by colonial or European disputes.

During the seventeenth century, New England towns parceled out land to individual families. In most cases, the original settlers practiced partible inheritance—that is, they subdivided land more or less equally among sons. By the eighteenth century, repeated subdivisions had left many plots of land too small to support a family. Sons who could not hope to inherit sufficient land to farm had to move away from the town where they were born.

During the eighteenth century, colonial governments in New England abandoned the seventeenth-century policy of granting land to towns. Needing revenue, the governments of both Connecticut and Massachusetts sold land directly to individuals, including speculators. Now money, rather than membership in a community bound by a church covenant, determined whether a person could obtain land. The new land policy eroded the seventeenth-century pattern of settlement. As colonists moved, they tended to settle on individual farms rather than in the towns and villages that characterized the seventeenth century. New Englanders still depended on their relatives and neighbors, but far more than in the seventeenth century, they regulated their behavior in newly settled areas by their own individual choices.

Farms, Fish, and Atlantic Trade

New England farmers grew food for their families, but their fields did not produce huge marketable surpluses. Instead of one big crop, a farmer grew many small ones. If farmers had extra, they sold to or traded with neighbors. By 1770, New Englanders had only one-fourth as much wealth per capita as free colonists in the southern colonies. As consumers, New England farmers participated in a diversified commercial economy that linked remote farms to markets throughout the Atlantic world. Merchants large and small stocked imported goods—British textiles, ceramics, and metal goods; Chinese tea; West Indian sugar; and Chesapeake tobacco. Farmers' needs supported local shoemakers, tailors, wheelwrights, and carpenters. Larger towns, especially Boston, housed skilled tradesmen such as cabinetmakers, silversmiths, and printers. Shipbuilders tended to do better than other artisans because they served the most dynamic sector of the New England economy.

Many New Englanders made their fortunes at sea, as they had since the seventeenth century. Fish accounted for more than a third of New England's eighteenth-century exports; livestock and timber made up another third. The West Indies absorbed two-thirds of all of New England's exports. Slaves on Caribbean sugar plantations ate dried, salted codfish caught by New England fishermen, filled barrels crafted from New England timber with molasses and refined sugar, and loaded those barrels aboard ships bound ultimately for Europe.

What changed in New England life and culture?	How were the middle colonies distinctive?	How did slavery become the defining feature of the southern colonies?	What were the unifying experiences for British American colonists?	Conclusion: What was the dual identity of British North American colonists?

Almost all of the rest of New England's exports went to Britain and continental Europe (**Map 5.2**). This Atlantic commerce benefited the entire New England economy, providing jobs for laborers and tradesmen as well as for ship captains, clerks, merchants, and sailors.

Merchants dominated Atlantic commerce. The largest and most successful New England merchants lived in Boston at the hub of trade between local folk and the international market. Merchants not only bought and sold goods, but they also owned and insured the ships that carried merchandise throughout the Atlantic world. Shrewd, diligent, and lucky merchants could make fortunes. The luxurious

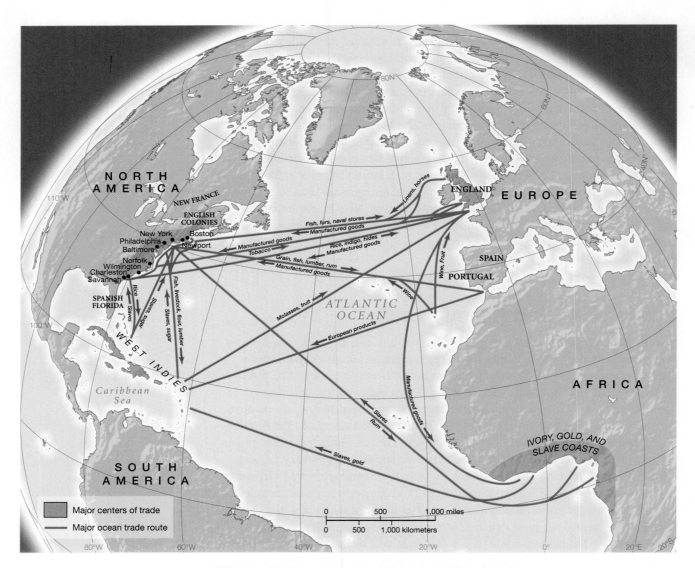

MAP 5.2 ■ North American Atlantic Trade in the Eighteenth Century
This map illustrates the economic outlook of the colonies in the eighteenth century—east toward the Atlantic world rather than west toward the interior of North America. The long distances involved in the Atlantic trade and the uncertainties of ocean travel suggest the difficulties Britain experienced governing the colonies and regulating colonial commerce.

CHAPTER LOCATOR | How and why did British North America change in the eighteenth century?

Boston homes of such men were an indication of the polarization of wealth that developed in Boston and other seaports during the eighteenth century. By 1770, the richest 5 percent of Bostonians owned about half the city's wealth; the poorest two-thirds of the population owned less than one-tenth.

While the rich got richer and everybody else had a smaller share of the total wealth, the incidence of genuine poverty did not change much. About 5 percent of New Englanders qualified for poor relief throughout the eighteenth century. Overall, colonists were better off than most people in England. A Connecticut traveler wrote from England in 1764, "We in New England know nothing of poverty and want, we have no idea of the thing, how much better do our poor people live than 7/8 of the people on this much famed island."

The contrast with English poverty had meaning because the overwhelming majority of New Englanders traced their ancestry to England. New England was more homogeneously English than any other colonial region. People of African ancestry (almost all of them slaves) numbered more than fifteen thousand by 1770, but they barely diversified the region's 97 percent white majority. In the Narragansett region of Rhode Island, large landowners imported numerous slaves to raise livestock. But most New Englanders had little use for slaves on their family farms. Instead, slaves were concentrated in towns, especially Boston, where most of them worked as domestic servants and laborers.

By 1770, the population, wealth, and commercial activity of New England differed from what they had been in 1700. Ministers still enjoyed high status, but Yankee traders had replaced Puritan saints as the symbolic New Englanders. Atlantic commerce competed with religious convictions in ordering New Englanders' daily lives.

QUICK REVIEW

How and why did New England society change in the eighteenth century?

| What changed in New England life and culture? | How were the middle colonies distinctive? | How did slavery become the defining feature of the southern colonies? | What were the unifying experiences for British American colonists? | Conclusion: What was the dual identity of British North American colonists? |

> How were the middle colonies distinctive?

Bethlehem, Pennsylvania

This view of the small community of Bethlehem, Pennsylvania, in 1757 dramatizes the profound transformation of the natural landscape wrought in the eighteenth century by highly motivated human labor. By carefully penning their livestock (lower center right) and fencing their fields (lower left), farmers safeguarded their livelihoods from the risks and disorders of untamed nature. Print Collection, Miriam and Ira D. Wallack Division of Art, Prints, and Photographs, The New York Public Library. Astor, Lenox, and Tilden Foundations.

> ► FOR MORE HELP ANALYZING THIS IMAGE, see the visual activity for this chapter in the Online Study Guide at bedfordstmartins.com/roarkunderstanding.

IN 1700, almost twice as many people lived in New England as in the middle colonies of Pennsylvania, New York, New Jersey, and Delaware. But by 1770, the population of the middle colonies had multiplied tenfold, mainly from an influx of German, Irish, Scottish, and other immigrants. Immigrants made the middle colonies a uniquely diverse society. By 1800, barely one-third of Pennsylvanians and less than half the total population of the middle colonies traced their ancestry to England.

German and Scots-Irish Immigrants

Germans made up the largest contingent of migrants from the European continent to the middle colonies. By 1770, about 85,000 Germans had arrived in the colonies. Most German immigrants came from what is now southwestern Germany, where, one observer noted, peasants were "not as well off as cattle elsewhere." German immigrants included numerous artisans and a few merchants, but the great majority were farmers and laborers. Economically, they represented "middling

CHAPTER LOCATOR | How and why did British North America change in the eighteenth century?

118 CHAPTER 5
THE CHANGING WORLD OF COLONIAL AMERICA

folk," neither the poorest (who could not afford the trip) nor the better-off (who did not want to leave). By the 1720s, Germans who had established themselves in the colonies wrote back to their friends and relatives, as one reported, "of the civil and religious liberties [and] privileges, and of all the goodness I have heard and seen." Such letters prompted still more Germans to pull up stakes and embark for America.

Similar motives propelled the Scots-Irish, who considerably outnumbered German immigrants. The "Scots-Irish" actually hailed from northern Ireland, Scotland, and northern England. Like the Germans, the Scots-Irish were Protestants, but with a difference. Most German immigrants worshipped in Lutheran or German Reformed churches; many others belonged to dissenting sects such as the Mennonites, Moravians, and Amish, whose adherents sought relief from the persecution they had suffered in Europe for their refusal to bear arms and to swear oaths, practices they shared with the Quakers. In contrast, the Scots-Irish tended to be militant Presbyterians who seldom hesitated to bear arms or swear oaths. Like German settlers, however, Scots-Irish immigrants were clannish, residing when they could among relatives or neighbors from the old country.

In the eighteenth century, wave after wave of Scots-Irish immigrants arrived, culminating in a flood of immigration in the years just before the American Revolution. Deteriorating economic conditions in northern Ireland, Scotland, and England pushed many toward America. Most of the immigrants were farm laborers or tenant farmers fleeing droughts, crop failures, high food prices, or rising rents. They came, they told inquisitive British officials, because of "poverty," "tyranny of landlords," and their desire to "do better in America."

Ship captains, aware of the hunger for labor in the colonies, eagerly signed up poor emigrants as **redemptioners**, a variant of indentured servants. A captain would agree to provide transportation to Philadelphia, where redemptioners would obtain the money to pay for their passage by borrowing it from a friend or

CHRONOLOGY

1733
– Benjamin Franklin begins publication of *Poor Richard's Almanack*.

1770
– The population of the colonies of Pennsylvania, New York, New Jersey, and Delaware has increased tenfold since 1700, largely the result of immigration.
– Germans make up the largest percentage of migrants from the European continent.
– The middle colonies' per capita consumption of imported goods from Britain has doubled since 1720.

redemptioners
▶ Immigrants who agreed to pay for their passage to America by borrowing from a friend or relative who was already in the colonies or by selling themselves as servants. Many German families came to Pennsylvania as redemptioners in the eighteenth century.

German Hymnal This manuscript hymnal, once owned by Benjamin Franklin, contains works and music created by Johann Conrad Beissel, the founder of the Seventh-Day Baptists and among the earliest musical composers in the colonies. The hymns evoke the Seventh-Day Baptists' vision of "The Bitter good, or . . . the Christian church here on earth, in the valley of sadness." Roger Foley/Library of Congress.

| What changed in New England life and culture? | **How were the middle colonies distinctive?** | How did slavery become the defining feature of the southern colonies? | What were the unifying experiences for British American colonists? | Conclusion: What was the dual identity of British North American colonists? |

relative who was already in the colonies or, as most did, by selling themselves as servants. Many redemptioners traveled in family groups, unlike impoverished Scots-Irish emigrants, who usually traveled alone and paid for their passage by contracting as indentured servants before they sailed to the colonies.

Redemptioners and indentured servants were packed aboard ships "as closely as herring," one migrant observed. Seasickness compounded by exhaustion, poverty, poor food, bad water, inadequate sanitation, and tight quarters encouraged the spread of disease. When one ship finally approached land, a traveler wrote, "everyone crawls from below to the deck . . . and people cry for joy, pray, and sing praises and thanks to God." Unfortunately, their troubles were far from over. Redemptioners and indentured servants had to stay on board until somebody came to purchase their labor. Unlike indentured servants, redemptioners negotiated independently with their purchasers about their period of servitude. Typically, a healthy adult redemptioner agreed to four years of labor. Indentured servants commonly served five, six, or seven years.

Pennsylvania: "The Best Poor [White] Man's Country"

New settlers, whether free or in servitude, poured into the middle colonies because they perceived unparalleled opportunities, particularly in Pennsylvania, "the best poor Man's Country in the World," as an indentured servant wrote in 1743. Although the servant reported that "the Condition of bought Servants is very hard" and masters often failed to live up to their promise to provide decent food and clothing, opportunity abounded because there was more work to be done than workers to do it.

Most servants toiled in Philadelphia, New York City, or one of the smaller towns or villages. From the masters' viewpoint, servants were a bargain. A master could purchase five or six years of a servant's labor for approximately the wages a common laborer would earn in four months. Wageworkers could walk away from their jobs when they pleased, and they did so often enough to be troublesome for employers. Servants, however, could not walk away; they were legally bound to work for their masters until their terms expired.

Since a slave cost at least three times as much as a servant, only affluent colonists could afford the long-term investment in slave labor. Most farmers in the middle colonies used family labor, not slaves. Wheat, the most widely grown crop, did not require more labor than farmers could typically muster from relatives, neighbors, and a hired hand or two. Consequently, although people of African ancestry (almost all slaves) increased to more than thirty thousand in the middle colonies by 1770, they accounted for only about 7 percent of the total population and much less outside the cities.

Most slaves came to the middle colonies and New England after a stopover in the West Indies. Very few came directly from Africa. Enough slaves arrived to prompt colonial assemblies to pass laws that punished slaves much more severely than servants for the same transgressions. But in cases of abuse, servants—unlike slaves—could charge masters with violating the terms of their indenture contracts. Small numbers of slaves managed to obtain their freedom.

CHAPTER LOCATOR | How and why did British North America change in the eighteenth century?

CHAPTER 5
120 THE CHANGING WORLD OF COLONIAL AMERICA

Patterns of Settlement, 1700–1770

But free African Americans did not escape whites' firm convictions about black inferiority and white supremacy.

Whites' racism and blacks' lowly social status made African Americans scapegoats for European Americans' suspicions and anxieties. In 1741, when arson and several unexplained thefts plagued New York City, officials suspected a murderous slave conspiracy and executed thirty-one slaves. Although slaves were certifiably impoverished, they were not among the poor for whom the middle colonies were reputed to be the best country in the world.

Immigrants swarmed to the middle colonies because of the availability of land. The Penn family encouraged immigration to bring in potential buyers for their enormous tracts of land in Pennsylvania. From the beginning, Pennsylvania followed a policy of negotiating with Indian tribes to purchase additional land. This policy reduced the violent frontier clashes more common elsewhere in the colonies.

Few colonists drifted beyond the northern boundaries of Pennsylvania. Owners of the huge estates in New York's Hudson valley preferred to rent rather than sell their land, and therefore they attracted fewer immigrants. The **Iroquois Indians** dominated the lucrative fur trade of the St. Lawrence valley and eastern Great Lakes, and they vigorously defended their territory from colonial encroachment.

The price of farmland depended on soil quality, access to water, distance from a market town, and extent of improvements. Since the cheapest land always lay at the margin of settlement, would-be farmers tended to migrate to promising areas

Iroquois Indians
▶ A confederation of five (and later six) tribes that dominated the fur trade of the St. Lawrence valley and the eastern Great Lakes in the first half of the eighteenth century.

Marten Van Bergen Farm
This rare 1730s painting by a local artist depicts the farm of Marten and Catarina Van Bergen, prosperous colonists in New York's Hudson valley. What ideas and attitudes are suggested by the clothing of the people in the painting? What do the design and construction of the house and outbuilding suggest about the influence of different cultures at the farm? Copyright © New York State Historical Association, Cooperstown, NY.

| What changed in New England life and culture? | **How were the middle colonies distinctive?** | How did slavery become the defining feature of the southern colonies? | What were the unifying experiences for British American colonists? | Conclusion: What was the dual identity of British North American colonists? |

just beyond already improved farms. By midcentury, settlement had reached the eastern slopes of the Appalachian Mountains, and newcomers spilled south down the fertile valley of the Shenandoah River into western Virginia and the Carolinas.

Farmers made the middle colonies the breadbasket of North America. They planted a wide variety of crops to feed their families, but they grew wheat in abundance. Flour milling was the number one industry and flour the number one export, constituting nearly three-fourths of all exports from the middle colonies. For farmers, the grain market in the Atlantic world proved risky but profitable, as grain prices rose steadily after 1720.

The standard of living in rural Pennsylvania was probably higher than in any other agricultural region of the eighteenth-century world. The comparatively widespread prosperity of all the middle colonies allowed the region's per capita consumption of imported goods from Britain to more than double between 1720 and 1770, far outstripping the per capita consumption of British goods in New England and the southern colonies.

At the crossroads of trade in wheat exports and British imports stood Philadelphia. By 1776, Philadelphia had a larger population than any other city in the entire British empire except London. Merchants occupied the top stratum of Philadelphia society. In a city where only 2 percent of the residents owned enough property to qualify to vote, merchants built grand homes and dominated local government. Many of Philadelphia's wealthiest merchants were Quakers, whose traits of industry, thrift, honesty, and sobriety encouraged the accumulation of wealth.

Benjamin Franklin

► (1706–1790) American writer, publisher, politician, and diplomat. Franklin published *Poor Richard's Almanack,* which advocated hard work, discipline, and thrift. He was also a deist, believing that God's work was reflected in science and nature.

In 1733, **Benjamin Franklin** began to publish *Poor Richard's Almanack,* which preached the likelihood of long-term rewards for tireless labor. Poor Richard's advice that "God gives all Things to Industry" might be considered the motto for the middle colonies. The promise of a worldly payoff made work a secular faith. Poor Richard advised, "Work as if you were to live 100 years, Pray as if you were to die Tomorrow." William Penn's Quaker utopia had become a center of worldly affluence. Quakers remained influential, but Franklin spoke for most colonists with his aphorisms of work, discipline, and thrift that echoed Quaker rules for outward behavior.

> **QUICK REVIEW**

Why did immigrants flood into Pennsylvania during the eighteenth century?

CHAPTER LOCATOR | How and why did British North America change in the eighteenth century?

How did slavery become the defining feature of the southern colonies?

Charleston Harbor This 1730s painting of Charleston, South Carolina, depicts the intersecting currents of international trade and local commerce in the variety of vessels conveying goods and people between ship and shore. More African slaves arrived in Charleston than in any other North American port, yet no slaves appear in this painting. Colonial Williamsburg Foundation.

BETWEEN 1700 AND 1770, the population of the southern colonies of Virginia, Maryland, North Carolina, South Carolina, and Georgia grew almost ninefold. By 1770, about twice as many people lived in the South as in either the middle colonies or New England. As elsewhere, natural increase and immigration accounted for the rapid population growth. Many Scots-Irish and German immigrants funneled from the middle colonies into the southern backcountry. Other immigrants were indentured servants (mostly English and Scots-Irish) who followed their seventeenth-century predecessors. But slaves made the most striking contribution to the booming southern colonies, transforming the racial composition of the population. Slavery became the defining characteristic of the southern colonies during the eighteenth century, shaping the region's economy, society, and politics.

The Atlantic Slave Trade and the Growth of Slavery

The number of southerners of African ancestry (nearly all of them slaves) rocketed from just over 20,000 in 1700 to well over 400,000 in 1770. The black population increased nearly three times faster than the South's briskly growing white population. Consequently, the proportion of southerners of African ancestry grew from 20 percent in 1700 to 40 percent in 1770.

Southern colonists clustered into two distinct geographic and agricultural zones. The colonies in the upper South, surrounding the Chesapeake Bay, specialized in growing tobacco. Throughout the eighteenth century, nine out of ten southern whites and eight out of ten southern blacks lived in the Chesapeake region. The upper South retained a white majority during the eighteenth century.

In the lower South, a much smaller cluster of colonists inhabited the coastal region and specialized in the production of rice and indigo (a plant used to make blue dye). Lower South colonists made up only 5 percent of the total population of

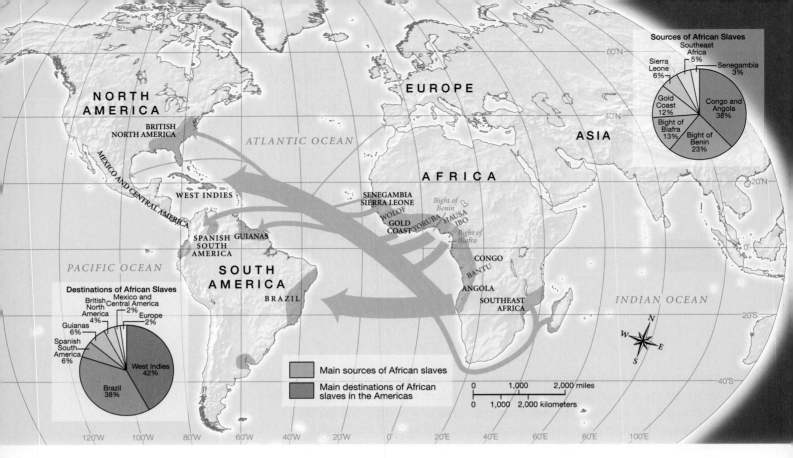

MAP 5.3 ■ The Atlantic Slave Trade

Although the Atlantic slave trade lasted from about 1450 to 1870, it peaked during the eighteenth century, when more than six million African slaves were imported to the New World. Only a small fraction of these slaves were taken to British North America. Most went to sugar plantations in Brazil and the Caribbean.

▶ FOR MORE HELP ANALYZING THIS MAP, see the map activity for this chapter in the Online Study Guide at bedfordstmartins.com/roarkunderstanding.

CHRONOLOGY

1711
– North Carolina is founded.

1732
– Georgia is founded.

1739
– Stono rebellion, an uprising by slaves in South Carolina.

1745
– Olaudah Equiano is born.

1770
– The southern colonies supply 90 percent of all North American exports to Britain.

the southern colonies in 1700 but inched upward to 15 percent by 1770. South Carolina was the sole British colony along the southern Atlantic coast until 1732, when Georgia was founded. (North Carolina, founded in 1711, was largely an extension of the Chesapeake region.) Blacks in South Carolina, in contrast to every other British mainland colony, outnumbered whites almost two to one; in some low-country districts, the ratio of blacks to whites exceeded ten to one.

The enormous growth in the South's slave population occurred through natural increase and the flourishing Atlantic slave trade (**Map 5.3** and **Table 5.1**). Slave ships brought almost 300,000 Africans to British North America between 1619 and 1780. Of these Africans, 95 percent arrived in the South, and 96 percent arrived during the eighteenth century. Most of them had been born into free families in villages located within a few hundred miles of the West African coast.

Although they shared African origins, they came from many different African cultures, including Akan, Angolan, Asante, Bambara, Gambian, Igbo, and Mandinga, among others. They spoke different languages, worshipped different deities, observed different rules of kinship, grew different crops, and recognized different rulers. The most important experience they had in common was enslavement. Captured in war, kidnapped, or sold into slavery by other Africans,

CHAPTER LOCATOR | How and why did British North America change in the eighteenth century?

TABLE 5.1 ■ Slave Imports, 1451–1870

Estimated Slave Imports to the Western Hemisphere	
1451–1600	275,000
1601–1700	1,341,000
1701–1810	6,100,000
1811–1870	1,900,000

they were brought to the coast, sold to African traders who assembled slaves for resale, and sold again to European or colonial slave traders or ship captains, who packed two hundred to three hundred or more aboard ships that carried them on the **Middle Passage** across the Atlantic and then sold them yet again to colonial slave merchants or southern planters.

Olaudah Equiano published an account of his enslavement that hints at the stories that might have been told by the millions of other Africans swept up in the slave trade. Equiano wrote that he was born in 1745 in the interior of what is now Nigeria. "I had never heard of white men or Europeans, nor of the sea," he recalled. One day when he was eleven years old, he was kidnapped by Africans, who sold him to other Africans, who in turn eventually sold him to a slave ship on the coast. Equiano feared that he was "going to be killed" and "eaten by those white men with horrible looks, red faces, and loose hair." Once the ship set sail, many of the slaves, crowded together in suffocating, filthy conditions, died from sickness. "The shrieks of the women and the groans of the dying rendered the whole a scene of horror almost inconceivable," Equiano recalled. Most of the slaves on the ship were sold in Barbados, but Equiano and a few others were shipped off to Virginia, where he "saw few or none of our native Africans and not one soul who could talk to me." Equiano felt isolated and "exceedingly miserable" because he "had no person to speak to that I could understand." Finally, the captain of a tobacco ship bound for England purchased Equiano, and he traveled as a slave between North America, England, and the West Indies for ten years until he succeeded in buying his freedom in 1766.

About 85 percent of the slaves brought into the southern colonies came directly from Africa, and almost all the ships that brought them (roughly 90 percent) belonged to British merchants. Most of the slaves on board were young adults, with men usually outnumbering women two to one. Children under the age of fourteen, like Equiano, typically accounted for no more than 10 to 15 percent of a cargo.

Middle Passage

▶ Name given to the journey across the Atlantic that brought African slaves to the Americas. Slave ships were packed with two hundred to three hundred slaves for their trip across the Atlantic. On average, about 15 percent of the slaves who began the journey died during the Middle Passage.

Olaudah Equiano

▶ Eighteenth-century West African who published an account of his enslavement and transport to North America. After buying his freedom in 1766, Equiano described the horrors of the Middle Passage, which bolstered the arguments of early advocates of the abolition of slavery.

The Deadly Middle Passage

Eighty-five percent of slaves brought into the southern colonies came directly from Africa.

Mortality during the Middle Passage varied considerably from ship to ship.

On average, about 15 percent of the slaves died.

In general, the longer the voyage lasted, the more people died.

Smallpox, dysentery, and acute dehydration were leading causes of death.

Men outnumbered women two to one.

Children usually accounted for no more than 10 to 15 percent of the cargo.

| What changed in New England life and culture? | How were the middle colonies distinctive? | **How did slavery become the defining feature of the southern colonies?** | What were the unifying experiences for British American colonists? | Conclusion: What was the dual identity of British North American colonists? |

Normally, an individual planter purchased at any one time a relatively small number of newly arrived Africans, or new Negroes, as they were called. New Negroes were often profoundly depressed, demoralized, and disoriented. Planters expected their other slaves—either those born into slavery in the colonies (often called country-born or creole slaves) or Africans who had arrived earlier—to help new Negroes become accustomed to their strange new surroundings. Planters' preferences for slaves from specific regions of Africa aided slaves' acculturation (or seasoning, as it was called) to the routines of bondage in the southern colonies. Chesapeake planters preferred slaves from Senegambia, the Gold Coast, or the Bight of Biafra, which combined accounted for 40 percent of all Africans imported to the Chesapeake. South Carolina planters favored slaves from the central African Congo and Angola regions, the origin of about 40 percent of the African slaves they imported (see Map 5.3, page 124). Although slaves within each of these regions spoke many different languages, enough linguistic and cultural similarities existed that they could usually communicate with other Africans from the same region.

Seasoning acclimated new Africans to the physical as well as the cultural environment of the southern colonies. Slaves who had just endured the Middle Passage were poorly nourished, weak, and sick. In this vulnerable state, they encountered the alien diseases of North America without having acquired immunities. As many as 10 to 15 percent of newly arrived Africans, sometimes more, died during their first year in the southern colonies. Nonetheless, the large number of newly enslaved Africans made the influence of African culture in the South stronger in the eighteenth century than ever before—or since.

While newly enslaved Africans poured into the southern colonies, slave mothers bore children, which caused the slave population in the South to grow rapidly. Slave owners encouraged these births. The growing number of slave babies set the southern colonies apart from other New World slave societies, where mortality rates were so high that deaths exceeded births. The high rate of natural increase in the southern colonies meant that by the 1740s, the majority of southern slaves were country-born.

Slave Labor and African American Culture

Southern planters expected slaves to work from sunup to sundown and beyond. George Washington wrote that his slaves should "be at their work as soon as it is light, work til it is dark, and be diligent while they are at it." The conflict between the masters' desire for maximum labor and the slaves' reluctance to do more than necessary made the threat of physical punishment a constant for eighteenth-century slaves. Masters preferred black slaves to white indentured servants, not just because slaves served for life but also because colonial laws did not limit the force masters could use against slaves. As a traveler observed in 1740, slaves resisted their masters' demands because of their "greatness of soul"—their stubborn unwillingness to conform to their masters' definition of them as merely slaves.

Olaudah Equiano

This portrait shows Equiano more than a decade after he had bought his freedom. The portrait evokes Equiano's successful acculturation to the customs of eighteenth-century England. His clothing and hairstyle reflect the fashions of a respectable young Englishman.
Library of Congress.

Some slaves escalated their acts of resistance to direct physical confrontation with the master, the mistress, or an overseer. But a hoe raised in anger, a punch in the face, or a desperate swipe with a knife led to swift and predictable retaliation by whites. Throughout the southern colonies, the balance of physical power rested securely in the hands of whites.

Rebellion occurred, however, at Stono, South Carolina, in 1739. Before dawn on a September Sunday, a group of about twenty slaves attacked a country store, killed the two storekeepers, and confiscated the store's guns, ammunition, and powder. Enticing other slaves to join, the group plundered and burned more than half a dozen plantations and killed more than twenty white men, women, and children. A mounted force of whites quickly suppressed the rebellion. They placed the rebels' heads atop mileposts along the road, grim reminders of the consequences of rebellion. The **Stono rebellion** illustrated that eighteenth-century slaves had no chance of overturning slavery and very little chance of defending themselves in any bold strike for freedom. After the rebellion, South Carolina legislators enacted repressive laws designed to guarantee that whites would always have the upper hand. No other similar uprisings occurred during the colonial period.

Slaves maneuvered constantly to protect themselves and to gain a measure of autonomy within the boundaries of slavery. In Chesapeake tobacco fields, most slaves were subject to close supervision by whites. In the lower South, the task system gave slaves some control over the pace of their work and some discretion in the use of the rest of their time. A "task" was typically defined as a certain area of ground to be cultivated or a specific job to be completed. A slave who completed the assigned task might use the remainder of the day, if any, to work in a garden, fish, hunt, spin, weave, sew, or cook. When masters sought to boost productivity by increasing tasks, slaves did what they could to defend their customary work assignments.

Eighteenth-century slaves also planted the roots of African American lineages that branch out to the present. Slaves expressed their humanity through the value they placed on family ties, and, as in West African societies, kinship structured slaves' relations with one another. Slave parents often gave a child the name of a grandparent, an aunt, or an uncle. In West Africa, kinship identified a person's place among living relatives and linked the person to ancestors in the past and to descendants in the future. Newly imported African slaves usually arrived alone, like Equiano, without kin. Often slaves who arrived from Africa on the same ship adopted one another as "brothers" and "sisters." Likewise, as new Negroes were seasoned and incorporated into existing slave communities, established families often adopted them as fictive kin.

When possible, slaves expressed many other features of their West African origins in their lives on New World plantations. They gave their children traditional dolls and African names such as Cudjo or Quash, Minda or Fuladi. They grew food crops they had known in Africa, such as yams and okra. They constructed huts with mud walls and thatched roofs similar to African residences. They fashioned banjos, drums, and other musical instruments, held dances, and observed funeral rites that echoed African practices. In these and many other ways, slaves drew upon their African heritages as much as the oppressive circumstances of slavery permitted.

Stono rebellion

▶ Slave uprising in Stono, South Carolina. In September 1739, a small group of slaves attacked a country store, plundered and burned more than half a dozen plantations, and killed more than twenty white colonists. After the uprising, South Carolina passed laws placing further restrictions on the activities and movements of slaves.

Doll Belonging to a Slave Child

This doll, recovered from an archaeological investigation of slaves' housing, was probably a gift from a slave parent or elder to a child, a token of the affection that linked kin groups among slaves. The Stagville Center, Division of Archives and History, North Carolina Department of Archives and History, North Carolina Department of Cultural Resources.

What changed in New England life and culture? | How were the middle colonies distinctive? | **How did slavery become the defining feature of the southern colonies?** | What were the unifying experiences for British American colonists? | Conclusion: What was the dual identity of British North American colonists?

Tobacco, Rice, and Prosperity

Slaves' labor bestowed prosperity on their masters, British merchants, and the monarchy. The southern colonies supplied 90 percent of all North American exports to Britain. Rice exports from the lower South exploded from less than half a million pounds in 1700 to eighty million pounds in 1770, nearly all of it grown by slaves. Exports of indigo also boomed. Tobacco was by far the most important export from British North America; by 1770, it represented almost one-third of all colonial exports and three-fourths of all Chesapeake exports. Under the provisions of the Navigation Acts (see chapter 4), nearly all of it went to Britain, where the monarchy collected a lucrative tax on each pound. British merchants then reexported more than 80 percent of the tobacco to the European continent, pocketing a nice markup for their troubles.

These products of slave labor made the southern colonies by far the richest in North America. The per capita wealth of free whites in the South was four times greater than that in New England and three times that in the middle colonies. At the top of the wealth pyramid stood the rice grandees of the lower South and the tobacco **gentry** of the Chesapeake. The vast differences in wealth among white southerners engendered envy and occasional tension between rich and poor, but remarkably little open hostility. Although racial slavery made a few whites much richer than others, it also gave those who did not get rich a powerful reason to feel similar (in race) to those who were so different (in wealth).

The slaveholding gentry dominated the politics and economy of the southern colonies. Property requirements prevented about 40 percent of white men in Virginia from voting for representatives to the House of Burgesses. In South Carolina, the property requirement was lower, and therefore most adult white men qualified to vote. In both colonies, voters elected members of the gentry to serve in the colonial legislature. The gentry passed political offices from generation to generation, building a self-perpetuating oligarchy—rule by the elite few—with the votes of their many humble neighbors.

The gentry also set the cultural standard in the southern colonies. They entertained lavishly, gambled regularly, and attended Anglican (Church of England) services more for social than for religious reasons. Above all, they cultivated the leisurely pursuit of happiness. They did not condone idleness, however. Their many pleasures and responsibilities as plantation owners kept them busy. Thomas Jefferson, a phenomenally productive member of the gentry, recalled that his earliest childhood memory was of being carried on a pillow by a family slave—a powerful image of the slave hands supporting the gentry's leisure and achievement.

gentry

▶ The social and political elite of the southern colonies who dominated society and politics. They worked to defuse social and political tensions between rich and poor whites by promoting a sense of solidarity with poor whites along racial lines.

> **QUICK REVIEW**

How did slavery shape the society and economy of the southern colonies?

CHAPTER LOCATOR | How and why did British North America change in the eighteenth century?

CHAPTER 5
128 THE CHANGING WORLD OF COLONIAL AMERICA

What were the unifying experiences for British American colonists?

THE SOCIETIES OF NEW ENGLAND, the middle colonies, and the southern colonies became more sharply differentiated during the eighteenth century, but colonists throughout British North America also shared unifying experiences that eluded settlers in the Spanish and French colonies. The first was economic. All three British colonial regions had their economic roots in agriculture. Colonists sold their distinctive products in markets that, in turn, offered a more or less uniform array of goods to consumers throughout British North America. A second unifying experience was a decline in the importance of religion. Some settlers called for a revival of religious intensity, but most people focused less on religion and more on the affairs of the world than they had in the seventeenth century. Third, white inhabitants throughout British North America became aware that they shared a distinctive identity as *British* colonists. Thirteen different governments presided over these North American colonies, but all of them answered to the British monarchy. British policies governed not only trade but also military and diplomatic relations with the Indians, French, and Spanish arrayed along colonial borderlands. Royal officials who expected loyalty from the colonists often had difficulty obtaining obedience. The British colonists asserted their prerogatives as British subjects to defend their special colonial interests.

1715
- Yamasee War pits Yamasee and Creek Indian allies of the French against British colonists in South Carolina.

1730s
- Jonathan Edwards promotes the religious movement known as the Great Awakening.

1740s
- George Whitefield preaches religious revival in North America.

1754
- Seven Years' War begins.

1769
- American Philosophical Society is founded.
- First Spanish mission in California, San Diego de Alcalá, is established.

1770
- Spanish mission and presidio are established at Monterey, California.

Commerce and Consumption

Colonial products spurred the development of mass markets throughout the Atlantic world. Colonial goods helped make it possible for ordinary people, not just the wealthy elite, to buy the things that they desired in addition to what they absolutely needed. Even news, formerly restricted mostly to a few people through face-to-face conversations or private letters, became an object of public consumption through the innovation of newspapers. With the appropriate stimulus, market demand seemed unlimited.

The Atlantic commerce that took colonial goods to markets in Britain brought consumer products back to the colonies. By midcentury, export-oriented industries in Britain were growing ten times faster than firms attuned to the home market. Most British exports went to the vast European market, where potential customers outnumbered those in the colonies by more than one hundred to one. But as European competition stiffened, colonial markets became increasingly important. British exports to North America multiplied eightfold between 1700 and 1770, outpacing the rate of population growth after midcentury. When the colonists' eagerness to consume exceeded their ability to pay, British exporters willingly extended credit, and colonial debts soared (**Figure 5.1**).

Despite the many differences among the colonists, the consumption of British exports built a certain material uniformity across region, religion, class, and status. Consumption of British exports made the colonists look and feel more British even though they lived at the edge of a wilderness an ocean away from Britain.

The rising tide of colonial consumption had other less visible but no less important consequences. Consumption presented women and men with a novel array of choices. As colonial consumers defined and expressed their desires with greater frequency during the eighteenth century, they became accustomed to thinking of themselves as individuals who had the power to make decisions that influenced the quality of their lives—attitudes of significance in the hierarchical world of eighteenth-century British North America.

Religion, Enlightenment, and Revival

Eighteenth-century colonists could choose from almost as many religions as consumer goods. Virtually all colonial religious denominations represented some form of Christianity, almost all of them Protestant. Slaves made up the largest group of non-Christians. A few slaves converted to Christianity in Africa or after they arrived in North America, but most continued to embrace elements of indigenous African religions. Roman Catholics concentrated in Maryland as they had since the seventeenth century, but even there they were outnumbered by Protestants.

The varieties of Protestant faith and practice ranged across a broad spectrum. The middle colonies and the southern backcountry included militant Baptists and Presbyterians. Huguenots who had fled persecution in Catholic France peopled congregations in several cities. In New England, old-style Puritanism splintered into strands of Congregationalism that differed over fine points of theological doctrine. The Congregational Church was the official established church in New England, and all residents paid taxes for its support. Throughout the plantation South and in urban centers such as Charleston, New York, and Philadelphia,

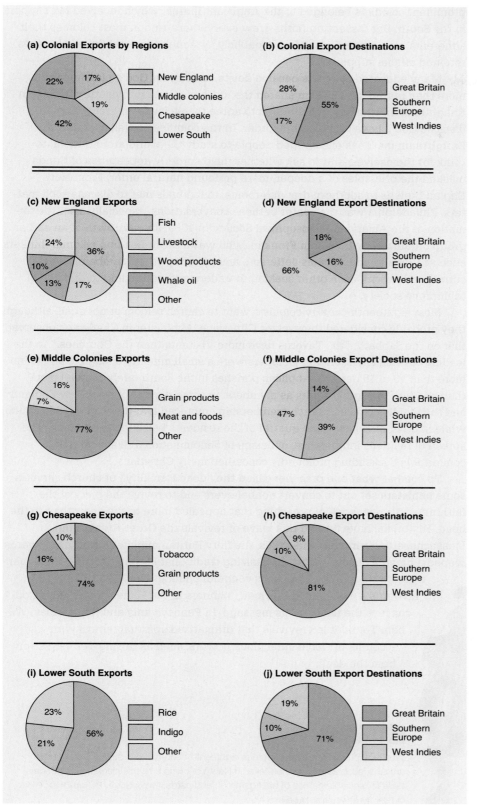

(a) Colonial Exports by Regions

- New England 17%
- Middle colonies 19%
- Chesapeake 42%
- Lower South 22%

(b) Colonial Export Destinations

- Great Britain 55%
- Southern Europe 17%
- West Indies 28%

(c) New England Exports

- Fish 36%
- Livestock 17%
- Wood products 13%
- Whale oil 10%
- Other 24%

(d) New England Export Destinations

- Great Britain 18%
- Southern Europe 16%
- West Indies 66%

(e) Middle Colonies Exports

- Grain products 77%
- Meat and foods 7%
- Other 16%

(f) Middle Colonies Export Destinations

- Great Britain 14%
- Southern Europe 39%
- West Indies 47%

(g) Chesapeake Exports

- Tobacco 74%
- Grain products 16%
- Other 10%

(h) Chesapeake Export Destinations

- Great Britain 81%
- Southern Europe 10%
- West Indies 9%

(i) Lower South Exports

- Rice 56%
- Indigo 21%
- Other 23%

(j) Lower South Export Destinations

- Great Britain 71%
- Southern Europe 10%
- West Indies 19%

FIGURE 5.1 ■ Colonial Exports, 1768–1772

These pie charts provide an overview of the colonial export economy of the 1760s. The first two show that almost two-thirds of colonial exports came from the South and that the majority of the colonies' exports went to Great Britain. The remaining charts illustrate the distinctive patterns of exports in each colonial region. What do these patterns reveal about regional variations in Britain's North American colonies? What do they suggest about Britain's economic interest in the colonies?

| What changed in New England life and culture? | How were the middle colonies distinctive? | How did slavery become the defining feature of the southern colonies? | What were the unifying experiences for British American colonists? | Conclusion: What was the dual identity of British North American colonists? |

deism

▶ Belief that God created a universe governed by natural laws and that those laws could be discovered through the use of reason. Many deists also rejected the possibility of supernatural events and of God's direct intervention in the lives of human beings. Deism was an outgrowth of the eighteenth-century Enlightenment.

Enlightenment

▶ Eighteenth-century cultural and intellectual movement that emphasized the power of reason and focused on improving human life in the here and now. Philadelphia was the center of the discussion of Enlightenment ideas in America, especially after the formation of the American Philosophical Society in 1769.

Great Awakening

▶ Early- to mid-eighteenth-century religious revival that attempted to convert nonbelievers and to revive the piety of the faithful through emotional, as opposed to rational, appeals. The revivals renewed the spiritual energies of thousands of colonists but did not substantially boost the total number of church members.

prominent colonists belonged to the Anglican Church, which received tax support in the South. But dissenting faiths grew everywhere, and in most colonies their adherents won the right to worship publicly, although the established churches retained official support.

Many educated colonists became deists, looking for God's plan in nature more than in the Bible. **Deism** shared the ideas of eighteenth-century European Enlightenment thinkers, who tended to agree that science and reason could disclose God's laws in the natural order. In the colonies as well as in Europe, **Enlightenment** ideas encouraged people to study the world around them, to think for themselves, and to ask whether the disorderly appearance of things masked the principles of a deeper, more profound natural order. From New England towns to southern drawing rooms, individuals met to discuss such matters. Philadelphia was the center of these conversations, especially after the formation of the American Philosophical Society in 1769, an outgrowth of an earlier group organized by Benjamin Franklin, who was a deist. Leading colonial thinkers such as Franklin and Thomas Jefferson, among many other members, corresponded with each other seeking to understand nature and to find ways to improve society.

Most eighteenth-century colonists went to church seldom or not at all, although they probably considered themselves Christians. A minister in Charleston observed that on the Sabbath, "the Taverns have more Visitants than the Churches." In the leading colonial cities, church members were a small minority of eligible adults, no more than 10 to 15 percent. Anglican parishes in the South rarely claimed more than one-fifth of eligible adults as members. In some regions of rural New England and the middle colonies, church membership embraced two-thirds of eligible adults, while in other areas, only one-quarter of the residents belonged to a church. The spread of religious indifference, of deism, of denominational rivalry, and of comfortable backsliding profoundly concerned many Christians.

To combat what one preacher called the "dead formality" of church services, some ministers set out to convert nonbelievers and to revive the piety of the faithful with a new style of preaching that appealed more to the heart than to the head. Historians have termed this wave of revivals the **Great Awakening**. In Massachusetts during the mid-1730s, the fiery Puritan minister Jonathan Edwards reaped a harvest of souls by reemphasizing traditional Puritan doctrines of humanity's utter depravity and God's vengeful omnipotence. The title of Edwards's most famous sermon, "Sinners in the Hands of an Angry God," conveys the flavor of his message. In Pennsylvania and New Jersey, William Tennent led revivals that dramatized spiritual rebirth with accounts of God's miraculous powers, such as raising Tennent's son from the dead.

Game Table

Wealth accumulated by prosperous eighteenth-century colonists supported urban artisans, such as the cabinetmaker in New York who built this elegant Chippendale table for sociable games of backgammon and cards. Photograph by Richard Cheek, Photo © 1984 The Metropolitan Museum of Art.

CHAPTER LOCATOR | How and why did British North America change in the eighteenth century?

132   CHAPTER 5   THE CHANGING WORLD OF COLONIAL AMERICA

The most famous revivalist in the eighteenth-century Atlantic world was **George Whitefield**. An Anglican, Whitefield preached to large audiences in England. Whitefield visited the North American colonies seven times, staying for more than three years during the mid-1740s and attracting tens of thousands to his sermons, including Benjamin Franklin and Olaudah Equiano. Whitefield's preaching transported many in his audience to emotion-choked states of religious ecstasy. About one revival he wrote, "The bitter cries and groans were enough to pierce the hardest heart. Some of the people were as pale as death; others were wringing their hands; others lying on the ground; others sinking into the arms of their friends; and most lifting their eyes to heaven, and crying to God for mercy."

Whitefield's successful revivals spawned many lesser imitations. Itinerant preachers, many of them poorly educated, toured the colonial backcountry after midcentury, echoing Whitefield's medium and message as best they could. Bathsheba Kingsley, a member of Jonathan Edwards's flock, preached the revival message informally—as did an unprecedented number of other women throughout the colonies—causing her congregation to brand her a "brawling woman" who had "gone quite out of her place."

The revivals awakened and refreshed the spiritual energies of thousands of colonists struggling with the uncertainties and anxieties of eighteenth-century America. In the end, the conversions at revivals did not substantially boost the total number of church members, but they did communicate the important message that every soul mattered, that men and women could choose to be saved, that individuals had the power to make a decision for everlasting life or death. Colonial revivals expressed in religious terms many of the same democratic and egalitarian values expressed in economic terms by colonists' patterns of consumption. Like consumption, revivals contributed to a set of common experiences that bridged colonial divides of faith, region, class, and status.

Borderlands and Colonial Politics in the British Empire

The plurality of peoples, faiths, and communities that characterized the North American colonies arose from the somewhat haphazard policies of the eighteenth-century British empire. Since the Puritan Revolution of the mid-seventeenth century, British monarchs had valued the colonies' contributions to trade and encouraged their growth and development. Unlike Spain and France—whose policies of excluding Protestants and foreigners kept the population of their North American colonial territories tiny—Britain kept the door to its colonies open to anyone, and tens of thousands of non-British immigrants settled in the North American colonies and raised families. The open door did not extend to trade, however, as the seventeenth-century Navigation Acts restricted colonial trade to British ships and traders. These policies evolved because they served the interests of the monarchy and of influential groups in Britain and the colonies. The policies also gave the colonists a common framework of political expectations and experiences.

At a minimum, British power defended the colonists from Indian, French, and Spanish enemies on their borders—as well as from foreign powers abroad. Each colony organized a militia, and privateers sailed from every port to prey on foreign

George Whitefield

▶ The most famous revivalist of the Great Awakening. Whitefield spoke before enormous audiences in both Britain and the colonies, visiting the North American colonies seven times and staying for more than three years during the mid-1740s. His success inspired numerous lesser imitators to tour the colonies, leading revival meetings of their own.

| What changed in New England life and culture? | How were the middle colonies distinctive? | How did slavery become the defining feature of the southern colonies? | What were the unifying experiences for British American colonists? | Conclusion: What was the dual identity of British North American colonists? |

133

Large Warships in European Navies, 1660–1760

The large warships in England's navy usually outnumbered those of rival nations from 1660 to 1760. During the eighteenth century, the British fleet grew dramatically, while the fleets of rival nations declined. The British monarchy paid the enormous cost of building, manning, and maintaining the largest European navy because defending commerce and communication with its far-flung colonies was fundamental to the integrity of its empire. Britain's North American colonies benefited from defense by the most powerful navy in the Atlantic. Why do you think British warships outnumbered those of their competitors?

= 10 warships

1660 · 1710 · 1760

England · France · Netherlands · Denmark

Note: Comparable data does not exist for Spain.

ships. But the British navy and army bore ultimate responsibility for colonial defense. (See "Global Comparison.")

Royal officials warily eyed the small North American settlements of New France and New Spain for signs of threats to the colonies. Alone, neither New France nor New Spain jeopardized British North America, but with Indian allies, they could become a potent force that kept colonists on their guard (**Map 5.4**). Native Americans' impulse to defend their territory from colonial incursions warred with their desire for trade, which tugged them toward the settlers. As a colonial official observed in 1761, "A modern Indian cannot subsist without Europeans. . . . [The European goods that were] only conveniency at first [have] now become necessity." To obtain such necessities as guns, ammunition, clothing, sewing utensils, and much more that was manufactured largely by the British, Indians trapped beavers, deer, and other furbearing animals throughout the interior.

Colonial traders and their respective empires competed to control the fur trade. British, French, Spanish, and Dutch officials monitored the trade to prevent their competitors from deflecting the flow of furs toward their own markets. Indians took advantage of this competition to improve their own prospects, playing one trader and empire off against another. Indian tribes and confederacies also competed among themselves for favored trading rights with one colony or another, a competition colonists encouraged.

The shifting alliances and complex dynamics of the fur trade struck a fragile balance along the frontier. The threat of violence from all sides was ever present, and the threat became reality often enough for all parties to be prepared for the worst. In the Yamasee War of 1715, Yamasee and Creek Indians—with French encouragement—mounted a coordinated attack against colonial settlements in South Carolina and inflicted heavy casualties. The Cherokee Indians, traditional enemies of the Creeks, refused to join the attack. Instead, they protected their access to British trade goods by allying with the colonists and turning the tide of battle.

Relations between Indians and colonists differed from colony to colony and from year to year. But the British colonists' fears kept them continually hoping for

CHAPTER LOCATOR | How and why did British North America change in the eighteenth century?

help from the British to keep the Indians at bay and to maintain the essential flow of trade. In 1754, the British colonists' endemic competition with the French flared into the Seven Years' War, also known as the French and Indian War (see chapter 6). Before the 1760s, neither the British colonists nor the British themselves developed a coherent policy toward the Indians. But both agreed that Indians made deadly enemies, profitable trading partners, and powerful allies. As a result, the British and their colonists kept an eye on the Spanish empire to the west and relations with the Indians there.

Russian hunters in search of seals and sea otters ventured along the Pacific coast from Alaska to California and threatened to become a permanent presence on New Spain's northern frontier. To block Russian access to present-day California, officials in New Spain mounted a campaign to build forts (called *presidios*) and missions there.

In 1769, an expedition headed by a military man, **Gaspar de Portolá**, and a Catholic priest, Junípero Serra, traveled north from Mexico to present-day San Diego, where they founded the first California mission, San Diego de Alcalá. They soon journeyed all the way to Monterey, which became the capital of Spanish California. There Portolá established a presidio in 1770 "to defend us from attacks by the Russians," he wrote. By 1772, Serra had founded other missions along the path from San Diego to Monterey.

One Spanish soldier praised the work of the missionaries, writing that "with flattery and presents [the missionaries] attract the savage Indians and persuade them to adhere to life in society and to receive instruction for a knowledge of the Catholic faith, the cultivation of the land, and the arts necessary for making the instruments most needed for farming." Yet for the Indians, the Spaniards' California missions had horrendous consequences, as they had elsewhere in the Spanish borderlands. European diseases decimated Indian populations, Spanish soldiers raped Indian women, and missionaries beat Indians and subjected them to near slavery. Indian uprisings against the Spaniards occurred repeatedly, but the presidios and missions endured as projections of the Spanish empire along the Pacific coast.

British attempts to exercise political power in their colonial governments met with success so long as British officials were on or very near the sea. Colonists acknowledged British authority to collect customs duties, inspect cargoes, and enforce trade regulations. But when royal officials tried to wield their authority in the internal affairs of the colonies on land, they invariably

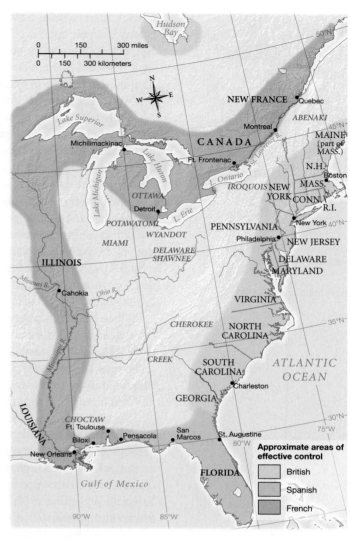

MAP 5.4 ■ Zones of Empire in Eastern North America
The British zone, extending west from the Atlantic coast, was much more densely settled than the zones under French, Spanish, and Indian control. The comparatively large number of British colonists made them more secure than the relatively few colonists in the vast regions claimed by France and Spain or the settlers living among the many Indian peoples in the huge area between the Mississippi River and the Appalachian Mountains. Yet the British colonists were not powerful enough to dominate the French, Spaniards, or Indians. Instead, they had to guard against attacks by powerful Indian groups allied with the French or Spaniards.

Gaspar de Portolá
▶ Spanish military leader who, beginning in 1769, began the establishment of Spanish missions in California, ostensibly to defend Spanish interests in the West from Russia. Eventually, these missions extended from San Diego to Monterey.

| What changed in New England life and culture? | How were the middle colonies distinctive? | How did slavery become the defining feature of the southern colonies? | What were the unifying experiences for British American colonists? | Conclusion: What was the dual identity of British North American colonists? |

Spanish Missions in California

encountered colonial resistance. A governor headed the government of each colony; he was appointed by the king in each of the nine royal colonies (Rhode Island and Connecticut selected their own governors) or by the proprietors in Maryland and Pennsylvania. The British envisioned colonial governors as mini-monarchs able to exert influence in the colonies much as the king did in Britain. But colonial governors were not kings, and the colonies were not Britain.

Eighty percent of colonial governors had been born in England, not in the colonies. Some governors stayed in England and delegated the details of colonial affairs to subordinates. Even the best-intentioned colonial governors had difficulty developing relations of trust and respect with influential colonists because their terms of office averaged just five years and could be terminated at any time. Colonial governors controlled few patronage positions in the colonies that could have helped them build political alliances. In obedience to Britain, colonial governors fought incessantly with the colonists' assemblies. They battled over governors' vetoes of colonial legislation, removal of colonial judges, creation of new courts, dismissal of the representative assemblies, and other local issues. Some governors developed a working relationship with the colonists' assemblies. But during the eighteenth century, the assemblies gained the upper hand.

Since British policies did not clearly define the colonists' legal powers, colonial assemblies seized the opportunity to make their own rules. Gradually, the assemblies established a strong tradition of representative government analogous, in their eyes, to the British Parliament. Voters often returned the same representatives to the assemblies year after year, building continuity in power and leadership that far exceeded that of the governor.

By 1720, colonial assemblies had won the power to initiate legislation, including tax laws and authorizations to spend public funds. Although all laws passed by the assemblies (except in Maryland, Rhode Island, and Connecticut) had to be approved by the governor and then by the Board of Trade in Britain, the difficulties in communication about complex subjects over long distances effectively ratified the assemblies' decisions. Often years passed before colonial laws were repealed by British authorities, and in the meantime, the assemblies' laws prevailed.

The heated political struggles between royal governors and colonial assemblies that occurred throughout the eighteenth century taught colonists a common set of political lessons. They learned to employ traditionally British ideas of representative government to defend their own colonial interests. They learned that power in the British colonies rarely belonged exclusively to the British government.

> QUICK REVIEW

How did commerce and consumption shape the collective identity of colonists in British North America during the eighteenth century?

CHAPTER LOCATOR | How and why did British North America change in the eighteenth century?

Courtesy, American Antiquarian Society.

Conclusion: What was the dual identity of British North American colonists?

DURING THE EIGHTEENTH CENTURY, a society that was both distinctively colonial and distinctively British emerged in British North America. Tens of thousands of immigrants and slaves gave the colonies an unmistakably colonial complexion and contributed to the colonies' growing population and expanding economy. People of different ethnicities and faiths sought their fortunes in the colonies, where land was cheap, labor was dear, and—as Benjamin Franklin preached—work promised to be rewarding. Indentured servants and redemptioners risked temporary periods of bondage for the potential reward of better opportunities in the colonies than on the Atlantic's eastern shore. Slaves endured lifetime servitude, which they neither chose nor desired but from which their masters greatly benefited.

Identifiably colonial products from New England, the middle colonies, and the southern colonies flowed to the West Indies and across the Atlantic. Back came unquestionably British consumer goods along with fashions in ideas, faith, and politics. The bonds of the British empire required colonists to think of themselves as British subjects and, at the same time, encouraged them to consider their status as colonists.

By 1750, British colonists in North America could not imagine that their distinctively dual identity—as British and as colonists—would soon become a source of intense conflict. But by 1776, colonists in British North America had to choose whether they were British or American.

SO NOW YOU KNOW

All of Britain's North American colonies experienced rapid change and growth over the course of the eighteenth century leading up to the American Revolution. While there were many variations among the colonies, colonial wars and British policies helped foster a growing sense of an *American* identity for many colonists.

CHAPTER 5 STUDY GUIDE

Online Study Guide
bedfordstmartins.com/roarkunderstanding

STEP 1

GETTING STARTED

Below are basic terms from this period in American history. Can you identify each term below and explain why it matters? To do this exercise online or to download this chart, visit bedfordstmartins.com/roarkunderstanding.

TERM	WHO OR WHAT & WHEN	WHY IT MATTERS
redemptioners, p. 119		
Iroquois Indians, p. 121		
Benjamin Franklin, p. 122		
Middle Passage, p. 125		
Olaudah Equiano, p. 125		
Stono rebellion , p. 127		
gentry, p. 128		
deism, p. 132		
Enlightenment, p. 132		
Great Awakening, p. 132		
George Whitefield, p. 133		
Gaspar de Portolá, p. 135		

STEP 2

MOVING BEYOND THE BASICS

The exercise below represents a more advanced understanding of the chapter material. In this exercise, identify the changes in colonial society between 1700 and 1770. Use the chart below to describe the economy, society, culture, and politics of the major regions of British North America in 1700 and 1770. What accounts for regional divergence over the course of the eighteenth century? To do this exercise online or to download this chart, visit bedfordstmartins.com/roarkunderstanding.

Region	Economy (imports and exports, jobs, wealth)	Population (ethnicity, race, class)	Culture—ways of life, values (including religious beliefs)	Colonial politics
New England in 1700				
New England in 1770				
Middle colonies in 1700				
Middle colonies in 1770				
Southern colonies in 1700				
Southern colonies in 1770				

Now that you have reviewed key elements of the chapter, take a step back and try to explain the big picture. Remember to use specific examples from the chapter in your answers. To do this exercise online, visit bedfordstmartins.com/roarkunderstanding.

NEW ENGLAND

► How did the economy of New England differ from that of other regions?

► Why did New England not attract as many immigrants as other areas did? How did that affect the social structure of the region?

THE MIDDLE COLONIES

► How did immigration shape the religious and ethnic diversity of the middle colonies? What factors led immigrants to settle in the middle colonies?

► How did Atlantic commerce, particularly colonial consumption, affect the middle colonies?

LOOKING BACKWARD, LOOKING AHEAD

► How did the relationship between the colonies and Britain in the eighteenth century differ from that of the seventeenth century?

► What were the most pressing sources of potential conflict between the colonies and Britain in 1770? What were the most important sources of cooperation and mutual dependence?

THE SOUTHERN COLONIES AND SPANISH CALIFORNIA

► What role did slavery play in the social and economic development of the South?

► How did slaves attempt to maintain their own culture and gain some control within the limits of slavery?

► Why did New Spain establish presidios and missions, and what were their consequences for Native Americans?

IN YOUR OWN WORDS

Imagine that you must explain chapter 5 to someone who hasn't read it. What would be the most important points to include and why?

6

THE MAKING OF AN AMERICAN REVOLUTION

1754–1775

> This chapter explores the efforts of the British government to tax and control the North American colonies in the decade following the Seven Years' War. It examines the resulting deterioration of relations between Britain and its American colonists, tracing the escalating colonial response from political protest, to open resistance, to war.

DID YOU KNOW?

Colonial women were prominent in protesting and resisting British policies.

> How did the Seven Years' War lay the groundwork for colonial crisis?

> Why did the American colonists find offense with the Sugar and Stamp Acts of 1763–1765?

> What were the colonial responses to the Townshend duties?

> What led to the escalation of tensions after 1772?

> What were the varieties of domestic insurrections in 1774–1775?

> Conclusion: What changes did Americans want in 1775?

Resistance to the Stamp Act. This contemporary engraving (ca. 1765) depicts an angry Boston crowd burning a pile of stamps in protest of the Stamp Act.

How did the Seven Years' War lay the groundwork for colonial crisis?

Washington's Journal, 1754

When George Washington returned from his first mission to the French, Governor Dinwiddie asked him to write a full report of what he had seen of the countryside, the Indians, and French troop strength. Dinwiddie printed Washington's report, along with his own letter and the French commander's defiant answer, in a thirty-two-page pamphlet that was soon reprinted in London. Huntington Library.

Seven Years' War
► War (1754–1762) between Britain and France that ended with British domination of North America. Known in America as the French and Indian War, the war spread in 1756 to encompass much of Europe, the Caribbean, and India. The cost of the war laid the foundation for colonial conflicts that would lead to the American Revolution.

FOR THE FIRST HALF of the eighteenth century, Britain was at war intermittently with France or Spain. In the 1750s, international tensions returned, this time over events originating in America. The conflict began in 1754 over contested land in the Ohio Valley. The result was the costly **Seven Years' War** (its British name—Americans called it the French and Indian War), which spread in 1756 to encompass much of Europe, the Caribbean, and even India. The British and their colonial allies won the war, but the immense costs of the conflict laid the groundwork for the imperial crisis of the 1760s between the British and the Americans.

French-British Rivalry in the Ohio Country

For several decades, French traders had cultivated alliances with the Indian tribes in the Ohio Country, a region they regarded as part of New France, establishing a profitable trade of manufactured goods for beaver furs (**Map 6.1**). But in the 1740s, aggressive Pennsylvania traders began to infringe on their territory. Adding to the tensions, a group of enterprising Virginians formed the Ohio Company in 1747 and advanced on the same land. Their hope for profit lay not in the fur trade but in land speculation, fueled by American population expansion.

In response to these incursions, the French sent soldiers to build a series of military forts to secure their trade routes and to create a western barrier to American expansion. In 1753, the royal governor of Virginia, Robert Dinwiddie,

CHAPTER LOCATOR | How did the Seven Years' War lay the groundwork for colonial crisis?

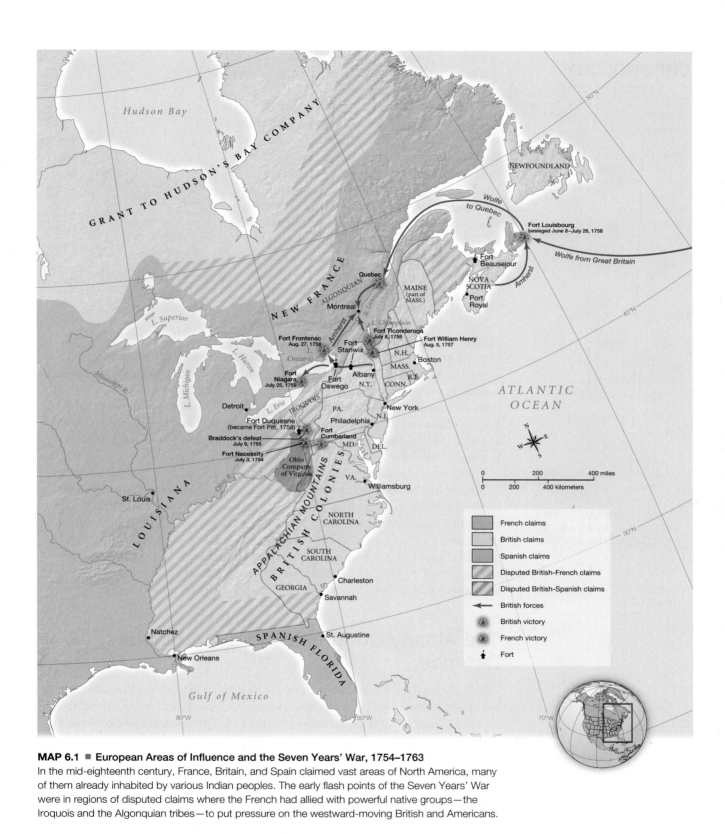

MAP 6.1 ■ European Areas of Influence and the Seven Years' War, 1754–1763
In the mid-eighteenth century, France, Britain, and Spain claimed vast areas of North America, many of them already inhabited by various Indian peoples. The early flash points of the Seven Years' War were in regions of disputed claims where the French had allied with powerful native groups—the Iroquois and the Algonquian tribes—to put pressure on the westward-moving British and Americans.

Why did the American colonists find offense with the Sugar and Stamp Acts of 1763–1765?	What were the colonial responses to the Townshend duties?	What led to the escalation of tensions after 1772?	What were the varieties of domestic insurrections in 1774–1775?	Conclusion: What changes did Americans want in 1775?

CHRONOLOGY

1747
- Ohio Company of Virginia is formed.

1754
- Seven Years' War begins in North America.
- Albany Congress proposes Plan of Union (never implemented).

1755
- Braddock is defeated in western Pennsylvania.

1757
- William Pitt fully commits Britain to war effort.

1760
- Montreal falls to British. George III becomes British king.

1763
- Treaty of Paris ends Seven Years' War.
- Pontiac's uprising increases tensions between Indians and British America.
- Proclamation of 1763 forbids colonists from settling west of the Appalachian Mountains.

himself a shareholder in the Ohio Company, sent a messenger to warn the French that they were trespassing on Virginia land.

The messenger on this dangerous mission was George Washington, twenty-one years old at the time. Washington returned from his mission with crucial intelligence about French military plans. Impressed, Dinwiddie appointed him to lead a small military expedition west to assert and, if need be, defend Virginia's claim. By early 1754, the French had built Fort Duquesne at the forks of the Ohio River; Washington's assignment was to chase the French away without actually being the aggressor.

In the spring of 1754, Washington set out with 160 Virginians and a small contingent of Mingo Indians, who were also concerned about the French military presence in the Ohio Country. The first battle of what would become known as the French and Indian War occurred early one May morning when the Mingo chief Tanaghrisson led a detachment of Washington's soldiers to a small French encampment in the woods. A brief skirmish left fourteen French-men wounded. While Washington struggled to communicate with the injured French commander, Tanaghrisson and his men intervened to kill and then scalp the wounded soldiers, including the commander, probably with the aim of inflaming hostilities between the French and the colonists.

This sudden massacre violated Washington's instructions to avoid being the aggressor and raised the stakes considerably. Fearing retaliation, Washington ordered his men to fortify their position; "Fort Necessity" was the result. Several hundred Virginian reinforcements arrived; but the Mingos, sensing disaster and displeased by Washington's style of command, fled. In early July, more than six hundred French soldiers aided by one hundred Shawnee and Delaware warriors attacked Fort Necessity, killing or wounding a third of Washington's men. The message was clear: The French would not depart from the disputed territory.

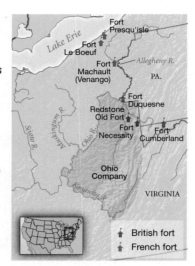

Ohio River Valley, 1753

British fort
French fort

The Albany Congress and Intercolonial Defense

British imperial leaders hoped to prevent the conflict in the Ohio Country from leading to a larger war. One obvious strategy was to strengthen British alliances with seemingly neutral Indian tribes. To this end, British authorities convened a colonial conference.

In June and July 1754, delegates from seven colonies met in Albany, New York. Also attending were Indians of the Iroquois Confederacy, an alliance of tribes inhabiting the central and western parts of present-day New York. Albany was the traditional meeting place of the Covenant Chain, first created in 1692 as a trade alliance of New York leaders and Mohawk Indians, the most easterly of the Iroquois Confederacy. In 1753, the Mohawk leader Hendrick accused the colonists of breaking the Covenant Chain. A prime goal of the Albany Congress was to

CHAPTER LOCATOR

How did the Seven Years' War lay the groundwork for colonial crisis?

► FOR MORE HELP ANALYZING THIS IMAGE, see the visual activity for this chapter in the Online Study Guide at bedfordstmartins.com/roarkunderstanding.

repair trade relations with the Mohawks and secure their help—or at least their neutrality—against the French threat.

Benjamin Franklin of Pennsylvania and Thomas Hutchinson of Massachusetts had more ambitious plans. They coauthored the Albany Plan of Union, a proposal for a unified colonial government limited to war, defense policies, and relations with Indians.

Key Features of the Albany Plan of Union

A president general was to be appointed by the crown.

A grand council was to meet annually to consider questions of war, peace, and trade with the Indians.

The plan reaffirmed Parliament's authority and was not a bid for enlarged autonomy of the colonies.

Not a single colony approved the Albany Plan. The Massachusetts assembly feared it was "a Design of gaining power over the Colonies," especially the power of taxation. Others objected that it would be impossible to agree on unified policies toward scores of quite different Indian tribes. The British government never backed the Albany Plan either, and soon after it appointed two superintendents of Indian affairs, one for the northern and another for the southern colonies, each with exclusive powers to negotiate treaties, trade, and land sales with all tribes.

The Albany Congress had very limited success. The Covenant Chain alliance with the Mohawk tribe was reaffirmed, but other Indian nations left without

Why did the American colonists find offense with the Sugar and Stamp Acts of 1763–1765?	What were the colonial responses to the Townshend duties?	What led to the escalation of tensions after 1772?	What were the varieties of domestic insurrections in 1774–1775?	Conclusion: What changes did Americans want in 1775?

pledging to help the British battle the French. Some of the Iroquois figured that the French military presence around the Great Lakes would discourage the westward push of American colonists and therefore better serve their interests.

The War and Its Consequences

By 1755, Washington's frontier skirmish had turned into a major mobilization of British and American troops against the French. The British expected a quick victory on three fronts. General Edward Braddock marched his army toward Fort Duquesne in western Pennsylvania. Farther north, British troops moved toward Fort Niagara, critically located between Lakes Erie and Ontario. And New Yorker William Johnson led forces north toward Lake Champlain, intending to defend the border against the French in Canada (see Map 6.1, page 143).

Unfortunately for the British, the French were prepared to fight and had cemented alliances with many Indian tribes throughout the region. In July 1755, Braddock's army of 2,000 British soldiers rode west with Washington and Virginia militiamen and were ambushed by 250 French soldiers and 640 Indian warriors. Nearly 1,000 on the British side were killed or wounded, including General Braddock. Washington, who was unhurt, was commended for his bravery and promoted to commander of the Virginia army.

For the next two years, British leaders stumbled badly, deploying inadequate numbers of undersupplied troops. What finally turned the war around was the rise to power in 1757 of William Pitt, Britain's prime minister, a man willing to commit massive resources to fight France and its ally Spain worldwide. In America, British troops aided by American soldiers captured Forts Duquesne, Niagara, and Ticonderoga and then the French cities of Quebec and finally Montreal, all from 1758 to 1760. The American colonists rejoiced, but the war expanded globally, with battles in the Caribbean, Austria, Prussia, and India. By the end of 1762, France and Spain capitulated, and the Treaty of Paris was signed in 1763.

In the complex peace negotiations that followed, Britain gained control of Canada, eliminating the French threat from the north. In addition, British and American title to the eastern half of North America was confirmed. But French territory west of the Mississippi River, including New Orleans, was transferred to Spain as compensation for Spain's assistance during the war. Most significantly, two sugar-producing French islands in the Caribbean were returned to France (**Map 6.2**).

One key group, the Indians, was ignored by the Treaty of Paris. With the French gone, the Indians lost the advantage of having two opponents to play off against each other, and they now had to cope with the westward-moving Americans. Indian policy would soon become a serious point of contention between the British government and the colonists.

The British credited the British army for their victory, while criticizing the inadequate and ungrateful support of the colonists. Fueling resentment, during the war colonial smugglers kept up the trade in beaver pelts with the French as well as an illegal molasses trade in the Caribbean. William Pitt was convinced that these activities "principally, if not alone, enabled France to sustain and protract this long and expensive war."

Colonists read the lessons of the war differently. American soldiers had turned out in force, they claimed, but had been relegated to grunt work by British

CHAPTER LOCATOR | How did the Seven Years' War lay the groundwork for colonial crisis?

CHAPTER 6
146 THE MAKING OF AN AMERICAN REVOLUTION, 1754–1775

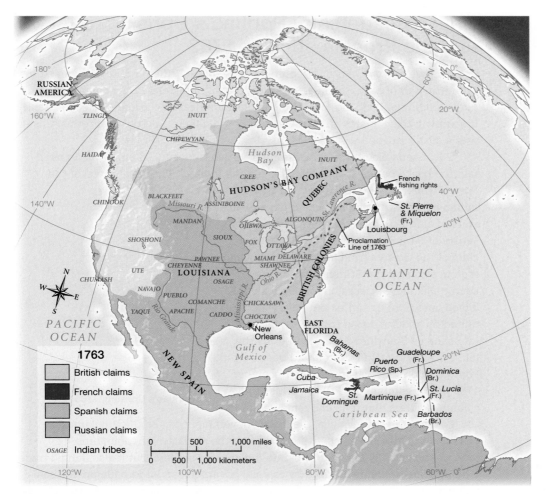

MAP 6.2 ■ North America after the Seven Years' War
In the peace treaty of 1763, France ceded to Britain its interior territory from Quebec to New Orleans, retaining fishing rights in the far north and several sugar islands in the Caribbean. France transferred to Spain its claim to extensive territory west of the Mississippi River.

▶ FOR MORE HELP ANALYZING THIS MAP, see the map activity for this chapter in the Online Study Guide at bedfordstmartins.com/roarkunderstanding.

leaders and subjected to unexpectedly harsh military discipline. General Braddock bragged to Benjamin Franklin that "these savages may, indeed, be a formidable enemy to your raw American militia, but upon the king's regular and disciplined troops, sir, it is impossible they should make any impression."

The human costs of the war were etched especially sharply in the minds of New England colonists. About one-third of all Massachusetts men between fifteen and thirty had seen service, and many families lost loved ones.

The enormous expense of the war cast another huge shadow over the victory. By 1763, Britain's national debt, double what it had been when Pitt took office, posed a formidable challenge to the next decade of leadership in Britain.

| Why did the American colonists find offense with the Sugar and Stamp Acts of 1763–1765? | What were the colonial responses to the Townshend duties? | What led to the escalation of tensions after 1772? | What were the varieties of domestic insurrections in 1774–1775? | Conclusion: What changes did Americans want in 1775? |

British Leadership, Pontiac's Uprising, and the Proclamation of 1763

In 1760, twenty-two-year-old George III came to the British throne and named his tutor, the Earl of Bute, the head of his cabinet of ministers. Bute committed blunders and did not last long, but he made one significant decision—to keep a standing army in the colonies after the war. In both financial and political terms, this was a costly move.

The ostensible reason for stationing British troops in America was to maintain the peace between the colonists and the Indians. The withdrawal of the French from North America had left their Indian allies—who did not accept defeat—in a state of alarm. Just three months after the Treaty of Paris was signed in 1763, Pontiac, chief of the Ottawa tribe in the northern Ohio region, attacked the British garrison near Detroit. Six more attacks on forts quickly followed, and frontier settlements were also raided by about a dozen tribes, leaving two thousand civilians dead or captured. By the fall, every fort west of Detroit had been seized. Pontiac's uprising was quelled in December 1763 by the combined efforts of British and colonial soldiers, but tensions remained high.

Pontiac's Uprising, 1763

Proclamation of 1763

▶ British proclamation forbidding colonists to settle west of the Appalachian Mountains. The Proclamation chiefly aimed to separate Indians and settlers, but it also limited trade with Indians to traders licensed by colonial governors, and it forbade private sales of Indian land.

To minimize the violence, the British government issued the **Proclamation of 1763**, forbidding colonists to settle west of the Appalachian Mountains. The Proclamation chiefly aimed to separate Indians and settlers, but it also limited trade with Indians to traders licensed by colonial governors, and it forbade private sales of Indian land. The Proclamation's language took care not to identify western lands as belonging to the Indians. And while other parts of the Proclamation of 1763 referred to American and even French colonists in Canada as "our loving subjects," the Indians were not described as British subjects.

The 1763 boundary proved impossible to enforce. Surging population growth had already sent many hundreds of settlers west of the Appalachians, and land speculators, such as those of Virginia's Ohio Company, had no desire to lose opportunities for profitable resale of their land grants. Bute's decision to post a standing army in the colonies was thus a cause for concern among western settlers, eastern speculators, and Indian tribes alike.

> **QUICK REVIEW**

How did the Seven Years' War erode relations between colonists and British authorities?

CHAPTER LOCATOR | How did the Seven Years' War lay the groundwork for colonial crisis?

George Grenville, Prime Minister 1763–1765

George Grenville gained the prime minister's job in 1763 at a point when King George was short of competent alternatives, but the king found him irksome: "When he has wearied me for two hours, he looks at his watch, to see if he may not tire me for an hour more," King George said. The king sacked him in July 1765 for being insolent, not for his controversial colonial policies. The Earl of Halifax, Garrowby, Yorkshire.

Why did the American colonists find offense with the Sugar and Stamp Acts of 1763–1765?

LORD BUTE LOST POWER in 1763, and King George turned to a succession of leaders throughout the 1760s, searching for a prime minister he could trust. A half dozen ministers in seven years took turns dealing with one basic, underlying British reality: A huge war debt needed to be serviced, and the colonists, as British subjects, should help pay it off. To many Americans, however, that proposition violated what they perceived to be their rights and liberties as British subjects, and it created resentment that eventually erupted in large-scale protests. The first provocative revenue acts were the work of Sir George Grenville, prime minister from 1763 to 1765.

Grenville's Sugar Act

To find revenue, George Grenville scrutinized the customs service, which monitored the shipping trade and collected all import and export duties. Grenville found that the salaries of customs officers cost the government four times what was collected in revenue. The shortfall was due in part to bribery and smuggling, so Grenville began to insist on rigorous attention to paperwork and a strict accounting of collected duties.

| Why did the American colonists find offense with the Sugar and Stamp Acts of 1763–1765? | What were the colonial responses to the Townshend duties? | What led to the escalation of tensions after 1772? | What were the varieties of domestic insurrections in 1774–1775? | Conclusion: What changes did Americans want in 1775? |

1764
- Parliament enacts Sugar (Revenue) Act.

1765
- Parliament enacts Stamp Act.
- Virginia Resolves assert the colony's exclusive right to tax its citizens.
- The newly formed Sons of Liberty engages in dozens of crowd actions.
- Stamp Act Congress, an intercolonial group, meets to consider political responses to Great Britain.

1766
- The British Parliament repeals the Stamp Act.

Sugar Act
► Officially called the Revenue Act, this 1764 British law lowered the duty on French molasses, making it more attractive for shippers to obey the law, and at the same time raised penalties for smuggling. Conflicts over the Sugar Act foreshadowed later colonial conflicts over taxation.

Stamp Act
► 1765 British law imposing a tax on all paper used for official documents and requiring an affixed stamp as proof that the tax had been paid. Unlike the Sugar Act, which regulated trade, the Stamp Act was designed simply to raise money. Widespread resistance to the Stamp Act led to its repeal in 1766.

virtual representation
► The theory that all British subjects were represented in Parliament, whether they had elected representatives in that body or not. American colonists rejected the theory of virtual representation, arguing that only direct representatives had the right to tax the colonists.

The hardest duty to enforce was the one imposed by the Molasses Act of 1733—a stiff tax of six pence per gallon on any molasses purchased from non-British sources. Rum-loving Americans, however, were eager to buy molasses from French Caribbean islands, and they had ignored the tax law for decades. Grenville's solution was the Revenue Act of 1764, popularly dubbed the **Sugar Act**. It lowered the duty on French molasses to three pence, making it more attractive for shippers to obey the law, and at the same time raised penalties for smuggling. The act appeared to be in the tradition of navigation acts meant to regulate trade, but Grenville's actual intent was to raise revenue.

The Sugar Act toughened enforcement policies. From now on, all British naval crews could act as impromptu customs officers, boarding suspicious ships and seizing cargoes found to be in violation. Smugglers caught without proper paperwork would be prosecuted, not in a local court with a friendly jury but in a vice admiralty court located in Nova Scotia, where a crown judge presided.

Grenville's hopes for the Sugar Act did not materialize. The small decrease in duty did not offset the attractions of smuggling, while the increased vigilance in enforcement led to several ugly confrontations in port cities. Reaction to the Sugar Act foreshadowed questions about Britain's right to tax Americans, but in 1764 objections to the act came principally from Americans in the shipping trades.

From the British point of view, the Proclamation of 1763 and the Sugar Act seemed to be reasonable efforts to administer the colonies. To the Americans, however, the British supervision appeared to be a disturbing intrusion into colonial practices.

The Stamp Act

In February 1765, Grenville escalated his revenue program with the **Stamp Act**, precipitating a major conflict between Britain and the colonies over Parliament's right to tax. The Stamp Act imposed a tax on all paper used for official documents—newspapers, pamphlets, court documents, licenses, wills, ships' cargo lists—and required an affixed stamp as proof that the tax had been paid. Unlike the Sugar Act, which regulated trade, the Stamp Act was designed simply to raise money. It affected nearly everyone who used any taxed paper but, most of all, users of official documents in the business and legal communities.

Anticipating that the stamp tax would be unpopular, Grenville delegated the administration of the act to Americans to avoid taxpayer hostility toward British enforcers. In each colony, local stamp distributors would be hired at a handsome salary of 8 percent of the revenue collected.

English tradition held that taxes were a gift of the people to their monarch, granted by the people's representatives. The king could not demand money; only the House of Commons could grant it. Grenville agreed with the notion of taxation by consent, but he argued that the colonists were already "virtually" represented in Parliament. The House of Commons, he insisted, represented all British subjects, wherever they were.

Colonial leaders emphatically rejected this view, arguing that **virtual representation** could not withstand the stretch across the Atlantic. The stamp tax itself, levied by a distant Parliament on unwilling colonies, illustrated the problem. In the words of a Maryland lawyer, virtual representation was "a mere cob-web, spread to catch the unwary, and entangle the weak."

CHAPTER LOCATOR

How did the Seven Years' War lay the groundwork for colonial crisis?

CHAPTER 6

150   THE MAKING OF AN AMERICAN REVOLUTION, 1754–1775

Resistance Strategies and Crowd Politics

News of the Stamp Act arrived in the colonies in April 1765, seven months before it was to take effect. There was time, therefore, to object. Governors were unlikely to challenge the law, for most of them owed their office to the king. Instead, the colonial assemblies took the lead; eight of them held discussions on the Stamp Act.

Virginia's assembly, the House of Burgesses, was the first. At the end of its May session, after two-thirds of the members had left, Patrick Henry, a young political newcomer, presented a series of resolutions on the Stamp Act, which were debated and passed, one by one. They became known as the Virginia Resolves. Henry's resolutions inched the assembly toward radical opposition to the Stamp Act. The first three stated the obvious: that Virginians were British citizens, that they enjoyed the same rights and privileges as Britons, and that self-taxation was one of those rights. The fourth resolution noted that Virginians had always taxed themselves, through their representatives in the House of Burgesses. The fifth took a radical leap by pushing the other four unexceptional statements to one logical conclusion—that the Virginia assembly alone had the right to tax Virginians.

Two more resolutions were debated as Henry pressed the logic of his case to the extreme. The sixth resolution denied legitimacy to any tax law originating outside Virginia, and a seventh boldly called anyone who disagreed with these propositions an enemy of Virginia. This was too much for the other representatives. They voted down resolutions six and seven and later rescinded their vote on number five as well.

Their caution hardly mattered, however, because newspapers in other colonies printed all seven Virginia Resolves, creating the impression that a daring first challenge to the Stamp Act had occurred. Consequently, other assemblies were willing to consider even more radical questions, such as this: By what authority could Parliament legislate for the colonies without also taxing them? No one disagreed, in 1765, that Parliament had legislative power over the colonists, who were, after all, British subjects. Several assemblies advanced the argument that there was a distinction between *external* taxes, imposed to regulate trade, and *internal* taxes, such as a stamp tax or a property tax, which could only be self-imposed.

Reaction to the Stamp Act ran far deeper than political debate in assemblies. Every person whose livelihood required official paper had to decide whether to comply with the act. The first organized resistance to the Stamp Act began in Boston in August 1765 under the direction of town leaders, chief among them Samuel Adams, John Hancock, and Ebenezer Mackintosh. Many other artisans, tradesmen, printers, tavern keepers, dockworkers, and sailors—the middling and lower orders—mobilized in resistance to the Stamp Act, taking the name "Sons of Liberty."

The plan hatched in Boston called for a large street demonstration highlighting a mock execution designed to convince Andrew Oliver, the designated stamp distributor, to resign. On August 14, 1765, a crowd of two thousand to three thousand demonstrators, led by the young shoemaker Mackintosh, hung an effigy of Oliver in a tree and then paraded it around town before finally beheading and burning it. In hopes of calming tensions, the royal governor Francis Bernard took no action. The next day Oliver resigned his office in a well-publicized announcement.

The demonstration provided lessons for everyone. Oliver learned that stamp distributors would be very unpopular people. Francis Bernard, the royal governor, learned the limitations of his power to govern, with no police force to call on. The demonstration's leaders learned that street action was effective. And hundreds

| Why did the American colonists find offense with the Sugar and Stamp Acts of 1763–1765? | What were the colonial responses to the Townshend duties? | What led to the escalation of tensions after 1772? | What were the varieties of domestic insurrections in 1774–1775? | Conclusion: What changes did Americans want in 1775? |

151

of ordinary men not only learned what the Stamp Act was all about but also gained pride in their ability to have a decisive impact on politics.

Twelve days later, a second crowd action showed how well these lessons had been learned. On August 26, a crowd visited the houses of three customs and court officials, breaking windows and raiding wine cellars. A fourth target was the finest dwelling in Massachusetts, owned by Thomas Hutchinson, lieutenant governor of Massachusetts and the chief justice of the colony's highest court. Rumors abounded that Hutchinson had urged Grenville to adopt the Stamp Act. Although he had actually done the opposite, Hutchinson refused to set the record straight, saying, "I am not obliged to give an answer to all the questions that may be put me by every lawless person." The crowd attacked his house, and by daybreak only the exterior walls were standing. Governor Bernard gave orders to call out the militia, but he was told that many militiamen were among the crowd.

The destruction of Hutchinson's house brought a temporary halt to protest activities in Boston. The town meeting issued a statement of sympathy for Hutchinson, but a large reward for the arrest and conviction of rioters failed to produce a single lead. Essentially, the opponents of the Stamp Act in Boston had triumphed; no one replaced Oliver as distributor. When the act took effect on November 1, ships without stamped permits continued to clear the harbor. Since he could not bring the lawbreakers to court, Hutchinson felt obliged to resign his office as chief justice. He remained lieutenant governor, however, and within five years he became the royal governor.

Liberty and Property

Boston's crowd actions of August sparked similar eruptions by groups calling themselves Sons of Liberty in nearly fifty towns throughout the colonies, and stamp distributors everywhere hastened to resign. One Connecticut distributor was forced by a crowd to throw his hat and powdered wig in the air while shouting a cheer for "Liberty and property!" In Charleston, South Carolina, the stamp distributor resigned after crowds burned effigies and chanted "Liberty! Liberty!"

Some colonial leaders, disturbed by the riots, sought a more moderate challenge to parliamentary authority. Twenty-seven delegates representing nine colonial assemblies met in New York City in October 1765 as the Stamp Act

CHAPTER LOCATOR | How did the Seven Years' War lay the groundwork for colonial crisis?

Congress. The result was a petition to the king and Parliament that closely resembled the first five Virginia Resolves, claiming that taxes were "free gifts of the people," which only the people's representatives could give. They dismissed virtual representation: "The people of these colonies are not, and from their local circumstances, cannot be represented in the House of Commons." At the same time, the delegates carefully affirmed their subordination to Parliament and their monarch in deferential language. Nevertheless, the Stamp Act Congress, by the mere fact of its meeting, advanced a radical potential—the notion of intercolonial political action.

The rallying cry of "Liberty and property" made perfect sense to many white Americans of all social ranks, who feared that the Stamp Act threatened their traditional right to liberty as British subjects. The liberty in question was the right to be taxed only by representative government. "Liberty and property" came from a trinity of concepts—"life, liberty, property"—that had come to be regarded as the birthright of freeborn British subjects since at least the seventeenth century. A powerful tradition of British political thought invested representative government with the duty to protect individual lives, liberties, and property against potential abuse by royal authority. Up to 1765, Americans had consented to accept Parliament as a body that represented them. But now, in this matter of taxation via stamps, Parliament seemed a distant body that had failed to protect Americans' liberty and property against royal authority.

Alarmed, some Americans began to speak and write about a plot by British leaders to enslave them. A Maryland writer warned that if the colonies lost "the right of exemption from all taxes without their consent," that loss would "deprive them of every privilege distinguishing freemen from slaves." The opposite meanings of *liberty* and *slavery* were clear to white Americans, but they stopped short of applying similar logic to enslaved black Americans. When a crowd of Charleston blacks paraded with shouts of "Liberty!" just a few months after white Sons of Liberty had done the same, the town militia turned out to break up the demonstration.

Politicians and merchants in Britain reacted with distress to the American demonstrations and petitions. Merchants particularly feared trade disruptions and pressured Parliament to repeal the Stamp Act. By late 1765, yet another new minister, the Marquess of Rockingham, headed the king's cabinet and sought a way to repeal the act without losing face. The solution came in March 1766: The Stamp Act was repealed, but with the repeal came the Declaratory Act, which asserted Parliament's right to legislate for the colonies "in all cases whatsoever." Perhaps the stamp tax had been inexpedient, but the power to tax—one prime case of a legislative power—was upheld.

QUICK REVIEW

What rights did many Americans feel were challenged by the Sugar Act and the Stamp Act? How did they express their disapproval of the acts?

Why did the American colonists find offense with the Sugar and Stamp Acts of 1763–1765?	What were the colonial responses to the Townshend duties?	What led to the escalation of tensions after 1772?	What were the varieties of domestic insurrections in 1774–1775?	Conclusion: What changes did Americans want in 1775?

What were the colonial responses to the Townshend duties?

Edenton Tea Ladies

American women in many communities renounced British apparel and tea during the early 1770s. Women in Edenton, North Carolina, publicized their pledge and drew hostile fire in the form of a British cartoon. The cartoon's message is that brazen women who meddled in politics would undermine their femininity. Library of Congress.

ROCKINGHAM did not last long as prime minister. By the summer of 1766, George III had persuaded William Pitt to resume that position. Pitt appointed Charles Townshend to be chancellor of the exchequer, the chief financial minister. Facing both the old war debt and the continuing cost of stationing British troops in America, Townshend turned again to taxation. His plan to raise revenue touched off coordinated boycotts of British goods in 1768 and 1769. Boston led the uproar, causing the British to send peacekeeping soldiers to assist the royal governor. The stage was thus set for the first fatalities in the brewing revolution.

The Townshend Duties

Townshend duties

▶ British law that established new duties on tea, glass, lead, paper, and painters' colors imported into the colonies, to be paid by the importer but passed on to consumers in the retail price. The Townshend duties (officially called the Revenue Act of 1767) led to boycotts and heightened tensions between Britain and the American colonies.

Townshend proposed new taxes in the old form of a navigation act. Officially called the Revenue Act of 1767, it established new duties on tea, glass, lead, paper, and painters' colors imported into the colonies, to be paid by the importer but passed on to consumers in the retail price. The **Townshend duties** were not especially burdensome, but the principle they embodied—taxation through trade duties—looked different to the colonists in the wake of the Stamp Act crisis. Although Americans once distinguished between external and internal taxes, accepting external duties as a means to direct the flow of trade, that distinction was wiped out by an external tax meant only to raise money. John Dickinson, a Philadelphia lawyer, articulated this view in a series of articles titled *Letters from a Farmer in Pennsylvania*, widely circulated in late 1767. "We are taxed without our consent. . . . We are therefore—SLAVES," Dickinson wrote, calling for "a total denial of the power of Parliament to lay upon these colonies any 'tax' whatever."

CHAPTER LOCATOR | How did the Seven Years' War lay the groundwork for colonial crisis?

CHAPTER 6

154   THE MAKING OF AN AMERICAN REVOLUTION, 1754–1775

A controversial provision of the Townshend duties directed that some of the revenue generated would pay the salaries of royal governors. Before 1767, local assemblies set the salaries of their own officials, giving them significant influence over crown-appointed officeholders. Townshend wanted to strengthen the governors' position as well as to curb the growing independence of the assemblies.

Massachusetts again took the lead in protesting the Townshend duties. Samuel Adams, now an elected member of the provincial assembly, argued that any form of parliamentary taxation was unjust because Americans were not represented in Parliament. Further, he argued that the new way to pay governors' salaries subverted the proper relationship between the people and their rulers. The assembly circulated a letter with Adams's arguments to other colonial assemblies for their endorsement. As with the Stamp Act Congress of 1765, colonial assemblies were starting to coordinate their protests.

In response to Adams's letter, the new man in charge of colonial affairs in Britain, Lord Hillsborough, instructed Massachusetts governor Bernard to dissolve the assembly if it refused to repudiate the letter. The assembly refused, by a vote of 92 to 17, and Bernard carried out his instruction. In the summer of 1768, Boston was in an uproar.

Nonconsumption and the Daughters of Liberty

The Boston town meeting led the way with nonconsumption agreements calling for a boycott of all British-made goods. Dozens of other towns passed similar resolutions in 1767 and 1768. For example, prohibited purchases in the town of New Haven, Connecticut, included imported carriages, furniture, lace, clocks, and textiles. The idea was to encourage home manufacture and to hurt trade, causing London merchants to pressure Parliament for repeal of the duties.

Nonconsumption agreements were very hard to enforce. With the Stamp Act, there was one hated item, a stamp, and a limited number of official distributors. In contrast, an agreement to boycott all British goods required serious personal sacrifices, sacrifices not everyone was prepared to make. A more direct blow to trade came from nonimportation agreements, but getting merchants to agree to these proved more difficult, because of fears that merchants in other colonies might continue to import goods and make handsome profits. Not until late 1768 could Boston merchants agree to suspend trade through a nonimportation agreement lasting one year starting January 1, 1769. Sixty signed the agreement. New York merchants soon followed suit, as did Philadelphia and Charleston merchants in 1769.

Many of the British products specified in nonconsumption agreements were household goods traditionally under the control of the "ladies." By 1769, male leaders in the patriot cause clearly understood that women's cooperation in nonconsumption and home manufacture was beneficial to their cause. The Townshend duties thus provided an unparalleled opportunity for encouraging female patriotism. During the Stamp Act crisis, Sons of Liberty took to the streets in protest. During the difficulties of 1768 and 1769, the Daughters of Liberty emerged, embodying the new idea that women might play a role in public affairs. Any woman could express affiliation with the colonial protest through conspicuous boycotts of British-made goods. In Boston, more than three hundred women signed a petition to abstain from tea, "sickness excepted," in order to "save this abused Country from Ruin and Slavery."

CHRONOLOGY

1767
- Parliament enacts Townshend duties.

1768
- British station troops in Boston.
- Merchants sign nonimportation agreements.

1770
- Boston Massacre.

| Why did the American colonists find offense with the Sugar and Stamp Acts of 1763–1765? | **What were the colonial responses to the Townshend duties?** | What led to the escalation of tensions after 1772? | What were the varieties of domestic insurrections in 1774–1775? | Conclusion: What changes did Americans want in 1775? |

Homespun cloth became a prominent symbol of patriotism. A young Boston girl learning to spin called herself "a daughter of liberty," noting that "I chuse to wear as much of our own manufactory as pocible." In the boycott period of 1768 to 1770, newspapers reported on spinning matches, or bees, in some sixty New England towns, in which women came together in public to make yarn. Newspaper accounts variously called the spinners "Daughters of Liberty" or "Daughters of Industry."

This surge of public spinning was related to the politics of the boycott, which infused traditional women's work with new political purpose. But the women spinners were not equivalents of the Sons of Liberty. The Sons marched in streets, burned effigies, threatened officials, and celebrated anniversaries of their successes with drinking in taverns. The Daughters manifested their patriotism quietly, in ways marked by piety, industry, and charity. The difference was due in part to cultural ideals of gender, which prized masculine self-assertion and feminine selflessness. It also was due to class. The Sons were a cross-class alliance, with leaders from the middling orders reliant on members of the lower ranks to fuel their crowds. The Daughters were genteel ladies used to buying British goods. The difference between the Sons and Daughters also speaks to two views of how best to challenge authority: violent threats and street actions, or the self-disciplined, self-sacrificing boycott of goods?

On the whole, the anti-British boycotts were a success. Imports fell by more than 40 percent; British merchants felt the pinch and let Parliament know it. Boston seemed overrun with anti-British sentiment, and both Lieutenant Governor Hutchinson and Governor Bernard concluded that British troops were necessary to restore order.

The Bloody Massacre Perpetrated in King Street, Boston, on March 5, 1770

This mass-produced engraving by Paul Revere sold for six pence per copy. In this patriot version of events, the soldiers fire on an unarmed crowd under orders of their captain. Among the five killed was Crispus Attucks, a black sailor, but Revere shows only whites among the casualties. Anne S. K. Brown Military Collection, Providence, R.I.

▶ FOR MORE HELP ANALYZING THIS IMAGE, see the visual activity for this chapter in the Online Study Guide at bedfordstmartins.com/roarkunderstanding.

CHAPTER LOCATOR | How did the Seven Years' War lay the groundwork for colonial crisis?

Military Occupation and "Massacre" in Boston

In the fall of 1768, three thousand uniformed troops arrived to occupy Boston. Although the situation was frequently tense, no major troubles occurred that winter and through most of 1769. But as January 1, 1770, approached, marking the end of the nonimportation agreement, it was clear that some merchants—such as Thomas Hutchinson's two sons, both importers—were ready to break the boycott.

Trouble began in January, when someone defaced the door of the Hutchinson brothers' shop with manure. In February, a crowd surrounded the house of customs official Ebenezer Richardson, who panicked and fired a musket, accidentally killing a young boy passing on the street. The Sons of Liberty mounted a massive funeral procession to mark this first instance of violent death in the struggle with Britain.

For the next week, tension gripped Boston. The climax came on Monday evening, March 5, 1770, when a crowd taunted eight British soldiers guarding the customs house. Onlookers threw snowballs and rocks and dared the soldiers to fire; finally one did. After a short pause, someone yelled "Fire!" and the other soldiers shot into the crowd, hitting eleven men, killing five of them.

In the immediate aftermath of the **Boston Massacre**, as the event quickly became called, Hutchinson (now acting governor after Bernard's recall to Britain) quickly removed the regiments to an island in the harbor to prevent further bloodshed, and he jailed Captain Thomas Preston and his eight soldiers for their own protection, promising they would be held for trial. Meanwhile, the Sons of Liberty staged elaborate martyrs' funerals for the five victims. Significantly, the one nonwhite victim, Crispus Attucks, shared equally in the public's veneration.

Crispus Attucks, a sailor and rope maker in his forties, was the son of an African man and a Natick Indian woman. A slave in his youth, he was at the time of his death a free laborer at the Boston docks. Attucks was one of the first American partisans to die in the American Revolution, and certainly the first African American.

The trial of the eight soldiers came in the fall of 1770. They were defended by two young Boston attorneys, Samuel Adams's cousin John Adams and Josiah Quincy. Because Adams and Quincy had direct ties to the leadership of the Sons of Liberty, their decision to defend the British soldiers at first seems odd. Beyond Adams's deep commitment to the principle that even unpopular defendants deserved a fair trial, there were strategic reasons to take on their defense. It showed that the Boston leadership was not lawless but could be seen as defenders of British liberty and law. The five-day trial resulted in acquittal for Preston and for all but two of the soldiers, who were convicted of manslaughter, branded on the thumbs, and released.

Boston Massacre

▶ March 1770 incident in Boston in which British soldiers fired on an American crowd, killing five and wounding six others. A five-day trial of the soldiers resulted in acquittal for all but two of them. The Boston Massacre became a rallying point for colonists who increasingly saw the British government as tyrannical and illegitimate.

QUICK REVIEW

Why were Boston's resistance to British policies and British reaction to this resistance so pronounced?

What led to the escalation of tensions after 1772?

Tossing the Tea

This colored engraving appeared in an English book published in 1789 recounting the history of North America from its earliest settlement to "becoming united, free, and independent states." This event was not dubbed the "Tea Party" until the 1830s, when a later generation celebrated the illegal destruction of the tea and made heroes out of the few surviving participants, by then in their eighties and nineties. Library of Congress.

IN THE SAME WEEK as the Boston Massacre, yet another new British prime minister, Frederick North, acknowledged the harmful impact of the boycott on trade and recommended repeal of the Townshend duties. Seeking peace with the colonies and prosperity for British merchants, North persuaded Parliament to remove all the duties except the tax on tea, kept as a symbol of Parliament's power. For nearly two years following repeal of the Townshend duties, peace seemed possible, but tense incidents in 1772, followed by a renewed struggle over the tea tax in 1773, precipitated a full-scale crisis that by 1775 resulted in war.

The Calm before the Storm

Repeal of the Townshend duties brought an end to nonimportation. Trade boomed in 1770 and 1771, driven by pent-up demand. Then in 1772, new troubles again brought the conflict with Britain into sharp focus. In Rhode Island, suspected smugglers burned the *Gaspée*, a Royal Navy ship. The British investigating commission announced that it would send suspects, if any were found, to Britain for trial on charges of high treason. This ruling seemed to fly in the face of the traditional English right to trial by a jury of one's peers.

When news of the *Gaspée* investigation spread, Patrick Henry, Thomas Jefferson, and Richard Henry Lee in the Virginia House of Burgesses proposed that a network of standing committees be established to link the colonial assemblies and facilitate the spread of alarming news. By mid-1773, every assembly except Pennsylvania's had its own **committees of correspondence**, linking hundreds of towns by express riders. These committees politicized ordinary townspeople, sparking a revolutionary language of rights and constitutional duties. They also bypassed the official flow of power and information through the colony's royal government.

committees of correspondence

▶ Committees first set up in Virginia in 1772 and in Massachusetts in 1773 to provide local forums for debate and to spread news about important political developments. These committees politicized ordinary townspeople, sparking a revolutionary language of rights and constitutional duties.

CHAPTER LOCATOR | How did the Seven Years' War lay the groundwork for colonial crisis?

The paramount incident shattering the relative calm of the early 1770s was the **Tea Act of 1773**. Americans had resumed buying the taxed British tea, but they were also smuggling large quantities of Dutch tea, cutting into the sales of Britain's East India Company. So Lord North proposed legislation giving favored status to the East India Company, allowing it to sell tea directly to government agents rather than through public auction to independent merchants. The hope was to lower the price of the East India tea, including the duty, below that of smuggled Dutch tea, motivating Americans to obey the law.

Tea in Boston Harbor

In the fall of 1773, news of the Tea Act reached the colonies. Parliamentary legislation to make tea inexpensive struck many colonists as a plot to trick Americans into buying the duted tea. The real goal, some argued, was the increased revenue, which would be used to pay the royal governors and judges.

But how to resist the Tea Act? Nonimportation was not viable, because the tea trade was too lucrative to expect merchants to give it up willingly. Consumer boycotts of duted tea seemed ineffective, because it was impossible to distinguish between duted tea and smuggled tea once it was in the teapot. The appointment of tea agents, parallel to the Stamp Act distributors, suggested one solution. In every port city, revived Sons of Liberty pressured tea agents to resign; without agents, governors yielded, and tea cargoes either landed without paperwork or were sent home.

Governor Hutchinson, however, would not bend any rules. Three ships bearing tea arrived in Boston in November 1773. They cleared customs and unloaded their other cargoes, but not the tea. Sensing the town's extreme tension, the captains wished to return to England, but Hutchinson would not grant them clearance to leave without paying the tea duty. He gave them twenty days to pay, after which time the tea would be confiscated.

For the full twenty days, pressure built in Boston. Daily mass meetings energized citizens from Boston and surrounding towns, alerted by the committees of correspondence. On the final day, December 16, a large crowd gathered at Old South Church to debate a course of action. No solution emerged at that meeting, but immediately following it, 100 to 150 men, disguised as Indians, boarded the ships and dumped thousands of pounds of tea into the harbor while a crowd of two thousand watched. In admiration, John Adams wrote: "This Destruction of the Tea is so bold, so daring, so firm, intrepid and inflexible, and it must have so important Consequences."

The Coercive Acts

In response, Lord North persuaded Parliament to issue the **Coercive (Intolerable) Acts**, four laws meant to punish Massachusetts for destroying the tea. A fifth act—the Quebec Act—had nothing to do with the four Coercive Acts, but it fed American fears by confirming the continuation of French civil law and government form, as well as Catholicism, for Quebec and by giving Quebec control of disputed land (and the lucrative fur trade) throughout the Ohio Valley. In America, these laws were soon known as the Intolerable Acts (**Table 6.1**).

The Intolerable Acts spread alarm in all the colonies. If Britain could squelch Massachusetts—change its charter, suspend local government, inaugurate military

Tea Act of 1773
▶ British act that gave favored status to the British East India Company, allowing it to sell tea directly to government agents rather than through public auction to independent merchants. The goal was to lower the price of the East India tea, including the duty, below that of smuggled Dutch tea, motivating Americans to obey the law. Resistance to the Tea Act led to the passage of the Coercive Acts and imposition of military rule in Massachusetts.

Coercive (Intolerable) Acts
▶ British acts of 1774 meant to punish Massachusetts for the destruction of a large amount of tea. Known in America as the Intolerable Acts, they led to open rebellion in the colonies.

Why did the American colonists find offense with the Sugar and Stamp Acts of 1763–1765?	What were the colonial responses to the Townshend duties?	**What led to the escalation of tensions after 1772?**	What were the varieties of domestic insurrections in 1774–1775?	Conclusion: What changes did Americans want in 1775?

TABLE 6.1 ■ The Coercive (Intolerable) Acts

1. Boston Port Act	Closed Boston harbor to all shipping as of June 1, 1774, until the destroyed tea was paid for. Britain's objective was to halt the commercial life of the city.
2. Massachusetts Government Act	Augmented the royal governor's powers. The governor could appoint the Massachusetts council, which before was elected. He could appoint and remove all judges, sheriffs, and officers of the court. Going forward, town meetings could be held only with the governor's approval.
3. Impartial Administration of Justice Act	Stipulated that any royal official accused of a capital crime would be tried in Britain. The act implied that there would be further violent confrontations between British soldiers and colonists.
4. Quartering Act	Permitted military commanders to lodge soldiers wherever necessary, even in private households, a step toward military rule in Massachusetts.
5. Quebec Act	Not directly related to the Coercive Acts, it gave control of disputed land throughout the Ohio Valley to Quebec.

rule, and on top of that give Ohio to Catholic Quebec—what liberties were secure? Fearful royal governors in half a dozen colonies dismissed the sitting assemblies, adding to the sense of urgency. A few of the assemblies defiantly continued to meet in new locations. Through the committees of correspondence, colonial leaders arranged to convene in Philadelphia in September 1774 to respond to the crisis.

Beyond Boston: Rural Massachusetts

By the time delegates assembled in Philadelphia, all of Massachusetts had arrived at the brink of open insurrection. With Thomas Gage, a British general, occupying the governorship and some three thousand troops controlling Boston, the revolutionary momentum shifted from urban radicals to rural farmers who protested the Massachusetts Government Act in dozens of spontaneous, dramatic showdowns. Some towns found creative ways to get around the prohibition on new town meetings, and others just ignored the law. Gage's call for elections for a new provincial assembly under his control sparked elections for a competing unauthorized assembly. In all counties except one, crowds of armed men converged to prevent the opening of county courts run by crown-appointed jurists. By late August 1774, farmers and artisans all over Massachusetts had effectively taken local control away from the crown.

One incident, the Powder Alarm, nearly provoked violence and showed how close New England farmers were to armed insurrection. Gage sent troops to capture a supply of gunpowder just outside Boston on September 1, and in the surprise and scramble of the attack, false news spread that the troops had fired on men defending the powder, killing six. Within twenty-four hours, several thousand armed men from Massachusetts and Connecticut streamed on foot to Boston seeking revenge. Once the error was corrected and the crisis defused, the men returned home peaceably. But Gage could no longer doubt the strength of rebellious sentiment.

CHAPTER LOCATOR

How did the Seven Years' War lay the groundwork for colonial crisis?

160 CHAPTER 6
THE MAKING OF AN AMERICAN REVOLUTION, 1754–1775

Ordinary Massachusetts citizens began serious planning for the crisis everyone assumed would come. Town militias stockpiled gunpowder "in case of invasion." Judges who had been willing crown appointees reversed their positions or started packing to leave. The new and unauthorized provincial assembly convinced towns to withhold tax money from the royal governor and divert it to military supplies. Gage beefed up fortifications around Boston and sent armed soldiers to stop meetings that quickly dispersed. Bolder action would have to wait until he could acquire a larger army.

The First Continental Congress

Every colony except Georgia sent delegates to Philadelphia in September 1774 to discuss the looming crisis in what was later called the **First Continental Congress**. Delegates sought to articulate their liberties as British subjects and the powers Parliament held over them, and they debated possible responses to the Coercive Acts. Some wanted a total ban on trade with Britain to force repeal, while others, especially southerners dependent on tobacco and rice exports, opposed halting trade. Samuel Adams and Patrick Henry were eager for a ringing denunciation of all parliamentary control. The conservative Joseph Galloway from Pennsylvania proposed a plan (quickly defeated) to create a secondary parliament in America to assist the British Parliament in ruling the colonies.

The congress met for seven weeks and produced a declaration of rights couched in traditional language: "We ask only for peace, liberty and security. We wish no diminution of royal prerogatives, we demand no new rights." But from Britain's point of view, the rights assumed already to exist were radical. Chief among them was the claim that Americans were not represented in Parliament and that therefore each colonial government had the sole right to govern and tax its own people.

To put pressure on Britain, the delegates agreed to a staggered and limited boycott of trade. To enforce the boycott, they called for a Continental Association, with chapters in each town variously called committees of public safety or of inspection, to monitor all commerce and punish suspected violators of the boycott. Its work done in a month, the congress disbanded in October, with agreement to convene the following May.

Britain's severe reaction to Boston's destruction of the tea finally succeeded in making many colonists from New Hampshire to Georgia realize that the problems of British rule went far beyond questions of taxation. The Coercive Acts infringed on liberty and denied self-government; they could not be ignored. With one colony already subordinated to military rule and a British army at the ready in Boston, the threat of a general war was on the doorstep.

First Continental Congress
▶ September 1774 gathering of colonial delegates in Philadelphia to discuss the crisis precipitated by the Coercive Acts. The congress met for seven weeks and produced a declaration of rights and an agreement to impose a limited boycott of trade with Britain.

QUICK REVIEW <

In what ways did colonial responses to British actions change after 1772?

| Why did the American colonists find offense with the Sugar and Stamp Acts of 1763–1765? | What were the colonial responses to the Townshend duties? | What led to the escalation of tensions after 1772? | What were the varieties of domestic insurrections in 1774–1775? | Conclusion: What changes did Americans want in 1775? |

What were the varieties of domestic insurrections in 1774–1775?

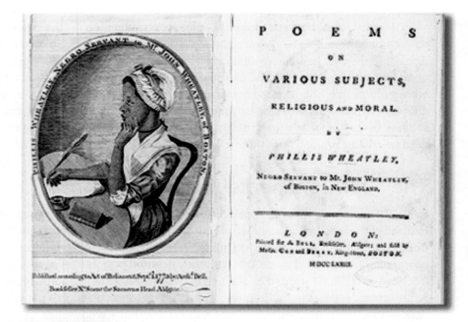

Phillis Wheatley's Title Page

Phillis, born in Africa, was sold into slavery to John Wheatley of Boston at age seven. She published her first poem at age twelve, in 1766. Her master took her to London in 1773, where this book was published, gaining her great literary notice. Library of Congress.

BEFORE THE SECOND CONTINENTAL CONGRESS could meet, violence and bloodshed came to Massachusetts. General Thomas Gage requested more troops from Britain and prepared to subdue rebellion. On the other side, New England farmers prepared to defend their homes against a power they feared was bent on enslaving them. To the south, a different and inverted version of the same story began to unfold, as thousands of enslaved black men and women seized an unprecedented opportunity to mount an insurrection of their own.

Lexington and Concord

During the winter of 1774–75, Americans pressed on with boycotts, hoping to force a repeal of the Coercive Acts, but pessimists stockpiled arms and ammunition. In Massachusetts, militia units known as minutemen prepared to respond at a minute's notice to any threat from the British troops in Boston.

Thomas Gage realized how desperate the British position was. The people, Gage wrote Lord North, were "numerous, worked up to a fury, and not a Boston rabble but the freeholders and farmers of the country." Gage requested twenty thousand reinforcements. He also strongly advised repeal of the Coercive Acts, but leaders in Britain could not admit failure. Instead, in mid-April 1775, they ordered Gage to arrest the troublemakers.

Gage quickly planned a surprise attack on a suspected ammunition storage site at Concord, a village eighteen miles west of Boston (**Map 6.3**). Near midnight

CHAPTER LOCATOR | How did the Seven Years' War lay the groundwork for colonial crisis?

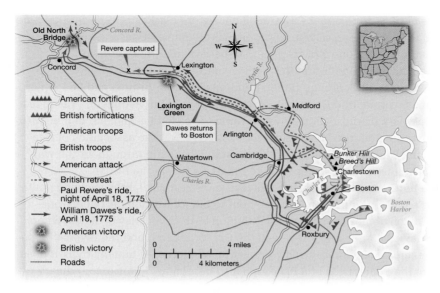

MAP 6.3 ■ Lexington and Concord, April 1775

Under pressure from Britain, some nine hundred British forces at Boston staged a raid on a suspected patriot arms supply in Concord, Massachusetts, starting the first battle of the Revolutionary War. The routes taken by Paul Revere and William Dawes to warn the patriots of the impending raid are marked.

CHRONOLOGY

1773
– Phillis Wheatley's *Poems on Various Subjects, Religious and Moral* is published in London.

1775
– General Gage is ordered to crack down on colonial resistance.

– Battles of Lexington and Concord.
– Lord Dunmore promises freedom to defecting slaves.
– Phillis Wheatley is freed by her master.
– Uprisings by slaves are discovered in New York, Maryland, and North Carolina.

on April 18, 1775, British soldiers moved west across the Charles River. Paul Revere and William Dawes raced ahead to alert the minutemen. When the soldiers got to Lexington, a village five miles east of Concord, they were met by some seventy armed men. The British commander barked out, "Lay down your arms, you damned rebels, and disperse." The militiamen hesitated and began to comply, but then someone—nobody knows who—fired. Within two minutes, eight Americans were dead and ten were wounded.

The British units continued their march to Concord, any pretense of surprise gone. Three companies of minutemen occupied the town center but offered no challenge to the British as they searched in vain for the ammunition. Finally, at Old North Bridge in Concord, troops and minutemen exchanged shots, killing two Americans and three British soldiers. As the British returned to Boston, militia units ambushed them, bringing the bloodiest fighting of the day. In the end, 273 British soldiers were wounded or dead; the toll for the Americans stood at about 95. It was April 19, 1775, and the war had begun.

Rebelling against Slavery

News of the battles of Lexington and Concord spread rapidly. Within eight days, Virginians had heard of the fighting, and, as Thomas Jefferson reflected, "a phrenzy of revenge seems to have seized all ranks of people." The royal governor of Virginia, Lord Dunmore, removed a large quantity of gunpowder from the Williamsburg powder house and put it on a ship, out of reach of the Virginians. Next, he threatened to arm slaves, if necessary, to ward off attacks by colonists.

In November 1775, seeking to frighten Virginia's planters, Dunmore issued an official proclamation promising freedom to defecting able-bodied slaves who would fight for the British. Dunmore had no intention, however, of liberating all

| Why did the American colonists find offense with the Sugar and Stamp Acts of 1763–1765? | What were the colonial responses to the Townshend duties? | What led to the escalation of tensions after 1772? | **What were the varieties of domestic insurrections in 1774–1775?** | Conclusion: What changes did Americans want in 1775? |

the slaves or of starting a real slave rebellion. Astute blacks noticed that Dunmore neglected to free his own slaves. A Virginia barber named Caesar declared that "he did not know any one foolish enough to believe him [Dunmore], for if he intended to do so, he ought first to set his own free."

By December 1775, around fifteen hundred slaves in Virginia had fled to Lord Dunmore, who armed them and called them his "Ethiopian Regiment." Camp diseases quickly set in, however, and when Dunmore sailed for England in mid-1776, he took just three hundred black survivors with him. But the association of freedom with the British authorities had been established, and throughout the war, thousands more southern slaves fled their masters to join the British.

In the northern colonies as well, slaves clearly recognized the evolving political struggle with Britain as an ideal moment to bid for freedom. A twenty-one-year-old Boston domestic slave called attention to the hypocrisy of slave owners in a 1774 newspaper essay: "How well the Cry for Liberty, and the reverse Disposition for exercise of oppressive Power over others agree,—I humbly think it does not require the Penetration of a Philosopher to Determine." This extraordinary young woman, **Phillis Wheatley**, had already gained international recognition through a book of poems published in London in 1773. Wheatley's poems spoke of "Fair Freedom" as the "Goddess long desir'd" by Africans enslaved in America. At the urging of his wife, Wheatley's master freed the young poet in 1775.

Wheatley's poetic ideas about freedom found concrete expression among other discontented groups. Some slaves in Boston petitioned Thomas Gage, promising to fight for the British if he would liberate them. Gage turned them down. In Ulster County, New York, along the Hudson River, a plot for an armed uprising that involved at least twenty slaves in four villages was discovered.

In Maryland, soon after the news of the Lexington battle arrived, blacks exhibited impatience with their status as slaves, causing one Maryland planter to report that "the insolence of the Negroes in this county is come to such a height, that we are under a necessity of disarming them. . . . We took about eighty guns, some bayonets, swords, etc." In North Carolina, a planned uprising was uncovered, and scores of slaves were arrested.

By 1783, when the Revolutionary War ended, as many as twenty thousand blacks had sought refuge with the British army. Most failed to achieve the liberation they were seeking. The British generally used them for menial labor, and disease, especially smallpox, devastated encampments of runaways. But some eight thousand to ten thousand persisted through the war and later, under the protection of the British army, left America to start new lives of freedom in Canada's Nova Scotia or Africa's Sierra Leone.

Phillis Wheatley

▶ A domestic slave in Boston who was also a published poet. Her writing drew attention to the hypocrisy of Americans' simultaneous embrace of slavery and the ideals of freedom in the years leading up to the American Revolution.

> **QUICK REVIEW**

What was the connection between rebelling against the British and rebelling against slavery?

CHAPTER LOCATOR | How did the Seven Years' War lay the groundwork for colonial crisis?

CHAPTER 6
164 THE MAKING OF AN AMERICAN REVOLUTION, 1754–1775

Picture Research Consultants & Archives.

THE SEVEN YEARS' WAR set the stage for the imperial crisis of the 1760s and 1770s by creating distrust between Britain and its colonies and by running up a huge deficit in the British treasury. The years 1763 to 1775 brought repeated attempts by the British government to subordinate the colonies into taxpaying partners in the larger scheme of empire.

American resistance grew slowly but steadily over those years. By 1775, events propelled many Americans to the conclusion that a concerted effort was afoot to deprive them of all their liberties, the most important of which were the right to self-taxation, the right to live free of an occupying army, and the right to self-rule. Hundreds of minutemen converged on Concord, prepared to die for those liberties. April 19 marked the start of their rebellion.

Another rebellion under way in 1775 was doomed to be short-circuited. Black Americans who had experienced actual slavery listened to shouts of "Liberty!" from white crowds and applied the language of revolution to their own circumstances. Defiance of authority was indeed contagious.

The emerging leaders of the patriot cause were mindful of a delicate balance they felt they had to strike. To energize the American public about the crisis with Britain, they had to politicize masses of men—and eventually women, too—and infuse them with a keen sense of their rights and liberties. But in doing so, they became fearful of the unintended consequences of teaching a vocabulary of rights and liberties.

Patriot leaders in 1765 wanted a correction, a restoration of an ancient liberty of self-taxation that Parliament seemed to be ignoring. But events from 1765 to 1775 convinced many that a return to the old ways was impossible. Challenging Parliament's right to tax had led, step-by-step, to challenging Parliament's right to legislate over the colonies in any matter. If Parliament's sovereignty was set aside, who actually had authority over the American colonies? By 1775, with the outbreak of fighting and the specter of slave rebellions, American leaders turned to the king for the answer to that question.

SO NOW YOU KNOW

Colonial women and men showed their opposition to British policies through a variety of collective actions, including boycotts and public demonstrations. By 1775, Britain's relationship with its American colonies reached a crisis point as armed conflict broke out in Lexington and Concord and American patriots began to consider independence as their best option.

CHAPTER 6 STUDY GUIDE

Online Study Guide
bedfordstmartins.com/roarkunderstanding

STEP 1
GETTING STARTED

Below are basic terms from this period in American history. Can you identify each term below and explain why it matters? To do this exercise online or to download this chart, visit bedfordstmartins.com/roarkunderstanding.

TERM	WHO OR WHAT & WHEN	WHY IT MATTERS
Seven Years' War, p. 142		
Proclamation of 1763, p. 148		
Sugar (Revenue) Act, p. 150		
Stamp Act, p. 150		
virtual representation, p. 150		
Townshend duties, p. 154		
Boston Massacre, p. 157		
committees of correspondence, p. 158		
Tea Act of 1773, p. 159		
Coercive (Intolerable) Acts, p. 159		
First Continental Congress, p. 161		
Phillis Wheatley, p. 162		

STEP 2
MOVING BEYOND THE BASICS

The exercise below represents a more advanced understanding of the chapter material. Examine the escalation of tensions between Britain and its North American colonies. Fill in the following chart by describing the key pieces of British legislation aimed at the colonies between 1763 and 1774, the British rationale for each act, and the colonial response. To do this exercise online or to download the chart, visit bedfordstmartins.com/roarkunderstanding.

Legislation	Provisions	British rationale	Colonial response
Proclamation of 1763			
Sugar (Revenue) Act			
Stamp Act			
Townshend duties			
Tea Act of 1773			
Coercive (Intolerable) Acts			

Now that you've reviewed various parts of the chapter, take a step back and try to see the big picture by answering these questions. Remember to use specific examples from the chapter in your answers. To do this exercise online, visit bedfordstmartins.com/roarkunderstanding.

THE SEVEN YEARS' WAR

▶ How did the outcome of the Seven Years' War change the European balance of power in North America?

▶ How did British and colonial views of the war and its consequences differ?

TAXING THE COLONIES

▶ Why did some colonists see British efforts to tax the colonies as illegitimate? How did the British justify their efforts to raise revenue?

▶ What different groups, both in the colonies and in Great Britain, encouraged Parliament to repeal various taxes? What were their motives?

THE ESCALATION OF THE CONFLICT

▶ Why was the Tea Act so provocative? How did some colonists protest its passage?

▶ How did the British response to these protests, and the colonial reaction, help put Britain and the colonies on the path toward war?

LOOKING BACKWARD, LOOKING AHEAD

▶ How did the relationship between Britain and its North American colonies before 1763 differ from the relationship after 1763?

▶ Was war between Britain and the colonies inevitable after 1774? Why or why not?

IN YOUR OWN WORDS

Imagine that you must explain chapter 6 to someone who hasn't read it. What would be the most important points to include and why?

7
FIGHTING THE AMERICAN REVOLUTION

1775–1783

> This chapter follows the course of the American Revolution from the Declaration of Independence in 1776 to the signing of the Treaty of Paris in 1783. It examines the events that led up to the Declaration of Independence, the early military strategies of both sides, the experience of war on the home front, the role of Indians and the French in the war, and the events that culminated in a seemingly improbable British defeat.

> Why did the Americans declare their independence?

> What initial challenges did the opposing armies face?

> What role did the home front play in the war?

> How were Native Americans and the French involved in the American Revolution?

> Why did the British southern strategy ultimately fail?

> Conclusion: Why did the British lose the American Revolution?

DID YOU KNOW?

In 1776, about three-fifths of the American colonists either supported the British or were undecided about independence.

A crowd pulls down the statue of King George III in New York City, July 9, 1776, following a formal reading of the Declaration of Independence.

Why did the Americans declare their independence?

Declaration of Independence Read to a Crowd

Printed copies of the Declaration of Independence were read aloud in public places throughout America in the week after July 4, 1776. Library of Congress.

ON MAY 10, 1775, nearly one month after the fighting at Lexington and Concord, the Second Continental Congress assembled in Philadelphia. The delegates at the congress immediately set to work on two crucial but contradictory tasks: to raise and supply an army and to explore reconciliation with Britain. To do the former, they needed soldiers and a commander, they needed money, and they needed to work out a declaration of war. To do the latter, however, they needed diplomacy to approach the king. But the king was not receptive, and by 1776, as the war progressed and hopes of reconciliation faded, delegates at the congress began to ponder the treasonous act of declaring independence.

Second Continental Congress

▶ Legislative body that governed the United States during the first several years of the Revolutionary War. The Second Continental Congress met for the first time in May 1775 and began preparing for war while pursuing the possibility of reconciliation with Britain. On July 4, 1776, with all hope of peaceful reconciliation with Britain gone, the congress declared independence.

Assuming Political and Military Authority

The delegates to the **Second Continental Congress** had to learn to know and trust one another. Moreover, they did not always agree. The Adams cousins John and Samuel defined the radical end of the spectrum, favoring independence. John Dickinson of Pennsylvania, no longer the eager revolutionary who wrote *Letters from a Farmer* in 1767 (see chapter 6), was now a moderate, seeking reconciliation with Britain. Benjamin Franklin was feared by some to be a British spy. Mutual suspicions flourished easily when the undertaking was so dangerous, opinions were so varied, and a misstep could spell disaster.

Most of the delegates were not yet prepared to break with Britain. Some felt that government without a king was unworkable, while others feared it might be

CHAPTER LOCATOR

> Why did the Americans declare their independence?

Abigail Adams

Abigail Smith Adams was twenty-two when she sat for this pastel portrait in 1766. Pearls and a lace collar anchor her femininity, while her facial expression projects a confidence and maturity not often credited to young women of the 1760s. A decade later, she was running the family's Massachusetts farm while her husband, John, attended the Continental Congress in Philadelphia. Her frequent letters gave him the benefit of her sage advice on politics and the war. Courtesy of the Massachusetts Historical Society.

suicidal to lose Britain's protection against its traditional enemies, France and Spain. Colonies that traded actively with Britain feared undermining their economies. Probably the vast majority of ordinary Americans were unable to envision complete independence from the monarchy.

The few men at the Continental Congress who did think that independence was desirable were, not surprisingly, from Massachusetts, the target of the Coercive Acts. Even so, those men knew that it was premature to push for a break with Britain. John Adams wrote his wife, Abigail, in June 1775: "America is a great, unwieldy body. Its progress must be slow. It is like a large fleet sailing under convoy. The fleetest sailors must wait for the dullest and slowest."

Yet swift action was needed, for the Massachusetts countryside was under threat of further attack. Even the hesitant moderates in the congress agreed that a military buildup was necessary. Around the country, militia units from New York to Georgia collected arms and drilled on village greens in anticipation. On June 14, the congress voted to create the Continental army, choosing a Virginian, **George Washington**, as commander in chief. Washington's appointment sent the clear message that there was widespread commitment to war beyond New England.

Next the congress drew up a document titled "A Declaration on the Causes and Necessity of Taking Up Arms," which rehearsed familiar arguments about the tyranny of Parliament and the need to defend English liberties. This declaration was first drafted by a young Virginia planter, Thomas Jefferson, a radical on the question of independence. The moderate John Dickinson, fearing that the declaration would offend Britain, was allowed to rewrite it. However, he left intact much of Jefferson's highly charged language about choosing "to die freemen rather than to live slaves."

To pay for the military buildup, the congress authorized a currency issue of $2 million. The Continental dollars were merely paper; they were not backed by gold or silver. The delegates somewhat naively expected that the currency would be accepted as valuable on trust as it spread in the population through the hands of soldiers, farmers, munitions suppliers, and beyond.

In just two months, the Second Continental Congress had created an army, declared war, and issued its own currency. It had taken on the major functions of a

George Washington

▶ Commander in chief of the Continental army. Washington had gained considerable military experience during the French and Indian War. Congress's selection of Washington, a Virginian, as commander in chief in 1775 also sent a clear signal that there was widespread commitment to war beyond New England.

| What initial challenges did the opposing armies face? | What role did the home front play in the war? | How were Native Americans and the French involved in the American Revolution? | Why did the British southern strategy ultimately fail? | Conclusion: Why did the British lose the American Revolution? |

legitimate government, both military and financial, without any legal basis for its authority. It had not yet, however, declared independence from the authority of the king.

Pursuing Both War and Peace

Three days after the congress established the army, one of the bloodiest battles of the Revolution occurred. The British commander in Boston, Thomas Gage, had recently received troop reinforcements, three talented generals (William Howe, John Burgoyne, and Henry Clinton), and new instructions to attack the Massachusetts rebels. But before Gage could take the offensive, the Americans fortified the hilly terrain of Charlestown, a peninsula just north of Boston, on the night of June 16, 1775.

General Howe insisted on a bold frontal assault, sending 2,500 soldiers across the water and up the hill in an intimidating but potentially costly attack. Three bloody assaults were needed before the British took the hill, the third succeeding mainly because the American ammunition supply gave out, and the defenders quickly retreated. The battle of Bunker Hill was thus a British victory, but an expensive one. On the British side, the dead numbered 226, with more than 800 wounded; the Americans suffered 140 dead, 271 wounded, and 30 captured.

Instead of pursuing the fleeing Americans, Howe retreated to Boston, unwilling to risk more raids into the countryside. If the British had had any grasp of the basic instability of the American units around Boston, they might have decisively defeated the Continental army in its infancy. Instead, they lingered in Boston, abandoning it without a fight nine months later.

A week after Bunker Hill, when General Washington arrived to take charge of the new Continental army, he found enthusiastic but undisciplined troops. Sanitation was an unknown concept, with inadequate latrines fouling the campground. Washington attributed the disarray to the New England custom of letting militia units elect their own officers, which he felt undermined deference. Washington quickly imposed more hierarchy and authority. "Discipline is the soul of the army," he stated.

While military plans moved forward, the Second Continental Congress pursued its contradictory objective: reconciliation with Britain. Delegates from the middle colonies (Pennsylvania, Delaware, and New York), whose merchants depended on trade with Britain, urged that channels for negotiation remain open. In July 1775, congressional moderates led by John Dickinson engineered an appeal to the king called the Olive Branch Petition. The petition affirmed loyalty to the monarchy and blamed all the troubles on the king's ministers and on Parliament. It proposed that the American colonial assemblies be recognized as individual parliaments under the umbrella of the monarchy. King George III rejected the Olive Branch Petition and heatedly condemned the Americans as traitors.

Thomas Paine, Abigail Adams, and the Case for Independence

Pressure for independence started to mount in January 1776, when a pamphlet titled *Common Sense* appeared in Philadelphia. Thomas Paine, its author, was an English artisan and coffeehouse intellectual who had come to America in the fall of

Battle of Bunker Hill, 1775

Common Sense

▶ Pamphlet written by Thomas Paine in 1776 that laid out the case for independence. In it, Paine rejected monarchy, advocating its replacement with republican government based on the consent of the people. The pamphlet sold more than 150,000 copies in a matter of weeks and influenced public opinion throughout the colonies.

CHAPTER LOCATOR | Why did the Americans declare their independence?

1774. With the encouragement of members of the Second Continental Congress, he wrote *Common Sense*.

In simple yet forceful language, Paine elaborated on the absurdities of the British monarchy. Why should one man, by accident of birth, claim extensive power over others? he asked. A king might be foolish or wicked. "One of the strongest natural proofs of the folly of hereditary right in kings," Paine wrote, "is that nature disapproves it; otherwise she would not so frequently turn it into ridicule by giving mankind *an ass for a lion.*" To replace monarchy, Paine advocated republican government based on the consent of the people. Rulers, according to Paine, were only representatives of the people, and the best form of government relied on frequent elections to achieve the most direct democracy possible.

Thomas Paine, a recent immigrant to America, wrote *Common Sense* to advance the debate on independence. Although the pamphlet sold more than 150,000 copies, he made no profit on it personally but instead donated proceeds to the Revolutionary cause. Shown here is George Washington's personal copy, with his name inscribed at the top. Boston Athenaeum.

Paine's pamphlet sold more than 150,000 copies in a matter of weeks. Newspapers reprinted it; men read it aloud in taverns and coffeehouses; John Adams sent a copy to his wife, Abigail, who passed it around to neighbors in Braintree, Massachusetts. New Englanders desired independence, but other colonies, under no immediate threat of violence, remained cautious.

Abigail Adams was impatient not only for independence but also for other legal changes that would revolutionize the new country. In a series of astute letters to her husband, she outlined obstacles and gave advice. She worried that southern slave owners might shrink from a war in the name of liberty: "I have sometimes been ready to think that the passion for Liberty cannot be Equally strong in the Breasts of those who have been accustomed to deprive their fellow Creatures of theirs." And in March 1776, she expressed her hope that women's legal status would improve under the new government: "In the new Code of Laws which I suppose it will be necessary for you to make I desire you would Remember the Ladies, and be more generous and favourable to them than your ancestors."

John Adams dismissed his wife's concerns. But to a male politician, Adams privately rehearsed the reasons why women (and free black men, propertyless men, and young people) should remain excluded from political participation. Even though he concluded that nothing should change, at least Abigail's letter had forced him to ponder the exclusion, something few men—or women—did in 1776.

Abigail Adams

► Wife of John Adams, Massachusetts delegate to the Second Continental Congress, and advocate for the improvement of women's legal status. In a series of astute letters to her husband, she outlined obstacles to independence and gave advice. She particularly urged John Adams to help end husbands' legal dominion over wives.

The Declaration of Independence

In addition to Paine's *Common Sense*, another factor hastening independence was the prospect of an alliance with France, Britain's archrival. France was willing to provide military supplies and naval power only if assured that the Americans would separate from Britain. By May, all but four colonies were agitating for a declaration.

| What initial challenges did the opposing armies face? | What role did the home front play in the war? | How were Native Americans and the French involved in the American Revolution? | Why did the British southern strategy ultimately fail? | Conclusion: Why did the British lose the American Revolution? |

The holdouts were Pennsylvania, Maryland, New York, and South Carolina, the latter two containing large loyalist populations. An exasperated Virginian wrote to his friend in the congress, "For God's sake, why do you dawdle in the Congress so strangely? Why do you not at once declare yourself a separate independent state?"

In early June, the Virginia delegation introduced a resolution calling for independence. The moderates still commanded enough support to postpone a vote on the measure until July. In the meantime, the congress appointed a committee, with Thomas Jefferson and others, to draft a longer document setting out the case for independence.

On July 2, after intense politicking, all but one state voted for independence; New York abstained. The congress then turned to the document drafted by Jefferson and his committee. Jefferson began with a preamble that articulated philosophical principles about natural rights, equality, the right of revolution, and the consent of the governed as the only true basis for government. He then listed more than two dozen specific grievances against King George. The congress passed over the preamble with little comment, as though startling ideas about natural rights, the equality of all men, and the consent of the governed were indeed "self-evident truths."

For two days, the congress wrangled over the list of grievances, especially the issue of slavery. Jefferson had included an impassioned statement blaming the king for slavery, which delegates from Georgia and South Carolina struck out. They had no intention of denouncing their labor system as an evil practice. But the congress let stand another of Jefferson's grievances, blaming the king for mobilizing "the merciless Indian Savages" into bloody frontier warfare, a reference to Pontiac's uprising (see chapter 6).

On July 4, the amendments to Jefferson's text were complete, and the congress formally adopted the **Declaration of Independence**. A month later, the delegates gathered to sign the official parchment copy. Four men, including John Dickinson, declined to sign; several others "signed with regret . . . and with many doubts," according to John Adams. The document was then printed, widely distributed, and read aloud in celebrations everywhere. (Printed copies did not include the signers' names, for they had committed treason, a crime punishable by death.) On July 15, the New York delegation switched from abstention to endorsement, making the vote on independence unanimous.

Declaration of Independence

▶ The formal declaration of separation from Britain adopted by the Second Continental Congress on July 4, 1776. A period of intense debate preceded the call for independence, as many moderates still hoped to reconcile with Britain. The document included a statement of philosophical principles and a list of grievances.

> **QUICK REVIEW**

Why were many Americans initially reluctant to pursue independence from Britain? What changed their minds?

Backcountry Riflemen

A German officer with the British army drew this sketch of two American riflemen, dressed in rustic hunting shirts and leggings. One wears moccasins; the other is barefoot. Their celebrated ability to hit small targets at great distances and their willingness to snipe from behind trees and aim particularly at officers made them a terror to the British. Ten companies of riflemen were recruited in 1775 from western Pennsylvania and Virginia. General Washington worried that they were too undisciplined to make good soldiers, but others suggested that the trademark hunting shirt should become the Continental army uniform for all soldiers, just for the fear it provoked in the enemy. Anne S. K. Brown Military Collection, Brown University Library.

What initial challenges did the opposing armies face?

BOTH SIDES APPROACHED the war for America with uneasiness. The Americans, with inexperienced militias, were opposing the mightiest military power in the world. Also, their country was not unified; many people remained loyal to Britain. The British faced serious obstacles as well. Their disdain for the fighting abilities of the Americans required reassessment in light of the Bunker Hill battle. The logistics of supplying an army with food across three thousand miles of water were daunting. And since the British goal was to regain allegiance, not to destroy and conquer, the army was often constrained in its actions.

The American Military Forces

Americans claimed that the initial months of war were purely defensive, triggered by the British invasion. But the war also quickly became a rebellion, an overthrowing of long-established authority. As both defenders and rebels, many Americans were highly motivated to fight, and the potential manpower that could be mobilized was, in theory, very great.

What initial challenges did the opposing armies face?	What role did the home front play in the war?	How were Native Americans and the French involved in the American Revolution?	Why did the British southern strategy ultimately fail?	Conclusion: Why did the British lose the American Revolution?

CHRONOLOGY

1775
- Americans lose battle of Quebec.

1776
- British take Manhattan.
- **December 25.** Washington captures German troops stationed along the Delaware River.

Continental army

▶ The army created in June 1775 by the Second Continental Congress to oppose the British. George Washington was selected as its commander in chief and given the task of turning a collection of local militias and untrained volunteers into a disciplined army. British reluctance to follow up early victories allowed the Continental army to develop into an effective fighting force.

Local defense in the colonies had long rested with a militia composed of all able-bodied men over age sixteen. Militias, however, were best suited for limited engagements, such as conflicts with Indians, not for extended wars. In forming the **Continental army**, the congress set enlistment at one year, but leaders soon learned that was inadequate to train and deploy soldiers. A three-year enlistment earned a new soldier a $20 bonus, while men who committed for the duration were promised a postwar land grant of one hundred acres. Over the course of the war, some 230,000 men enlisted, about one-quarter of the white male adult population.

Women also served in the Continental army, cooking, washing, and nursing the wounded. Close to 20,000 "camp followers," as they were called, served during the war. Children also tagged along, and babies were born in the camps.

Black Americans were at first excluded from the Continental army. But as manpower needs increased, northern states welcomed free blacks into service; slaves in some states could serve with their masters' permission. About 5,000 black men served in the Revolutionary War on the rebel side, nearly all from the northern states. Black soldiers sometimes were segregated into separate units, and, while some of these men were draftees, others were clearly inspired by ideals of freedom in a war against tyranny. For example, twenty-three blacks gave "Liberty," "Freedom," and "Freeman" as their surnames at the time of enlistment.

Military service helped politicize Americans during the early stages of the war. But as the war heated up and recruiters demanded commitment, some Americans discovered that apathy had its dangers as well. Anyone who refused to serve ran the risk of being called a traitor to the cause. Military service became a prime way of demonstrating political allegiance.

The American army was at times raw and inexperienced, and often woefully undermanned. It never had the precision and discipline of European professional armies. But it was never as bad as the British continually assumed.

The British Strategy

The American strategy was straightforward—to repulse and defeat an invading army. The British strategy was not as clear. Britain wanted to put down a rebellion and restore monarchical power in the colonies, but the question was how to accomplish this. A decisive defeat of the Continental army was essential but not sufficient to end the rebellion, for the British would still have to contend with an armed and motivated insurgent population. Furthermore, there was no single political nerve center whose capture would spell certain victory. The Continental Congress moved from place to place, staying just out of reach of the British. During the course of the war, the British captured and occupied every major port city, but that brought no serious loss to the Americans, 95 percent of whom lived in the countryside.

Britain's task was to restore the old governments, not to destroy an enemy country. British generals were reluctant to ravage the countryside, confiscate food, or burn villages. With thirteen distinct political entities to capture, pacify, and restore to the crown, stretching from New Hampshire to Georgia, Britain needed a large land army to do the job. Without the willingness to seize food from the locals, the British needed hundreds of supply ships—hence their desire to

CHAPTER LOCATOR | Why did the Americans declare their independence?

capture the ports. The British strategy also assumed that many Americans remained loyal to the king and would come to their aid.

The overall British plan was a divide-and-conquer approach, focusing first on New York, the state judged to have the greatest number of loyal subjects. New York offered a geographic advantage as well: Control of the Hudson River would allow the British to isolate New England. British armies could descend from Canada and move up from New York City along the Hudson River into western Massachusetts. If Massachusetts could be driven to surrender, New Jersey and Pennsylvania would fall in line, the British thought, because of loyalist strength. Virginia was a problem, like Massachusetts, but the British were confident that the Carolinas would help them isolate and subdue Virginia.

Quebec, New York, and New Jersey

In late 1775, an American expedition was launched to capture the cities of Montreal and Quebec before British reinforcements could arrive (**Map 7.1**). This offensive was a clear sign that the war was not purely a reaction to the invasion of Massachusetts. A force of New York Continentals commanded by General

A View of the Attack on Fort Washington

An eyewitness sketched this scene of Hessian troops attacking Fort Washington in mid-November 1775. The fort, manned by 3,000 American soldiers, sat on well-secured high ground between the Harlem and Hudson rivers. General Washington watched the attack in despair from Fort Lee, on the New Jersey side of the Hudson. The Phelps Stokes Collection, Miriam and Ira D. Wallach Division of Arts, Prints, and Photographs, The New York Public Library. Astor, Lenox, and Tilden Foundations.

| What initial challenges did the opposing armies face? | What role did the home front play in the war? | How were Native Americans and the French involved in the American Revolution? | Why did the British southern strategy ultimately fail? | Conclusion: Why did the British lose the American Revolution? |

MAP 7.1 ■ **The War in the North, 1775–1778** After the early battles in Massachusetts in 1775, rebel forces invaded Canada but failed to capture Quebec. A large British army landed in New York in August 1776, turning New Jersey into a continual battle site in 1777 and 1778. Burgoyne arrived from England to secure Canada and attempted to pinch off New England along the Hudson River, but he was stopped at Saratoga in 1777 in the key battle of the early war.

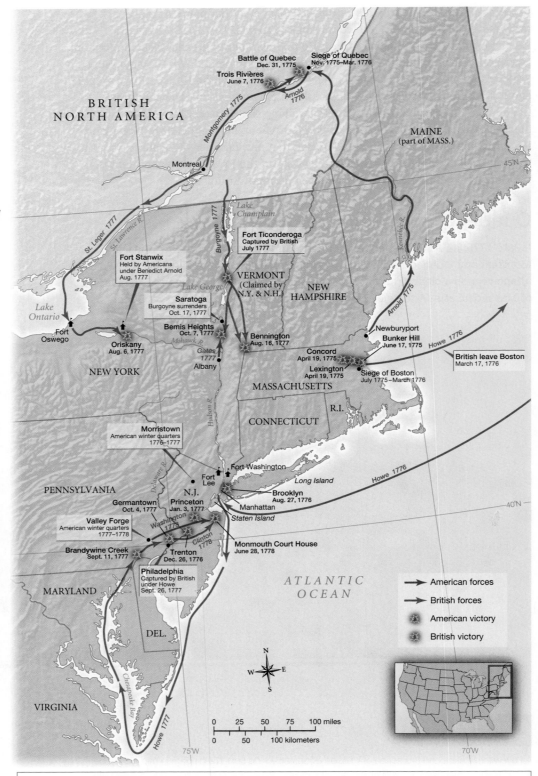

BRITISH NORTH AMERICA

Siege of Quebec
Nov. 1775–Mar. 1776

Battle of Quebec
Dec. 31, 1775

Trois Rivières
June 7, 1776

Arnold 1776

Montgomery 1775

MAINE
(part of MASS.)

Montreal

St. Leger 1777

St. Lawrence R.

Lake Champlain

Burgoyne 1777

Fort Ticonderoga
Captured by British
July 1777

Fort Stanwix
Held by Americans
under Benedict Arnold
Aug. 1777

VERMONT
(Claimed by
N.Y. & N.H.)

NEW HAMPSHIRE

Kennebec R.

Arnold 1775

Lake George

Saratoga
Burgoyne surrenders
Oct. 17, 1777

Lake Ontario

Fort Oswego

Oriskany
Aug. 6, 1777

Bemis Heights
Oct. 7, 1777

Mohawk R.

Gates 1777

Albany

NEW YORK

Bennington
Aug. 16, 1777

Newburyport

Bunker Hill
June 17, 1775

Concord
April 19, 1775

Lexington
April 19, 1775

Siege of Boston
July 1775–March 1776

Howe 1776

British leave Boston
March 17, 1776

MASSACHUSETTS

CONNECTICUT

R.I.

Hudson R.

Morristown
American winter quarters
1776–1777

Fort Washington

Fort Lee

Delaware R.

PENNSYLVANIA

Germantown
Oct. 4, 1777

N.J.

Princeton
Jan. 3, 1777

Washington 1776

Manhattan

Staten Island

Brooklyn
Aug. 27, 1776

Long Island

Howe 1776

Valley Forge
American winter quarters
1777–1778

Clinton 1778

Brandywine Creek
Sept. 11, 1777

Trenton
Dec. 26, 1776

Monmouth Court House
June 28, 1778

Philadelphia
Captured by British
under Howe
Sept. 26, 1777

MARYLAND

DEL.

ATLANTIC OCEAN

Chesapeake Bay

VIRGINIA

Howe 1777

American forces
British forces
American victory
British victory

N W E S

0   25   50   75   100 miles
0   50   100 kilometers

75°W   70°W
45°N
40°N

► FOR MORE HELP ANALYZING THIS MAP, see the map activity for this chapter in the Online Study Guide at bedfordstmartins.com/roarkunderstanding.

CHAPTER LOCATOR

Why did the Americans declare their independence?

Richard Montgomery took Montreal easily in September 1775 and then advanced on Quebec. Meanwhile, a second contingent of Continentals led by Colonel Benedict Arnold moved north through Maine to Quebec. Arnold and Montgomery jointly attacked Quebec in December but failed to take the city. Worse yet, they encountered smallpox, which killed more men than had battles.

The main action of the first year of the war came not in Canada, however, but in New York. In August 1776, some 45,000 British troops (including 8,000 German mercenaries, called Hessians) under the command of General Howe landed south of New York City. General Washington had anticipated this move and had relocated his army of 20,000 south from Massachusetts. The battle of Long Island, in late August 1776, pitted the well-trained British "redcoats" (slang referring to their red uniforms) against a very green Continental army. Howe attacked, inflicting many casualties. Howe failed to press forward, however, perhaps remembering the costly victory of Bunker Hill, and Washington evacuated his troops to Manhattan Island.

Washington knew it would be hard to hold Manhattan, so he withdrew farther north to two forts on either side of the Hudson River. For two months, the armies engaged in limited skirmishing, but in November, Howe finally captured Fort Washington and Fort Lee, taking nearly 3,000 prisoners. Washington retreated quickly across New Jersey into Pennsylvania. Again Howe unaccountably failed to press his advantage. Instead, he parked his German troops in winter quarters along the Delaware River. Perhaps he knew that many of the Continental soldiers' enlistment periods ended on December 31, making him confident the Americans would not attack him. He was wrong.

On December 25, Washington stealthily moved his army across the Delaware River and at dawn made a quick capture of the unsuspecting German soldiers. This impressive victory lifted the sagging morale of the patriot side. For the next two weeks, Washington remained on the offensive, capturing supplies in a clever attack on British units at Princeton. Soon he was safe in Morristown, in northern New Jersey, where he settled his army for the winter.

All in all, in the first year of declared war, the rebellious Americans had a few proud moments but also many worries. The inexperienced Continental army had barely hung on in the New York campaign. Washington had shown exceptional daring and admirable restraint, but what really saved the Americans was the repeated reluctance of the British to follow through militarily when they had the advantage.

QUICK REVIEW

Why did the British initially exercise restraint in their efforts to defeat the rebellious colonies?

| What initial challenges did the opposing armies face? | What role did the home front play in the war? | How were Native Americans and the French involved in the American Revolution? | Why did the British southern strategy ultimately fail? | Conclusion: Why did the British lose the American Revolution? |

> What role did the home front play in the war?

BATTLEFIELDS ALONE did not determine the outcome of the war. Struggles on the home front were equally important. In 1776, each community contained small numbers of highly committed people on both sides and far larger numbers who were uncertain about whether independence was worth a war. Both persuasion and force were used to gain the allegiance of the many neutrals. The struggle to secure political allegiance was complicated greatly by a shaky wartime economy. The creative financing of the fledgling government brought hardships as well as opportunities, forcing Americans to confront new manifestations of virtue and corruption.

Patriotism at the Local Level

Committees of correspondence, of public safety, and of inspection dominated the political landscape in patriot communities. These committees took on more than customary local governance; they enforced boycotts, picked army draftees, and policed suspected traitors. They sometimes invaded homes to search for contraband goods such as British tea or textiles.

Loyalists were dismayed by the increasing show of power by patriots. A man in Westchester, New York, described his response to intrusions by committees: "Choose your committee or suffer it to be chosen by a half dozen fools in your neighborhood—open your doors to them—let them examine your tea-cannisters and molasses-jugs, and your wives' and daughters' petty coats—bow and cringe and tremble and quake—fall down and worship our sovereign lord the mob. . . . Should any pragmatical committee-gentleman come to my house and give himself airs, I shall show him the door." Oppressive or not, the local committees were rarely challenged. Their persuasive powers convinced many middle-of-the-road citizens that neutrality was not a comfortable option.

Another group new to political life—white women—increasingly demonstrated a capacity for patriotism as wartime hardships dramatically altered their work routines. Many wives whose husbands were away on military or political service took on masculine duties. Their competence to tend farms and make business decisions encouraged some to assert competence in politics as well. Eliza Wilkinson managed a South Carolina plantation and talked revolutionary politics with women friends. "None were greater politicians than the several knots of ladies who met together," she remarked, alert to the unusual turn female conversations had taken. "We commenced perfect statesmen." Women from prominent Philadelphia families took more direct action, forming the Ladies Association in 1780 to collect money for Continental soldiers. A published broadside, "The Sentiments of an American Woman," defended their female patriotism: "The time is arrived to display the same sentiments which animated us at the beginning of the Revolution, when we renounced the use of teas [and] when our republican and laborious hands spun the flax."

The Loyalists

Around one-fifth of the American population remained loyal to the crown in 1776, and another two-fifths tried to stay neutral. In general, **loyalists** had strong cultural and economic ties to England; they thought that social stability depended on a government anchored by monarchy and aristocracy. Perhaps most of all, they feared democratic tyranny. They understood that dissolving the automatic respect that subjects had for their king could lead to a society in which deference to one's social betters might come under challenge. Patriots seemed to them to be unscrupulous, violent, self-interested men who simply wanted power for themselves.

Pockets of loyalism existed everywhere—in New England, in the middle colonies, in the backcountry of the southern colonies, and out beyond the Appalachian Mountains in Indian country (**Map 7.2**). The most visible loyalists (called Tories by their enemies) were royal officials. Wealthy merchants gravitated toward loyalism to maintain the trade protections of navigation acts and the British navy. Conservative urban lawyers admired the stability of British law and order. Some colonists chose loyalism simply to oppose traditional adversaries. Backcountry Carolina farmers leaned toward loyalism out of resentment of the power of the pro-revolution gentry. And, of course, southern slaves had their own resentments and looked to Britain in hope of freedom.

Many Indian tribes hoped to remain neutral at the war's start, seeing the conflict as a civil war between the English and Americans. Eventually, however, most were drawn in, many taking the British side. The powerful Iroquois Confederacy divided: The Mohawk, Cayuga, Seneca, and Onondaga peoples lined up with the British; the Oneida and Tuscarora tribes aided Americans. One young Mohawk leader, **Thayendanegea** (known also by his English name, **Joseph Brant**), traveled to England in 1775 to complain to King George about cheating American settlers. "It is very hard when we have let the King's subjects have so much of our lands for so little value," he wrote, "they should want to

CHRONOLOGY

1775
- **June.** The Second Continental Congress declares all loyalists traitors.
- Mohawk leader Joseph Brant travels to England to pledge support for the British side.

1776
- New York City loyalists circulate a "Declaration of Dependence" in rebuttal to the declaration of the Second Continental Congress.

1778
- Colonial committees of public safety fix prices on essential goods.

loyalists
▶ Colonists who remained loyal to Britain during the Revolutionary War. Around one-fifth of the American population remained loyal to the crown in 1776. Colonists remained loyal to Britain for many reasons, and loyalists could be found in every region of the country.

Joseph Brant (Thayendanegea)
▶ Mohawk leader who fought for the British during the Revolutionary War. Brant pledged Indian support for the king in exchange for protection from encroaching settlers. Brant led the Senecas and Mohawks to victory over German settlers living in the Mohawk Valley and Oneida Indians in the battle of Oriskany.

| What initial challenges did the opposing armies face? | **What role did the home front play in the war?** | How were Native Americans and the French involved in the American Revolution? | Why did the British southern strategy ultimately fail? | Conclusion: Why did the British lose the American Revolution? |

181

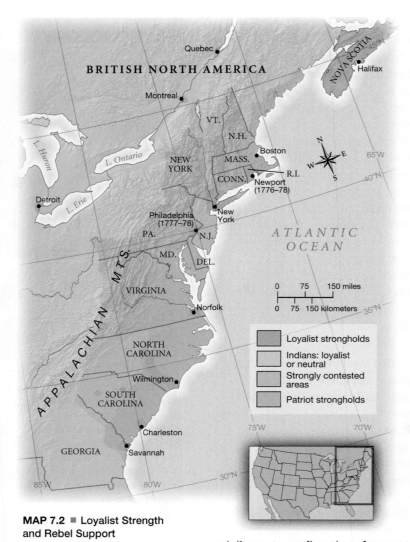

MAP 7.2 ■ Loyalist Strength and Rebel Support
The exact number of loyalists can never be known. No one could have made an accurate count at the time, and political allegiance often shifted with the wind. This map shows the regions of loyalist strength on which the British relied—most significantly, the lower Hudson valley and the Carolina Piedmont.

cheat us in this manner of the small spots we have left for our women and children to live on." Brant pledged Indian support for the king in exchange for protection from encroaching settlers. In the Ohio Country, parts of the Shawnee and Delaware tribes started out pro-American but shifted to the British side by 1779 in the face of repeated betrayals by American settlers and soldiers.

Loyalists were most vocal between 1774 and 1776, when the possibility of a full-scale rebellion against Britain was still uncertain. They challenged the emerging patriot side in pamphlets and newspapers. In New York City, 547 loyalists signed and circulated a broadside titled "A Declaration of Dependence" in rebuttal to the congress's July 4, 1776, declaration, denouncing the "most unnatural, unprovoked Rebellion that ever disgraced the annals of Time."

Who Is a Traitor?

In June 1775, the Second Continental Congress declared all loyalists to be traitors. Over the next year, state laws defined as treason acts such as provisioning the British army, saying anything that undermined patriot morale, and discouraging men from enlisting in the Continental army. Punishments ranged from house arrest and suspension of voting privileges to confiscation of property and deportation. Sometimes self-appointed committees of Tory-hunters bypassed the judicial niceties and terrorized loyalists, raiding their houses or tarring and feathering them.

Were wives of loyalists also traitors? When loyalist families fled the country, their property was typically confiscated. But if the wife stayed, courts usually allowed her to keep one-third of the property, the amount due her if widowed, and confiscated the rest. A wife who fled with her husband might have little choice in the matter. After the Revolution, descendants of refugee loyalists filed several lawsuits to regain property that had entered the family through the mother's inheritance. In 1805, the American son of loyalist refugee Anna Martin recovered her dowry property on the grounds that she had no independent will to be a loyalist.

Tarring and feathering, property confiscation, deportation, terrorism—to the loyalists, such denials of liberty of conscience and of freedom to own private property proved that democratic tyranny was more to be feared than the monarchical variety. A Boston loyalist named Mather Byles aptly expressed this point: "They call me a brainless Tory, but tell me . . . which is better—to be ruled by one tyrant three thousand miles away, or by three thousand tyrants not a mile away?" Byles was soon sentenced to deportation.

CHAPTER LOCATOR | Why did the Americans declare their independence?

Throughout the war, probably 7,000 to 8,000 loyalists fled to England, and 28,000 found haven in Canada. But many chose to remain in the new United States and swing with the changing political winds. In some instances, that proved difficult. In New Jersey, for example, 3,000 Jerseyites felt protected (or scared) enough by the occupying British army in 1776 to swear an oath of allegiance to the king. But then General Howe drew back to New York City, leaving them to the mercy of local patriot committees. British strategy depended on using loyalists to hold occupied territory, but the New Jersey experience showed how poorly that strategy was carried out.

Financial Instability and Corruption

Wars cost money—for arms and ammunition, for food and uniforms, for soldiers' pay. The Continental Congress printed money, but its value quickly deteriorated because the congress held no reserves of gold or silver to back the currency. States began printing paper money to pay for wartime expenses, further complicating the economy.

As the currency depreciated, the congress turned to other means to procure supplies and labor. One method was to borrow hard money (gold or silver coins) from wealthy men in exchange for certificates of debt (public securities) promising repayment with interest. The certificates of debt were similar to present-day government bonds. To pay soldiers, the congress issued land-grant certificates, written promises of acreage usually located in frontier areas such as central Maine or eastern Ohio. Both the public securities and the land-grant certificates quickly became forms of negotiable currency. These certificates soon depreciated, too.

Depreciating currency inevitably led to rising prices, as sellers compensated for the falling value of the money. The wartime economy of the late 1770s, with its unreliable currency and price inflation, was extremely demoralizing to Americans everywhere. In 1778, in an effort to impose stability, local committees of public safety began to fix prices on essential goods such as flour. Inevitably, some turned this unstable situation to their advantage. Money that fell fast in value needed to be spent quickly; being in debt was suddenly advantageous because the debt could be repaid in devalued currency. A brisk black market sprang up in prohibited luxury imports, such as tea, sugar, textiles, and wines, even though these items came from Britain. A New Hampshire delegate to the congress denounced the trade: "We are a crooked and perverse generation, longing for the fineries and follies of those Egyptian task masters from whom we have so lately freed ourselves."

QUICK REVIEW

Why did some colonists promote rebellion while others remained loyal to Britain?

| What initial challenges did the opposing armies face? | What role did the home front play in the war? | How were Native Americans and the French involved in the American Revolution? | Why did the British southern strategy ultimately fail? | Conclusion: Why did the British lose the American Revolution? |

How were Native Americans and the French involved in the American Revolution?

Death of Jane McCrea

This 1804 painting by John Vanderlyn memorializes the martyr legend of Jane McCrea. Daughter of an American patriot family in northern New York, McCrea was in love with a young American loyalist who joined Burgoyne's army. In July 1777, she eloped to join her fiancé, guided by Indians sent by the British to escort her. But she was killed on the short journey—either shot in the crossfire of battle, as the British claimed, or murdered by savage Indians allied with the British, in the patriots' version. Wadsworth Athenaeum, Hartford.

▶ FOR MORE HELP ANALYZING THIS IMAGE, see the visual activity for this chapter in the Online Study Guide at bedfordstmartins.com/roarkunderstanding.

IN EARLY 1777, about the best that could be said was that General Washington had skillfully avoided defeat. The minor victories in New Jersey lent only faint optimism to the American side. Meanwhile, British troops moved south from Quebec in an effort to take control of the Hudson River. Their presence drew the Continental army up into central New York, polarizing Indian tribes of the Iroquois nation and turning the Mohawk Valley into a bloody war zone. By 1779, tribes in western New York and in the Ohio Valley were fully involved in the war. Most sided with the British, and while the Americans had some success in this period, such as the victory at Saratoga, the involvement of Indians and the continuing strength of the British forced the Americans to look to France for help.

Burgoyne's Army and the Battle of Saratoga

In 1777, British general John Burgoyne and a considerable army began the squeeze on the Hudson River valley. His goal was to capture Albany, near the intersection of the Hudson and Mohawk rivers (see Map 7.1, page 178). Accompanied by 1,000 camp followers (cooks, laundresses, musicians) and some 400 Indian warriors, Burgoyne's army of 7,800 men did not travel light. Food had to be packed in, not only for people but also for the 400 horses needed to haul heavy artillery. The British continued to move south, but the large army moved slowly on primitive roads through dense forests. The logical second step in isolating New England should have been to advance troops up the Hudson from New York City to meet Burgoyne. American surveillance indicated that General

CHAPTER LOCATOR | Why did the Americans declare their independence?

Howe in Manhattan was readying his men for a major move in August 1777. But Howe surprised everyone by sailing south to attack Philadelphia.

To reinforce Burgoyne, British troops from Montreal came from the east along the Mohawk River, aided by Mohawks and Senecas of the Iroquois Confederacy. The British were counting on loyalism among the numerous German colonists living in the Mohawk Valley. A hundred miles west of Albany, they encountered American Continental soldiers at Fort Stanwix and laid siege, causing local German militiamen, joined by a few Oneida Indians, to rush to the Continentals' support. Mohawk chief Joseph Brant led the Senecas and Mohawks in an ambush on the Germans and the Oneidas in a narrow ravine called Oriskany, killing nearly 500 out of 840 of them. On Brant's side, some 90 warriors were killed. The defenders of Fort Stanwix ultimately repelled the British and Indians and forced them to retreat (see Map 7.1, page 178). These deadly battles were complexly multiethnic, pitting Indians against Indians, German Americans against German mercenaries, New York patriots against New York loyalists, and English Americans against British soldiers.

The British retreat at Fort Stanwix deprived General Burgoyne of the additional troops he expected. Camped at a small village called Saratoga, he was isolated, with food supplies dwindling and men deserting. The American commander, General Horatio Gates, began moving his army toward him. Burgoyne decided to attack first, and the British prevailed, but at the great cost of 600 dead or wounded. Three weeks later, an American attack on Burgoyne's forces at Saratoga cost the British another 600 men and most of their cannons. Burgoyne finally surrendered on October 17, 1777.

General Howe, meanwhile, had succeeded in occupying Philadelphia in September 1777. Figuring that the Saratoga loss was balanced by the capture of Philadelphia, the British government proposed a negotiated settlement—not including independence—to end the war. The Americans refused.

But supplies of arms and food for the rebel army were precariously low. Washington moved his troops into winter quarters at Valley Forge, just west of Philadelphia. Quartered in drafty huts, the men lacked blankets, boots, stockings, and food. Some 2,000 men at Valley Forge died of disease; another 2,000 deserted over the bitter six-month encampment.

Washington blamed the citizenry for lack of support; indeed, evidence of corruption and profiteering was abundant. Army suppliers too often provided defective food, clothing, and gunpowder. One shipment of bedding arrived with blankets one-quarter their customary size. Food supplies arrived rotten. As one Continental officer said, "The people at home are destroying the Army by their conduct much faster than Howe and all his army can possibly do by fighting us."

The War in Indian Country

Between the fall of 1777 and the summer of 1778, the fighting on the Atlantic coast slowed. But in the interior western areas—the Mohawk Valley, the Ohio Valley, and Kentucky—the war of Indians against the American rebels heated up.

The ambush and slaughter at Oriskany in August 1777 marked the beginning of three years of terror for the inhabitants of the Mohawk Valley. Loyalists and Indians engaged in raids on farms throughout 1778, capturing or killing the residents. In retaliation, American militiamen destroyed Joseph Brant's village but failed to capture any warriors. A month later, Brant's warriors attacked the town of Cherry Valley, killing 16 soldiers and 32 civilians.

CHRONOLOGY

1777
- Ambush at Oriskany.
- British occupy Philadelphia.
- British surrender at Saratoga.
- Continental army endures winter at Valley Forge.

1778
- France enters war on American side.
- Mohawk Valley sees terrorism by both sides.
- White Eyes negotiates treaty with Americans; later dies mysteriously.

1779
- Sullivan's campaign destroys forty Iroquois villages in New York.
- Virginia and Kentucky militiamen take Forts Kaskaskia and Vincennes.

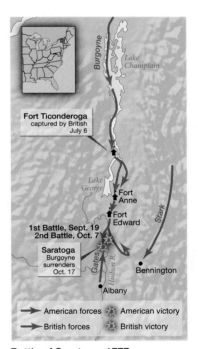

Battle of Saratoga, 1777

What initial challenges did the opposing armies face?

What role did the home front play in the war?

How were Native Americans and the French involved in the American Revolution?

Why did the British southern strategy ultimately fail?

Conclusion: Why did the British lose the American Revolution?

The following summer, General Washington authorized a campaign to wreak "total destruction and devastation" on all the Iroquois villages of central New York. Some 4,500 troops commanded by General John Sullivan implemented a campaign of terror in the fall of 1779. Forty Indian towns met with total obliteration; the soldiers looted and torched the dwellings and then burned cornfields and orchards. In a few towns, women and children were slaughtered, but in most, the inhabitants managed to escape, fleeing to the British at Fort Niagara. Thousands of Indian refugees, sick and starving, camped around the fort in one of the most miserable winters on record.

Much farther to the west, beyond Fort Pitt, another complex story of alliances and betrayals between American militiamen and Indians unfolded. Some 150,000 native people lived between the Appalachian Mountains and the Mississippi River. Most sided with the British, but a portion of the Shawnee and Delaware tribes at first sought peace with the Americans. In mid-1778, the Delaware chief White Eyes negotiated a treaty at Fort Pitt, pledging Indian support for the Americans in exchange for supplies and trade goods. But escalating violence undermined the agreement. That fall, when American soldiers killed two friendly Shawnee chiefs, Cornstalk and Red Hawk, the Continental Congress hastened to apologize, as did the governors of Pennsylvania and Virginia, but the soldiers who stood trial for the murders were acquitted. Two months later, White Eyes, nominally an ally of and an informant for the Americans, died under mysterious circumstances, almost certainly murdered by militiamen, who repeatedly had trouble honoring distinctions between allied and enemy Indians.

West of the Appalachian Mountains, Indian raiders from north of the Ohio River, in alliance with the British, repeatedly attacked white settlements such as Boonesborough (in present-day Kentucky) (**Map 7.3**). In retaliation, a young Virginian, George Rogers Clark, led Virginia and Kentucky militiamen into what is now Illinois, attacking and taking the British fort at Kaskaskia in 1779. Clark's men wore native clothing—hunting shirts and breechcloths—but their dress was not a sign of solidarity with the Indians. When they attacked British-held Fort Vincennes in 1779, Clark's troops tomahawked Indian captives and threw their still-live bodies into the river in a gory spectacle witnessed by the redcoats. "To excel them in barbarity is the only way to make war upon Indians," Clark announced.

By 1780, very few Indians remained neutral. Violent raids by Americans drove Indians into the arms of the British at Detroit and Niagara, or into the arms of the Spaniards, who still held much of the land west of the Mississippi River. For those who stayed near their native lands, chaos and confusion prevailed. Rare as it was, Indian support for the American side occasionally emerged out of a strategic sense that the Americans were unstoppable in their westward pressure and that it was better to work out an alliance than to lose in a war. But American treatment of even friendly Indians showed that there was no winning strategy for them.

The French Alliance

On their own, the Americans could not have defeated Britain, especially as pressure from hostile Indians increased. Essential help arrived as a result of the victory at Saratoga, which convinced the French to enter the war; a formal alliance was signed in February 1778. France recognized the United States as an independent nation and promised full military and commercial support. Most

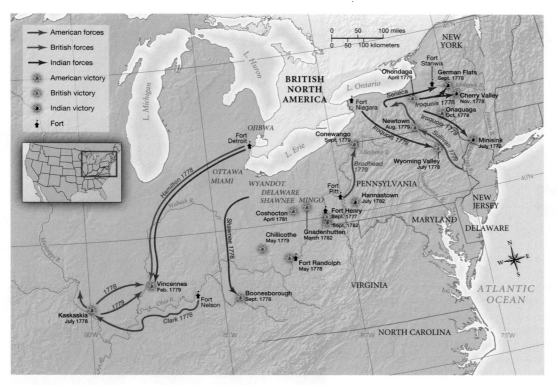

MAP 7.3 ■ **The Indian War in the West, 1777–1782**
The American Revolution involved many Indian tribes, most of them supporting the British. Iroquois Indians, with British aid, attacked American towns in New York's Mohawk Valley throughout 1778. In 1779, the Continental army marched on forty Iroquois villages in central New York and destroyed them. Shawnee and Delaware Indians to the west of Fort Pitt tangled with American militia units in 1779, while tribes supported by the British at Fort Detroit conducted raids on Kentucky settlers, who hit back with raids of their own. George Rogers Clark led Kentucky militiamen against Indians and British in the Illinois region. Sporadic fighting continued in the West through 1782, ending with Indian attacks on Hannastown, Pennsylvania, and Fort Henry on the Ohio River. By the late 1780s, occasional fighting resumed, sparked by American settlers pressing west onto Indian land.

crucial was the French navy, which could challenge British supplies and troops at sea and aid the Americans in taking and holding prisoners of war.

Well before 1778, however, the French had provided cannons, muskets, gunpowder, and highly trained military advisers to the Americans. From the French perspective, the main attraction of an alliance was the opportunity it provided to defeat archrival Britain. A victory would also open pathways to trade and perhaps result in France's acquiring the coveted British West Indies. Even American defeat would not be a disaster for France if the war lasted many years and drained Britain of men and money.

QUICK REVIEW <

Why was French assistance so crucial to the American cause?

| What initial challenges did the opposing armies face? | What role did the home front play in the war? | **How were Native Americans and the French involved in the American Revolution?** | Why did the British southern strategy ultimately fail? | Conclusion: Why did the British lose the American Revolution? |

Why did the British southern strategy ultimately fail?

An enthusiast for American liberty, the young French nobleman Lafayette came to the United States in 1777 at age twenty to volunteer his services to General Washington. After proving his leadership in several northern campaigns, he went to Virginia in 1781 to fight Cornwallis. Near Richmond, he met James, a slave belonging to William Armistead, who loaned him to Lafayette. At the siege of Yorktown, James, pretending to be an escaped slave, infiltrated the British command, giving them misinformation and bringing crucial intelligence back to Lafayette. James obtained his freedom in 1786 after Lafayette wrote a letter on his behalf to the Virginia assembly. Art Gallery, Williams Center, Lafayette College.

WHEN FRANCE JOINED the war, some British officials wondered whether the fight was worth continuing. A troop commander, arguing for an immediate negotiated settlement, shrewdly observed that "we are far from an anticipated peace, because the bitterness of the rebels is too widespread, and in regions where we are masters the rebellious spirit is still in them. The land is too large, and there are too many people. The more land we win, the weaker our army gets in the field." The commander of the British navy argued for abandoning the war, and even Lord North, the prime minister, agreed. But the king was determined to crush the rebellion, and he encouraged a new strategy for victory focusing on the southern colonies, thought to be more persuadably loyalist. It was a brilliant but desperate plan, and ultimately unsuccessful.

Georgia and South Carolina

The new strategy called for British forces to abandon New England and focus on the South, with its valuable crops and its large slave population, a destabilizing factor that might keep rebellious white southerners in line. Georgia and the Carolinas appeared to hold large numbers of loyalists, providing a base for the British to recapture the southern colonies one by one, before moving north to the middle colonies and New England.

Georgia, the first target, fell at the end of December 1778 (**Map 7.4**). A small army of British soldiers occupied Savannah and Augusta, and a new royal governor and loyalist assembly were quickly installed. The British in Georgia

CHAPTER LOCATOR | Why did the Americans declare their independence?

quickly organized twenty loyal militia units, and 1,400 Georgians swore an oath of allegiance to the king. So far, the southern strategy looked as if it might work.

Next came South Carolina. The Continental army put ten regiments into the port city of Charleston to defend it from attack by British troops shipped south from New York under the command of General Henry Clinton, Howe's replacement as commander in chief. For five weeks in early 1780, the British laid siege to the city and took it in May 1780, capturing 3,300 American soldiers.

Clinton returned to New York, leaving the task of pacifying the rest of South Carolina to General Charles Cornwallis and 4,000 troops. A bold commander, Lord Cornwallis quickly chased out the remaining Continentals and established military rule of South Carolina by midsummer. He purged rebels from government office and disarmed rebel militias. Exports of rice, South Carolina's main crop, resumed, and pardons were offered to Carolinians willing to prove their loyalty by taking up arms for the British.

By August, American troops arrived from the North to strike back at Cornwallis. General Gates, the hero of Saratoga, led 3,000 troops, many of them newly recruited militiamen, into battle against Cornwallis at Camden, South Carolina, on August 16. The militiamen panicked at the sight of the approaching British cavalry, however, and fled. When regiment leaders tried to regroup the next day, only 700 soldiers showed up. The battle of Camden was a devastating defeat for the Americans.

Britain's southern strategy succeeded in 1780 in part because of information about American troop movements secretly conveyed by an American officer,

CHRONOLOGY

1780
- British take Charleston, South Carolina.
- French army arrives in Newport, Rhode Island.
- British win battle of Camden.
- Benedict Arnold is exposed as traitor.
- Americans win battle of King's Mountain.

1781
- British forces invade Virginia.
- French fleet blockades Chesapeake Bay.
- Cornwallis surrenders at Yorktown; concedes British defeat.

1783
- Treaty of Paris ends war; United States gains all land to Mississippi River.

MAP 7.4 ■ The War in the South, 1780–1781
After taking Charleston in May 1780, the British advanced into South Carolina and the foothills of North Carolina, leaving a bloody civil war in their wake. When the American general Horatio Gates and his men fled from the humiliating battle of Camden, Gates was replaced by General Nathanael Greene and General Daniel Morgan, who pulled off major victories at King's Mountain and Cowpens. The British general Cornwallis then moved north and invaded Virginia, but he was bottled up and finally overpowered at Yorktown in the fall of 1781.

| What initial challenges did the opposing armies face? | What role did the home front play in the war? | How were Native Americans and the French involved in the American Revolution? | **Why did the British southern strategy ultimately fail?** | Conclusion: Why did the British lose the American Revolution? |

Benedict Arnold

▶ American general who plotted to sell military secrets to the British. The hero of several American battles, Arnold felt he had not got his due in either honor or financial reward for his service. Sometime in 1779, he opened secret negotiations with the British. His treason was discovered in the fall of 1780 when the Americans captured a man carrying plans of West Point's defense from Arnold to the British.

Benedict Arnold. The hero of several American battles, Arnold was a deeply insecure man who never felt he got his due. Sometime in 1779, he opened secret negotiations with General Clinton in New York, trading information for money and hinting that he could deliver far more of value. When General Washington made him commander of West Point, a new fort on the Hudson River sixty miles north of New York City, Arnold's plan crystallized. West Point controlled the Hudson; its capture might well have meant victory for the British.

Arnold's plot to sell a West Point victory to the British was foiled in the fall of 1780 when Americans captured the man carrying plans of the fort's defense from Arnold to Clinton. News of Arnold's treason created shock waves. Arnold represented all of the patriots' worst fears about themselves: greedy self-interest, like that of the war profiteers; the unprincipled abandonment of war aims, like that of turncoat southern Tories; panic, like that of the terrified soldiers at Camden. But instead of demoralizing the Americans, Arnold's treachery revived their commitment to the patriot cause. Vilifying Arnold allowed Americans to stake out a wide distance between themselves and dastardly conduct. It inspired a renewal of patriotism at a particularly low moment.

Guerrilla Warfare in the South

Shock over Gates's defeat at Camden and Arnold's treason revitalized rebel support in western South Carolina, an area that Cornwallis thought was pacified and loyal. The backcountry of the South soon became the site of guerrilla warfare. In hit-and-run attacks, both sides burned and ravaged not only opponents' property but also the property of anyone claiming to be neutral. Loyalist militia units organized by the British were met by fierce rebel militia units. In South Carolina, some 6,000 rebels met loyalist units in bloody engagements. Guerrilla warfare soon spread to Georgia and North Carolina. Both sides committed atrocities and plundered property, clear deviations from standard military practice.

The British southern strategy depended on sufficient loyalist strength to hold reconquered territory as Cornwallis's army moved north. The backcountry civil war proved this assumption false. The Americans won few major battles in the South, but they ultimately succeeded by harassing the British forces and preventing them from foraging for food. Cornwallis moved the war into North Carolina in the fall of 1780 because the North Carolinians were supplying the South Carolina rebels with arms and men (see Map 7.4, page 189). Then news of a massacre of loyalist units by 1,400 frontier riflemen at the battle of King's Mountain, in western South Carolina, sent him hurrying back. The British were stretched too thin to hold even two colonies.

Surrender at Yorktown

By early 1781, the war was going very badly for the British. Their defeat at King's Mountain was quickly followed by a second major defeat at the battle of Cowpens in South Carolina in January 1781. Cornwallis retreated to North Carolina and thence to Virginia, where he captured Williamsburg in June. A raiding party proceeded to Charlottesville, the seat of government, capturing members of the Virginia assembly, but not Governor Thomas Jefferson, who escaped the soldiers by a mere ten minutes. These minor victories allowed Cornwallis to imagine he

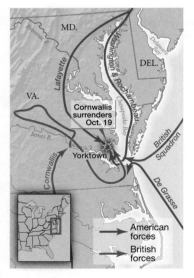

Siege of Yorktown, 1781

CHAPTER LOCATOR | Why did the Americans declare their independence?

was succeeding in Virginia. He next marched to Yorktown, near the Chesapeake Bay, expecting backup troops by ship from British headquarters in New York City.

At this juncture, the French-American alliance came into play. Already, French regiments commanded by the Comte de Rochambeau had joined General Washington in Newport, Rhode Island, in mid-1780, and now in 1781 warships under the Comte de Grasse sailed from France. Washington, Rochambeau, and de Grasse fixed their attention on the Chesapeake Bay. The French fleet got there ahead of the British troop ships from New York; a five-day naval battle left the French navy in control of the Virginia coast. This proved to be the decisive factor in ending the war, because the French ships prevented any rescue of Cornwallis's army.

On land, General Cornwallis and his 7,500 troops faced a combined French and American army of 16,000. For twelve days, the Americans and French bombarded the British fortifications at the **battle of Yorktown**; Cornwallis ran low on food and ammunition. An American observer noted that "the enemy, from want of forage, are killing off their horses in great numbers. Six or seven hundred of these valuable animals have been killed." Realizing that escape was impossible, Cornwallis surrendered on October 19, 1781.

battle of Yorktown
▶ October 1781 battle that sealed American victory in the Revolutionary War. American troops and a French fleet trapped the British army under the command of General Charles Cornwallis at Yorktown, Virginia. The war dragged on for two more years after Cornwallis's surrender on October 19, 1781, but the ultimate outcome was never again in doubt.

"The Ballance of Power," 1780 This cartoon was published in England soon after Spain and the Netherlands declared an alliance with France to support the war in America. On the left, Britannia, a female figure representing Great Britain, cannot be moved by all the lightweights on the right side of the scale. France wears a ruffled shirt, Spain has a feather in his hat, and a Dutch boy has just hopped on, saying, "I'll do anything for Money." The forlorn Indian maiden, the standard icon representing America in the eighteenth century, sits on the scale, wailing, "My Ingratitude is Justly punished." The poem printed below the cartoon predicts, "The Americans too will with Britons Unite." *Print Collection, Miriam and Ira D. Wallach Division of Art, Prints, and Photographs, The New York Public Library. Astor, Lenox, and Tilden Foundations.*

▶ FOR MORE HELP ANALYZING THIS IMAGE, see the visual activity for this chapter in the Online Study Guide at bedfordstmartins.com/roarkunderstanding.

| What initial challenges did the opposing armies face? | What role did the home front play in the war? | How were Native Americans and the French involved in the American Revolution? | **Why did the British southern strategy ultimately fail?** | Conclusion: Why did the British lose the American Revolution? |

191

What began as a promising southern strategy in 1778 turned into a discouraging defeat. British attacks in the South had energized American resistance, as did the timely exposure of Benedict Arnold's treason. The arrival of the French fleet sealed the fate of Cornwallis at the battle of Yorktown, and major military operations came to a halt.

The Losers and the Winners

The surrender at Yorktown spelled the end for the British, but two more years of skirmishes ensued. Frontier areas in Kentucky, Ohio, and Illinois blazed with battles pitting Americans against various Indian tribes. The British army still occupied three coastal cities, including New York City, and an augmented Continental army stayed at the ready.

The peace treaty took six months to negotiate. Commissioners from America, Britain, and France met in Paris and worked out the terms of peace. First and foremost, Britain recognized American independence. Other terms set the western boundary of the new country at the Mississippi River and guaranteed that creditors on both sides could collect debts owed them in sterling money, a provision especially important to British merchants. The **Treaty of Paris** was signed on September 3, 1783.

Like the treaty ending the Seven Years' War, this treaty ignored the Indians as players in the conflict. As one American told the Shawnee people, "Your Fathers the English have made Peace with us for themselves, but forgot you their Children, who Fought with them, and neglected you like Bastards." Indian lands were assigned to the victors as though they were uninhabited. Some Indian refugees fled west into present-day Missouri and Arkansas; others, such as Joseph Brant's Mohawks, relocated to Canada. But significant numbers remained within the new United States, occupying their traditional homelands in areas west and north of the Ohio River. For them, the Treaty of Paris brought no peace at all; their longer war against the Americans would extend at least until 1795 and for some until 1813. Their ally, Britain, conceded defeat, but the Indians did not.

With the treaty finally signed, the British began their evacuation of New York, Charleston, and Savannah, a process complicated by the sheer numbers involved—soldiers, fearful loyalists, and runaway slaves by the thousands. In New York City, more than 27,000 soldiers and 30,000 loyalists sailed on hundreds of ships for England in the late fall of 1783.

Treaty of Paris

▶ September 3, 1783, treaty that ended the Revolutionary War. The treaty acknowledged America's independence, set the western boundary of the new country, guaranteed that creditors on both sides could collect debts owed them in sterling money, and promised the quick withdrawal of British troops from American soil. Like the treaty ending the Seven Years' War, the Treaty of Paris failed to recognize Indians as players in the conflict.

> **QUICK REVIEW**

Why did the British southern strategy ultimately fail?

CHAPTER LOCATOR | Why did the Americans declare their independence?

Picture Research Consultants & Archives.

Conclusion: Why did the British lose the American Revolution?

THE BRITISH BEGAN the war for America convinced that they could not lose. They had the best-trained army and navy in the world; they were familiar with the landscape from the Seven Years' War; they had the support of most of the native tribes of the backcountry; and they easily captured every port city of consequence in America. Probably one-fifth of the population was loyalist, and another two-fifths were undecided. Why, then, did the British lose?

One continuing problem the British faced was the uncertainty of supplies. The army depended on a steady stream of supply ships from home, and insecurity about food helps explain their reluctance to pursue the Continental army aggressively. A further obstacle was their continual misuse of loyalist energies. Any plan to repacify the colonies required the cooperation of the loyalists, but the British repeatedly left them to the mercy of vengeful rebels. French aid also helps explain the British defeat. Even before the formal alliance, French artillery and ammunition proved vital to the Continental army. After 1780, the French army fought alongside the Americans, and the French navy made the Yorktown victory possible. Finally, the British abdicated civil power in the colonies in 1775 and 1776, when royal officials fled to safety, and they never really regained it. The basic British goal—to turn back the clock to imperial rule—receded into impossibility as the war dragged on.

The Revolution profoundly disrupted the lives of Americans everywhere. It was a war for independence from Britain, but it was more. It was a war that required men and women to think about politics and the legitimacy of authority. The rhetoric employed to justify the revolution against Britain put words such as *liberty*, *tyranny*, *slavery*, *independence*, and *equality* into common usage. These words carried far deeper meanings than a mere complaint over taxation without representation. The Revolution unleashed a dynamic of equality and liberty that was largely unintended and unwanted by many of the American leaders of 1776. But that dynamic emerged as a potent force in American life in the decades to come.

SO NOW YOU KNOW

Only two-fifths of the colonists fully supported the idea of American independence in 1776. But by 1783, that minority became a majority that created new government structures, defeated the British army and its allies, and revolutionized the ways most Americans thought about politics and the ideas of liberty and equality.

What initial challenges did the opposing armies face?

What role did the home front play in the war?

How were Native Americans and the French involved in the American Revolution?

Why did the British southern strategy ultimately fail?

Conclusion: Why did the British lose the American Revolution?

CHAPTER 7 STUDY GUIDE

Online Study Guide
bedfordstmartins.com/roarkunderstanding

STEP 1
GETTING STARTED

Below are basic terms from this period in American history. Can you identify each term below and explain why it matters? To do this exercise online or to download this chart, visit bedfordstmartins.com/roarkunderstanding.

TERM	WHO OR WHAT & WHEN	WHY IT MATTERS
Second Continental Congress, p. 170		
George Washington, p. 171		
Common Sense, p. 172		
Abigail Adams, p. 173		
Declaration of Independence, p. 174		
Continental army, p. 176		
loyalists, p. 181		
Joseph Brant (Thayendanegea), p. 181		
Benedict Arnold, p. 190		
battle of Yorktown, p. 191		
Treaty of Paris (1783), p. 192		

STEP 2
MOVING BEYOND THE BASICS

The exercise below represents a more advanced understanding of the chapter material. The following chart divides the war into three periods. Fill in the chart by providing details of the American strategy, the British strategy, key events, and major battles for each of the periods. When you are finished, ask yourself how and why each side's strategy shifted or changed. Why were the Americans ultimately victorious? To do this exercise online or to download this chart, visit bedfordstmartins.com/roarkunderstanding.

Period	American strategy	British strategy	Key events	Major battles/ victor
June 1775–December 1776				
January 1777–February 1778				
March 1778–September 1783				

STEP

3

PUTTING IT ALL TOGETHER

Now that you have reviewed key elements of the chapter, take a step back and try to explain the big picture by answering these questions. Remember to use specific examples from the chapter in your answers. To do this exercise online, visit bedfordstmartins.com/roarkunderstanding.

DECLARING INDEPENDENCE

► Why were so many Americans divided about the question of independence from Britain?
► What factors contributed to the decision by the Continental Congress to declare independence in July 1776?

THE FIRST TWO YEARS OF WAR

► What challenges did the Americans face in the first year of the war? How successful were they in meeting them?
► What impact did other European powers and Indian peoples have on the course of the war?

AMERICAN VICTORY

► Why did the British switch to the southern strategy? Why did it fail?
► Is it more accurate to say that the Americans won the Revolutionary War or that the British lost it? Why?

LOOKING BACKWARD, LOOKING AHEAD

► When did the chain of events that culminated in the establishment of an independent United States begin? In 1763? In 1776? In 1783? At another date? Present evidence to support your answer.
► What challenges did the United States face as it emerged victorious from the Revolutionary War?

IN YOUR OWN WORDS

Imagine that you must explain chapter 7 to someone who hasn't read it. What would be the most important points to include and why?

8
BUILDING A REPUBLIC

1775–1789

> This chapter explores the events and debates that led to the formulation and ratification of the Constitution, the legal foundation of American government after 1788. It examines the challenges the country faced in the 1780s, the efforts of the states to define freedom and citizenship, and the process that led to the abandonment of the Articles of Confederation and the ratification of the United States Constitution.

> What kind of government did the Articles of Confederation create?

> How did the states define freedom and citizenship?

> Why did the Articles of Confederation fail?

> How did the U.S. Constitution increase federal power?

> What were the obstacles to ratification of the Constitution?

> Conclusion: What was the "republican remedy"?

DID YOU KNOW?

Immediately after the American Revolution, the first federal government had no power of taxation.

George Washington presides over the Constitutional Convention. Philadelphia, 1787.

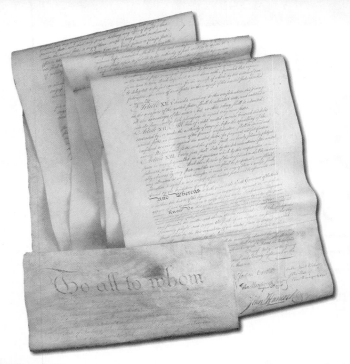

What kind of government did the Articles of Confederation create?

Articles of Confederation

Delegates to the Second Continental Congress hammered out the Articles of Confederation over many months in 1776 and 1777. Once the congress agreed on it, the plan was printed and distributed to state legislatures for ratification, a process that took nearly five years because it required the assent of all thirteen. National Archives.

BEGINNING IN 1775 and continuing for five years after declaring independence, the Second Continental Congress lacked a formal constitutional basis for its governance. Delegates first had to work out a plan of government that embodied Revolutionary principles. With monarchy gone, where would sovereignty lie? What would be the nature of representation? Who would hold the power of taxation? Who should vote? Who should rule? The resulting plan, called the **Articles of Confederation**, proved to be surprisingly difficult to implement, mainly because the thirteen states had serious disagreements about how to manage areas to the west whose political ownership was contested. Once the Articles were finally ratified, the confederation government seemed to many to be far less relevant or interesting than the state governments.

Articles of Confederation

▶ The constitutional basis for national government from 1781 to 1788. The Articles defined the Union as a loose confederation of states existing mainly to foster a common defense. The Articles provided for no executive and limited congress's authority to tax, leaving the preponderance of political power in the hands of the states.

Congress, Confederation, and the Problem of Western Lands

Only after declaring independence did the Continental Congress turn its attention to creating a written document that would specify what powers the congress had and by what authority it existed. There was widespread agreement on key government powers: pursuing war and peace, conducting foreign relations, regulating trade, and running a postal service. But there was serious disagreement about the powers of the congress over the western boundaries of the states. Virginia and Connecticut, for example, had old colonial charters that located their western boundaries at the Mississippi River. States without extensive land claims insisted on redrawing those colonial boundaries.

CHAPTER LOCATOR | What kind of government did the Articles of Confederation create?

This was no mere quarrel over lines on a map. In the 1780s, more than 100,000 Americans had moved west of the Appalachian Mountains, and another 100,000 were moving from eastern towns to newly opened land in northern Vermont and western New York and Pennsylvania, as well as to Kentucky, Georgia, and beyond. Who owned the land, who protected it, and who governed it? These were major and pressing questions.

Congress reached agreement on a proposal for the Articles of Confederation in November 1777. The Articles defined the union as a loose confederation of states, characterized as "a firm league of friendship" existing mainly to foster a common defense. The structure of the government paralleled that of the existing Continental Congress. There was no national executive (that is, no president) and no national judiciary. Each state delegation cast a single vote in congress. Routine decisions in the congress required a simple majority of seven states; for momentous decisions, such as declaring war, nine states needed to agree. To approve or amend the Articles required the unanimous consent both of the thirteen state delegations and of the thirteen state legislatures.

On the delicate question of taxes, necessary to finance the war, the Articles provided an ingenious but troublesome solution. Each state was to contribute in proportion to the property value of the state's land. Large and populous states would give more than small or sparsely populated states. The actual taxes would be levied by the state legislatures, not by the congress, to preserve the Revolution's principle of taxation only by direct representation. However, no mechanism compelled states to pay.

The lack of centralized authority in the confederation government was exactly what many state leaders wanted in the late 1770s. A league of states with rotating personnel, no executive branch, no power of taxation, and a requirement of unanimity for any major change seemed to be a good way to keep government in check. Yet there were problems. The requirement for unanimous approval stalled the acceptance of the Articles for four additional years. The key dispute involved lands west of the existing states (**Map 8.1**). Five states, all lacking land claims, insisted that the congress preserve western lands as a national domain that would eventually constitute new states. The other eight states refused to yield their colonial-era claims and opposed giving the congress power to alter boundaries.

The eight land-claiming states were ready to sign the Articles of Confederation in 1777. Three states without claims, Rhode Island, Pennsylvania, and New Jersey, eventually capitulated and signed, "not from a Conviction of the Equality and Justness of it," said a New Jersey delegate, "but merely from an absolute Necessity there was of complying to save the Continent." But Delaware and Maryland continued to hold out. In 1779, the disputants finally compromised: Any land a state volunteered to relinquish would become the national domain. When James Madison and Thomas Jefferson ceded Virginia's huge land claim in 1781, the Articles were at last unanimously approved.

The western lands issue demonstrated that powerful interests divided the thirteen new states. The apparent unity of purpose inspired by fighting the war against Britain papered over sizable cracks in the new confederation.

Running the New Government

No fanfare greeted the long-awaited inauguration of the new government. The congress continued to sputter along, its problems far from solved by the signing of the

CHRONOLOGY

1775
- Second Continental Congress begins to meet.

1777
- Articles of Confederation are sent to states.

1781
- Articles of Confederation are ratified.
- Creation of executive departments.

How did the states define freedom and citizenship? | Why did the Articles of Confederation fail? | How did the U.S. Constitution increase federal power? | What were the obstacles to ratification of the Constitution? | Conclusion: What was the "republican remedy"?

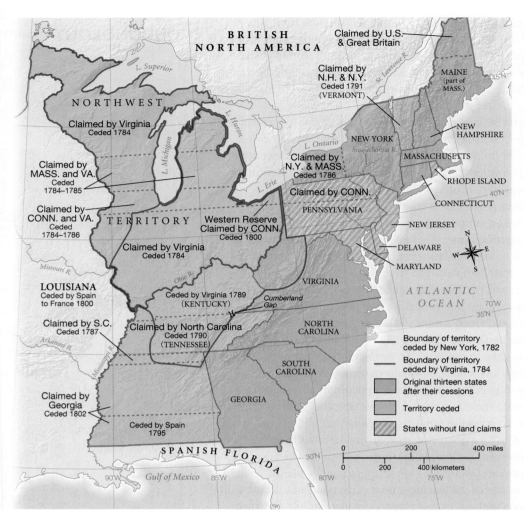

MAP 8.1 ▪ Cession of Western Lands, 1782–1802
The thirteen new states found it hard to ratify the Articles of Confederation without settling their conflicting land claims in the West, an area larger than the original states and occupied by Indian tribes. The five states objecting to the Articles' silence over western lands policy were Maryland, Delaware, New Jersey, Rhode Island, and Pennsylvania.

BRITISH NORTH AMERICA

Claimed by U.S. & Great Britain

Claimed by N.H. & N.Y. Ceded 1791 (VERMONT)

MAINE (part of MASS.)

L. Superior

NORTHWEST

Claimed by Virginia Ceded 1784

NEW HAMPSHIRE

L. Michigan

L. Huron

L. Ontario

Susquehanna R.

NEW YORK

Claimed by MASS. and VA. Ceded 1784–1785

MASSACHUSETTS

Claimed by N.Y. & MASS. Ceded 1786

RHODE ISLAND

L. Erie

Claimed by CONN.

CONNECTICUT

Claimed by CONN. and VA. Ceded 1784–1786

TERRITORY

Western Reserve Claimed by CONN. Ceded 1800

PENNSYLVANIA

NEW JERSEY

Claimed by Virginia Ceded 1784

DELAWARE

Missouri R.

Ohio R.

MARYLAND

LOUISIANA Ceded by Spain to France 1800

Ceded by Virginia 1789 (KENTUCKY)

Cumberland Gap

VIRGINIA

ATLANTIC OCEAN

Claimed by S.C. Ceded 1787

Claimed by North Carolina Ceded 1790 (TENNESSEE)

NORTH CAROLINA

Arkansas R.

Mississippi R.

SOUTH CAROLINA

Claimed by Georgia Ceded 1802

Ceded by Spain 1795

GEORGIA

SPANISH FLORIDA

Gulf of Mexico

Boundary of territory ceded by New York, 1782
Boundary of territory ceded by Virginia, 1784
Original thirteen states after their cessions
Territory ceded
States without land claims

0   200   400 miles
0   200   400 kilometers

Articles. Lack of a quorum often hampered day-to-day activities. Many politicians preferred to devote their energies to state governments, especially when the congress seemed deadlocked or, worse, irrelevant. It also did not help that the congress had no permanent home. During the war, when the British army threatened Philadelphia, the congress relocated to small Pennsylvania towns such as Lancaster and York and then to Baltimore. After hostilities ceased, the congress moved from Trenton to Princeton to Annapolis to New York City.

To address the difficulties of an inefficient congress, executive departments of war, finance, and foreign affairs were created in 1781 to handle purely administrative functions. When the department heads were ambitious, they could exercise considerable executive power. The Articles of Confederation had deliberately refrained from setting up an executive branch, but a modest one was being invented by necessity.

> **QUICK REVIEW**

Why was the confederation government's authority so limited?

CHAPTER LOCATOR | What kind of government did the Articles of Confederation create?

Widow from Essex County

Mrs. Elizabeth Alexander Stevens was married to John Stevens, a New Jersey delegate to the Continental Congress in 1783. Widowed in 1792, she would have then been eligible to vote in state elections according to New Jersey's unique enfranchisement of property-holding women. The widow Stevens died in 1799, before suffrage was redefined to be the exclusive right of males. New Jersey Historical Society.

IN THE FIRST DECADE of independence, the states were sovereign and all-powerful. Relatively few functions, such as declaring war and peace, had been transferred to the confederation government. As Americans discarded their British identity, they thought of themselves instead as Virginians or New Yorkers or Rhode Islanders. Familiar and close to home, state governments claimed the allegiance of citizens and became the arena in which the Revolution's innovations would first be tried.

The State Constitutions

In May 1776, the congress recommended that all states draw up constitutions based on "the authority of the people." By 1778, ten states had done so, and three more (Connecticut, Massachusetts, and Rhode Island) had adopted and updated their original colonial charters. A shared feature of all the state constitutions was the conviction that government ultimately rests on the consent of the governed. Political writers in the late 1770s embraced the concept of republicanism as the underpinning of the new governments. Republicanism meant more than popular elections and representative institutions. For some, republicanism invoked a way of thinking about who leaders should be: autonomous, virtuous citizens who placed civic values above private interests. For others, it suggested direct

| How did the states define freedom and citizenship? | Why did the Articles of Confederation fail? | How did the U.S. Constitution increase federal power? | What were the obstacles to ratification of the Constitution? | Conclusion: What was the "republican remedy"? |

1776
- Virginia adopts first state bill of rights.

1778
- State constitutions are completed.

1780
- Pennsylvania institutes gradual emancipation.

1781
- Slaves Mum Bett and Quok Walker successfully sue for freedom in Massachusetts.

1782–1790
- Virginia, Delaware, and Maryland relax state manumission laws.

1783
- Massachusetts extends suffrage to taxpaying free blacks.

1784–1804
- Gradual emancipation laws are passed in Rhode Island, Connecticut, New York, and New Jersey.

bills of rights

▶ Lists of basic individual liberties that governments could not violate. Virginia debated and passed the first bill of rights in June 1776, and other states borrowed from its language. These lists usually included general rights to life, liberty, and property, and specific rights to freedom of speech, freedom of the press, and trial by jury.

democracy, with nothing standing in the way of the will of the people. For all, it meant government that promoted the people's welfare.

Widespread agreement about the virtues of republicanism went hand in hand with the idea that republics could succeed only in relatively small units so that the people could make sure their interests were being served. Nearly every state continued the colonial practice of a two-chamber assembly but greatly augmented the powers of the lower house. Two states, Pennsylvania and Georgia, abolished the more elite upper house altogether, and most states severely limited the term and powers of the governor.

Six of the state constitutions included **bills of rights**—lists of basic individual liberties that government could not abridge. Virginia debated and passed the first bill of rights in June 1776, and many of the other states borrowed from it. Along with inherent rights, closely resembling the inalienable rights to "life, liberty, and the pursuit of happiness" claimed in the Declaration of Independence, these documents included more specific rights to freedom of speech, freedom of the press, and trial by jury.

Who Are "the People"?

When the Continental Congress called for state constitutions based on "the authority of the people," and when the Virginia bill of rights granted "all men" certain rights, who was meant by "the people"? Who exactly were the citizens of this new country, and how far would the principle of democratic government extend? Different people answered these questions differently, but in the 1770s certain limits to full political participation by all Americans were widely agreed upon.

One limit was defined by property. In nearly every state, voters and political candidates had to meet varying property qualifications. Only property owners were presumed to possess the necessary independence of mind to make wise political choices. Are not propertyless men, asked John Adams, "too little acquainted with public affairs to form a right judgment, and too dependent upon other men to have a will of their own?"

Property qualifications probably disfranchised from one-quarter to one-half of adult white males in all the states. Not all of them took their nonvoter status quietly. One Maryland man wondered what was so special about being worth £30, the property threshold for voting in that state: "Every poor man has a life, a personal liberty, and a right to his earnings; and is in danger of being injured by government in a variety of ways." Why then restrict such a man from voting? Others pointed out that propertyless men were fighting and dying in the Revolutionary War; surely they were expressing an active concern about politics. Finally, a few radical voices challenged the notion that wealth was correlated with good citizenship; maybe the opposite was true. But ideas like this were outside the mainstream. The writers of the new constitutions, themselves men of property, viewed the right to own and preserve property as a central principle of the Revolution.

Another exclusion from voting—women—was so ingrained that few stopped to question it. Yet the logic of allowing propertied females to vote did occur to a handful of well-placed women. Abigail Adams wrote to her husband, John, in 1782, "Even in the freest countrys our property is subject to the controul and disposal of our partners, to whom the Laws have given a sovereign Authority.

CHAPTER LOCATOR | What kind of government did the Articles of Confederation create?

Deprived of a voice in Legislation, obliged to submit to those Laws which are imposed upon us, is it not sufficient to make us indifferent to the publick Welfare?"

Only three states specified that voters had to be male, so powerful was the unspoken assumption that only men could vote. Still, in one state, small numbers of women began to turn out at the polls in the 1780s. New Jersey's constitution of 1776 enfranchised all free inhabitants worth more than £50, language that in theory opened the door to free blacks as well as unmarried women who met the property requirement. (Married women owned no property, for by law their husbands held title to everything.) In 1790, only about 1,000 free black adults of both sexes lived in New Jersey, a state with a population of 184,000. The number of unmarried adult white women was probably also small and comprised mainly widows. In view of the property requirement, the voter blocs enfranchised under this law were minuscule. Still, this highly unusual situation lasted until 1807, when a new state law specifically disfranchised both blacks and women. Henceforth, independence of mind, that essential precondition of voting, was redefined to be sex- and race-specific.

In the 1780s, voting everywhere was class-specific because of the property restrictions. John Adams urged the framers of the Massachusetts constitution not even to discuss the scope of suffrage but simply to adopt the traditional colonial property qualifications. If suffrage is brought up for debate, he warned, "there will be no end of it. New claims will arise; women will demand a vote; lads from twelve to twenty-one will think their rights not enough attended to; and every man who has not a farthing, will demand an equal voice with any other."

Equality and Slavery

Restrictions on political participation did not mean that propertyless people enjoyed no civil rights and liberties. The various state bills of rights applied to all free individuals. No matter how poor, a free person was entitled to life, liberty, property, and freedom of conscience. Unfree people, however, were another matter.

The author of the Virginia bill of rights was George Mason, a plantation owner with 118 slaves. When drafting the right that "All men are by nature equally free and independent," Mason did not have slaves in mind; he instead was asserting that white Americans were the equals of the British and could not be denied the liberties of British citizens. Other Virginia legislators, worried about misinterpretations, added a qualifying phrase: that all men "when they enter into a state of society" have inherent rights. As one legislator wrote, with relief, "Slaves, not being constituent members of our society, could never pretend to any benefit from such a maxim."

One month later, the Declaration of Independence used essentially the same phrase about equality, this time without the modifying clause about entering society. Two state constitutions, for Pennsylvania and Massachusetts, also picked it up. In Massachusetts, one town suggested rewording the draft constitution to read "All men, whites and blacks, are born free and equal." The suggestion was not implemented.

Nevertheless, after 1776, the ideals of the Revolution about natural equality and liberty began to erode the institution of slavery. Often, enslaved blacks led the challenge. In 1777, several Massachusetts slaves petitioned the state

| How did the states define freedom and citizenship? | Why did the Articles of Confederation fail? | How did the U.S. Constitution increase federal power? | What were the obstacles to ratification of the Constitution? | Conclusion: What was the "republican remedy"? |

PAUL CUFFE

CAPTAIN CUFFE

1812.

legislature, claiming a "natural & unalienable right to that freedom which the great Parent of the Universe hath bestowed equally on all mankind." They modestly asked for freedom for their children at age twenty-one and were turned down. In 1779, similar petitions in Connecticut and New Hampshire met with no success. Seven Massachusetts freemen, including the mariner brothers Paul and John Cuffe, refused to pay taxes for three years on the grounds that they could not vote and so were not represented. The Cuffe brothers landed in jail in 1780 for tax evasion, but their petition to the Massachusetts legislature spurred the extension of suffrage to taxpaying free blacks in 1783.

Another way to bring the issue before lawmakers was to sue in court. In 1781, a woman called Elizabeth Freeman (Mum Bett) was the first to win freedom in a Massachusetts court, basing her case on the just-passed state constitution that declared "all men are born free and equal." Later that year, another Massachusetts slave, Quok Walker, charged his master with assault and battery, arguing that he was a free man under that same constitutional phrase. Walker won and was set free, a decision confirmed in an appeal to the state's superior court in 1783. Several similar cases followed, and by 1789 slavery had been effectively abolished by a series of judicial decisions in Massachusetts.

State legislatures acted more slowly. Pennsylvania enacted a gradual emancipation law in 1780. Only infants born to a slave mother on or after March 1, 1780, would be freed, but not until age twenty-eight. Thus no current slave in Pennsylvania could gain freedom until 1808, while those born before 1780 remained slaves. Not until 1847 did Pennsylvania fully abolish slavery. But slaves did not wait for such slow implementation. Untold numbers in Pennsylvania simply

CHAPTER LOCATOR | What kind of government did the Articles of Confederation create?

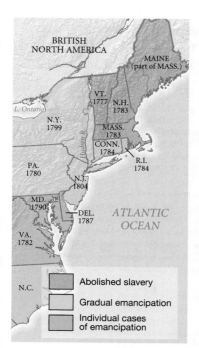

BRITISH
NORTH AMERICA

MAINE
(part of MASS.)

VT.
1777 N.H.
1783

L. Ontario

N.Y.
1799

MASS.
1783

CONN.
1784

PA.
1780

R.I.
1784

N.J.
1804

MD.
1790

DEL.
1787

ATLANTIC
OCEAN

VA.
1782

N.C.

Hudson R.

Abolished slavery

Gradual emancipation

Individual cases
of emancipation

**Legal Changes to Slavery,
1777–1804**

ran away and asserted their freedom, sometimes with the help of sympathetic whites. One
estimate holds that more than half of young
slave men in Philadelphia joined the ranks of
free blacks, and by 1790, free blacks outnumbered slaves in Pennsylvania two to one.

Between 1784 and 1804, Rhode Island, Connecticut, New York, and New Jersey followed
Pennsylvania's lead and adopted gradual emancipation laws. Gradual emancipation illustrates
the tension between radical and conservative
implications of republican ideology. Republican
government protected people's liberties and
property, yet slaves were both people and property. Gradual emancipation balanced the civil
rights of blacks and the property rights of their
owners by delaying the promise of freedom.

South of Pennsylvania, in Delaware, Maryland, and Virginia, where slavery was so important to the economy, emancipation bills were
rejected. All three states, however, eased legal
restrictions and allowed individual acts of
emancipation for adult slaves below the age of
forty-five under new manumission laws. By 1790, close to 10,000 newly freed Virginia slaves had formed local free black communities complete with schools and
churches.

In the deep South—the Carolinas and Georgia—freedom for slaves was
unthinkable among whites. Yet several thousand slaves had defected to the
British during the war, and between 3,000 and 4,000 left with the British at the
war's conclusion. Adding northern blacks evacuated from New York City in 1783,
the probable total of emancipated blacks who left the United States was between
8,000 and 10,000. Some went to Canada, some to England, and some to Sierra
Leone on the west coast of Africa. Many hundreds took refuge with the Seminole
and Creek Indians, becoming permanent members of their communities in
Spanish Florida and western Georgia.

Although all these instances of emancipation were gradual, small, and certainly incomplete, their symbolic importance was enormous. Every state from
Pennsylvania north acknowledged that slavery was fundamentally inconsistent
with Revolutionary ideology; "all men are created equal" was beginning to
acquire real force as a basic principle.

**Slave Populations of
Pennsylvania, New York,
and New Jersey in 1800**

Pennsylvania: 1,700

New York: 20,000

New Jersey: 12,000

QUICK REVIEW <

What were the limits of rights and freedom
within the various states?

| How did the states define freedom and citizenship? | Why did the Articles of Confederation fail? | How did the U.S. Constitution increase federal power? | What were the obstacles to ratification of the Constitution? | Conclusion: What was the "republican remedy"? |

205

Why did the Articles of Confederation fail?

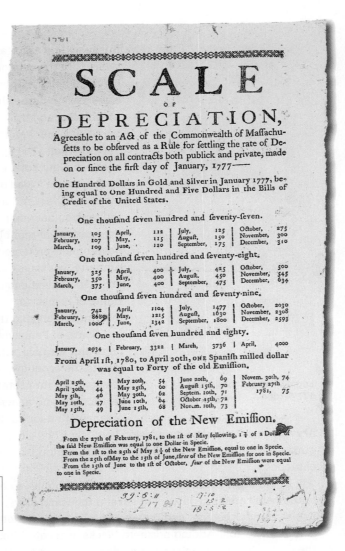

1781

SCALE
OF
DEPRECIATION,

Agreeable to an Act of the Commonwealth of Massachusetts to be observed as a Rule for settling the rate of Depreciation on all contracts both publick and private, made on or since the first day of January, 1777——

One Hundred Dollars in Gold and Silver in January 1777, being equal to One Hundred and Five Dollars in the Bills of Credit of the United States.

One thousand seven hundred and seventy-seven.

January,	105	April,	112	July,	125	October,	275
February,	107	May,	115	August,	150	November,	300
March,	109	June,	120	September,	175	December,	310

One thousand seven hundred and seventy-eight.

January,	325	April,	400	July,	425	October,	500
February,	350	May,	400	August,	450	November,	545
March,	375	June,	400	September,	475	December,	634

One thousand seven hundred and seventy-nine.

January,	742	April,	1104	July,	1477	October,	2030
February,	868	May,	1215	August,	1630	November,	2308
March,	1000	June,	1342	September,	1800	December,	2593

One thousand seven hundred and eighty.

| January, | 2934 | February, | 3322 | March, | 3736 | April, | 4000 |

From April 1st, 1780, to April 20th, ONE Spanish milled dollar was equal to Forty of the old Emission.

April 25th,	42	May 20th,	54	June 20th,	69	Novem. 30th, 74
April 30th,	44	May 25th,	60	August 15th,	70	February 27th
May 5th,	46	May 30th,	62	Septem. 10th,	71	1781, 75
May 10th,	47	June 10th,	64	October 15th,	72	
May 15th,	49	June 15th,	68	Novem. 10th,	73	

Depreciation of the New Emission.

From the 27th of February, 1781, to the 1st of May following, 1¾ of a Dollar of the said New Emission was equal to one Dollar in Specie.
From the 1st to the 25th of May 2½ of the New Emission, equal to one in Specie.
From the 25th of May to the 15th of June, three of the New Emission for one in Specie.
From the 15th of June to the 1st of October, four of the New Emission were equal to one in Specie.

39:6:11
[17 81]
17:10
15 2
18:3 2

Scale of Depreciation

This chart shows the declining monthly value of two emissions of paper dollars from January 1777 to October 1781 as stipulated by the government of Massachusetts. In January 1777, 105 paper dollars were equal in buying power to $100 in silver or gold. In April 1780, 4,000 paper dollars were needed to equal the buying power of $100 in gold or silver. Such a chart was needed when debtors and creditors settled accounts contracted at one time and paid off later in greatly depreciated dollars. Courtesy, American Antiquarian Society.

▶ FOR MORE HELP ANALYZING THIS IMAGE, see the visual activity for this chapter in the Online Study Guide at bedfordstmartins.com/roarkunderstanding.

IN 1783, the confederation government faced three interrelated concerns: paying down the large war debt, making formal peace with the Indians, and dealing with western settlement. From 1784 to 1786, the congress struggled mightily with these three issues. Some leaders were gripped by a sense of crisis, fearing that the Articles of Confederation were too weak. Others defended the Articles as the best guarantee of liberty because real governance occurred at the state level, closer to the people. A major outbreak of civil disorder in western Massachusetts quickly crystallized the debate and propelled the critics of the Articles into decisive and far-reaching action.

Financial Chaos and Paper Money

Seven years of war produced a chaotic economy in the 1780s. The confederation and the individual states had run up huge war debts financed by printing paper money and borrowing from private sources. Some $400 million to $500 million in paper currency had been injected into the economy, and prices and wages fluctuated wildly. Private debt and rapid expenditure flourished, and as Massachusetts

CHAPTER LOCATOR | What kind of government did the Articles of Confederation create?

laborer William Manning described, "jails were crowded with debtors." A serious postwar depression settled in by the mid-1780s and did not lift until the 1790s.

The confederation government itself was in a terrible financial fix. Continental dollars had lost almost all value. Desperate times required desperate measures. The congress chose Robert Morris, Philadelphia merchant and newly reelected delegate, to be superintendent of finance. From 1781 to 1784, he took charge of the confederation's economic problems.

To augment the government's revenue, Morris first proposed a 5 percent impost (an import tax). Since the Articles of Confederation did not authorize taxation, an amendment was needed, but unanimous agreement proved impossible. Rhode Island and New York, whose bustling ports provided ample state revenue, preferred to keep their money for themselves.

Morris's next idea was the creation of the Bank of North America. This private bank would enjoy a special relationship with the confederation, holding the government's hard money (gold and silver coins), as well as private deposits, and providing it with short-term loans. The bank's contribution to economic stability came in the form of banknotes, pieces of paper inscribed with a dollar value. Unlike paper money, banknotes were backed by hard money in the bank's vaults and thus would not depreciate. Congress voted to approve the bank in 1781. But the bank had limited success in curing the confederation's economic woes because it issued very little currency, and its charter was allowed to expire in 1786.

The government formed by the Articles of Confederation tried but failed to resuscitate the economy in the 1780s. Because the Articles reserved most economic functions to the states, the congress was helpless to tax trade, control inflation, curb the flow of state-issued paper money, or pay the mounting public debt. However, the confederation had one source of enormous potential wealth: the huge western territories, attractive to the fast-growing white population but inhabited by Indians.

The Treaty of Fort Stanwix

Since the Indians had not participated in the Treaty of Paris of 1783, the confederation government hoped to formalize treaties ending ongoing hostilities between Indians and settlers and securing land cessions. The most pressing problem was the land inhabited by the Iroquois Confederacy, a league of six tribes, now claimed by the states of New York and Massachusetts based on their colonial charters.

At issue was the revenue stream that land sales would generate: which government would get it? The congress summoned the Iroquois to a meeting in October 1784 at Fort Stanwix, on the upper reaches of the Mohawk River. The Articles of Confederation gave the congress (as opposed to individual states) the right to manage diplomacy, war, and "all affairs with the Indians, not members of any of the States." But New York's governor seized on this ambiguous language to claim that the Iroquois were in fact "members" of his state, and called his own meeting with the Iroquois at Fort Stanwix in September. Suspecting that New York might be superseded by the congress, the most important chiefs declined to come and instead sent deputies without authority to negotiate. The Mohawk leader Joseph Brant shrewdly identified the problem of divided authority that afflicted the confederation government: "Here lies some Difficulty in our Minds, that there should be two separate bodies to manage these Affairs." No deal was struck with New York.

CHRONOLOGY

1781
- Bank of North America is chartered.

1784
- Treaty of Fort Stanwix with Iroquois Confederacy.

1785
- Ordinance of 1785 maps western lands into squares.

1786-1787
- Shays's Rebellion protesting taxes in Massachusetts leads to call for a constitutional convention.

1787
- Northwest Ordinance establishes a three-step process for new states to enter the Union.

| How did the states define freedom and citizenship? | **Why did the Articles of Confederation fail?** | How did the U.S. Constitution increase federal power? | What were the obstacles to ratification of the Constitution? | Conclusion: What was the "republican remedy"? |

Treaty of Fort Stanwix

Treaty of Fort Stanwix
▶ October 1784 treaty between the United States and the Iroquois Confederacy. The Americans demanded a return of prisoners of war, recognition of the confederation's authority to negotiate, and cession of a strip of land from Fort Niagara due south. The Americans took hostages until the terms of the treaty were met. This act, combined with the fact that many affected tribes were not present at the negotiations, led some Indians to later disavow the treaty.

Three weeks later, U.S. commissioners opened proceedings at Fort Stanwix with the Seneca chief Cornplanter and Captain Aaron Hill, a Mohawk leader, accompanied by six hundred Indians from the six tribes. The U.S. commissioners arrived with a security detail of one hundred New Jersey militiamen. The Americans demanded a return of prisoners of war; recognition of the confederation's authority to negotiate, rather than that of individual states; and an all-important cession of a strip of land from Fort Niagara due south, which established U.S.-held territory adjacent to the border with Canada. This crucial change enclosed the Iroquois land within the United States and made it impossible for the Indians to claim to be *between* the United States and Canada. When the tribal leaders balked, one of the commissioners sternly replied, "You are mistaken in supposing that, having been excluded from the treaty *between* the United States and the King of England, you are become a free and independent nation and may make what terms you please. It is not so. You are a subdued people."

In the end, the treaty was signed, gifts were given, and six high-level Indian hostages were kept at the fort awaiting the release of the American prisoners taken during the Revolutionary War, mostly women and children. In addition, a significant side deal sealed the release of much of the Seneca tribe's claim to the Ohio Valley to the United States. This move was a major surprise and disappointment to the Delaware, Mingo, and Shawnee Indians who lived there. In the months to come, tribes not at the meeting tried to disavow the **Treaty of Fort Stanwix** as a document signed under coercion by virtual hostages. But the confederation government ignored those complaints and made plans to survey and develop the Ohio Territory.

New York's governor shrewdly figured that the congress's power to implement the treaty terms was limited. The confederation had little money, and its leadership was stretched. So New York began surveying and then selling the very land it had failed to secure by individual treaty with the Iroquois. As that fact became generally known, it pointed up the weakness of the confederation government. One Connecticut leader wondered, "What is to defend us from the ambition and rapacity of New-York, when she has spread over that vast territory, which she claims and holds? Do we not already see in her the seeds of an over-bearing ambition?"

Land Ordinances and the Northwest Territory

The congress ignored western New York and turned instead to the Ohio Valley to make good on the promise of western expansion. Delegate Thomas Jefferson, charged with drafting a policy, proposed dividing the territory north of the Ohio River and east of the Mississippi—called the Northwest Territory—into nine new states with evenly spaced east-west boundaries and townships ten miles square. He advocated giving the land to settlers, rather than selling it, arguing that future property taxes on the improved land would be payment enough. Jefferson's aim was to encourage rapid and democratic settlement, to build a nation of freeholders (as opposed to renters), and to discourage land speculation. Jefferson also insisted on representative governments in the new states; they would not become colonies of the older states. Finally, Jefferson's draft prohibited slavery in the nine new states.

The congress adopted parts of Jefferson's plan in the Ordinance of 1784: the rectangular grid, the nine new states, and the guarantee of self-government and eventual statehood. What the congress found too radical was the proposal to give

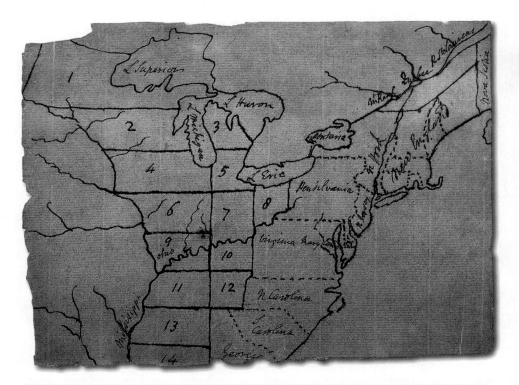

Thomas Jefferson sketched out borders for nine new states in his initial plan for the Northwest Territory in 1784 and additional anticipated states south of the Ohio River. Straight lines and right angles held a strong appeal for him. But such regularity ignored inconvenient geographic features such as rivers and even more inconvenient political facts such as Indian territorial claims. William L. Clements Library.

▶ FOR MORE HELP ANALYZING THIS IMAGE, see the visual activity for this chapter in the Online Study Guide at bedfordstmartins.com/roarkunderstanding.

away the land; the national domain was the confederation's only source of independent wealth. The slavery prohibition also failed, by a vote of seven to six states.

A year later, the congress revised the legislation with procedures for mapping and selling the land. The Ordinance of 1785 called for three to five states, divided into townships six miles square, further divided into thirty-six sections of 640 acres, each section enough for four family farms (**Map 8.2**). Property was thus reduced to easily mappable squares. Land would be sold by public auction at a minimum price of one dollar an acre, with highly desirable land bid up for more. Two further restrictions applied: The minimum purchase was 640 acres, and payment must be in hard money or in certificates of debt from Revolutionary days. This effectively meant that the land's first purchasers would be prosperous speculators. The grid of invariant squares further enhanced speculation, allowing buyers and sellers to operate without ever setting foot on the acreage. The commodification of land had been taken to a new level.

Speculators usually held the land for resale rather than inhabiting it. Thus they avoided direct contact with the most serious obstacle to settlement: the dozens of Indian tribes that claimed the land as their own. The treaty signed at Fort Stanwix in 1784 was followed by the Treaty of Fort McIntosh in 1785, which similarly coerced partial cessions of land from the Delaware, Huron, and Miami tribes. Finally, in 1786, a united Indian meeting near Detroit issued an ultimatum: No cession would be valid without the unanimous consent of the tribes. The Indians advised the United States to "prevent your surveyors and other people from coming upon our side of the Ohio river." For two more decades, violent Indian wars in Ohio and Indiana would continue to impede white settlement (see chapter 9).

| How did the states define freedom and citizenship? | **Why did the Articles of Confederation fail?** | How did the U.S. Constitution increase federal power? | What were the obstacles to ratification of the Constitution? | Conclusion: What was the "republican remedy"? |

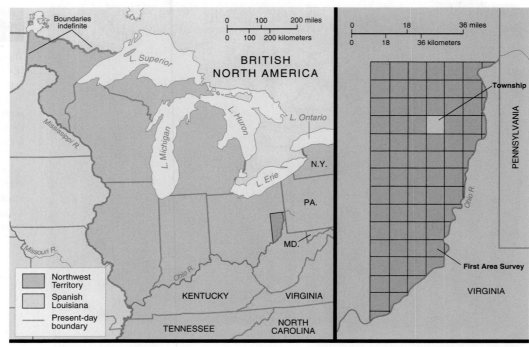

MAP 8.2 ■ The Northwest Territory and the Ordinance of 1785

Surveyors mapping the eastern edge of the Northwest Territory followed the Ordinance of 1785, using the stars as well as poles and chains (standard surveying equipment) to run boundary lines. The result was a blanket of six-mile-square townships, subdivided into one-mile squares each containing sixteen 40-acre farms.

(Map labels: Boundaries indefinite; L. Superior; L. Michigan; L. Huron; L. Ontario; L. Erie; BRITISH NORTH AMERICA; Mississippi R.; Missouri R.; Ohio R.; N.Y.; PA.; MD.; KENTUCKY; VIRGINIA; TENNESSEE; NORTH CAROLINA; 0 100 200 miles; 0 100 200 kilometers; Township; First Area Survey; PENNSYLVANIA; VIRGINIA; Ohio R.; 0 18 36 miles; 0 18 36 kilometers)

Legend: Northwest Territory / Spanish Louisiana / Present-day boundary

Northwest Ordinance

▶ Land act of 1787 that set forth the process by which settled territories would become states. The law stipulated that as the population of a territory increased, it would move step-by-step closer to full statehood. It also banned slavery in the Northwest Territory. The Northwest Ordinance was intended to guarantee that the United States would not become a colonial power over western lands.

In 1787, a third land act, called the **Northwest Ordinance**, set forth a three-stage process by which settled territories would advance to statehood. As the population of a territory increased, it would move step-by-step closer to full statehood. At all three territorial stages, the inhabitants were subject to taxation to support the Union, in the same manner as were the original states.

The Northwest Ordinance of 1787 and the Path to Statehood

Phase One	Congress appoints officials for a sparsely populated territory who adopt a legal code and appoint local magistrates to administer justice.
Phase Two	When the free male population of voting age and landowning status (fifty acres) reaches 5,000, the territory elects its own legislature and sends a nonvoting delegate to the congress.
Phase Three	When the population of voting citizens reaches 60,000, the territory writes a state constitution and applies for full admission to the Union.

The Northwest Ordinance of 1787 was perhaps the most important legislation passed by the confederation government. It ensured that the new United States, so recently released from colonial dependency, would not itself become a colonial power—at least not with respect to white citizens. The mechanism it established allowed for the successful and orderly expansion of the United States across the continent in the next century.

Nonwhites were not forgotten or neglected in the 1787 ordinance. The brief document acknowledged the Indian presence in the Northwest Territory and promised that "the utmost good faith shall always be observed towards the Indians; their lands and property shall never be taken from them without their consent; and, in their property, rights, and liberty, they shall never be invaded or

CHAPTER LOCATOR | What kind of government did the Articles of Confederation create?

disturbed, unless in just and lawful wars authorized by Congress." The 1787 ordinance further pledged that "laws founded in justice and humanity, shall from time to time be made for preventing wrongs being done to them, and for preserving peace and friendship with them." Such promises were full of noble intentions, but they were not generally honored in the decades to come.

Jefferson's original and remarkable suggestion to prohibit slavery in the Northwest Territory resurfaced in the 1787 ordinance, passing this time without any debate. Probably the addition of a fugitive slave provision in the act set southern congressmen at ease: Escaped slaves caught north of the Ohio River would be returned south. The ordinance thus acknowledged and supported slavery even as it prohibited it in one region. Further, abundant territory south of the Ohio remained available for the spread of slavery. Still, the prohibition of slavery in the Northwest Territory perpetuated the dynamic of gradual emancipation in the North. North-South sectionalism based on slavery was slowly taking shape.

Shays's Rebellion, 1786–1787

Without an impost amendment, and with public land sales projected but not yet realized, the confederation turned to the states in the 1780s to contribute revenue voluntarily. Struggling with their own war debts, most state legislatures were reluctant to tax their constituents too heavily. Massachusetts, however, had a fiscally conservative legislature dominated by the coastal commercial centers. For four years, the legislature passed tough tax laws that called for payment in hard money, not cheap paper. Farmers in the western two-thirds of the state found it increasingly difficult to comply and repeatedly petitioned against what they called oppressive taxation. In July 1786, when the legislature adjourned, having yet again ignored their complaints, dissidents held a series of conventions and called for revisions to the state constitution to promote democracy, eliminate the elite upper house, and move the capital farther west in the state.

Still unheard in Boston, the dissidents targeted the county courts, the local symbol of state authority. In the fall of 1786, several thousand armed men marched on courthouses in six Massachusetts counties and forced judges to close their courts until the state constitution was revised. Sympathetic local militias did not intervene. The insurgents were not predominantly poor or debt-ridden farmers; they included veteran soldiers and officers in the Continental army as well as town leaders. One was a farmer and onetime army captain, Daniel Shays.

The governor of Massachusetts, James Bowdoin, once a protester against British taxes, now characterized the western dissidents as illegal rebels. He vilified Shays as the chief leader, and a Boston newspaper claimed that Shays planned to burn Boston to the ground and overthrow the government. Another former radical, Samuel Adams, took the extreme position that "the man who dares rebel against the laws of a republic ought to suffer death." The dissidents challenged the aging revolutionaries' assumption that popularly elected governments would always be fair and just.

Members of the Continental Congress worried that the Massachusetts insurgency was spinning out of control. In October, the congress attempted to triple the size of the federal army, but fewer than 100 men enlisted. So Governor Bowdoin raised a private army, gaining the services of some 3,000 men, with pay provided by wealthy and fearful Boston merchants.

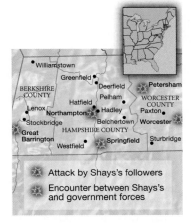

Shays's Rebellion, 1786–1787

| How did the states define freedom and citizenship? | **Why did the Articles of Confederation fail?** | How did the U.S. Constitution increase federal power? | What were the obstacles to ratification of the Constitution? | Conclusion: What was the "republican remedy"? |

Daniel Shays and Job Shattuck

A Boston almanac of 1787 yields the only rough depiction of Daniel Shays in existence. Shays is standing with another rebel leader, Job Shattuck, from the town of Groton. This particular almanac series was quite pro-Constitution in 1788, so very likely this picture was intended to mock the rebels by showing them in fancy uniforms and armed with swords, trappings beyond their presumed lowly means. National Portrait Gallery, Smithsonian Institution/Art Resource, NY.

Shays's Rebellion

▶ Uprising (1786–1787) led by Massachusetts farmer and former soldier Daniel Shays. Centered in western Massachusetts, the uprising was sparked by what dissidents considered the oppressive policies of the eastern elites who controlled the state's government. Shays's Rebellion caused leaders throughout the country to worry about the confederation's ability to handle civil disorder.

In January 1787, the insurgents learned of the private army marching their way, and 1,500 of them moved to capture a federal armory in Springfield to obtain weapons. But a militia band loyal to the state government beat them to the weapons facility and met their attack with gunfire; 4 rebels were killed and another 20 wounded. The final and bloodless encounter came in February at Petersham, where Bowdoin's army surprised the rebels and took 150 prisoners; the others fled into the woods but were soon rounded up and jailed.

In the end, 2 men were executed for rebellion; 16 more sentenced to hang were reprieved at the last moment on the gallows. Some 4,000 men gained leniency by confessing their misconduct and swearing an oath of allegiance to the state. A special Disqualification Act prohibited the penitent rebels from voting, holding public office, serving on juries, working as schoolmasters, or operating taverns for up to three years.

Shays's Rebellion caused leaders throughout the country to worry about the confederation's ability to handle civil disorder. Inflammatory Massachusetts newspapers wrote about bloody mob rule and the possibility of similar uprisings in other states. New York lawyer John Jay wrote to George Washington, "Our affairs seem to lead to some crisis, some revolution—something I cannot foresee or conjecture. I am uneasy and apprehensive; more so than during the war." Benjamin Franklin, in his eighties, shrewdly observed that in 1776, Americans had feared "an excess of power in the rulers" but now the problem was perhaps "a defect of obedience" in the subjects. Among such leaders, the sense of crisis in the confederation had greatly deepened.

> **QUICK REVIEW**

How were the issues of war debt, Indian policy, and western land settlement interconnected in the 1780s?

CHAPTER LOCATOR | What kind of government did the Articles of Confederation create?

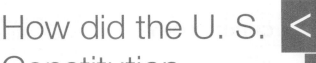

How did the U. S. Constitution increase federal power?

The Pennsylvania Statehouse

The constitutional convention assembled at the Pennsylvania statehouse in the summer of 1787. Despite the heat, the delegates nailed the windows shut to eliminate the chance of being heard by eavesdroppers, so intent were they on secrecy. The building is now called Independence Hall in honor of the signing of the Declaration of Independence there in 1776. Historical Society of Pennsylvania.

SHAYS'S REBELLION PROVOKED an odd mixture of fear and hope that the government under the Articles of Confederation was losing its grip on power. A small circle of Virginians decided to try one last time to augment the powers granted to the government by the Articles. Their call for a meeting to discuss trade regulation led to a total reworking of the national government.

From Annapolis to Philadelphia

The Virginians, led by James Madison, convinced the confederation congress to allow a meeting of delegates at Annapolis, Maryland, in September 1786, to try again to revise the trade regulation powers of the Articles. Only five states participated, and they rescheduled the meeting for Philadelphia in May 1787. The congress reluctantly endorsed the Philadelphia meeting and limited its scope to "the sole and express purpose of revising the Articles of Confederation." But at least one representative at the Annapolis meeting had more ambitious plans. Alexander Hamilton of New York hoped the Philadelphia meeting would do whatever was necessary to strengthen the federal government.

The fifty-five men who assembled at Philadelphia in May 1787 for the **constitutional convention** were generally those who had already concluded that there were weaknesses in the Articles of Confederation. Patrick Henry, author of

constitutional convention
► May 1787 meeting in Philadelphia to revise the Articles of Confederation. Going well beyond their original mandate, the delegates at the convention crafted a new basis for the government of the United States, the Constitution. The Constitution greatly enhanced the power of the federal government.

How did the states define freedom and citizenship?	Why did the Articles of Confederation fail?	How did the U.S. Constitution increase federal power?	What were the obstacles to ratification of the Constitution?	Conclusion: What was the "republican remedy"?

1787

- **May.** Constitutional convention convenes in Philadelphia. Virginia Plan proposes a two-house legislature and three branches of government.
- **June.** New Jersey plan proposes a single-house legislature and a three-man presidency.
- **July.** Great Compromise breaks a stalemate at the constitutional convention, and the basic features of the Constitution emerge.
- **September.** Constitutional convention approves the U.S. Constitution and sends it to the states for ratification.

Virginia Plan

► Plan presented at the constitutional convention by James Madison that set out a three-branch government composed of a two-chamber legislature, a powerful executive, and a judiciary. Under Madison's plan, representation in both houses of the congress would be tied to population, all but eliminating the voice of small states in national government.

New Jersey Plan

► Alternative plan presented by New Jersey delegates of the constitutional convention. The plan retained the confederation principle that the national government was an assembly of states, maintained the existing single-house congress of the Articles of Confederation in which each state had one vote, and created a plural presidency to be shared by three men elected by the congress from its membership. This proposal gave the new congress sweeping powers, including the right to tax, regulate trade, and use force on unruly state governments.

the Virginia Resolves in 1765 and more recently state governor, refused to go to the convention, saying he "smelled a rat." Rhode Island refused to send delegates. Two New York representatives left in dismay in the middle of the convention, leaving Alexander Hamilton as the sole delegate from New York.

The Delegates to the Constitutional Convention

All were white men.
None were artisans or day laborers, or even farmers of middling wealth.
Two-thirds of the delegates were lawyers.
The majority had served in the confederation congress.
Half had been officers in the Continental army.
Seven had been governors of their states.

The Virginia and New Jersey Plans

The convention worked in secrecy so that the men could freely explore alternatives without fear that their honest opinions would come back to haunt them. The Virginia delegation first laid out a fifteen-point plan for a complete restructuring of the government. This **Virginia Plan** was a total repudiation of the principle of a confederation of states. Largely the work of Madison, the plan set out a three-branch government composed of a two-chamber legislature, a powerful executive, and a judiciary. It practically eliminated the voices of the smaller states by pegging representation in both houses of the congress to population. The theory was that government operated directly on people, not on states. Among the breathtaking powers assigned to the congress were the rights to veto state legislation and to coerce states militarily to obey national laws. To prevent the congress from having absolute power, the executive and judiciary could jointly veto its actions.

In mid-June, a delegate from New Jersey, after caucusing with delegates from other small states, unveiled an alternative proposal. The **New Jersey Plan**, as it was called, maintained the existing single-house congress of the Articles of Confederation in which each state had one vote. Acknowledging the need for an executive, it created a plural presidency to be shared by three men elected by the congress from among its membership. Where it sharply departed from the existing government was in the sweeping powers it gave to the new congress: the right to tax, regulate trade, and use force on unruly state governments. In favoring national power over states' rights, it aligned itself with the Virginia Plan. But the New Jersey Plan retained the confederation principle that the national government was to be an assembly of states, not of people.

For two weeks, delegates debated the two plans, focusing on the key issue of representation. The small-state delegates conceded that one house in a two-house legislature could be apportioned by population, but they would never agree that both houses could be. Madison was equally vehement about bypassing representation by state, which he viewed as the fundamental flaw in the Articles.

The debate seemed deadlocked, and for a while the convention was "on the verge of dissolution, scarce held together by the strength of a hair," according to

CHAPTER LOCATOR | What kind of government did the Articles of Confederation create?

214 CHAPTER 8 BUILDING A REPUBLIC, 1775–1789

one delegate. Only in mid-July did the so-called Great Compromise break the stalemate and produce the basic structural features of the emerging United States Constitution. Proponents of the competing plans agreed on a bicameral legislature.

Representation in the lower house, the House of Representatives, would be apportioned by population, and representation in the upper house, the Senate, would come from all the states equally, with each state represented by two independently voting senators. Representation by population turned out to be an ambiguous concept once it was subjected to rigorous discussion. Who counted? Were slaves, for example, people or property? As people, they would add weight to the southern delegations in the House of Representatives, but as property they would add to the tax burdens of those states. What emerged was the compromise known as the **three-fifths clause**: All free persons plus "three-fifths of all other Persons" constituted the numerical base for the apportionment of representatives.

Using "all other Persons" as a substitute for "slaves" indicates the discomfort delegates felt in acknowledging in the Constitution the existence of slavery. But though slavery was nowhere named, nonetheless it was recognized, guaranteed, and thereby perpetuated by the U.S. Constitution.

Democracy versus Republicanism

The delegates in Philadelphia made a distinction between *democracy* and *republicanism* new to the American political vocabulary. Pure democracy was now taken to be a dangerous thing. As a Massachusetts delegate put it, "The evils we experience flow from the excess of democracy." The delegates still favored republican institutions, but they created a government that gave direct voice to the people only in the House and that granted a check on that voice to the Senate, a body of men elected not by direct popular vote but by the state legislatures. Senators served for six years, with no limit on reelection; they were protected from the whims of democratic majorities, and their long terms fostered experience and maturity in office.

Similarly, the presidency evolved into a powerful office out of the reach of direct democracy. The delegates devised an electoral college whose only function was to elect the president and vice president. Each state's legislature would choose the electors, whose number was the sum of representatives and senators for the state. The president thus would owe his office not to the Congress, the

City Tavern

Philadelphia's City Tavern, built in 1773, became a favorite gathering place for the delegates to the Constitutional Convention in the summer of 1787. The men who wrote the Constitution took meals and drinks at the tavern. Rare Book Department, The Free Library of Philadelphia.

three-fifths clause

▶ Clause in the Constitution that stipulated that all free persons plus "three-fifths of all other persons" would constitute the numerical base for the apportionment of representatives. The clause was a compromise designed to resolve the issue of how slaves would be counted for purposes of representation and taxation. The clause tacitly acknowledged the existence of slavery in the United States.

| How did the states define freedom and citizenship? | Why did the Articles of Confederation fail? | **How did the U.S. Constitution increase federal power?** | What were the obstacles to ratification of the Constitution? | Conclusion: What was the "republican remedy"? |

states, or the people, but to a temporary assemblage of distinguished citizens who could vote their own judgment on the candidates.

The framers had developed a far more complex form of federal government than that provided by the Articles of Confederation. To curb the excesses of democracy, they devised a government with limits and checks on all three of its branches. They set forth a powerful president who could veto legislation passed in Congress, but they gave Congress power to override presidential vetoes. They set up a national judiciary to settle disputes between states and citizens of different states. They separated the branches of government not only by functions and by reciprocal checks but also by deliberately basing the election of each branch on different universes of voters—voting citizens (the House), state legislators (the Senate), and the electoral college (the presidency). The convention carefully listed the powers of the president and of Congress. The president could initiate policy, propose legislation, and veto acts of Congress; he could command the military and direct foreign policy; and he could appoint the entire judiciary, subject to Senate approval. Congress held the purse strings: the power to levy taxes, to regulate trade, and to coin money and control the currency. States were expressly forbidden to issue paper money. Two more powers of Congress—to "provide for the common defence and general Welfare" of the country and "to make all laws which shall be necessary and proper" for carrying out its powers—provided elastic language that came closest to Madison's wish to grant sweeping powers to the new government.

While no one was entirely satisfied with every line of the Constitution, only three dissenters refused to sign the document. The Constitution specified a mechanism for ratification that avoided the dilemma faced earlier by the confederation government: Nine states, not all thirteen, had to ratify it, and special ratifying conventions elected only for that purpose, not state legislatures, would make the crucial decision. On September 17, the convention passed the Constitution and sent it to the states for ratification.

> **QUICK REVIEW**

What problems with the Articles of Confederation did the delegates to the constitutional convention seek to rectify?

CHAPTER LOCATOR | What kind of government did the Articles of Confederation create?

216 CHAPTER 8
BUILDING A REPUBLIC, 1775–1789

What were the obstacles to ratification of the Constitution?

The Looking Glass for 1787

This pro-Federalist cartoon depicts the debate over the ratification of the Constitution. On the left, Federalists pull a stuck cart toward the shining sun. To the right, anti-Federalists pull it toward stormy skies. Library of Congress.

THE PROCESS of ratifying the Constitution was highly contentious. In the three most populous states—Virginia, Massachusetts, and New York—substantial majorities opposed a powerful new national government. North Carolina and Rhode Island refused to call ratifying conventions. Seven of the eight remaining states were easy victories for the Constitution, but securing the approval of the ninth proved difficult. Pro-Constitution forces, called Federalists, had to strategize very shrewdly to defeat anti-Constitution forces, called Antifederalists.

The Federalists

Proponents of the Constitution moved into action swiftly. To silence the criticism that they had gone beyond their charge, they sent the document to the congress. The congress withheld explicit approval but resolved to send the Constitution to the states for their consideration. The pro-Constitution forces shrewdly secured another advantage by calling themselves **Federalists**. Their opponents became known as **Antifederalists**, a label that made them sound defensive and negative, lacking a program of their own.

To gain momentum, the Federalists targeted the states most likely to ratify quickly. Delaware ratified the Constitution in early December, and Pennsylvania, New Jersey, and Georgia followed within a month (**Map 8.3**). Delaware and New Jersey were small states surrounded by more powerful neighbors; a government that would regulate trade and set taxes according to population was an attractive

Federalists
▶ Supporters of ratification of the Constitution. Federalists believed that a stronger national government was vital to the country's survival. Leading Federalists included John Adams, Alexander Hamilton, and George Washington.

Antifederalists
▶ Opponents of ratification of the Constitution. Antifederalists feared that the Constitution would create a potentially tyrannical government, out of touch with the needs of the citizens of individual states and localities. One widespread objection to the Constitution was its omission of any guarantees of individual liberties in a bill of rights like those contained in many state constitutions.

How did the states define freedom and citizenship?	Why did the Articles of Confederation fail?	How did the U.S. Constitution increase federal power?	**What were the obstacles to ratification of the Constitution?**	Conclusion: What was the "republican remedy"?

217

CHRONOLOGY

1787
- Constitutional convention meets in Philadelphia.
- **October.** Publication of *The Federalist Papers* begins.
- **December.** Delaware is the first state to ratify Constitution.

1788
- New Hampshire and Virginia ratify Constitution, with New Hampshire providing the ninth and decisive vote.
- **July.** New York ratifies Constitution.

1789
- **November.** North Carolina ratifies Constitution.

1790
- **May.** Rhode Island ratifies Constitution.

proposition. Georgia sought the protection that a stronger national government would afford against hostile Indians and Spanish Florida to the south.

Another three easy victories came in Connecticut, Maryland, and South Carolina. As in Pennsylvania, merchants, lawyers, and urban artisans in general favored the new Constitution, as did large landowners and slaveholders. This tendency for the established political elite to be Federalist enhanced the prospects of victory. Antifederalists in these states tended to be rural, western, and noncommercial, men whose access to news was limited and whose participation in state government was tenuous.

Massachusetts was the only early state that gave the Federalists difficulty. The vote to select the ratification delegates decidedly favored the Antifederalists, whose strength lay in the western areas of the state, home to Shays's Rebellion. One rural delegate from Worcester County voiced widely shared suspicions: "These lawyers and men of learning and money men that talk so finely, and gloss over matters so smoothly, to make us poor illiterate people swallow down the pill, expect to get into Congress themselves; they expect to be the managers of the Constitution and get all the power and all the money into their own hands, and then they will swallow up all us little folks." Nevertheless, the Antifederalists' lead was slowly eroded by a vigorous newspaper campaign. In the end, the Federalists won by a very slim margin and only with promises that amendments to the Constitution would be taken up in the first Congress.

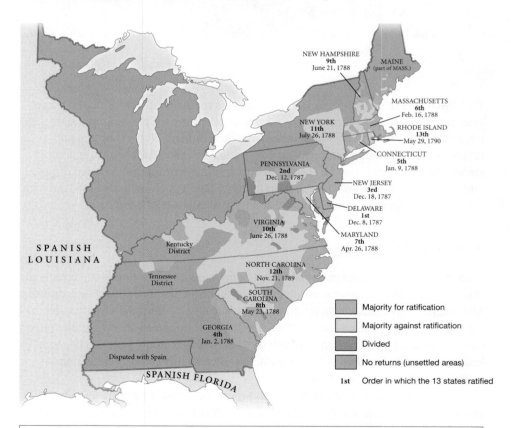

MAP 8.3 ■ **Ratification of the Constitution, 1788–1790**
Populated areas cast votes for delegates to state ratification conventions. This map shows Antifederalist strength generally concentrated in backcountry, noncoastal, and non-urban areas, but with significant exceptions (for example, Rhode Island).

▶ FOR MORE HELP ANALYZING THIS MAP, see the map activity for this chapter in the Online Study Guide at bedfordstmartins.com/roarkunderstanding.

CHAPTER LOCATOR | What kind of government did the Articles of Confederation create?

By May 1788, eight states had ratified; only one more was needed. North Carolina and Rhode Island were hopeless for the Federalist cause, and New Hampshire seemed nearly as bleak. More worrisome was the failure to win over the largest and most important states, Virginia and New York.

The Antifederalists

The Antifederalists were a composite group, united mainly in their desire to block the Constitution. Although much of their strength came from backcountry areas long suspicious of eastern elites, many Antifederalist leaders came from the same social background as Federalist leaders. The Antifederalists also drew strength in states already on sure economic footing, such as New York, which could afford to remain independent. Probably the biggest appeal of the Antifederalists' position lay in the long-nurtured fear that distant power might infringe on people's liberties.

But by the time eight states had ratified the Constitution, the Antifederalists faced a difficult task. First, they were no longer defending the status quo now that the momentum lay with the Federalists. Second, it was difficult to defend the confederation government with its admitted flaws. Even so, they remained genuinely fearful that the new government would be too distant from the people and could thus become corrupt or tyrannical. "The difficulty, if not impracticability, of exercising the equal and equitable powers of government by a single legislature over an extent of territory that reaches from the Mississippi to the western lakes, and from them to the Atlantic ocean, is an insuperable objection to the adoption of the new system," wrote Mercy Otis Warren, an Antifederalist woman writing under the alias "A Columbia Patriot."

The new government was indeed distant. In the proposed House of Representatives, the only directly democratic element of the Constitution, one member represented some 30,000 people. How could that member really know or communicate with his whole constituency, Antifederalists worried. They also worried that representatives would always be elites and thus "ignorant of the sentiments of the middling and much more of the lower class of citizens, strangers to their ability, unacquainted with their wants, difficulties, and distress," as one Maryland man said.

The Federalists generally agreed that the elite would be favored for national elections. Indeed, they did not envision a government constituted of every class of people. "Fools and knaves have voice enough in government already," argued one Federalist, without being guaranteed representation in proportion to their total population. Alexander Hamilton claimed that mechanics and laborers preferred to have their social betters represent them. Antifederalists disagreed: "In reality, there will be no part of the people represented, but the rich. . . . It will literally be a government in the hands of the few to oppress and plunder the many."

Antifederalists fretted over many specific features of the Constitution. The most widespread objection, however, was the Constitution's glaring omission of any guarantees of individual liberties in a bill of rights like those contained in many state constitutions.

Despite Federalist campaigns in the large states, it was a small state—New Hampshire—that provided the decisive ninth vote for ratification on June 21, 1788. Federalists there succeeded in getting the convention postponed from February to June and conducted an intense and successful lobbying effort on specific delegates in the interim.

How did the states define freedom and citizenship? | Why did the Articles of Confederation fail? | How did the U.S. Constitution increase federal power? | **What were the obstacles to ratification of the Constitution?** | Conclusion: What was the "republican remedy"?

219

The Big Holdouts: Virginia and New York

Four states still remained outside the new union, and a glance at a map demonstrated the necessity of pressing the Federalist case in the two largest, Virginia and New York (see Map 8.3, page 218). In Virginia, an influential Antifederalist group led by Patrick Henry and George Mason made the outcome uncertain. The Federalists finally won ratification by proposing twenty specific amendments that the new government would promise to consider.

New York voters tilted toward the Antifederalists out of a sense that a state so large and powerful need not relinquish so much authority to the new federal government. But New York was also home to some of the most persuasive Federalists. Starting in October 1787, Alexander Hamilton collaborated with James Madison and New York lawyer John Jay on a series of eighty-five essays on the political philosophy of the new Constitution published in New York newspapers and later republished as *The Federalist Papers*. The essays set out the failures of the Articles of Confederation and offered an analysis of the complex nature of the Federalist position. In one of the most compelling essays, number 10, Madison challenged the Antifederalists' conviction that republican government had to be small-scale. Madison argued that a large and diverse population was itself a guarantee of liberty. In a national government, no single faction could ever be large enough to subvert the freedom of other groups. "Extend the sphere, and you take in a greater variety of parties and interests; you make it less probable that a majority of the whole will have a common motive to invade the rights of other citizens," Madison asserted. He called it "a republican remedy for the diseases most incident to republican government."

At New York's ratifying convention, Antifederalists predominated, but impassioned debate and lobbying—plus the dramatic news of Virginia's ratification—finally tipped the balance to the Federalists. New York's ratification ensured the legitimacy of the new government. It took another year and a half for Antifederalists in North Carolina to come around. Rhode Island held out until May 1790, and even then it ratified by only a two-vote margin.

In less than twelve months, the U.S. Constitution was both written and ratified. The Federalists had faced a formidable task, but by building momentum and assuring consideration of a bill of rights, they carried the day.

> **QUICK REVIEW**

Why did Antifederalists oppose the Constitution?

CHAPTER LOCATOR | What kind of government did the Articles of Confederation create?

CHAPTER 8
220 BUILDING A REPUBLIC, 1775–1789

The Granger Collection, New York.

Conclusion: What was the "republican remedy"?

THE PERIOD DISCUSSED in this chapter began in 1775 with a confederation government that could barely be ratified because of its requirement of unanimity, but there was no reaching unanimity on the western lands, an impost, or the proper way to respond to unfair taxation in a republican state. The new Constitution offered a different approach to these problems by loosening the grip of impossible unanimity and by embracing the ideas of a heterogeneous public life and a carefully balanced government that together would prevent any one part of the public from tyrannizing another. The genius of James Madison was to anticipate that diversity of opinion was not only an unavoidable reality but also a hidden strength of the new society beginning to take shape. This is what he meant in *Federalist* essay number 10 when he spoke of the "republican remedy" for the troubles most likely to befall a government in which the people are the source of authority.

Despite Madison's optimism, political differences remained keen and worrisome to many. The Federalists still hoped for a society in which leaders of exceptional wisdom would discern the best path for public policy. They looked backward to a society of hierarchy, rank, and benevolent rule by an aristocracy of talent, but they created a government with forward-looking checks and balances as a guard against corruption, which they figured would most likely emanate from the people. The Antifederalists also looked backward, but to an old order of small-scale direct democracy and local control, in which virtuous people kept a close eye on potentially corruptible rulers. The Antifederalists feared a national government led by distant, self-interested leaders who needed to be held in check. In the 1790s, these two conceptions of republicanism and of leadership would be tested in real life.

SO NOW YOU KNOW

In the aftermath of the American Revolution, the new United States faced mounting conflicts over western settlement and taxation, questions that the government under the Articles of Confederation could not resolve. The result was the constitutional convention, which hammered out the Constitution of the United States. This document shaped a new federal government that was both more balanced and more powerful.

| How did the states define freedom and citizenship? | Why did the Articles of Confederation fail? | How did the U.S. Constitution increase federal power? | What were the obstacles to ratification of the Constitution? | **Conclusion: What was the "republican remedy"?** |

Online Study Guide
bedfordstmartins.com/roarkunderstanding

STEP

1

GETTING
STARTED

Below are basic terms from this period in American history. Can you identify each term below and explain why it matters? To do this exercise online or to download this chart, visit bedfordstmartins.com/roarkunderstanding.

TERM	WHO OR WHAT & WHEN	WHY IT MATTERS
Articles of Confederation, p. 198		
bills of rights, p. 202		
Treaty of Fort Stanwix, p. 208		
Northwest Ordinance, p. 210		
Shays's Rebellion, p. 212		
constitutional convention, p. 213		
Virginia Plan, p. 214		
New Jersey Plan, p. 214		
three-fifths clause, p. 215		
Federalists, p. 217		
Antifederalists, p. 217		

STEP

2

MOVING
BEYOND
THE
BASICS

The exercise below represents a more advanced understanding of the chapter material. Compare the government established by the Articles of Confederation with the government established by the U.S. Constitution. Fill in the chart below with the powers and responsibilities of Congress, the executive branch, the judiciary, and the states under the Articles of Confederation and under the Constitution. What were the important differences between the two documents? What weaknesses in the Articles were corrected? What groups were most in favor of creating a stronger central government and why? To do this exercise online or to download this chart, visit bedfordstmartins.com/roarkunderstanding.

	Powers and responsibilities under Articles of Confederation	Powers and responsibilities under U.S. Constitution
Congress		
Executive branch		
Federal judiciary		
States		

Now that you have reviewed key elements of the chapter, take a step back and try to explain the big picture by answering these questions. Remember to use specific examples from the chapter in your answers. To do this exercise online, visit bedfordstmartins.com/roarkunderstanding.

THE ARTICLES OF CONFEDERATION

▶ How did the confederation government deal with the problem of western lands?

▶ What do the state constitutions drawn up during the confederation period tell us about the range of political opinion during the Revolutionary War and the years immediately following?

THE CREATION OF A NEW CONSTITUTION

▶ What forces and events combined to produce momentum for the creation of a new constitution?

▶ What political compromises were embodied in the Constitution?

LOOKING BACKWARD, LOOKING AHEAD

▶ How did pre-revolutionary experiences with colonial legislatures and the British government shape the Articles of Confederation? The United States Constitution?

▶ What issues were left unresolved by the framers of the Constitution? Why?

THE FIGHT FOR RATIFICATION

▶ Where was support for the Constitution strongest? Where was it weakest? Why?

▶ Why did the Federalists ultimately prevail over the Antifederalists? What were the Federalists' most important weapons in the debate over the Constitution?

IN YOUR OWN WORDS

Imagine that you must explain chapter 8 to someone who hasn't read it. What would be the most important points to include and why?

Peter Lacour delin.   A. Doolittle Sculp.

FEDERAL HALL
The Seat of Congress

Printed & Sold by A. Doolittle New-Haven 1790

9
FORMING THE NEW NATION

1789–1800

> This chapter explores the early attempts to translate the rules and guidelines established by the Constitution into a functioning government and political system. It examines the efforts to achieve political stability in the wake of the ratification of the Constitution, Alexander Hamilton's plans to bring economic stability to the federal government, and the external threats and internal rivalries that led to the emergence of party politics.

> What were the sources of political stability in Federalist America?

> What was Hamilton's plan to solidify the government's fiscal position?

> What external threats did the United States face in the 1790s?

> How did partisan rivalries shape the politics of the late 1790s?

> Conclusion: Why did the new nation ultimately form political parties?

DID YOU KNOW?

George Washington proposed that he, and future presidents, should be addressed as "His High Mightiness."

George Washington takes the oath of office. Federal Hall, Philadelphia, April 30, 1789.

What were the sources of political stability in Federalist America?

▶ FOR MORE HELP ANALYZING THIS IMAGE, see the visual activity for this chapter in the Online Study Guide at bedfordstmartins.com/roarkunderstanding.

AFTER THE STRUGGLES of the 1780s, the most urgent task in establishing the new government was to secure stability. Leaders sought ways to heal old divisions, and the first presidential election offered the means to do that in the person of George Washington, who enjoyed widespread veneration. People trusted him to exercise the untested and perhaps elastic powers of the presidency.

Congress had important work as well in initiating the new government. Congress quickly agreed on the Bill of Rights, which answered the concerns of many Antifederalists. Beyond politics, cultural change in the area of gender also enhanced political stability. The private virtue of women was mobilized to bolster the public virtue of male citizens; republicanism was forcing a rethinking of women's relation to the state.

Washington Inaugurates the Government

George Washington was elected president in February 1789 by a unanimous vote of the electoral college. Washington perfectly embodied the republican ideal of disinterested, public-spirited leadership. Indeed, he cultivated that image through astute ceremonies such as the dramatic surrender of his sword to the Continental Congress at the end of the war, symbolizing the subservience of military power to the law.

CHAPTER LOCATOR | What were the sources of political stability in Federalist America?

226 CHAPTER 9
FORMING THE NEW NATION, 1789–1800

Once in office, Washington calculated his moves, knowing that every step set a precedent and that any misstep could be dangerous for the fragile government. Congress debated a title for Washington, such as "His Highness, the President of the United States of America and Protector of Their Liberties" and "His Majesty, the President"; Washington favored "His High Mightiness." But in the end, republican simplicity prevailed. The final title was simply "President of the United States of America," and the established form of address became "Mr. President."

Washington's genius in establishing the presidency lay in his capacity for implanting his own reputation for integrity into the office itself. In the political language of the day, he was "virtuous," meaning that he took pains to elevate the public good over private interest and projected honesty and honor over ambition. At all times, he remained aloof, resolute, and dignified. He encouraged pomp and ceremony to create respect for the office, traveling with six horses to pull his coach, hosting formal balls, and surrounding himself with uniformed servants. He even held weekly "levees," as European monarchs did, hour-long audiences granted to distinguished visitors (including women), at which Washington appeared attired in black velvet, with a feathered hat and a polished sword. The president and his guests bowed, avoiding the egalitarian familiarity of a handshake. But he always managed, perhaps just barely, to avoid the extreme of royal splendor.

Washington chose talented and experienced men to preside over the newly created Departments of War, Treasury, and State.

Washington's cabinet

Secretary of state	Thomas Jefferson
Secretary of the treasury	Alexander Hamilton
Secretary of war	Henry Knox
Attorney general	Edmund Randolph
Chief justice of the Supreme Court	John Jay

Soon Washington began to hold regular meetings with these men, thereby establishing the precedent of a presidential cabinet. No one anticipated that two decades of party turbulence would emerge from the brilliant but explosive mix of Washington's first cabinet.

The Bill of Rights

An important piece of business for the First Congress, meeting in 1789, was the passage of the **Bill of Rights**. Seven states had ratified the Constitution on the condition that guarantees of individual liberties and limitations to federal power be swiftly incorporated. The Federalists of 1787 had thought an enumeration of rights unnecessary, but in 1789 Congressman James Madison understood that healing the divisions of the 1780s was of prime importance. "It will be a desirable thing to extinguish from the bosom of every member of the community, any apprehensions that there are those among his countrymen who wish to deprive them of the liberty for which they valiantly fought and honorably bled."

CHRONOLOGY

1789
– George Washington is inaugurated first president.
– First Congress meets.

1790
– Judith Sargent Murray publishes "On the Equality of the Sexes."

1791
– States ratify the Bill of Rights.

Bill of Rights
▶ The first ten amendments to the Constitution, ratified between 1789 and 1791. The First through Eighth Amendments dealt with individual liberties, and the Ninth and Tenth concerned the boundary between federal and state authority. Passage of the Bill of Rights was critical to healing the political divisions of the 1780s.

What was Hamilton's plan to solidify the government's fiscal position?

What external threats did the United States face in the 1790s?

How did partisan rivalries shape the politics of the late 1790s?

Conclusion: Why did the new nation ultimately form political parties?

Drawing on existing state constitutions with bills of rights, Madison enumerated guarantees of freedom of speech, press, and religion; the right to petition and assemble; and the right to be free from unwarranted searches and seizures. One amendment asserted the right to keep and bear arms in support of a "well-regulated militia," to which Madison added, "but no person religiously scrupulous of bearing arms, shall be compelled to render military service in person." That provision for what a later century would call "conscientious objector" status failed to gain acceptance in Congress.

In September 1789, Congress approved a set of twelve amendments and sent them to the states for approval; by 1791, ten were eventually ratified. The First through Eighth Amendments dealt with individual liberties, and the Ninth and Tenth concerned the boundary between federal and state authority.

Still, not everyone was entirely satisfied. State ratifying conventions had submitted some eighty proposed amendments. Congress never considered proposals to change structural features of the new government, and Madison had no intention of reopening debates about the length of the president's term or the power to levy excise taxes.

Significantly, no one complained about one striking omission in the Bill of Rights: the right to vote. Only much later was voting seen as a fundamental liberty requiring protection by constitutional amendment—indeed, by four amendments. The Constitution deliberately left the definition of voters to the states because of the existing wide variation in local voting practices. Most of these practices were based on property qualifications, but some touched on religion and, in one unusual case (New Jersey), on sex and race (see chapter 8).

The Republican Wife and Mother

The exclusion of women from political activity did not mean they had no civic role or responsibility. A flood of periodical articles in the 1790s by both male and female writers reevaluated courtship, marriage, and motherhood in light of republican ideals. Tyrannical power in the ruler, whether king or husband, was declared a thing of the past. Affection, not duty, bound wives to their husbands and citizens to their government. In republican marriages, the writers claimed, women had the capacity to reform the morals and manners of men. One male author promised women that "the solidity and stability of the liberties of your country rest with you; since Liberty is never sure, 'till Virtue reigns triumphant. . . . While you thus keep our country virtuous, you maintain its independence."

Until the 1790s, public virtue was strictly a masculine quality. But another sort of virtue enlarged in importance: sexual chastity, a private asset prized as a feminine quality. Essayists of the 1790s explicitly advised young women to use sexual virtue to increase public virtue in men. "Love and courtship . . . invest a lady with more authority than in any other situation that falls to the lot of human beings," one male essayist proclaimed. If women spurned selfish suitors, they could promote good morals more than any social institution could, essayists promised.

Republican ideals also cast motherhood in a new light. Throughout the 1790s, advocates for female education, still a controversial proposition, argued that education would produce better mothers, who in turn would produce better citizens, a concept historians call republican motherhood. Benjamin Rush, a Pennsylvania physician and educator, called for female education because "our

CHAPTER LOCATOR | What were the sources of political stability in Federalist America?

CHAPTER 9
228 FORMING THE NEW NATION, 1789–1800

ladies should be qualified . . . in instructing their sons in the principles of liberty and government." A series of essays by Judith Sargent Murray of Massachusetts favored education that would remake women into self-confident, rational beings. Her first essay, published in 1790, was boldly titled "On the Equality of the Sexes." In a subsequent essay on education, she reassured readers that educated women "will not be assuming; the characteristic trait [sweetness] will still remain." Even Murray had to justify female education in the context of family duty.

Although women's obligations as wives and mothers were now infused with political meaning, traditional gender relations remained unaltered. The analogy between marriage and civil society worked precisely because of the self-subordination inherent in the term *virtue*. Men should put the public good first, before selfish desires, just as women must put their husbands and families first, before themselves. Women might gain literacy and knowledge, but only in the service of improved domestic duty. In Federalist America, wives and citizens alike should feel affection for and trust in their rulers; neither should ever rebel.

QUICK REVIEW

How did political leaders in the 1790s attempt to overcome the divisions of the 1780s?

What was Hamilton's plan to solidify the government's fiscal position?	What external threats did the United States face in the 1790s?	How did partisan rivalries shape the politics of the late 1790s?	Conclusion: Why did the new nation ultimately form political parties?

> What was Hamilton's plan to solidify the government's fiscal position?

Alexander Hamilton, by John Trumbull

Hamilton was confident, handsome, audacious, brilliant, and very hardworking. Ever slender, in marked contrast to the more corpulent leaders of his day, he posed for this portrait in 1792, at the age of thirty-seven and at the height of his power. Yale University Art Gallery.

Alexander Hamilton

▶ Secretary of the Treasury during the presidency of George Washington. Starting in 1790, Hamilton embarked on an innovative and controversial plan to solidify the government's economic base. His proposals for the creation of a national bank, dealing with the national debt, and the promotion of domestic manufacturing all met with considerable opposition and contributed to the rise of partisan politics in the 1790s.

COMPARED TO THE severe financial instability of the 1780s, the 1790s brimmed with opportunity, as seen in increased agricultural trade and improvements in transportation and banking. In 1790, the federal government moved from New York City to Philadelphia, a more central location with a substantial mercantile class. There, Secretary of the Treasury **Alexander Hamilton** embarked on his innovative and controversial plan to solidify the government's economic base.

Agriculture, Transportation, and Banking

Dramatic increases in international grain prices motivated American farmers to boost agricultural production for the export trade. Europe's rising population needed grain, and the French Revolutionary and Napoleonic Wars, which engulfed Europe for a dozen years after 1793, severely compromised production there. From the Connecticut River valley to the Chesapeake, farmers planted more wheat, generating new jobs for millers, coopers, dockworkers, and ship and wagon builders.

Cotton production also underwent a boom, spurred by market demand and a mechanical invention. Limited amounts of smooth-seed cotton had long been grown in the coastal areas of the South, but this variety of cotton did not prosper in the drier inland regions. Greenseed cotton grew well inland, but its rough seeds stuck to the cotton fibers and were labor-intensive to remove. In 1793, Yale graduate Eli Whitney devised a machine called a gin that easily separated out the seeds; cotton production soared.

A surge of road building also stimulated the economy. Before 1790, one road connected Maine to Georgia, but with the establishment of the U.S. Post Office in 1792,

CHAPTER LOCATOR | What were the sources of political stability in Federalist America?

230 CHAPTER 9
FORMING THE NEW NATION, 1789–1800

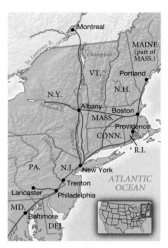

Major Roads in the 1790s

road mileage sextupled to facilitate the transport of mail. Private companies also built toll roads, the first of which was the Lancaster Turnpike of 1794, connecting Philadelphia with Lancaster, Pennsylvania. Another turnpike linked Boston with Albany, New York. Farther inland, a major road extended southwest down the Shenandoah Valley, while another joined Richmond, Virginia, with the Tennessee towns of Knoxville and Nashville.

By 1800, a dense network of dirt, gravel, and plank roadways connected towns in southern New England and the Middle Atlantic states, spurring commercial stage companies to regularize and speed up passenger traffic. A trip from New York to Boston took four days; from New York to Philadelphia, less than two (**Map 9.1**). In 1790, Boston had only three stagecoach companies; by 1800, there were twenty-four.

A third development signaling economic resurgence was the growth of commercial banking. During the 1790s, the number of banks nationwide multiplied tenfold, from three to twenty-nine in 1800. Banks drew in money chiefly through the

CHRONOLOGY

1790
– Hamilton issues his *Report on Public Credit*.
– Congress approves Hamilton's debt plan.

1791
– Congress and president charter Bank of the United States.
– Hamilton issues his *Report on Manufactures*.
– Congress passes whiskey tax.

1792
– U.S. Post Office is established.

1793
– War breaks out between France and Britain.
– Eli Whitney patents the cotton gin.

1794
– Whiskey Rebellion.

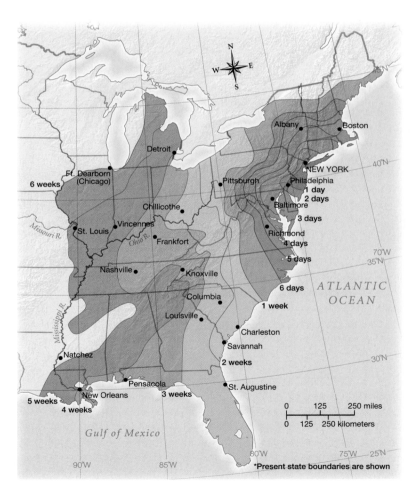

MAP 9.1 ■ Travel Times from New York City in 1800
Notice that travel out of New York extends over a much greater distance in the first week than in subsequent weeks. In one week, a traveler could get to Pittsburgh, but it would take another four weeks to go a comparable distance west of that city. River corridors in the West and East speeded up travel—but only if one were going downriver. Also notice that travel by sea (north and south along the coast) was much faster than land travel.

What was Hamilton's plan to solidify the government's fiscal position?	What external threats did the United States face in the 1790s?	How did partisan rivalries shape the politics of the late 1790s?	Conclusion: Why did the new nation ultimately form political parties?

sale of stock. They then made loans in the form of banknotes, paper currency backed by the gold and silver that stockholders paid in. Because banks issued two or three times as much money in banknotes as they held in hard money, they were creating new money for the economy.

The U.S. population expanded along with economic development, propelled by large average family size and better than adequate food and land resources. As measured by the first two federal censuses in 1790 and 1800, the population grew from 3.9 million to 5.3 million, an increase of 35 percent.

The Public Debt and Taxes

The upturn in the economy, plus the new taxation powers of the government, suggested that the government might soon repay its wartime debt, amounting to more than $52 million owed to foreign and domestic creditors. But Hamilton had a different plan. He issued a *Report on Public Credit* in January 1790, recommending that the debt be funded—but not repaid immediately—at full value. This meant that old certificates of debt would be rolled over into new bonds, which would earn interest until they were retired several years later. There would still be a public debt, but it would be secure, giving its holders a direct financial stake in the

Report on Public Credit

▶ Alexander Hamilton's January 1790 report recommending that the national debt be funded— but not repaid immediately—at full value. Hamilton's goal was to make the new country creditworthy, not debt-free. Critics of his plan complained that it would benefit speculators, and not the country, and that it would lead to higher taxes.

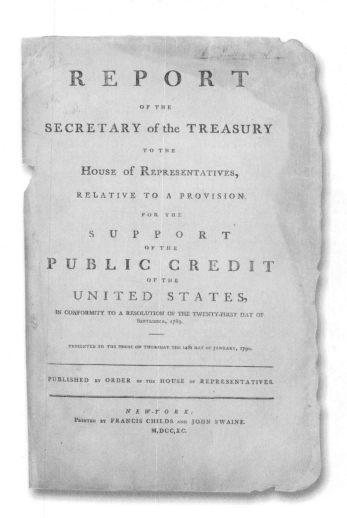

REPORT

OF THE

SECRETARY of the TREASURY

TO THE

House of REPRESENTATIVES,

RELATIVE TO A PROVISION

FOR THE

SUPPORT

OF THE

PUBLIC CREDIT

OF THE

UNITED STATES,

IN CONFORMITY TO A RESOLUTION OF THE TWENTY-FIRST DAY OF
SEPTEMBER, 1789.

PRESENTED TO THE HOUSE ON THURSDAY THE 14th DAY OF JANUARY, 1790.

PUBLISHED BY ORDER OF THE HOUSE OF REPRESENTATIVES.

NEW-YORK:
PRINTED BY FRANCIS CHILDS AND JOHN SWAINE.
M,DCC,XC.

Hamilton's *Report on Public Credit*

Hamilton wrote this report in just over three months, in response to a resolution by Congress. He proposed funding the debt, rolling it over into a new debt instead of paying it off. The Gilder Lehrman Collection, Pierpont Morgan Library.

new government. The bonds would circulate, injecting millions of dollars of new money into the economy. "A national debt if not excessive will be to us a national blessing; it will be a powerfull cement of our union," Hamilton wrote to a financier. Hamilton's goal was to make the new country creditworthy, not debt-free.

Funding the debt in full was controversial because speculators had already bought up debt certificates cheaply, and Hamilton's report touched off further speculation. Philadelphia and New York speculators sent agents into backcountry regions looking for certificates of debt whose unwary owners were ignorant about the proposed face-value funding.

Hamilton compounded controversy with his proposal to add to the federal debt another $25 million that some state governments still owed to individuals. During the war, states had obtained supplies by issuing IOUs to farmers, merchants, and moneylenders. Some states, such as Virginia and New York, had paid off these debts entirely. Others, such as Massachusetts, had partially paid them off through heavy taxation of the people. About half the states had made little headway. Hamilton called for the federal government to assume these state debts and combine them with the federal debt, in effect consolidating federal power over the states.

Congressman James Madison strenuously objected to putting windfall profits in the pockets of speculators. He instead proposed a complex scheme to pay both the original holders of the federal debt and the speculators, each at fair fractions of the face value. He also strongly objected to assumption of all the states' debts. A large debt was dangerous, Madison warned, especially because it would lead to high taxation. Secretary of State Jefferson also was fearful of Hamilton's proposals. "No man is more ardently intent to see the public debt soon and sacredly paid off than I am. This exactly marks the difference between Colonel Hamilton's views and mine, that I would wish the debt paid tomorrow; he wishes it never to be paid, but always to be a thing where with to corrupt and manage the legislature." A solution to this impasse arrived when Jefferson invited Hamilton and Madison to dinner. Hamilton secured the reluctant Madison's promise to restrain his opposition. In return, Hamilton pledged to back efforts to locate the nation's new capital city in the South, along the Potomac River, an outcome that was sure to please Virginians. In early July 1790, Congress voted for the Potomac site, and in late July, Congress passed Hamilton's debt proposal without significant modification.

The First Bank of the United States and the *Report on Manufactures*

The second and third major elements of Hamilton's economic plan were his proposal to create a national Bank of the United States and his program to encourage domestic manufacturing. Arguing that banks were the "nurseries of national wealth," Hamilton modeled his bank plan on European central banks, such as the Bank of England, a private corporation that used its government's money to invigorate the British economy. According to Hamilton's plan, the central bank was to be capitalized at $10 million, a sum larger than all the hard money in the entire nation. The federal government would hold 20 percent of the bank's stock, making the bank in effect the government's fiscal agent, holding its revenues derived from import duties, land sales, and various other taxes. The other 80 percent of the bank's capital would come from private investors, who could buy stock in the bank with either

| What was Hamilton's plan to solidify the government's fiscal position? | What external threats did the United States face in the 1790s? | How did partisan rivalries shape the politics of the late 1790s? | Conclusion: Why did the new nation ultimately form political parties? |

233

hard money (silver or gold) or federal securities. Because of its size and the privilege of being the only national bank, the central bank would help stabilize the economy by exerting control over credit, interest rates, and the value of the currency.

Concerned that a few rich bankers might have undue influence over the economy, Madison tried but failed to stop the plan in Congress. Jefferson advised President Washington that the Constitution did not permit Congress to charter banks. Hamilton, however, pointed out that the Constitution gave Congress specific powers to regulate commerce and a broad right "to make all laws which shall be necessary and proper for carrying into execution the foregoing powers." Washington sided with Hamilton and signed the Bank of the United States into law in February 1791, with a charter allowing it to operate for twenty years.

When the bank's privately held stock went on sale in Philadelphia, Boston, and New York City in July, it sold out in a few hours, touching off a period of speculation in resale that lasted a month and drew in many hundreds of urban merchants and artisans. A discouraged Madison reported that in New York, "the Coffee House is an eternal buzz with the gamblers," some of them self-interested congressmen intent on "public plunder." Stock prices shot upward but then crashed in mid-August. Hamilton shrewdly managed to cushion the crash to an extent, but Jefferson worried about the risk to morality inherent in gambling in stocks: "The spirit of gaming, once it has seized a subject, is incurable. The tailor who has made thousands in one day, tho' he has lost them the next, can never again be content with the slow and moderate earnings of his needle."

The third component of Hamilton's plan was issued in December 1791 in the *Report on Manufactures*, a proposal to encourage the production of American-made goods. Domestic manufacturing was in its infancy, and Hamilton aimed to mobilize the new powers of the federal government to grant subsidies to manufacturers and to impose moderate tariffs on those same products from overseas. Hamilton's plan targeted manufacturing of iron goods, arms and ammunition, coal, textiles, wood products, and glass. Among the blessings of manufacturing, he counted the new employment opportunities that would open to children and unmarried young women, who he assumed were underutilized in agricultural societies. The *Report on Manufactures*, however, was never approved by Congress. Many confirmed agriculturalists in Congress feared that manufacturing was a curse rather than a blessing. Madison and Jefferson in particular were alarmed by stretching the "general welfare" clause of the Constitution to include public subsidies to private businesses.

The Whiskey Rebellion

Hamilton's plan to restore public credit required new taxation to pay the interest on the large national debt. In deference to the merchant class, Hamilton did not propose a general increase in import duties, nor did he propose land taxes, which would have fallen hardest on the nation's wealthiest landowners. Instead, he convinced Congress in 1791 to pass a 25 percent excise tax on whiskey, to be paid by farmers when they brought their grain to the distillery, then passed on to individual whiskey consumers in the form of higher prices.

Not surprisingly, the new excise tax proved unpopular with grain farmers in the western regions and whiskey drinkers everywhere. In 1791, farmers in Kentucky and the western parts of Pennsylvania, Virginia, Maryland, and the

CHAPTER LOCATOR | What were the sources of political stability in Federalist America?

CHAPTER 9
234   FORMING THE NEW NATION, 1789–1800

Carolinas forcefully conveyed to Congress their resentment of Hamilton's tax. One farmer complained that he already paid half his grain to the local distillery for distilling his rye, and now the distiller was taking the new whiskey tax out of the farmer's remaining half. This "reduces the balance to less than one-third of the original quantity. If this is not an oppressive tax, I am at a loss to describe what is so," the farmer wrote. Congress responded with modest modifications to the tax in 1792, but even so, discontent was rampant. Simple evasion of the law was the most common response. In some places, crowds threatened to tar and feather federal tax collectors, and distilleries underreported their production. Four counties in Pennsylvania established committees of correspondence and held assemblies to carry their message to Congress. Hamilton admitted to Congress that the revenue was far less than anticipated. But rather than abandon the law, he tightened up the prosecution of tax evaders.

In western Pennsylvania, Hamilton had one ally, a stubborn tax collector named John Neville, who refused to quit even after a group of spirited farmers burned him in effigy. In May 1794, Neville filed charges against seventy-five farmers and distillers for tax evasion. His action touched off the **Whiskey Rebellion**. In July, he and a federal marshal were ambushed in Allegheny County by a group of forty men. Neville's house was then burned to the ground by a crowd estimated at five hundred, and one man in the crowd was killed. At the end of July, seven thousand Pennsylvania farmers planned a march—or perhaps an attack, some thought—on Pittsburgh to protest the hated tax.

In response, President Washington nationalized the Pennsylvania militia and set out, with Hamilton at his side, at the head of thirteen thousand soldiers. A worried Philadelphia newspaper criticized the show of force: "Shall Pennsylvania be converted into a human slaughter house because the dignity of the United States will not admit of conciliatory measures? Shall torrents of blood be spilled to support an odious excise system?" But in the end, no blood was spilled. By the time the army arrived in late September, the demonstrators had dispersed. Twenty men were rounded up as rebels and charged with high treason, but only two were convicted, and both were soon pardoned by Washington.

Had the federal government overreacted? Thomas Jefferson thought so; he saw the event as a replay of Shays's Rebellion of 1786, when a protest against government taxation had been met with unreasonable government force (see chapter 8). The rebel farmers agreed; they felt entitled to protest oppressive taxation. Hamilton and Washington, however, thought that laws passed by a republican government must be obeyed. The Whiskey Rebellion presented an opportunity for the new federal government to flex its muscles and stand up to civil disorder.

Whiskey Rebellion

▶ July 1794 uprising by farmers and distillers in western Pennsylvania in response to efforts to enforce an unpopular excise tax on whiskey. When angry farmers gathered to march on Pittsburgh to protest the tax, George Washington led an army of thirteen thousand soldiers to Pennsylvania to suppress the rebellion. Some thought that Washington overreacted, but Washington defended his actions as necessary to preserve the rule of law. No battle was fought; the dissidents dispersed.

QUICK REVIEW <

Why were Hamilton's economic policies controversial?

| What was Hamilton's plan to solidify the government's fiscal position? | What external threats did the United States face in the 1790s? | How did partisan rivalries shape the politics of the late 1790s? | Conclusion: Why did the new nation ultimately form political parties? |

What external threats did the United States face in the 1790s?

This painting by an unknown artist of the 1790s purports to depict the signing of the Treaty of Greenville in 1795. The treaty was signed by General Anthony Wayne, Chief Little Turtle of the Miami tribe, and Chief Tarhe the Crane of the Wyandot tribe. One Indian of the three pictured seems to be gesturing with emphasis, as if to dictate terms to the Americans, but in fact the treaty was most favorable to the United States. Chicago Historical Society.

WHILE THE WHISKEY REBELS challenged federal leadership from within the country, disorder threatened the United States from external sources as well. From 1790 onward, serious trouble brewed in three directions. To the west, a powerful confederation of Indian tribes in the Ohio Country resisted white encroachment, resulting in a brutal war. At the same time, conflicts between the major European powers forced Americans to take sides and nearly pulled the country into another war. And to the south, a Caribbean slave rebellion raised fears that racial war would be imported to the United States.

To the West: The Indians

In the 1783 Treaty of Paris, Britain had yielded all land east of the Mississippi River to the United States without regard to the resident Indian population. The 1784 Treaty of Fort Stanwix (see chapter 8) had attempted to solve that omission by establishing terms between the new confederation government and native peoples, but the key tribes of the Ohio Valley—the Shawnee, Delaware, and Miami—had not been involved in those negotiations. To confuse matters further, British troops still occupied half a dozen forts in the northwest, protecting an

CHAPTER LOCATOR | What were the sources of political stability in Federalist America?

ongoing fur trade between British traders and Indians and thereby sustaining Indians' claims to that land.

The doubling of the American population from two million in 1770 to nearly four million in 1790 greatly intensified the pressure for western land. Several thousand settlers a year moved down the Ohio River in the mid-1780s. Most headed for Kentucky on the south bank of the river, but some looked north to Indian country. By the late 1780s, government land sales in eastern Ohio had commenced, although actual settlement lagged.

Meanwhile, the U.S. Army entered the western half of Ohio, where white settlers did not dare to go. Fort Washington, built on the Ohio River in 1789 at the site of present-day Cincinnati, became the command post for three major invasions of Indian country (**Map 9.2**). General Josiah Harmar, under orders to subdue the Indians of western Ohio, marched with 1,400 men into Ohio's northwest region in the fall of 1790, burning Indian villages. His inexperienced troops were ambushed by Miami and Shawnee Indians led by their chiefs, Little Turtle and Blue Jacket. Harmar lost one-eighth of his soldiers.

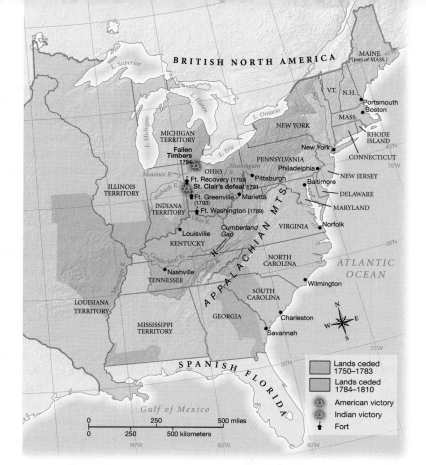

MAP 9.2 ■ Western Expansion and Indian Land Cessions to 1810
By the first decade of the nineteenth century, intense Indian wars had resulted in significant cessions of land to the U.S. government by treaty.

▶ FOR MORE HELP ANALYZING THIS MAP, see the map activity for this chapter in the Online Study Guide at bedfordstmartins.com/roarkunderstanding.

Harmar's defeat spurred efforts to clear Ohio for permanent American settlement. General Arthur St. Clair, the military governor of the Northwest Territory, had pursued peaceful tactics in the 1780s, signing treaties with Indians for land in eastern Ohio. In the fall of 1791, in the wake of Harmar's bungled operation, St. Clair led two thousand men north from Fort Washington to claim Ohio territory from the Miami and Shawnee tribes. Along the route, St. Clair's men quickly built two forts, named for Hamilton and Jefferson. However, when the Indians attacked at daybreak on November 4 at the headwaters of the Wabash River, St. Clair's army was not protected by fortifications.

Before noon, 55 percent of the Americans were dead or wounded. "The savages seemed not to fear anything we could do," wrote an officer afterward. "The ground was literally covered with the dead." The Indians captured valuable weaponry, scalped and dismembered the dying, and pursued fleeing survivors for miles. With more than nine hundred lives lost, this was the most stunning American loss in the history of the U.S.-Indian wars. Grisly tales of St. Clair's defeat increased the level of terror that Americans brought to their confrontations with the Indians.

Washington doubled the U.S. military presence in Ohio and appointed a new commander, General Anthony Wayne of Pennsylvania. About the Ohio natives, Wayne wrote, "I have always been of the opinion that we never should have a permanent peace with those Indians until they were made to experience our superiority." Throughout 1794, Wayne's army engaged in skirmishes with Shawnee,

| What was Hamilton's plan to solidify the government's fiscal position? | What external threats did the United States face in the 1790s? | How did partisan rivalries shape the politics of the late 1790s? | Conclusion: Why did the new nation ultimately form political parties? |

CHRONOLOGY

1789
- Fort Washington is erected in western Ohio.
- French Revolution begins.

1790
- Shawnee and Miami Indians in Ohio defeat General Josiah Harmar.

1791
- Ohio Indians defeat General Arthur St. Clair.
- Haitian Revolution begins.

1793
- War breaks out between France and Britain.
- Washington issues Neutrality Proclamation.

1794
- Ohio Valley Indians suffer major defeat in battle of Fallen Timbers.

1795
- Treaty of Greenville settles conflict with Ohio Valley Indians.
- Jay Treaty settles conflict with Great Britain.

Treaty of Greenville
▶ 1795 treaty between the United States and various Indian tribes. The United States gave the tribes treaty goods valued at $25,000 and promised additional annual shipments of goods. In exchange, the Indians ceded most of Ohio to the Americans. The treaty brought only temporary peace to the region.

Delaware, and Miami Indians. Chief Little Turtle of the Miami tribe advised negotiation; in his view, Wayne's large army looked overpowering. But Blue Jacket of the Shawnees counseled continued warfare, and his view prevailed. The decisive action came in August 1794 at the battle of Fallen Timbers, near the Maumee River. The confederated Indians—mainly Ottawas, Potawatomis, Shawnees, and Delawares, numbering around eight hundred—ambushed the Americans but were underarmed, and Wayne's troops made effective use of their guns and bayonets. The Indians withdrew and sought refuge at nearby Fort Miami, still held by the British. Their former allies locked the gate and refused protection. The surviving Indians fled to the woods, their ranks decimated.

Fallen Timbers was a major defeat for the Indians. The Americans had destroyed cornfields and villages on the march north, and with winter approaching, the Indians' confidence was sapped. They reentered negotiations in a much less powerful bargaining position. In 1795, about a thousand Indians representing nearly a dozen tribes met with Wayne and other American emissaries to work out the **Treaty of Greenville**. The Americans offered treaty goods (calico shirts, axes, knives, blankets, kettles, mirrors, ribbons, thimbles, and abundant wine and liquor casks) worth $25,000 and promised additional shipments every year. The government's idea was to create a dependency on American goods to keep the Indians friendly. In exchange, the Indians ceded most of Ohio to the Americans; only the northwest part of the territory was reserved solely for the Indians.

The treaty brought temporary peace to the region, but it did not restore a peaceful life to the Indians. The annual allowance from the United States too often came in the form of liquor. "More of us have died since the Treaty of Greenville than we lost by the years of war before, and it is all owing to the introduction of liquor among us," said Chief Little Turtle in 1800. "This liquor that they introduce into our country is more to be feared than the gun and tomahawk."

Across the Atlantic: France and Britain

While Indian battles engaged the American military in the west, another war overseas to the east was also closely watched. Since 1789, revolution had been raging in France. At first, the general American reaction was positive. As monarchy and privilege were overthrown in France, towns throughout America celebrated the victory of the French people with civic feasts and public festivities. Dozens of pro-French political clubs, called democratic or republican societies, sprang up around the country.

Many American women exhibited solidarity with revolutionary France by donning sashes and cockades made with ribbons of red, white, and blue. Pro-French headgear for committed women included an elaborate turban, leading one horrified Federalist newspaper editor to chastise the "fiery frenchified dames" thronging Philadelphia's streets. In Charleston, South Carolina, a pro-French pageant in 1793 united two women as partners, one representing France and the other America. The women repudiated their husbands "on account of ill treatment" and pledged mutual "union and friendship," while a gun salute sealed the pledge. Most likely, this ceremony was not the country's first civil union but instead a richly metaphorical piece of street theater in which the spurned husbands represented Britain.

Anti–French Revolution sentiments also ran deep. Vice President John Adams, who lived in France in the 1780s, trembled to think of radicals in France

CHAPTER LOCATOR | What were the sources of political stability in Federalist America?

CHAPTER 9
238 FORMING THE NEW NATION, 1789–1800

or America. "Too many Frenchmen, after the example of too many Americans, pant for the equality of persons and property," Adams said. "The impracticability of this, God Almighty has decreed, and the advocates for liberty, who attempt it, will surely suffer for it."

Support for the French Revolution remained a matter of personal conviction until 1793, when Britain and France went to war and French versus British loyalty became a critical foreign policy debate. France had helped America substantially during the American Revolution, and the confederation government had signed an alliance in 1778 promising aid if France were ever under attack. Americans optimistic about the eventual outcome of the French Revolution wanted to deliver on that promise. Others, including those shaken by the report of the guillotining of thousands of French people, as well as those with strong commercial ties to Britain, sought ways to stay neutral.

In May 1793, President Washington issued the Neutrality Proclamation, which contained friendly assurances to both sides, in an effort to stay out of European wars. Yet American ships continued to trade between the French West Indies and France. In late 1793 and early 1794, the British expressed their displeasure by capturing more than three hundred of these vessels near the West Indies. Clearly, something had to be done to assert American power.

President Washington sent John Jay, the chief justice of the Supreme Court and a man of strong pro-British sentiments, to England to negotiate commercial relations in the British West Indies and secure compensation for the seizure of American ships. In addition, Jay was supposed to resolve several long-standing problems. Southern planters wanted reimbursement for the slaves liberated by the British army during the war, and western settlers wanted Britain to vacate the frontier forts still occupied because of their proximity to the Indian fur trade.

Jay returned from his diplomatic mission in 1795 with a treaty that no one could love. First, the **Jay Treaty** failed to address the captured cargoes or the lost property in slaves. Second, it granted the British a lenient eighteen months to withdraw from the frontier forts, as well as continued rights in the fur trade. (The provision disheartened the Indians just then negotiating the Treaty of Greenville in Ohio. It was a significant factor in their decision to make peace.) Finally, the treaty called for repayment with interest of the debts that some American planters still owed to British firms dating from the Revolutionary War. In exchange for such generous terms, Jay secured limited trading rights in the West Indies and agreement that some issues—boundary disputes with Canada and the damage and loss claims of shipowners—would be decided later by arbitration commissions.

When newspapers published the terms of the treaty, powerful opposition quickly emerged. In Massachusetts, this graffito appeared on a wall: "Damn John Jay! Damn everyone who won't damn John Jay! Damn everyone who won't stay up all night damning John Jay!" Bonfires in many places burned effigies of Jay and copies of the treaty. Nevertheless, the treaty passed the Senate in 1795 by a vote of 20 to 10. Some representatives in the House, led by Madison, tried to undermine the Senate's approval by insisting on a separate vote on the funding provisions of the treaty, on the grounds that the House controlled all money bills. Finally, in 1796, the House approved funds to implement the various commissions mandated by the treaty, but by only a three-vote margin. The bitter vote in both houses of Congress divided along the same lines as the Hamilton-Jefferson split on economic policy.

French Dress Style: Woman with Cockade

In the early 1790s, some Americans showed enthusiasm for the French Revolution by wearing a tricolor cockade—a distinctive bow made from red, white, and blue ribbons. Bibliothèque Nationale de France.

Jay Treaty

▶ 1795 treaty between the United States and England. John Jay was sent by President Washington to negotiate commercial relations in the British West Indies and secure compensation for the seizure of American ships. In addition, Jay was supposed to press for the reimbursement of southern planters for the slaves set free by the British army during the war and for the removal of British soldiers from frontier forts still occupied because of their proximity to the Indian fur trade. The resulting treaty was seen as too favorable to the British and was widely unpopular.

What was Hamilton's plan to solidify the government's fiscal position? | What external threats did the United States face in the 1790s? | How did partisan rivalries shape the politics of the late 1790s? | Conclusion: Why did the new nation ultimately form political parties?

239

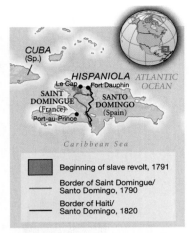

Haitian Revolution, 1791–1804

Haitian Revolution

▶ A complex conflict lasting from 1791 to 1804 and involving many participants, including the diverse population of Haiti and, eventually, three European countries. As a result of the revolution, Haiti became an independent country, and slavery was outlawed within its borders. The Haitian Revolution fueled fears among white southerners that their own slaves might rise to ignite a bloody race war.

To the South: The Haitian Revolution

In addition to the Indian wars in Ohio and the European wars across the Atlantic, a third bloody conflict to the south polarized and even terrorized many Americans in the 1790s. The western third of the large Caribbean island of Hispaniola, just to the east of Cuba, became engulfed in revolution starting in 1791. The eastern portion of the island was a Spanish colony called Santo Domingo; the western part was the French Saint Domingue. War raged in Saint Domingue for more than a decade, resulting in 1804 in the birth of the Republic of Haiti, the first and only independent black state to arise out of a successful slave revolution.

The **Haitian Revolution** was a complex event involving many participants, including the diverse local population and, eventually, three European countries. Some 30,000 whites ruled the island in 1790, running sugar and coffee plantations with close to half a million enslaved blacks, two-thirds of them of African birth. The white French colonists were not the only plantation owners, however. About 28,000 free mixed-race people (*gens de couleur*) also lived in Saint Domingue; they owned one-third of the island's plantations and nearly a quarter of the slave labor force. Despite their economic status, these mixed-race planters were barred from political power, but they aspired to it.

The French Revolution of 1789 was the immediate catalyst for rebellion in this already tense society. First, white colonists challenged the white royalist government in an effort to link Saint Domingue with the new revolutionary government in France. Next, the mixed-race planters rebelled in 1791, demanding equal civil rights with the whites. No sooner was this revolt viciously suppressed than another part of the island exploded as thousands of enslaved blacks armed with machetes and torches wreaked devastation and slaughter. In 1793, the civil war escalated to include French, Spanish, and British troops fighting the inhabitants and also one another. Slaves led by Toussaint L'Ouverture in alliance with Spain occupied the northern regions of the island, leaving a thousand plantations in ruins and tens of thousands of people dead. Thousands of white and mixed-race planters, along with some of their slaves, fled to Spanish Louisiana and southern cities in the United States.

White Americans followed the revolution in horror through newspapers and refugees' accounts. A few sympathized with the impulse for liberty, but many more feared that violent black insurrection might spread to the United States. Many black American slaves also followed the revolution, for the news of the success of a first-ever massive revolution by slaves traveled quickly in this oral culture.

The Haitian Revolution provoked naked fear of a race war in white southerners. Jefferson, agonizing over the contagion of liberty in 1797, wrote another Virginia slaveholder that "if something is not done, and soon done, we shall be the murderers of our own children . . . ; the revolutionary storm, now sweeping the globe, will be upon us, and happy if we make timely provision to give it an easy passage over our land. From the present state of things in Europe and America, the day which brings our combustion must be near at hand; and only a single spark is wanting to make that day to-morrow."

> **QUICK REVIEW**

What connections did Americans make between events overseas and domestic stability in the 1790s?

CHAPTER LOCATOR | What were the sources of political stability in Federalist America?

How did partisan rivalries shape the politics of the late 1790s?

Cartoon of the Matthew Lyon Fight in Congress

The political tensions of 1798 were not merely intellectual. A February session in Congress degenerated from name-calling to a brawl. Roger Griswold, a Connecticut Federalist, called Matthew Lyon, a Vermont Republican, a coward. Lyon responded with some well-aimed spit, the first departure from the gentleman's code of honor. Griswold responded by raising his cane to Lyon, whereupon Lyon grabbed nearby fire tongs to beat back his assailant. Library of Congress.

► FOR MORE HELP ANALYZING THIS IMAGE, see the visual activity for this chapter in the Online Study Guide at bedfordstmartins.com/roarkunderstanding.

BY THE MID-1790s, polarization over the French Revolution, Haiti, the Jay Treaty, and Hamilton's economic plans had led to two distinct and consistent rival political groups: **Federalists** and **Republicans**. Federalist leaders supported Britain in foreign policy and commercial interests at home, while Republicans rooted for liberty in France and worried about monarchical Federalists at home. The labels did not yet describe full-fledged political parties, which were still thought to be a sign of failure of the experiment in government. Washington's decision not to seek a third term led to serious partisan electioneering in the presidential and congressional elections of 1796. Federalist John Adams won the presidency, but party strife accelerated over failed diplomacy in France, bringing the United States to the brink of war. Pro-war and antiwar antagonism created a major crisis over political free speech, militarism, and fears of sedition and treason.

The Election of 1796

Washington struggled to appear to be above party politics, and in his farewell address, he stressed the need to maintain a "unity of government" reflecting a unified body politic. He also urged the country to "steer clear of permanent alliances with any portion of the foreign world." The leading contenders for his position, John Adams of

Federalists
► One of the two dominant political groups that emerged in the 1790s. Federalist leaders supported Britain in foreign policy and commercial interests at home. Prominent Federalists included George Washington, Alexander Hamilton, and John Adams.

Republicans
► One of the two dominant political groups that emerged in the 1790s. Republicans supported the revolutionaries in France and worried about monarchical Federalists at home. Prominent Republicans included Thomas Jefferson and James Madison.

What was Hamilton's plan to solidify the government's fiscal position?	What external threats did the United States face in the 1790s?	How did partisan rivalries shape the politics of the late 1790s?	Conclusion: Why did the new nation ultimately form political parties?

CHRONOLOGY

1796
– Federalist John Adams is elected second president.

1797
– XYZ affair between France and the United States.

1798
– Quasi-War with France erupts.
– Alien and Sedition Acts crack down on dissidents.
– Virginia and Kentucky Resolutions assert that states have the right to nullify federal laws.

1800
– Republican Thomas Jefferson is elected third president.

Massachusetts and Thomas Jefferson of Virginia, in theory agreed with him, but around them raged a party contest split along pro-British versus pro-French lines.

The leading Federalists informally caucused and chose Adams as their candidate, with Thomas Pinckney of South Carolina to run with him. The Republicans settled on Aaron Burr of New York to pair with Jefferson. The Constitution did not anticipate parties and tickets. Instead, each electoral college voter could cast two votes for any two candidates, but on only one ballot. The top vote-getter became president, and the next-highest assumed the vice presidency. (This procedural flaw was corrected by the Twelfth Amendment, adopted in 1804.) With only one ballot, careful maneuvering was required to make sure that the chief rivals for the presidency did not land in the top two spots.

A failed effort by Alexander Hamilton to influence the outcome of the election landed the country in just such a position. Hamilton did not trust Adams; he preferred Pinckney, and he tried to influence electors to throw their support to the South Carolinian. But his plan backfired: Adams was elected president with 71 electoral votes; Jefferson came in second with 68 and thus became vice president. Pinckney got 59 votes, while Burr trailed with 30.

Adams's inaugural speech pledged neutrality in foreign affairs and respect for the French people, which made Republicans hopeful. To please Federalists, Adams retained three cabinet members from Washington's administration—the secretaries of state, treasury, and war. But the three were Hamilton loyalists, passing off Hamilton's judgments and advice as their own to the unwitting Adams. Vice President Jefferson extended a conciliatory hand to Adams, but the Hamiltonian cabinet ruined the honeymoon. Jefferson's advice was spurned, and he withdrew from active counsel of the president.

The XYZ Affair

From the start, Adams's presidency was in crisis. France retaliated for the British-friendly Jay Treaty by abandoning its 1778 alliance with the United States. French

John Adams

In 1793, a year after painting a portrait of the youthful secretary of the treasury Alexander Hamilton (see page 230), John Trumbull painted Vice President John Adams, then age fifty-eight. National Portrait Gallery, Smithsonian Institution/ Art Resources, NY.

CHAPTER LOCATOR | What were the sources of political stability in Federalist America?

CHAPTER 9
242 FORMING THE NEW NATION, 1789–1800

privateers—armed private vessels—started detaining American ships carrying British goods; by March 1797, more than three hundred American vessels had been seized. To avenge these insults, Federalists started murmuring openly about war with France. Adams preferred negotiations and dispatched a three-man commission to France in the fall of 1797. When the three commissioners arrived in Paris, French officials would not receive them. Finally, the French minister of foreign affairs, Talleyrand, sent three French agents—unnamed and later known to the American public as X, Y, and Z—to the American commissioners with the information that $250,000 might grease the wheels of diplomacy and that a $12 million loan to the French government would be the price of a peace treaty. Incensed, the commissioners brought news of the bribery attempt to the president.

Americans reacted to the **XYZ affair** with shock and anger. Even staunch pro-French Republicans began to reevaluate their allegiance. The Federalist-dominated Congress appropriated money for an army of ten thousand soldiers and repealed all prior treaties with France. In 1798, twenty naval warships launched the United States into its first undeclared war, called the Quasi-War by historians to underscore its uncertain legal status. The main scene of action was the Caribbean, where more than one hundred French ships were captured.

There was no home-front unity in this time of undeclared war; antagonism only intensified between Federalists and Republicans. Republican newspapers heaped abuse on Adams. Pro-French mobs roamed the capital, and Adams, fearing for his personal safety, stocked weapons in his presidential quarters. Federalists, too, went on the offensive. In Newburyport, Massachusetts, they lit a huge bonfire and burned issues of the state's Republican newspapers. One Federalist editor ominously declared that "he who is not for us is against us."

The Alien and Sedition Acts

With tempers so dangerously high and fears that political dissent was perhaps akin to treason, Federalist leaders moved to muffle the opposition. In mid-1798, Congress passed the Sedition Act, which not only made conspiracy and revolt illegal but also penalized speaking or writing anything that defamed the president or Congress. Criticizing government leaders became a criminal offense. One Federalist warned of the threat that existed "to overturn and ruin the government by publishing the most shameless falsehoods against the representatives of the people." In all, twenty-five men, almost all Republican newspaper editors, were charged with sedition; twelve were convicted.

Congress also passed two Alien Acts. The first extended the waiting period for an alien to achieve citizenship from five to fourteen years and required all aliens to register with the federal government. The second empowered the president in time of war to deport or imprison without trial any foreigner suspected of being a danger to the United States. The clear intent of these laws was to harass French immigrants already in the United States and to discourage others from coming.

Republicans strongly opposed the **Alien and Sedition Acts** on the grounds that they were in conflict with the Bill of Rights, but they did not have the votes to revoke the acts in Congress, nor could the federal judiciary, dominated by Federalist judges, be counted on to challenge them. Jefferson and Madison turned to the state legislatures, the only other competing political arena, to press their opposition. Each man drafted a set of resolutions condemning the acts and had the

XYZ affair

▶ 1797 scandal in which an American commission sent to negotiate with France was rebuffed for refusing to pay a substantial bribe. When the incident became public, the United States entered into an undeclared war with France, known as the Quasi-War. The Quasi-War led to intensified antagonism between Federalists and Republicans.

Alien and Sedition Acts

▶ 1798 acts passed by the Federalist Congress to suppress political dissent. The Sedition Act not only made conspiracy and revolt illegal but also penalized speaking or writing anything that defamed the president or Congress. The two Alien Acts extended the waiting period for an alien to achieve citizenship from five to fourteen years, required all aliens to register with the federal government, and empowered the president in time of war to deport or imprison without trial any foreigner suspected of being a danger to the United States. The Alien and Sedition Acts reflected the highly partisan politics and war hysteria of the late 1790s.

What was Hamilton's plan to solidify the government's fiscal position?

What external threats did the United States face in the 1790s?

How did partisan rivalries shape the politics of the late 1790s?

Conclusion: Why did the new nation ultimately form political parties?

243

legislatures of Virginia and Kentucky present them to the federal government in late fall 1798. The Virginia and Kentucky Resolutions tested the novel argument that state legislatures have the right to judge the constitutionality of federal laws and to nullify laws that infringe on the liberties of the people as defined in the Bill of Rights. The resolutions made little dent in the Alien and Sedition Acts, but the idea of a state's right to nullify federal law did not disappear. It would resurface several times in decades to come, most notably in a major tariff dispute in 1832 and in the sectional arguments that led to the Civil War.

Amid all the war hysteria and sedition fears in 1798, President Adams regained his balance. He was uncharacteristically restrained in pursuing opponents under the Sedition Act, and he finally refused to declare war on France, as extreme Federalists wished. He also shrewdly realized that France was not eager for war and that a peaceful settlement might be close at hand. In January 1799, a peace initiative from France arrived in the form of a letter assuring Adams that diplomatic channels were open again and that new commissioners would be welcomed in France.

Adams accepted this overture and appointed new negotiators. By late 1799, the Quasi-War with France had subsided, and in 1800 the negotiations resulted in a treaty declaring "a true and sincere friendship" between the United States and France. But Federalists were not pleased; Adams lost the support of a significant part of his own party and sealed his fate as the first one-term president of the United States.

The election of 1800 was openly organized along party lines. The self-designated national leaders of each group met to handpick their candidates for president and vice president. Adams's chief opponent was Thomas Jefferson. When the election was finally over, President Jefferson mounted the inaugural platform to announce, "We are all republicans, we are all federalists," an appealing rhetoric of harmony appropriate to an inaugural address. But his formulation perpetuated a denial of the validity of party politics, a denial that ran deep in the founding generation of political leaders.

> QUICK REVIEW

How did war between Britain and France intensify political division in the United States?

CHAPTER LOCATOR | What were the sources of political stability in Federalist America?

244 CHAPTER 9
FORMING THE NEW NATION, 1789–1800

Courtesy, The Henry Francis du Pont Winterthur Museum.

Conclusion: Why did the new nation ultimately form political parties?

AMERICAN POLITICAL LEADERS began operating the new government in 1789 with great hopes of unifying the country and overcoming selfish factionalism. The enormous trust in President Washington was the central foundation for those hopes, and Washington did not disappoint, becoming a model Mr. President with a blend of integrity and authority. Stability was further aided by easy passage of the Bill of Rights (to appease Antifederalists) and by attention to cultivating a virtuous citizenry of upright men supported and rewarded by republican womanhood. Yet the hopes of the honeymoon period soon turned to worries and then fears as major political disagreements flared up.

At the core of the conflict was a group of talented men—Hamilton, Madison, Jefferson, and Adams—so recently allies but now opponents. They diverged over Hamilton's economic program, over relations with the British and the Jay Treaty, over the French and Haitian revolutions, and over preparedness for war abroad and free speech at home. Hamilton was perhaps the driving force in these conflicts, but the antagonism was not about mere personality. Parties were taking shape not around individuals, but around principles, such as ideas about what constituted enlightened leadership, how powerful the federal government should be, who was the best ally in Europe, and when oppositional political speech turned into treason.

In his inaugural address of 1800, Jefferson offered his conciliatory assurance that Americans were at the same time "all republicans" and "all federalists," suggesting that both groups shared two basic ideas—the value of republican government, in which power derived from the people, and the value of the unique federal system of shared governance structured by the Constitution. But by 1800, *Federalist* and *Republican* defined competing philosophies of government. For the next two decades, these two groups would battle each other, each fearing that the success of the other might bring the demise of the country.

SO NOW YOU KNOW

Even though Washington had originally favored "His High Mightiness" as the title by which the president should be addressed, ultimately the established form of address became "Mr. President." Washington, a "virtuous" man in the language of the day, maintained dignity and even encouraged ceremonialism, but in the end he helped shape the presidency in a way that signaled new republican ideals.

What was Hamilton's plan to solidify the government's fiscal position?

What external threats did the United States face in the 1790s?

How did partisan rivalries shape the politics of the late 1790s?

Conclusion: Why did the new nation ultimately form political parties?

> CHAPTER 9 STUDY GUIDE

Online Study Guide
bedfordstmartins.com/roarkunderstanding

STEP 1 GETTING STARTED

Below are basic terms from this period in American history. Can you identify each term below and explain why it matters? To do this exercise online or to download this chart, visit bedfordstmartins.com/roarkunderstanding.

TERM	WHO OR WHAT & WHEN	WHY IT MATTERS
Bill of Rights, p. 227		
Alexander Hamilton, p. 230		
Report on Public Credit, p. 232		
Whiskey Rebellion, p. 235		
Treaty of Greenville, p. 238		
Jay Treaty, p. 239		
Haitian Revolution, p. 240		
Federalists, p. 241		
Republicans, p. 241		
XYZ affair, p. 243		
Alien and Sedition Acts, p. 243		

STEP 2 MOVING BEYOND THE BASICS

The exercise below represents a more advanced understanding of the chapter material. Assess the growing split between the Federalists and the Republicans in the late eighteenth century. Fill in the chart below by describing the Federalist and Republican positions and opinions on the key issues of the period. What core assumptions and beliefs informed the policies and positions of each group? Is it accurate to describe the two groups as political parties? Why or why not? To do this exercise online or to download this chart, visit bedfordstmartins.com/roarkunderstanding.

	Federalists	Republicans
States' rights		
Government influence on economy		
Social and political hierarchy		
Relations with Britain		
Relations with France		

Now that you've reviewed various parts of the chapter, take a step back and try to see the big picture by answering these questions. Remember to use specific examples from the chapter in your answers. To do this exercise online, visit bedfordsmartins.com/roarkunderstanding.

DOMESTIC AFFAIRS

► What important precedents did George Washington set? How did he use the presidency to bring political stability to the country?

► How did Hamilton imagine the future of the United States? How did his vision conflict with that of Jefferson?

NATIONAL SECURITY

► What were the most important threats to America's national security in the 1790s? How did the Washington and Adams administrations respond to those threats?

► How did the French Revolution contribute to the split between Federalists and Republicans in the United States?

FEDERALISTS AND REPUBLICANS

► What led to the factionalizing of American politics in the 1790s?

► How did the development of political factions affect the country domestically? In its external affairs?

LOOKING BACKWARD, LOOKING AHEAD

► How did the government Washington headed differ from the government created by the Articles of Confederation?

► What steps had been taken toward the creation of national political parties by 1800? What steps were still required before a true party system was in place?

IN YOUR OWN WORDS

Imagine that you must explain chapter 9 to someone who hasn't read it. What would be the most important points to include and why?

WE OWE ALLEGIANCE TO NO CRO

10
A MATURING REPUBLIC

1800–1824

> This chapter explores the changing political landscape in America from the election of Thomas Jefferson in 1800 to the election of John Quincy Adams in 1824. It examines the foreign and domestic challenges and opportunities that shaped American politics in the early nineteenth century, as well the shifting political culture that resulted in the expansion of suffrage for white men, the disfranchisement of most of their black counterparts, and new educational opportunities for American women.

> How did Thomas Jefferson radically transform the presidency?

> What were the challenges and successes of the Madison presidency?

> To what extent did women's status change in the early Republic?

> Why did partisan conflict increase during the administrations of Monroe and Adams?

> Conclusion: How did republican simplicity become complex?

DID YOU KNOW?

The Department of State had a grand total of eight employees during Thomas Jefferson's first term as president.

"We Owe Allegiance to No Crown," by American sailor John A. Woodside, ca. 1815–1820.

> How did Thomas Jefferson radically transform the presidency?

Thomas Jefferson, by John Trumbull

When the young widower Thomas Jefferson lived in Paris in the late 1780s, he distributed three copies of this miniature portrait as affectionate gifts, one to his daughter Martha, another to a very attractive (but married) American woman in London, and the third to a British woman, also married. A much younger fourth woman in Paris shared his residence: his slave Sally Hemings, attendant to Jefferson's two daughters. Early in Jefferson's presidency, a scandal erupted when a journalist charged that Jefferson had fathered several children by Sally Hemings. DNA evidence, when combined with historical evidence about Jefferson's whereabouts at the start of each of Hemings's six pregnancies, makes a powerful case that Jefferson fathered some and probably all of her children. Monticello/Thomas Jefferson Memorial Foundation, Inc.

Thomas Jefferson
▶ Republican president of the United States from 1801 to 1809 who presided over the Louisiana Purchase, Lewis and Clark's exploration of the West, and precarious relations with Britain and France. He brought the presidency more in line with his own republican values by limiting the size of the federal government and displaying modest simplicity in affairs of state.

THE ELECTION OF 1800, decided in the House of Representatives, stoked fears that party divisions would ruin the country. A panicky Federalist newspaper in Connecticut predicted that **Thomas Jefferson's** victory would produce a civil war and usher in a reign of "murder, robbery, rape, adultery and incest." Similar fears were expressed in the South, where a slave uprising seemed a possible outcome of Jefferson's victory.

Although nothing so dramatic occurred, Jefferson did radically transform the presidency, away from the Federalists' vision of a powerful executive branch and toward republican simplicity and limited government. Yet even Jefferson found that circumstances sometimes required him to draw on the expansive powers of the presidency. The rise of Napoleon in France brought France and Britain into open warfare again in 1803, creating unexpected opportunities and challenges for Jefferson. One major opportunity arrived in the spectacular purchase from

CHAPTER LOCATOR | How did Thomas Jefferson radically transform the presidency?

France of the Louisiana Territory; a significant challenge arose when pirates threatened American ships off the north coast of Africa and when British and French naval forces nipped at American ships—and American honor—in the Atlantic Ocean.

Turbulent Times: Election and Rebellion

The result of the election of 1800 remained uncertain from polling time in November to repeated roll call votes in the House of Representatives in February 1801. Federalist John Adams was no longer in the presidential race once it got to the House. Instead, the contest was between Thomas Jefferson and his running mate, Senator Aaron Burr of New York. Republican voters in the electoral college slipped up, giving Jefferson and Burr an equal number of votes, an outcome possible because of the single balloting to choose both president and vice president. (To fix this problem, the Twelfth Amendment to the Constitution, adopted in 1804, provided for distinct ballots for the two offices.) The vain and ambitious Burr declined to concede, so the sitting Federalist-dominated House of Representatives got to choose the president (**Map 10.1**).

Some Federalists preferred Burr, believing that he was susceptible to Federalist pressure. But the influential Alexander Hamilton, though no friend of Jefferson, recognized that Burr would be more dangerous in the presidency. Jefferson was a "contemptible hypocrite" in Hamilton's opinion, but at least he was not corrupt. (In 1804, Burr shot and killed Hamilton in a formal but illegal duel.) Thirty-six ballots and six days later, Jefferson got the votes he needed to win the presidency. This election demonstrated a remarkable feature of the new government: No matter how hard fought the campaign, the leadership of the nation could shift from one group to its rivals in a peaceful transfer of power.

As the country struggled over its white leadership crisis, a twenty-four-year-old blacksmith named Gabriel, the slave of Thomas Prossor, plotted rebellion in Virginia. Inspired by the Haitian Revolution (see chapter 9), Gabriel was said to be organizing a thousand slaves to march on the state capital of Richmond and take the governor, James Monroe, hostage. On the appointed day, however, a few nervous slaves went to the authorities with news of Gabriel's rebellion, and within days, scores of implicated conspirators were jailed and brought to trial.

CHRONOLOGY

1800
- Republicans Thomas Jefferson and Aaron Burr tie in electoral college.
- Fears of slave rebellion led by Gabriel in Virginia result in twenty-seven executions.

1801
- House of Representatives elects Thomas Jefferson president after thirty-six ballots.

1803
- In *Marbury v. Madison*, the U.S. Supreme Court rules that it can declare laws unconstitutional.
- Rivals Britain and France warn United States not to ship war-related goods to the other.
- United States purchases the Louisiana Territory from France.

1804–1806
- Lewis and Clark expedition to the Louisiana Territory travels to the Pacific Ocean.

1807
- British attack and search the American ship *Chesapeake*.
- Embargo Act bans importation of British goods.

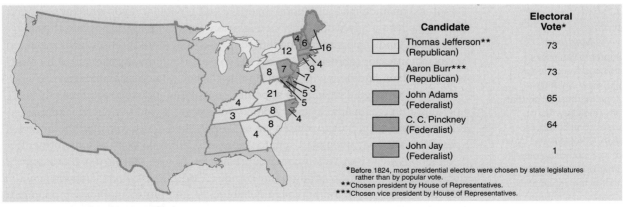

Candidate	Electoral Vote*
Thomas Jefferson** (Republican)	73
Aaron Burr*** (Republican)	73
John Adams (Federalist)	65
C. C. Pinckney (Federalist)	64
John Jay (Federalist)	1

*Before 1824, most presidential electors were chosen by state legislatures rather than by popular vote.
**Chosen president by House of Representatives.
***Chosen vice president by House of Representatives.

MAP 10.1 ■ The Election of 1800

What were the challenges and successes of the Madison presidency?

To what extent did women's status change in the early Republic?

Why did partisan conflict increase during the administrations of Monroe and Adams?

Conclusion: How did republican simplicity become complex?

One of the jailed rebels compared himself to the most venerated icon of the early Republic: "I have nothing more to offer than what General Washington would have had to offer, had he been taken by the British and put to trial by them." Such talk worried white Virginians, and in fall of 1800, twenty-seven black men were hanged for allegedly contemplating rebellion. Finally, Jefferson advised Governor Monroe to halt the hangings. "The world at large will forever condemn us if we indulge a principle of revenge," Jefferson wrote.

The Jeffersonian Vision of Republican Simplicity

Once elected, Thomas Jefferson turned his attention to establishing his administration in clear contrast to the Federalists. For his inauguration, he dressed in everyday clothing to strike a tone of republican simplicity, and he walked to the Capitol for the modest swearing-in ceremony. As president, he scaled back Federalist building plans for Washington and cut the government budget.

Martha Washington and Abigail Adams had received the wives of government officials at weekly teas, thereby cementing social relations in the governing class. But Jefferson, a longtime widower, disdained female gatherings and avoided the women of Washington City. He abandoned George Washington's practice of holding weekly formal receptions. He preferred small dinner parties with carefully chosen politicos, either all Republicans or all Federalists (and all male). At these intimate dinners, the president exercised influence and strengthened informal relationships that would help him govern.

Jefferson was no Antifederalist. He had supported the Constitution in 1788. But events of the 1790s had caused him to worry about the stretching of powers in the executive branch. Jefferson had watched with distrust as Hamiltonian policies refinanced the public debt, established a national bank, and secured commercial ties with Britain (see chapter 9). These policies seemed to Jefferson to promote the interests of greedy speculators and profiteers at the expense of the rest of the country. In Jefferson's vision, the source of true liberty in America was the independent farmer, someone who owned and worked his land both for himself and for the market.

Jefferson set out to dismantle Federalist innovations. He reduced the size of the army by a third, and he limited the navy to six ships. With the consent of Congress, he abolished all federal taxes based on population or whiskey. Government revenue would now derive solely from customs duties and the sale of western land. This strategy benefited the South, where three-fifths of the slaves counted for representation but not for taxation now. By the end of his first term, Jefferson had deeply reduced Hamilton's cherished national debt.

Faced with 217 last-minute appointments of Federalists to various judicial and military posts made by John Adams, Jefferson refused to honor those not yet fully processed. One disappointed job seeker, William Marbury, sued the new secretary of state, James Madison, for failure to make good on the appointment. This action gave rise to a landmark Supreme Court case, *Marbury v. Madison*, decided in 1803. The Court ruled that although Marbury's commission was valid and the new president should have delivered it, the Court could not compel him to do so. The Court found that the grounds of Marbury's suit, resting in the Judiciary

Marbury v. Madison
▶ 1803 Supreme Court case that established the concept of judicial review when Chief Justice John Marshall ruled that parts of the Judiciary Act of 1789 were in conflict with the Constitution. The Supreme Court assumed legal authority to nullify acts of other branches of the government in this rebalancing of power between Congress and the judiciary.

CHAPTER LOCATOR | How did Thomas Jefferson radically transform the presidency?

CHAPTER 10
252 A MATURING REPUBLIC, 1800–1824

Act of 1789, were in conflict with the Constitution. Thus, for the first time, the Court acted to disallow a law on the grounds that it was unconstitutional.

A properly limited federal government, according to Jefferson, was responsible merely for running a postal system, maintaining the federal courts, staffing lighthouses, collecting customs duties, and conducting a census once every ten years. Government jobs were kept to a minimum. The president had one private secretary, a young man named Meriwether Lewis, to help with his correspondence, and Jefferson paid him out of his own pocket. The Department of State employed only 8 people: Secretary James Madison, 6 clerks, and a messenger. The Treasury Department was by far the largest unit, with 73 revenue commissioners, auditors, and clerks, plus 2 watchmen. The entire payroll of the executive branch amounted to a mere 130 people in 1801.

The Promise of the West: The Louisiana Purchase and the Lewis and Clark Expedition

Jefferson's government was small, but his ambitions for the trans-Mississippi West were great. A large expanse of the Great Plains had been transferred from France to Spain under the 1763 Treaty of Paris. Spain never controlled or settled it, and Spanish power in North America remained precarious everywhere outside New Orleans. In an effort to augment population, Spain encouraged American farmers to move west across the Mississippi River, and by 1801, Americans made up a sizable minority of the population around New Orleans. Publicly, Jefferson protested the luring of Americans to Spanish territory, but privately he welcomed it: "I wish a hundred thousand of our inhabitants would accept the invitation; it will be the means of delivering to us peaceably, what may otherwise cost us a war."

In 1802, rumors reached Jefferson that Spain had struck a secret bargain with far more powerful France to transfer all of Spain's trans-Mississippi territory to Napoleon in exchange for land in Italy. Jefferson was so alarmed that he instructed Robert R. Livingston, America's minister in France, to try to buy New Orleans. When Livingston hinted that the United States might seize it if buying was not an option, the French negotiator asked him to name his price for the entire Louisiana Territory from the Gulf of Mexico north to Canada. Livingston shrewdly stalled and within days accepted the bargain price of $15 million (**Map 10.2**). In late 1803, the American army took formal control of the Louisiana Territory, and the United States nearly doubled in size.

Even before the **Louisiana Purchase**, Jefferson had his eye on the trans-Mississippi West. In early 1803, he had arranged congressional funding for a secret scientific and military mission into Indian territory. Jefferson appointed twenty-eight-year-old Meriwether Lewis, his secretary, to head the expedition, instructing him to investigate Indian cultures, to collect plant and animal specimens, and to chart the geography of the West. Congress wanted the expedition to scout locations for military posts, negotiate fur trade agreements, and identify river routes to the West.

For his co-leader, Lewis chose Kentuckian William Clark, a veteran of the 1790s Indian wars. Lewis and Clark, along with their crew of forty-five, left St. Louis in the spring of 1804, working their way northwest up the Missouri River. They camped for the winter at a Mandan village in what is now central North Dakota.

Louisiana Purchase

▶ 1803 purchase of French territory in the United States that stretched from the Gulf of Mexico to Canada. The Louisiana Purchase nearly doubled the size of the United States and opened the way for future American expansion west.

What were the challenges and successes of the Madison presidency?

To what extent did women's status change in the early Republic?

Why did partisan conflict increase during the administrations of Monroe and Adams?

Conclusion: How did republican simplicity become complex?

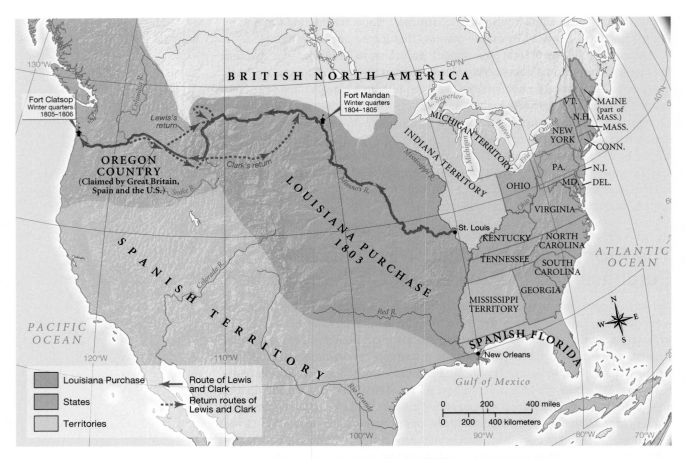

MAP 10.2 ■ The Louisiana Purchase and the Lewis and Clark Expedition
Robert Livingston's bargain buy of 1803 far exceeded his initial assignment to acquire the city of
New Orleans. New England Federalists, worried that their geographically based power in the federal
government would someday be eclipsed by the West, voted against the purchase. The Indians
who inhabited the vast region, unaware that their land had been claimed by either the French or the
Americans, got their first look at Anglo-American and African American men when the Lewis and
Clark expedition explored the territory in 1804–1806.

> ► FOR MORE HELP ANALYZING THIS MAP, see the map activity for this chapter in the Online
> Study Guide at bedfordstmartins.com/roarkunderstanding.

Lewis and Clark expedition

► 1804–1806 expedition led
by Meriwether Lewis and
William Clark that explored the
trans-Mississippi West on behalf
of the U.S. government. The
expedition's mission was to
scout locations for military posts,
negotiate fur trade agreements,
and identify river routes to the
West. The expedition made
Lewis and Clark heroes and
focused the nation's attention
on the potential of western
expansion.

The following spring, they headed west, accompanied by a sixteen-year-old
Shoshoni woman named Sacajawea. Kidnapped by Mandans at about age ten,
she had been sold to a French trapper as a slave/wife. Hers was not a unique
story among Indian women; such women knew several languages, making them
valuable translators and mediators. Further, Sacajawea and her new baby
allowed the American expedition to appear peaceful to suspicious tribes. As
Lewis wrote in his journal, "No woman ever accompanies a war party of Indians
in this quarter."

The **Lewis and Clark expedition** reached the Pacific Ocean at the mouth of
the Columbia River in November 1805. When Lewis and Clark returned home the
following year, they were greeted as national heroes. They had established favorable relations with dozens of Indian tribes; they had collected invaluable informa-

CHAPTER LOCATOR | How did Thomas Jefferson
radically transform the
presidency?

Grizzly Bear Claw Necklace

Lewis and Clark collected hundreds of Indian artifacts on their expedition, including this bear claw necklace presented by Shoshoni warriors in the Rocky Mountains. The thirty-eight impressive claws, each three to four inches long, are strung together by rawhide thongs: At least two grizzly bears were killed to create the necklace. This was no simple task: Male grizzlies are large—six to seven feet tall and five hundred to nine hundred pounds—and aggressive. It seems certain that a sense of the bears' power would be bestowed on the wearer. Peabody Museum of Archaeology and Ethnology, Harvard University.

tion on the peoples, soils, plants, animals, and geography of the West; and they had inspired a nation of restless explorers and solitary imitators.

Challenges Overseas: The Barbary Wars

Around the same time, events in the western Mediterranean led to the first declaration of war against the United States by a foreign power. For well over a century, four Muslim states on the northern coast of Africa—Morocco, Algiers, Tunis, and Tripoli, called the Barbary States by Americans—controlled all Mediterranean shipping traffic by demanding large annual payments (called "tribute") for safe passage. Countries electing not to pay found their ships at risk for seizure. By the mid-1790s, the United States was paying $50,000 a year.

American Commerce in the Mediterranean

Mediterranean trade involved about a hundred American merchant ships annually.

Exports to the region included lumber, tobacco, sugar, and rum.

Imports from the region included raisins, figs, capers, and opium for medicinal use.

Some 20 percent of all American exports went to the Middle East.

In May 1801, when the pasha (military head) of Tripoli failed to secure a large increase in his tribute, he declared war on the United States. Jefferson had long considered such payments extortion, and he sent four warships to the Mediterranean to protect U.S. shipping. From 1801 to 1803, U.S. frigates engaged in skirmishes with Barbary privateers.

Then, in late 1803, the USS *Philadelphia* ran aground near Tripoli harbor and was captured along with its crew. In retaliation, a U.S. naval ship commanded by navy lieutenant Stephen Decatur sailed into the harbor after dark and set the *Philadelphia* on fire, making Decatur an instant hero in America. A later foray into the harbor to try to blow up the entire Tripoli fleet with a bomb-laden boat failed when the explosives detonated prematurely, killing eleven Americans.

In 1804, William Eaton, an American officer stationed in Tunis, felt the humiliation of his country's ineffectiveness. He wrote to Secretary of State James

| What were the challenges and successes of the Madison presidency? | To what extent did women's status change in the early Republic? | Why did partisan conflict increase during the administrations of Monroe and Adams? | Conclusion: How did republican simplicity become complex? |

255

Madison to ask for a thousand marines to invade Tripoli. Madison rejected the plan and another scheme to ally with the pasha's exiled brother to effect a regime change. On his own, Eaton contacted the brother, assembled a force of four hundred men (most of them Egyptian mercenaries), and marched them over five hundred miles of desert for a surprise attack on Tripoli's second-largest city. Amazingly, he succeeded. The pasha of Tripoli yielded, released the prisoners taken from the *Philadelphia*, and negotiated a treaty with the United States. Peace with the other Barbary States came in a second treaty in 1812.

More Transatlantic Troubles: Impressment and Embargo

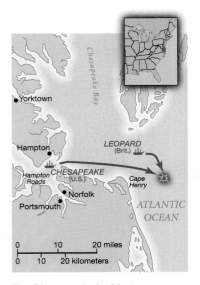

The *Chesapeake* Incident, June 22, 1807

Jefferson easily retained the presidency in the election of 1804, winning 162 electoral votes to the 14 won by Federalist Charles Cotesworth Pinckney of South Carolina. But governing in his second term was not easy, because of seriously escalating tensions between the United States and both France and Britain. Beginning in 1803, both European rivals, embroiled in a war with each other, repeatedly warned the United States not to ship arms to the other. Britain acted on these threats in 1806, stopping U.S. ships to inspect cargoes for military aid to France and seizing suspected deserters from the British navy, along with many Americans. Ultimately, 2,500 U.S. sailors were "impressed" (taken by force) by the British. In retaliation against the impressment of U.S. sailors, Jefferson convinced Congress to pass nonimportation laws banning certain British-made goods.

Jefferson found one event particularly provoking. In June 1807, the American ship *Chesapeake*, harboring some British deserters, was ordered to stop by the British frigate *Leopard*. The *Chesapeake* refused, and the *Leopard* opened fire, killing three Americans—right at the mouth of the Chesapeake Bay, well within U.S. territory. In response, Congress passed the Embargo Act of 1807, banning all importation of British goods into the country. All foreign ports were declared off-limits to American merchants to discourage illegal trading through secondary ports. Though a drastic measure, the embargo was meant to forestall war by forcing concessions from the British through economic pressure.

The Embargo Act of 1807 was a disaster. From 1790 to 1807, U.S. exports had increased fivefold, but the embargo brought commerce to a standstill. In New England, the heart of the shipping industry, unemployment rose. Grain plummeted in value, river traffic halted, tobacco rotted in the South, and cotton went unpicked. Protest petitions flooded Washington. The federal government suffered, too, for import duties were a significant source of revenue. Jefferson paid political costs as well. The Federalist Party, weakened by its poor showing in the election of 1804, began to revive.

> ## QUICK REVIEW

How did Jefferson attempt to undo the Federalist innovations of earlier administrations?

CHAPTER LOCATOR | How did Thomas Jefferson radically transform the presidency?

What were the challenges and successes of the Madison presidency?

Dolley Madison, by Gilbert Stuart

The "presidentress" of the Madison administration sat for this official portrait in 1804. She wears an empire-style dress, at the height of French fashion in 1804 and a style worn by many women at the coronation of the emperor Napoleon in Paris. The hallmarks of such a dress were a light fabric (muslin or chiffon), short sleeves, a high waistline from which the fabric fell straight to the ground, and usually a low, open neckline, as shown here. © White House Historical Association.

IN MID-1808, Jefferson indicated that he would not run for a third term. Secretary of State James Madison was chosen by the Republican caucuses—informal political groups that orchestrated the selection of candidates. The Federalist caucuses again chose Charles Cotesworth Pinckney. Madison won, but Pinckney received 47 electoral votes, nearly half of Madison's total. Support for the Federalists remained centered in New England, and Republicans still held the balance of power nationwide.

Women in Washington City

Although women could not vote and supposedly left politics to men, the female relatives of Washington politicians took on several overtly political functions that greased the wheels of the affairs of state. They networked through dinners, balls, receptions, and the intricate custom of "calling," in which men and women paid brief visits at each other's homes. Webs of friendship and influence in turn facilitated female political lobbying. It was not uncommon for women in this social set to write letters of recommendation for men seeking government work.

When James Madison became president, **Dolley Madison**, called by some the "presidentress," struck a balance between queenliness and republican openness. She dressed the part in resplendent clothes, opening three elegant rooms in the executive mansion for a weekly party called "Mrs. Madison's crush" or "squeeze." In contrast to George and Martha Washington's stiff, brief receptions, the Madisons' parties went on for hours, with scores or even hundreds of guests milling about, talking, and eating. Members of Congress, cabinet officers, distinguished guests, envoys from foreign countries, and their womenfolk attended with regularity. Mrs. Madison's squeeze was an essential event for gaining political access, trading information, and establishing informal channels that would smooth the governing process.

Dolley Madison
► Wife of President James Madison and center of Washington's social scene during his presidency. She was called by some the "presidentress." Her social gatherings were important political events at which the Washington elite would gather to gain political access, trade information, and establish informal channels that would smooth the governing process.

| What were the challenges and successes of the Madison presidency? | To what extent did women's status change in the early Republic? | Why did partisan conflict increase during the administrations of Monroe and Adams? | Conclusion: How did republican simplicity become complex? |

1808
- Republican James Madison is elected president; Dolley Madison is soon dubbed "presidentress."

1811
- Battle of Tippecanoe ends uprising by Native Americans in the old Northwest.

1812
- United States declares war on Great Britain.

1813
- Tecumseh dies at battle of the Thames.

1814
- British attack Washington, D.C.
- New England Federalists meet at Hartford Convention.

1815
- U.S. troops led by Andrew Jackson defeat British at the battle of New Orleans.

Tecumseh

▶ Shawnee chief who, along with this brother Tenskwatawa (known as the Prophet), built a pan-Indian confederacy in the first decade of the nineteenth century to resist further white encroachment on Indian lands. The two promoted a potent blend of spiritual regeneration and political unity that attracted thousands of followers. Tecumseh was killed in 1813 while fighting on the British side in the War of 1812.

In 1810–1811, the Madisons' house acquired its present name, the White House. The many guests at the weekly parties experienced simultaneously the splendor of the executive mansion and the atmosphere of republicanism that made it accessible to so many. Dolley Madison, ever an enormous political asset to her rather shy husband, understood well the symbolic function of the White House to enhance the power and legitimacy of the presidency.

Indian Troubles in the West

While the Madisons cemented alliances at home, difficulties with Britain and France overseas and with Indians in the old Northwest continued to increase. In the Ohio Country, the Shawnee chief **Tecumseh** and his brother Tenskwatawa (known as the Prophet) actively solidified a pan-Indian confederacy to resist further white encroachment on Indian lands. The two promoted a potent blend of spiritual regeneration and political unity that attracted thousands of followers. At the same time, the more northern tribes renewed their ties with supportive British agents and fur traders in Canada, a potential source of food and weapons. If the United States went to war with Britain, there would clearly be serious repercussions on the frontier.

Shifting demographics put the Indians under pressure. The 1810 census counted some 230,000 Americans in Ohio, while another 40,000 inhabited the territories of Indiana, Illinois, and Michigan. The Indian population of the same area was much smaller, probably about 70,000.

Up to 1805, Indiana's territorial governor, William Henry Harrison, had negotiated a series of treaties in a divide-and-conquer strategy aimed at extracting Indian lands for paltry payments. But with the rise to power of Tecumseh and his brother Tenskwatawa, the Prophet, Harrison's strategy faltered. A fundamental part of Tecumseh's message was the assertion that all Indian lands were held in common by all the tribes. "No tribe has the right to sell [these lands], even to each

Tenskwatawa, by George Catlin

Tenskwatawa, the Prophet, and his brother Tecumseh led the spiritual and political efforts of a number of Indian tribes to resist land-hungry Americans moving west in the decade before the War of 1812. Artist George Catlin portrays the Prophet wearing beaded necklaces, metal arm- and wristbands, and earrings. National Museum of American Art, Washington, D.C./ Art Resource, NY.

CHAPTER LOCATOR | How did Thomas Jefferson radically transform the presidency?

other, much less to strangers . . . ," Tecumseh said. "Sell a country! Why not sell the air, the great sea, as well as the earth? Didn't the Great Spirit make them all for the use of his children?" In 1809, while Tecumseh was away on a recruiting trip, Harrison assembled the leaders of the Potawatomi, Miami, and Delaware tribes to negotiate the Treaty of Fort Wayne. After promising (falsely) that this was the last cession of land the United States would seek, Harrison secured three million acres at about two cents per acre.

When he returned, Tecumseh was furious with both Harrison and the tribal leaders. Leaving his brother in charge at his headquarters of Prophetstown on Tippecanoe River, the Shawnee chief left to seek alliances with tribes in the South. In November 1811, Harrison decided to attack Prophetstown with a thousand men. The two-hour battle resulted in the deaths of sixty-two Americans and forty Indians before the Prophet's forces fled. The Americans won the battle of Tippecanoe, but Tecumseh was now more ready than ever to make war on the United States.

Battle of Tippecanoe, 1811

The War of 1812

The Indian conflicts in the old Northwest soon merged into the wider conflict with Britain now known as the **War of 1812**. Between 1809 and 1812, President Madison teetered between declaring either Britain or France America's primary enemy, as attacks by both countries on U.S. ships continued. In 1809, Congress replaced Jefferson's embargo with the Non-Intercourse Act, which prohibited trade only with Britain and France and their colonies, thus opening up other trade routes to alleviate somewhat the anguish of shippers, farmers, and planters. By 1811, the country was seriously divided and on the verge of war.

The new Congress seated in March 1811 contained several dozen young Republicans from the West and South who would come to be known as the War Hawks. Led by thirty-four-year-old Henry Clay from Kentucky and twenty-nine-year-old John C. Calhoun from South Carolina, they welcomed a war with Britain both to justify attacks on the Indians and to bring an end to impressment. Many were also expansionists, looking to occupy Florida and threaten Canada. Clay was elected Speaker of the House. Calhoun won a seat on the Foreign Relations Committee. The War Hawks approved major defense expenditures, and the army soon quadrupled in size.

In June 1812, Congress declared war on Great Britain in a vote divided along sectional lines: New England and some Middle Atlantic states opposed the war, fearing its effect on commerce, while the South and West were strongly for it. Ironically, Britain had just announced that it would stop the search and seizure of American ships, but the war momentum would not be slowed. The Foreign Relations Committee issued an elaborate justification titled *Report on the Causes and Reasons for War*, written mainly by Calhoun and containing extravagant language about Britain's "lust for power," "unbounded tyranny," and "mad ambition." These were fighting words in a war that was in large measure about insult and honor.

The War Hawks proposed an invasion of Canada, confidently predicting victory in four weeks. Instead, the war lasted two and a half years, and Canada never fell. The northern invasion turned out to be one of a series of blunders that revealed America's grave unpreparedness for war against the unexpectedly powerful British and Indian forces (**Map 10.3**). By the fall of 1812, the outlook was grim.

War of 1812

▶ War between the United States and Great Britain. After years of attacks on American vessels abroad, the War Hawks pushed for the United States to declare war on Britain to end impressment of Americans, legitimize attacks on Indians in the West, and pursue expansionist impulses. In June 1812, Congress declared war on Great Britain. The War Hawks proposed an invasion of Canada and expected quick success; instead, the conflict dragged on for two and a half years. The Treaty of Ghent ended the war in late 1814, although the final battle in New Orleans occurred in early 1815: Americans yielded on impressment and relinquished any claims to Canada, and the British stopped giving aid to Indians.

| What were the challenges and successes of the Madison presidency? | To what extent did women's status change in the early Republic? | Why did partisan conflict increase during the administrations of Monroe and Adams? | Conclusion: How did republican simplicity become complex? |

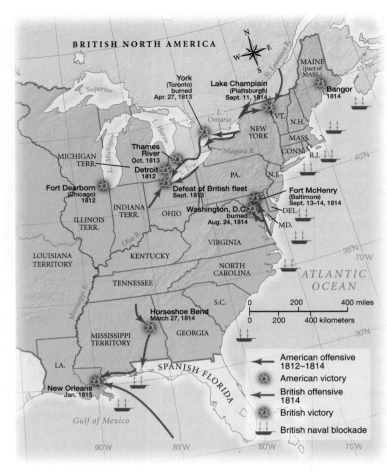

MAP 10.3 ■ The War of 1812
During the War of 1812, battles were fought along the Canadian border and in the Chesapeake region. The most important American victory came in New Orleans two weeks after a peace agreement had been signed in Europe.

Worse, the New England states were slow to raise troops, and some New England merchants carried on illegal trade with Britain. The fall presidential election pitted Madison against DeWitt Clinton of New York, nominally a Republican but able to attract the Federalist vote. Clinton picked up all of New England's electoral votes, with the exception of Vermont's, and also took New York, New Jersey, and part of Maryland. Madison won in the electoral college, 128 to 89, but his margin of victory was considerably smaller than in 1808.

In late 1812 and early 1813, the tide began to turn in the Americans' favor. First came some reassuring victories at sea. Then the Americans attacked York (now Toronto) and burned it in April 1813. A few months later, Commodore Oliver Hazard Perry defeated the British fleet at the western end of Lake Erie. Emboldened, General Harrison drove an army into Canada from Detroit and in October 1813 defeated the British and Indians at the battle of the Thames, where Tecumseh was killed.

Creek Indians in the South who had allied with Tecumseh's confederacy were also plunged into war. Some 10,000 living in the Mississippi Territory put up a spirited fight against U.S. forces for ten months. But the Creek War ended suddenly in March 1814 when a general named Andrew Jackson led 2,500 Tennessee militiamen in a bloody attack called the Battle of Horseshoe Bend. More than 550 Indians were killed, and several hundred more died trying to escape across a river. Later that year, General Jackson extracted a treaty relinquishing thousands of square miles of Creek land to the United States.

Washington City Burns: The British Offensive

In August 1814, British ships sailed into the Chesapeake Bay, landing five thousand troops and throwing the capital into a panic. The British troops entered the city and burned the White House, the Capitol, a newspaper office, and a well-stocked arsenal. Instead of trying to hold the city, the British headed north and attacked Baltimore, but a fierce defense by the Maryland militia thwarted that effort.

In another powerful offensive that same month, British troops marched from Canada into New York State, but a series of mistakes cost them a naval skirmish at Plattsburgh on Lake Champlain, and they retreated to Canada. Five months later, another large British army landed in lower Louisiana and, in early January 1815, encountered General Andrew Jackson and his militia just outside New Orleans. Jackson's forces carried the day, and Jackson instantly became known as the hero of the battle of New Orleans. No one in the United States knew that negotiators in Europe had signed a peace agreement two weeks earlier.

The Treaty of Ghent, signed in December 1814, settled few of the surface issues that had led to war. Neither country could claim victory, and no land changed hands. Instead, the treaty reflected a mutual agreement to give up certain goals. The Americans dropped their plea for an end to impressments, which in any case subsided as soon as Britain and France ended their war in 1815. They also gave up any claim to Canada. The British agreed to stop all aid to the Indians. Nothing was said about shipping rights.

Antiwar Federalists in New England could not gloat over the war's ambiguous conclusion because of an ill-timed and seemingly unpatriotic move on their part. The region's leaders had convened a secret meeting in Hartford, Connecticut, in December 1814 to discuss a series of proposals aimed at reducing the South's political power and breaking Virginia's lock on the presidency. The Federalists at Hartford even discussed secession from the Union but rejected that path. Coming just as peace was achieved, however, the Hartford Convention looked very unpatriotic. The Federalist Party never recovered, and within a few years, it was reduced to a shadow of its former self, even in New England.

Proposals Supported at the Hartford Convention

Abolition of the Constitution's three-fifths clause as a basis of representation.
Requirement of a two-thirds vote instead of a simple majority for imposing embargoes, admitting states, or declaring war.
Limit of one term for presidents.
Prohibition of the election of successive presidents from the same state.

No one really won the War of 1812. The war did, however, give rise to a new spirit of American nationalism. The paranoia over British tyranny that contributed to the outbreak of war was replaced by pride in a more equal relationship with the old mother country. Indeed, in 1817 the two countries signed the Rush-Bagot disarmament treaty (named after its two negotiators), which limited each country to a total of four naval vessels, each with just a single cannon, to patrol the vast watery border between them.

The biggest winners in the War of 1812 were the War Hawks, who took up the banner of the Republican Party and carried it in new, expansive directions. These young politicians favored trade, western expansion, internal improvements, and the energetic development of new economic markets. The biggest losers of the war were the Indians. Tecumseh was dead, his brother the Prophet was discredited, the prospects of an Indian confederacy were dashed, the Creeks' large homeland was seized, and the British protectors were gone.

QUICK REVIEW <

Why did Congress declare war on Great Britain in 1812?

| What were the challenges and successes of the Madison presidency? | To what extent did women's status change in the early Republic? | Why did partisan conflict increase during the administrations of Monroe and Adams? | Conclusion: How did republican simplicity become complex? |

To what extent did women's status change in the early Republic?

Emma Hart Willard, leading proponent of advanced education for girls, projects a calm composure and assurance in this portrait. Emma Willard School.

DOLLEY MADISON'S pioneering role as "presidentress" showed that elite women could assume an active presence in civic affairs. But, as with the 1790s cultural compromise that endorsed female education to make women into better wives and mothers (see chapter 9), Mrs. Madison and her female circle practiced politics to further their husbands' careers. There was little talk of the "rights of woman." Indeed, from 1800 to 1825, key institutions central to the shaping of women's lives—the legal system, marriage, and religion—proved fairly resistant to change. Nonetheless, the trend toward increased commitment to female education that began in the 1780s and 1790s, continued in the first decades of the nineteenth century.

feme covert

▶ Legal doctrine grounded in British common law that held that a wife's civic life was completely subsumed by her husband's. This meant that a married woman could not own property, make contracts, sue or be sued, or keep her own wages; even her children legally belonged to her husband. The doctrine shaped women's social and legal status in the early Republic despite a few departures from British law, such as limited provisions for divorce.

Women and the Law

In English common law, wives had no independent legal or political personhood. The legal doctrine of **feme covert** (covered woman) held that a wife's civic life was completely subsumed by her husband's. A wife had to obey her husband; her property was his, her domestic and sexual services were his, and even their children were legally his. Wives had no right to keep their wages or to make contracts. State legislatures passed up the opportunity to rewrite the laws of domestic relations even though they redrafted other British laws in light of republican principles.

The one aspect of family law that changed in the early Republic was divorce. Before the Revolution, only New England jurisdictions recognized a limited right to divorce; by 1820, every state except South Carolina did so. However, divorce was uncommon and in many states could be obtained only by petition to the

CHAPTER LOCATOR | How did Thomas Jefferson radically transform the presidency?

state's legislature, a daunting obstacle for many ordinary people. A mutual wish to terminate a marriage was never sufficient grounds for a legal divorce. A New York judge affirmed that "it would be aiming a deadly blow at public morals to decree a dissolution of the marriage contract merely because the parties requested it. Divorces should never be allowed, except for the protection of the innocent party, and for the punishment of the guilty." States upheld the institution of marriage both to protect persons they thought of as naturally dependent (women and children) and to regulate the use and inheritance of property. Legal enforcement of marriage as an unequal relationship played a major role in maintaining gender inequality in the nineteenth century.

Single adult women could own and convey property, make contracts, initiate lawsuits, and pay taxes. They could not vote (except in New Jersey before 1807), serve on juries, or practice law, so their civil status was limited. Single women's economic status was often limited as well, by custom as much as by law. Unless they had inherited adequate property or could live with married siblings, single adult women in the early Republic were very often poor.

None of the legal institutions that structured white gender relations applied to black slaves. Treated as property, they could not freely consent to any contractual obligations, including marriage. The protective features of state-sponsored unions were thus denied to black men and women in slavery. But this also meant that slave unions did not establish unequal power relations between partners backed by the force of law, as did marriages among the free.

Women and Church Governance

In most Protestant denominations around 1800, white women made up the majority of congregants. Yet church leadership generally rested in men's hands. There were some exceptions, however. In Baptist congregations in New England, women joined men on church governance committees that hired ministers, admitted members, and debated doctrinal points. Quakers, too, had a history of recognizing women's spiritual talents. Some were accorded the status of minister, capable of leading and speaking in Quaker meetings.

Between 1790 and 1820, a small and highly unusual set of women actively engaged in open preaching. Most were from Freewill Baptist groups centered in New England and upstate New York. Others came from small Methodist sects, and yet others rejected any formal religious affiliation. Probably fewer than a hundred such women existed, but several dozen traveled beyond their local communities, creating converts and controversy.

The best-known such woman was Jemima Wilkinson, who called herself "the Publick Universal Friend." After a near-death experience from a high fever, Wilkinson proclaimed her body no longer female or male but the incarnation of the "Spirit of Light." She dressed in men's clothes, wore her hair in a masculine style, shunned gender-specific pronouns, and preached openly in Rhode Island and Philadelphia. In the early nineteenth century, Wilkinson established a town called New Jerusalem in western New York with some 250 followers.

The decades from 1790 to the 1820s marked a period of unusual confusion, ferment, and creativity in American religion. New denominations blossomed, new styles of religiosity gripped adherents, and an extensive periodical press devoted to religion popularized all manner of theological and institutional innovations.

CHRONOLOGY

1790–1820
– In an era of religious ferment, a small number of women engage in open preaching.

1821
– Emma Willard founds the Troy Female Seminary in New York.

1822
– Catharine Beecher founds the Hartford Seminary in Connecticut for female students.

1830
– By this time, nearly two hundred female academies are operating in the United States.

What were the challenges and successes of the Madison presidency?

To what extent did women's status change in the early Republic?

Why did partisan conflict increase during the administrations of Monroe and Adams?

Conclusion: How did republican simplicity become complex?

263

Congregations increasingly attracted female participation, often eclipsing the number of male congregants. In such a climate, gender subordination came into question here and there among the most radically democratic of the churches. But the presumption of male authority over women was deeply entrenched in American culture. Even denominations that had allowed women to participate in church governance began to pull back, and most churches reinstated patterns of hierarchy along gender lines.

Female Education

First in the North and then in the South, states and localities began investing in public schools to create the educated citizenry thought necessary in a republic. Young girls attended district schools, sometimes along with boys or, in rural areas, more often in separate summer sessions. By 1830, girls had made rapid gains, in many places approaching male literacy rates.

More advanced female education came from a growing number of private academies. Judith Sargent Murray, the Massachusetts author who had called for equality of the sexes around 1790 (see chapter 9), predicted in 1800 that "a new era in female history" would emerge because "**female academies** are everywhere establishing." Some dozen female academies were established in the 1790s, and by 1830 that number had grown to nearly two hundred.

The three-year curriculum included both ornamental arts and solid academics. The former strengthened female gentility: drawing, needlework, music, and French conversation. The academic subjects included English grammar, literature, history, the natural sciences, geography, and elocution (the art of effective public speaking). Academy catalogs show that, by the 1820s, the courses and reading lists at the top female academies equaled those at male colleges such as Harvard, Yale, Dartmouth, and Princeton. The girls at these academies studied Latin, rhetoric, logic, theology, moral philosophy, algebra, geometry, and even chemistry and physics.

Two of the best-known female academies were the Troy Female Seminary in New York, founded by Emma Willard in 1821, and the Hartford Seminary in Connecticut, founded by Catharine Beecher in 1822. Both prepared their students to teach, on the grounds that women made better teachers than men did. Author Harriet Beecher Stowe, educated at her sister's school and then a teacher there, agreed: "If men have more knowledge they have less talent at communicating it. Nor have they the patience, the long-suffering, and gentleness necessary to superintend the formation of character."

The most immediate value of advanced female education lay in the self-cultivation and confidence it provided. Female graduation exercises showcased speeches and recitations performed in front of a mixed-sex audience of family, friends, and local notables. Academies also took care to promote a pleasing female modesty. Female pedantry or intellectual immodesty triggered the stereotype of the "bluestocking," a British term of hostility for a too-learned woman doomed to fail in the marriage market.

By the mid-1820s, the total annual enrollment at the female academies and seminaries equaled male enrollment at the five dozen male colleges in the United States. Both groups accounted for only about 1 percent of their age cohorts in the country at large, indicating that advanced education was clearly limited to a privileged few. Most female graduates in time married and raised families, but

female academies

▶ Private schools that began providing advanced education to teenage girls in the late 1700s. A dozen or so female academies were formed in the 1790s, and by 1830 there were almost two hundred such schools. The girls at these academies were primarily daughters of elite families and received instruction in ornamental arts (drawing, needlework, music, dancing) as well as in academic subjects such as English grammar, literature, history, geography, and the natural sciences.

CHAPTER LOCATOR | How did Thomas Jefferson radically transform the presidency?

264 CHAPTER 10 A MATURING REPUBLIC, 1800–1824

first many of them became teachers at academies and district schools. A large number also became authors, contributing essays and poetry to newspapers, editing periodicals, and publishing novels. The new attention to the training of female minds laid the foundation for major changes in the gender system as girl students of the 1810s matured into adult women of the 1830s.

▶ FOR MORE HELP ANALYZING THIS IMAGE, see the visual activity for this chapter in the Online Study Guide at bedfordstmartins.com/roarkunderstanding.

QUICK REVIEW <

How did the civil status of American women and men differ in the early Republic?

| What were the challenges and successes of the Madison presidency? | **To what extent did women's status change in the early Republic?** | Why did partisan conflict increase during the administrations of Monroe and Adams? | Conclusion: How did republican simplicity become complex? |

Why did partisan conflict increase during the administrations of Monroe and Adams?

Election Sewing Box Everyday household objects could become vehicles for the expression of political partisanship. Here a sewing box sporting John Quincy Adams's face allowed its owner—almost certainly a woman—to proclaim her sympathy for the Adams Republicans. On the top of the Adams box sits a velvet pincushion (not visible here) printed with the slogan "Be Firm for Adams." Collection of Janice L. and David J. Frent.

IN 1816, JAMES MONROE beat Federalist Rufus King of New York, garnering 183 electoral votes to King's 34. In 1820, Republican Monroe was reelected with all but one electoral vote. At the state level, increasing voter engagement sparked a drive for universal white male suffrage. The collapse of the Federalist Party ushered in an apparent period of one-party rule, but politics remained highly contentious, with many factors promoting increased partisanship. Put to the test of practical circumstances, the one-party political system failed and then fractured.

From Property to Democracy

Up to 1820, presidential elections occurred in the electoral college, at a remove from ordinary voters. The excitement generated by state elections, however, created pressure for greater democratization of presidential elections.

In the 1780s, twelve of the original thirteen states enacted property qualifications based on the theory that only male freeholders—landowners, as distinct from tenants or servants—had sufficient independence of mind to be entrusted with the vote. Of course, not everyone accepted that restricted idea of the people's role in government (see chapter 8). In the 1790s, Vermont became the first state to enfranchise all adult males, and four other states soon broadened suffrage considerably by allowing all taxpayers to vote. Between 1800 and 1830, greater democratization became a lively issue both in established states and in new states emerging in the West.

In new states, small populations together with yet smaller numbers of large property owners meant that few men could vote under typical restrictive property qualifications. Congress initially set a fifty-acre freehold as the threshold for voting, but in Illinois, fewer than three hundred men met that test at the time of

CHAPTER LOCATOR | How did Thomas Jefferson radically transform the presidency?

statehood. When Indiana, Illinois, and Mississippi became states, their constitutions granted suffrage to all taxpayers. Five additional new western states abandoned property and taxpayer qualifications altogether.

The most heated battles over suffrage occurred in eastern states, where expanding numbers of commercial men, renters, and mortgage holders of all classes contended with entrenched landed elites who, not surprisingly, favored the status quo. Still, by 1820, a half dozen states passed suffrage reform. Some stopped short of complete manhood suffrage, instead tying the vote to tax status or militia service. In the remainder of the states, the defenders of landed property qualifications managed to delay expanded suffrage for two more decades. But it was increasingly hard to persuade the disfranchised that landowners alone had a stake in government. Proponents of the status quo began to argue instead that the "industry and good habits" necessary to achieve a propertied status in life were what gave landowners the right character to vote. Rejecting that position, one delegate to New York's constitutional convention said, "More integrity and more patriotism are generally found in the labouring class of the community than in the higher orders." Owning land was no more predictive of wisdom and good character than it was of a person's height or strength, said another.

Both sides of the debate generally agreed that character mattered, and many ideas for ensuring an electorate of proper wisdom came up for discussion. The exclusion of paupers and felons convicted of "infamous crimes" found favor in legislation in many states. Literacy tests and raising the voting age to a figure in the thirties were debated but ultimately discarded. In one exceptional moment, at the Virginia convention in 1829, a delegate wondered aloud why unmarried women over the age of twenty-one could not vote; he was quickly silenced with the argument that all women lacked the "free agency and intelligence" necessary for wise voting.

Free black men's enfranchisement generated much discussion at all the conventions. Under existing freehold qualifications, a small number of propertied black men could vote; universal or taxpayer suffrage would inevitably enfranchise many more. Many delegates at the various state conventions spoke against that extension, claiming that blacks as a race lacked prudence, independence, and knowledge. With the exception of New York, which retained the existing property qualification for black voters as it removed it for whites, the general pattern was one of expanded suffrage for whites and a total eclipse of suffrage for blacks.

The Missouri Compromise

The politics of race produced perhaps the most divisive issue during Monroe's term. In February 1819, Missouri applied for statehood. Since 1815, four other states had joined the Union (Indiana, Mississippi, Illinois, and Alabama) following the blueprint laid out by the Northwest Ordinance of 1787. But Missouri posed a problem. Although much of its area was on the same latitude as the free state of Illinois, its territorial population included ten thousand slaves brought there by southern planters.

The problem led a New York congressman, James Tallmadge Jr., to propose two amendments to the statehood bill. The first stipulated that slaves born in Missouri after statehood would be free at age twenty-five, and the second declared that no new slaves could be imported into the state. Tallmadge's model was New York's gradual emancipation law of 1799. It did not strip slave owners of their

CHRONOLOGY

1816
- Republican James Monroe is elected president.

1820
- Missouri Compromise allows Missouri to enter the Union as a slave state and Maine to enter as a free state and sets a boundary for future slave states.

1823
- Monroe Doctrine asserts that the Western Hemisphere should be free from European interference.

1825
- John Quincy Adams is elected president by House of Representatives in a bitterly contested election.

| What were the challenges and successes of the Madison presidency? | To what extent did women's status change in the early Republic? | **Why did partisan conflict increase during the administrations of Monroe and Adams?** | Conclusion: How did republican simplicity become complex? |

267

current property, and it allowed them full use of the labor of newborn slaves well into their prime productive years. Still, southern congressmen objected because in the long run the amendments would make Missouri a free state, presumably no longer allied with southern economic and political interests. Just as southern economic power rested on slave labor, southern political power drew extra strength from the slave population because of the three-fifths rule. In 1820, the South owed seventeen of its seats in the House of Representatives to its slave population.

Tallmadge's amendments passed in the House by a close and sharply sectional vote of North against South. The ferocious debate led a Georgia representative to observe that the question had started "a fire which all the waters of the ocean could not extinguish. It can be extinguished only in blood." The Senate, with an even number of slave and free states, voted down the amendments, and Missouri statehood was postponed until the next congressional term.

In 1820, a compromise emerged. Maine, once part of Massachusetts, applied for statehood as a free state, balancing against Missouri as a slave state. The Senate further agreed that the southern boundary of Missouri—latitude 36°30'—extended west, would become the permanent line dividing slave from free states, guaranteeing the North a large area where slavery was banned (**Map 10.4**). The House also approved the **Missouri Compromise**, thanks to expert deal brokering by Kentucky's Henry Clay. The whole package passed because seventeen northern congressmen decided that minimizing sectional conflict was the best course and voted with the South.

President Monroe and former president Jefferson at first worried that the Missouri crisis would reinvigorate the Federalist Party as the party of the North. But even ex-Federalists agreed that the split between free and slave states was too danger-

Missouri Compromise

▶ 1820 congressional compromise engineered by Henry Clay that allowed Missouri to enter the Union as a slave state and Maine to enter as a free state. The compromise also established Missouri's southern border as the permanent line dividing slave from free states. The Missouri Compromise calmed tensions in the short run but did nothing to resolve the underlying issue of the future of slavery in the United States.

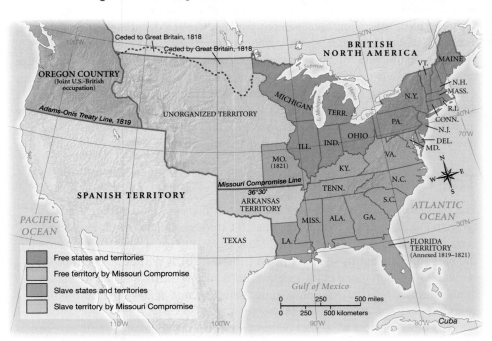

MAP 10.4 ■ The Missouri Compromise, 1820
After a difficult battle in Congress, Missouri entered the Union in 1821 as part of a package of compromises. Maine was admitted as a free state to balance slavery in Missouri, and a line drawn at latitude 36°30' put most of the rest of the Louisiana Territory off-limits to slavery in the future.

CHAPTER LOCATOR | How did Thomas Jefferson radically transform the presidency?

A View of St. Louis from an Illinois Town, 1835

Just fifteen years after the Missouri Compromise, St. Louis was already a booming city, having gotten its start in the eighteenth century as a French fur-trading village. In this 1835 view, commercial buildings and steamships line the riverfront; a ferry on the Illinois shore prepares to transport travelers across the Mississippi River. Black laborers (in the foreground) handle loading tasks. Illinois was a free state; Missouri, where the ferry will land, was a slave state. *A View of St. Louis from an Illinois Town*, 1835: Private collection.

> ▶ FOR MORE HELP ANALYZING THIS IMAGE, see the visual activity for this chapter in the Online Study Guide at bedfordstmartins.com/roarkunderstanding.

ous a fault line to be permitted to become a shaper of national politics. When new parties did develop in the 1830s, they took pains to bridge geography, each party developing a presence in both North and South. Monroe and Jefferson also worried about the future of slavery. Both understood slavery to be deeply problematic, but, as Jefferson said, "we have the wolf by the ears, and we can neither hold him, nor safely let him go. Justice is in one scale, and self-preservation in the other."

The Monroe Doctrine

New foreign policy challenges arose even as Congress struggled with the slavery issue. In 1816, U.S. troops led by General Andrew Jackson invaded Spanish Florida in search of Seminole Indians harboring escaped slaves. Once there, Jackson declared himself the commander of northern Florida, demonstrating his power in

| What were the challenges and successes of the Madison presidency? | To what extent did women's status change in the early Republic? | Why did partisan conflict increase during the administrations of Monroe and Adams? | Conclusion: How did republican simplicity become complex? |

1818 by executing two British men who he claimed were dangerous enemies. In asserting rule over the territory, and in executing the two British subjects on Spanish land, Jackson had gone too far. Privately, President Monroe was distressed and pondered court-martialing Jackson, prevented only by Jackson's immense popularity as the hero of the battle of New Orleans. Instead, John Quincy Adams, the secretary of state, negotiated with Spain the Adams-Onís Treaty, which delivered Florida to the United States in 1819. In exchange, the Americans agreed to abandon any claim to Texas or Cuba. Southerners viewed this as a large concession, having eyed both places as potential acquisitions for future slave states.

Spain at that moment was preoccupied with its colonies in South America. One after another, Chile, Colombia, Peru, and finally Mexico declared themselves independent in the early 1820s. To discourage Spain or France from reconquering these colonies, Monroe in 1823 formulated a declaration of principles on South America, known in later years as the **Monroe Doctrine**. The president warned that "the American Continents, by the free and independent condition which they have assumed and maintain, are henceforth not to be considered as subjects for future colonization by any European power." Any attempt to interfere in the Western Hemisphere would be regarded as "the manifestation of an unfriendly disposition towards the United States." In exchange for noninterference by Europeans, Monroe pledged that the United States would stay out of European struggles.

The Election of 1824

Monroe's nonpartisan administration was the last of its kind, a throwback to eighteenth-century ideals, as was Monroe, with his powdered wig and knee breeches. Monroe's cabinet contained men of sharply different philosophies, all calling themselves Republicans. Secretary of State **John Quincy Adams** represented the urban Northeast; South Carolinian John C. Calhoun spoke for the planter aristocracy as secretary of war; and William H. Crawford of Georgia, secretary of the treasury, was a proponent of Jeffersonian states' rights and limited federal power. Even before the end of Monroe's first term, these men and others began to maneuver for the election of 1824.

Crucially helping them to maneuver were their wives, who accomplished some of the work of modern campaign managers by courting men—and women—of influence. Louisa Catherine Adams had a weekly party for guests numbering in the hundreds. The somber Adams lacked charm—"I am a man of reserved, cold, austere, and forbidding manners," he once wrote—but his abundantly charming (and hardworking) wife made up for that. She attended to the etiquette of social calls, sometimes making two dozen in a morning, and counted sixty-eight members of Congress as her regular guests.

John Quincy Adams (and Louisa Catherine) were ambitious for the presidency, but so were others. Candidate Henry Clay, Speaker of the House and negotiator of the Treaty of Ghent with Britain in 1814, promoted a new "American System," a package of protective tariffs to encourage manufacturing and federal expenditures for internal improvements such as roads and canals. Treasurer William Crawford was a favorite of Republicans from Virginia and New York, even after he suffered an incapacitating stroke in mid-1824. Calhoun was another serious contender, having served in Congress and in several cabinets. A southern

Monroe Doctrine
▶ 1823 declaration by President James Monroe that the United States would regard any attempt by an external power to interfere in the Western Hemisphere as a hostile act. In exchange for noninterference by Europeans, Monroe pledged that the United States would stay out of European struggles. The Monroe Doctrine became the foundation of U.S. foreign policy with respect to the Western Hemisphere.

John Quincy Adams
▶ Secretary of state during James Monroe's administration. In 1819, he negotiated the Adams-Onís Treaty with Spain, which gave the United States control over Florida in exchange for relinquishing U.S. claims to Texas and Cuba. Adams also served as president from 1825 to 1829, at which time it became clear that he lacked the political skills necessary to manage the fractures in his cabinet or to advance his legislative goals.

CHAPTER LOCATOR | How did Thomas Jefferson radically transform the presidency?

CHAPTER 10
270 A MATURING REPUBLIC, 1800–1824

planter, he attracted northern support for his backing of internal improvements and protective tariffs.

The final candidate was an outsider and a latecomer: General Andrew Jackson of Tennessee. Jackson had far less national political experience than the others, but he enjoyed great celebrity from his military career. When Jackson's supporters put his name forward for the presidency, voters in the West and South reacted with enthusiasm. Adams was dismayed, while Calhoun dropped out of the race.

Along with democratizing the vote, eighteen states had put the power to choose members of the electoral college directly in the hands of voters, making the 1824 election the first one to have a popular vote tally for the presidency. Jackson proved by far to be the most popular candidate, winning 153,544 votes. Adams was second with 108,740, Clay won 47,136 votes, and Crawford garnered 46,618.

In the electoral college, Jackson received 99 votes, Adams 84, Crawford 41, and Clay 37 (**Map 10.5**). Jackson lacked a majority, so the House of Representatives stepped in for the second time in U.S. history. Each congressional delegation had one vote; according to the Constitution's Twelfth Amendment, only the top three candidates joined the runoff. Thus Henry Clay was out of the race and in a position to bestow his support on another candidate.

Jackson's supporters later characterized the election of 1824 as the "corrupt bargain." Clay backed Adams, and Adams won by one vote in the House in February 1825. Clay's support made sense on several levels. Despite strong mutual dislike, he and Adams agreed on issues such as federal support to build roads and canals. Moreover, Clay was uneasy with Jackson's volatile temperament and unstated political views and with Crawford's diminished capacity. What made

MAP 10.5 ■ The Election of 1824

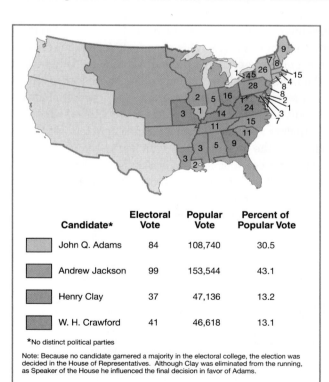

Candidate*	Electoral Vote	Popular Vote	Percent of Popular Vote
John Q. Adams	84	108,740	30.5
Andrew Jackson	99	153,544	43.1
Henry Clay	37	47,136	13.2
W. H. Crawford	41	46,618	13.1

*No distinct political parties

Note: Because no candidate garnered a majority in the electoral college, the election was decided in the House of Representatives. Although Clay was eliminated from the running, as Speaker of the House he influenced the final decision in favor of Adams.

| What were the challenges and successes of the Madison presidency? | To what extent did women's status change in the early Republic? | Why did partisan conflict increase during the administrations of Monroe and Adams? | Conclusion: How did republican simplicity become complex? |

Clay's decision look "corrupt" was that immediately after the election, Adams offered to appoint Clay secretary of state—and Clay accepted.

In fact, there probably was no concrete bargain; Adams's subsequent cabinet appointments demonstrated his lack of political astuteness. But Andrew Jackson felt that the election had been stolen from him, and he wrote bitterly that "the Judas of the West [Clay] has closed the contract and will receive the thirty pieces of silver."

The Adams Administration

John Quincy Adams, like his father, was a one-term president. His career had been built on diplomacy, not electoral politics, and his political horse sense was not well developed. With his cabinet choices, he welcomed his opposition into his inner circle. He asked Crawford to stay on in the Treasury. He retained an openly pro-Jackson postmaster general even though that position controlled thousands of nationwide patronage appointments. He even asked Jackson to become secretary of war. With Calhoun as vice president (elected without opposition by the electoral college) and Clay at the State Department, the whole argumentative crew would have been thrust into the executive branch. Crawford and Jackson had the good sense to decline the appointments.

Adams had lofty ideas for federal action during his presidency, and the plan he put before Congress was sweeping. Adams called for federally built roads, canals, and harbors. He proposed a national university in Washington as well as government-sponsored scientific research. He wanted to build observatories to advance astronomical knowledge and to promote precision in timekeeping, and he backed a decimal-based system of weights and measures. In all these endeavors, Adams believed he was continuing the legacy of Jefferson and Madison, using the powers of government to advance knowledge. But his opponents feared he was too Hamiltonian, using federal power inappropriately to advance commercial interests.

Lacking the give-and-take political skills required to gain congressional support, Adams was unable to implement much of his program. He scorned the idea of courting voters to gain support and using the patronage system to enhance his power. He often made appointments to placate enemies rather than to reward friends. A story of a toast offered to the president may well have been mythical, but it came to summarize Adams's precarious hold on leadership. A dignitary raised a glass and said, "May he strike confusion to his foes," to which another voice scornfully chimed in, "as he has already done to his friends."

> **QUICK REVIEW**

How did the collapse of the Federalist Party influence the administrations of James Monroe and John Quincy Adams?

CHAPTER LOCATOR | How did Thomas Jefferson radically transform the presidency?

CHAPTER 10
272 A MATURING REPUBLIC, 1800–1824

Picture Research Consultants & Archives.

Conclusion: How did republican simplicity become complex?

THE JEFFERSONIAN REPUBLICANS tried at first to undo much of what the Federalists had created in the 1790s, but their promise of a simpler government gave way to the complexities of domestic and foreign issues. The sudden acquisition of the Louisiana Purchase promised land and opportunity to settlers but also complicated the country's political future with the issues central to the Missouri Compromise. Antagonism from both foreign and Indian nations led to complex and costly policies, culminating in the War of 1812.

The war elevated to national prominence General Andrew Jackson, whose popularity with voters in the 1824 election surprised traditional politicians and threw the one-party rule of Republicans into a tailspin. John Quincy Adams had barely assumed office in 1825 before the election campaign of 1828 was off and running. Appeals to the people—the mass of white male voters—would be the hallmark of all elections after 1824. It was a game Adams could not easily play.

Politics in this entire period was a game that women could not play either. Except for the political wives of Washington, women, whether white or free black, had no place in government. Male legislatures maintained women's feme covert status, keeping wives dependent on husbands. A few women found a pathway to greater personal autonomy through religion. Meanwhile, the routine inclusion of girls in public schools and the steady spread of female academies planted seeds that would blossom into a major transformation of gender in the 1830s and 1840s.

The War of 1812 started another chain of events that would prove momentous in later decades. Jefferson's long embargo and Madison's wartime trade stoppages gave strong encouragement to American manufacturing, momentarily protected from competition with British factories. When peace returned in 1815, the years of independent development burst forth into a period of sustained economic growth that continued nearly unabated into the mid-nineteenth century.

SO NOW YOU KNOW

When he took office in 1801, Thomas Jefferson promised to counter the influence of the Federalists and to restore smaller, simpler government. But the increasing complexity of domestic and international issues in the early 1800s actually required Jefferson and his Republican successors to expand the federal government's size and influence.

What were the challenges and successes of the Madison presidency?

To what extent did women's status change in the early Republic?

Why did partisan conflict increase during the administrations of Monroe and Adams?

Conclusion: How did republican simplicity become complex?

CHAPTER 10 STUDY GUIDE

Online Study Guide
bedfordstmartins.com/roarkunderstanding

STEP 1 GETTING STARTED

Below are basic terms from this period in American history. Can you identify each term below and explain why it matters? To do this exercise online or to download this chart, visit bedfordstmartins.com/roarkunderstanding.

TERM	WHO OR WHAT & WHEN	WHY IT MATTERS
Thomas Jefferson, p. 250		
Marbury v. Madison, p. 252		
Louisiana Purchase, p. 253		
Lewis and Clark expedition, p. 254		
Dolley Madison, p. 257		
Tecumseh, p. 258		
War of 1812, p. 259		
feme covert, p. 262		
female academies, p. 264		
Missouri Compromise, p. 268		
Monroe Doctrine, p. 270		
John Quincy Adams, p. 270		

STEP 2 MOVING BEYOND THE BASICS

The exercise below represents a more advanced understanding of the chapter material. Explore the key events of the presidents in the early nineteenth century, using the results to formulate an accurate and insightful overview of their administrations. Fill in the chart below by describing the important aspects and developments of each administration, and the results those policies produced. What core assumptions and beliefs informed each president's policies and positions? How did each successive president change the presidency? To do this exercise online or to download this chart, visit bedfordstmartins.com/roarkunderstanding.

Aspects and developments	Jefferson	Madison	Monroe	J. Q. Adams
Power of the presidency				
Expansion of the nation				
Domestic affairs				
Foreign affairs				
Difficulties				
Successes				

STEP

3

PUTTING IT ALL TOGETHER

Now that you have reviewed key elements of the chapter, take a step back and try to explain the big picture by answering these questions. Remember to use specific examples from the chapter in your answers. To do this exercise online, visit bedfordstmartins.com/roarkunderstanding.

JEFFERSON AND REPUBLICANISM

▶ Why did Jefferson believe that western expansion was so important? How did he encourage expansion?

▶ How did foreign policy issues shape the Jefferson presidency?

MADISON AND THE WAR OF 1812

▶ Where was support for the War of 1812 strongest? Where was it weakest? Why?

▶ How did the status of women change in the early decades of the nineteenth century? In what ways did some women exert political influence?

MONROE, ADAMS, AND PARTISANSHIP

▶ What forces led to the expansion of the franchise in the early nineteenth century?

▶ In what ways did the election of 1824 mark a turning point in American politics?

LOOKING BACKWARD, LOOKING AHEAD

▶ How did the partisanship of the 1820s differ from the partisanship of the 1790s? What explains the changes you note?

▶ What problems were solved by the Missouri Compromise? What tensions and conflicts were left unresolved?

IN YOUR OWN WORDS

Imagine that you must explain chapter 10 to someone who hasn't read it. What would be the most important points to include and why?

11
THE EXPANDING REPUBLIC

1815–1840

> This chapter explores the causes and consequences of the market revolution, examining its impact on American social and cultural life. It also traces the political development of the United States between 1828 and 1840, noting the connections between political events and their larger social, cultural, and economic context.

> What caused the market revolution?

> What changes in national politics were reflected in the election of 1828?

> What was Andrew Jackson's impact on the presidency?

> How did the market revolution transform social and cultural life?

> Why was Martin Van Buren a one-term president?

> Conclusion: Age of Jackson or era of reform?

DID YOU KNOW?

Before 1815, it cost as much to ship a crate over thirty miles of domestic roads in the United States as it did to send it across the Atlantic Ocean.

The Clermont. Robert Fulton's steamboat travels up the Hudson River from New York City.

> What caused the market revolution?

The Erie Canal at Lockport

When the Erie Canal was completed in 1825, it was impressive not only for its length of 350 miles but also for its elevation. Eighty-three locks were required to move canal boats over the combined ascent and descent of 680 feet. The biggest challenge came at Lockport, 20 miles northeast of Buffalo, where the canal traversed a steep slate escarpment by means of five double locks, which slowed traffic considerably. The village of Lockport grew up here to service waiting passengers and crews. Library of Congress.

THE RETURN OF PEACE in 1815 unleashed powerful forces that revolutionized the organization of the economy. Spectacular changes in transportation facilitated the movement of commodities, information, and people, while textile mills and other factories created many new jobs, especially for young unmarried women. Innovations in banking, legal practices, and tariff policies promoted swift economic growth.

This was not yet an industrial revolution, as was beginning in Britain, but rather a market revolution fueled by traditional sources—water, wood, beasts of burden, and human muscle. What was new was the accelerated pace of economic activity and the scale of the distribution of goods. The new nature and scale of production and consumption changed Americans' economic behavior, attitudes, and expectations.

Improvements in Transportation

Before 1815, transportation in the United States was slow and expensive; it cost as much to ship a crate over thirty miles of domestic roads as it did to send it across

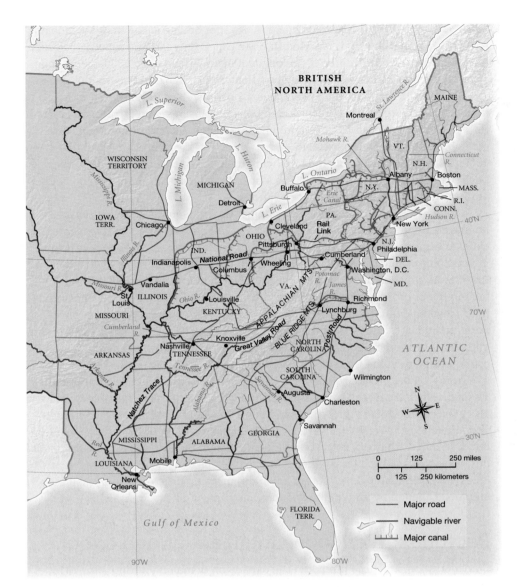

MAP 11.1 ■ Routes of Transportation in 1840
By the 1830s, transportation advances had cut travel times significantly. By way of the Erie Canal, goods and people could move from New York City to Buffalo in four days, a trip that had taken two weeks by road in 1800. Similarly, the trip from New York to New Orleans, which had taken four weeks in 1800, could now be accomplished in less than half that time on steamboats plying the western rivers.

CHRONOLOGY

1807
– Robert Fulton's *Clermont* sets off steamboat craze.

1816
– Second Bank of the United States is chartered.

1819
– Economic panic leads to the loss of property and jobs for thousands.

1821
– Mill town of Lowell, Massachusetts, is founded.

1825
– Erie Canal is completed in New York, extending 350 miles between Albany and Buffalo.

1829
– Baltimore and Ohio Railroad starts laying track.

1834
– Female mill workers strike in Lowell, Massachusetts, and again in 1836.

the Atlantic Ocean. A stagecoach trip from Boston to New York took four days. But between 1815 and 1840, networks of roads, canals, steamboats, and finally railroads dramatically raised the speed and lowered the cost of travel (**Map 11.1**).

Improved transportation moved goods into wider markets. It moved passengers, too, broadening their horizons and allowing young people as well as adults to take up new employment in cities or factory towns. Transportation also facilitated the flow of political information via the U.S. mail. Enhanced public transport was expensive and produced uneven economic benefits, so presidents from Jefferson to Monroe were reluctant to fund it with federal dollars. Instead, private investors pooled resources and chartered transport companies, receiving significant subsidies and monopoly rights from state governments. Turnpike and roadway mileage increased dramatically after 1815, reducing shipping costs. Stagecoach companies proliferated, and travel time on main routes was cut in half.

Water travel was similarly transformed. In 1807, Robert Fulton's steam-propelled boat, the *Clermont*, churned up the Hudson River from New York City to

| What changes in national politics were reflected in the election of 1828? | What was Andrew Jackson's impact on the presidency? | How did the market revolution transform social and cultural life? | Why was Martin Van Buren a one-term president? | Conclusion: Age of Jackson or era of reform? |

Albany, touching off a steamboat craze. A voyager on one of the first steamboats to go down the Mississippi reported that the Chickasaw Indians called the vessel a "fire canoe" and considered it "an omen of evil." By the early 1830s, more than seven hundred steamboats were in operation on the Ohio and Mississippi rivers.

Steamboats were not benign advances, however. The urgency to cut travel time led to overstoked furnaces, sudden boiler explosions, and terrible mass fatalities. Another huge cost, to the environment, was the deforestation brought by steamboats, which had to load fuel—"wood up"—every twenty miles or so. By the 1830s, the banks of many main rivers were denuded of trees, and forests miles back from the rivers fell to the ax. The smoke from wood-burning steamboats created America's first significant air pollution.

Canals were another major innovation of the transportation revolution. Pennsylvania in 1815 and New York in 1817 commenced major state-sponsored canal enterprises. Pennsylvania's Schuylkill Canal stretched 108 miles west from Philadelphia when it was completed in 1826. Much more impressive was the **Erie Canal**, finished in 1825, covering 350 miles between Albany and Buffalo and linking the port of New York City with the entire Great Lakes region. Wheat and flour moved east, household goods and tools moved west, and passengers went in both directions. By the 1830s, the cost of shipping by canal fell to less than a tenth of the cost of overland transport, and New York City quickly became the premier commercial city in the United States.

In the 1830s, private railroad companies began to give canals competition. The nation's first railroad, the Baltimore and Ohio, laid thirteen miles of track in 1829. During the 1830s, three thousand more miles of track materialized nationwide. Rail lines in the 1830s were generally short, on the order of twenty to one hundred miles. They did not yet provide an efficient distribution system for goods, but passengers flocked to experience the marvelous speeds of fifteen to twenty miles per hour. Railroads and other advances in transportation made possible enormous change by unifying the country culturally and economically.

Factories, Workingwomen, and Wage Labor

Transportation advances promoted the expansion of manufacturing after 1815, creating an ever-expanding market for goods. The two leading industries, textiles and shoes, altered methods of production and labor relations. Textile production was greatly spurred by the development of water-driven machinery built near fast-coursing rivers. Shoe manufacturing, still using the power and skill of human hands, involved only a reorganization of production. Shoes and textiles pulled young women into wage-earning labor for the first time.

The earliest textile factory was built by English immigrant Samuel Slater in Pawtucket, Rhode Island, in the 1790s. By 1815, nearly 170 spinning mills had been built along New England rivers. In British manufacturing cities, entire families worked in low-wage, health-threatening factories. In contrast, American factories targeted young women as employees; they were cheap to hire because of their limited employment options. "Mill girls" would retire to marriage, replaced by fresh recruits earning beginners' wages.

In 1821, a group of Boston entrepreneurs founded the town of Lowell on the Merrimack River, centralizing all aspects of cloth production: combing, shrinking, spinning, weaving, and dyeing. By 1836, the eight Lowell mills employed more

Erie Canal
▶ Canal finished in 1825, covering 350 miles between Albany and Buffalo and linking the port of New York City with the entire Great Lakes region. Aided by the canal, New York City quickly became the premier commercial city in the United States. The Erie Canal was a powerful example of the economic impact of the transportation revolution.

CHAPTER LOCATOR | What caused the market revolution?

than five thousand young women, who lived in carefully managed company-owned boardinghouses.

Life in the Lowell Mills

Rules: church attendance mandatory, drinking and unsupervised courtship prohibited, dorms locked at 10 p.m.

Wages: typically $2 to $3 for a seventy-hour week.

Work: tending noisy power looms in hot and humid rooms.

Young women embraced factory work as a means to earn spending money and build savings before marriage. Also welcome was the unprecedented, though still limited, personal freedom of living in an all-female social space, away from parents and domestic tasks. In the evening, the women could engage in self-improvement activities, such as attending lectures or writing for the company's periodical, the *Lowell Offering*.

In the mid-1830s, worldwide changes in the cotton market impelled mill owners to speed up work and decrease wages. The workers protested, emboldened by their communal living arrangement and by their relative independence as temporary employees. In 1834 and again in 1836, hundreds of women at the Lowell mills went out on strike. All over New England, female mill workers led strikes and formed unions. In 1834, mill women in Dover, New Hampshire, denounced their owners for trying to turn them into "slaves": "However freely the epithet of 'factory slaves' may be bestowed upon us, we will never deserve it by a base and cringing submission to proud wealth or haughty insolence." Their assertiveness surprised many, but ultimately the ease of replacing them undermined their bargaining power, and owners in the 1840s began to shift to immigrant families as their primary labor source.

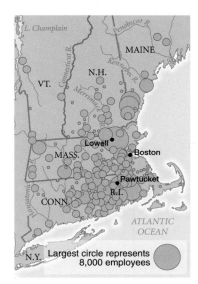

Cotton Textile Industry, ca. 1840

Mill Worker Tending a Power Loom, 1850

This daguerreotype (the earliest form of photograph) shows a young woman tending a power loom in a textile mill. In the 1830s, women weavers generally tended two machines at a time. In the 1840s, some companies increased the workload to four. American Textile History Museum.

What changes in national politics were reflected in the election of 1828?

What was Andrew Jackson's impact on the presidency?

How did the market revolution transform social and cultural life?

Why was Martin Van Buren a one-term president?

Conclusion: Age of Jackson or era of reform?

The shoe manufacturing industry centered in eastern New England reorganized production and hired women, including wives, as shoebinders. Male shoemakers still cut the leather and made the soles in shops, but female shoebinders working from home now stitched the upper parts of the shoes. Working from home meant that wives could still perform their domestic chores. But they earned money to contribute to family income, which was unusual for most wives in that period.

In the economically turbulent 1830s, shoebinder wages fell. Unlike mill workers, female shoebinders worked in isolation, a serious hindrance to organized protest. In Lynn, Massachusetts, a major shoemaking center, women used female church networks to organize resistance. The Lynn shoebinders who demanded higher wages in 1834 built on a collective sense of themselves as women. "Equal rights should be extended to all—to the weaker sex as well as the stronger," they wrote in a document establishing the Female Society of Lynn.

In the end, the Lynn shoebinders' protests failed to achieve wage increases. At-home workers all over New England continued to accept low wages, and even in Lynn, many women shied away from organized protest, preferring to situate their work in the context of family duty (helping their husbands to finish the shoes) instead of market relations.

Bankers and Lawyers

Entrepreneurs like the Lowell factory owners relied on innovations in the banking system to finance their ventures. Between 1814 and 1816, the number of state-chartered banks in the United States more than doubled from fewer than 90 to 208. By 1830, there were 330, and by 1840 hundreds more. Banks stimulated the economy by making loans to merchants and manufacturers and by enlarging the money supply. Borrowers were issued loans in the form of banknotes—certificates unique to each bank—that were used as money for all transactions. Neither federal nor state governments issued paper money, so banknotes became the country's currency.

second Bank of the United States

▶ National bank chartered in 1816. The rechartering of the bank was a major issue in Andrew Jackson's reelection campaign in 1832. Efforts by Daniel Webster and Henry Clay to use Jackson's opposition to the bank against him backfired, helping Jackson win the election and put an end to the bank.

Bankers exercised great power over the economy, and the most powerful bankers sat on the board of directors for the **second Bank of the United States**, headquartered in Philadelphia. The twenty-year charter of the first Bank of the United States had expired in 1811. The second Bank of the United States, with eighteen branches throughout the country, opened for business in 1816 under another twenty-year charter. The rechartering of this bank would become a major issue in the 1832 presidential campaign.

Lawyer-politicians too exercised economic power, by refashioning commercial law to enhance the prospects of private investment. In 1811, states started to rewrite their laws of incorporation (allowing the chartering of businesses by states), and the number of corporations expanded rapidly, from about twenty in 1800 to eighteen hundred by 1817. Incorporation protected individual investors from being held liable for corporate debts. State lawmakers also wrote laws of eminent domain, empowering states to buy land for roads and canals even from unwilling sellers. In such ways, entrepreneurial lawyers of the 1820s and 1830s created the legal foundation for an economy that favored ambitious individuals interested in maximizing their own wealth.

Not everyone applauded these developments. **Andrew Jackson**, himself a skillful lawyer turned politician, spoke for a large and mistrustful segment of the population when he warned about the potential abuses of power "which the mon-eyed interest derives from a paper currency which they are able to control, from the multitude of corporations with exclusive privileges which they have suc-ceeded in obtaining in the different states, and which are employed altogether for their benefit." Jacksonians believed that ending government-granted privileges was the way to maximize individual liberty and economic opportunity.

Booms and Busts

One aspect of the economy that the lawyer-politicians could not control was the threat of financial collapse. In 1819 and again in the 1830s, boom times of high inflation and speculative investment were punctured by sharp economic reces-sions called "panics." Some blamed the panic of 1819 on the second Bank of the United States for failing to control state banks that had suspended specie payments—the exchange of gold or silver for banknotes—in their eagerness to expand the economic bubble. By mid-1818, when the Bank of the United States called in its loans and insisted that the state banks do likewise, the contracting of the money supply sent tremors throughout the economy. The crunch was made worse by a financial crisis in Europe in the spring of 1819. Overseas, prices for American cotton, tobacco, and wheat plummeted by more than 50 percent. Thus, when the banks began to call in their outstanding loans, American debtors involved in the commodities trade could not come up with the money. The intri-cate web of credit and debt relationships meant that almost everyone with even a toehold in the new commercial economy was affected by the panic. Thousands of Americans lost their savings and property, and unemployment estimates suggest that half a million people lost their jobs.

Recovery took several years. Unemployment declined, but bitterness lingered, ready to be stirred up by politicians in the decades to come. The dangers of a sys-tem dependent on extensive credit were now clear. In one folksy formulation that circulated around 1820, a farmer compared credit to "a man pissing in his breeches on a cold day to keep his arse warm—very comfortable at first but I dare say . . . you know how it feels afterwards."

By the mid-1820s, the economy was back on track, driven by increases in pro-ductivity, consumer demand for goods, and international trade. Despite the panic of 1819, credit financing continued to fuel the system. A network of credit and debt relations grew dense by the 1830s in a system that encouraged speculation and risk taking. A pervasive optimism about continued growth supported the elaborate system, but a single business failure could produce many innocent vic-tims. Well after the panic of 1819, an undercurrent of anxiety about rapid eco-nomic change continued to shape the political views of many Americans.

Andrew Jackson

▶ U.S. president from 1829 to 1837 whose tough, unrefined frontier image helped define the age. His presidency coincided with the democratization of American politics. He presided over the removal of Indians from most of the eastern states and the destruction of the second Bank of the United States.

QUICK REVIEW <

What role did state governments play in stimulating the market revolution?

| What changes in national politics were reflected in the election of 1828? | What was Andrew Jackson's impact on the presidency? | How did the market revolution transform social and cultural life? | Why was Martin Van Buren a one-term president? | Conclusion: Age of Jackson or era of reform? |

> What changes in national politics were reflected in the election of 1828?

Campaign Poster for 1828 Election

This poster praises Andrew Jackson as a war hero and a "man of the people" and reminds readers that Jackson, who won the largest popular vote in 1824, did not stoop to "bargain for the presidency," as John Quincy Adams presumably had in his dealings with Henry Clay. © Collection of the New-York Historical Society.

JUST AS THE MARKET REVOLUTION held out the promise, if not the reality, of economic opportunity for all who worked, the political transformation of the 1830s held out the promise of political opportunity for hundreds of thousands of new voters. During Andrew Jackson's presidency (1829–1837), the second American party system took shape. Not until 1836, however, would the parties have distinct names and consistent programs transcending the particular personalities running for office. Over those years, more men could and did vote, responding to new methods of arousing voter interest.

Popular Politics and Partisan Identity

The election of 1828, pitting Andrew Jackson against John Quincy Adams, was the first presidential contest in which the popular vote determined the outcome. In twenty-two out of twenty-four states, voters—not state legislatures—designated the number of electors committed to a particular candidate. More than a million voters participated, three times the number in 1824 and nearly half the free male population. Throughout the 1830s, voter turnout continued to rise and reached 70 percent in some localities, partly because of the disappearance of property qualifications in all but three states and partly because of heightened political interest.

The 1828 election inaugurated new campaign styles. State-level candidates routinely gave speeches at rallies, picnics, and banquets. Adams and Jackson still declined such appearances as undignified, but Henry Clay of Kentucky, campaigning for Adams, earned the nickname "the Barbecue Orator." Campaign rhetoric became more informal and even blunt. The Jackson camp established many

CHAPTER LOCATOR | What caused the market revolution?

TABLE 11.1 ■ The Growth of Newspapers, 1820–1840

	1820	1830	1835	1840
U.S. population (in millions)	9.6	12.8	15.0	17.1
Number of newspapers published	500	800	1,200	1,400
Daily newspapers	42	65	—	138

KEY FACTORS

The Election of 1828
- It was the first presidential race in which the popular vote determined the outcome.
- Nearly half the free male population voted, three times as many as voted in the 1824 election.
- It was the first national election to be dominated by character issues.

Hickory Clubs, trading on Jackson's popular nickname, "Old Hickory," from a common Tennessee tree suggesting resilience and toughness.

Partisan newspapers in ever-larger numbers defined issues and publicized political personalities as never before (**Table 11.1**). Party leaders dispensed subsidies and other favors to secure the support of papers, even in remote towns and villages. In New York State, where party development was most advanced, a pro-Jackson group called the Bucktails controlled fifty weekly publications.

Politicians at first identified themselves as Jackson or Adams men, honoring the fiction of Republican Party unity. By 1832, however, the terminology had evolved to National Republicans, favoring federal action to promote commercial development, and Democratic Republicans, who promised to be responsive to the will of the majority. Between 1834 and 1836, National Republicans came to be called Whigs, while those in Jackson's party became simply the Democrats.

The Election of 1828 and the Character Issue

The campaign of 1828 was the first national election dominated by scandal and character questions. They became central issues because voters used them to comprehend the kind of public official each man would make. Character issues conveyed in shorthand larger questions about morality, honor, and discipline. Jackson and Adams presented two radically different styles of manhood.

John Quincy Adams was vilified by his opponents as an elitist, a bookish academic, and even a monarchist. They attacked his "corrupt bargain" of 1824—the alleged election deal between Adams and Henry Clay (see chapter 10). Adams's supporters countered by playing on Jackson's fatherless childhood to portray him as the bastard son of a prostitute. Worse, the circumstances around his marriage to Rachel Donelson Robards in 1791 gave rise to the story that Jackson was a seducer and an adulterer, having married a woman whose divorce from her first husband was not entirely legal. Pro-Adams newspapers howled that Jackson was sinful and impulsive, while portraying Adams as pious, learned, and virtuous.

Editors in favor of Adams played up Jackson's violent temper, as evidenced by his participation in many duels, brawls, and canings. Jackson's supporters used the same stories to project Old Hickory as a tough frontier hero who knew how to command obedience. As for learning, Jackson's rough frontier education gave him a "natural sense," wrote a Boston editor, that "can never be acquired by reading books—it can only be acquired, in perfection, by reading men."

Jackson won a sweeping victory, with 56 percent of the popular vote and 178 electoral votes to Adams's 83 (**Map 11.2**). Old Hickory took most of the South and West and carried Pennsylvania and New York as well; Adams carried the remainder of the East. Jackson's vice president was **John C. Calhoun**, who had just served as vice president under Adams but had broken with Adams's policies.

John C. Calhoun
▶ Vice president under John Quincy Adams and Andrew Jackson. Calhoun was a leading advocate of South Carolina's statement of nullification. When Jackson ignored Calhoun's views on the subject, Calhoun resigned and became a senator to better serve the interests of his state.

| What changes in national politics were reflected in the election of 1828? | What was Andrew Jackson's impact on the presidency? | How did the market revolution transform social and cultural life? | Why was Martin Van Buren a one-term president? | Conclusion: Age of Jackson or era of reform? |

285

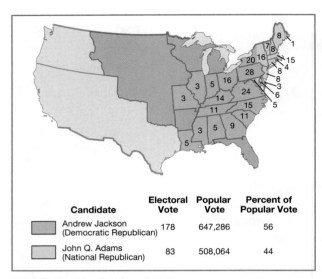

Candidate	Electoral Vote	Popular Vote	Percent of Popular Vote
Andrew Jackson (Democratic Republican)	178	647,286	56
John Q. Adams (National Republican)	83	508,064	44

MAP 11.2 ■ The Election of 1828

Whigs

▶ Political party that evolved out of the National Republicans between 1834 and 1836. The Whigs' power base was in the Northeast. They supported federal action to promote commercial development and generally looked favorably on the reform movements associated with the Second Great Awakening.

Democrats

▶ Political party that evolved out of the Democratic Republicans between 1834 and 1836. The Democrats were strongest in the South and West. Closely associated with Andrew Jackson, the Democrats embraced Jackson's vision of limited government, expanded political participation for white men, and the promotion of an ethic of individualism.

After 1828, national politicians no longer deplored the existence of political parties. They were coming to see that parties mobilized and delivered voters, sharpened candidates' differences, and created party loyalty that surpassed loyalty to individual candidates and elections. Adams and Jackson clearly symbolized the competing ideas of the emerging parties: a moralistic, top-down party (the **Whigs**) ready to make major decisions to promote economic growth competing against a contentious, energetic party (the **Democrats**) ready to embrace liberty-loving individualism.

Jackson's Democratic Agenda

Jackson's supporters went wild at his March 1829 inauguration. Thousands cheered his ten-minute inaugural address, the shortest in history. An open reception at the White House turned into a near riot as well-wishers jammed the premises, used windows as doors, stood on furniture for a better view of the great man, and broke thousands of dollars' worth of china and glasses. During his presidency, Jackson continued to offer unprecedented hospitality to the public. The courteous Jackson, committed to his image as president of the "common man," held audiences with unannounced visitors throughout his two terms.

Past presidents had tried to lessen party conflict by including men of different factions in their cabinets, but Jackson would have only loyalists. For secretary of state, the key job, he tapped New Yorker Martin Van Buren, one of the shrewdest politicians of the day. Throughout the federal government, from postal clerks to ambassadors, Jackson replaced competent civil servants with party loyalists. Jackson's appointment practices came to be known as the spoils system.

Jackson's agenda quickly emerged. He favored a Jeffersonian limited federal government, fearing that intervention in the economy inevitably favored some groups at the expense of others. He therefore opposed federal support of transportation and grants of monopolies and charters that privileged wealthy investors. Like Jefferson, he anticipated the rapid settlement of the country's interior, where land sales would spread economic democracy to settlers. Thus, establishing a federal policy to remove the Indians had high priority. Jackson was freer than previous presidents with the use of the presidential veto power over Congress. In 1830, he vetoed a Congress-backed highway project in Maysville, Kentucky, Henry Clay's home state. The Maysville Road veto articulated Jackson's principled stand that citizens' tax dollars could be spent only on projects of a "general, not local" character.

> **QUICK REVIEW**

What role did character play in the 1828 presidential campaign?

CHAPTER LOCATOR | What caused the market revolution?

What was Andrew Jackson's impact on the presidency?

Andrew Jackson as "the Great Father"

In 1828, a new process of cheap commercial lithography found immediate application in a colorful presidential campaign aimed at capturing popular votes, and with it, a rich tradition of political cartoons was born. Jackson inspired at least five dozen satirical cartoons centering on caricatures of him. Strikingly, only one of them featured his Indian policy, controversial as it was, and only a single copy still exists. William L. Clements Library.

▶ FOR MORE HELP ANALYZING THIS IMAGE, see the visual activity for this chapter in the Online Study Guide at bedfordstmartins.com/roarkunderstanding.

IN HIS TWO TERMS AS PRESIDENT, Andrew Jackson worked to implement his vision of a politics of opportunity for all white men. To open land for white settlement, he favored the relocation of all eastern Indian tribes. He confronted John C. Calhoun and South Carolina when that state tried to nullify the tariff of 1828. Disapproving of all government-granted privilege, Jackson challenged and defeated the Bank of the United States. In all this, he greatly enhanced the power of the presidency.

Indian Policy and the Trail of Tears

Probably nothing defined Jackson's presidency more than his efforts to solve what he saw as the Indian problem. Thousands of Indians lived in the South and the old Northwest, and many remained in New England and New York. In his first message to Congress in 1829, Jackson declared that removing the Indians to territory west of the Mississippi was the only way to save them. White civilization destroyed Indian resources and thus doomed the Indians, he claimed: "That this fate surely awaits them if they remain within the limits of the states does not admit of a doubt. Humanity and national honor demand that every effort should be made to avert so great a calamity." Jackson never publicly wavered from this seemingly noble theme, returning to it in his next seven annual messages.

Prior administrations had experimented with different Indian policies. Starting in 1819, Congress funded missionary associations eager to "civilize" native

| What changes in national politics were reflected in the election of 1828? | **What was Andrew Jackson's impact on the presidency?** | How did the market revolution transform social and cultural life? | Why was Martin Van Buren a one-term president? | Conclusion: Age of Jackson or era of reform? |

1828
- Congress passes Tariff of Abominations.
- Democrat Andrew Jackson is elected president.

1830
- Indian Removal Act establishes process for relocating eastern Indian tribes west of the Mississippi River.

1832
- Sauk and Fox Indians led by Chief Black Hawk are massacred by state militias.
- Supreme Court rules in *Worcester v. Georgia* that the Cherokee nation is a distinct community not subject to Georgia state law.
- Jackson vetoes charter renewal of Bank of the United States.

1833
- South Carolina leaders declare nullification of federal tariffs.

1838
- Trail of Tears: Cherokees are forced to relocate.

Indian Removal Act of 1830
▶ Act that provided funds for relocating eastern tribes west of the Mississippi. The act embodied Jackson's preferred solution to the "Indian problem," the mandatory expulsion of all Indians from the then-existing states. Indians resisted in numerous ways, but, in the end, most were forced to comply with the terms of the act.

peoples by converting them to Christianity and to whites' agricultural practices. The federal government had pursued aggressive treaty making with many tribes, dealing with the Indians as foreign nations (see chapter 10). In contrast, Jackson saw Indians as subjects of the United States, and he did not approve of assimilation. In his 1833 message to Congress, he wrote, "They have neither the intelligence, the industry, the moral habits, nor the desire of improvement which are essential. . . . Established in the midst of a superior race . . . they must necessarily yield to the force of circumstances and ere long disappear." Congress backed Jackson's goal of relocating eastern tribes west of the Mississippi and passed the **Indian Removal Act of 1830**. About 100 million acres of eastern land would be vacated for eventual white settlement under this act authorizing ethnic expulsion (**Map 11.3**).

The Indian Removal Act generated widespread controversy. Newspapers, public lecturers, and local clubs debated the expulsion law. In an unprecedented move, thousands of northern white women signed anti-removal petitions, directly challenging the prevailing assumption that women could not be political actors.

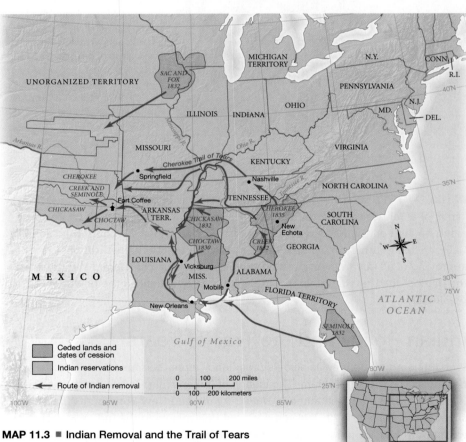

MAP 11.3 ■ Indian Removal and the Trail of Tears
The federal government under President Andrew Jackson pursued a vigorous policy of Indian removal in the 1830s. Tribes were forcibly moved west to land known as Indian Territory (present-day Oklahoma). As many as a quarter of the Cherokee Indians died on the route known as the Trail of Tears in 1838.

> ▶ FOR MORE HELP ANALYZING THIS MAP, see the map activity for this chapter in the Online Study Guide at bedfordstmartins.com/roarkunderstanding.

Between 1830 and 1832, women's petitions rolled into Washington, arguing specifically that the Cherokee Indians of Georgia were a sovereign people on the road to Christianity and entitled to stay on their land. Jackson ignored the petitions.

For the northern tribes, their numbers diminished by years of war, gradual removal was already well under way. But not all the Indians went quietly. In 1832 in western Illinois, Black Hawk, a leader of the Sauk and Fox Indians who had fought in alliance with Tecumseh in the War of 1812 (see chapter 10, page 257), resisted removal. Volunteer militias attacked and chased the Indians into southern Wisconsin, where, after several skirmishes and a deadly battle (later called the Black Hawk War), Black Hawk was captured and four hundred of his people were massacred.

The large southern tribes—the Creek, Chickasaw, Choctaw, and Cherokee—proved even more resistant to removal. Georgia Cherokees had already taken several assimilationist steps. Aided by dedicated missionaries, these leaders had adopted written laws, including, in 1827, a constitution modeled on the U.S. Constitution. Two hundred of the wealthiest Cherokee men had intermarried with whites, adopting white styles of housing, dress, and cotton agriculture, including the ownership of slaves. They developed a written alphabet and published a newspaper and Christian prayer books in their language. These features helped make their cause attractive to the northern white women who petitioned the government on their behalf. Yet most of the seventeen thousand Cherokees maintained cultural continuity with past traditions.

In 1831, when Georgia announced its plans to seize all Cherokee property, the tribal leadership took their case to the U.S. Supreme Court. In *Worcester v. Georgia* (1832), the Supreme Court upheld the territorial sovereignty of the Cherokee people, recognizing their existence as "a distinct community, occupying its own territory, in which the laws of Georgia can have no force." An angry President Jackson ignored the Court and pressed the Cherokee tribe to move west: "If they now refuse to accept the liberal terms offered, they can only be liable for whatever evils and difficulties may arise. I feel conscious of having done my duty to my red children."

The Cherokee tribe remained in Georgia for two more years without significant violence. Then, in 1835, a small, unauthorized faction of the acculturated leaders signed a treaty selling all the tribal lands to the state, which rapidly resold the land to whites. Most Cherokees refused to move, so in May 1838, the deadline for voluntary evacuation, federal troops arrived to remove them. Under armed guard, the Cherokees embarked on a 1,200-mile journey west that came to be called the **Trail of Tears.** Nearly a quarter of the Cherokees died en route from the hardship. Survivors joined the fifteen thousand Creek, twelve thousand Choctaw, five thousand Chickasaw, and several thousand Seminole Indians also forcibly relocated to Indian Territory (which became the state of Oklahoma in 1907).

In his farewell address to the nation in 1837, Jackson professed his belief in the benefit of Indian removal: "This unhappy race . . . are now placed in a situation where we may well hope that they will share in the blessings of civilization and be saved from the degradation and destruction to which they were rapidly hastening while they remained in the states." Perhaps Jackson genuinely believed that removal was necessary, but for the forcibly removed tribes, the costs of relocation were high.

Trail of Tears
► Forced westward journey of Cherokees from their homes in Georgia. After the Cherokees resisted Georgia's efforts to remove them for almost a decade, federal troops in 1838 forced them to leave after a small, unauthorized faction of the tribe signed away all of the Cherokee lands. Nearly a quarter of the Cherokees died during the 1,200-mile trip; the survivors joined other Indian groups forcibly relocated to Indian Territory in present-day Oklahoma.

What changes in national politics were reflected in the election of 1828? | **What was Andrew Jackson's impact on the presidency?** | How did the market revolution transform social and cultural life? | Why was Martin Van Buren a one-term president? | Conclusion: Age of Jackson or era of reform?

289

The Tariff of Abominations and Nullification

Because it advanced his Indian policy, Jackson supported Georgia's right to ignore the Supreme Court's decision in *Worcester v. Georgia*. But in another pressing question of states' rights, Jackson contested South Carolina's attempt to ignore federal tariff policy.

Federal tariffs as high as 33 percent on imports such as textiles and iron goods had been passed in 1816 and again in 1824 in an effort to shelter new American manufacturers from foreign competition. Some southern congressmen opposed the steep tariffs, fearing they would decrease overseas shipping and thereby hurt cotton exports. In 1828, Congress passed a revised tariff that came to be known as the Tariff of Abominations. A bundle of conflicting duties, some as high as 50 percent, the legislation contained provisions that both pleased and angered every economic and sectional interest.

South Carolina in particular suffered from the Tariff of Abominations. Worldwide prices for cotton had declined in the late 1820s, and the falloff in shipping caused by the high tariffs further hurt the South. In 1828, a group of South Carolina politicians headed by John C. Calhoun advanced a doctrine called **nullification.** They argued that when Congress overstepped its powers, states had the right to nullify Congress's acts. As precedents, they pointed to the Virginia and Kentucky Resolutions of 1798, intended to invalidate the Alien and Sedition Acts (see chapter 9). Congress had erred in using tariff policy to benefit specific industries, they claimed; tariffs should be used only to raise revenue.

On assuming the presidency in 1829, Jackson ignored the South Carolina statement of nullification and shut out Calhoun, his new vice president, from influence or power. Tariff revisions in early 1832 brought little relief to the South. Calhoun resigned the vice presidency and became a senator to better serve his state. Finally, strained to their limit, South Carolina leaders declared federal tariffs null and void in their state as of February 1, 1833.

In response, Jackson sent armed ships to Charleston harbor and threatened to invade the state. He pushed through Congress the Force Bill, defining the Carolina stance as treason and authorizing military action to collect federal tariffs. At the same time, Congress moved quickly to pass a revised tariff that was more acceptable to the South. On March 1, 1833, Congress passed both the new tariff and the Force Bill. South Carolina then withdrew its nullification of the old tariff—and then nullified the Force Bill. It was a symbolic gesture, since Jackson's show of muscle was no longer necessary.

Yet the question of federal power versus states' rights was far from settled. The implied threat behind nullification was secession, a position articulated in 1832 by some South Carolinians whose concerns went beyond tariff policy. In the 1830s, the political moratorium on discussions of slavery agreed on at the time of the Missouri Compromise (see chapter 10) was coming unglued, and new northern voices opposed to slavery gained increasing attention. If and when a northern-dominated federal government decided to end slavery, the South Carolinians thought, the South should nullify such laws, or remove itself from the Union.

The Bank War and Economic Boom

Along with the tariff and nullification, President Jackson fought another political battle, over the Bank of the United States. With twenty-nine branches, the bank

nullification

▶ The doctrine that when Congress overstepped its powers, states had the right to nullify Congress's acts. South Carolina advanced the doctrine of nullification in 1828 in response to passage of the Tariff of Abominations. A show of force by Andrew Jackson, combined with revision of the objectionable tariff, prompted South Carolina to withdraw its nullification.

handled the federal government's deposits, extended credit and loans, and issued banknotes. Jackson, however, thought the bank concentrated undue economic power in the hands of a few.

National Republican (Whig) senators Daniel Webster and Henry Clay, the National Republican candidate for president in 1832, decided to force the issue. They convinced the bank to apply for charter renewal in 1832, well before the fall election, even though the existing charter ran until 1836. They fully expected that Congress's renewal would be vetoed by Jackson, that the unpopular veto would cause Jackson to lose the election, and that the bank would survive on an override vote by a new Congress swept into power on the anti-Jackson tide.

At first, the plan seemed to work. The bank applied for rechartering, Congress voted to renew, and Jackson issued his veto. But it was a brilliantly written veto, presenting Jackson as the champion of the democratic masses. "Many of our rich men have not been content with equal protection and equal benefits, but have besought us to make them richer by act of Congress," Jackson wrote.

Fistfight between Andrew Jackson and Nicholas Biddle This 1834 cartoon represents President Andrew Jackson squaring off against Nicholas Biddle, the director of the Bank of the United States. To Biddle's left are his seconds, Daniel Webster and Henry Clay. Behind the president is Vice President Martin Van Buren. Whiskey and port wine lubricate the action. The Library Company of Philadelphia.

| What changes in national politics were reflected in the election of 1828? | **What was Andrew Jackson's impact on the presidency?** | How did the market revolution transform social and cultural life? | Why was Martin Van Buren a one-term president? | Conclusion: Age of Jackson or era of reform? |

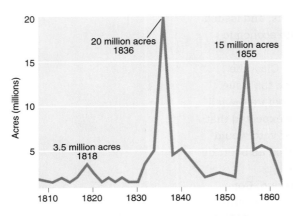

FIGURE 11.1 ■ **Western Land Sales, 1810–1860**
Land sales peaked in the 1810s, 1830s, and 1850s as
Americans rushed to speculate in western land sold by
the federal government. The surges in 1818 and 1836
demonstrate the volatile, speculative economy that
suddenly collapsed in the panics of 1819 and 1837.

Jackson's translation of the bank controversy into a language of class antagonism and egalitarian ideals resonated
with many Americans. Jackson won 55 percent of the popular
vote and 219 electoral votes to Clay's 49. Jackson's party still
controlled Congress, so no override was possible. The second
Bank of the United States would cease to exist after 1836.

Jackson, however, wanted to destroy the bank sooner.
Calling it a "monster," he ordered the sizable federal deposits
to be removed from its vaults and redeposited into Democratic-
inclined state banks. In retaliation, the Bank of the United
States raised interest rates and called in loans. This action
caused a brief decline in the economy in 1833 and actually
enhanced Jackson's claim that the bank was too powerful
for the good of the country.

Unleashed and unregulated, the economy went into high
gear in 1834. Just at this moment, an excess of silver from
Mexican mines made its way into American banks, giving
bankers license to print ever more banknotes. From 1834 to
1837, inflation soared; prices of basic goods rose more than 50
percent. States quickly chartered hundreds of new private banks, each issuing its
own banknotes. Entrepreneurs borrowed and invested money, and the webs of
credit and debt relationships that were the hallmark of the American economy
grew denser yet. The market in western land sales also heated up. In 1834, about
4.5 million acres of the public domain had been sold, the highest annual volume
since 1818. By 1836, the total reached an astonishing 20 million acres.

In one respect, the economy attained an admirable goal: The national debt
disappeared, and from 1835 to 1837, for the only time in American history, the
government had a monetary surplus. But much of that surplus consisted of
questionable bank currencies—"bloated, diseased" currencies, in Jackson's vivid
terminology. While the boom was on, however, few stopped to worry about the
consequences if and when the bubble burst.

> **QUICK REVIEW**

What were the most significant policies of Andrew Jackson's presidency?

CHAPTER LOCATOR | What caused the market revolution?

The Talcott Family at Home, 1832 Folk art depicting family life became popular and affordable in the early Republic. Samuel Talcott, twenty-eight, a farmer in Madison County, New York, poses with his wife, Betsey, twenty; his recently widowed mother, Mary, seventy; and daughters Clarissa, three, and Emily, three months. The couple wear quite fashionable clothes: Betsey's enormous sleeves are a hallmark of the 1830s, as is Samuel's "cutaway" waistcoat with its stiff, high collar. Abby Aldrich Rockefeller Folk Art Center, Williamsburg, Va.

How did the market revolution transform social and cultural life?

THE GROWING ECONOMY, booming by the mid-1830s, transformed social and cultural life. For many families, especially in the commercialized Northeast, standards of living rose, consumption patterns changed, and the nature and location of work were altered. All this had a direct impact on the duties of men and women and on the training of youths for the economy of the future.

Along with economic change came an unprecedented revival of evangelical religion known as the Second Great Awakening. Among the most serious adherents of evangelical Protestantism were men and women of the new merchant classes. Not content with individual perfection, many of these people sought to perfect society as well, by defining excessive alcohol consumption, nonmarital sex, and slavery as three major evils of modern life in need of correction.

The Family and Separate Spheres

The centerpiece of new ideas about gender relations was the notion that husbands found their status and authority in the new world of work, leaving wives to tend the hearth and home. Sermons, advice books, periodicals, and novels reinforced the idea that men and women inhabited separate spheres and had separate duties. "To woman it belongs . . . to elevate the intellectual character of her household [and] to kindle the fires of mental activity in childhood," wrote Mrs. A. J. Graves in a popular book titled *Advice to American Women.* For men, in

What changes in national politics were reflected in the election of 1828?

What was Andrew Jackson's impact on the presidency?

How did the market revolution transform social and cultural life?

Why was Martin Van Buren a one-term president?

Conclusion: Age of Jackson or era of reform?

Changing Trends in Age at First Marriage for Women

Average age at first marriage is a remarkably sensitive indicator of social, economic, and cultural factors in all societies. In general, conditions favoring low age at marriage for women are those that provide young couples with early financial support: abundant affordable farmland, co-residence with parents, or steady employment for men at a wage that can support a family. Factors that postpone marriage include a lack of farmland, deterioration in male employment prospects, a changed economy requiring more years of pre-job education and training, or enhanced employment for women, which makes the job market more attractive than the marriage market. The low mean ages in this table reflect abundant farmland (1800, United States), factory wage labor (1800, England), and serfdom (1850, Russia). In Europe and the United States, age of first marriage for women rose steeply in the nineteenth century. The northeastern United States led the way in the 1820s and 1830s. Can you suggest reasons why? One immediate consequence of later marriage was a decline in completed family size, since brides shaved two years off their exposure to the risk of pregnancy. Finally, demographers note that in some cases, rising age at first marriage is accompanied by rising rates of nonmarriage, sometimes as high as 20 percent. How might these two trends be connected?

	Nineteenth Century		Twentieth Century		
	1800	*1850*	*1900*	*1960*	*2000*
United States	21	23	23	20	25
England	20	24	24	22	28
Netherlands	—	28	26	25	28
Russia	—	19	—	25	22

Note: Dates are approximate. Dashes indicate a lack of reliable information.

contrast, "the absorbing passion for gain, and the pressing demands of business, engross their whole attention." In particular, the home, now the exclusive domain of women, was sentimentalized as the source of intimacy, love, and safety, a refuge from the cruel and competitive world of market relations.

Some new aspects of society gave substance to this formulation of separate spheres. Men's work was undergoing profound change after 1815 and increasingly brought cash to the household, especially in the manufacturing and urban Northeast. Farmers and tradesmen sold products in a market, and bankers, bookkeepers, shoemakers, and canal diggers got pay envelopes. Furthermore, many men now worked away from the home, at an office or a store.

A woman's domestic role was more complicated than the cultural prescriptions indicated. (See "Global Comparison.") Although the vast majority of married white women did not hold paying jobs, their homes required time-consuming labor. But the advice books treated housework as a loving familial duty, thus rendering it invisible in an economy that evaluated work by how much cash it generated. In reality, many wives contributed to family income by taking in boarders or sewing for cash. Wives in the poorest classes, including most free black wives, did not have the luxury of husbands earning adequate wages; for them, work as servants or laundry workers helped augment family income.

Idealized notions about the feminine home and the masculine workplace gained acceptance in the 1830s because of the cultural ascendancy of the commercialized Northeast, with its domination of book and periodical publication. Beyond white families of the middle and upper classes, however, these new gender ideals had limited applicability. Despite their apparent authority in printed material of the period, they were never all-pervasive.

The Education and Training of Youths

The market economy required expanded opportunities for training youths of both sexes. By the 1830s, in both the North and the South, state-supported public school systems were the norm, designed to produce pupils of both sexes able, by age twelve to fourteen, to read, write, and participate in marketplace calculations. Literacy rates for white females climbed dramatically, rivaling the rates for white males for the first time. The fact that taxpayers paid for children's education created an incentive to seek an inexpensive teaching force. By the 1830s, school districts replaced male teachers with young female teachers, for, as a Massachusetts report on education put it, "females can be educated cheaper, quicker, and better, and will teach cheaper after they are qualified."

Advanced education continued to expand in the 1830s, with an additional two dozen colleges for men and several more female seminaries offering education on a par with the male colleges. Still, only a very small percentage of young people attended institutions of higher learning. The vast majority of male youths left public school at age fourteen to apprentice in specific trades or to embark on business careers by seeking entry-level clerkships. Young girls headed for mill towns or cities in unprecedented numbers, seeking work in the expanding service sector as seamstresses and domestic servants. Changes in patterns of youth employment meant that large numbers of youngsters escaped the watchful eyes of their parents, a cause of great concern for the moralists of the era.

The Second Great Awakening

A newly invigorated version of Protestantism gained momentum in the 1820s and 1830s as the economy reshaped gender and age relations. The earliest manifestations of this fervent piety appeared in 1801 in Kentucky, when a crowd of ten thousand people camped out on a hillside at Cane Ridge for a revival meeting that lasted several weeks. By the 1810s and 1820s, "camp meetings" had spread to the Atlantic seaboard states.

The gatherings attracted women and men hungry for a more immediate access to spiritual peace, one not requiring years of soul-searching. One eyewitness reported that "some of the people were singing, others praying, some crying for mercy. . . . At one time I saw at least five hundred swept down in a moment as if a battery of a thousand guns had been opened upon them, and then immediately followed shrieks and shouts that rent the very heavens."

From 1800 to 1820, church membership doubled in the United States, much of it among the evangelical groups. Methodists, Baptists, and Presbyterians formed the core of the new movement. Women more than men were attracted to the evangelical movement, and wives and mothers typically recruited husbands and sons to join them.

The ministry of Charles Grandison Finney embodied the **Second Great Awakening**. Finney lived in western New York, where the completion of the Erie

CHRONOLOGY

1817
– American Colonization Society is founded.

1826
– American Temperance Society is founded.

1829
– David Walker's *Appeal . . . to the Coloured Citizens of the World* is published.

1830–1831
– Charles Grandison Finney preaches in Rochester, New York.

1831
– William Lloyd Garrison starts *Liberator*.

1832
– New England Anti-Slavery Society is founded.

1833
– New York and Philadelphia antislavery societies are founded.
– New York Female Moral Reform Society is founded.

1836
– American Temperance Union is founded.

Second Great Awakening
▶ Unprecedented revival of evangelical religion in the 1820s and 1830s. The revival attracted men and women who, in the face of the changes wrought by the market revolution, sought new and immediate sources of spiritual solace. The Second Great Awakening was also a major force behind the reform movements of the era, inspiring efforts to combat drinking, sexual sin, and slavery.

| What changes in national politics were reflected in the election of 1828? | What was Andrew Jackson's impact on the presidency? | **How did the market revolution transform social and cultural life?** | Why was Martin Van Buren a one-term president? | Conclusion: Age of Jackson or era of reform? |

295

▶ FOR MORE HELP ANALYZING THIS IMAGE, see the visual activity for this chapter in the Online Study Guide at bedfordstmartins.com/roarkunderstanding.

Charles G. Finney and His Broadway Tabernacle

The Reverend Charles Grandison Finney took his evangelical movement to New York City in the early 1830s, operating first out of a renovated theater. In 1836, the Broadway Tabernacle was built for his pastorate. In its use of space, the tabernacle resembled a theater more than a traditional church.
Oberlin College Archives, Oberlin, Ohio.

American Temperance Society

▶ Organization founded in 1826 by Lyman Beecher that warned that drinking led to poverty, idleness, crime, and family violence. Adopting the methods of evangelical ministers, temperance lecturers traveled the country expounding the damage of drink. The temperance movement had considerable success, contributing to a sharp drop in American alcohol consumption.

Canal in 1825 fundamentally altered the social and economic landscape overnight. Growth and prosperity came with less admirable side effects, such as prostitution, drinking, and gaming. Finney saw New York canal towns as ripe for evangelical awakening. In Rochester, he sustained a six-month revival through the winter of 1830–31, generating thousands of converts.

Finney's message was directed primarily at the business classes and pressed for public-spirited outreach to the less-than-perfect to foster their salvation. Evangelicals promoted Sunday schools to bring piety to children; they battled to end mail delivery, stop public transport, and close shops on Sundays to honor the Sabbath. Many women formed missionary societies that distributed millions of Bibles and religious tracts. Through such avenues, evangelical religion offered women expanded spheres of influence. Finney adopted the tactics of Jacksonian-era politicians—publicity, argumentation, rallies, and speeches—to sell his cause. His object, he said, was to get Americans to "vote in the Lord Jesus Christ as the governor of the Universe."

The Temperance Movement and the Campaign for Moral Reform

Evangelical fervor animated vigorous campaigns to eliminate alcohol abuse and eradicate sexual sin. Millions of Americans took the temperance pledge to abstain from strong drink, and thousands became involved in efforts to end prostitution.

Alcohol consumption had risen steadily in the decades up to 1830. All classes imbibed. A lively saloon culture fostered masculine camaraderie along with extensive alcohol consumption among laborers, while in elite homes, the after-dinner whiskey or sherry was commonplace. Colleges before 1820 routinely served students a pint of ale with meals, and the military included rum in the daily ration.

Average Annual Alcohol Consumption in 1830

Nine gallons of hard liquor.
Thirty gallons of hard cider, beer, and wine.

Organized opposition to drinking first surfaced in the 1810s among health and religious reformers. In 1826, Lyman Beecher, a Connecticut minister of an "awakened" church, founded the **American Temperance Society**, which warned that drinking led to poverty, idleness, crime, and family violence. Adopting the methods of evangelical ministers, temperance lecturers traveled the country expounding the damage of drink. By 1833, some six thousand local affiliates of the American Temperance Society boasted more than a million members.

CHAPTER LOCATOR | What caused the market revolution?

In 1836, leaders of the temperance movement regrouped into a new society, the American Temperance Union, which demanded total abstinence from its adherents. The intensified war against alcohol moved beyond individual moral suasion into the realm of politics as reformers sought to deny taverns liquor licenses. By 1845, temperance advocates had put an impressive dent in alcohol consumption, which diminished to one-quarter of the per capita consumption of 1830.

More controversial than temperance was a social movement called "moral reform," which first aimed at public morals in general but quickly narrowed to a campaign to eradicate sexual sin. In 1833, a group of Finneyite women started the New York Female Moral Reform Society. Its members insisted that uncontrolled male sexual expression posed a serious threat to society in general and to women in particular. Within five years, more than four thousand auxiliary groups of women had sprung up, mostly in New England, New York, Pennsylvania, and Ohio.

In its analysis of sexual sin and its conviction that women had a duty to speak out about unspeakable things, the Moral Reform Society pushed the limits of what even the men in the evangelical movement could tolerate. Yet these women did not regard themselves as radicals. They were simply pursuing the logic of a gender system that defined home protection and morality as women's special sphere and a religious conviction that called for the eradication of sin.

Organizing against Slavery

More radical still was the movement in the 1830s to abolish the sin of slavery. Previously, the American Colonization Society, founded in 1817 by Maryland and Virginia planters, aimed to promote gradual individual emancipation of slaves followed by colonization in Africa. By the early 1820s, several thousand ex-slaves had been transported to Liberia on the West African coast. But not surprisingly, newly freed men and women were often not eager to emigrate; their African roots were three or more generations in the past. Colonization was too gradual (and expensive) to have much impact on American slavery.

Around 1830, northern challenges to slavery intensified, beginning in free black communities. In 1829, a Boston printer named David Walker published *An Appeal . . . to the Coloured Citizens of the World*, which condemned racism, invoked the egalitarian language of the Declaration of Independence, and hinted at racial violence if whites did not change their prejudiced ways. In 1830, at the inaugural National Negro Convention meeting in Philadelphia, forty blacks from nine states discussed the racism of American society and proposed emigration to Canada. In 1832 and 1833, a twenty-eight-year-old black woman named Maria Stewart delivered public lectures on slavery and racial prejudice to black audiences in Boston. Her lectures gained wider circulation when they were published in a national publication called the *Liberator*.

The *Liberator*, founded in 1831 in Boston, took antislavery agitation to new heights. Its founder and editor, **William Lloyd Garrison**, advocated immediate abolition: "On this subject, I do not wish to think, or speak, or write, with moderation. No! No! Tell a man whose house is on fire to give a moderate alarm; tell him to moderately rescue his wife from the hands of the ravisher; tell the mother to gradually extricate her babe from the fire into which it has fallen;—but urge me not to use moderation in a cause like the present." In 1832, Garrison's supporters started the New England Anti-Slavery Society.

William Lloyd Garrison
▶ Leading advocate of the immediate abolition of slavery. Garrison founded his abolitionist newspaper, the *Liberator*, in 1831 and, along with his supporters, started the New England Anti-Slavery Society in 1832. Garrison played a key role in the growing antislavery movement of the 1830s and 1840s.

| What changes in national politics were reflected in the election of 1828? | What was Andrew Jackson's impact on the presidency? | How did the market revolution transform social and cultural life? | Why was Martin Van Buren a one-term president? | Conclusion: Age of Jackson or era of reform? |

297

Garrison, Thompson, and Phillips

George Thompson (middle) was a leading figure in the successful campaign to abolish slavery in Britain and its West Indies colonies in 1833. William Lloyd Garrison (left) welcomed Thompson to the United States in 1835 and promoted his speaking tour in Garrison's antislavery newspaper, the *Liberator*. Boston lawyer Wendell Phillips (right) heard Thompson speak and was inspired to make abolition his lifework. This picture dates from 1850, when Thompson returned to the United States. Historical Library of Swarthmore College.

Similar groups were organized in Philadelphia and New York in 1833. Soon a dozen antislavery newspapers and scores of antislavery lecturers were spreading the word and inspiring the formation of new local societies, which numbered thirteen hundred by 1837. Confined entirely to the North, their membership totaled a quarter of a million men and women.

Many white northerners, even those who opposed slavery, were not prepared to embrace the abolitionist call for emancipation. From 1834 to 1838, there were more than a hundred eruptions of serious mob violence against abolitionists and free blacks.

Women played a prominent role in abolition, just as they did in moral reform and evangelical religion. They formed women's auxiliaries and held fairs to sell handmade crafts to support male lecturers in the field. They circulated antislavery petitions, presented to the U.S. Congress with tens of thousands of signatures. Up to 1835, women's petitions were framed as respectful memorials to Congress about the evils of slavery, but by mid-decade these petitions used urgent language to call for political action.

When a southern planter's daughter named Angelina Grimké wrote to Garrison about her personal repugnance for slavery, he published the letter in the *Liberator* and brought her overnight fame. In 1837, Grimké and her older sister, Sarah, became antislavery lecturers targeting women, but their powerful eyewitness speeches attracted male audiences as well. This caused leaders of the Congregational Church in Massachusetts to ban the Grimkés from their pulpits, because women should not presume to instruct men.

In the late 1830s, the cause of abolition divided the nation as no other issue did. Even among abolitionists, significant divisions emerged. Angelina and Sarah Grimké, radicalized by the controversy over their speaking tour, began to write and speak about woman's rights. They were opposed by moderate abolitionists who were unwilling to mix the new and contentious issue of woman's rights with their first cause, the rights of blacks.

The many men and women active in reform movements in the 1830s found their initial inspiration in evangelical Protestantism's dual message: Salvation was open to all, and society needed to be perfected. Their activist mentality squared well with the interventionist tendencies of the Whig Party forming in opposition to Andrew Jackson's Democrats.

> **QUICK REVIEW**

How did idealized roles for men and women change in the 1830s? What impact did these have on the rise of evangelical Protestantism and social reform movements?

Panic of 1837 Cartoon A sad family with an unemployed father faces sudden privation in this cartoon showing the consequences of the panic of 1837. The wife and children complain of hunger, the house is stripped nearly bare, and rent collectors loom in the doorway. Faint pictures on the wall show Andrew Jackson and Martin Van Buren presiding over the economic devastation of the family. Library of Congress.

BY THE MID-1830s, a vibrant and tumultuous political culture occupied center stage of American life. Andrew Jackson's vice president and successor, the northerner Martin Van Buren, inherited a strong Democratic organization, but he faced doubts from slave-owning Jacksonians and outright opposition from increasingly combative Whigs. Van Buren was a skilled politician, but there was little he could do in the face of economic collapse. A shattering panic in 1837, followed by another panic in 1839, brought the country its worst economic depression yet.

| What changes in national politics were reflected in the election of 1828? | What was Andrew Jackson's impact on the presidency? | How did the market revolution transform social and cultural life? | Why was Martin Van Buren a one-term president? | Conclusion: Age of Jackson or era of reform? |

1835
- Abolitionist literature is burned in Charleston, South Carolina.

1836
- Democrat Martin Van Buren is elected president.
- Congress adopts "gag rule" forbidding antislavery petitions from being entered into the public record.

1837–1839
- Economic panics lead to runs on banks, business failures, and a deflated economy.

1840
- Whig William Henry Harrison is elected president.

The Politics of Slavery

Sophisticated party organization was the specialty of Martin Van Buren. He earned the nickname "the Little Magician" for his consummate political skills. First a senator and then a governor, he became Jackson's secretary of state and then his running mate in 1832.

Jackson clearly favored Van Buren for the nomination in 1836, but starting in 1832, the major political parties had developed nominating conventions to choose their candidates. In 1835, Van Buren got the convention nod unanimously, to the dismay of his archrival, Calhoun, who then worked to discredit Van Buren among southern proslavery Democrats. Van Buren spent months assuring them that he was a "northern man with southern principles."

Calhoun was able to stir up trouble for Van Buren because, in 1835, southerners were increasingly alarmed by the rise of northern antislavery sentiment. When, in late 1835, abolitionists prepared to circulate in the South a million pamphlets condemning slavery, a mailbag of their literature was hijacked at the post office in Charleston, South Carolina, and ceremoniously burned along with effigies of leading abolitionists.

The petitioning tactics of abolitionists escalated sectional tensions. When the number of antislavery petitions presented to Congress grew into the hundreds, proslavery congressmen responded by passing a "gag rule" in 1836. The gag rule prohibited entering the documents into the public record on the grounds that what the abolitionists prayed for was unconstitutional and, further, an assault on the rights of white southerners, as one South Carolina representative put it.

Van Buren shrewdly seized on the conflict between abolitionists and their opponents to express his prosouthern sympathies. Abolitionists were "fanatics," he repeatedly claimed, possibly under the influence of "foreign agents" (British abolitionists). He promised that if he was elected president, he would not allow any interference in southern "domestic institutions."

Elections and Panics

Although the elections of 1824, 1828, and 1832 clearly bore the stamp of Jackson's personality, by 1836 the party apparatus was sufficiently developed to give Van Buren, a backroom politician, a shot at the presidency. Local and state committees existed throughout the country, and more than four hundred newspapers were Democratic partisans.

The Whigs had also built state-level organizations and cultivated newspaper loyalty. They had no top contender with nationwide support, so three regional candidates opposed Van Buren: Senator Daniel Webster of Massachusetts, Senator Hugh Lawson White of Tennessee, and the aging General William Henry Harrison, now residing in Ohio. Not one of the three candidates had the ability to win the presidency, but together they came close to denying Van Buren a majority vote and throwing the election into the House of Representatives.

In the end, Van Buren won with 170 electoral votes, while the other three received a total of 113. Although Van Buren had pulled together a national Democratic Party with wins in both the North and the South, he had done it at the cost of committing northern Democrats to the proslavery agenda. And running three candidates had maximized the Whigs' success by drawing Whigs into office at the state level.

CHAPTER LOCATOR | What caused the market revolution?

When Van Buren took office in March 1837, the financial markets were already quaking; by April, the country was plunged into crisis. The causes of the panic of 1837 were multiple and far-ranging. Bad harvests in Europe and a large trade imbalance between Britain and the United States caused the Bank of England to start calling in loans to American merchants. Failures in various crop markets and a 30 percent downturn in international cotton prices fed the growing disaster. Frightened citizens thronged the banks to try to get their money out, and businesses rushed to liquefy their remaining assets to pay off debts. Prices of stocks, bonds, and real estate fell 30 to 40 percent. The credit market tumbled like a house of cards.

Some Whig leaders were certain that Jackson's antibank and hard-money policies were responsible for the ruin. New Yorker Philip Hone, a wealthy Whig, called the Jackson administration "the most disastrous in the annals of the country" for its "wicked interference" in banking and monetary matters. Others framed the devastation as retribution for the frenzy of speculation that had gripped the nation. A religious periodical in Boston hoped that Americans would now moderate their greed: "We were getting to think that there was no end to the wealth, and could be no check to the progress of our country; that economy was not needed, that prudence was weakness." Others identified the competitive, profit-maximizing capitalist system as the cause and looked to Britain and France for new socialist ideas calling for the common ownership of the means of production.

The panic of 1837 subsided by 1838, but in 1839, another run on the banks and ripples of business failures deflated the economy, creating a second panic. President Van Buren called a special session of Congress to consider creating an independent treasury system to perform some of the functions of the defunct Bank of the United States. Such a system, funded by government deposits, would deal only in hard money and would exert a powerful moderating influence on inflation and the credit market. But Van Buren encountered strong resistance in Congress, even among Democrats. The treasury system finally won approval in 1840, but by then Van Buren's chances of winning a second term in office were virtually nil.

In 1840, the Whigs settled on William Henry Harrison to oppose Van Buren. The campaign drew on voter involvement as no presidential campaign ever had. The Whigs borrowed tricks from the Democrats: Harrison was touted as a common man born in a log cabin (in reality, he was born on a Virginia plantation), and his Indian-fighting days, now thirty years behind him, were played up to give him a Jacksonian aura. Whigs staged festive rallies around the country, drumming up mass appeal with candlelight parades and song shows, and women participated in rallies as never before. Some 78 percent of eligible voters cast ballots, the highest percentage ever in American history. Harrison took 53 percent of the popular vote and won 234 electoral college votes to Van Buren's 60. A Democratic editor lamented, "We have taught them how to conquer us!"

QUICK REVIEW <

What impact did the economy have on national life in the late 1830s?

> Conclusion: Age of Jackson or era of reform?

ECONOMIC TRANSFORMATIONS loom large in explaining the fast-paced changes of the 1830s. Transportation advances put goods and people in circulation, augmenting urban growth and helping to create a national culture, and water-powered manufacturing began to change the face of wage labor. Trade and banking mushroomed, and western land once occupied by Indians was auctioned off in a landslide of sales. Two periods of economic downturn—including the panic of 1819 and the panics of 1837 and 1839—offered sobering lessons about speculative fever.

Andrew Jackson symbolized this age of opportunity for many. His fame as an aggressive general, an Indian fighter, a champion of the common man, and a defender of slavery attracted growing numbers of voters to the emergent Democratic Party, which championed personal liberty, free competition, and egalitarian opportunity for all white men.

Jackson's constituency was challenged by a small but vocal segment of the population troubled by serious moral problems that Jacksonians preferred to ignore. Inspired by the Second Great Awakening, reformers targeted personal vices (illicit sex and intemperance) and social problems (prostitution, poverty, and slavery) and joined forces with evangelicals and wealthy lawyers and merchants (from the North and South) who appreciated a national bank and protective tariffs. The Whig Party was the party of activist moralism and state-sponsored entrepreneurship. Whig voters were, of course, male, but thousands of reform-minded women broke new ground by signing political petitions on the issues of Indian removal and slavery.

National politics in the 1830s were more divisive than at any time since the 1790s. The new party system of Democrats and Whigs reached far deeper into the electorate than had the Federalists and Republicans. Politics acquired immediacy and excitement, causing nearly four out of five white men to cast ballots in 1840.

High rates of voter participation would continue into the 1840s and 1850s. Unprecedented urban growth, westward expansion, and early industrialism marked those decades, sustaining the Democrat-Whig split in the electorate. But critiques of slavery, concerns for free labor, and an emerging protest against women's second-class citizenship complicated the political scene of the 1840s, leading to third-party political movements. One of these third parties, called the Republican Party, would achieve dominance in 1860 with the election of an Illinois lawyer, Abraham Lincoln, to the presidency.

The Granger Collection, New York.

SO NOW YOU KNOW

Before 1815, transportation in the United States was slow and expensive, but by 1840, networks of roads, canals, and even railroads began to unify the country culturally and economically. Improved transportation also brought improved communication, which energized new voters, created new party loyalties, and brought new issues such as temperance, moral reform, and abolition into American politics.

| What changes in national politics were reflected in the election of 1828? | What was Andrew Jackson's impact on the presidency? | How did the market revolution transform social and cultural life? | Why was Martin Van Buren a one-term president? | Conclusion: Age of Jackson or era of reform? |

CHAPTER 11 STUDY GUIDE

Online Study Guide
bedfordstmartins.com/roarkunderstanding

STEP 1 GETTING STARTED

Below are basic terms from this period in American history. Can you identify each term below and explain why it matters? To do this exercise online or to download this chart, visit bedfordstmartins.com/roarkunderstanding.

TERM	WHO OR WHAT & WHEN	WHY IT MATTERS
Erie Canal, p. 280		
second Bank of the United States, p. 282		
Andrew Jackson, p. 283		
John C. Calhoun, p. 285		
Whigs, p. 286		
Democrats, p. 286		
Indian Removal Act of 1830, p. 288		
Trail of Tears, p. 289		
nullification, p. 290		
Second Great Awakening, p. 295		
American Temperance Society, p. 296		
William Lloyd Garrison, p. 297		

STEP 2 MOVING BEYOND THE BASICS

The exercise below represents a more advanced understanding of the chapter material. Fill in the following chart by describing the key developments that combined to create the market revolution and by assessing the impact of each development. When you are finished, consider the relationship between each of the developments. How did improved transportation facilitate industrialization? How did the advent of factories alter labor relations? How did financial innovations contribute to economic volatility? To do this exercise online or to download this chart, visit bedfordstmartins.com/roarkunderstanding.

	Key developments	Societal and political effects
Improvements in transportation		
New methods of production		
Changes in the workforce and in labor relations		
Financial innovations		
Changes in commercial law		
Increased economic volatility		

Now that you have reviewed key elements of the chapter, take a step back and try to explain the big picture by answering these questions. Remember to use specific examples from the chapter in your answers. To do this exercise online, visit bedfordstmartins.com/roarkunderstanding.

THE MARKET REVOLUTION

▶ Why were improvements in transportation so crucial to America's economic growth and development in the early nineteenth century?

▶ What changes in workers' lives and status accompanied industrialization?

THE AGE OF JACKSON

▶ What does Andrew Jackson's rise to the presidency tell us about popular politics in the 1820s?

▶ How did Andrew Jackson change the presidency? How did he see and manipulate the relationship among the president, Congress, and the courts?

LOOKING BACKWARD, LOOKING AHEAD

▶ How did the second American party system differ from the first party system? How did it differ from the partisanship of the 1790s?

▶ How do the reform movements of the 1820s and 1830s shed light on the causes of the sectional tensions that would dominate the 1840s and 1850s?

THE ERA OF REFORM

▶ How did the Second Great Awakening lead to a variety of social reform movements? What impact did these various reform movements have on politics and society in the 1830s?

▶ What role did women play in the reform movements of the early nineteenth century?

IN YOUR OWN WORDS

Imagine that you must explain chapter 11 to someone who hasn't read it. What would be the most important points to include and why?

12
THE NEW WEST AND FREE NORTH

1840–1860

> This chapter explores the factors that propelled American economic growth and territorial expansion in the mid-nineteenth-century West and North. Rapid growth shaped the nation's economy and geographic boundaries as well as political debates and movements for social reform. This era of growth contributed to emerging tensions between the free-labor economy and slavery.

> What factors contributed to America's "industrial evolution"?

> Who benefited from America's economic growth?

> What factors spurred westward expansion?

> Why did the United States go to war with Mexico?

> How did reform efforts change after 1840?

> Conclusion: How was white freedom in the West and North defined?

DID YOU KNOW?

In 1860, the United States had about as many miles of railroad track as the rest of the world combined.

War news from Mexico. In 1848, artist Richard Caton Woodville imagined this scene of a man reading of the war.

> What factors contributed to America's "industrial evolution"?

Westward the Star of Empire Takes Its Way—near Council Bluffs, Iowa This painting by Andrew Melrose depicts the mid-nineteenth-century landscape of agricultural and technological progress. Museum of the American West, Autry National Center, 92.147.1.

▶ FOR MORE HELP ANALYZING THIS IMAGE, see the visual activity for this chapter in the Online Study Guide at bedfordstmartins.com/roarkunderstanding.

DURING THE 1840s AND 1850s, Americans experienced a profound economic transformation that had been under way since the start of the nineteenth century. Since 1800, the total output of the U.S. economy had multiplied twelvefold. Four fundamental changes in American society fueled this remarkable economic growth.

First, millions of Americans moved from farms to towns and cities. Second, the number of Americans who worked in factories, mainly in urban centers, grew to about 20 percent of the labor force by 1860. This trend contributed to the nation's economic growth because, in general, factory workers produced twice as much (per unit of labor) as agricultural workers.

Third, a shift from water power to steam as a source of energy raised productivity, especially in factories and transportation. Between 1840 and 1860, coal production multiplied eightfold, cutting prices in half and permitting coal-fired steam engines to power ever more factories, railroads, and ships.

A fourth fundamental change propelling America's economic development was the rise in agricultural productivity, which nearly doubled between 1800 and 1860. More than any other single factor, agricultural productivity spurred the nation's economic growth.

Historians often refer to this cascade of changes in farms, cities, factories, power, and transportation as an industrial revolution. However, these changes did not cause an abrupt discontinuity in America's economy or society. The United States remained overwhelmingly rural and agricultural. Old methods of production continued alongside new ones. By 1860, the muscles of people and

CHAPTER LOCATOR

What factors contributed to America's "industrial evolution"?

work animals still provided thirty times more energy for manufacturing than did steam power. The changes in the American economy during the 1840s and 1850s might better be termed "industrial evolution."

Agriculture and Land Policy

As farmers pushed westward in their quest for cheap land, they encountered the Midwest's comparatively treeless prairie. Rich prairie soils yielded bumper crops, enticing farmers to migrate to the Midwest by the tens of thousands between 1830 and 1860. The populations of Indiana, Illinois, Michigan, Wisconsin, and Iowa exploded tenfold between 1830 and 1860, four times faster than the growth of the nation as a whole.

Labor-saving improvements in farm implements also hiked agricultural productivity. In 1837, John Deere patented a strong, smooth steel plow that sliced through prairie soil so cleanly that farmers called it the "singing plow." Deere's company became the leading plow manufacturer in the Midwest, turning out more than ten thousand plows a year by the late 1850s.

Improvements in wheat harvesting also multiplied farmers' productivity. In 1850, most farmers harvested wheat by hand, cutting two or three acres a day with backbreaking labor. In the 1840s, Cyrus McCormick and others experimented with designs for mechanical reapers, and by the 1850s, an inexpensive McCormick reaper allowed a farmer to harvest twelve acres a day. Most continued to cut their grain by hand, but improved reapers and plows, usually powered by horses or oxen, allowed farmers to cultivate more land, doubling the corn and wheat harvests between 1840 and 1860.

Federal land policy made possible the agricultural productivity that fueled the nation's economy. Up to 1860, the United States continued to be land-rich and labor-poor. Territorial acquisitions made the nation a great deal richer in land, adding more than a billion acres with the Louisiana Purchase (see chapter 10) and the annexation of Florida, Oregon, and vast territories following the Mexican-American War (see page 323). The federal government made most of this land available for purchase to attract settlers and to generate revenue. Speculators found ways to claim large tracts of the most desirable plots and sell them to settlers at a profit. But millions of ordinary farmers bought federal land for just $1.25 an acre, or $50 for a forty-acre farm, which could support a family. Millions of other farmers squatted on unclaimed federal land. By making land available to millions of Americans on relatively easy terms, the federal government achieved the goal of attracting settlers to the new territories in the West, which in due course joined the Union as new states. Above all, federal land policy fueled the increase in agricultural productivity that underlay the nation's impressive economic growth.

Manufacturing and Mechanization

In contrast to the United States, Britain and other European countries had land-poor, labor-rich economies; there, meager opportunities in agriculture kept factory laborers plentiful and wages low. In the United States, western expansion and government land policies buoyed agriculture, keeping millions of people on

CHRONOLOGY

1800–1860
– American agricultural productivity nearly doubles.

1837
– John Deere patents steel plow.

1840s
– Practical mechanical reapers are created.

1840–1860
– American coal production multiplies eightfold.
– American corn and wheat harvests double.

1844
– Samuel F. B. Morse demonstrates telegraph.

| Who benefited from America's economic growth? | What factors spurred westward expansion? | Why did the United States go to war with Mexico? | How did reform efforts change after 1840? | Conclusion: How was white freedom in the West and North defined? |

309

the farm and thereby limiting the supply of workers for manufacturing and elevating wages. Because of this relative shortage of workers, manufacturers searched constantly for ways to save labor.

Mechanization allowed manufacturers to produce more with less labor. The practice of manufacturing and then assembling interchangeable parts spread from gun making to other industries and became known as the **American system**. Standardized parts produced by machine allowed manufacturers to employ unskilled workers, who were much cheaper and more readily available than highly trained craftsmen. A visitor to a Springfield, Massachusetts, gun factory in 1842 noted, for example, that standardized parts made the trained gunsmith's "skill of the eye and the hand, [previously] acquired by practice alone . . . no longer indispensable." Even in heavily mechanized industries, factories remained fairly small; few had more than twenty or thirty employees.

Manufacturing and agriculture meshed into a dynamic national economy. New England led the nation in manufacturing, shipping goods such as guns, clocks, plows, and axes west and south, while southern and western states sent commodities such as wheat, pork, whiskey, tobacco, and cotton north and east. Manufacturers produced for the huge domestic market rather than for export. To protect their access to domestic consumers, manufacturers supported tariffs on goods imported from foreign countries. The burgeoning national economy was further fueled by the growth of the railroads, which linked farms and factories in new ways.

Railroads: Breaking the Bonds of Nature

Railroads seemed to break the bonds of nature. When canals and rivers froze in winter or became impassable during summer droughts, trains steamed ahead. When becalmed sailing ships went nowhere, locomotives kept on chugging, averaging more than twenty miles an hour during the 1850s. Above all, railroads gave cities not blessed with canals or navigable rivers a way to compete for rural trade. The massive expansion of American railroads helped catapult the nation into position as the world's second-greatest industrial power, after Great Britain (**Map 12.1**).

In addition to speeding transportation, railroads propelled the growth of other industries, such as iron and communications. Iron production grew five times faster than the population during the decades up to 1860, in part to meet railroads' demand. Railroads also stimulated the fledgling telegraph industry. In 1844, Samuel F. B. Morse demonstrated the potential of his telegraph by transmitting an electronic message along forty miles of wire strung between Washington, D.C., and Baltimore. By 1861, more than fifty thousand miles of wire stretched

The Railroad Boom of the 1850s

1850: 9,000 miles of railroad track in the United States, almost two-thirds of it in New England.

1860: 30,000 miles of railroad track in the United States, with several railroads spanning the Mississippi River.

By 1860, the United States has approximately as much railroad track as the rest of the world combined.

American system

▶ The practice of manufacturing and then assembling interchangeable parts. A system that spread quickly across American industries, the use of standardized parts allowed American manufacturers to employ cheap unskilled workers.

The Telegraph

Samuel F. B. Morse is credited with inventing the telegraph because of his patent in June 1840, but, as one contemporary observed, Morse's talent consisted of "combining and applying the discoveries of others in the invention of a particular instrument and process for telegraphic purposes." Morse sent the first message in 1844 on this telegraph using a code he devised that represented each letter and number with dots and dashes.
Division of Political History, Smithsonian Institution, Washington, D.C.

CHAPTER LOCATOR | What factors contributed to America's "industrial evolution"?

CHAPTER 12
310 THE NEW WEST AND FREE NORTH, 1840–1860

MAP 12.1 ■ Railroads in 1860
Railroads were a crucial component of the revolutions in transportation and communications that transformed nineteenth-century America. The railroad system reflected the differences in the economies of the North and South.

across the continent to the Pacific Ocean, often alongside railroad tracks, making trains safer and more efficient and accelerating communications of all sorts.

Private corporations built and owned almost all railroads, in contrast to government ownership of railroads common in other industrial nations. But privately owned American railroads received massive government aid, especially federal land grants. By 1860, Congress had granted railroads more than twenty million acres of federal land, thereby underwriting construction costs and promoting the expansion of the rail network, the settlement of federal land, and the integration of the domestic market.

The railroad boom of the 1850s signaled the growing industrial might of the American economy. But railroads, like other industries, succeeded because they served both farms and cities. Despite this growth, in 1860, most Americans were far more familiar with horses than with locomotives.

QUICK REVIEW <

How did the United States become a leading industrial power in the nineteenth century?

| Who benefited from America's economic growth? | What factors spurred westward expansion? | Why did the United States go to war with Mexico? | How did reform efforts change after 1840? | Conclusion: How was white freedom in the West and North defined? |

> Who benefited from America's economic growth?

Miner with Pick, Pan, and Shovel This young man exhibits the spirit of individual effort that was the foundation of free-labor ideals. Hard work with these tools, the picture suggests, promised rewards and maybe riches. Collection of Matthew Isenburg.

THE NATION'S IMPRESSIVE economic performance did not reward all Americans equally. Native-born white men tended to do better than immigrants. With few exceptions, women were excluded from opportunities open to men. In the North and West, slavery was slowly eliminated in the half century after the American Revolution, but most free African Americans were relegated to dead-end jobs as laborers and servants. Discrimination against immigrants, women, and free blacks did not trouble most white men. With certain notable exceptions, they considered it proper and just.

The Free-Labor Ideal: Freedom Plus Labor

During the 1840s and 1850s, leaders throughout the North and West emphasized a set of ideas that seemed to explain why the changes under way in their society benefited some people more than others. They referred again and again to the advantages of what they termed free labor, that is to say, laborers who were not slaves. By the 1850s, free-labor ideas described a social and economic ideal that accounted for both the successes and the shortcomings of the economy and society taking shape in the North and the West.

CHAPTER LOCATOR

What factors contributed to America's "industrial evolution"?

Spokesmen for the **free-labor ideal** celebrated hard work, self-reliance, and independence. They proclaimed that the door to success was open not just to those who inherited wealth or status but also to self-made men. Free labor, Abraham Lincoln argued, was "the just and generous, and prosperous system, which opens the way for all—gives hope to all, and energy, and progress, and improvement of condition to all." Free labor permitted farmers and artisans to enjoy the products of their own labor, and it also benefited wageworkers. "The prudent, penniless beginner in the world," Lincoln asserted, "labors for wages awhile, saves a surplus with which to buy tools or land, for himself; then labors on his own account another while, and at length hires another new beginner to help him."

The free-labor ideal affirmed an egalitarian vision of human potential. Advocates stressed the importance of universal education. (See "Global Comparison," page 314.) By 1860, many cities and towns had public schools that boasted that up to 80 percent of children ages seven to thirteen attended school for at least a few weeks each year. In rural areas, where the labor of children was more difficult to spare, schools typically enrolled no more than half the school-age children. Lessons included more than arithmetic, penmanship, and a smattering of other subjects. Textbooks and teachers—most of whom were young women—drummed into students the lessons of the free-labor system: self-reliance, discipline, and, above all else, hard work. "Remember that all the ignorance, degradation, and misery in the world is the result of indolence and vice," one textbook intoned. In school and out, free-labor ideology emphasized labor as much as freedom.

Economic Inequality

The opportunities presented by the expanding economy made a few men rich. Most Americans, however, measured success in more modest terms. The average wealth of adult white men in the North in 1860 barely topped $2,000. Nearly half of American men had no wealth at all; about 60 percent owned no land. Because property possessed by married women was normally considered to belong to their husbands, women had less wealth than men. Free African Americans had still less; 90 percent of them were propertyless.

Free-labor spokesmen considered these economic inequalities a natural outgrowth of freedom—the inevitable result of some individuals being more able and willing to work and luckier. These inequalities also demonstrate the gap between the promise and the performance of the free-labor ideal. Economic growth permitted many men to move from being landless squatters to landowning farmers and from being hired laborers to independent, self-employed producers. But many more Americans remained behind, landless and working for wages.

Seeking out new opportunities in pursuit of free-labor ideals created restless social and geographic mobility. While fortunate people rose far beyond their social origins, others shared the misfortune of a merchant who, an observer noted, "has been on the sinking list all his life." In search of better prospects, roughly two-thirds of the rural population moved every decade, and population turnover in cities was even greater. This constant coming and going weakened community ties to neighbors and friends and threw individuals even more on their own resources in times of trouble.

CHRONOLOGY

1840s–1850s
– Free-labor ideal develops to describe the economic and social successes and shortcomings in the North and the West.

1840–1860
– Almost 4.5 million immigrants arrive in the United States, three-fourths of them from Ireland and Germany.

free-labor ideal
▶ Social and economic ideal popular in the 1840s and 1850s that attributed success to the hard work and self-reliance of free laborers working in a democratic society. The free-labor ideal affirmed an egalitarian vision of human potential. Most free-labor advocates, however, did not include women and racial minorities in their vision of American individualism.

| Who benefited from America's economic growth? | What factors spurred westward expansion? | Why did the United States go to war with Mexico? | How did reform efforts change after 1840? | Conclusion: How was white freedom in the West and North defined? |

313

Nineteenth-Century School Enrollment and Literacy Rates

In the first half of the nineteenth century, school enrollment and literacy rates in northern and western Europe and the United States were high compared with those in the rest of the world. U.S. figures would be even higher but for the South, where fewer than 10 percent of black slaves were literate and whites were less likely to attend school than in the North. The ability to read and write facilitates communication, business transactions, acquisition of skills, and perhaps even greater openness to change, all building blocks of rapid economic growth. But mass literacy has not always been a prerequisite for economic development. When England underwent industrialization between 1780 and 1830, fewer than half of the nation's children attended school. By 1850, England was the world's greatest industrial power, but where did it rank in literacy? Literacy levels may actually have fallen in Lancashire, a region of England that experienced great industrial growth, as children went to work in factories rather than attend school.

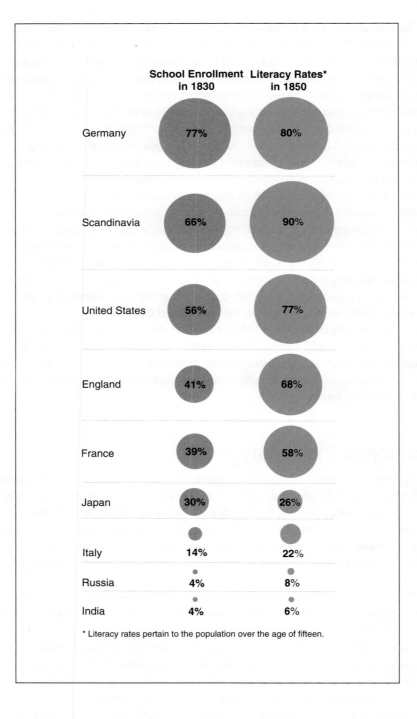

	School Enrollment in 1830	Literacy Rates* in 1850
Germany	77%	80%
Scandinavia	66%	90%
United States	56%	77%
England	41%	68%
France	39%	58%
Japan	30%	26%
Italy	14%	22%
Russia	4%	8%
India	4%	6%

* Literacy rates pertain to the population over the age of fifteen.

Immigrants and the Free-Labor Ladder

The risks and uncertainties of free labor did not deter millions of immigrants from entering the United States during the 1840s and 1850s. Almost 4.5 million immigrants arrived between 1840 and 1860, six times more than had come during the previous two decades. By 1860, foreign-born residents made up about one-eighth of the U.S. population.

CHAPTER LOCATOR

What factors contributed to America's "industrial evolution"?

Nearly three out of four immigrants who arrived in the United States between 1840 and 1860 came from Germany and Ireland. The vast majority of the 1.4 million Germans who entered during these years were skilled tradesmen and their families. German tradesmen settled mostly in the Midwest, often congregating in cities. Roughly a quarter of German immigrants were farmers, some of whom settled in Texas. On the whole, German Americans occupied the middle stratum of independent producers celebrated by free-labor spokesmen.

Irish immigrants, in contrast, entered at the bottom of the free-labor ladder and struggled to climb up. Nearly 1.7 million Irish immigrants arrived between 1840 and 1860, nearly all of them desperately poor and often weakened by hunger and disease. Potato blight struck Ireland in 1845 and returned repeatedly in subsequent years, spreading a catastrophic famine throughout the island. Many of the lucky ones crowded into the holds of ships and set out for America, where they congregated in northeastern cities. As one immigrant group declared, "All we want is to get out of Ireland; we must be better anywhere than here." Roughly three out of four Irish immigrants worked as laborers or domestic servants. Almost all Irish immigrants were Catholic, a fact that set them apart from the overwhelmingly Protestant native-born residents. Many natives regarded the Irish as hard-drinking, obstreperous, half-civilized folk. Such views lay behind the discrimination reflected in job announcements that commonly stated, "No Irish need apply."

In America's labor-poor economy, Irish laborers could earn more in one day than in several weeks in Ireland, if they could find work there. In America, one immigrant explained in 1853, there was "plenty of work and plenty of wages plenty to eat and no land lords thats enough what more does a man want." But some immigrants wanted more, especially respect and decent working conditions. One immigrant complained that he was "a slave for the Americans as the generality of the Irish . . . are."

Such testimony illustrates that the free-labor system, whether for immigrants or native-born laborers, often did not live up to its optimistic promise. Many wage laborers could not realistically aspire to become independent, self-sufficient property holders, despite the claims of free-labor proponents.

QUICK REVIEW

What values underlay the free-labor ideal?

| Who benefited from America's economic growth? | What factors spurred westward expansion? | Why did the United States go to war with Mexico? | How did reform efforts change after 1840? | Conclusion: How was white freedom in the West and North defined? |

What factors spurred westward expansion?

Pioneer Family on the Trail West

In 1860, W. G. Chamberlain photographed these unidentified travelers momentarily at rest by the upper Arkansas River in Colorado. Traveling in family groups created additional challenges for Americans moving west. Denver Public Library, Western History Division # F3226.

▶ FOR MORE HELP ANALYZING THIS IMAGE, see the visual activity for this chapter in the Online Study Guide at bedfordstmartins.com/roarkunderstanding.

UNTIL THE 1840s, the overwhelming majority of Americans lived east of the Mississippi River. Native Americans inhabited the plains, deserts, and rugged coasts to the west. The British claimed the Oregon Country, and the Mexican flag flew over the vast expanse of the Southwest. But by 1850, the boundaries of the United States stretched to the Pacific, and the nation had more than doubled in size. By 1860, the great migration had carried four million Americans west of the Mississippi River.

Manifest Destiny

Most Americans believed that the superiority of their institutions and white culture bestowed on them a God-given right to spread their civilization across the continent. They imagined the West as a wilderness, empty and undeveloped. If they recognized Indians and Mexicans at all, they dismissed them as mere obstacles to American progress. The West provided young men especially an arena in which to "show their manhood." Americans' belief in their own superiority had been bolstered by the United States' amazing success. Most Americans believed that the West could only be improved by the spread of their civilization.

In 1845, a New York political journal edited by John L. O'Sullivan coined the term **manifest destiny** as the latest justification for American expansionism. O'Sullivan called on Americans to resist any foreign power—British, French, or Mexican—that attempted to thwart "the fulfillment of our manifest destiny to overspread the continent allotted by Providence for the free development of our yearly multiplying millions . . . [and] for the development of the great experiment of liberty and federative self-government entrusted to us." Almost overnight, the phrase *manifest destiny* swept the nation, framing the conquest of the West as part of a divine plan.

manifest destiny

▶ Term coined in 1845 by John L. O'Sullivan to justify American expansion. O'Sullivan claimed that it was Americans' "manifest destiny" to move westward, bringing with them their values and civilization. Manifest destiny framed the American conquest of the West as part of a divine plan.

CHAPTER LOCATOR | What factors contributed to America's "industrial evolution"?

As important as national pride and racial arrogance were to manifest destiny, economic gain made up its core. Land hunger drew hundreds of thousands of average Americans westward. Some politicians, moreover, had become convinced that national prosperity depended on capturing the rich trade of the Far East. To trade with Asia, the United States needed Pacific coast ports. "The sun of civilization must shine across the sea: socially and commercially," Missouri senator Thomas Hart Benton declared. The United States and Asia must "talk together, and trade together. Commerce is a great civilizer." In the 1840s, American economic expansion came wrapped in the rhetoric of uplift and civilization.

Oregon and the Overland Trail

The Oregon Country—a vast region bounded on the west by the Pacific Ocean, on the east by the Rocky Mountains, on the south by the forty-second parallel, and on the north by Russian Alaska—was claimed by both the United States and Britain. Unable to agree which country had the stronger claim, the United States and Great Britain decided in 1818 on a "joint occupation" that would leave Oregon "free and open" to settlement by both countries. A handful of American fur traders and "mountain men" roamed the region in the 1820s.

By the late 1830s, settlers began to trickle along the **Oregon Trail** (**Map 12.2,** page 318). The first wagon trains headed west in 1841, and by 1843 about 1,000 emigrants a year set out from Independence, Missouri. By 1869, when the first transcontinental railroad was completed, approximately 350,000 migrants had traveled west to the Pacific in wagon trains.

Emigrants encountered a quarter of a million Plains Indians. Some Native Americans were farmers who lived peaceful, sedentary lives, but a majority were horse-mounted, nomadic, nonagricultural peoples whose warriors symbolized the "savage Indian" in the minds of whites.

Horse Cultures of the Great Plains

Central plains: Sioux, Cheyenne, Shoshoni, and Arapaho
Southern plains: Kiowa, Wichita, and Comanche

Horses, which had been brought to North America by Spaniards in the sixteenth century, permitted the Plains tribes to become highly mobile hunters of buffalo. They came to depend on buffalo for nearly everything—food, clothing, shelter, and fuel. Competition for buffalo led to war between the tribes. Young men were introduced to warfare early, learning to ride ponies at breakneck speed while firing off arrows and, later, rifles with astounding accuracy. "A Comanche on his feet is out of his element," observed western artist George Catlin, "but the moment he lays his hands upon his horse, his *face* even becomes handsome, and he gracefully flies away like a different being."

The Plains Indians struck fear in the hearts of whites on the wagon trains. But Native Americans had far more to fear from whites. Indians killed fewer than four hundred emigrants on the trail between 1840 and 1860, while whites brought alcohol and deadly epidemics of smallpox, measles, cholera, and scarlet fever. Moreover, whites killed the buffalo, often slaughtering them for sport. The buffalo

CHRONOLOGY

1836
– Texas declares independence from Mexico.

1841
– First wagon trains head west on Oregon Trail.

1845
– Term *manifest destiny* is coined.

1846
– Bear Flag Revolt in California.

1847
– Mormons settle in Utah.

1850
– Mormon community is annexed to United States as Utah Territory.

1851
– Conference in Laramie, Wyoming, marks the beginning of government policy of concentration for Plains Indians.

1857
– U.S. troops invade Salt Lake City in Mormon War.

Oregon Trail
▶ Route from Independence, Missouri, to Oregon traveled by American settlers starting in the late 1830s. Despite the fears of American migrants, disease and accidents caused many more deaths along the trail than did Indian attacks. By 1869, approximately 350,000 migrants had traveled west along the Oregon Trail to the Pacific in wagon trains.

| Who benefited from America's economic growth? | **What factors spurred westward expansion?** | Why did the United States go to war with Mexico? | How did reform efforts change after 1840? | Conclusion: How was white freedom in the West and North defined? |

317

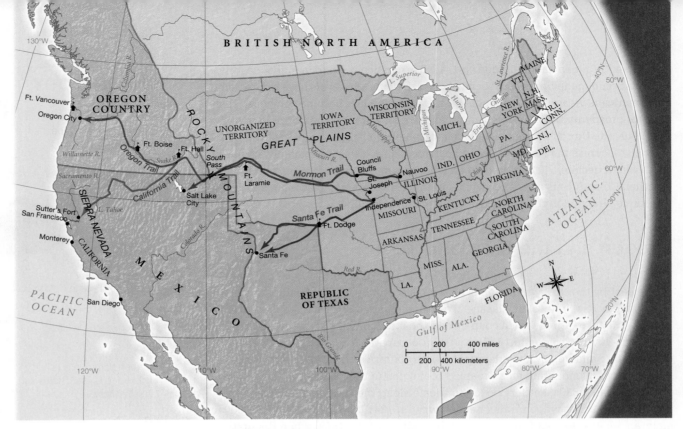

MAP 12.2 ■ Major Trails West
In the 1830s, wagon trains began snaking their way to the Southwest and the Pacific coast. Deep ruts, some of which can still be seen today, soon marked the most popular routes.

Plains Indians and Trails West in the 1840s and 1850s

still numbered some twelve million in 1860, but the herds were shrinking rapidly, intensifying conflict among the Plains tribes.

Emigrants insisted that the federal government provide them with more protection. The government constructed a chain of forts along the Oregon Trail (see Map 12.2). More important, it adopted a new Indian policy: "concentration." In 1851, the government called the Plains tribes to a conference at Fort Laramie, Wyoming. Government negotiators persuaded the chiefs to sign agreements that cleared a wide corridor for wagon trains by restricting Native Americans to specific areas that whites promised they would never violate. This policy of concentration became the seedbed for the subsequent policy of reservations. But whites would not keep out of Indian territory, and Indians would not easily give up their traditional ways of life. Struggle for control of the West meant warfare for decades to come.

Still, Indians threatened emigrants less than life on the trail did. The men, women, and children who headed west each spring could count on at least six months of grueling travel. The pioneers endured parching heat, drought, treacherous rivers, disease, physical and emotional exhaustion, and, if the snows closed the mountain passes before they got through, freezing and starvation. Such tribulations led one miserable woman, trying to keep her children dry in a rainstorm and to calm them as they listened to Indian shouts, to wonder "what had possessed my husband, anyway, that he should have thought of bringing us away out through this God forsaken country."

Men usually found Oregon "one of the greatest countries in the world." From "the Cascade mountains to the Pacific, the whole country can be cultivated," exclaimed one eager settler. When women reached Oregon, they found that

CHAPTER LOCATOR

What factors contributed to America's "industrial evolution"?

neighbors were scarce and things were in a "primitive state." Necessity blurred the traditional division between men's and women's work. "I am maid of all traids," one busy woman remarked in 1853. Work seemed unending. "I am a very old woman," declared twenty-nine-year-old Sarah Everett. "My face is thin sunken and wrinkled, my hands bony withered and hard." Another settler observed, "A woman that can not endure almost as much as a horse has no business here." Yet despite the ordeal of the trail and the difficulties of starting from scratch, emigrants kept coming.

The Mormon Exodus

Not every wagon train heading west was bound for the Pacific Slope. One remarkable group of religious emigrants halted near the Great Salt Lake in what was then Mexican territory. The Mormons deliberately chose the remote site as a refuge. After years of persecution in the East, they fled west to find religious freedom and communal security.

In 1830, Joseph Smith Jr., who was only twenty-four, published *The Book of Mormon* and founded the Church of Jesus Christ of Latter-Day Saints (the Mormons). A decade earlier, the upstate New York farm boy had begun to experience revelations that were followed, he said, by a visit from an angel who led him to golden tablets buried near his home. *The Book of Mormon*, as the tablets' text came to be known, told the story of an ancient Hebrew civilization in the New World and predicted the appearance of an American prophet who would reestablish Jesus Christ's kingdom in America. Converts, repulsed by antebellum America's social turmoil and rampant materialism, flocked to the new church.

Neighbors branded Mormons heretics and drove Smith and his followers from New York to Ohio, then to Missouri, and finally in 1839 to Nauvoo, Illinois, where they built a prosperous community. But a rift in the church developed after Smith sanctioned "plural marriage" (polygamy). Non-Mormons caught wind of the controversy and eventually arrested Smith and his brother. On June 27, 1844, a mob stormed the jail and shot both men dead.

The embattled church turned to an extraordinary new leader, Brigham Young, who oversaw a great exodus. In 1846, traveling in 3,700 wagons, 12,000 Mormons made their way to eastern Iowa, then the following year to their new home beside the Great Salt Lake. Young described the region as a barren waste, "the paradise of the lizard, the cricket and the rattlesnake." Within ten years, however, the Mormons developed an irrigation system that made the desert bloom and, under Young's stern leadership, built a thriving community.

In 1850, the Mormon kingdom was annexed to the United States as Utah Territory. The nation's attention focused on Utah in 1852 when Brigham Young announced that many Mormons practiced polygamy. Young's statement caused a popular outcry that forced the U.S. government to establish its authority in Utah. In 1857, 2,500 U.S. troops invaded Salt Lake City in a bloodless occupation that was known as the Mormon War. The invasion did not, however, dislodge the Mormon Church from its central place in Utah.

The Mexican Borderlands

In the Mexican Southwest, westward-moving Anglo-American pioneers con-fronted northern-moving Spanish-speaking frontiersmen, resulting in a collision of national cultures, interests, and aspirations. Independent from Spain since 1821,

| Who benefited from America's economic growth? | **What factors spurred westward expansion?** | Why did the United States go to war with Mexico? | How did reform efforts change after 1840? | Conclusion: How was white freedom in the West and North defined? |

319

MAP 12.3 ■ Texas and Mexico
in the 1830s

As Americans spilled into lightly
populated and loosely governed
northern Mexico, Texas and then
other Mexican provinces became
contested territory.

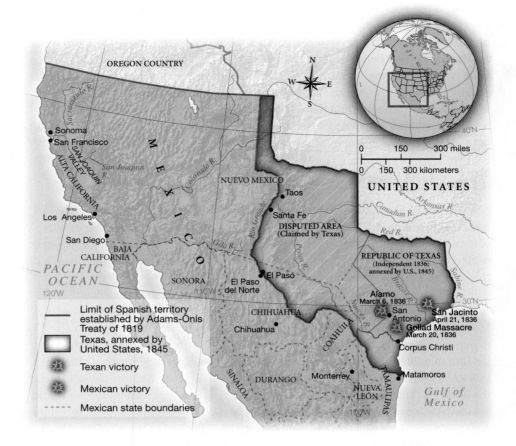

Mexico was a vast country that stretched from the Gulf of Mexico to the Pacific
and from the Oregon Country to Guatemala (**Map 12.3**). But Mexico's northern
provinces were sparsely populated, and the young nation found it increasingly
difficult to defend its borderlands, especially when faced with a northern neighbor
convinced of its superiority and bent on territorial acquisition.

The American assault began quietly. In the 1820s, Anglo-American trappers,
traders, and settlers drifted into Mexico's far northern provinces. Santa Fe, a
remote outpost in the province of New Mexico, became a magnet for American
enterprise. Each spring, American traders gathered at Independence, Missouri,
for the long trek southwest along the Santa Fe Trail (see Map 12.2, page 318).
They crammed their wagons with inexpensive American manufactured goods and
returned home with Mexican silver, furs, and mules.

The Mexican province of Texas attracted a flood of Americans who had settlement, not long-distance trade, on their minds (see Map 12.3). Wanting to populate
and develop its northern territory, the Mexican government granted the American
Stephen F. Austin a huge tract of land along the Brazos River. In the 1820s, Austin
became the first Anglo-American *empresario* (colonization agent) in Texas, offering
land at only ten cents an acre. Thousands of Americans poured across the border.
Most were Southerners who brought cotton and slaves with them.

By the 1830s, the settlers had established a thriving plantation economy in
Texas. Americans numbered 35,000, while the *Tejano* (Spanish-speaking) population was less than 8,000. Few Anglo-American settlers were Roman Catholic,
spoke Spanish, or cared about assimilating into Mexican culture. Afraid of losing

CHAPTER LOCATOR

What factors contributed
to America's "industrial
evolution"?

Texas to the new arrivals, the Mexican government in 1830 banned further immigration to Texas from the United States and outlawed the introduction of additional slaves. The Anglo-Americans made it clear that they wanted to be rid of the "despotism of the sword and the priesthood" and to govern themselves. In Mexico City, however, General Antonio López de Santa Anna seized political power and set about restoring order to the northern frontier.

When the Texan settlers rebelled, Santa Anna ordered the Mexican army northward. In February 1836, the army arrived at the outskirts of San Antonio, where a small band of rebels had taken refuge in a former Franciscan mission known as the Alamo. Santa Anna sent wave after wave of his 2,000-man army crashing against the walls until the attackers finally broke through and killed all 187 rebels. A few weeks later, outside the small town of Goliad, Mexican forces captured a garrison of Texans and proceeded to execute almost 400 of the men as "pirates and outlaws." In April 1836, at San Jacinto, General Sam Houston's army adopted the massacre of Goliad as a battle cry and crushed Santa Anna's troops. The Texans had succeeded in establishing the Lone Star Republic, and the following year, the United States recognized the independence of Texas from Mexico.

Earlier, in 1824, in an effort to increase Mexican migration to the province of California, the Mexican government granted *ranchos*—huge estates devoted to cattle raising—to new settlers. *Rancheros* ruled over near-feudal empires worked by Indians whose condition sometimes approached that of slaves. Not satisfied, the rancheros coveted the vast lands controlled by the Franciscan missions. In 1834, they persuaded the Mexican government to confiscate the missions and make their lands available to new settlement, a development that accelerated the decline of the California Indians.

Despite the efforts of the Mexican government, California in 1840 had a population of only 7,000 Mexican settlers and 380 non-Mexican settlers. Among the non-Mexicans were Americans who championed manifest destiny and sought to woo American emigrants to California. In the 1840s, wagon after wagon left the Oregon Trail to head southwest on the California Trail, alarming Mexican officials (see Map 12.2, page 318). Many Americans hoped California would someday become part of the United States. As a New York newspaper put it in 1845, "Let the tide of emigration flow toward California and the American population will soon be sufficiently numerous to play the Texas game."

In 1846, American settlers in the Sacramento Valley took matters into their own hands. Prodded by John C. Frémont, a former army captain and explorer who had arrived with a party of sixty buckskin-clad frontiersmen spoiling for a fight, the Californians raised an independence movement known as the Bear Flag Revolt. By then, James K. Polk, a champion of aggressive expansion, sat in the White House.

Texas War for Independence, 1836

QUICK REVIEW

Why did westward migration expand dramatically in the mid-nineteenth century?

| Who benefited from America's economic growth? | **What factors spurred westward expansion?** | Why did the United States go to war with Mexico? | How did reform efforts change after 1840? | Conclusion: How was white freedom in the West and North defined? |

Why did the United States go to war with Mexico?

Polk and Dallas Banner, 1844 In 1844, Democratic presidential nominee James K. Polk and vice presidential nominee George M. Dallas campaigned under this cotton banner. The extra star spilling over into the red and white stripes symbolizes Polk's vigorous support for annexing the huge slave republic of Texas, which had declared its independence from Mexico eight years earlier. Collection of Janice L. and David J. Frent.

ALTHOUGH EMIGRANTS acted as the advance guard of American empire, acquiring territory in the West required political action. In the 1840s, the politics of expansion became entangled with sectionalism and the slavery question. Texas, Oregon, and the Mexican borderlands thrust the United States into a dangerous diplomatic crisis with Great Britain and a full-scale war with Mexico.

The Politics of Expansion

Texans had sought admission to the Union almost since winning their independence from Mexico in 1836. But any suggestion of adding another slave state to the Union outraged most Northerners. Moreover, annexing Texas risked precipitating war, because Mexico had never relinquished its claim to its lost province.

President John Tyler, who became president in April 1841 when William Henry Harrison died one month after taking office, understood that Texas was a dangerous issue but decided to risk annexing the Lone Star Republic. In April 1844, when he laid an annexation treaty before the Senate, howls of protest erupted across the North. Future Massachusetts senator Charles Sumner deplored the "insidious" plan to annex Texas and to carve from it "great slaveholding states." The Senate soundly rejected the treaty, and it appeared that Tyler had succeeded only in inflaming sectional conflict.

The issue of Texas had not died down by the 1844 election. In an effort to appeal to northern voters, the Whig nominee for president, Henry Clay, came out against the annexation of Texas. "Annexation and war with Mexico are identical," he declared. The Democrats chose Tennessean **James K. Polk**, who was strongly in favor of annexation. To make annexation palatable to Northerners, the Democrats shrewdly yoked Texas to Oregon, thus tapping the desire for expansion in the free states of the North as well as in the slave states of the South. The Democratic platform called for the "reannexation of Texas" and the "reoccupation of Oregon," suggesting erroneously that the United States was merely reasserting

James K. Polk

▶ The tenth president of the United States. The Democrat Polk was elected in 1844. His support for the annexation of Texas was the key issue in the election against Whig nominee Henry Clay. Polk made the annexation of Texas more acceptable to northern voters by tying it to the acquisition of the vast Oregon territory from the British.

CHAPTER LOCATOR | What factors contributed to America's "industrial evolution"?

existing rights. When Clay waffled, hinting that he might accept the annexation of Texas, his retreat succeeded only in alienating antislavery opinion in the North. In the November election, Polk received 170 electoral votes and Clay 105.

One month after the election, President Tyler announced that the triumph of the Democratic Party provided a mandate for the annexation of Texas "promptly and immediately." In February 1845, after a fierce debate between antislavery and proslavery forces, Congress approved a joint resolution offering the Republic of Texas admission to the United States. Texas entered as the fifteenth slave state.

Tyler delivered Texas, but Polk had promised Oregon, too. Westerners particularly demanded that the new president make good on the Democrats' pledge "Fifty-four Forty or Fight"—that is, all of Oregon, right up to Alaska (54°40' was the southern latitude of Russian Alaska). But Polk was close to war with Mexico and could not afford a war with Britain over U.S. claims in Canada. He renewed an old offer to divide Oregon along the forty-ninth parallel. When Britain accepted the compromise, some Americans cried betrayal, but most celebrated the agreement, which gave the nation an enormous territory peacefully. When the Senate finally approved the treaty in June 1846, the United States and Mexico were already at war.

The Mexican-American War, 1846–1848

From the day he entered the White House, Polk craved Mexico's remaining northern provinces: California and New Mexico, land that today makes up California, Nevada, Utah, most of New Mexico and Arizona, and parts of Wyoming and Colorado. Polk hoped to buy the territory, but when the Mexicans refused to sell, he concluded that military force would be needed to realize the United States' manifest destiny.

Polk had already ordered General **Zachary Taylor** to march his 4,000-man army 150 miles south from its position on the Nueces River, the southern boundary of Texas according to the Mexicans, to the banks of the Rio Grande, the boundary claimed by Texans (**Map 12.4**). The Mexicans saw the American advance as aggression, and on April 25, Mexican cavalry attacked a party of American soldiers, killing or wounding sixteen and capturing the rest. Even before news of the battle arrived in Washington, Polk had obtained his cabinet's approval of a war message.

On May 11, 1846, the president told Congress, "Mexico has passed the boundary of the United States, has invaded our territory, and shed American blood upon American soil." Thus "war exists, and, notwithstanding all our efforts to avoid it, exists by the act of Mexico herself." Congress passed a declaration of war and began raising an army. Faced with the nation's first foreign war, Polk called for volunteers. Eventually, more than 112,000 white Americans (blacks were banned) joined the army to fight in Mexico.

Despite the flood of volunteers, the war divided the nation. Northern Whigs in particular condemned the war. The Massachusetts legislature claimed that the war was being fought for the "triple object of extending slavery, of strengthening the slave power, and of obtaining control of the free states." Antislavery, antiwar Whigs kept up the attack throughout the conflict.

Polk planned a short war in which U.S. armies would occupy Mexico's northern provinces and defeat the Mexican army in a decisive battle or two, after which Mexico would sue for peace and the United States would keep the territory its

1841
- Vice President John Tyler becomes president when William Henry Harrison dies.

1844
- Democrat James K. Polk is elected president.

1845
- United States annexes Texas, which enters Union as slave state.

1846
- Congress declares war on Mexico.
- United States and Great Britain agree to divide Oregon Country.

1848
- Treaty of Guadalupe Hidalgo ends Mexican-American War.

1849
- California gold rush begins.

Zachary Taylor
▶ U.S. general who led the American fight in northern Mexico in the Mexican-American War (1846–1848). His aggression on the battlefield played a major role in crushing Mexico. In 1849, Taylor succeeded James K. Polk as the president of the United States.

Who benefited from America's economic growth? | What factors spurred westward expansion? | **Why did the United States go to war with Mexico?** | How did reform efforts change after 1840? | Conclusion: How was white freedom in the West and North defined?

323

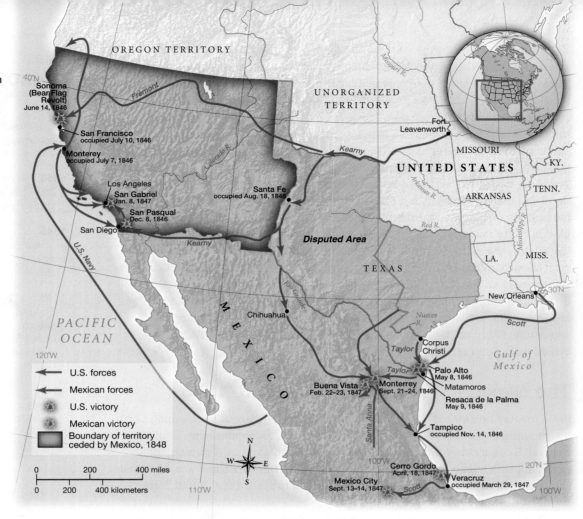

MAP 12.4 ■ The Mexican-American War, 1846–1848
American and Mexican soldiers skirmished across much of northern Mexico, but the major battles took place between the Rio Grande and Mexico City.

Map labels:
OREGON TERRITORY
40°N
Sonoma (Bear Flag Revolt) June 14, 1846
Frémont
San Francisco occupied July 10, 1846
Monterey occupied July 7, 1846
Los Angeles
San Gabriel Jan. 8, 1847
San Pasqual Dec. 6, 1846
San Diego
Kearny
PACIFIC OCEAN
120°W
UNORGANIZED TERRITORY
Missouri R.
Fort Leavenworth
Kearny
MISSOURI
UNITED STATES
KY.
Colorado R.
Santa Fe occupied Aug. 18, 1846
Arkansas R.
ARKANSAS
TENN.
Disputed Area
Red R.
Mississippi R.
LA.
MISS.
TEXAS
U.S. Navy
MEXICO
Rio Grande
Chihuahua
Nueces R.
New Orleans
30°N
Scott
Corpus Christi
Taylor
Gulf of Mexico
Taylor
Palo Alto May 8, 1846
Matamoros
Buena Vista Feb. 22–23, 1847
Monterrey Sept. 21–24, 1846
Resaca de la Palma May 9, 1846
Santa Anna
Tampico occupied Nov. 14, 1846
Cerro Gordo April, 18, 1847
Veracruz occupied March 29, 1847
Mexico City Sept. 13–14, 1847
Scott
110°W
100°W
20°N
100°W

Legend:
→ U.S. forces
→ Mexican forces
✳ U.S. victory
✳ Mexican victory
▨ Boundary of territory ceded by Mexico, 1848

0 200 400 miles
0 200 400 kilometers

N W E S

armies occupied. At first, Polk's strategy seemed to work. In May 1846, Zachary Taylor's troops drove south from the Rio Grande and routed the Mexican army, first at Palo Alto, then at Resaca de la Palma (see Map 12.4). Polk rewarded Taylor for his victories by making him commander of the Mexican campaign.

A second prong of the campaign centered on Colonel Stephen Watts Kearny, who led a 1,700-man army from Missouri into New Mexico. Without firing a shot, U.S. forces took Santa Fe in August 1846. Kearny then marched into San Diego three months later, encountering a major Mexican rebellion against American rule. In January 1847, after several clashes and severe losses, the U.S. forces occupied Los Angeles. California and New Mexico were in American hands.

By then, Taylor had driven deep into the interior of Mexico. In September 1846, he took the city of Monterrey. Taylor then pushed his 5,000 troops southwest, where the Mexican hero of the Alamo, General Antonio López de Santa Anna, was concentrating an army of 21,000. On February 23, 1847, Santa Anna's troops attacked Taylor at Buena Vista. The Americans suffered heavy casualties, but the Mexicans suffered even greater losses (some 3,400 dead, wounded, and missing, compared with 650 Americans). During the night, Santa Anna withdrew his battered army, much to the "profound disgust of the troops," one Mexican officer remembered. "They are filled with grief that they were going to lose the benefit of all the sacrifices that they had made; that the conquered field would be abandoned, and that the victory would be given to the enemy."

CHAPTER LOCATOR   What factors contributed to America's "industrial evolution"?

This family had its portrait taken in 1847, in the middle of the war. Mexican civilians were vulnerable to atrocities committed by the invading army. Volunteers, a large portion of the American troops, received little training and resisted discipline. The "lawless Volunteers stop at no outrage," Brigadier General William Worth declared. "Innocent blood has been basely, cowardly, and barbarously shed in cold blood."

Mexican Family, unknown, ca. 1847, Daguerreotype, Amon Carter Museum, Fort Worth, Texas.

Victory in Mexico

Although the Americans won battle after battle, President Polk's strategy misfired. Despite heavy losses on the battlefield, Mexico refused to trade land for peace. One American soldier captured the Mexican mood: "They cannot submit to be deprived of California after the loss of Texas, and nothing but the conquest of their Capital will force them to such a humiliation." Polk had arrived at the same conclusion. While Taylor occupied the north, General Winfield Scott would land an army on the Gulf coast of Mexico and march 250 miles inland to Mexico City. Polk's plan entailed enormous risk because Scott would have to cut himself off from supplies and lead his men deep into enemy country against a much larger army.

An amphibious landing on March 9, 1847, near Veracruz put some 10,000 American troops ashore, and the city surrendered two weeks later. In early April 1847, the U.S. Army moved westward. After the defeat at Buena Vista, Santa Anna had returned to Mexico City, where he rallied his troops and marched them east to set a trap for Scott in the mountain pass at Cerro Gordo. The American victory in the ensuing battle was so complete that Scott gloated to Taylor, "Mexico no longer has an army." But Santa Anna, ever resilient, again rallied the Mexican army. Some 30,000 troops took up defensive positions on the outskirts of Mexico City and began melting down church bells to cast new cannons.

In August, Scott began his assault on the Mexican capital. The fighting proved the most brutal of the war. Santa Anna backed his army into the city, fighting each step of the way. At the battle of Churubusco, the Mexicans took 4,000 casualties in a single day and the Americans more than 1,000. At the castle of Chapultepec, American troops scaled the walls and fought the Mexican defenders hand to hand. After Chapultepec, Mexico City officials persuaded Santa Anna to evacuate the city to save it from destruction, and on September 14, 1847, General Winfield Scott rode in triumphantly.

On February 2, 1848, American and Mexican officials signed the **Treaty of Guadalupe Hidalgo** in Mexico City. Mexico agreed to give up all claims to Texas

Treaty of Guadalupe Hidalgo

▶ February 1848 treaty that brought the Mexican-American War to an end. Mexico agreed to give up all claims to Texas north of the Rio Grande and to cede the provinces of New Mexico and California to the United States. The United States agreed to pay Mexico $15 million and to assume $3.25 million in claims that American citizens had against Mexico.

| Who benefited from America's economic growth? | What factors spurred westward expansion? | Why did the United States go to war with Mexico? | How did reform efforts change after 1840? | Conclusion: How was white freedom in the West and North defined? |

north of the Rio Grande and to cede the provinces of New Mexico and California—more than 500,000 square miles—to the United States (see Map 12.4, page 324). The United States agreed to pay Mexico $15 million and to assume $3.25 million in claims that American citizens had against Mexico.

The American triumph had enormous consequences. Less than three-quarters of a century after its founding, the United States had achieved its self-proclaimed manifest destiny to stretch from the Atlantic to the Pacific (**Map 12.5**). It would enter the industrial age with vast new natural resources and a two-ocean economy, while Mexico faced a sharply diminished economic future.

Golden California

Another consequence of the Mexican defeat was that California gold poured into American, not Mexican, pockets. In January 1848, James Marshall discovered gold in the American River in the foothills of the Sierra Nevada. Marshall's discovery set off the **California gold rush**. Between 1849 and 1852, more than 250,000 "forty-niners," as the would-be miners were known, descended on the Golden State.

California gold rush
▶ Gold rush set off by James Marshall's discovery of gold in the foothills of the Sierra Nevada in January 1848. Between 1849 and 1852, more than 250,000 "forty-niners," as the would-be miners were known, descended on California. As a result of the gold rush, California quickly attracted sufficient population to apply for statehood.

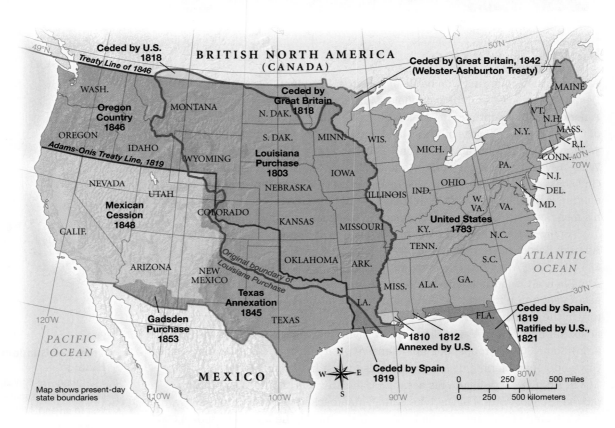

MAP 12.5 ■ Territorial Expansion by 1860
Less than a century after its founding, the United States spread from the Atlantic seaboard to the Pacific coast. War, purchase, and diplomacy had gained a continent.

▶ FOR MORE HELP ANALYZING THIS MAP, see the map activity for this chapter in the Online Study Guide at bedfordstmartins.com/roarkunderstanding.

CHAPTER LOCATOR | What factors contributed to America's "industrial evolution"?

News of the gold strike quickly spread around the world. Soon, a stream of men of various races and nationalities, all bent on getting rich, arrived in California. Only a few struck it rich. Men faced miserable living conditions, sometimes sheltering in holes and brush lean-tos. They also faced cholera and scurvy, exorbitant prices for food (eggs cost a dollar apiece), deadly encounters with claim jumpers, and endless backbreaking labor. Miners could find only temporary relief in the saloons, gambling dens, and brothels that flourished in the mining camps.

By 1853, San Francisco had grown into a raw, booming city of 50,000 that depended as much on gold as did the mining camps inland. Like all the towns that dotted the San Joaquin and Sacramento valleys, it suffered from overcrowding, fire, crime, and violence. But enterprising individuals had learned that there was money to be made tending to the needs of the miners. Hotels, saloons, restaurants, laundries, and stores of all kinds exchanged services and goods for miners' gold.

In 1851, the Committee of Vigilance determined to bring order to the city. Members pledged that "no thief, burglar, incendiary or assassin shall escape punishment, either by the quibbles of the law, the insecurity of prisons, the carelessness or corruption of the police, or a laxity of those who pretended to administer justice." Lynchings proved that the committee meant business. Gunfights declined, but many years would pass before anyone pacified San Francisco.

Establishing civic order was made more difficult by California's diversity and Anglo bigotry. The Chinese attracted special scrutiny. By 1851, 25,000 Chinese lived in California, and many Anglos were convinced that they were not fit citizens of the Golden State. As early as 1852, opponents demanded a halt to Chinese immigration. Chinese leaders in San Francisco fought back. Admitting deep cultural differences, they insisted that "in the important matters we are good men. We honor our parents; we take care of our children; we are industrious and peaceable; we trade much; we are trusted for small and large sums; we pay our debts; and are honest, and of course must tell the truth." Their protestations offered little protection, however, and racial violence persisted.

Chinese Man

This daguerreotype of an unidentified Chinese man was made by Isaac Wallace Baker, a photographer who traveled through California's mining camps in his wagon studio. One of the earliest known portraits of an Asian in California, the portrait shows a proud man boldly displaying his queue (long braid). This was almost certainly an act of defiance, for Anglos ridiculed Chinese cultural traditions, and vigilantes chased down men who wore queues. Copyright the Dorothea Lange Collection, Oakland Museum of California, City of Oakland. Gift of Paul S. Taylor.

QUICK REVIEW

What were the consequences of the U.S. victory in the war with Mexico?

| Who benefited from America's economic growth? | What factors spurred westward expansion? | Why did the United States go to war with Mexico? | How did reform efforts change after 1840? | Conclusion: How was white freedom in the West and North defined? |

327

How did reform efforts change after 1840?

Abolitionist Meeting This rare daguerreotype was made by Ezra Greenleaf Weld in August 1850 at an abolitionist meeting in Cazenovia, New York. Frederick Douglass, who had escaped from slavery in Maryland twelve years earlier, is seated on the platform next to the woman at the table. One of the nation's most brilliant and eloquent abolitionists, Douglass also supported equal rights for women. Collection of the J. Paul Getty Museum, Malibu, Calif.

WHILE MANIFEST DESTINY, the Mexican-American War, and the California gold rush transformed the nation's geography, many Americans sought personal and social reform. The emphasis on self-discipline and individual effort at the core of the free-labor ideal led Americans to believe that insufficient self-control caused the major social problems of the era. The evangelical temperament—a conviction of righteousness coupled with energy, self-discipline, and faith that the world could be improved—animated most reformers.

A few activists pointed out that certain fundamental injustices lay beyond the reach of individual self-control. Transcendentalists and utopians believed that perfection could be attained only by rejecting the competitive, individualistic

CHAPTER LOCATOR | What factors contributed to America's "industrial evolution"?

values of mainstream society. Woman's rights activists and abolitionists sought to reverse the subordination of women and to eliminate the enslavement of blacks by changing laws and social institutions as well as attitudes and customs.

The Pursuit of Perfection: Transcendentalists and Utopians

A group of New England writers who came to be known as transcendentalists believed that individuals should conform neither to the dictates of the materialistic world nor to the dogma of formal religion. Instead, people should look within themselves for truth and guidance. Ralph Waldo Emerson, the leading transcendentalist, proclaimed that the power of the solitary individual was nearly limitless. Henry David Thoreau, Margaret Fuller, and other transcendentalists agreed with Emerson that "if the single man plant himself indomitably on his instincts, and there abide, the huge world will come round to him." In many ways, the confident egoism of transcendentalism represented less an alternative to mainstream values than an exaggerated form of the rampant individualism of the age.

Unlike transcendentalists who sought to turn inward, a few reformers tried to change the world by organizing utopian communities as alternatives to prevailing social arrangements. Some communities set out to become models of perfection whose success would point the way toward a better life for everyone. During the 1840s, more than two dozen communities organized around the ideas of Charles Fourier, a French critic of contemporary society. Members of Fourierist phalanxes, as these communities were called, believed that individualism and competition were evils that denied the basic truth that "men . . . are brothers and not competitors." Phalanxes aspired to replace competition with harmonious cooperation based on the communal ownership of property. But Fourierist communities failed to realize their lofty goals, and few survived more than two or three years.

The Oneida community went beyond the Fourierist notion of communalism. John Humphrey Noyes, the charismatic leader of Oneida, believed that American society's commitment to private property made people greedy and selfish. Noyes claimed that the root of private property lay in marriage, in men's conviction that their wives were their exclusive property. Drawing from a substantial inheritance, Noyes organized the Oneida community in New York in 1848 to abolish marital property rights through the practice of what he called "complex marriage." Sexual intercourse was not restricted to married couples but was permitted between any consenting man and woman in the community. Noyes also required all members to relinquish their economic property to the community. Oneida's sexual and economic communalism attracted several hundred members, but most of their neighbors considered Oneidans adulterers, blasphemers, and worse. Yet the practices that set Oneida apart from its mainstream neighbors strengthened the community, and it survived long after the Civil War.

Woman's Rights Activists

Women participated in the many reform activities that grew out of evangelical churches. Women church members outnumbered men two to one and worked to

CHRONOLOGY

1840s
- More than two dozen communities organize around the ideas of Charles Fourier.

1843
- Henry Highland Garnet calls for slaves to rise in insurrection in "Liberty or Death."

1848

- Oneida community is organized in New York.
- First U.S. woman's rights convention takes place at Seneca Falls, New York.

1849
- Harriet Tubman escapes from slavery.

1848–1860
- Nearly two dozen other woman's rights conventions call for suffrage and an end to discrimination against women.

| Who benefited from America's economic growth? | What factors spurred westward expansion? | Why did the United States go to war with Mexico? | **How did reform efforts change after 1840?** | Conclusion: How was white freedom in the West and North defined? |

329

Elizabeth Cady Stanton

Women's rights leader Elizabeth Cady Stanton, pictured here with two of her sons, knew firsthand the joys and frustrations of domestic life as she sought to expand women's political, moral, and social responsibilities beyond the confines of the home. Collection of Rhoda Jenkins.

Elizabeth Cady Stanton

▶ Activist and reformer who played a key role in the first national woman's rights convention in the United States at Seneca Falls, New York. Stanton and other reformers sought fair pay and expanded employment opportunities for women by appealing to free-labor ideology. While the efforts of woman's rights activists produced little tangible gain in the short run, they inspired many women to challenge the barriers that limited their opportunities.

put their religious ideas into practice by joining peace, temperance, antislavery, and other societies. Involvement in reform organizations gave a few women activists practical experience in such political arts as speaking in public, running meetings, drafting resolutions, and circulating petitions. Along with such experience came confidence. The abolitionist Lydia Maria Child pointed out in 1841 that "those who urged women to become missionaries and form tract societies . . . have changed the household utensil to a living energetic being and they have no spell to turn it into a broom again."

In 1848, about three hundred reformers led by **Elizabeth Cady Stanton** and Lucretia Mott gathered at Seneca Falls, New York, for the first national woman's rights convention in the United States. As Stanton recalled, "The general discontent I felt with women's portion as wife, mother, housekeeper, physician, and spiritual guide, [and] the wearied anxious look of the majority of women impressed me with a strong feeling that some active measure should be taken to right the wrongs of society in general, and of women in particular." The **Seneca Falls Declaration of Sentiments** proclaimed that "the history of mankind is a history of repeated injuries and usurpations on the part of man toward woman, having in direct object the establishment of an absolute tyranny over her." In the style of the Declaration of Independence (see appendix I, page A-1), the Seneca Falls declaration demanded that women "have immediate admission to all the rights and privileges which belong to them as citizens of the United States," particularly the "inalienable right to the elective franchise."

Nearly two dozen other woman's rights conventions assembled before 1860, repeatedly calling for suffrage and an end to discrimination against women. But women had difficulty receiving a respectful hearing, much less achieving legislative action. Even so, the Seneca Falls declaration served as a pathbreaking manifesto of dissent against male supremacy and of support for woman suffrage, and it inspired many women to challenge the barriers that limited their opportunities.

Stanton and other activists sought fair pay and expanded employment opportunities for women by appealing to free-labor ideology. Woman's rights advocate Paula Wright Davis urged Americans to stop discriminating against able and enterprising women: "Let [women] . . . open a Store, . . . plant and tend an Orchard, . . . learn any of the lighter mechanical Trades, . . . study for a Profession, . . . be called to the lecture-room, [and] . . . the Temperance rostrum . . . [and] let her be appointed [to serve in the Post Office]." Some women pioneered in these and many other occupations during the 1840s and 1850s. Woman's rights activists also succeeded in protecting married women's rights to their own wages and property in New York in 1860. But discrimination against women persisted, as most men believed that free-labor ideology required no compromise of male supremacy.

Seneca Falls Declaration of Sentiments

▶ Declaration issued in 1848 at the first national woman's rights convention in the United States. The declaration described the history of mankind as the history of the oppression of women and demanded that women receive all the same rights and privileges of American citizenship as men. Nearly two dozen other woman's rights conventions assembled between 1848 and 1860, repeatedly calling for suffrage and an end to discrimination against women.

Abolitionists and the American Ideal

During the 1840s and 1850s, abolitionists continued to struggle to draw the nation's attention to the plight of slaves and the need for emancipation. Former slaves **Frederick Douglass**, Henry Bibb, and Sojourner Truth lectured to reform audiences throughout the North about the cruelties of slavery. Abolitionists published newspapers, held conventions, and petitioned Congress, but they never attracted a mass following among white Americans. Many white Northerners became convinced that slavery was wrong, but they still believed that blacks were inferior. Many other white Northerners shared the common view of white Southerners that slavery was necessary and even desirable. The geographic expansion of the nation during the 1840s offered abolitionists an opportunity to link their unpopular ideal to a goal that many white Northerners found much more attractive—limiting the geographic expansion of slavery, an issue that moved to the center of national politics during the 1850s (see chapter 14).

Black leaders rose to prominence in the abolitionist movement during the 1840s and 1850s. Frederick Douglass, Henry Highland Garnet, William Wells Brown, Martin R. Delany, and others became impatient with white abolitionists' appeals to the conscience of the white majority. In 1843, Garnet urged slaves to choose "Liberty or Death" and rise in insurrection against their masters, an idea that alienated almost all white people and carried little influence among slaves.

Frederick Douglass

▶ Former slave and a leader in the abolitionist movement. During the 1840s and 1850s, Douglass and other black abolitionists lectured to reform audiences throughout the North about the cruelties of slavery. In time, Douglass became impatient with the slow and cautious approach of white abolitionists and began to advocate a more aggressive assault on the institution of slavery.

| Who benefited from America's economic growth? | What factors spurred westward expansion? | Why did the United States go to war with Mexico? | How did reform efforts change after 1840? | Conclusion: How was white freedom in the West and North defined? |

To express their own uncompromising ideas, black abolitionists founded their own newspapers and held their own antislavery conventions, although they still cooperated with sympathetic whites.

The commitment of black abolitionists to battling slavery grew out of their own experiences with white supremacy. The 250,000 free African Americans in the North and West constituted less than 2 percent of the total population in 1860. Pervasive racial discrimination both handicapped and energized black abolitionists. Some cooperated with the efforts of the American Colonization Society to send freed slaves and other black Americans to Liberia in West Africa. Others sought to move to Canada, Haiti, or someplace else, convinced that, as an African American from Michigan wrote, "it is impracticable, not to say impossible, for the whites and blacks to live together, and upon terms of social and civil equality, under the same government." Most black American leaders refused to embrace emigration and worked against racial prejudice in their own communities, organizing campaigns against segregation, particularly in transportation and education.

Outside the public spotlight, free African Americans in the North and West contributed to the antislavery cause by quietly aiding fugitive slaves. **Harriet Tubman** escaped from slavery in Maryland in 1849 and repeatedly risked her freedom and her life to return to the South to escort slaves to freedom. When the opportunity arose, free blacks in the North provided fugitive slaves with food, a safe place to rest, and a helping hand. An outgrowth of the antislavery sentiment, this "underground railroad" ran mainly through black neighborhoods, black churches, and black homes.

Harriet Tubman
▶ Former slave who contributed to the antislavery cause by aiding fugitive slaves. Tubman escaped from slavery in Maryland in 1849 and repeatedly risked her freedom and her life to return to the South to escort slaves to freedom. The "underground railroad" she worked on ran mainly through black neighborhoods, black churches, and black homes.

> **QUICK REVIEW**

Why were women especially prominent in many nineteenth-century reform efforts?

CHAPTER LOCATOR | What factors contributed to America's "industrial evolution"?

National Gallery of Art, Washington, D.C.

Conclusion: How was white freedom in the West and North defined?

DURING THE 1840s AND 1850s, a cluster of interrelated developments—steam power, railroads, and the growing mechanization of agriculture and manufacturing—meant greater economic productivity, a burst of output from farms and factories, and prosperity for many. Diplomacy and war handed the United States 1.2 million square miles and more than 1,000 miles of Pacific coastline. One prize of manifest destiny, California, almost immediately rewarded its new owners with tons of gold. To most Americans, new territory and vast riches were appropriate accompaniments to the nation's stunning economic progress.

To those in the West and North, industrial evolution confirmed the choice they had made to eliminate slavery and to promote free labor as the key to independence, equality, and prosperity. Like Abraham Lincoln, millions of Americans could point to their personal experiences as evidence of the practical truth of the free-labor ideal. But millions of others had different stories to tell. They knew that in the free-labor system, poverty and wealth continued to rub shoulders. By 1860, more than half of the nation's free-labor workforce still toiled for someone else. Free-labor enthusiasts denied that the problems were inherent in the country's social and economic systems. Instead, they argued, most social ills—including poverty and dependency—sprang from individual deficiencies. Consequently, many reformers focused on self-control and discipline, on avoiding sin and alcohol. Other reformers focused on woman's rights and slavery. They challenged widespread conceptions of male supremacy and black inferiority, but neither group managed to overcome the prevailing free-labor ideology based on individualism, racial prejudice, and notions of male superiority.

By midcentury, the nation was half slave and half free, and each region was animated by different economic interests, cultural values, and political aims. Not even the victory over Mexico could bridge the deepening divide between North and South.

SO NOW YOU KNOW

The United States experienced an amazing railroad boom in the first half of the nineteenth century. Railroads were at the heart of America's economic growth before the Civil War. They stimulated old industries and helped to create new ones, aided westward expansion, and connected communities across the United States to expanding national and international markets.

| Who benefited from America's economic growth? | What factors spurred westward expansion? | Why did the United States go to war with Mexico? | How did reform efforts change after 1840? | Conclusion: How was white freedom in the West and North defined? |

> CHAPTER 12 STUDY GUIDE

Online Study Guide
bedfordstmartins.com/roarkunderstanding

STEP 1 GETTING STARTED

Below are basic terms from this period in American history. Can you identify each term below and explain why it matters? To do this exercise online or to download this chart, visit bedfordstmartins.com/roarkunderstanding.

TERM	WHO OR WHAT & WHEN	WHY IT MATTERS
American system, p. 310		
free-labor ideal, p. 313		
manifest destiny, p. 316		
Oregon Trail, p. 317		
James K. Polk, p. 322		
Zachary Taylor, p. 323		
Treaty of Guadalupe Hidalgo, p. 325		
California gold rush, p. 326		
Elizabeth Cady Stanton, p. 330		
Seneca Falls Declaration of Sentiments, p. 331		
Frederick Douglass, p. 331		
Harriet Tubman, p. 332		

STEP 2 MOVING BEYOND THE BASICS

The exercise below represents a more advanced understanding of the chapter material. Fill in the following chart by describing key economic developments and their contributions to industrialization. When you have finished filling in the chart, ask yourself how each development was influenced by the others. How, for example, did increases in agricultural production contribute to the growth of manufacturing? How, in turn, did new industrial processes and products aid agricultural production? To do this exercise online or to download this chart, visit bedfordstmartins.com/roarkunderstanding.

	Key developments	Consequences/who benefited
Agricultural technology		
Federal land policy		
Mechanization and energy sources		
Railroads		

STEP

3

PUTTING IT ALL TOGETHER

Now that you've reviewed various parts of the chapter, take a step back and try to see the big picture by answering these questions. Remember to use specific examples from the chapter in your answers. To do this exercise online, visit bedfordstmartins.com/roarkunderstanding.

INDUSTRIAL DEVELOPMENT AND WESTWARD EXPANSION

► What were the social consequences of American industrial development in the first half of the nineteenth century?

► What role did American nationalism and economic opportunity play in promoting westward expansion?

THE MEXICAN-AMERICAN WAR

► Where was support for war with Mexico strongest? Where was there the least support? Why?

► How did victory in the Mexican-American War contribute to rising tensions over slavery?

REFORM

► What common concerns linked the reform movements of the 1840s and 1850s?

► What role did women play in reform movements in the decades before the Civil War?

LOOKING BACKWARD, LOOKING AHEAD

► How had America's economy and society changed between 1800 and 1860?

► How did American expansion and industrial development contribute to the sectional conflicts that culminated in the Civil War?

IN YOUR OWN WORDS

Imagine that you must explain chapter 12 to someone who hasn't read it. What would be the most important points to include and why?

13

UNDERSTANDING THE SLAVE SOUTH

1820–1860

> This chapter explores the emergence and development of a distinctive slave society in the American South. It examines the causes and consequences of the divergence of the North and the South, the social world of the slave South, and the impact of slavery on internal southern politics.

> Why and how did the South become so different from the North?

> What was plantation life like for masters and mistresses?

> What was plantation life like for slaves?

> What place did free blacks occupy in southern society?

> How did nonslaveholding southern whites work and live?

> How did slavery shape southern politics?

> Conclusion: How did slavery come to define the South?

DID YOU KNOW?

By 1860, the South contained more slaves than all the other slave societies in the New World combined.

Slave quarters. This early photograph depicts a slave family in Savannah, Georgia, ca. 1860.

Why and how did the South become so different from the North?

The *Henry Frank*, New Orleans

The steamboat *Henry Frank* sits dangerously overloaded with cotton bales at the New Orleans levee in 1854. The magnitude of the cotton trade in the South's largest city and major port is difficult to capture. Six years earlier, a visitor, Solon Robinson, had expressed awe: "It must be seen to be believed; and even then, it will require an active mind to comprehend acres of cotton bales standing upon the levee, while miles of drays [carts] are constantly taking it off to the cotton presses. . . . Boats are constantly arriving, so piled up with cotton, that the lower tier of bales on deck are in the water." Amid the mountains of cotton, few Southerners doubted that cotton was king. Historic New Orleans Collection.

> ▶ FOR MORE HELP ANALYZING THIS IMAGE, see the visual activity for this chapter in the Online Study Guide at bedfordstmartins.com/roarkunderstanding.

FROM THE EARLIEST SETTLEMENTS, inhabitants of the southern colonies had shared a great deal with northern colonists. Most whites in both sections were British and Protestant, spoke a common language, and shared pride in their victorious revolution against British rule. The creation of the new nation under the Constitution in 1789 forged political ties that bound all Americans. The beginnings of a national economy fostered economic interdependence and communication across regional boundaries. White Americans everywhere celebrated the achievements of the prosperous young nation, and they looked forward to its seemingly boundless future.

Despite these national similarities, Southerners and Northerners grew increasingly different. The French political observer Alexis de Tocqueville believed he knew why. "I could easily prove," he asserted in 1831, "that almost all the differences which may be noticed between the character of the Americans in the Southern and Northern states have originated in slavery." Slavery made the South different, and it was the differences between the North and the South, not the similarities, that increasingly shaped antebellum American history.

CHAPTER LOCATOR | Why and how did the South become so different from the North? | What was plantation life like for masters and mistresses?

CHAPTER 13
338 UNDERSTANDING THE SLAVE SOUTH, 1820–1860

The Upper and Lower South

Upper South
Lower South

Cotton Kingdom, Slave Empire

In the first half of the nineteenth century, millions of Americans migrated west. In the South, the stampede began after the Creek War of 1813–1814, which divested the Creek Indians of 24 million acres and initiated the government campaign to remove Indian people living east of the Mississippi River to the West (see chapters 10 and 11). Southerners—planters, small farmers, and herders and drovers—pushed westward relentlessly, until by midcentury the South encompassed nearly a million square miles. Contemporaries spoke of this vast region as the Lower South, those states where cotton was dominant, and the Upper South, where cotton was less important.

The South's climate and geography were ideally suited for the cultivation of cotton. By the 1830s, cotton fields stretched from southern Virginia to central Texas. Heavy migration led to statehood for Arkansas in 1836 and for Texas and Florida in 1845. Production soared from 300,000 bales in 1830 to nearly 5 million in 1860, when the South produced three-fourths of the world's supply. The

CHRONOLOGY

1813–1814
- Creek War opens Indian land to white settlement.

1820s–1830s
- Southern legislatures enact slave codes to strengthen slavery.
- Southern intellectuals fashion systematic defense of slavery.

1830
- Southern slaves number approximately two million.

1836
- Arkansas is admitted to Union as slave state.

1840
- Cotton accounts for more than 60 percent of American exports.

1845
- Texas and Florida are admitted to Union as slave states.

1860
- Southern slaves number nearly four million, one-third of the South's population.

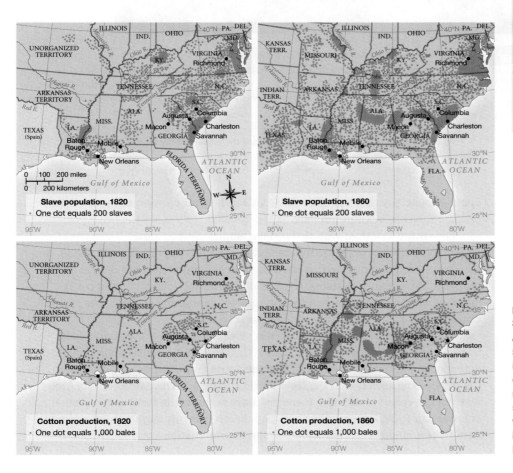

Slave population, 1820
One dot equals 200 slaves

Slave population, 1860
One dot equals 200 slaves

Cotton production, 1820
One dot equals 1,000 bales

Cotton production, 1860
One dot equals 1,000 bales

MAP 13.1 ■ Cotton Kingdom, Slave Empire: 1820 and 1860
As the production of cotton soared, the slave population increased dramatically. Slaves continued to toil in tobacco and rice fields along the Atlantic seaboard, but increasingly they worked on cotton plantations in Alabama, Mississippi, and Louisiana.

What was plantation life like for slaves?	What place did free blacks occupy in southern society?	How did nonslaveholding southern whites work and live?	How did slavery shape southern politics?	Conclusion: How did slavery come to define the South?

The Price of Blood This 1868 painting by T. S. Noble depicts a transaction between a slave trader and a rich planter. The trader nervously pretends to study the contract, while the planter waits impatiently for the completion of the sale. The planter's mulatto son, who is being sold, looks away. The children of white men and slave women were property and could be sold by the father/master. Morris Museum of Art, Augusta, Ga.

> ► FOR MORE HELP ANALYZING THIS IMAGE, see the visual activity for this chapter in the Online Study Guide at bedfordstmartins.com/roarkunderstanding.

cotton kingdom

► Term for the South that reflected the dominance of cotton in the southern economy. Cotton was particularly important in the tier of states from South Carolina west to Texas. The spread of cotton cultivation in the first half of the nineteenth century was the key factor in the growth of slavery.

South—especially that tier of states from South Carolina west to Texas—had become the **cotton kingdom** (**Map 13.1,** page 339).

The cotton kingdom was also a slave empire. Slaves grew 75 percent of the crop on plantations, toiling in gangs under the direct supervision of whites. As cotton agriculture expanded westward, whites shipped nearly a million slaves out of the Atlantic seaboard states. Victims of this brutal domestic slave trade marched hundreds of miles southwest to new plantations in the Lower South. Cotton, slaves, and plantations moved west together.

As cotton production expanded, the slave population grew enormously. Southern slaves numbered fewer than 700,000 in 1790, about 2 million in 1830, and almost 4 million by 1860. By 1860, the South contained more slaves than all the other slave societies in the New World combined. The extraordinary growth was not the result of the importation of slaves, which the federal government outlawed in 1808. Instead, the slave population grew through natural reproduction. By the nineteenth century, most slaves were native-born Southerners.

CHAPTER LOCATOR | Why and how did the South become so different from the North? | What was plantation life like for masters and mistresses?

CHAPTER 13
340 UNDERSTANDING THE SLAVE SOUTH, 1820–1860

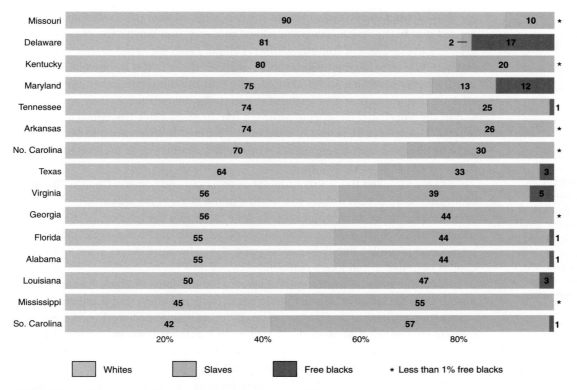

Missouri	90			10	*
Delaware	81		2 —	17	
Kentucky	80			20	*
Maryland	75		13	12	
Tennessee	74		25		1
Arkansas	74		26		*
No. Carolina	70		30		*
Texas	64		33		3
Virginia	56		39		5
Georgia	56		44		*
Florida	55		44		1
Alabama	55		44		1
Louisiana	50		47		3
Mississippi	45		55		*
So. Carolina	42		57		1

20% 40% 60% 80%

☐ Whites   ☐ Slaves   ■ Free blacks   * Less than 1% free blacks

FIGURE 13.1 ■ Black and White Population in the South, 1860
Blacks represented a much larger fraction of the population in the South than in the North, but considerable variation existed from state to state. Only one Missourian in ten, for example, was black, while Mississippi and South Carolina had black majorities. States in the Upper South were "whiter" than states in the Lower South, despite the Upper South's greater number of free blacks.

The South in Black and White

By 1860, one in every three Southerners was black (approximately 4 million blacks and 8 million whites) (**Figure 13.1**). The presence of large numbers of African Americans had profound consequences for the South. Southern culture—language, food, music, religion, and even accents—was in part shaped by blacks. But the most direct consequence of the South's biracialism was southern whites' commitment to white supremacy. Northern whites believed in racial superiority, too, but their dedication to white supremacy lacked the intensity and urgency increasingly felt by white Southerners who lived among millions of blacks who had every reason to hate them and to strike back.

Attacks on slavery after 1820 jolted southern slaveholders into an awareness that they lived in a dangerous world. As the only slave society embedded in an egalitarian, democratic republic, the South made extraordinary efforts to strengthen slavery. State legislatures constructed **slave codes** (laws) that required the total submission of slaves. As the Louisiana code stated, a slave "owes his master . . . a respect without bounds, and an absolute obedience." The laws also underlined the authority of all whites, not just masters. Any white could "correct" slaves who did not stay "in their place."

slave codes
▶ Laws enacted in southern states that required the total submission of slaves. Attacks by antislavery activists convinced southern legislators that they had to do everything in their power to strengthen the institution. They were joined in their efforts by intellectuals who argued that slavery was a just and beneficial practice.

What was plantation life like for slaves?	What place did free blacks occupy in southern society?	How did nonslaveholding southern whites work and live?	How did slavery shape southern politics?	Conclusion: How did slavery come to define the South?

Intellectuals joined legislators in the campaign to strengthen slavery. They argued that in the South slaves were legal property, and wasn't the protection of property the bedrock of American liberty? History also endorsed slavery, they claimed. Weren't the great civilizations—such as those of the Hebrews, Greeks, and Romans—slave societies? They claimed that the Bible, properly interpreted, also sanctioned slavery. Old Testament patriarchs owned slaves, they observed, and in the New Testament, Paul returned the runaway slave Onesimus to his master. Proslavery spokesmen played on the fears of Northerners and Southerners alike by charging that giving blacks equal rights would lead to the sexual mixing of the races, or **miscegenation**.

miscegenation
▶ The sexual mixing of the races. Proslavery spokesmen played on the fears of whites when they suggested that giving blacks equal rights would lead to miscegenation. In reality, the power dynamics of slavery led to considerable sexual abuse of black women by their white masters.

Others attacked the North's free-labor economy and society. George Fitzhugh of Virginia argued that behind the North's grand slogans lay a heartless philosophy: "Every man for himself, and the devil take the hindmost." He contrasted the North's vicious free-labor system with the humane relations that he claimed prevailed between masters and slaves because slaves were valuable capital that masters sought to protect.

But at the heart of the defense of slavery lay the claim of black inferiority. Rather than exploitative, slavery was a mass civilizing effort that lifted lowly blacks from barbarism and savagery, taught them disciplined work, and converted them to soul-saving Christianity. According to Virginian Thomas R. Dew, most slaves were grateful. He declared that "the slaves of a good master are his warmest, most constant, and most devoted friends."

Whites gradually moved away from defending slavery as a "necessary evil"—the halfhearted argument popular in Jefferson's day—and toward an aggressive defense of slavery as a "positive good." John C. Calhoun, an influential southern politician, declared that in the states where slavery had been abolished, "the condition of the African, instead of being improved, has become worse," while in the slave states, the Africans "have improved greatly in every respect."

Black slavery encouraged southern whites to unify around race rather than to divide by class. Because of racial slavery, Georgia attorney Thomas R. R. Cobb observed, every white Southerner "feels that he belongs to an elevated class. It matters not that he is no slaveholder; he is not of the inferior race; he is a freeborn citizen." Consequently, the "poorest meets the richest as an equal; sits at his table with him; salutes him as a neighbor; meets him in every public assembly, and stands on the same social platform." In the South, Cobb boasted, "there is no war of classes." In reality, slavery did not create perfect harmony among whites or ease every strain along class lines. But by providing every white Southerner membership in the ruling race, slavery helped whites bridge differences in wealth, education, and culture.

The Plantation Economy

planter
▶ A substantial landowner who tilled his estate with twenty or more slaves. Planters dominated the social and political world of the South. Their values and ideology influenced the values and ideology of all southern whites, slaveholders and nonslaveholders alike.

As important as slavery was in unifying white Southerners, only about a quarter of the white population lived in slaveholding families. Most slaveholders owned fewer than five slaves. Only about 12 percent of slave owners owned twenty or more, the number of slaves that historians consider necessary to distinguish a **planter** from a farmer. Nevertheless, planters dominated the southern economy. In 1860, 52 percent of the South's slaves lived and worked on plantations. Plantation slaves produced more than 75 percent of the South's export crops, the backbone of the region's economy.

CHAPTER LOCATOR | Why and how did the South become so different from the North? | What was plantation life like for masters and mistresses?

342 CHAPTER 13 UNDERSTANDING THE SLAVE SOUTH, 1820–1860

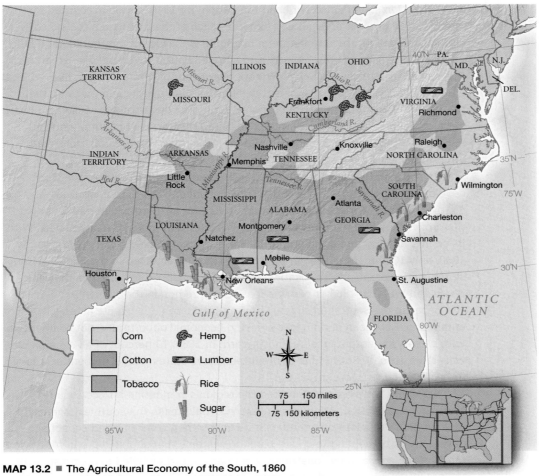

MAP 13.2 ■ The Agricultural Economy of the South, 1860
Cotton dominated the South's agricultural economy, but the region grew a
variety of crops and was largely self-sufficient in foodstuffs.

▶ FOR MORE HELP ANALYZING THIS MAP, see the map activity for this chapter in the Online
Study Guide at bedfordstmartins.com/roarkunderstanding.

The South's major cash crops—tobacco, sugar, rice, and cotton—grew on plantations (**Map 13.2**). Tobacco, the original plantation crop in North America, had shifted westward in the nineteenth century from the Chesapeake to Tennessee and Kentucky. Large-scale sugar production began in 1795, when Étienne de Boré built a modern sugar mill in what is today New Orleans, and sugar plantations were confined almost entirely to Louisiana. Commercial rice production began in the seventeenth century, and like sugar, rice was confined to a small geographic area, a narrow strip of coast stretching from the Carolinas into Georgia.

By the nineteenth century, cotton was king of the South's plantation crops. Cotton became commercially significant in the 1790s after the invention of a new cotton gin by Eli Whitney dramatically increased the production of raw cotton. Cotton was relatively easy to grow and took little capital to get started. Thus small farmers as well as planters grew cotton. But planters, whose fields were worked by slaves, produced three-quarters of the South's cotton, and cotton made planters rich.

What was plantation life like for slaves?	What place did free blacks occupy in southern society?	How did nonslaveholding southern whites work and live?	How did slavery shape southern politics?	Conclusion: How did slavery come to define the South?

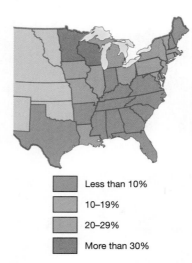

Less than 10%

10–19%

20–29%

More than 30%

Immigrants as a Percent of State Populations, 1860

Plantation slavery also enriched the nation. By 1840, cotton accounted for more than 60 percent of American exports. Much of the profit from the sale of cotton overseas returned to planters, but some went to northern middlemen who bought, sold, insured, warehoused, and shipped cotton to the mills in Great Britain and elsewhere. As one New York merchant observed, "Cotton has enriched all through whose hands it has passed." As middlemen invested their profits in the booming northern economy, industrial development received a burst of much-needed capital. Furthermore, southern plantations benefited northern industry by providing an important market for textiles, agricultural tools, and other manufactured goods.

The economies of the North and South steadily diverged. While the North developed a mixed economy—agriculture, commerce, and manufacturing—the South remained overwhelmingly agricultural. Year after year, planters funneled the profits they earned from land and slaves back into more land and slaves. With its capital flowing into agriculture, the South did not develop many factories. By 1860, only 10 percent of the nation's industrial workers lived in the South. Without significant economic diversification, the South developed fewer cities than the North and West. In 1860, it was the least urban region in the country.

Because the South had so few cities and industrial jobs, it attracted small numbers of European immigrants. Seeking economic opportunity, not competition with slaves, immigrants steered northward. In 1860, 13 percent of all Americans were born abroad. But in nine of the fifteen slave states, only 2 percent or less of the population was foreign-born.

Not every Southerner celebrated the region's commitment to cotton and slaves. Diversification, reformers promised, would make the South economically independent and more prosperous. State governments encouraged economic development by helping to create banking systems that supplied credit for a wide range of projects and by constructing railroads, but they failed to create some of the essential services modern economies required. By the mid-nineteenth century, for example, no southern legislature had created a statewide public school system.

Northerners claimed that slavery was a backward labor system, and compared with Northerners, Southerners invested less of their capital in industry, transportation, and public education. But plantations were profitable, and planters' decisions to reinvest in agriculture ensured the momentum of the plantation economy and the political and social relationships rooted in it.

> QUICK REVIEW

Why did the nineteenth-century southern economy remain primarily agricultural?

CHAPTER LOCATOR | Why and how did the South become so different from the North? | What was plantation life like for masters and mistresses?

344 CHAPTER 13 UNDERSTANDING THE SLAVE SOUTH, 1820–1860

Obviously prosperous and looking like a man accustomed to giving orders and being obeyed, this patriarch poses around 1848 with his young daughters and their nurse. Collection of the J. Paul Getty Museum, Malibu, Calif.

What was plantation life like for masters and mistresses?

NOWHERE WAS THE CONTRAST between northern and southern life more vivid than on the plantations of the South. The plantation was the home of masters, mistresses, and slaves (**Figure 13.2,** page 347). Slavery shaped the lives of all the plantation's inhabitants, from work to leisure activities, but it affected each group differently. A hierarchy of rigid roles and duties governed relationships. Presiding was the master, who ruled his wife, children, and slaves, none of whom had many legal rights, and all of whom were designated by the state as dependents under his dominion and protection.

A Typical Plantation

Located on a patchwork of cleared fields and dense forests.

Included several structures:

- "Big house": The residence of the master and his family.
- Slave quarter: The cluster of cabins where slaves lived.
- Outbuildings: Scattered buildings such as storehouses, barns, and specialized buildings for crop processing.
  - Infirmary and chapel for slaves, sometimes found on large plantations.

What was plantation life like for slaves?	What place did free blacks occupy in southern society?	How did nonslaveholding southern whites work and live?	How did slavery shape southern politics?	Conclusion: How did slavery come to define the South?

Plantation Masters
- Often characterized their roles in terms of paternalism.
- On larger plantations, hired overseers to supervise slaves in the field.
- Were increasingly interested in extending the lives of slave property.

Plantation Mistresses
- Were expected to conform to gender norms for white women.
- Lived within a system that both glorified and subordinated them.
- Lived privileged lives but also experienced discontent.

overseer

▶ Person hired by a planter to supervise the labor of slaves. The use of overseers allowed planters to concentrate on marketing, finance, and general affairs of the plantation.

paternalism

▶ The theory of slavery that emphasized reciprocal duties and obligations between planters and their slaves. Southern planters denied that slavery was brutal and exploitative; instead, they argued that they were Christian guardians who had the responsibility of caring for a childlike, dependent people.

Plantation Masters

Whereas smaller planters supervised the labor of their slaves themselves, larger planters hired **overseers** who went to the fields with the slaves, leaving the planters free to concentrate on marketing, finance, and general affairs of the plantation. Planters also found time to escape to town to discuss cotton prices, to the courthouse and legislature to debate politics, and to the woods to hunt and fish.

Increasingly, planters characterized their mastery in terms of what they called "Christian guardianship" and what historians have called **paternalism**. As owners of blacks, masters argued, they had the responsibility of caring for a childlike, dependent people. In 1814, Thomas Jefferson captured the essence of the advancing ideal: "We should endeavor, with those whom fortune has thrown on our hands, to feed & clothe them well, protect them from ill usage, require such reasonable labor only as is performed voluntarily by freemen, and be led by no repugnancies to abdicate them, and our duties to them." A South Carolina rice planter insisted, "I manage them as my children."

Paternalism was part propaganda and part self-delusion. But it was also economically shrewd. Masters increasingly recognized slaves as valuable assets. As one planter declared in 1849, "It behooves those who own them to make them last as long as possible." One consequence of this paternalism and economic self-interest was a small improvement in slaves' welfare. Diet improved, although nineteenth-century slaves still ate mainly fatty pork and cornmeal. Housing improved, although slave cabins were still small and in poor condition. Clothing improved, although slaves seldom received much more than two crude outfits a year and perhaps a pair of cheap shoes. In the fields, workdays remained sunup to sundown, but planters often provided a rest period in the heat of the day. And most owners ceased the colonial practice of punishing slaves by branding and mutilation.

Paternalism should not be mistaken for kindness and goodwill. It encouraged better treatment because it made economic sense to provide at least minimal care for valuable slaves. Nor did paternalism require that planters put aside their whips. State laws gave masters nearly "uncontrolled authority over the body" of the slave, according to one North Carolina judge. With its notion that slavery imposed on masters a burden and a duty, paternalism provided slaveholders with a means of rationalizing their rule. But it also provided some slaves with leverage in controlling the conditions of their lives. Slaves learned to manipulate the slaveholder's need to see himself as a good master. To avoid a reputation as a cruel tyrant, planters sometimes negotiated with slaves, rather than just resorting to the whip. Masters sometimes granted slaves small garden plots in which they could work for themselves after working all day in the fields, or they gave slaves a few days off and a dance when they had gathered the last of the cotton.

Virginia statesman Edmund Randolph argued that slavery created in white southern men a "quick and acute sense of personal liberty" and a "disdain for every abridgement of personal independence." Indeed, prickly individualism and aggressive independence became crucial features of the southern concept of honor. Defending honor became a male passion. Andrew Jackson's mother reportedly told her son, "Never tell a lie, nor take what is not your own, nor sue anybody for slander or assault and battery. *Always settle them cases yourself.*"

Southerners also expected an honorable gentleman to be a proper patriarch. Nowhere in America was masculine power more accentuated. Planters brooked

CHAPTER LOCATOR | Why and how did the South become so different from the North? | What was plantation life like for masters and mistresses?

CHAPTER 13
346 UNDERSTANDING THE SLAVE SOUTH, 1820–1860

no opposition from any of their dependents, black or white. The master's absolute dominion sometimes led to miscegenation. As long as slavery gave white men extraordinary power, slave women were forced to submit to the sexual appetites of the men who owned them.

In time, as the children of one elite family married the children of another, ties of blood and kinship, as well as economic interest and ideology, linked planters to one another. Conscious of what they shared as slaveholders, planters worked together to defend their common interests. The values of the big house—slavery, honor, male domination—washed over the boundaries of plantations and flooded all of southern life.

Plantation Mistresses

Like their northern counterparts, southern ladies were expected to possess the feminine virtues of piety, purity, chastity, and obedience within the context of marriage, motherhood, and domesticity. The ideal southern lady was the perfect complement to her husband, the commanding patriarch. For women, this image of the southern lady was no blessing. **Chivalry**—the South's romantic ideal of male-female relationships—glorified the lady while it subordinated her. Chivalry's underlying assumptions about the weakness of women and the protective authority of men resembled the paternalistic defense of slavery.

Indeed, the most articulate spokesmen for slavery also vigorously defended the subordination of women. George Fitzhugh insisted that "a woman, like children, has but one right and that is the right to protection. The right to protection involves the obligation to obey. A husband, a lord and master, nature designed for every woman. . . . If she be obedient she stands little danger of maltreatment." Just as the slaveholder's mastery was written into law, so too were the paramount rights of husbands. Married women lost almost all their property rights to their husbands. Women throughout the nation found divorce difficult, but southern women found it almost impossible.

Daughters of planters confronted chivalry's demands at an early age. Their education aimed at fitting them to become southern ladies. Elite women began courting at a young age and married early. Kate Carney exaggerated only slightly when she despaired in her diary: "Today, I am seventeen, getting quite old, and am not married." Yet marriage meant turning their fates over to their husbands and making enormous efforts to live up to their region's lofty ideal.

Proslavery advocates claimed that slavery freed white women from drudgery. Surrounded "by her domestics," declared Thomas R. Dew, "she ceases to be a mere beast of burden" and "becomes the cheering and animating center of the family circle." In reality, however, having servants required the plantation mistress to work long hours. She managed the big house, directly supervising as many as a dozen slaves. She assigned them tasks each morning, directed their work throughout the day, and punished them when she found fault.

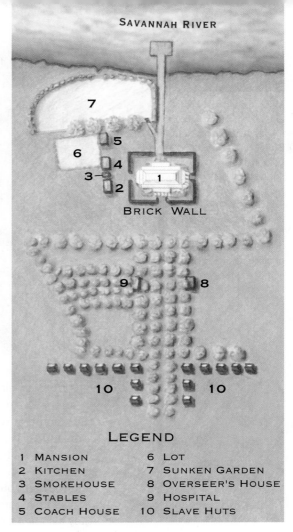

SAVANNAH RIVER

BRICK WALL

LEGEND

1	MANSION	6	LOT
2	KITCHEN	7	SUNKEN GARDEN
3	SMOKEHOUSE	8	OVERSEER'S HOUSE
4	STABLES	9	HOSPITAL
5	COACH HOUSE	10	SLAVE HUTS

FIGURE 13.2 ■ A Southern Plantation

Slavery determined how masters laid out their plantations, where they situated their "big houses" and slave quarters, and what kinds of buildings they constructed. This model of a plantation shows the overseer's house poised in a grove of oak trees halfway between the owner's mansion and the slave huts. The placement of the mansion at the end of an extended road leading up from the river underscored the owner's affluence and authority. Adapted from *Back of the Big House: The Architecture of Plantation Slavery* by John Michael Vlach. Copyright © 1993 by the University of North Carolina Press. Reprinted with permission of the University of North Carolina Press. Original illustration property of the Historical American Buildings Survey, a division of the National Park Service.

chivalry

▶ The South's romantic ideal of male-female relationships. The ideal southern lady was the perfect complement to her husband, the commanding patriarch. Chivalry's underlying assumptions about the weakness of women and the protective authority of men resembled the paternalistic defense of slavery.

| What was plantation life like for slaves? | What place did free blacks occupy in southern society? | How did nonslaveholding southern whites work and live? | How did slavery shape southern politics? | Conclusion: How did slavery come to define the South? |

347

Bird Store, New Orleans

Most elite women in the antebellum South lived isolated existences on rural plantations. But when they visited cities, they liked to shop. Here a wealthy mother and daughter shop for a pet in a New Orleans bird store. Elite white women themselves were, in a way, like birds kept in golden cages. Could it be that they were attracted to the thought of owning birds of their own, something they could care for, train, and control? Historic New Orleans Collection.

Whereas masters used their status as slaveholders as a springboard into public affairs, mistresses' lives were circumscribed by the plantation. Masters left the plantation when they pleased, but mistresses needed chaperones to travel. Women spent most days at home, where they often became lonely. In 1853, Mary Kendall wrote how much she enjoyed her sister's letter: "For about three weeks I did not have the pleasure of seeing one white female face, there being no white family except our own upon the plantation."

As members of slaveholding families, mistresses lived privileged lives. But they also had significant grounds for discontent. No feature of plantation life generated more anguish among mistresses than miscegenation. Mary Boykin Chesnut of Camden, South Carolina, confided in her diary, "Ours is a monstrous system, a wrong and iniquity. Like the patriarchs of old, our men live all in one house with their wives and their concubines; and the mulattos one sees in every family partly resemble the white children. Any lady is ready to tell you who is the father of all the mulatto children in everybody's household but her own. Those, she seems to think drop from the clouds."

Most planters' wives, including Chesnut, accepted slavery. After all, the mistress's world rested on slave labor, just as the master's did. By acknowledging the realities of male power, mistresses enjoyed the rewards of their class and race. But these rewards came at a price. Still, the heaviest burdens of slavery fell not on those who lived in the big house, but on those who toiled to support them.

> ## QUICK REVIEW

Why did the ideology of paternalism gain currency among planters in the nineteenth century?

CHAPTER LOCATOR | Why and how did the South become so different from the North? | What was plantation life like for masters and mistresses?

What was plantation life like for slaves?

Slave Quarter, South Carolina

On large plantations, several score of African Americans lived in cabins that were often arranged along what slaves called "the street." The dwellings in this picture were better built than the typical rickety, one-room, dirt-floored slave cabin. During the daylight hours of the workweek, when most men and women labored in the fields, the quarter was mostly empty. At night and on Sundays, it was a busy place. Collection of the New-York Historical Society.

ON MOST PLANTATIONS, only a few hundred yards separated the big house and the slave quarter. There, slaves drew together and built lives of their own. They created families, worshipped God, and developed an African American community and culture. Individually and collectively, slaves found subtle and not so subtle ways to resist their bondage.

Despite the rise of plantations, a substantial minority of slaves lived and worked elsewhere. Most labored on small farms. But by 1860, almost half a million slaves (one in eight) did not work in agriculture at all. Some were employed in towns and cities as domestics, day laborers, bakers, barbers, tailors, and more. Others, far from urban centers, toiled as fishermen, lumbermen, and railroad workers. Slaves could also be found in most of the South's factories. Nevertheless, a majority of slaves (52 percent) counted plantations as their workplaces and homes.

Work

Ex-slave Albert Todd recalled, "Work was a religion that we were taught." Whites enslaved blacks for their labor, and all slaves who were capable of productive labor worked. Former slave Carrie Hudson recalled that children who were "knee high to a duck" were sent to the fields to carry water to thirsty workers or to pro-tect ripening crops from hungry birds. Others helped in the slave nursery, caring for children even younger than themselves, or in the big house, where they swept

1822
– Denmark Vesey, a free black man in Charleston, South Carolina, is accused of planning a slave revolt.

1831
– Nat Turner's rebellion in Virginia.

In 1860:
– One in eight slaves does not work in agriculture.
– The majority of slaves (52 percent) live on plantations.
– An overwhelming majority of plantation slaves work as field hands.
– One in ten slaves is a house servant.

slave driver
▶ Slave who was a kind of foreman whose primary task was driving other slaves to work harder in the fields. Probably no more than one male slave in a hundred worked in this capacity. Some drivers were harsh, but others showed restraint when they could.

Isaac Jefferson

In this 1845 daguerreotype, seventy-year-old Isaac Jefferson proudly poses in the apron he wore while practicing his crafts as a tinsmith and nail maker. Slaves of Thomas Jefferson, he, his wife, and their two children were deeded to Jefferson's daughter Mary when she married in 1797. Isaac worked at Jefferson's home, Monticello, until 1820, when he moved to Petersburg, Virginia. Special Collections Department, University of Virginia Library.

floors or shooed flies in the dining room. When slave boys and girls reached the age of eleven or twelve, masters sent most of them to the fields, where they learned farmwork by laboring alongside their parents. After a lifetime of labor, old women left the fields to care for the small children and spin yarn, and old men moved on to mind livestock and clean stables.

The overwhelming majority of plantation slaves worked as field hands. Planters sometimes assigned men and women to separate gangs, the women working at lighter tasks and the men doing the heavy work of clearing and breaking the land. But women also did heavy work. "I had to work hard," Nancy Boudry remembered, and "plow and go and split wood just like a man." The backbreaking labor and the monotonous routines caused one ex-slave to observe that the "history of one day is the history of every day."

A few slaves (about one in ten) became house servants. Nearly all of those (nine out of ten) were women. House servants enjoyed somewhat less physically demanding work than field hands, but they were constantly on call, with no time that was entirely their own. Since no servant could please constantly, most bore the brunt of white frustration and rage. Ex-slave Jacob Branch of Texas remembered, "My poor mama! Every washday old Missy give her a beating."

Even rarer than house servants were skilled artisans. In the cotton South, no more than one slave in twenty (almost all men) worked in a skilled trade. Most were carpenters or blacksmiths. Slave craftsmen took pride in their skills and often exhibited the independence of spirit that caused slaveholder James H. Hammond of South Carolina to declare in disgust that when a slave became a skilled artisan, "he is more than half freed." Skilled slave fathers took pride in teaching their crafts to their sons. "My pappy was one of the black smiths and worked in the shop," John Mathews remembered. "I had to help my pappy in the shop when I was a child and I learnt how to beat out the iron and make wagon tires, and make plows."

Rarest of all slave occupations was that of **slave driver**. Probably no more than one male slave in a hundred worked in this capacity. Their primary task was driving other slaves to work harder in the fields. In some drivers' hands, the whip never rested. Ex-slave Jane Johnson of South Carolina called her driver the "meanest man, white or black, I ever see." But other drivers showed all the

CHAPTER LOCATOR | Why and how did the South become so different from the North? | What was plantation life like for masters and mistresses?

CHAPTER 13
350 UNDERSTANDING THE SLAVE SOUTH, 1820–1860

restraint they could. "Ole Gabe didn't like that whippin' business," West Turner of Virginia remembered. "When Marsa was there, he would lay it on 'cause he had to. But when old Marsa wasn't lookin', he never would beat them slaves."

Normally, slaves worked from what they called "can to can't," from "can see" in the morning to "can't see" at night. Even with a break at noon for a meal and rest, it made for a long day. For slaves, Lewis Young recalled, "work, work, work, 'twas all they do."

Family, Religion, and Community

From dawn to dusk, slaves worked for the master, but at night, when the labor was done, and all day Sunday and usually Saturday afternoon, slaves were left largely to themselves. They used this limited time to develop and enjoy what mattered most: family, religion, and community. One of the most important consequences of slaves' limited autonomy was the preservation of the family. No laws recognized slave marriage, and therefore no master or slave was legally obligated to honor the bond. Nevertheless, plantation records show that slave marriages were often long-lasting. The primary cause of the ending of slave marriages was death, just as it was in white families. But the second most frequent cause was the sale of the husband or wife, something no white family ever had to fear.

In 1858, a South Carolina slave named Abream Scriven wrote a letter to his wife, who lived on a neighboring plantation. "My dear wife," he began, "I take the pleasure of writing you . . . with much regret to inform you I am Sold to man by the name of Peterson, a Treader and Stays in New Orleans." Scriven promised to send some things when he got to his new home in Louisiana, but he admitted that he was not sure how he would "get them to you and my children." He asked his wife to "give my love to my father and mother and tell them good Bye for me. And if we do not meet in this world I hope to meet in heaven. . . . My dear wife for you and my children my pen cannot express the griffe I feel to be parted from you all." He closed with words no master would have permitted in a slave's marriage vows: "I remain your truly husband until Death." The letter makes clear Scriven's love for his family; it also demonstrates slavery's massive assault on family life in the quarter.

Religion also provided slaves with a refuge and a reason for living. Evangelical Baptists and Methodists had great success in converting slaves from their African beliefs. By the mid-nineteenth century, perhaps as many as one-quarter of all slaves claimed church membership, and many of the rest would not have objected to being called Christians. Planters promoted Christianity in the quarter because they believed that the slaves' salvation was part of their obligation and that religion made slaves more obedient. But slaves had little use for the religion offered them by their masters. "That old white preacher just was telling us slaves to be good to our masters," one ex-slave said with a chuckle. "We ain't cared a bit about that stuff he was telling us 'cause we wanted to sing, pray, and serve God in our own way."

Meeting in their cabins or secretly in the woods, slaves created an African American Christianity that served their needs, not the masters'. Laws prohibited teaching slaves to read, but a few could read enough to struggle with the Bible. They interpreted the Christian message themselves. Rather than obedience, their faith emphasized justice. Slaves believed that the injustices of this world would

| What was plantation life like for slaves? | What place did free blacks occupy in southern society? | How did nonslaveholding southern whites work and live? | How did slavery shape southern politics? | Conclusion: How did slavery come to define the South? |

351

be settled in the next. "The idea of a revolution in the conditions of the whites and blacks is the corner-stone" of the slaves' religion, recalled one ex-slave. But the slaves' faith also spoke to their experiences in this world. In the Old Testament, they discovered Moses, who delivered his people from slavery, and in the New Testament, they found Jesus, who offered a message of equality and of salvation to all.

Christianity did not entirely drive out traditional African beliefs. Even slaves who were Christians sometimes continued to believe that conjurers, witches, and spirits possessed the power to injure and protect. Moreover, slaves' Christian music, preaching, and rituals reflected the influence of Africa, as did many of their secular activities, such as wood carving, quilt making, and storytelling. But by the mid-nineteenth century, black Christianity had assumed a central place in slaves' quest for freedom. In the words of one spiritual, "O my Lord delivered Daniel / O why not deliver me too?"

Resistance and Rebellion

Slaves did not suffer slavery passively. They were, as whites said, "troublesome property." Slaves understood that accommodation to what they could not change was the price of survival, but in a hundred ways, they protested their bondage. Theoretically, the master was all-powerful and the slave powerless. But sustained by their families, religion, and community, slaves engaged in day-to-day resistance against their enslavers.

The spectrum of slave resistance ranged from mild to extreme. Protest in the fields included putting rocks in their cotton bags before having them weighed and feigning illness. Slaves broke so many hoes that owners outfitted the tools with oversized handles. Slaves so mistreated the work animals that masters switched from horses to mules, which could absorb more abuse. Although slaves worked hard in the master's fields, they also sabotaged his interests.

Running away was a common form of protest. Except along the borders with northern states and with Mexico, escape to freedom was almost impossible. Most runaways could hope to escape only for a few days. Seeking temporary respite from hard labor or avoiding punishment, they usually stayed close to their plantations, keeping to the deep woods or swamps and slipping back into the quarter at night to get food.

Although resistance was common, outright rebellion—a violent assault on slavery by large numbers of slaves—was very rare. The scarcity of revolts in the South reflected the fact that conditions gave rebels almost no chance of success. By 1860, whites in the South outnumbered blacks two to one and were heavily armed. Moreover, communication between plantations was difficult, and the South provided little protective wilderness into which rebels could retreat and defend themselves.

Nat Turner's rebellion illustrates the inevitable consequences of even the most ferocious uprising. **Nat Turner** was born a slave in Southampton County, Virginia. In the early morning of August 22, 1831, Turner set out with six trusted friends to punish slave owners. The rebels killed all of the white men, women, and children they encountered. By noon, they had visited eleven farms and slaughtered fifty-seven whites. Along the way, they had added fifty or sixty men to their army. Word spread quickly, and soon the militia and hundreds of local

Nat Turner

▶ Leader of an 1831 slave uprising in Virginia. Turner and his followers killed fifty-seven whites before the rebellion was suppressed. The ferocity of the white counterattack that put down the uprising illustrates the futility of slave revolts and helps explain their rarity.

CHAPTER LOCATOR | Why and how did the South become so different from the North? | What was plantation life like for masters and mistresses?

CHAPTER 13
352 UNDERSTANDING THE SLAVE SOUTH, 1820–1860

whites gathered. By the next day, whites had captured or killed all of the rebels except Turner, who hid out for about ten weeks before being captured in nearby woods. Within a week, he was tried, convicted, and executed. By then, forty-five slaves had stood trial, twenty had been convicted and hanged, and another ten had been banished from Virginia. Frenzied whites had killed another hundred or more blacks—insurgents and innocent bystanders—in their counterattack against the rebellion.

Despite the rarity of slave revolts, whites believed that they were surrounded by conspiracies to rebel. In 1822, whites in Charleston accused **Denmark Vesey**, a free black carpenter, of conspiring with plantation slaves to slaughter Charleston's white inhabitants. The authorities rounded up scores of suspects, who, prodded by torture and the threat of death, implicated others in the plot "to riot in blood, outrage, and rapine." Although the city fathers never found any weapons and Vesey and most of the accused steadfastly denied the charges of conspiracy, officials hanged thirty-five black men, including Vesey, and banished another thirty-seven blacks from the state.

Despite steady resistance and occasional rebellion, slaves did not have the power to end their bondage. Nonetheless, slaves fought back physically, culturally, and spiritually. They not only survived bondage but also created a vibrant African American culture that buoyed them up during long hours in the fields and brought them joy and hope in the few hours they had to themselves.

Denmark Vesey

▶ A free black carpenter who, in 1822, was accused of planning a slave uprising in Charleston, South Carolina. Although no weapons were found and Vesey and most of the accused denied the charges, thirty-five black men were hanged, including Vesey, and another thirty-seven blacks were banished from the state. The event illustrates the deep fear southern whites had of slave conspiracies.

QUICK REVIEW ◀

What types of resistance did slaves participate in, and why did slave resistance rarely take the form of rebellion?

| What was plantation life like for slaves? | What place did free blacks occupy in southern society? | How did nonslaveholding southern whites work and live? | How did slavery shape southern politics? | Conclusion: How did slavery come to define the South? |

What place did free blacks occupy in southern society?

Freedom Paper

This legal document attests to the free status of the Reverend John F. Cook of Washington, D.C., his daughter Mary, and his son George. Cook was a free black man who kept his "freedom paper" in this watertight tin, which he probably carried with him at all times. Free blacks had to be prepared to prove their free status anytime a white man challenged them, for southern law presumed that a black person was a slave unless he or she could prove otherwise. Moorland-Spingarn Research Center, Howard University, Washington, D.C.

NOT EVERY BLACK SOUTHERNER was a slave. In 1860, some 260,000 (approximately 6 percent) of the region's 4.1 million African Americans were free (see Figure 13.1, page 341). What is surprising is not that their numbers were small but that they existed at all. According to the emerging racial thinking, blacks were supposed to be slaves. Blacks who were free stood out, and whites made them more and more the targets of oppression. Free blacks stood precariously between slavery and full freedom, on what a free black artisan in Charleston characterized in 1848 as "a middle ground." But they made the most of their freedom, and a few found success despite the restrictions placed on them by white Southerners.

Precarious Freedom

The population of free blacks swelled after the Revolution, when the natural rights philosophy of the Declaration of Independence and the egalitarian message of evangelical Protestantism joined to challenge slavery. A brief flurry of **emancipation**—the act of freeing from slavery—visited the Upper South, where the ideological assault on slavery coincided with a deep depression in the tobacco economy. By 1810, free blacks in the South numbered more than 100,000.

In the 1820s and 1830s, state legislatures acted to stem the growth of the free black population and to shrink the liberty of those blacks who had gained their freedom. Laws denied masters the right to free their slaves. Other laws humiliated and restricted free blacks, increasingly subjecting free blacks to the same laws as slaves. They could not testify under oath in a court of law or serve on

emancipation

▶ The act of freeing slaves. Emancipation occurred in significant numbers in the Upper South after the American Revolution, and by 1810 there were more than 100,000 free blacks in the South.

CHAPTER LOCATOR | Why and how did the South become so different from the North? | What was plantation life like for masters and mistresses?

CHAPTER 13
354 UNDERSTANDING THE SLAVE SOUTH, 1820–1860

juries. Like slaves, they were liable to whipping. Free blacks were forbidden to strike whites, even to defend themselves. "Free negroes belong to a degraded caste of society," a South Carolina judge said in 1848. "They are in no respect on a perfect equality with the white man. . . . They ought, by law, to be compelled to demean themselves as inferiors."

Limits on Free Blacks

Subjected to special taxes.
Prohibited from interstate travel.
Denied the right to have schools.
Denied the right to participate in politics.
Required to carry "freedom papers" to prove they were not slaves.

Laws confined most free African Americans to a constricted life of poverty and dependence. Typically, free blacks were rural, uneducated, unskilled agricultural laborers and domestic servants. Opportunities of all kinds—for work, education, or community—were slim.

Achievement despite Restrictions

Despite increasingly harsh laws and stepped-up persecution, free African Americans made the most of the advantages their status offered. Unlike slaves, free blacks could legally marry. They could protect their families from arbitrary disruption and pass on their heritage of freedom to their children. Freedom also meant that they could choose occupations and own property. For most, however, these economic rights proved only theoretical, for a majority of the South's free blacks remained propertyless.

Still, some free blacks escaped the poverty and degradation whites thrust on them. Particularly in the cities of Charleston, Savannah, Mobile, and New Orleans, a small elite of free blacks emerged. Urban whites enforced restrictive laws only sporadically, allowing free blacks room to maneuver. The free black elite, which consisted overwhelmingly of light-skinned African Americans who worked at skilled trades, operated schools for their children and traveled in and out of their states, despite laws forbidding both activities. They worshipped with whites (in separate seating) in the finest churches and lived scattered about in white neighborhoods, not in ghettos. And like elite whites, some owned slaves.

Most free blacks neither became slaveholders nor sought to raise a slave rebellion, as whites accused Denmark Vesey of doing. Rather, most free blacks simply tried to preserve their freedom, which was under increasing attack. Unlike blacks in the North whose freedom was secure, free blacks in the South clung to a precarious freedom by seeking to impress whites with their reliability, economic contributions, and good behavior.

CHRONOLOGY

1810
– More than 100,000 free blacks are living in the South.

1820s–1830s
– Southern state legislatures pass laws to limit the number of free blacks and the rights accorded to them.

1860
– 260,000 (6 percent of total) southern blacks are free.

QUICK REVIEW <

In what ways did the South's free black population stand on a "middle ground"?

What was plantation life like for slaves?	What place did free blacks occupy in southern society?	How did nonslaveholding southern whites work and live?	How did slavery shape southern politics?	Conclusion: How did slavery come to define the South?

How did nonslaveholding southern whites work and live?

Gathering Corn in Virginia

In this romanticized agricultural scene, painter Felix O. C. Darley depicts members of a white farm family gathering its harvest by hand. In reality, growing corn was hard work. The artist, however, is less concerned with realism than with extolling rural family labor as virtuous and noble. Darley surrounds the southern yeomen with an aura of republican independence, dignity, and freedom. Warner Collection of Gulf States Paper Corporation.

MOST WHITES IN THE SOUTH did not own slaves. In 1860, more than six million of the South's eight million whites lived in slaveless households. Some slaveless whites lived in cities and worked as artisans, mechanics, and traders. Others lived in the country and worked as storekeepers, parsons, and schoolteachers. But most "plain folk" were small farmers. Perhaps three out of four were **yeomen**, small farmers who owned their own land. In an important sense, the South had more than one white yeomanry. The huge southern landscape provided space enough for two yeoman societies, separated roughly along geographic lines: plantation belt yeomen and upcountry yeomen. And some rural slaveless whites were not yeomen; they owned no land at all and were sometimes desperately poor.

yeomen

▶ Small farmers who owned their own land. Perhaps three out of four nonslaveholding southern farmers were yeomen. The South contained two distinct yeoman societies, separated roughly along geographic lines: plantation belt yeomen and upcountry yeomen. Planters took great pains to win the loyalty and support of the region's yeomen.

The Cotton Belt

Plantation Belt Yeomen

Plantation belt yeomen lived within the orbit of the planter class. Small farmers grew mainly food crops, particularly corn, but they also devoted a portion of their land to cotton. The small farmers' cotton tied them to planters. Unable to afford cotton gins or baling presses of their own, they relied on slave owners to gin and bale their cotton. With no link to merchants in the port cities, plantation belt yeomen also turned to better-connected planters to ship and sell their cotton. A network of relationships laced small farmers and planters together. Planters hired out surplus slaves to ambitious yeomen who wanted to expand cotton production. They sometimes chose overseers from among the sons of local farm families. Plantation mistresses occasionally nursed ailing neighbors. Male yeomen helped police slaves by riding in slave patrols, which nightly scoured country roads to make certain that no slaves were moving about without permission. On Sundays,

CHAPTER LOCATOR | Why and how did the South become so different from the North? | What was plantation life like for masters and mistresses?

356 CHAPTER 13 UNDERSTANDING THE SLAVE SOUTH, 1820–1860

plantation dwellers and plain folk came together in church to worship and afterward lingered to gossip and to transact small business.

Plantation belt yeomen may have envied, and at times even resented, wealthy slaveholders, but small farmers learned to accommodate. Planters made accommodation easier by going out of their way to behave as good neighbors and avoid direct exploitation of slaveless whites in their community. As a consequence, rather than raging at the oppression of the planter regime, the typical plantation belt yeoman sought entry into it.

Upcountry Yeomen

By contrast, the hills and mountains of the South resisted the spread of slavery and plantations. In the western parts of Virginia, North Carolina, and South Carolina; in northern Georgia and Alabama; and in eastern Tennessee and Kentucky, the higher elevation, colder climate, rugged terrain, and poor transportation made it difficult for commercial agriculture to make headway. As a result, yeomen dominated these isolated areas, and planters and slaves were scarce.

At the core of this upcountry society was the sturdy farm family working its own patch of land; raising hogs, cattle, and sheep; and seeking self-sufficiency and independence. Toward that end, all members of the family worked, their tasks depending on their sex and age. Husbands labored in the fields, and with their sons, they cleared, plowed, planted, and cultivated primarily food crops. Women and their daughters labored primarily in and about the cabin. Male and female tasks were equally crucial to the farm's success, but as in other white southern households, the domestic sphere was subordinated to the will of the male patriarch.

The typical upcountry yeoman also grew a little cotton or tobacco, but food production was more important than cash crops. Not much currency changed hands in the upcountry, and barter was common. Farm families also joined together in logrolling, house and barn raising, and cornhusking.

The few upcountry folks who owned slaves usually had only two or three. As a result, slaveholders had much less social and economic power, and yeomen had more. But the upcountry did not oppose slavery. As long as upcountry plain folk were free to lead their own lives, they defended slavery and white supremacy just as staunchly as other white Southerners.

Poor Whites

Although hardworking, landholding small farmers made up the majority of white Southerners, Northerners had a different image of southern society. They believed that slavery had condemned most whites to poverty and backwardness. One antislavery advocate charged that the South harbored three classes: "the slaves on whom devolves all the regular industry, the slaveholders who reap all the fruits, and an idle and lawless rabble who live dispersed over vast plains little removed from absolute barbarism."

Contrary to northern opinion, only about one in four nonslaveholding rural white men was landless and very poor. Some worked as tenants, renting land and struggling to make a go of it. Others survived by herding pigs and cattle. And still others worked for meager wages, ditching, mining, logging, and laying track for railroads. A Georgian remembered that his "father worked by the day when ever he could get work."

Although they sat at the bottom of the white pecking order, poor whites were ambitious people eager to climb into the yeomanry. The Lipscomb family illustrates

KEY FACTORS

– More than six million of the South's eight million whites owned no slaves.
– Approximately three out of four nonslaveholding southern whites were small farmers who owned their own land (yeomen).
– In the southern upcountry, slaves and plantations were rare.

Upcountry of the South

| What was plantation life like for slaves? | What place did free blacks occupy in southern society? | **How did nonslaveholding southern whites work and live?** | How did slavery shape southern politics? | Conclusion: How did slavery come to define the South? |

357

the possibility of upward mobility. In 1845, Smith and Sally Lipscomb and their children abandoned their worn-out land in South Carolina for Benton County, Alabama. "Benton is a mountainous country but ther is a heep of good levil land to tend in it," Smith wrote back to his brother. Alabama, Smith said, "will be better for the rising generation if not for ourselves but I think it will be the best for us all that live any length of time."

Because the Lipscombs had no money to buy land, they squatted on seven unoccupied acres. With the help of neighbors, they built a 22-by-24-foot cabin, a detached kitchen, and two stables. From daylight to dark, Smith and his sons worked the land, and the first year they produced enough food for the table and several bales of cotton. Sally contributed to the family's income by selling home-made shirts and socks. In time, the Lipscombs bought land and joined the Baptist church, completing their transformation to respectable yeomen.

Many poor whites succeeded in climbing the economic ladder, but in the 1850s upward mobility slowed. The cotton boom of that decade caused planters to expand their operations, driving the price of land beyond the reach of poor families.

The Culture of the Plain Folk

Situated on scattered farms and in tiny villages, rural plain folk lived isolated lives. Life revolved around family, neighbors, the local church, and perhaps a country store. Work occupied most hours, but plain folk still found time for pleasure. "Dancing they are all fond of," a visitor to North Carolina discovered, "especially when they can get a fiddle, or bagpipe." The most popular pastimes of men and boys were fishing and hunting. A traveler in Mississippi recalled that his host sent "two of his sons, little fellows that looked almost too small to shoulder a gun," for food. "In a few hours we were feasting on delicious venison, trout and turtle."

Plain folk did not usually associate "book learning" with the basic needs of life. A northern woman visiting the South in the 1850s observed, "Education is not extended to the masses here as at the North." Private academies charged fees that yeomen could not afford, and public schools were scarce. Although most people managed to pick up the "three R's," approximately one southern white man in five was illiterate in 1860, and the rate for white women was even higher. "People here prefer talking to reading," a Virginian remarked. Telling stories, reciting ballads, and singing hymns were important activities in yeoman culture.

Plain folk spent more hours in revival tents than in classrooms. Not all rural whites were religious, but many were, and the most characteristic feature of their evangelical Christian faith was the revival. Revivalism crossed denominational lines, but Baptists and Methodists adopted it most readily and by midcentury had become the South's largest religious groups. By emphasizing free choice and individual worth, the plain folk's religion was hopeful and affirming. Hymns and spirituals provided guides to right and wrong. Above all, hymns spoke of the eventual release from worldly sorrows and the assurance of eternal salvation.

> **QUICK REVIEW**

How did the lives of plantation belt
and upcountry yeomen differ?

CHAPTER LOCATOR | Why and how did the South become so different from the North? | What was plantation life like for masters and mistresses?

358 CHAPTER 13 UNDERSTANDING THE SLAVE SOUTH, 1820–1860

Gen. James Chesnut, Jr., C.S.A.

James Chesnut

James Chesnut came from a family with a large number of slaves and thus represents the power of slaveholders in southern politics. He served in the South Carolina state legislature for years before becoming a U.S. senator in 1858. He resigned in 1860 and became a colonel in the Confederate army during the Civil War. Courtesy of South Carolina Library, University of South Carolina, Columbia.

BY THE MID-NINETEENTH CENTURY, all southern white men—planters and plain folk alike—had gained the vote. Nonetheless, political power remained unevenly distributed. The nonslaveholding white majority wielded less political power than their numbers indicated. The slaveholding white minority wielded more. Self-conscious, cohesive, and with a well-developed sense of class interest, slaveholders were active in politics and made demands of state governments. As a result, they received significant benefits. Nonslaveholding whites were concerned mainly with preserving their liberties and keeping their taxes low. Collectively, they asked government for little of an economic nature, and they received little.

Slaveholders sometimes worried about nonslaveholders' loyalty to slavery, but the majority of whites accepted the planters' argument that the existing social order served all Southerners' interests. White men in the South fought furiously about many things, but they agreed that they should take land from Indians, promote agriculture, uphold white supremacy and masculine privilege, and defend slavery from its enemies.

The Democratization of the Political Arena

The political reforms that swept the nation in the first half of the nineteenth century reached deeply into the South. Southerners eliminated the wealth and property requirements that had once restricted political participation. Most southern states also removed the property requirements for holding state offices. To be sure, undemocratic features lingered. Plantation districts still wielded disproportionate power in several state legislatures. Nevertheless, southern politics took place within an increasingly democratic political structure.

White male suffrage ushered in an era of vigorous electoral competition in the South. As politics became aggressively democratic, it also grew fiercely partisan. From the 1830s to the 1850s, Whigs and Democrats battled for the electorate's favor. Both parties presented themselves as the plain white folk's best friend.

In 1860:
- All southern white men can vote.
- Slaveholding white men are most active in politics and are far more likely to hold political office than those without slaves.

Planter Power

Whether Whig or Democrat, southern officeholders were likely to be slave owners, often owning large numbers of slaves. The democratization of politics in the nineteenth century meant that more ordinary citizens participated in elections, but yeomen did not throw the planters out.

Upper-class dominance of southern politics reflected the elite's success in persuading the yeoman majority that what was good for slaveholders was also good for them. In reality, the South had, on the whole, done well by the plain folk. Most had farms of their own. They participated as equals in a democratic political system. They enjoyed an elevated social status, above all blacks and in theory equal to all other whites. They commanded patriarchal authority over their households. And as long as slavery existed, they could dream of joining the planter class.

Most slaveholders took pains to win the plain folk's trust and to nurture their respect. One South Carolinian told his wealthy neighbor that he had a bright political future because he never thought himself "too good to sit down & talk to a poor man." Mary Boykin Chesnut complained about the fawning attention her husband, U.S. senator from South Carolina, showed to poor men, including one who had "mud sticking up through his toes."

Georgia politics illustrate how well planters protected their interests in state legislatures. In 1850, about half of the state's revenues came from taxes on slaves, the characteristic form of planter wealth. However, the tax rate on slaves was only about one-fifth the rate on land. Moreover, planters benefited far more than other groups from public spending. Financing railroads—which carried cotton to market—was the largest state expenditure. The legislature also established low tax rates on land, the characteristic form of yeoman wealth, which meant that the typical yeoman's annual tax bill was small. Still, relative to their wealth, large slaveholders paid less than did other whites. Relative to their numbers, they got more in return. Slaveholding legislators protected planters' interests while giving the impression of protecting the small farmers' interests as well.

The South's elite defended slavery in other ways. In the 1830s, whites decided that slavery was too important to debate. To end free speech on the slavery question, powerful whites dismissed slavery's critics from college faculties, drove them from pulpits, and hounded them from political life. Sometimes antislavery Southerners fell victim to vigilantes and mob violence.

In the South, therefore, the rise of the common man occurred alongside the continuing, even growing, power of the planter class. Rather than pitting slaveholders against nonslaveholders, elections remained an effective means of binding the region's whites together. Elections affirmed the sovereignty of white men, whether planter or plain folk, and the subordination of African Americans. Those twin themes played well among white women as well. Though unable to vote, white women supported equality for whites and slavery for blacks. In the antebellum South, the politics of slavery helped knit together all of white society.

> **QUICK REVIEW**

How did planters benefit from their control of state legislatures?

CHAPTER LOCATOR | Why and how did the South become so different from the North? | What was plantation life like for masters and mistresses?

CHAPTER 13
360 UNDERSTANDING THE SLAVE SOUTH, 1820–1860

Collection of the New-York Historical Society.

Conclusion: How did slavery come to define the South?

BY THE EARLY NINETEENTH CENTURY, northern states had either abolished slavery or put it on the road to extinction, while southern states were building the largest slave society in the New World. Regional differences increased over time, not merely because the South became more and more dominated by slavery, but also because developments in the North rapidly propelled it in a very different direction.

One-third of the South's population was enslaved by 1860. Bondage saddled blacks with enormous physical and spiritual burdens: hard labor, harsh treatment, broken families, and, most important, the denial of freedom itself. Although degraded and exploited, they were not defeated. Out of African memories and New World realities, blacks created a life-affirming African American culture that sustained and strengthened them. Defined as property, they refused to be reduced to things. Perceived as inferior beings, they rejected the notion that they were natural slaves.

Slavery was crucial to the South's distinctiveness and to the loyalty and regional identification of its whites. The South was not merely a society with slaves; it had become a slave society. Slavery shaped the region's economy, culture, social structure, and politics. Whites south of the Mason-Dixon line believed that racial slavery was necessary and just. By making all blacks a pariah class, all whites gained a measure of equality and harmony.

Racism did not erase all stress along class lines. Anxious slaveholders continued to worry that yeomen would defect from the proslavery consensus. But during the 1850s, a far more ominous division emerged—that between "slave states" and "free states."

SO NOW YOU KNOW

By 1860, slaves made up one-third of the South's population. Slaves were degraded and exploited by their owners, but they also created their own African American culture, which strengthened and sustained them. Slavery shaped the South's economy, culture, social structure, and politics and made it very different from the North.

What was plantation life like for slaves?	What place did free blacks occupy in southern society?	How did nonslaveholding southern whites work and live?	How did slavery shape southern politics?	Conclusion: How did slavery come to define the South?

> CHAPTER 13 STUDY GUIDE

Online Study Guide
bedfordstmartins.com/roarkunderstanding

STEP 1

GETTING STARTED

Below are basic terms from this period in American history. Can you identify each term below and explain why it matters? To do this exercise online or to download this chart, visit bedfordstmartins.com/roarkunderstanding.

TERM	WHO OR WHAT & WHEN	WHY IT MATTERS
cotton kingdom, p. 340		
slave codes, p. 341		
miscegenation, p. 342		
planter, p. 342		
overseer, p. 346		
paternalism, p. 346		
chivalry, p. 347		
slave driver, p. 350		
Nat Turner, p. 352		
Denmark Vesey, p. 353		
emancipation, p. 354		
yeomen, p. 356		

STEP 2

MOVING BEYOND THE BASICS

The exercise below represents a more advanced understanding of the chapter material. Fill in the following chart by describing key characteristics and trends in the North (see chapter 12) and the South in the nineteenth century. When you have finished filling in your chart, ask yourself what role slavery played in creating the split between North and South. How did slavery shape white racial attitudes in both the North and the South? To do this exercise online or to download this chart, visit bedfordstmartins.com/roarkunderstanding.

Key characteristics and trends	North	South
Agriculture		
Urbanization/industrialization		
White racial attitudes		
Economic diversity/labor		
Population/immigration		

STEP 3

PUTTING IT ALL TOGETHER

Now that you've reviewed various parts of the chapter, take a step back and try to see the big picture by answering these questions. Remember to use specific examples from the chapter in your answers. To do this exercise online, visit bedfordstmartins.com/roarkunderstanding.

REGIONAL DIVERGENCE

▶ How and why did the economies of the North and South steadily diverge over the course of the first half of the nineteenth century?

▶ How did the presence of large numbers of African Americans shape southern culture?

PLANTATION LIFE

▶ How did plantation owners see the relationship between master and slave? How did slavery shape other social relationships in the antebellum South?

▶ In what ways did slaves create communities for themselves and develop methods to resist their bondage?

SOUTHERN SOCIETY AND POLITICS

▶ How did southern yeomen see themselves and their place in southern society? How was slavery a part of that place?

▶ How did slavery shape southern politics?

Gen. James Chesnut, Jr., C.S.A.

LOOKING BACKWARD, LOOKING AHEAD

▶ How did southern slave society change from the eighteenth to nineteenth centuries?

▶ Why did many white Southerners come to believe that slavery had to be preserved at any cost? How might that have influenced national politics?

IN YOUR OWN WORDS

Imagine that you must explain chapter 13 to someone who hasn't read it. What would be the most important points to include and why?

ANNIHILATI

TO TRAITORS

THE EAGLE'S NEST.

"THE UNION: IT MUST AND SHALL BE PRESERVED."

14

THE HOUSE DIVIDED

1846–1861

> This chapter explores the politics of slavery in the tumultuous decades before the Civil War. It examines the ways the recurring issue of the expansion of slavery into newly acquired territory deepened sectional divisions, undermined old political parties, made room for new parties, and, ultimately, led to secession and civil war.

> How did the acquisition of land from Mexico contribute to sectional tensions?

> What factors helped unravel the balance between slave and free states?

> How did the party system change in the 1850s?

> Why did northern fear of the "Slave Power" intensify in the 1850s?

> What caused some southern states to secede after the election of 1860?

> Conclusion: Why did political compromise fail?

DID YOU KNOW?

Uncle Tom's Cabin was the first American novel to sell a million copies.

The Eagle's Nest. This 1861 cartoon by E.B. Kellogg of Hartford, Connecticut, makes his position clear in the subtitle: "The Union! It Must and Shall Be Preserved."

How did the acquisition of land from Mexico contribute to sectional tensions?

Oak Home Farm, San Joaquin County, California

The discovery of gold in California initiated a stampede west, but not everyone wanted to be a prospector. In 1860, an unknown artist painted this idyllic view of the farm of W. I. Overhiser in California's fertile San Joaquin Valley. Thousands of miles away, farmers compared farmsteads like Overhiser's with their own. Many judged life more bountiful in the West and trekked across the country to try to strike it rich in western agriculture. University of California at Berkeley, Bancroft Library.

BETWEEN 1846 AND 1848, the nation grew by 1.2 million square miles, an incredible two-thirds. Victory in the Mexican-American War brought vast new territories in the West into the United States. The gold rush of 1849 transformed California into a booming economy (see chapter 12). The 1850s witnessed new "rushes," for gold in Colorado and silver in Nevada's Comstock Lode, and people from around the world flocked to the West. But it quickly became clear that Northerners and Southerners had very different visions of the West, particularly the place of slavery in its future. Still, Congress in 1850 patched together a settlement that Americans hoped would be permanent.

The Wilmot Proviso and the Expansion of Slavery

Most Americans agreed that the Constitution left the issue of slavery to the individual states to decide. Northern states had done away with slavery, while southern states had retained it. But what about slavery in the nation's territories? The Constitution states that "Congress shall have power to . . . make all needful rules and regulations respecting the territory . . . belonging to the United States." The debate about slavery, then, turned toward Congress.

Mexican Cession, 1848

CHAPTER LOCATOR | How did the acquisition of land from Mexico contribute to sectional tensions?

Slavery in the Territories: Contradictory Precedents

1787: Northwest Ordinance bans slavery north of the Ohio River.

1803: Congress allows slavery to remain in the newly acquired Louisiana Territory.

1820: The Missouri Compromise prohibits slavery in part of the Louisiana Territory but allows it in the rest.

The spark for the national debate was provided in August 1846 by a Democratic representative from Pennsylvania, David Wilmot, who proposed that Congress bar slavery from all lands acquired in the war with Mexico. Regardless of party affiliation, Northerners lined up behind the **Wilmot Proviso**. Many supported free soil, by which they meant territory in which slavery would be prohibited, because they wanted to preserve the West for free labor, for hardworking, self-reliant free men, not for slaveholders and slaves. But support also came from those who were simply anti-South. New slave territories would eventually mean new slave states, and they opposed magnifying the political power of Southerners. Wilmot himself said his proposal would blunt "the *power* of slaveholders" in the national government.

Additional support for free soil came from Northerners who were hostile to blacks and wanted to reserve new land for whites. Wilmot himself declared, "I would preserve for free white labor a fair country, a rich inheritance, where the sons of toil, of my own race and own color, can live without the disgrace which association with negro slavery brings upon free labor." It is no wonder that some called the Wilmot Proviso the "White Man's Proviso."

The thought that slavery might be excluded outraged white Southerners. Like Northerners, they regarded the West as a ladder for economic and social opportunity. They also believed that the exclusion of slavery was a slap in the face to southern veterans of the Mexican-American War. "When the war-worn soldier returns home," one Alabaman asked, "is he to be told that he cannot carry his property to the country won by his blood?"

Southern leaders also sought to maintain political parity with the North to protect the South's interests, especially slavery. The need seemed especially urgent in the 1840s, when the North's population and wealth were booming. James Henry Hammond of South Carolina predicted that ten new states would be carved from the acquired Mexican land. If free soil won, the North would "ride over us roughshod" in Congress, he claimed. "Our only safety is in *equality* of POWER."

Because Northerners had a majority in the House, they easily passed the Wilmot Proviso. In the Senate, however, where slave states outnumbered free states fifteen to fourteen, Southerners defeated it. Senator John C. Calhoun of South Carolina denied that Congress had the constitutional authority to exclude slavery from the nation's territories. Whereas Wilmot demanded that Congress slam shut the door to slavery, Calhoun called on Congress to hold the door wide open.

In 1847, Senator Lewis Cass of Michigan offered a compromise through the doctrine of **popular sovereignty**, by which the people who settled the territories would decide for themselves slavery's fate. This solution, Cass argued, sat squarely in the American tradition of democracy and local self-government. Popular sovereignty's most attractive feature was its ambiguity about the precise moment when

CHRONOLOGY

1846
- Wilmot Proviso prohibiting the expansion of slavery into territory acquired from Mexico is introduced in Congress.

1847
- Wilmot Proviso is defeated in Senate.
- Compromise of "popular sovereignty" is offered allowing the people of the territories to decide the issue of slavery.

1848
- Free-Soil Party is founded.
- Whig Zachary Taylor is elected president.

1849
- California gold rush begins.

1850
- Taylor dies; Vice President Millard Fillmore becomes president.
- Compromise of 1850 becomes law.

Wilmot Proviso

▶ Proposal put forward by Representative David Wilmot of Pennsylvania in August 1846 to ban slavery in territory acquired as a result of the Mexican-American War. The proviso enjoyed widespread support in the North, but many Southerners saw it as an attack on their economic and political interests.

| What factors helped unravel the balance between slave and free states? | How did the party system change in the 1850s? | Why did northern fear of the "Slave Power" intensify in the 1850s? | What caused some southern states to secede after the election of 1860? | Conclusion: Why did political compromise fail? |

popular sovereignty

▶ The principle that the people of a given territory should resolve the issue of slavery in the territory themselves by a popular vote. First advanced by Senator Lewis Cass of Michigan in 1847, popular sovereignty initially appeared to offer a compromise on the slavery question. In the end, popular sovereignty did little to resolve sectional tensions, and its application in Kansas in 1856 actually led to violence.

settlers could determine slavery's fate. Northern advocates believed that the decision on slavery could be made as soon as the first territorial legislature assembled. With free-soil majorities likely because of the North's greater population, they would shut the door to slavery almost before the first slave arrived. Southern supporters believed that popular sovereignty guaranteed that slavery would be unrestricted throughout the entire territorial period. Only at the very end, when settlers in a territory drew up a constitution and applied for statehood, could they decide the issue of slavery. By then, slavery would have sunk deep roots. As long as the matter of timing remained vague, popular sovereignty gave hope to both sides.

When Congress ended its session in 1848, no plan had won a majority in both houses. Northerners who demanded no new slave territory anywhere, ever, and Southerners who demanded entry for their slave property into all territories, or else, staked out their extreme positions. Unresolved in Congress, the territorial question naturally became an issue in the presidential election of 1848.

The Election of 1848

When President Polk chose not to seek reelection, the Democratic convention nominated Lewis Cass of Michigan, the man most closely associated with popular sovereignty. The Whigs nominated a Mexican-American War hero, General Zachary Taylor. The Whigs declined to adopt a party platform, betting that the combination of a military hero and total silence on the slavery issue would unite their divided party. Taylor, who owned more than one hundred slaves on plantations in Mississippi and Louisiana, was hailed by Georgia politician Robert Toombs as a "Southern man, a slaveholder, a cotton planter."

Antislavery Whigs balked and looked for an alternative. Senator Charles Sumner called for a major political realignment, "one grand Northern party of Freedom." In the summer of 1848, antislavery Whigs and antislavery Democrats founded the Free-Soil Party, nominating a Democrat, Martin Van Buren, for president and a Whig, Charles Francis Adams, for vice president. The platform boldly proclaimed, "Free soil, free speech, free labor, and free men."

The November election dashed the hopes of the Free-Soilers. They did not carry a single state. Taylor won the all-important electoral college vote 163 to 127, carrying eight of the fifteen slave states and seven of the fifteen free states (**Map 14.1**).

General Taylor Cigar Case

This papier-mâché cigar case portrays General Zachary Taylor, Whig presidential candidate in 1848, in a colorful scene from the Mexican-American War. Shown here as a dashing, elegant officer, Taylor was in fact a short, thickset, and roughly dressed Indian fighter who had spent his career commanding small frontier garrisons. The inscription reminds voters that Taylor was a victor in the first four battles fought in the war and directs attention away from the fact that in politics, he was a rank amateur. Collection of Janice L. and David Frent.

CHAPTER LOCATOR | How did the acquisition of land from Mexico contribute to sectional tensions?

(Wisconsin had entered the Union earlier in 1848 as the fifteenth free state.) Northern voters were not yet ready for Sumner's "one grand Northern party of Freedom," but the struggle over slavery in the territories had shaken the major parties badly.

Debate and Compromise

Believing that he could avoid further sectional strife if California and New Mexico skipped the territorial stage, new president Zachary Taylor in 1849 encouraged the settlers to apply for admission to the Union as states. Predominantly antislavery, the settlers began writing free-state constitutions. "For the first time," Mississippian Jefferson Davis lamented, "we are about permanently to destroy the balance of power between the sections."

Congress convened in December 1849, beginning one of the most contentious and most significant sessions in its history. President Taylor urged Congress to admit California as a free state immediately and to admit New Mexico, which lagged behind a few months, as soon as it applied. Southerners exploded. A North Carolinian declared that Southerners who would "consent to be thus degraded and enslaved, ought to be whipped through their fields by their own negroes."

At this juncture, Senator Henry Clay of Kentucky stepped in to offer a series of resolutions meant to answer and balance "all questions in controversy between the free and slave states, growing out of the subject of slavery." Admit California as a free state, he proposed, but organize the rest of the Southwest without restrictions on slavery. Require Texas to abandon its claim to parts of New Mexico, but compensate it by assuming its preannexation debt. Abolish the domestic slave trade in Washington, D.C., but confirm slavery itself in the nation's capital. Reassert Congress's lack of authority to interfere with the interstate slave trade, and enact a more effective fugitive slave law.

Both antislavery advocates and "fire-eaters" (as radical Southerners who urged secession from the Union were called) savaged Clay's plan. Senator Salmon P. Chase of Ohio ridiculed it as "sentiment for the North, substance for the South." Senator Henry S. Foote of Mississippi denounced it as more offensive to the South than the speeches of abolitionists William Lloyd Garrison, Wendell Phillips, and Frederick Douglass combined. The most ominous response came from John C. Calhoun, who argued that the fragile political unity of North and South depended on continued equal representation in the Senate, which Clay's plan for a free California destroyed. "As things now stand," he said in February 1850, the South "cannot with safety remain in the Union."

Senator Daniel Webster of Massachusetts then addressed the Senate. Like Clay, Webster defended compromise. He told Northerners that the South had legitimate complaints, but he told Southerners that secession from the Union would mean civil war. Referring to the Wilmot Proviso, he argued that a legal ban on slavery in the territories was unnecessary because the harsh climate effectively prohibited the expansion of cotton and slaves into the new American Southwest.

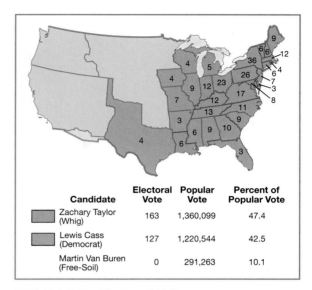

Candidate	Electoral Vote	Popular Vote	Percent of Popular Vote
Zachary Taylor (Whig)	163	1,360,099	47.4
Lewis Cass (Democrat)	127	1,220,544	42.5
Martin Van Buren (Free-Soil)	0	291,263	10.1

MAP 14.1 ■ The Election of 1848

What factors helped unravel the balance between slave and free states?	How did the party system change in the 1850s?	Why did northern fear of the "Slave Power" intensify in the 1850s?	What caused some southern states to secede after the election of 1860?	Conclusion: Why did political compromise fail?

Free state or territory
Slave state
Opened to slavery by principle of popular sovereignty
• Slave trade ended

MAP 14.2 ■ The Compromise of 1850
The patched-together sectional agreement was both clumsy and unstable. Few Americans—in either North or South—supported all five parts of the Compromise.

Free-Soil forces recoiled from what they saw as Webster's desertion. Senator William H. Seward of New York responded that Webster's and Clay's compromise with slavery was "radically wrong and essentially vicious." He rejected Calhoun's argument that Congress lacked the constitutional authority to exclude slavery from the territories. In any case, Seward said, there was a "higher law than the Constitution"—the law of God—to ensure freedom in all the public domain. Claiming that God was a Free-Soiler did nothing to cool the superheated political atmosphere.

In May, the Senate considered a bill that joined Clay's resolutions into a single comprehensive package. Clay bet that a majority of Congress wanted compromise and that the members would vote for the package. But the strategy backfired. Free-Soilers and proslavery Southerners voted down the comprehensive plan.

Fortunately for those who favored a settlement, Senator Stephen A. Douglas, a rising Democratic star from Illinois, broke the bill into its parts and skillfully ushered each through Congress. The agreement Douglas won in September 1850 was very much the one Clay had proposed in January. California entered the Union as a free state. New Mexico and Utah became territories where slavery would be decided by popular sovereignty. Texas accepted its boundary with New Mexico and received $10 million from the federal government. Congress ended the slave trade in the District of Columbia but enacted a more stringent fugitive slave law. In September, Millard Fillmore, who had become president when Zachary Taylor died in July, signed into law each bill, collectively known as the **Compromise of 1850 (Map 14.2)**. The nation breathed a sigh of relief. The Compromise preserved the Union and peace for the moment.

Compromise of 1850
▶ Collection of laws passed in 1850 meant to resolve the dispute over the spread of slavery in the territories. Key elements of the Compromise of 1850 included the admission of California as a free state and the passage of the Fugitive Slave Act. The Compromise of 1850 began to unravel almost immediately after its passage, as sectional tensions continued to rise.

> **QUICK REVIEW**

What provisions of the Compromise of 1850 might have eased sectional tensions and why?

CHAPTER LOCATOR | How did the acquisition of land from Mexico contribute to sectional tensions?

What factors helped unravel the balance between slave and free states?

The Modern Medea In 1855, a slave family—Robert Garner; his twenty-two-year-old wife, Margaret; their four children; and his parents—fled Kentucky. Margaret's owner tracked them to a cabin in Ohio. Thinking that her children would be returned to slavery, Margaret seized a butcher knife and cut the throat of her two-year-old daughter. She was turning on her other children when slave catchers burst in and captured her. Abolitionists claimed that the act revealed the horror of slavery; defenders of slavery argued that the deed proved that slaves were savages. This 1867 painting shows Margaret standing over the bodies of two boys. Artist Thomas Satterwhite Noble departed from history in order to allude to the Greek myth of Medea, who killed her two children to spite her husband. *Harper's Weekly*, May 18, 1867/Picture Research Consultants & Archives.

▶ FOR MORE HELP ANALYZING THIS IMAGE, see the visual activity for this chapter in the Online Study Guide at bedfordstmartins.com/roarkunderstanding.

THE COMPROMISE OF 1850 began to come apart almost immediately. The implementation of the Fugitive Slave Act and the publication of Harriet Beecher Stowe's *Uncle Tom's Cabin* combined to inflame antislavery feeling in the North. Congress did its part to undo the Compromise as well. In 1854, Congress passed the Kansas-Nebraska Act, once again opening up the question of slavery in the territories, the deadliest of all sectional issues.

The Fugitive Slave Act

The issue of runaway slaves was as old as the Constitution, which contained a provision for the return of any "person held to service or labor in one state" who escaped to another. In 1793, a federal law authorized slave owners to enter other states to recapture their slave property. Proclaiming the 1793 law a license to kidnap free blacks, northern states in the 1830s began passing "personal liberty laws" that provided fugitives with some protection.

What factors helped unravel the balance between slave and free states?	How did the party system change in the 1850s?	Why did northern fear of the "Slave Power" intensify in the 1850s?	What caused some southern states to secede after the election of 1860?	Conclusion: Why did political compromise fail?

Some northern communities also formed vigilance committees to help runaways. Each year, a few hundred slaves escaped into free states and found friendly northern "conductors" who put them on board the underground railroad, which was not a railroad at all but a series of secret "stations" (hideouts) on the way to Canada (see chapter 12).

Furious about northern interference, Southerners in 1850 insisted on the stricter fugitive slave law that was passed as part of the Compromise. According to the **Fugitive Slave Act**, to seize an alleged slave, a slaveholder simply had to appear before a commissioner and swear that the runaway was his. The commissioner earned $10 for every individual returned to slavery but only $5 for those set free. Most galling to Northerners, the law stipulated that all citizens were expected to assist officials in apprehending runaways.

In Boston in February 1851, an angry crowd overpowered federal marshals and snatched a runaway named Shadrach from a courtroom, put him on the underground railroad, and whisked him off to Canada. Three years later, when another Boston crowd rushed the courthouse in a failed attempt to rescue Anthony Burns, who had recently fled slavery in Richmond, a guard was shot dead. To white Southerners, it seemed that antislavery fanatics had whipped Northerners into a frenzy of massive resistance.

Actually, the overwhelming majority of fugitives claimed by slaveholders were reenslaved peacefully. But brutal enforcement of the unpopular law had a radicalizing effect in the North, particularly in New England. To Southerners, it seemed that Northerners had betrayed the Compromise. "The continued existence of the United States as one nation," warned the *Southern Literary Messenger*, "depends upon the full and faithful execution of the Fugitive Slave Bill."

Uncle Tom's Cabin

As unsettling as the Fugitive Slave Act was, even more Northerners were turned against slavery by a novel. Harriet Beecher Stowe, a Northerner who had never set foot on a plantation, made the South's slaves into flesh-and-blood human beings for many of her readers. A member of a famous clan of preachers, teachers, and reformers, Stowe despised the slave catchers and wrote to expose the sin of slavery. Published as a book in 1852, **Uncle Tom's Cabin, or Life among the Lowly** sold 300,000 copies in its first year and more than 2 million copies within ten years. Stowe's characters leaped from the page. Here was the gentle slave Uncle Tom, a Christian saint who forgave those who beat him to death; the courageous slave Eliza, who fled with her child across the frozen Ohio River; and the fiendish overseer Simon Legree, whose Louisiana plantation was a nightmare of torture and death. Northerners shed tears and sang praises to *Uncle Tom's Cabin*.

What Northerners accepted as truth, however, Southerners denounced as slander. Virginian George F. Holmes proclaimed Stowe a member of the "Woman's Rights" and "Higher Law" schools and dismissed the novel as a work of "intense fanaticism." Although it is impossible to measure precisely the impact of a novel on public opinion, *Uncle Tom's Cabin* clearly helped to crystallize northern sentiment against slavery and to confirm white Southerners' suspicion that they no longer received any sympathy in the free states. Other writers—

Fugitive Slave Act
▶ A law included in the Compromise of 1850 to help attract southern support for the legislative package. Its strict provisions for capturing runaway slaves provoked outrage in the North and contributed to intensified antislavery sentiment in the region.

Uncle Tom's Cabin, or Life among the Lowly
▶ Antislavery novel written by Harriet Beecher Stowe and published in 1852. The book sold two million copies within ten years. It helped to solidify northern sentiment against slavery and to confirm white Southerners' sense that they no longer had any sympathy in the free states.

CHAPTER LOCATOR | How did the acquisition of land from Mexico contribute to sectional tensions?

ex-slaves who knew life in slave cabins firsthand—also produced stinging indictments of slavery. Solomon Northup's compelling *Twelve Years a Slave* (1853) sold 27,000 copies in two years, and the powerful *Narrative of the Life of Frederick Douglass, as Told by Himself* (1845) eventually sold more than 30,000 copies. But no work touched the North's conscience like Stowe's novel.

The Kansas-Nebraska Act

As the 1852 election approached, the Democrats and Whigs sought to close the sectional rifts that had opened within their parties. For their presidential nominee, the Democrats turned to Franklin Pierce of New Hampshire. Pierce's well-known sympathy with southern views on public issues caused his northern critics to include him among the "doughfaces," northern men malleable enough to champion southern causes. Adopting the formula that had worked in 1848, the Whigs chose another Mexican-American War hero, General Winfield Scott of Virginia. But the Whigs' northern and southern factions were hopelessly divided, and the party suffered a humiliating defeat. The Democrat Pierce carried twenty-seven states to Scott's four and won the electoral college vote 254 to 42 (Map 14.4, page 376). The Free-Soil Party lost almost half of the voters who had turned to it in the tumultuous political atmosphere of 1848.

Eager to leave the sectional controversy behind, the new president turned swiftly to foreign expansion. Pierce's major objective was Cuba, but when anti-slavery Northerners blocked Cuba's acquisition to keep more slave territory from entering the Union, he turned his attention to Mexico. In 1853, diplomat James Gadsden negotiated a $15 million purchase of some 30,000 square miles of land in present-day Arizona and New Mexico. The Gadsden Purchase stemmed from Pierce's desire for a southern transcontinental railroad to California. Inevitably in the 1850s, the contest for a transcontinental railroad route evolved into a sectional contest over slavery.

Gadsden Purchase, 1853

Illinois's Democratic senator Stephen A. Douglas badly wanted the transcontinental railroad for Chicago, and he was the chair of the Senate Committee on Territories. Any railroad that ran west from Chicago would pass through a region that Congress in 1830 had designated a "permanent" Indian reserve. Douglas proposed giving this vast area between the Missouri River and the Rocky Mountains an Indian name, Nebraska, and then throwing the Indians out. Once the region achieved territorial status, whites could survey and sell the land, establish a civil government, and build a railroad.

Nebraska lay within the Louisiana Purchase and, according to the Missouri Compromise of 1820, was closed to slavery (see chapter 10). Douglas needed southern votes to pass his Nebraska legislation, but Southerners had no incentive to create another free territory or to help a northern city win the transcontinental railroad. Southerners, however, agreed to help if Congress organized Nebraska

| What factors helped unravel the balance between slave and free states? | How did the party system change in the 1850s? | Why did northern fear of the "Slave Power" intensify in the 1850s? | What caused some southern states to secede after the election of 1860? | Conclusion: Why did political compromise fail? |

MAP 14.3 ■ The Kansas-Nebraska Act, 1854
Americans hardly thought twice about dispossessing the Indians of land guaranteed them by treaty, but many worried about the outcome of repealing the Missouri Compromise and opening up the region to slavery.

Kansas-Nebraska Act

▶ 1854 law championed by Stephen A. Douglas that removed Indians from Nebraska Territory, divided the territory into Kansas and Nebraska, and stipulated that the issue of slavery in each of the new territories would be decided on the basis of popular sovereignty. Implementation of the measure led to bloody fighting between pro- and antislavery forces in Kansas.

according to popular sovereignty. That meant giving slavery a chance in Nebraska Territory and reopening the dangerous issue of the expansion of slavery.

In January 1854, Douglas introduced his bill to organize Nebraska Territory, leaving to the settlers themselves the decision about slavery. At southern insistence, Douglas added an explicit repeal of the Missouri Compromise. Free-Soilers branded Douglas's plan "a gross violation of a sacred pledge" and an "atrocious plot" to transform free land into a "dreary region of despotism, inhabited by masters and slaves."

Undaunted, Douglas skillfully shepherded the explosive bill through Congress in May 1854. Nine-tenths of the southern members (Whigs and Democrats) and half of the northern Democrats cast votes in favor of the bill. Like Douglas, most northern supporters believed that popular sovereignty would make Nebraska free territory. In its final form, the **Kansas-Nebraska Act** divided the huge territory in two: Nebraska and Kansas (**Map 14.3**). With this act, the government pushed the Plains Indians farther west, making way for farmers and railroads.

> **QUICK REVIEW**

Why did the desire for a transcontinental railroad turn into a debate over slavery in the 1850s?

CHAPTER LOCATOR | How did the acquisition of land from Mexico contribute to sectional tensions?

John and Jessie Frémont Poster

The election of 1856 marked the first time a candidate's wife appeared on campaign items. In this poster, Jessie Frémont and her husband, John, the Republican Party's presidential nominee, ride spirited horses. The scene emphasizes their youth (John was forty-three; Jessie, thirty-one), their vigor, and their outdoor exuberance. Smart and ambitious, Jessie helped plan her husband's campaign, coauthored his election biography, and drew northern women into political activity as never before. Museum of American Political Life.

How did the party system change in the 1850s? <

SINCE THE RISE of the Whig Party in the early 1830s, Whigs and Democrats had organized and channeled political conflict in the nation. This party system dampened sectionalism and strengthened the Union. To achieve national political power, the Whigs and Democrats had to retain their strength in both the North and the South. And strength in both regions required that parties compromise and find positions acceptable to both wings. But the Kansas-Nebraska controversy shattered this stabilizing political system. In place of two national parties with bisectional strength, the mid-1850s witnessed the development of one party heavily dominated by one section and another party entirely limited to the other section. The new party system thwarted political compromise and promoted political polarization.

The Old Parties: Whigs and Democrats

As early as the Mexican-American War, members of the Whig Party had clashed over the future of slavery in annexed Mexican lands. By 1852, the Whig Party could please its proslavery southern wing or its antislavery northern wing but not both. The Whigs' miserable showing in the election of 1852 made clear that they were no longer a strong national party. By 1856, after more than two decades of contesting the Democrats, they were hardly a party at all (**Map 14.4**).

What factors helped unravel the balance between slave and free states?	How did the party system change in the 1850s?	Why did northern fear of the "Slave Power" intensify in the 1850s?	What caused some southern states to secede after the election of 1860?	Conclusion: Why did political compromise fail?

1848

Candidate	Electoral Vote	Popular Vote	Percent of Popular Vote
Zachary Taylor (Whig)	163	1,360,099	47.4
Lewis Cass (Democrat)	127	1,220,544	42.5
Martin Van Buren (Free-Soil)	0	291,263	10.1

1852

Candidate	Electoral Vote	Popular Vote	Percent of Popular Vote
Franklin Pierce (Democrat)	254	1,601,274	50.9
Winfield Scott (Whig)	42	1,386,580	44.1
John P. Hale (Free-Soil)	5	155,825	5.0

1856

Candidate	Electoral Vote	Popular Vote	Percent of Popular Vote
James Buchanan (Democrat)	174	1,838,169	45.3
John C. Frémont (Republican)	114	1,341,264	33.1
Millard Fillmore (American)	8	874,534	21.6

1860

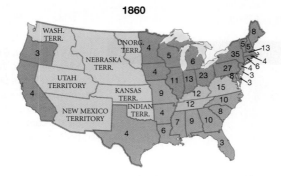

Candidate	Electoral Vote	Popular Vote	Percent of Popular Vote
Abraham Lincoln (Republican)	180	1,866,452	39.9
John C. Breckinridge (Southern Democrat)	72	847,953	18.1
Stephen A. Douglas (Northern Democrat)	12	1,375,157	29.4
John Bell (Constitutional Union)	39	590,631	12.6

MAP 14.4 ■ Political Realignment, 1848–1860

In 1848, slavery and sectionalism began taking their toll on the country's party system. The Whig Party was an early casualty. By 1860, national parties—those that contended for votes in both North and South—had been replaced by regional parties.

> ▶ FOR MORE HELP ANALYZING THIS MAP, see the map activity for this chapter in the Online Study Guide at bedfordstmartins.com/roarkunderstanding.

The collapse of the Whig Party left the Democrats as the country's only national party. Although the Democrats were not immune to the disruptive pressures of the territorial question, they discovered in popular sovereignty a doctrine that many Democrats could support. Even so, popular sovereignty very nearly undid the party. When Stephen Douglas applied the doctrine to the part of the Louisiana Purchase where slavery had been barred, he divided northern Democrats and destroyed the dominance of the Democratic Party in the free states. After 1854, even though the Democrats were a southern-dominated party, they remained a national political organization. Gains in the South more than balanced Democratic losses in the North. During the 1850s, Democrats elected two presidents and won majorities in Congress in almost every election.

The breakup of the Whigs and the disaffection of significant numbers of northern Democrats set many Americans politically adrift. As they searched for new political harbors, Americans found that the death of the old party system created a multitude of fresh political alternatives.

CHRONOLOGY

1854
– American (Know-Nothing) Party emerges.
– Republican Party is founded.

1855
– Height of Know-Nothings' political success.

1856
– Democrat James Buchanan is elected president.

The New Parties: Know-Nothings and Republicans

Out of the confusion, two parties emerged as true contenders for national prominence. One grew out of the slavery controversy, a coalition of indignant antislavery Northerners. The other arose from an entirely different split in American society, between Roman Catholic immigrants and native Protestants.

The wave of immigrants that arrived in America from 1845 to 1855 led some Protestant Americans to believe that the Republic would soon be dominated by Roman Catholics from Ireland and Germany. In the 1850s, nativists (individuals who were anti-immigrant) began to organize, first into secret fraternal societies and then in 1854 into a political party. Recruits swore never to vote for either foreign-born or Roman Catholic candidates and not to reveal any information about the organization. When questioned, they said, "I know nothing." Officially, they were the American Party, but most Americans called them Know-Nothings.

Campaign Flag of the Know-Nothing Party

Convinced that the incendiary issue of slavery had blinded Americans to the greater dangers of uncontrolled immigration and foreign influence, the Know-Nothings nominated Millard Fillmore for president in 1856. Milwaukee County Historical Society.

What factors helped unravel the balance between slave and free states?	How did the party system change in the 1850s?	Why did northern fear of the "Slave Power" intensify in the 1850s?	What caused some southern states to secede after the election of 1860?	Conclusion: Why did political compromise fail?

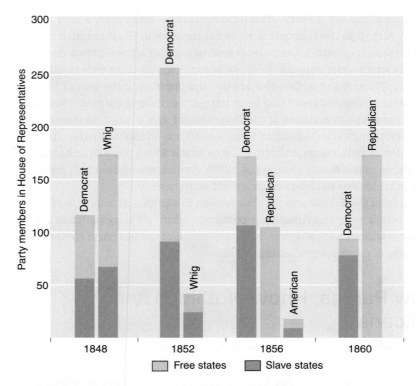

FIGURE 14.1 ■ Changing Political Landscape, 1848–1860

The polarization of American politics between free states and slave states occurred in little more than a decade.

The Know-Nothings exploded onto the political stage in 1854 and 1855 with a series of dazzling successes. They captured state legislatures in the Northeast, West, and South and claimed dozens of seats in Congress. By 1855, an observer might reasonably have concluded that the Know-Nothings had emerged as the successor to the Whigs.

The Know-Nothings were not the only new party making noise, however. One of the new antislavery organizations provoked by the Kansas-Nebraska Act called itself the **Republican Party**. The Republicans attempted to unite all those who opposed the extension of slavery into any territory of the United States (see **Figure 14.1**).

The Republican creed tapped into the basic beliefs and values of the northern public. Slavery, the Republicans believed, degraded the dignity of white labor by associating work with blacks and servility. They warned that the insatiable slaveholders of the South, whom antislavery Northerners called the "Slave Power," were conspiring through their control of the Democratic Party to expand slavery, subvert liberty, and undermine the Constitution.

Only if slavery was restricted to the South, Republicans believed, could the system of free labor flourish elsewhere. In the North, one Republican declared in 1854, "every man holds his fortune in his own right arm; and his position in society, in life, is to be tested by his own individual character" (see chapter 12). Powerful images of liberty and opportunity attracted a wide range of Northerners to the Republican cause.

Republican Party

▶ Antislavery party formed in 1854 in the wake of the passage of the Kansas-Nebraska Act. The Republicans attempted to unite all those who opposed the extension of slavery into any territory of the United States. In 1860, Abraham Lincoln won the presidency running as the Republican candidate.

CHAPTER LOCATOR | How did the acquisition of land from Mexico contribute to sectional tensions?

Women as well as men rushed to the new Republican Party. Indeed, three women helped found the party in Ripon, Wisconsin, in 1854. Although they could not vote before the Civil War and suffered from a raft of other legal handicaps, women nevertheless participated in partisan politics by writing campaign literature, marching in parades, giving speeches, and lobbying voters. Women's antislavery fervor attracted them to the Republican Party, and participation in party politics in turn nurtured the woman's rights movement. Susan B. Anthony, who attended Republican meetings throughout the 1850s, found that her political activity made her disfranchisement all the more galling. She and other women in the North worked on behalf of antislavery and to secure both woman suffrage and the right of married women to control their own property.

The Election of 1856

The election of 1856 revealed that the Republicans had become the Democrats' main challenger, and slavery in the territories, not nativism, was the election's principal issue. When the Know-Nothings insisted on a platform that endorsed the Kansas-Nebraska Act, most of the Northerners walked out, and the party came apart. The few Know-Nothings who remained nominated ex-president Millard Fillmore.

The Republicans adopted a platform that focused almost exclusively on "making every territory free." For president, they nominated the soldier and California adventurer John C. Frémont. Frémont lacked political credentials, but his wife, Jessie Frémont, the daughter of Senator Thomas Hart Benton of Missouri, knew the political map as well as her husband knew the western trails. Though careful to maintain a proper public image, the young mother and antislavery zealot helped attract voters and draw women into politics.

The Democrats, successful in 1852 in bridging sectional differences by nominating a northern man with southern principles, chose another "doughface," James Buchanan of Pennsylvania. They took refuge in the ambiguity of popular sovereignty and portrayed the Republicans as extremists ("Black Republican Abolitionists") whose support for the Wilmot Proviso risked pushing the South out of the Union.

The Democratic strategy carried the day for Buchanan. Buchanan won 174 electoral college votes against Frémont's 114 and Fillmore's 8 (see Map 14.4, page 376). But the big news was what the press called the "glorious defeat" of the Republicans. Despite being a brand-new party and purely sectional, Frémont and the Republicans had seriously challenged the Democrats for national power. Sectionalism had fashioned a new party system, one that spelled danger for the Republic. Indeed, war had already broken out between proslavery and antislavery forces in distant Kansas Territory.

QUICK REVIEW

Why did the Whig Party disintegrate in the 1850s?

| What factors helped unravel the balance between slave and free states? | How did the party system change in the 1850s? | Why did northern fear of the "Slave Power" intensify in the 1850s? | What caused some southern states to secede after the election of 1860? | Conclusion: Why did political compromise fail? |

Why did northern fear of the "Slave Power" intensify in the 1850s?

Armed Settlers near Lawrence, Kansas Armed with rifles, knives, swords, and pistols, these tough antislavery men gathered for a photograph near Lawrence in 1856. Kansas State Historical Society.

EVENTS IN KANSAS TERRITORY provided the young Republican organization with an enormous boost and help explain its strong showing in the election of 1856. Republicans organized around the premise that the slaveholding South provided a profound threat to "free soil, free labor, and free men," and now Kansas reeled with violence that Republicans argued was southern in origin. In fact, everywhere Republicans looked in the 1850s, they saw what they believed was evidence of the South's drive toward tyranny and minority rule.

"Bleeding Kansas"

Three days after the House of Representatives approved the Kansas-Nebraska Act in 1854, Senator William H. Seward of New York boldly challenged the South. "Come on then, Gentlemen of the Slave States," he cried, "since there is no escaping your challenge, I accept it in behalf of the cause of freedom. We will engage in competition for the virgin soil of Kansas, and God give the victory to the side which is stronger in numbers as it is in right."

In both North and South, emigrant aid societies sprang up to promote settlement from free states or slave states. Missourians, already bordered on the east by the free state of Illinois and on the north by the free state of Iowa, especially thought it important to secure Kansas for slavery. Thousands of rough frontiersmen, egged on by Missouri senator David Rice Atchison, invaded Kansas. "There are eleven hundred coming over from Platte County to vote," Atchison reported, "and if that ain't

CHAPTER LOCATOR | How did the acquisition of land from Mexico contribute to sectional tensions?

enough we can send five thousand—enough to kill every God-damned abolitionist in the Territory." Not surprisingly, proslavery candidates swept the territorial elections in November 1854. When Kansas's first territorial legislature met, it enacted a raft of proslavery laws. Ever-pliant President Pierce endorsed the work of the fraudulently elected legislature. Free-soil Kansans did not. They elected their own legislature, which promptly banned both slaves and free blacks from the territory. Organized into two rival governments and armed to the teeth, Kansans verged on civil war.

Fighting broke out on the morning of May 21, 1856, when several hundred proslavery men raided the town of Lawrence, the center of free-state settlement. The "Sack of Lawrence," as free-soil forces called it, inflamed northern opinion. Elsewhere in Kansas, news of the events in Lawrence provoked **John Brown**, a free-soil settler, to announce that "it was better that a score of bad men should die than that one man who came here to make Kansas a Free State should be driven out" and to lead the posse that massacred five allegedly proslavery settlers along Pottawatomie Creek. After that, guerrilla war engulfed the territory.

Just as "Bleeding Kansas" gave the fledgling Republican Party fresh ammunition for its battle against the Slave Power, so too did an event that occurred in the national capital. In May 1856, Senator Charles Sumner of Massachusetts delivered a speech titled "The Crime against Kansas," which included a scalding personal attack on South Carolina senator Andrew P. Butler. Sumner described Butler as a "Don Quixote" who had taken as his mistress "the harlot, slavery."

Preston Brooks, a young South Carolina member of the House and a kinsman of Butler, felt compelled to defend the honor of both his relative and his state. On May 22, Brooks entered the Senate, where he found Sumner working at his desk. He beat Sumner over the head with his cane until Sumner lay bleeding and unconscious on the floor. Brooks resigned his seat in the House, only to be promptly reelected. In the North, the southern hero became an arch-villain. Like "Bleeding Kansas," "Bleeding Sumner" provided the Republican Party with a potent symbol of the South's "twisted and violent civilization."

The *Dred Scott* Decision

Political debate over slavery in the territories became so heated in part because the Constitution lacked precision on the issue. In 1857, in the case of *Dred Scott v. Sandford*, the Supreme Court announced its understanding of the meaning of the Constitution regarding slavery in the territories. The Court's decision demonstrated that it was not immune from the sectional and partisan passions that convulsed the land.

In 1833, an army doctor bought the slave *Dred Scott* in St. Louis, Missouri, and took him as his personal servant to Fort Armstrong, Illinois, and then to Fort

"Bleeding Kansas," 1850s

CHRONOLOGY

1856
– "Bleeding Kansas."
– Congressman Preston Brooks canes Senator Charles Sumner in the Senate chambers.
– Pottawatomie massacre.

1857
– In the *Dred Scott* decision, the U.S. Supreme Court rules the Missouri Compromise unconstitutional and declares that blacks are not U.S. citizens.

1858
– Abraham Lincoln and Stephen A. Douglas debate slavery during the Illinois Senate race.

John Brown

▶ Militant abolitionist who led the Pottawatomie massacre in "Bleeding Kansas" in 1856 and the October 16, 1859, raid on Harpers Ferry, Virginia. Brown hoped his raid would spark a general slave uprising, but his invasion failed, and he was captured. His subsequent execution made him a martyr and a hero to many in the North.

| What factors helped unravel the balance between slave and free states? | How did the party system change in the 1850s? | Why did northern fear of the "Slave Power" intensify in the 1850s? | What caused some southern states to secede after the election of 1860? | Conclusion: Why did political compromise fail? |

Dred Scott

This portrait of Dred Scott was painted in 1857, the year of the Supreme Court's decision. Although the Court rejected his suit, Scott gained his freedom in May 1857 when a white man purchased and freed Scott and his family. Collection of the New-York Historical Society.

***Dred Scott* decision**

▶ 1857 Supreme Court decision that ruled the Missouri Compromise of 1820 unconstitutional. The case centered on Dred Scott, a slave who claimed that his travels with his master into free states made him and his family free. Ruling against Scott, the Court denied the federal government the right to exclude slavery in the territories and declared that African Americans were not citizens. The decision infuriated many in the North and contributed to the growing strength of the Republican Party.

Snelling in Wisconsin Territory. Back in St. Louis in 1846, Scott, with the help of white friends, sued to prove that he and his family were legally entitled to their freedom. Scott argued that living in Illinois, a free state, and Wisconsin, a free territory, had made his family free, and that they remained free even after returning to Missouri, a slave state.

In 1857, the U.S. Supreme Court ruled seven to two against Scott. Chief Justice Roger B. Taney, who hated Republicans and detested racial equality, wrote the Court's majority opinion. First, the Court ruled in the *Dred Scott* decision that Scott could not legally claim violation of his constitutional rights because he was not a citizen of the United States. When the Constitution was written, Taney said, blacks "were regarded as beings of an inferior order . . . so far inferior, that they had no rights which the white man was bound to respect." Second, the laws of Dred Scott's home state, Missouri, determined his status, and thus his travels in free areas did not make him free. Third, Congress's power to make "all needful rules and regulations" for the territories did not include the right to prohibit slavery. The Court explicitly declared the Missouri Compromise unconstitutional, even though it had already been voided by the Kansas-Nebraska Act.

The Taney Court's extreme proslavery decision outraged Republicans. By denying the federal government the right to exclude slavery in the territories, it cut the legs out from under the Republican Party. Moreover, as the *New York Tribune* lamented, the decision cleared the way for "all our Territories . . . to be ripened into Slave States." Particularly frightening to African Americans in the North was the Court's declaration that free blacks were not citizens and had no rights.

In essence, the Court's decision validated an extreme statement of the South's territorial rights. John C. Calhoun's claim that Congress had no authority to exclude slavery became the law of the land. White Southerners cheered, but the *Dred Scott* decision actually strengthened the young Republican Party.

CHAPTER LOCATOR | How did the acquisition of land from Mexico contribute to sectional tensions?

Indeed, that "outrageous" decision, one Republican argued, was "the best thing that could have happened." It provided dramatic evidence of the Republicans' claim that a hostile Slave Power conspired against northern liberties.

Prairie Republican: Abraham Lincoln

The *Dred Scott* case provided Republican politicians with fresh challenges and fresh opportunities. **Abraham Lincoln** had long since put behind him his log-cabin beginnings in Kentucky and Indiana. Now living in Springfield, Illinois, Lincoln earned good money as a lawyer, but politics was his life. "His ambition was a little engine that knew no rest," observed his law partner William Herndon. Lincoln had served as a Whig in the Illinois state legislature and in the House of Representatives, but he had not held public office since 1849.

Convinced that slavery was a "great moral wrong" and an "unqualified evil to the negro, the white man, and the State," Lincoln condemned Douglas's Kansas-Nebraska Act of 1854 for giving slavery a new life, and in 1856 he joined the Republican Party. He accepted that the Constitution permitted slavery in those states where it existed, but he believed that Congress could contain its spread. In time, Lincoln believed, plantation slavery would wither and Southerners would end slavery themselves.

Lincoln held what were, for his times, moderate racial views. Although he denounced slavery and defended black humanity, he also viewed black equality as impractical and unachievable. "Negroes have natural rights . . . as other men have," he said, "although they cannot enjoy them here." Insurmountable white prejudice made it impossible to extend full citizenship to blacks in America, he believed. Freeing blacks and allowing them to remain in this country would lead to a race war. In Lincoln's mind, social stability and black progress required that slavery end and that blacks leave the country.

Lincoln envisioned the western territories as "places for poor people to go to, and better their conditions." But slavery's expansion threatened free men's basic right to succeed. The Kansas-Nebraska Act and the *Dred Scott* decision persuaded him that slaveholders were engaged in a dangerous conspiracy to nationalize slavery. The next step, Lincoln warned, would be "another Supreme Court decision, declaring that the Constitution of the United States does not permit a State to exclude slavery from its limits." Unless the citizens of Illinois woke up, he warned, the Supreme Court would make "Illinois a slave State."

In Lincoln's view, the nation could not "endure, permanently half slave and half free." Either opponents of slavery would arrest its spread and place it on the "course of ultimate extinction," or its advocates would see that it became legal in "*all* the States, *old* as well as *new*—*North* as well as *South*." Lincoln's convictions that slavery was wrong and that Congress must stop its spread formed the core of the Republican ideology. Lincoln so impressed his fellow Republicans in Illinois that in 1858 they chose him to challenge the nation's premier Democrat, who was seeking reelection to the U.S. Senate.

The Lincoln-Douglas Debates

When Stephen Douglas learned that the Republican Abraham Lincoln would be his opponent for the Senate, he observed: "He is the strong man of the party—full of wit, facts, dates—and the best stump speaker, with his droll ways and dry jokes, in

Abraham Lincoln

▶ Successful lawyer who served as a Whig politician in Illinois in the 1840s and rose to national prominence in the newly formed Republican Party. Lincoln denounced slavery and defended black humanity, but he also accepted that the Constitution permitted slavery in the states where it already existed. His election as U.S. president in 1860 caused seven states to secede from the Union by February 1861 and spurred the creation of the Confederate States of America.

What factors helped unravel the balance between slave and free states?

How did the party system change in the 1850s?

Why did northern fear of the "Slave Power" intensify in the 1850s?

What caused some southern states to secede after the election of 1860?

Conclusion: Why did political compromise fail?

383

the West. He is as honest as he is shrewd, and if I beat him my victory will be hardly won."

Not only did Douglas have to contend with a formidable foe, but he also carried the weight of a burden not of his own making. The previous year, the nation's economy had experienced a sharp downturn. As a Democrat, Douglas had to go before the voters as a member of the party whose policies stood accused of causing the panic of 1857.

Douglas's response to another crisis in 1857, however, helped shore up his standing in Illinois. Proslavery forces in Kansas met in the town of Lecompton, drafted a proslavery constitution, and applied for statehood. Everyone knew that free-soilers outnumbered proslavery settlers, but President Buchanan instructed Congress to admit Kansas as the sixteenth slave state. Senator Douglas broke with the Democratic administration and denounced the Lecompton constitution; Congress killed the Lecompton bill. (When Kansans reconsidered the Lecompton constitution in an honest election, they rejected it six to one. Kansas entered the Union in 1861 as a free state.) By denouncing the fraudulent proslavery constitution, Douglas declared his independence from the South and, he hoped, made himself acceptable at home.

A relative unknown and a decided underdog in the Illinois election, Lincoln challenged Douglas to debate him face-to-face. The two met seven times for what would become a legendary series of debates. Thousands stood straining to see and hear as the two candidates debated the crucial issues of the age—slavery and freedom.

Lincoln badgered Douglas with the question of whether he favored the spread of slavery. He tried to force Douglas into the damaging admission that the Supreme Court had repudiated Douglas's own territorial solution, popular sovereignty. At Freeport, Illinois, Douglas admitted that settlers could not now pass legislation barring slavery, but he argued that they could ban slavery just as effectively by not passing protective laws, such as those found in slave states. Southerners condemned Douglas's "Freeport Doctrine" and charged him with trying to steal the victory they had gained with the *Dred Scott* decision. Lincoln chastised his opponent for his "don't care" attitude about slavery, for "blowing out the moral lights around us."

Douglas worked the racial issue. He called Lincoln an abolitionist and an egalitarian enamored of "our colored brethren." Put on the defensive, Lincoln reaffirmed his faith in white rule: "I will say, then, that I am not, nor ever have been, in favor of bringing about in any way the social and political equality of the white and black race." But Lincoln was no negrophobe, and he tried to steer the debate back to what he considered the true issue: the morality and future of slavery. "Slavery is wrong," Lincoln repeated, because "a man has the right to the fruits of his own labor."

As Douglas predicted, the election was hard-fought and closely contested, with Douglas pulling out a narrow victory. But the **Lincoln-Douglas debates** thrust Lincoln, the prairie Republican, into the national spotlight.

Lincoln-Douglas debates
▶ Series of debates on the issue of slavery and freedom between Democrat Stephen Douglas and Republican Abraham Lincoln, held as part of the 1858 Illinois senatorial race. Douglas won the election, but the debates helped catapult Lincoln to national attention.

> **QUICK REVIEW**

Why did the *Dred Scott* decision strengthen northern suspicions of a "Slave Power" conspiracy?

CHAPTER LOCATOR | How did the acquisition of land from Mexico contribute to sectional tensions?

What caused some southern states to secede after the election of 1860?

Abraham Lincoln

Lincoln actively sought the Republican presidential nomination in 1860. While in New York City to give a political address, he had his photograph taken by Mathew Brady. "While I was there I was taken to one of the places where they get up such things," Lincoln explained, sounding more innocent than he was, "and I suppose they got my shadow, and can multiply copies indefinitely." The Lincoln Museum, Fort Wayne, Indiana, #0-17.

LINCOLN'S THESIS that the "slavocracy" conspired to make slavery a national institution now seems exaggerated. But from the northern perspective, the Kansas-Nebraska Act, the Brooks-Sumner affair, the *Dred Scott* decision, and the Lecompton constitution amounted to irrefutable evidence of the South's aggressiveness. White Southerners, of course, saw things differently. They were the ones who were under siege, they declared. Signs were everywhere that the North planned to use its numerical advantage to attack slavery, and not just in the territories. Republicans had made it clear that they were unwilling to accept the *Dred Scott* ruling as the last word on the issue of slavery expansion. And John Brown's attempt to incite a slave insurrection in Virginia in 1859 proved that Northerners would stop at nothing to achieve their aims.

Talk of leaving the Union had been heard for years, but until the final crisis, Southerners had used secession as a ploy to gain concessions within the Union, not to destroy it. Then the 1850s delivered powerful blows to Southerners'

What factors helped unravel the balance between slave and free states?

How did the party system change in the 1850s?

Why did northern fear of the "Slave Power" intensify in the 1850s?

What caused some southern states to secede after the election of 1860?

Conclusion: Why did political compromise fail?

CHRONOLOGY

1859
- John Brown raids Harpers Ferry, Virginia, in an attempt to incite a slave uprising.

1860
- Republican Abraham Lincoln is elected president.
- South Carolina secedes from Union.

1861
- Six other Lower South states secede.
- The Confederate States of America is formed.
- Lincoln takes office.

confidence that they could remain Americans and protect slavery. When the Republican Party won the White House in 1860, many Southerners concluded that they would have to leave.

John Brown's Raid and Its Aftermath

After his participation in the Pottawatomie Creek massacre, John Brown slipped out of Kansas and reemerged in the East. More than ever, he was a man on fire for abolition. He spent thirty months begging money to support his vague plan for military operations against slavery, raising enough money to gather a small band of antislavery warriors.

On the night of October 16, 1859, Brown took his war against slavery into the South. With only twenty-one men, including five African Americans, he invaded Harpers Ferry, Virginia, believing his attack would spark a general slave uprising. It did not. His band seized the town's armory and rifle works, but the invaders were immediately surrounded, first by local militia and then by Colonel Robert E. Lee, who commanded the U.S. troops in the area. When Brown refused to surrender, federal soldiers charged with bayonets. Seventeen men, two of whom were slaves, lost their lives. Although a few of Brown's raiders escaped, federal forces killed ten (including two of his sons) and captured seven, among them Brown.

For his attack on Harpers Ferry, John Brown stood trial for treason, murder, and incitement of slave insurrection. On December 2, 1859, Virginia executed Brown. In life, he was a ne'er-do-well, but he died with courage and dignity. He told his wife that he was "determined to make the utmost possible out of a defeat." He told the court: "If it is deemed necessary that I should forfeit my life for the furtherance of the ends of justice, and mingle my blood further with the blood of . . . millions in this slave country whose rights are disregarded by wicked, cruel, and unjust enactments, I say, let it be done."

After Brown's death, northern denunciation of Brown as a dangerous fanatic gave way to grudging respect. Some even celebrated his "splendid martyrdom." Abolitionist Lydia Maria Child likened Brown to Christ and declared that he made "the scaffold . . . as glorious as the Cross of Calvary." Some abolitionists explicitly endorsed Brown's resort to violence. Abolitionist William Lloyd Garrison, who usually professed pacifism, announced, "I am prepared to say 'success to every slave insurrection at the South and in every country.'"

Most Northerners did not advocate bloody rebellion, however. Still, when northern churches marked John Brown's execution with tolling bells, hymns, and prayer vigils, white Southerners contemplated what they had in common with Northerners. With the presidential election only months away, Georgia senator Robert Toombs announced solemnly that Southerners must "never permit this Federal government to pass into the traitorous hands of the black Republican party."

Republican Victory in 1860

At the Democratic convention in Charleston in April 1860, fire-eating Southerners denounced Stephen Douglas and demanded a platform that included federal protection of slavery in the territories. When the delegates, led by northern Democrats, approved a platform with popular sovereignty, representatives from the

CHAPTER LOCATOR | How did the acquisition of land from Mexico contribute to sectional tensions?

386 CHAPTER 14 THE HOUSE DIVIDED, 1846–1861

John Brown Going to His Hanging, by Horace Pippin, 1942

The grandparents of Horace Pippin, a Pennsylvania artist, were slaves. His grandmother witnessed the hanging of John Brown, and this painting recalls the scene she so often described to him. Pennsylvania Academy of Fine Arts, Philadelphia. John Lambert Fund.

▶ FOR MORE HELP ANALYZING THIS IMAGE, see the visual activity for this chapter in the Online Study Guide at bedfordstmartins.com/roarkunderstanding.

entire Lower South and Arkansas left the convention. The remaining Democrats adjourned to meet a few weeks later in Baltimore, where they nominated Douglas for president.

When southern Democrats met, they nominated Vice President John C. Breckinridge of Kentucky and approved a platform with a federal slave code. Southern moderates, however, refused to support Breckinridge. They formed the Constitutional Union Party to provide voters with a Unionist choice. Instead of adopting a platform and confronting the slavery question, the Constitutional Union Party merely approved a vague resolution pledging "to recognize no political principle other than *the Constitution . . . the Union . . . and the Enforcement of the Laws.*" For president, they picked former senator John Bell of Tennessee.

| What factors helped unravel the balance between slave and free states? | How did the party system change in the 1850s? | Why did northern fear of the "Slave Power" intensify in the 1850s? | What caused some southern states to secede after the election of 1860? | Conclusion: Why did political compromise fail? |

The Republicans smelled victory, but they estimated that they needed to carry nearly all the free states to win. To make their party more appealing, they expanded their platform beyond antislavery. They hoped that free homesteads, a protective tariff, a transcontinental railroad, and a guarantee of immigrant political rights would provide an economic and social agenda broad enough to unify the North. While reasserting their commitment to stop the spread of slavery, they also denounced John Brown's raid as "among the gravest of crimes" and confirmed the security of slavery in the South.

The foremost Republican, William H. Seward, was a poor match for this even-handed platform. He had made enemies with his radical statements, including the claims that there was a "higher law" than the Constitution (God's law) and that there was an "irrepressible conflict" between slavery and freedom. Lincoln, however, since bursting onto the national scene in 1858, had demonstrated his clear purpose, good judgment, and moderate opinions. That, and his residence in Illinois, a crucial state, made him attractive to the party. On the third ballot, the delegates at the nominating convention chose Lincoln. Defeated by Douglas in a state contest less than two years earlier, Lincoln now stood ready to take him on for the presidency.

The election of 1860 was like none other in American politics. It took place in the midst of the nation's severest crisis. Four major candidates crowded the presidential field. Rather than a four-cornered contest, however, the election broke into two contests, each with two candidates. In the North, Lincoln faced Douglas; in the South, Breckinridge confronted Bell.

On November 6, 1860, Lincoln swept all of the eighteen free states except New Jersey, which split its electoral votes between him and Douglas. Although Lincoln received only 39 percent of the popular vote, he won easily in the electoral college with 180 votes, 28 more than he needed for victory (**Map 14.5**). The reason Lincoln won was not because his opposition was splintered. Even if the votes of his three

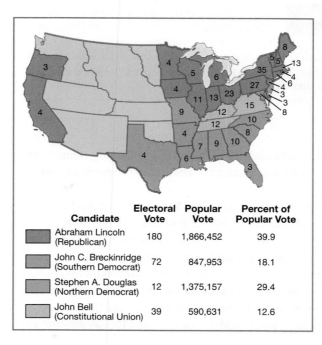

Candidate	Electoral Vote	Popular Vote	Percent of Popular Vote
Abraham Lincoln (Republican)	180	1,866,452	39.9
John C. Breckinridge (Southern Democrat)	72	847,953	18.1
Stephen A. Douglas (Northern Democrat)	12	1,375,157	29.4
John Bell (Constitutional Union)	39	590,631	12.6

MAP 14.5 ■ The Election of 1860

CHAPTER LOCATOR | How did the acquisition of land from Mexico contribute to sectional tensions?

opponents had been combined, Lincoln still would have won. He won because his votes were concentrated in the free states, which contained a majority of electoral votes. Ominously, however, Breckinridge, running on a southern-rights platform, won the entire Lower South, plus Delaware, Maryland, and North Carolina.

Secession Winter

Anxious Southerners immediately began debating their next step. Although Breckinridge had carried the South, a vote for "southern rights" was not necessarily a vote for secession. Besides, slightly more than half of the Southerners who had voted had cast ballots for Douglas and Bell, two stout defenders of the Union.

Southern Unionists tried to calm the fears that Lincoln's election triggered. Former congressman Alexander Stephens of Georgia asked what Lincoln had done to justify something as extreme as secession. Had he not promised to respect slavery where it existed? Moreover, secession might lead to war, which would loosen the hinges of southern society and possibly even open the door to slave insurrection. "Revolutions are much easier started than controlled," he warned. "I consider slavery much more secure in the Union than out of it."

Secessionists emphasized the dangers of delay. "Mr. Lincoln and his party assert that this doctrine of equality applies to the negro," former Georgia governor Howell Cobb declared, "and necessarily there can exist no such thing as property in our equals." Lincoln's election without a single electoral vote from the South meant that Southerners were no longer able to defend themselves within the Union, Cobb argued. Why wait, he asked, for the abolitionists to attack? As for war, there would be none. The Union was a voluntary compact, and Lincoln would not coerce patriotism. If Northerners did resist with force, secessionists argued, one southern woodsman could whip five of Lincoln's greasy mechanics.

For all their differences, southern whites agreed that they had to defend slavery. John Smith Preston of South Carolina spoke for the overwhelming majority when he declared, "The South cannot exist without slavery." They disagreed about whether the mere presence of a Republican in the White House made it necessary to exercise what they considered a legitimate right to secede.

The debate about what to do was briefest in South Carolina; it seceded from the Union on December 20, 1860. By February 1861, the six other Lower South states had followed suit. In February, representatives from South Carolina, Georgia, Florida, Alabama, Mississippi, Louisiana, and Texas met in Montgomery, Alabama, where they celebrated the birth of the Confederate States of America. **Jefferson Davis** became president, and Alexander Stephens, who had spoken so eloquently about the dangers of revolution, became vice president.

Lincoln's election had split the Union. Now secession split the South. Seven slave states seceded during the winter, but the eight slave states of the Upper South rejected secession, at least for the moment. The Upper South had a smaller stake in slavery. Barely half as many white families in the Upper South held slaves (21 percent) as in the Lower South (37 percent). Slaves represented twice as large a percentage of the population in the Lower South (48 percent) as in the Upper South (23 percent). Consequently, whites in the Upper South had fewer fears that Republican ascendancy meant economic catastrophe, social chaos, and racial war.

Jefferson Davis
▶ Member of the U.S. Senate from Mississippi who became president of the Confederate States of America in 1861.

| What factors helped unravel the balance between slave and free states? | How did the party system change in the 1850s? | Why did northern fear of the "Slave Power" intensify in the 1850s? | What caused some southern states to secede after the election of 1860? | Conclusion: Why did political compromise fail? |

Secession of the Lower South, December 1860–February 1861

Lincoln would need to do more than just be elected to provoke them into secession.

The nation had to wait until March 4, 1861, when Lincoln took office, to see what he would do. After his election, Lincoln chose to stay in Springfield and to say nothing. "Lame-duck" president James Buchanan sat in Washington and did nothing. In Congress, efforts at cobbling together a peace-saving compromise came to nothing.

At his swearing-in ceremony, Lincoln began his inaugural address with reassurances to the South. He had "no lawful right" to interfere with slavery where it existed, he declared again, adding for emphasis that he had "no inclination to do so." Conciliatory about slavery, Lincoln proved inflexible about the Union. The Union, he declared, was "perpetual." Secession was "anarchy" and "legally void." The Constitution required him to execute the law "in all the States."

The decision for civil war or peace rested in the South's hands, Lincoln said. "You can have no conflict, without being yourselves the aggressors. *You* have no oath registered in Heaven to destroy the government, while *I* shall have the most solemn one to 'preserve, protect, and defend' it."

> **QUICK REVIEW**

Why did some southern states secede immediately after Lincoln's election?

CHAPTER LOCATOR | How did the acquisition of land from Mexico contribute to sectional tensions?

Library of Congress.

THE EAGLE'S NEST.
"THE UNION IT MUST AND SHALL BE PRESERVED"

Conclusion: Why did political compromise fail?

AS THEIR ECONOMIES, societies, and cultures diverged in the nineteenth century, Northerners and Southerners expressed different concepts of the American promise and the place of slavery within it. Their differences crystallized into political form in 1846 when David Wilmot proposed banning slavery in any territory won in the Mexican-American War. Discovery of gold and other precious metals in the West added urgency to the controversy over slavery in the territories. Although Congress addressed the issue with the Compromise of 1850, the consequences of the Fugitive Slave Act and the publication of *Uncle Tom's Cabin* hardened northern sentiments against slavery and confirmed southern suspicions of northern ill will. The bloody violence that erupted in Kansas in 1856 and the incendiary *Dred Scott* decision in 1857 further eroded hope for a solution to this momentous question.

During the extended crisis of the Union that stretched from 1846 to 1861, the slavery question was interwoven with national politics. The traditional Whig and Democratic parties struggled to hold together, while new parties, most notably the Republican Party, emerged. Politicians fixed their attention on the expansion of slavery, but from the beginning, the nation recognized that the controversy had less to do with slavery in the territories than with the future of slavery in America.

For more than seventy years, statesmen had found compromises that accepted slavery and preserved the Union. But as each section grew increasingly committed to its labor system and the promise it offered, Americans discovered that accommodation had limits. In 1859, John Brown's militant antislavery pushed white Southerners to the edge. In 1860, Lincoln's election convinced whites in the Lower South that slavery and the society they had built on it were at risk in the Union, and they seceded. It remained to be seen whether disunion would mean war.

135,000 SETS. 270,000 VOLUMES SOLD.
UNCLE TOM'S CABIN
FOR SALE HERE.
The Greatest Book of the Age.

SO NOW YOU KNOW

Uncle Tom's Cabin was America's first million-selling book, but it was by no means the only antislavery book. Other writers, such as Solomon Northup and Frederick Douglass, both of whom had firsthand knowledge of being enslaved, also made impassioned cases against slavery. The sectional tensions that the debate over slavery created threatened civil war.

What factors helped unravel the balance between slave and free states?

How did the party system change in the 1850s?

Why did northern fear of the "Slave Power" intensify in the 1850s?

What caused some southern states to secede after the election of 1860?

Conclusion: Why did political compromise fail?

CHAPTER 14 STUDY GUIDE

Online Study Guide
bedfordstmartins.com/roarkunderstanding

STEP 1 GETTING STARTED

Below are basic terms from this period in American history. Can you identify each term below and explain why it matters? To do this exercise online or to download this chart, visit bedfordstmartins.com/roarkunderstanding.

TERM	WHO OR WHAT & WHEN	WHY IT MATTERS
Wilmot Proviso, p. 367		
popular sovereignty, p. 368		
Compromise of 1850, p. 370		
Fugitive Slave Act, p. 372		
Uncle Tom's Cabin, p. 372		
Kansas-Nebraska Act, p. 374		
Republican Party, p. 378		
John Brown, p. 381		
Dred Scott decision, p. 382		
Abraham Lincoln, p. 383		
Lincoln-Douglas debates, p. 384		
Jefferson Davis, p. 389		

STEP 2 MOVING BEYOND THE BASICS

The exercise below represents a more advanced understanding of the chapter material. Use the following chart to sketch the political landscape of the 1850s. First, describe the groups and regions where the Democratic, Whig, Republican, and American parties found their greatest support. Then describe each party's position on slavery, expansion, and immigration. When you are finished, see if you can make connections between each party's supporters and the positions the party took on important issues. How did slavery help transform the American political landscape? To do this exercise online or to download this chart, visit bedfordstmartins.com/roarkunderstanding.

Party	Who supported this party?	Position on slavery	Views on expansion	Perspectives on immigration
Democratic Party				
Whig Party				
Republican Party				
American (Know-Nothing) Party				

Now that you've reviewed various parts of the chapter, take a step back and try to see the big picture by answering these questions. Remember to use specific examples from the chapter in your answers. To do this exercise online, visit bedfordstmartins.com/roarkunderstanding.

EXPANSION AND SECTIONALISM

► Why was the Wilmot Proviso so controversial? What did the response to the Proviso reveal about the diverging visions of America in the North and in the South?

► Why was the expansion of slavery not only a moral issue for abolitionists but also an economic concern to both Northerners and Southerners?

POLITICAL INSTABILITY

► Why did the Compromise of 1850 ultimately fail?

► What were the consequences of the events of the 1840s and 1850s for America's political parties? How did the party system change under the pressure of the sectional divide?

THE ROAD TO SECESSION

► If most Northerners and Southerners wanted to avoid war, why did war come?

► Why did so many Southerners see the election of Abraham Lincoln as a threat to their way of life? Why did more than half of the southern electorate vote for pro-Union candidates?

LOOKING BACKWARD, LOOKING AHEAD

► Why, in the early nineteenth century, was compromise on the issue of slavery possible? Why did so many reject compromise in the 1840s and 1850s?

► What consequences might Southerners have imagined would follow from secession? What might have led them to underestimate Lincoln's determination to fight for the Union?

IN YOUR OWN WORDS

Imagine that you must explain chapter 14 to someone who hasn't read it. What would be the most important points to include and why?

15
THE CRUCIBLE OF WAR

1861–1865

> This chapter traces the course of the Civil War. It explores the connections between events on the battlefield and political, social, and economic developments on the home fronts, explains how the war became a fight for black freedom, and examines why the North ultimately prevailed.

> How did the war begin?

> Why did each side expect to win?

> How did each side fare in the early years of the war?

> Why did the war for union become a fight for black freedom?

> What problems did the Confederacy face at home?

> How did the war affect the economy and politics of the North?

> How did the Union finally win the war?

> Conclusion: In what ways was the Civil War a "Second American Revolution"?

DID YOU KNOW?

During the Civil War, 71 percent of northern African American men of military age served in the Union army.

"Price Raid," October 1864. This 1865 illustration by Samuel J. Reader shows a regiment of Kansas Militia captured by Confederate soldiers in Texas. Reader was one of the captives.

How did the war begin?

Fort Sumter Bombardment Located on an artificial island inside the entrance to Charleston harbor, Fort Sumter had walls eight to twelve feet thick. The fort was so undermanned that when Confederate shells began raining down on April 12, U.S. troops could answer back with only a few of the fort's forty-eight guns. Minnesota Historical Society.

ABRAHAM LINCOLN faced the worst crisis in the history of the nation: disunion. He revealed his strategy on March 4, 1861, in his inaugural address, which was firm yet conciliatory. First, he tried to avoid any act that would push the skittish Upper South (North Carolina, Virginia, Maryland, Delaware, Kentucky, Tennessee, Missouri, and Arkansas) out of the Union. Second, he sought to reassure the seceding Lower South (South Carolina, Georgia, Florida, Alabama, Mississippi, Louisiana, and Texas) that the Republicans would not abolish slavery. Lincoln believed that Unionists there would assert themselves and overturn the secession decision.

His counterpart, Jefferson Davis, fully intended to establish the Confederate States of America as an independent republic. Without additional states, however, the Confederacy would have little hope of long-term survival. Davis watched for opportunities to add new stars to the Confederate flag.

Neither man sought war; both wanted to achieve their objectives peacefully. As Lincoln later observed, "Both parties deprecated war, but one of them would

CHAPTER LOCATOR | How did the war begin? | Why did each side expect to win? | How did each side fare in the early years of the war?

396 CHAPTER 15 THE CRUCIBLE OF WAR, 1861–1865

make war rather than let the nation survive, and the other would *accept* war rather than let it perish. And the war came."

Attack on Fort Sumter

Major Robert Anderson and some eighty U.S. soldiers occupied **Fort Sumter**, which was perched on a tiny island at the entrance to Charleston harbor. By the end of March 1861, Anderson and his men were running dangerously short of food. In the first week of April, Lincoln authorized a peaceful expedition to bring supplies, but not military reinforcements, to the fort. The president understood that he risked war, but his plan honored his inaugural promises to defend federal property and to avoid using military force unless first attacked. Masterfully, Lincoln had shifted the fateful decision of war or peace to Jefferson Davis.

On April 9, Davis and his cabinet met to consider the situation in Charleston harbor. After sharp debate, Davis sent word to Confederate troops in Charleston to take the fort before the relief expedition arrived. Thirty-three hours of bombardment on April 12 and 13 reduced the fort to rubble. On April 14, Major Anderson offered his surrender. The Confederates had Fort Sumter, but they also had war.

On April 15, when Lincoln called for 75,000 militiamen to serve for ninety days to put down the rebellion, several times that number enlisted. Stephen A. Douglas, the recently defeated Democratic candidate for president, pledged his support. "There are only two sides to the question," he said. "Every man must be for the United States or against it. There can be no neutrals in this war, *only patriots—or traitors.*" But the people of the Upper South found themselves torn.

The Upper South Chooses Sides

In the Upper South, many who only months earlier had rejected secession now embraced the Confederacy. To vote against southern independence was one thing, to fight fellow Southerners another. Thousands felt betrayed, believing that Lincoln had promised to achieve a peaceful reunion by waiting patiently for Unionists to retake power in the seceding states. One man furiously denounced the conflict as a "politician's war," conceding that "this is no time now to discuss the causes, but it is the duty of all who regard Southern institutions of value to side with the South, make common cause with the Confederate States and sink or swim with them."

In the end, Virginia, Arkansas, Tennessee, and North Carolina joined the Confederacy (**Map 15.1**). But in the border states of Delaware, Maryland, Kentucky, and Missouri, Unionism triumphed. Only in Delaware, where slaves accounted for less than 2 percent of the population, was the victory easy. In Maryland, Lincoln suspended the writ of habeas corpus, essentially setting aside constitutional guarantees that protect citizens from arbitrary arrest and detention, and he ordered U.S. troops into Baltimore. Maryland's legislature rejected secession.

The struggle turned violent in the West. In Missouri, Unionists won a narrow victory, but southern-sympathizing guerrilla bands roamed the state for the duration of the war, terrorizing civilians and soldiers alike. In Kentucky, Unionists

CHRONOLOGY

1861
- **March**. Lincoln's inauguration.
- Fort Sumter begins to run low on supplies.
- **April**. Lincoln authorizes resupply of Fort Sumter.
- Attack on Fort Sumter.
- Lincoln calls up 75,000 militiamen to put down rebellion.
- **April–May**. Virginia, North Carolina, Arkansas, and Tennessee join the Confederacy.

Fort Sumter

▶ Union fort on an island at the entrance to Charleston harbor in South Carolina. When, in early April 1861, President Lincoln made clear his intention to resupply Fort Sumter, the Confederates responded by attacking and capturing the fort. The attack on Fort Sumter marked the beginning of the Civil War.

| Why did the war for union become a fight for black freedom? | What problems did the Confederacy face at home? | How did the war affect the economy and politics of the North? | How did the Union finally win the war? | Conclusion: In what ways was the Civil War a "Second American Revolution"? |

MAP 15.1 ■ Secession, 1860–1861
After Lincoln's election, the fifteen slave states debated what to do. Seven states quickly left the Union, four left after the firing on Fort Sumter, and four remained loyal to the Union.

Legend:
- Seceded before fall of Fort Sumter
- Seceded after fall of Fort Sumter
- Slave state loyal to Union
- Free state
- Territory
- 1 Order of secession

also narrowly defeated secession, but the prosouthern minority claimed otherwise.

Lincoln understood that the border states—particularly Kentucky—contained indispensable resources, population, and wealth and also controlled major rivers and railroads. "I think to lose Kentucky is nearly the same as to lose the whole game," Lincoln said. "Kentucky gone, we can not hold Missouri, nor, as I think, Maryland. These all against us, . . . we would as well consent to separation at once."

In the end, only eleven of the fifteen slave states joined the Confederate States of America. Moreover, the four seceding Upper South states contained significant numbers of people who felt little affection for the Confederacy. Dissatisfaction was so rife in the western counties of Virginia that in 1863, citizens there voted to create the separate state of West Virginia, loyal to the Union. Still, the acquisition of four new states greatly strengthened the Confederacy's drive for national independence.

> **QUICK REVIEW**

Why did the attack on Fort Sumter force the Upper South to choose sides?

CHAPTER LOCATOR | How did the war begin? | **Why did each side expect to win?** | How did each side fare in the early years of the war?

CHAPTER 15
398 THE CRUCIBLE OF WAR, 1861–1865

Why did each side expect to win?

Union Ordnance, Yorktown, Virginia

As the North successfully harnessed its enormous industrial capacity to meet the needs of the war, cannons, mortars, and shells poured out of its factories. A fraction of that abundance is seen here at Yorktown in 1862, ready for transportation to Union troops in the field. Library of Congress.

▶ FOR MORE HELP ANALYZING THIS IMAGE, see the visual activity for this chapter in the Online Study Guide at bedfordstmartins.com/roarkunderstanding.

ONLY SLAVEHOLDERS had a direct economic stake in preserving slavery, but most whites in the Confederacy defended the institution, the way of life built on it, and the Confederate nation. The degraded and subjugated status of blacks elevated the status of the poorest whites. One Southerner declared, "It is enough that one simply belongs to the superior and ruling race, to secure consideration and respect." Moreover, Yankee "aggression" was no longer a mere threat; it was real and at the South's door.

For Northerners, the South's failure to accept the democratic election of a president and its firing on the nation's flag challenged the rule of law, the authority of the Constitution, and the ability of the people to govern themselves. As an Indiana soldier told his wife, a "good government is the best thing on earth. Property is nothing without it, because it is not protected."

At the outset of the war, Yankees took heart from their superior numbers and resources, but the rebels believed they had advantages that nullified every northern strength. Both sides mobilized swiftly in 1861, and each devised what it believed would be a winning military and diplomatic strategy.

How They Expected to Win

The Union had overwhelming advantages in population, wealth, resources, and industrial capacity (**Figure 15.1**, page 400). Southerners knew they bucked the military odds, but hadn't the liberty-loving colonists in 1776 also done so? "Britain could not conquer three million," a Louisianan proclaimed, and "the world cannot conquer the South." The justice of their cause and the toughness of their people would overcome their material deficits.

The South's confidence also rested on its belief that northern prosperity depended on the South's cotton. Without cotton, New England textile mills would

Confederate Expectations
- "King Cotton" could help create alliances based on Europe's (especially Britain's) reliance on cotton imports.
- Defensive war strategy meant the South could win simply by outlasting the Union.
- President Jefferson Davis was an experienced military commander.

Union Expectations
- Superior navy could blockade trade between the Confederacy and Europe.
- Superior numbers meant a larger army.
- Greater industrial capacity meant a stronger army.
- President Abraham Lincoln appointed well-qualified men to key positions in government.

stand idle. Without planters purchasing northern manufactured goods, northern factories would fail. And without the foreign exchange earned by the overseas sales of cotton, the financial structure of the entire Yankee nation would collapse.

Cotton would also make Europe a powerful ally of the Confederacy, Southerners reasoned. Of the 900 million pounds of cotton Britain imported annually, more than 700 million pounds came from the South. If the supply was interrupted, sheer economic need would make Britain (and perhaps France) a Confederate ally. And because the British navy ruled the seas, the North would find Britain a formidable foe.

The Confederacy devised a military strategy to exploit its advantages and minimize its liabilities. It recognized that a Union victory required the North to defeat and subjugate the South, but a Confederate victory required only that the South stay at home, blunt invasions, avoid battles that risked annihilating its army, and outlast the North's will to fight. When an opportunity presented itself, the South would strike the invaders.

The Lincoln administration countered with a strategy designed to take advantage of its superior resources. Lincoln declared a naval blockade of the Confederacy to deny it the ability to sell cotton abroad, giving the South far fewer dollars to pay for war goods. Lincoln also ordered the Union army into Virginia, at the same time planning a march through the Mississippi valley that would cut the Confederacy in two.

Lincoln and Davis Mobilize

Mobilization required effective political leadership, and at first glance, the South appeared to have the advantage. Jefferson Davis brought to the Confederate presidency a distinguished political career, including experience in the U.S.

FIGURE 15.1 ■ Resources of the Union and Confederacy
The Union's enormous statistical advantages failed to convince Confederates that their cause was doomed.

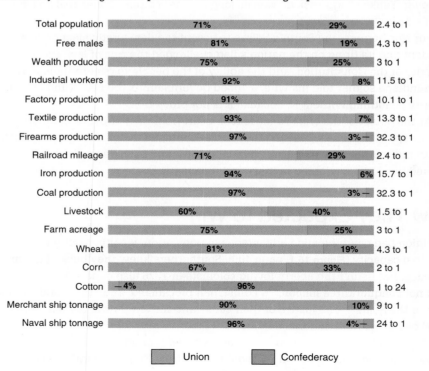

	Union	Confederacy	
Total population	71%	29%	2.4 to 1
Free males	81%	19%	4.3 to 1
Wealth produced	75%	25%	3 to 1
Industrial workers	92%	8%	11.5 to 1
Factory production	91%	9%	10.1 to 1
Textile production	93%	7%	13.3 to 1
Firearms production	97%	3%	32.3 to 1
Railroad mileage	71%	29%	2.4 to 1
Iron production	94%	6%	15.7 to 1
Coal production	97%	3%	32.3 to 1
Livestock	60%	40%	1.5 to 1
Farm acreage	75%	25%	3 to 1
Wheat	81%	19%	4.3 to 1
Corn	67%	33%	2 to 1
Cotton	4%	96%	1 to 24
Merchant ship tonnage	90%	10%	9 to 1
Naval ship tonnage	96%	4%	24 to 1

CHAPTER LOCATOR	How did the war begin?	Why did each side expect to win?	How did each side fare in the early years of the war?

Senate. He was also a West Point graduate, a combat veteran of the Mexican-American War, and a former secretary of war.

In contrast, Abraham Lincoln brought to the White House one term in the House of Representatives and almost no administrative experience. His sole brush with anything military was as a captain in the militia in the Black Hawk War, a brief struggle in Illinois in 1832 in which whites expelled the last Indians from the state.

Davis, however, proved to be less than he appeared. Although he worked hard, he had no gift for military strategy yet intervened often in military affairs. He was an even less able political leader. Quarrelsome and proud, he had an acid tongue that made enemies the Confederacy could ill afford.

With Lincoln, the North got far more than met the eye. He proved himself a master politician and a superb leader. When forming his cabinet, Lincoln appointed the ablest men, no matter that they were often his chief rivals and critics. He appointed Salmon P. Chase secretary of the treasury knowing that Chase had presidential ambitions. As secretary of state, he chose his chief opponent for the Republican nomination in 1860, William H. Seward. Despite his civilian background, Lincoln displayed an innate understanding of military strategy.

As Lincoln and Davis began gathering their armies, Confederates had to build almost everything from scratch, and Northerners had to channel their superior numbers and industrial resources to the war. On the eve of the war, the federal army numbered only 16,000 men. One-third of the officers followed the example of the Virginian Robert E. Lee, resigning their commissions and heading south. The U.S. Navy was in better shape. Forty-two ships were in service, and a large merchant marine would in time provide more ships and sailors for the Union cause.

The Confederacy made prodigious efforts to build new factories to supply its armies, but with only limited success. Even when factories managed to produce what the soldiers needed, southern railroads often could not deliver the goods. And each year, more railroads were captured, destroyed, or left in disrepair. Food production proved less of a problem, but food sometimes rotted before it reached the soldiers. The one bright spot was the Confederacy's Ordnance Bureau, headed by Josiah Gorgas, a near miracle worker when it came to manufacturing gunpowder, cannons, and rifles.

Recruiting and supplying huge armies required enormous new revenues. At first, the Union and the Confederacy sold war bonds, which essentially were loans from patriotic citizens. In addition, both sides turned to taxes. Eventually, both began printing paper money. Inflation soared, but the Confederacy suffered more because it financed a greater part of its wartime costs through the printing press. Prices in the Union rose by about 80 percent during the war, while inflation in the Confederacy topped 9,000 percent.

Within months of the bombardment of Fort Sumter, both sides found men to fight and ways to supply them. But the underlying strength of the northern economy gave the Union the decided advantage, and Northerners became itchy for action that would smash the rebellion. Horace Greeley's *New York Tribune* began to chant: "Forward to Richmond! Forward to Richmond!"

QUICK REVIEW <

Why did the South believe it could win the war despite its material disadvantages?

| Why did the war for union become a fight for black freedom? | What problems did the Confederacy face at home? | How did the war affect the economy and politics of the North? | How did the Union finally win the war? | Conclusion: In what ways was the Civil War a "Second American Revolution"? |

401

How did each side fare in the early years of the war?

The Battle of Savage's Station, by Robert Knox Sneden, 1862

Artist Robert Sneden captured an early Confederate assault in what became known as the Seven Days Battle. Over the next three years, Sneden produced hundreds of vivid drawings and eventually thousands of pages of remembrance, providing one of the most complete accounts of a Union soldier's Civil War experience. 1996, Lora Robbins Collection of Virginia Art, Virginia Historical Society.

▶ FOR MORE HELP ANALYZING THIS IMAGE, see the visual activity for this chapter in the Online Study Guide at bedfordstmartins.com/roarkunderstanding.

DURING THE FIRST YEAR AND A HALF of the war, armies fought major campaigns in both the East and the West. As Yankee and rebel armies pounded each other on land, the navies fought on the seas and on the rivers of the South. In Europe, Confederate and U.S. diplomats competed for advantage in the corridors of power. All the while, casualties on both sides mounted.

Stalemate in the Eastern Theater

In the summer of 1861, Lincoln ordered the Union army assembling outside Washington to attack the Confederates defending Manassas, a railroad junction in Virginia about thirty miles southwest of Washington. On July 21, the army forded Bull Run, a branch of the Potomac River, and engaged the southern forces (**Map 15.2**). But southern reinforcements blunted the Union attack and then counterattacked. What began as an orderly Union retreat turned into a panicky stampede.

The significance of the **battle of Bull Run** (or **Manassas**, as Southerners called the battle) lay in the lessons Northerners and Southerners drew from it. For Southerners, it confirmed the superiority of rebel fighting men and the inevitability of Confederate nationhood. While victory fed southern pride, defeat sobered Northerners. It was a major setback, admitted the *New York Tribune*, but "let us go to work, then, with a will." Within four days of the disaster, President Lincoln authorized the enlistment of 1 million men for three years.

battle of Bull Run (Manassas)

▶ The first major engagement of the Civil War. Union and Confederate troops met on July 21, 1861, at Manassas, Virginia, thirty miles southwest of Washington, D.C. The Confederate victory over a larger Union force convinced many in the South that they would win the war, at the same time as it demonstrated to Northerners that victory would not be quick or easy.

CHAPTER LOCATOR | How did the war begin? | Why did each side expect to win? | **How did each side fare in the early years of the war?**

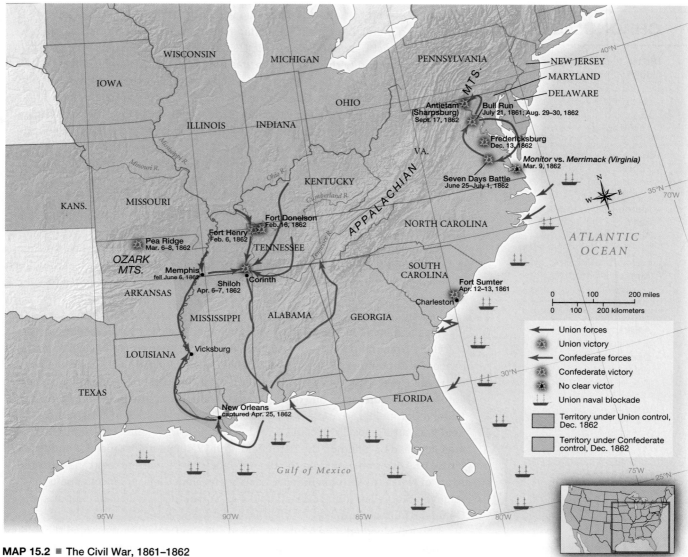

MAP 15.2 ■ The Civil War, 1861–1862
While most eyes were focused on the eastern theater, especially the ninety-mile stretch of land between Washington, D.C., and the Confederate capital of Richmond, Virginia, Union troops were winning strategic victories in the West.

Lincoln also appointed **George B. McClellan** commander of the newly named Army of the Potomac. A superb administrator and organizer, McClellan whipped his dispirited soldiers into shape, but he was reluctant to send them into battle. For all his energy, McClellan lacked decisiveness. Lincoln wanted a general who would advance, take risks, and fight, but McClellan went into winter quarters. "If General McClellan does not want to use the army I would like to *borrow* it," Lincoln declared in frustration.

Finally, in May 1862, McClellan launched his long-awaited offensive. He transported his highly polished army, now 130,000 strong, to the mouth of the James River and began slowly moving up the Yorktown peninsula toward Richmond. When he was within six miles of the Confederate capital, General Joseph Johnston hit him like a hammer. In the assault, Johnston was wounded

George B. McClellan
▶ General appointed to the command of the Army of the Potomac following the Union defeat at the battle of Bull Run in July 1861. McClellan was an able administrator and organizer, but he was indecisive and reluctant to take risks. Lincoln relieved him of his command twice. In 1864, McClellan ran against Lincoln for the presidency as a Democratic candidate.

| Why did the war for union become a fight for black freedom? | What problems did the Confederacy face at home? | How did the war affect the economy and politics of the North? | How did the Union finally win the war? | Conclusion: In what ways was the Civil War a "Second American Revolution"? |

CHRONOLOGY

1861
- **July**. Union forces are routed at Bull Run.
- George McClellan is appointed commander of the Army of the Potomac.

1862
- **February**. Grant captures Fort Henry and Fort Donelson.
- **March**. Union victory at battle of Pea Ridge.
- **April**. Battle of Shiloh in Tennessee ends Confederate bid to control Mississippi valley.
- **August**. Union forces are again defeated at second battle of Bull Run (Manassas).
- **September**. Battle of Antietam stops Lee's advance into Maryland.
- **December**. Confederate victory at battle of Fredericksburg

Peninsula Campaign, 1862

and was replaced by **Robert E. Lee**, who would become the South's most celebrated general. Lee named his command the Army of Northern Virginia.

The contrast between Lee and McClellan could hardly have been greater. McClellan brimmed with conceit; Lee was courteous and reserved. On the battlefield, McClellan grew timid, and Lee became audaciously, even recklessly, aggressive. And Lee had at his side military men of real talent: Thomas J. Jackson, nicknamed "Stonewall" for holding the line at Manassas, and James E. B. ("Jeb") Stuart, a twenty-nine-year-old cavalry commander who rode circles around Yankee troops.

Lee's assault initiated the Seven Days Battle (June 25–July 1) and began McClellan's retreat down the peninsula. By the time McClellan reached safety, 30,000 men from both sides had died or been wounded. Although Southerners suffered twice as many casualties as Northerners did, Lee had saved Richmond. Lincoln fired McClellan and replaced him with General John Pope.

In August, north of Richmond, at the second battle of Bull Run, Lee's smaller army battered Pope's forces and sent them scurrying back to Washington. Lincoln ordered Pope to Minnesota to pacify the Indians and restored McClellan to command.

Sensing that he had the enemy on the ropes, Lee pushed his army across the Potomac and invaded Maryland. A victory on northern soil would dislodge Maryland from the Union, Lee reasoned, and might even cause Lincoln to sue for peace. On September 17, 1862, McClellan's forces engaged Lee's army at Antietam Creek (see Map 15.2, page 403). With "solid shot . . . cracking skulls like eggshells," according to one observer, the armies went after each other. At Miller's Cornfield, the firing was so intense that "every stalk of corn in the . . . field was cut as closely as could have been done with a knife." By nightfall, 6,000 men lay dead or dying on the battlefield, and 17,000 more had been wounded. The **battle of Antietam** would be the bloodiest day of the war and sent the battered Army of Northern Virginia limping back home. Nonetheless, Lincoln again removed McClellan from command of the Army of the Potomac and appointed General Ambrose Burnside.

Though bloodied, Lee found an opportunity in December to punish the enemy at Fredericksburg, Virginia, where Burnside's 122,000 Union troops faced 78,500 Confederates dug in behind a stone wall on the heights above the Rappahannock River. Half a mile of open ground separated the armies. "A chicken could not live on that field when we open on it," a Confederate artillery officer predicted. Yet Burnside ordered a disastrous frontal assault. The battle of Fredericksburg was one of the Union's worst defeats. As 1862 ended, the North seemed no nearer to ending the rebellion than it had been when the war began.

Union Victories in the Western Theater

While most eyes focused on events in the East, the decisive early encounters of the war were taking place between the Appalachian Mountains and the Ozarks (see Map 15.2, page 403). Confederates wanted Missouri and Kentucky, states they claimed but did not control. Federals wanted to split Arkansas, Louisiana, and Texas from the Confederacy by taking control of the Mississippi River and to occupy Tennessee, one of the Confederacy's main producers of food, mules, and iron—all vital resources.

CHAPTER LOCATOR	How did the war begin?	Why did each side expect to win?	How did each side fare in the early years of the war?

Before Union forces could march on Tennessee, they needed to secure Missouri to the west. Union troops swept across Missouri to the border of Arkansas, where in March 1862 they encountered a 16,000-man Confederate army, which included three regiments of Indians from the Five Civilized Tribes in Indian Territory. The Union victory at the battle of Pea Ridge left Missouri free of Confederate troops, but guerrilla bands led by the notorious William Clarke Quantrill and "Bloody Bill" Anderson burned, tortured, scalped, and murdered Union civilians and soldiers until the final year of the war.

Even farther west, Confederate armies sought to fulfill Jefferson Davis's vision of a slaveholding empire stretching all the way to the Pacific. Both sides recognized the immense value of the gold and silver mines of California, Nevada, and Colorado. A quick strike by Texas troops took Santa Fe, New Mexico, in the winter of 1861–62. Then in March 1862, a band of Colorado miners ambushed and crushed southern forces at Glorieta Pass, outside Santa Fe, effectively ending the Confederate campaign in the far West.

The principal western battles took place in Tennessee, where General **Ulysses S. Grant** emerged as the key northern commander. "The art of war is simple," Grant said. "Find out where your enemy is, get at him as soon as you can and strike him as hard as you can, and keep moving on." Grant's philosophy of war as attrition would take a huge toll in human life, but it played to the North's superiority in manpower.

In February 1862, operating in tandem with U.S. Navy gunboats, Grant captured Fort Henry on the Tennessee River and Fort Donelson on the Cumberland (see Map 15.2, page 403). Defeat forced the Confederates to withdraw from all of Kentucky and most of Tennessee, but Grant followed.

On April 6, Confederate general Albert Sidney Johnston's army surprised him at Shiloh Church in Tennessee. Grant's troops were badly mauled the first day, but Grant remained cool and brought up reinforcements throughout the night.

Battle of Glorieta Pass, 1862

Robert E. Lee

▶ Commander of the Army of Northern Virginia. Lee was the South's most renowned general, and his skill played a key role in the Confederacy's successes against the much larger Union army.

battle of Antietam

▶ Battle fought in Maryland on September 17, 1862, between Union forces led by George McClellan and Confederate troops under the command of Robert E. Lee. The battle, a Union victory that left 6,000 dead and 17,000 wounded, was the bloodiest day of the war.

Ulysses S. Grant

▶ General in chief of all Union armies from March 1864 until the end of the war. Grant was a veteran of the Mexican-American War and made his name in the western theater in the early years of the Civil War. His strategy of waging a relentless war of attrition resulted in high casualties on both sides, but also in Union victory.

Major Battles of the Civil War, 1861–1862

April 12–13, 1861	Attack on Fort Sumter
July 21, 1861	First battle of Bull Run (Manassas)
February 6, 1862	Battle of Fort Henry
February 16, 1862	Battle of Fort Donelson
March 6–8, 1862	Battle of Pea Ridge
March 9, 1862	Battle of the *Merrimack* (the *Virginia*) and the *Monitor*
March 26, 1862	Battle of Glorieta Pass
April 6–7, 1862	Battle of Shiloh
May–July 1862	McClellan's peninsula campaign
June 6, 1862	Fall of Memphis
June 25–July 1, 1862	Seven Days Battle
August 29–30, 1862	Second battle of Bull Run (Manassas)
September 17, 1862	Battle of Antietam
December 13, 1862	Battle of Fredericksburg

Why did the war for union become a fight for black freedom?	What problems did the Confederacy face at home?	How did the war affect the economy and politics of the North?	How did the Union finally win the war?	Conclusion: In what ways was the Civil War a "Second American Revolution"?

The next morning, the Union army counterattacked, driving the Confederates before it. The battle of Shiloh was terribly costly to both sides; there were 20,000 casualties, among them General Johnston. Grant later said that after Shiloh, he "gave up all idea of saving the Union except by complete conquest."

Although no one knew it at the time, Shiloh ruined the Confederacy's bid to control the theater of operations in the West. The Yankees quickly captured the strategic town of Corinth, Mississippi; the river city of Memphis; and the South's largest city, New Orleans. By the end of 1862, the far West and most—but not all—of the Mississippi valley lay in Union hands. At the same time, the outcome of the struggle in another theater of war was also becoming clearer.

The Atlantic Theater

When the war began, the U.S. Navy's blockade fleet was much too small for the task and was thus ineffective. But as the Union built more ships and the size of the fleet increased, the Union navy dramatically improved its score. Despite its best efforts, the Confederacy never found a way to break the Union blockade. Each month, the Union fleet tightened its noose. By 1865, the blockaders were intercepting about half of the southern ships attempting to break through. The Confederacy was sealed off, with devastating results.

War at Sea

Unable to match the growth of the U.S. fleet, the Confederates experiment with ironclad warships.
The wooden Confederate warship *Merrimack* is refitted with armor plate and rechristened *Virginia*.
March 8, 1862: The *Virginia* sinks two wooden federal ships, killing at least 240 Union sailors.
March 9, 1862: The battle between the *Virginia* and the federal ironclad *Monitor* ends in a draw.

International Diplomacy

What the Confederates could not achieve on the seas, they sought to achieve through international diplomacy. The Confederates based their hope for European support on King Cotton. In theory, cotton-starved European nations would have no choice but to break the Union blockade and recognize the Confederacy. Southern hopes were not unreasonable, for at the height of the "cotton famine" in 1862, when 2 million British workers were unemployed, Britain tilted toward recognition. Along with several other European nations, Britain granted the Confederacy "belligerent" status, which enabled it to buy goods and build ships in European ports. But no country challenged the blockade or recognized the Confederate States of America as a nation.

King Cotton diplomacy failed for several reasons. A bumper cotton crop in 1860 meant that British textile manufacturers had plenty of cotton throughout 1861. In 1862, when a cotton shortage did occur, European manufacturers found new sources in India, Egypt, and elsewhere. (See "Global Comparison.")

King Cotton diplomacy
▶ Confederate diplomatic strategy centered on starving Britain and France of cotton and forcing them to side with the Confederacy. A bumper cotton crop in 1860, the emergence of new sources of cotton outside the South, and the issuing of the Emancipation Proclamation all contributed to the failure of King Cotton diplomacy.

CHAPTER LOCATOR | How did the war begin? | Why did each side expect to win? | How did each side fare in the early years of the war?

CHAPTER 15
406 THE CRUCIBLE OF WAR, 1861–1865

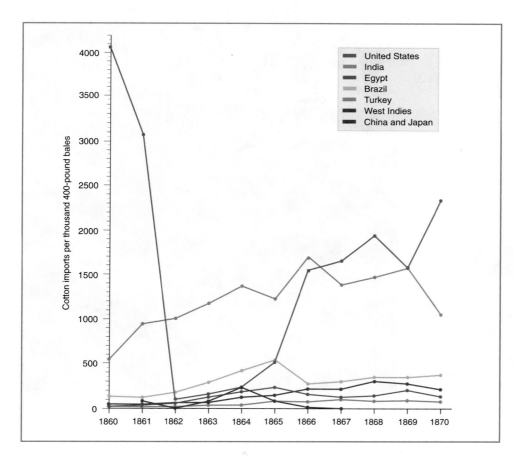

European Cotton Imports, 1860–1870

In 1860, the South enjoyed a near monopoly in supplying cotton to Europe's textile mills, but the Civil War almost entirely halted its exports. Figures for Europe's importation of cotton for 1861 to 1865 reveal one of the reasons the Confederacy's King Cotton diplomacy failed: Europeans found other sources of cotton. Which countries were most important in filling the void? When the war ended in 1865, cotton production resumed in the South, and exports to Europe again soared. Did the South regain its near monopoly? How would you characterize the United States' competitive position five years after the war?

In addition, the development of a brisk trade between the Union and Britain—British war materiel for American grain and flour—helped offset the decline in textiles and encouraged Britain to remain neutral.

Europe's temptation to intervene disappeared for good in 1862. Union military successes in the West made Britain and France think twice about linking their fates to the struggling Confederacy. Moreover, in September 1862, Lincoln announced a new policy that made an alliance with the Confederacy an alliance with slavery—a commitment the French and British, who had outlawed slavery in their empires and looked forward to its eradication worldwide, were not willing to make. After 1862, the South's cause was linked irrevocably with slavery and reaction, and the Union's cause was linked with freedom and democracy.

QUICK REVIEW

What successes and failures did the Union and the Confederacy experience in 1861 and 1862?

Why did the war for union become a fight for black freedom?	What problems did the Confederacy face at home?	How did the war affect the economy and politics of the North?	How did the Union finally win the war?	Conclusion: In what ways was the Civil War a "Second American Revolution"?

Why did the war for union become a fight for black freedom?

African Americans served as sailors in the federal military long before they were permitted to become soldiers. Blacks initially served only as coal heavers, cooks, and stewards, but within a year, some black sailors joined their ships' gun crews. National Archives.

FOR A YEAR AND A HALF, Lincoln insisted that the North fought strictly to save the Union and not to abolish slavery. Despite Lincoln's repeated pronouncements, however, the war for union became a war for African American freedom. Each month the conflict dragged on, it became clearer that the Confederate war machine depended heavily on slavery. Rebel armies used slaves to build fortifications, haul materiel, tend horses, and perform camp chores. On the home front, slaves labored in ironworks and shipyards, and they grew the food that fed both soldiers and civilians. Union military commanders and politicians alike gradually realized that to defeat the Confederacy, the North would have to destroy slavery.

From Slaves to Contraband

Lincoln detested human bondage, but as president he felt compelled to act prudently in the interests of the Union. He doubted his right under the Constitution to tamper with the "domestic institutions" of any state, even states in rebellion. An astute politician, Lincoln also worked within the tight limits of public opinion. The issue of black freedom was particularly explosive in the loyal border states, where slaveholders threatened to jump into the arms of the Confederacy at even the hint of emancipation.

Black freedom also raised alarms in the free states. The Democratic Party gave notice that emancipation would make the war strictly a Republican affair. Moreover, many white Northerners were not about to risk their lives to satisfy what they considered abolitionist "fanaticism." "We Won't Fight to Free the Nigger," one popular banner read. They feared that emancipation would propel "two or three million semi-savages" northward, where they would crowd into white neighborhoods, compete for white jobs, and mix with white "sons and daughters."

Yet proponents of emancipation pressed Lincoln as relentlessly as the anti-emancipation forces. The Republican-dominated Congress declined to leave slavery policy entirely in President Lincoln's hands. In August 1861, Congress approved the Confiscation Act, which allowed the seizure of any slave employed directly by the Confederate military. It also prohibited slavery in the territories and abolished slavery in Washington, D.C. Democrats and border-state representatives voted against even these mild measures.

Slaves, not politicians, became the most insistent force for emancipation. By escaping their masters by the tens of thousands and running away to Union lines, they put slavery on the North's wartime agenda. Runaways forced Northerners to answer a crucial question: Were the runaways now free, or were they still slaves who, according to the fugitive slave law, had to be returned to their masters? At first, Yankee military officers sent the fugitives back. But Union armies needed laborers, and some officers accepted the runaways and put them to work. At Fort Monroe, Virginia, General Benjamin F. Butler refused to turn them over to their owners, calling them contraband of war, meaning "confiscated property." Congress made Butler's practice national policy in March 1862 when it forbade the return of fugitive slaves to their masters. Slaves were still not legally free, but there was a tilt toward emancipation.

Lincoln's policy of noninterference with slavery gradually crumbled. To calm Northerners' racial fears, Lincoln offered colonization, the deportation of African Americans from the United States to Haiti, Panama, or elsewhere. Congress voted a small amount of money to underwrite colonization, but after one miserable experiment on a small island in the Caribbean, practical limitations and stiff black opposition sank further efforts.

While Lincoln was developing his own antislavery initiatives, he snuffed out actions that he believed would jeopardize northern unity. He was particularly alert to Union commanders who tried to dictate slavery policy from the field. In August 1861, when John C. Frémont, former Republican presidential nominee and now commander of federal troops in Missouri, freed the slaves belonging to Missouri rebels, Lincoln forced the general to revoke his edict. The following May, when General David Hunter freed the slaves in Georgia, South Carolina, and Florida, Lincoln countermanded his order. Increasingly, Lincoln found it impossible to control federal policy on slavery.

From Contraband to Free People

On August 22, 1862, Lincoln replied to an angry abolitionist who demanded that he attack slavery. "My paramount objective in this struggle *is* to save the Union," Lincoln said deliberately, "and is *not* either to save or destroy slavery. If I could save the Union without freeing *any* slave I would do it, and if I could save it by freeing *all* the slaves I would do it; and if I could save it by freeing some and leaving others alone I would also do that." Thus, Lincoln announced that he would emancipate every slave if doing so would preserve the Union.

CHRONOLOGY

1861
- **August**. First Confiscation Act.

1862
- **March**. Congress forbids the return of fugitive slaves to their masters.
- **July**. Second Confiscation Act.
- Militia Act.
- **September**. Preliminary Emancipation Proclamation.
- **November**. Democrats gain thirty-four congressional seats in midterm election.

1863
- **January**. Emancipation Proclamation becomes law.

| Why did the war for union become a fight for black freedom? | What problems did the Confederacy face at home? | How did the war affect the economy and politics of the North? | How did the Union finally win the war? | Conclusion: In what ways was the Civil War a "Second American Revolution"? |

By the summer of 1862, events were tumbling rapidly toward emancipation. On July 17, Congress adopted the second Confiscation Act. The first had confiscated slaves employed by the Confederate military; the second declared all slaves of rebel masters "forever free of their servitude." In theory, this breathtaking measure freed most Confederate slaves, for slaveholders formed the backbone of the rebellion. Congress had traveled far since the war began.

Lincoln had, too. He now saw emancipation as a "military necessity, absolutely essential to the preservation of the Union." On September 22, Lincoln issued his preliminary **Emancipation Proclamation** promising freedom to slaves in areas still in rebellion on January 1, 1863. The limitations of the proclamation— it exempted the loyal border states and the Union-occupied areas of the Confederacy—caused some to ridicule the act. The *Times* (London) observed cynically, "Where he has no power Mr. Lincoln will set the negroes free, where he retains power he will consider them as slaves." But Lincoln had no power to free slaves in loyal states, and invading Union armies would liberate slaves in the Confederacy as they advanced.

By presenting emancipation as a "military necessity," Lincoln hoped he had disarmed his conservative critics. Emancipation would deprive the Confederacy of valuable slave laborers, shorten the war, and thus save lives. Democrats, however, fumed that the "shrieking and howling abolitionist faction" had captured the White House. In the November 1862 elections, the Democrats gained thirty-four congressional seats. House Democrats quickly proposed a resolution branding emancipation "a high crime against the Constitution." The Republicans, who maintained narrow majorities in both houses of Congress, barely beat it back.

As promised, on New Year's Day 1863, Lincoln issued the final Emancipation Proclamation. In addition to freeing the slaves in the rebel states, the edict also committed the federal government to the fullest use of African Americans to defeat the Confederate enemy.

War of Black Liberation

Even before Lincoln proclaimed emancipation a Union war aim, African Americans in the North had volunteered to fight. But the War Department, doubtful of their abilities and fearful of white reaction to serving side by side with them, refused to make black men soldiers. Instead, the army employed black men as manual laborers; black women sometimes found employment as laundry workers and cooks.

As Union casualty lists lengthened, Northerners gradually and reluctantly turned to African Americans. With the Militia Act of July 1862, Congress authorized enrolling blacks in "any military or naval service for which they may be found competent." After the Emancipation Proclamation, whites were fighting and dying for black freedom, and few insisted that blacks remain out of harm's way behind the lines. Indeed, whites insisted that blacks share the danger, especially after March 1863, when Congress resorted to the draft to fill the Union army.

The military was far from color-blind, and black soldiers suffered discrimination and abuse. Still, when the war ended, 179,000 African American men had served in the Union army, and, in time, whites allowed blacks to put down their shovels and to shoulder rifles. At the battles of Port Hudson and Milliken's Bend on the Mississippi River and at Fort Wagner in Charleston harbor, black courage

Emancipation Proclamation

▶ Presidential proclamation issued on January 1, 1863, declaring all slaves in Confederate-controlled territory free. The limitations of the proclamation—it exempted the loyal border states and the Union-occupied areas of the Confederacy—caused some to ridicule the act. Nonetheless, the Emancipation Proclamation made the Civil War a war to free slaves.

CHAPTER LOCATOR | How did the war begin? | Why did each side expect to win? | How did each side fare in the early years of the war?

CHAPTER 15
410 THE CRUCIBLE OF WAR, 1861–1865

Company E, 4th U.S. Colored Infantry, Fort Lincoln, Virginia

The Lincoln administration was slow to accept black soldiers into the Union army, in part because of lingering doubts about their ability to fight. But Colonel Thomas W. Higginson, the white commander of the Union's First South Carolina Infantry, which was made up of former slaves, celebrated his men's courage: "No officer in this regiment now doubts that the key to the successful prosecution of this war lies in the unlimited employment of black troops. . . . Instead of leaving their homes and families to fight they are fighting for their homes and families." Before the war was over, ex-slaves and free blacks filled 145 Union regiments. Library of Congress.

under fire finally dispelled notions that African Americans could not fight. More than 38,000 black soldiers died in the Civil War, a mortality rate that was higher than that of white troops. Blacks played a crucial role in the triumph of the Union and the destruction of slavery in the South.

African Americans in Uniform

African American soldiers were:

- Segregated into black regiments.

- Paid substantially less than whites.

- Denied the opportunity to become commissioned officers.

- Punished by the army as if they were slaves.

- Often assigned to labor battalions rather than to combat units.

African Americans comprised 10 percent of all Union soldiers.

In the free states, 71 percent of black men ages eighteen to forty-five fought for the Union.

More than 130,000 black soldiers came from the slave states.

Approximately 100,000 ex-slaves fought for the Union.

QUICK REVIEW

Why did Lincoln feel compelled to issue the Emancipation Proclamation?

Why did the war for union become a fight for black freedom?	What problems did the Confederacy face at home?	How did the war affect the economy and politics of the North?	How did the Union finally win the war?	Conclusion: In what ways was the Civil War a "Second American Revolution"?

> What problems did the Confederacy face at home?

Southern Women Women such as these North Carolinians were expected to shift their energies from family to the southern cause. Most served by sewing uniforms, knitting socks, and rolling bandages at home. Some worked in newly founded hospitals nursing the sick and wounded. As the war ground on, southern women had their hands full trying to keep their families fed and safe. Museum of the Confederacy, Richmond, Virginia.

MONSTROUS LOSSES ON THE BATTLEFIELD nearly bled the Confederacy to death. White Southerners on the home front also suffered, even at the hands of their own government. Efforts by the Davis administration in Richmond to centralize power in order to fight the war effectively convinced some men and women that the Confederacy had betrayed them. Wartime economic changes hurt everyone, some more than others. By 1863, planters and yeomen who had stood together began to drift apart. Most disturbing of all, slaves became open participants in the destruction of slavery and the Confederacy.

Revolution from Above

Jefferson Davis faced the task of building an army and a navy from almost nothing, supplying them from inadequate factories, and paying for the war from a nonexistent treasury. Finding eager soldiers proved easiest. Hundreds of officers defected from the U.S. Army, and hundreds of thousands of eager young rebels volunteered to follow them.

The Confederacy's economy and finances proved tougher problems. Because of the Union blockade, the government had no choice but to build an industrial sector itself. The government also harnessed private companies, such as the huge

CHAPTER LOCATOR | How did the war begin? | Why did each side expect to win? | How did each side fare in the early years of the war?

CHAPTER 15
412 THE CRUCIBLE OF WAR, 1861–1865

Tredegar Iron Works in Richmond, to the war effort. Paying for the war became the most difficult task. A flood of paper money caused debilitating inflation. By 1863, people in Charleston paid ten times more for food than they had paid at the start of the war. The Confederacy manufactured much more than most people imagined possible, but it never produced all that the South needed.

Richmond's war-making effort brought unprecedented government intrusion into the private lives of Confederate citizens. In April 1862, the Confederate Congress passed the first conscription (draft) law in American history. All able-bodied white males between the ages of eighteen and thirty-five (later seventeen and fifty) were liable to serve in the rebel army. The government adopted a policy of impressment, which allowed officials to confiscate food, horses, and wagons from private citizens and to pay for them at below-market rates. After March 1863, the Confederacy legally impressed slaves, employing them as military laborers.

Richmond's centralizing efforts ran head-on into the South's traditional values of states' rights and unfettered individualism. The states lashed out at what Georgia governor Joseph E. Brown denounced as the "dangerous usurpation by Congress of the reserved right of the States." Richmond and the states struggled for control of money, supplies, and soldiers, with damaging consequences for the war effort.

Hardship Below

Hardships on the home front fell most heavily on the poor. The draft stripped yeoman farms of men, leaving the women and children to grow what they ate. Inflation and shortages afflicted the entire population, but the rich lost luxuries while the poor lost necessities. In the spring of 1863, bread riots broke out in a dozen cities and villages across the South. "Men cannot be expected to fight for the Government that permits their wives & children to starve," one Southerner observed. Although a few wealthy individuals shared their bounty and the Confederate and state governments made efforts at social welfare, every attempt fell short. When the war ended, one-third of the soldiers had already gone home. A Mississippi deserter explained, "We are poor men and are willing to defend our country but our families [come] first."

Yeomen perceived a profound inequality of sacrifice. The draft law permitted a man who had money to hire a substitute to take his place. Moreover, the "twenty-Negro law" exempted one white man on every plantation with twenty or more slaves. The government intended this law to provide protection for white women and to see that slaves tended the crops, but yeomen perceived it as rich men's evasion of military service. A Mississippian complained that stay-at-home planters sent their slaves into the fields to grow cotton while in plain view "poor soldiers' wives are plowing with *their own* hands to make a subsistence for them-selves and children—while their husbands are suffering, bleeding and dying for their country." In fact, most slaveholders went off to war, but the extreme suffering of common folk and the relative immunity of planters increased class friction.

The Richmond government hoped that the crucible of war would mold a region into a nation. Officials promoted a southern nationalism to "excite in our citizens an ardent and enduring attachment to our Government and its institutions." Clergymen assured their congregations that God had blessed slavery and

CHRONOLOGY

1862
- The South faces various war-related problems: inadequate manufacturing, inflation, shortages of food and other necessities, and government impressment of civilian goods.
- Confederate Congress passes the first conscription (draft) law in American history.

1863
- Riots break out in a dozen southern cities and villages because of the high cost of food.

Why did the war for union become a fight for black freedom?	**What problems did the Confederacy face at home?**	How did the war affect the economy and politics of the North?	How did the Union finally win the war?	Conclusion: In what ways was the Civil War a "Second American Revolution"?

the new nation. Patriotic songwriters, poets, authors, and artists extolled southern culture. Jefferson Davis asked citizens to observe national days of fasting and prayer. But these efforts failed to win over thousands of die-hard Unionists, and animosity between yeomen and planters increased rather than decreased. The war also threatened to rip the southern social fabric along its racial seam.

The Disintegration of Slavery

Slaves took advantage of the upheaval of war to reach for freedom. Some half a million of the South's 4 million slaves ran away to Union military lines. More than 100,000 runaways took up arms as federal soldiers and sailors and attacked slavery directly. Other men and women stayed in the slave quarter, where they staked their claim to more freedom.

War disrupted slavery in many ways. Almost immediately, it called the master away, leaving the mistress to assume responsibility for the plantation. But mistresses could not maintain traditional standards of slave discipline in wartime, and the balance of power shifted. Slaves got to the fields late, worked indifferently, and quit early. Some slaveholders responded violently; most saw no alternative but to strike bargains—offering gifts or part of the crop—to keep slaves at home and at work. Slaveholders had believed that they "knew" their slaves, but they learned that they did not. When the war began, a North Carolina woman praised her slaves as "diligent and respectful." When it ended, she said, "As to the idea of a *faithful servant, it is all a fiction.*"

> **QUICK REVIEW**

How did wartime hardship in the South contribute to class animosity?

CHAPTER LOCATOR | How did the war begin? | Why did each side expect to win? | How did each side fare in the early years of the war?

CHAPTER 15
414   THE CRUCIBLE OF WAR, 1861–1865

U.S. Sanitary Commission, Brandy Station, Virginia, 1863 The burden of caring for millions of Union soldiers was more than the government could shoulder. Private initiative in the form of the U.S. Sanitary Commission brought additional medical attention to the Union wounded and boosted the comfort and morale of soldiers in the camps. National Archives.

How did the war affect the economy and politics of the North?

ALTHOUGH THE NORTH was largely untouched by the fighting, Northerners could not avoid being touched by the war. Almost every family had a son, husband, father, or brother in uniform. Moreover, total war blurred the distinction between home front and battlefield. As in the South, men marched off to fight, but preserving the country was also women's work. For civilians as well as soldiers, for women as well as men, war was transforming.

The need to build and fuel the Union war machine boosted the economy. The Union sent nearly 2 million men into the military and still increased production in almost every area. But because the rewards and burdens of patriotism were distributed unevenly, the North experienced sharp, even violent, divisions. Workers confronted employers, whites confronted blacks, and Democrats confronted Republicans. Still, Northerners on the home front remained fervently attached to the Union.

The Government and the Economy

When the war began, the United States had no national banking system, no national currency, and no federal income tax. But the secession of eleven slave states cut the Democrats' strength in Congress in half, allowing the Republicans to put all of these things in place. By revolutionizing the country's banking, monetary, and tax structures, the Republicans generated enormous economic power.

Why did the war for union become a fight for black freedom? | What problems did the Confederacy face at home? | **How did the war affect the economy and politics of the North?** | How did the Union finally win the war? | Conclusion: In what ways was the Civil War a "Second American Revolution"?

1861–1865
- War boosts industrial and agricultural production.

1862
- **February**. Legal Tender Act.
- **May**. Homestead Act.
- Department of Agriculture is created.
- **July**. Pacific Railroad Act.
- **September.** Lincoln takes steps to suppress dissent.

1863
- **February**. National Banking Act.
- **March**. Congress authorizes draft.
- **July**. New York City draft riots.
- Land-Grant College Act (Morrill Act).

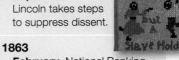

The Republican Economic Program

The Legal Tender Act (February 1862) creates a national currency.

The National Banking Act (February 1863) establishes a system of national banks.

Congress also enacts a series of sweeping tax laws, including the first income tax.

The Republicans' wartime legislation also aimed at integrating the West more thoroughly into the Union. In May 1862, Congress approved the Homestead Act, which offered 160 acres of public land to settlers who would live and labor on it. The Homestead Act bolstered western loyalty and in time resulted in more than a million new farms. The Pacific Railroad Act in July 1862 provided massive federal assistance for building a transcontinental railroad that ran from Omaha to San Francisco when completed in 1869. Congress further bound East and West by subsidizing the Pony Express mail service and a transcontinental telegraph.

Two additional initiatives had long-term economic consequences. Congress created the Department of Agriculture and passed the Land-Grant College Act (also known as the Morrill Act after its sponsor, Representative Justin Morrill of Vermont), which set aside public land to support universities that emphasized "agriculture and mechanical arts." The Lincoln administration immeasurably strengthened the North's effort to win the war, but its ideas also permanently changed the nation.

Women and Work on the Home Front

More than a million farm men were called to the military, placing additional burdens on farm women. "I met more women driving teams on the road and saw more at work in the fields than men," a visitor to Iowa reported in the fall of 1862. Rising production testified to their success in plowing, planting, and harvesting. Rapid mechanization assisted farm women in their new roles. Cyrus McCormick sold 165,000 of his reapers during the war years. The combination of high prices for farm products and increased production ensured that war brought prosperity to the rural North.

In cities, women stepped into jobs vacated by men, particularly in manufacturing, and also into essentially new occupations such as government secretaries and clerks. Women made up about one-quarter of the manufacturing workforce when the war began and one-third when it ended. As more and more women entered the workforce, employers cut wages. In 1864, New York seamstresses working fourteen-hour days earned only $1.54 a week. Urban workers resorted increasingly to strikes, but their protests rarely succeeded.

Most middle-class white women stayed home and contributed to the war effort in traditional ways. They sewed, wrapped bandages, and sold homemade goods at local fairs to raise money to aid the soldiers. Other women expressed their patriotism in an untraditional way, defying prejudices about female delicacy by volunteering to nurse the wounded. Many northern female volunteers worked through the U.S. Sanitary Commission, a civilian organization that bought and distributed clothing, food, and medicine and recruited doctors and nurses.

CHAPTER LOCATOR | How did the war begin? | Why did each side expect to win? | How did each side fare in the early years of the war?

CHAPTER 15
416   THE CRUCIBLE OF WAR, 1861–1865

Some volunteers went on to become paid military nurses. Dorothea Dix, well known for her efforts to reform insane asylums, was named superintendent of female nurses in April 1861. Eventually, some 3,000 women served under her. Most nurses worked in hospitals behind the battle lines, but some, like Clara Barton, who later founded the American Red Cross, worked in battlefield units. Women who served in the war went on to lead the postwar movement to establish training schools for female nurses.

Politics and Dissent

At first, the bustle of economic and military mobilization seemed to silence politics, but bipartisan unity did not last. Within a year, Democrats were labeling the Republican administration a "reign of terror," and Republicans were calling Democrats the party of "Dixie, Davis, and the Devil."

In September 1862, in an effort to stifle opposition to the war, Lincoln placed under military arrest any person who discouraged enlistments, resisted the draft, or engaged in "disloyal" practices. Before the war ended, his administration imprisoned nearly 14,000 individuals, most in the border states. The majority of the prisoners were not northern Democratic opponents but Confederates, blockade runners, and citizens of foreign countries, and most of those arrested gained quick release. Still, the administration's heavy-handed tactics did suppress free speech.

When the Republican-dominated Congress enacted the draft law in March 1863, Democrats had another grievance. The law required that all men between the ages of twenty and forty-five enroll and make themselves available for a lottery that would decide who went to war. It also allowed a draftee to hire a substitute or simply to pay a $300 fee and get out of his military obligation. As in the South, common folk could be heard chanting, "A rich man's war and a poor man's fight."

Linking the draft and emancipation, Democrats argued that Republicans employed an unconstitutional means (the draft) to achieve an unconstitutional end (emancipation). In the summer of 1863, antidraft, antiblack mobs went on rampages in northern cities. In July in New York City, Democratic Irish workingmen erupted in four days of rioting. The **New York City draft riots** killed at least 105 people, most of them black.

Racist mobs failed to subordinate African Americans, however. Free black leaders had lobbied aggressively for emancipation, and after Lincoln's proclamation, they pushed for equality in the North. They won a few small victories, but significant progress toward black equality would have to wait until the war ended.

New York City draft riots
► Four days of rioting in July 1863 triggered by efforts to enforce the military draft. The antidraft, antiblack mob was dominated by Democratic Irish workingmen. Some 105 people were killed, most of them black. The riots reflected growing northern discontent with the war.

QUICK REVIEW <

What were the most important changes that occurred in the North during the war?

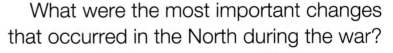

Why did the war for union become a fight for black freedom? | What problems did the Confederacy face at home? | **How did the war affect the economy and politics of the North?** | How did the Union finally win the war? | Conclusion: In what ways was the Civil War a "Second American Revolution"?

Ruins of Richmond

As the Confederate government evacuated Richmond during the evening of April 2, 1865, demolition squads set fire to everything that had military or industrial value. Huge explosions devastated the arsenal, the ruins of which are shown here. As one witness observed, "The old war-scarred city seemed to prefer annihilation to conquest." Library of Congress.

siege of Vicksburg

▶ A six-week siege by General Grant that came to an end on July 4, 1863, when the 30,000 Confederate troops holding the city surrendered. Victory at Vicksburg gave the Union control of the entire Mississippi River. Together with Gettysburg, Vicksburg marked a major turning point in the war.

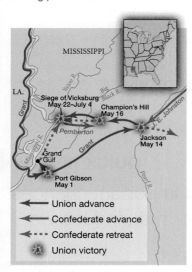

Union advance
Confederate advance
Confederate retreat
Union victory

Vicksburg Campaign, 1863

I**N THE EARLY MONTHS OF 1863,** the Union's prospects looked bleak, and the Confederate cause stood at high tide. Then, in July 1863, the tide began to turn. The military man most responsible for this shift was Ulysses S. Grant. Elevated to supreme command, Grant knit together a powerful war machine that integrated a sophisticated command structure, modern technology, and complex logistics and supply systems. Grant's plan was simple: Killing more of the enemy than he kills of you equaled "the complete overthrow of the rebellion."

The North ground out the victory battle by bloody battle. Still, Southerners were not deterred. The fighting escalated in the last two years of the war. As national elections approached in the fall of 1864, Lincoln expected a war-weary North to reject him. Instead, northern voters declared their willingness to continue the war in the defense of the ideals of union and freedom.

Vicksburg and Gettysburg

Vicksburg, Mississippi, situated on the eastern bank of the Mississippi River, stood between Union forces and complete control of the river. Union forces under Grant lay siege to the city in an effort to starve out the enemy. The **siege of Vicksburg** lasted six weeks, coming to an end on July 4, 1863, when nearly 30,000 rebels marched out of Vicksburg, stacked their arms, and surrendered unconditionally. A Yankee captain wrote home to his wife: "The backbone of the Rebellion is this day broken. The Confederacy is divided. . . . Vicksburg is ours. The Mississippi River is opened, and Gen. Grant is to be our next President."

CHAPTER LOCATOR | How did the war begin? | Why did each side expect to win? | How did each side fare in the early years of the war?

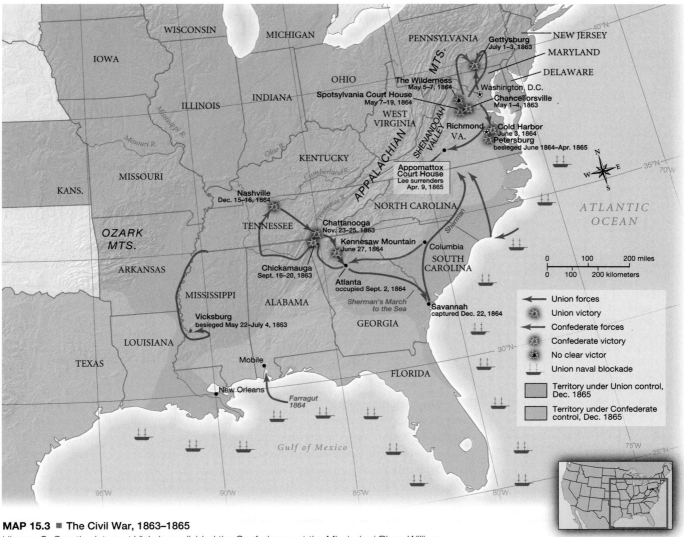

MAP 15.3 ■ The Civil War, 1863–1865
Ulysses S. Grant's victory at Vicksburg divided the Confederacy at the Mississippi River. William Tecumseh Sherman's march from Chattanooga to Savannah divided it again. In northern Virginia, Robert E. Lee fought fiercely, but Grant's larger, better-supplied armies prevailed.

> ▶ FOR MORE HELP ANALYZING THIS MAP, see the map activity for this chapter in the Online Study Guide at bedfordstmartins.com/roarkunderstanding.

On the same Fourth of July, word arrived that Union forces had defeated General Lee at Gettysburg, Pennsylvania (**Map 15.3**). Emboldened by his victory at Chancellorsville in May, Lee and his 75,000-man army had invaded Pennsylvania. On June 28, Union forces under General George G. Meade intercepted the Confederates at the small town of Gettysburg, where Union soldiers occupied the high ground. In three days of furious fighting from July 1 to July 3, the Confederates failed to dislodge the Yankees. The **battle of Gettysburg** cost Lee more than one-third of his army—28,000 casualties. On the night of July 4, 1863, he marched his battered army back to Virginia.

battle of Gettysburg
▶ Battle fought at Gettysburg, Pennsylvania (July 1–3, 1863), between Union forces under General Meade and Confederate forces under General Lee. The Union emerged victorious, and Lee lost more than one-third of his men. Together with Vicksburg, Gettysburg marked a major turning point in the war.

| Why did the war for union become a fight for black freedom? | What problems did the Confederacy face at home? | How did the war affect the economy and politics of the North? | **How did the Union finally win the war?** | Conclusion: In what ways was the Civil War a "Second American Revolution"? |

1863
- **July**. Vicksburg falls to Union forces.
- Lee is defeated at battle of Gettysburg.

1864
- **March**. Grant is appointed Union general in chief.
- **May–June**. Wilderness campaign.
- **September**. Atlanta falls to Sherman.
- **November**. Lincoln is reelected.
- **December**. Savannah falls to Sherman.

1865
- **April 2–3**. Fall of Petersburg and Richmond.
- **April 9**. Lee surrenders to Grant at Appomattox Court House.
- **April 15**. Lincoln dies from bullet wound; Andrew Johnson becomes president.

Major Battles of the Civil War, 1863–1865

May 1–4, 1863	Battle of Chancellorsville
July 1–3, 1863	Battle of Gettysburg
July 4, 1863	Fall of Vicksburg
September 16–20, 1863	Battle of Chickamauga
November 23–25, 1863	Battle of Chattanooga
May 5–7, 1864	Battle of the Wilderness
May 7–19, 1864	Battle of Spotsylvania Court House
June 3, 1864	Battle of Cold Harbor
June 27, 1864	Battle of Kennesaw Mountain
September 2, 1864	Fall of Atlanta
November–December 1864	Sheridan sacks Shenandoah Valley Sherman's March to the Sea
December 15–16, 1864	Battle of Nashville
December 22, 1864	Fall of Savannah
April 2–3, 1865	Fall of Petersburg and Richmond
April 9, 1865	Lee surrenders at Appomattox Court House

The twin disasters at Vicksburg and Gettysburg were the turning point of the war. It is hindsight, however, that permits us to see the pair of battles as decisive. At the time, the Confederacy still controlled the heartland of the South, and war-weariness threatened to erode the North's will to win before Union armies could destroy the Confederacy's ability to go on.

Grant Takes Command

In September 1863, Union general William Rosecrans placed his army in a dangerous situation in Chattanooga, Tennessee, where he had retreated after defeat at the battle of Chickamauga (see Map 15.3, page 419). Rebels surrounded the disorganized bluecoats and threatened to starve them into submission. Grant, now commander of Union forces between the Mississippi River and the Appalachians, arrived in Chattanooga in October. Within weeks, he opened an effective supply line, broke the siege, and routed the Confederate army. The victory at Chattanooga on November 25 opened the door to Georgia. In March 1864, Lincoln asked Grant to come east to become the general in chief of all Union armies.

In Washington, General Grant implemented his grand strategy for a war of attrition. He ordered a series of simultaneous assaults from Virginia all the way to Louisiana. Two actions proved particularly significant. In one, General William Tecumseh Sherman, Grant's successor in the West, plunged southeast toward Atlanta. In the other, Grant, commanding the Army of the Potomac, went head-to-head with Lee in Virginia for almost four straight weeks.

Twice as many Union soldiers as rebel soldiers died in four weeks of fighting in Virginia in May and June, but because Lee had only half as many troops as Grant,

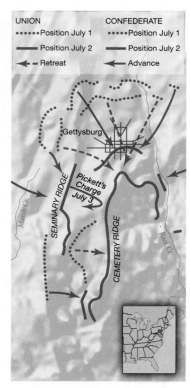

UNION
- •••••Position July 1
- —— Position July 2
- ◄— Retreat

CONFEDERATE
- •••••Position July 1
- —— Position July 2
- ◄— Advance

Gettysburg

SEMINARY RIDGE

Pickett's Charge July 3

CEMETERY RIDGE

Marsh Cr.

Rock Cr.

Battle of Gettysburg, July 1–3, 1863

CHAPTER LOCATOR | How did the war begin? | Why did each side expect to win? | How did each side fare in the early years of the war?

CHAPTER 15
420 THE CRUCIBLE OF WAR, 1861–1865

his losses were equivalent to Grant's. Grant knew that the South could not replace the losses. Moreover, the campaign carried Grant to the outskirts of Petersburg, just south of Richmond, where he abandoned the costly tactic of the frontal assault and began a siege that immobilized both armies and dragged on for nine months.

Grant's War of Attrition in Virginia (May–June 1864)

Battle of the Wilderness 18,000 Union dead, 11,000 Confederate dead.

Battle of Spotsylvania 18,000 Union dead, 10,000 Confederate dead.

Battle of Cold Harbor 13,000 Union dead, 5,000 Confederate dead.

Simultaneously, Sherman invaded Georgia. Grant instructed Sherman to "get into the interior of the enemy's country as far as you can, inflicting all the damage you can against their War resources." Skillful maneuvering, constant skirmishing, and one pitched battle, at Kennesaw Mountain, brought Sherman to Atlanta, which fell on September 2.

Intending to "make Georgia howl," Sherman marched out of Atlanta on November 15, heading for Savannah, 285 miles away on the Atlantic coast. One veteran remembered, "[We] destroyed all we could not eat, stole their niggers, burned their cotton & gins, spilled their sorghum, burned & twisted their R. Roads and raised Hell generally." **Sherman's March to the Sea** aimed at destroying white Southerners' will to continue the war. When Sherman's troops entered an undefended Savannah in mid-December, the general telegraphed Lincoln that he had "a Christmas gift" for him. A month earlier, Union voters had bestowed on the president an even greater gift.

Sherman's March to the Sea

▶ Military campaign from September through December 1864 in which Union forces under General Sherman marched from Atlanta, Georgia, to the coast at Savannah. Carving a path of destruction as it progressed, Sherman's army aimed at destroying white Southerners' will to continue the war.

The Election of 1864

In the summer of 1864, with Sherman temporarily checked outside Atlanta and Grant bogged down in the siege of Petersburg, the Democratic Party smelled victory in the fall elections. Lincoln himself concluded, "It seems exceedingly probable that this administration will not be re-elected."

The Democrats were badly divided, however. "Peace" Democrats insisted on an armistice, while "war" Democrats supported the conflict but opposed Republican means of fighting it. The party tried to paper over the chasm by nominating a war candidate, General George McClellan, but adopting a peace platform that demanded that "immediate efforts be made for a cessation of hostilities." Republicans denounced the peace plank as a plan that "virtually proposed to surrender the country to the rebels in arms against us."

The capture of Atlanta in September turned the political tide in favor of the Republicans. Lincoln received 55 percent of the popular vote, but his electoral margin was a whopping 212 to McClellan's 21. Lincoln's party won a resounding victory, one that gave him a mandate to continue the war until slavery and the Confederacy were dead.

The Confederacy Collapses

As 1865 dawned, military disaster littered the Confederate landscape. With the destruction of John B. Hood's army at Nashville in December 1864, the interior of

| Why did the war for union become a fight for black freedom? | What problems did the Confederacy face at home? | How did the war affect the economy and politics of the North? | How did the Union finally win the war? | Conclusion: In what ways was the Civil War a "Second American Revolution"? |

the Confederacy lay in Yankee hands (see Map 15.3, page 419). Sherman's troops, resting momentarily in Savannah, eyed South Carolina hungrily. Farther north, Grant had Lee's army pinned down in Petersburg, a few miles from Richmond.

Some Confederates turned their backs on the rebellion. News from the battle-field made it difficult not to conclude that the Yankees had beaten them. Soldiers' wives begged their husbands to return home to keep their families from starving, and the stream of deserters grew dramatically. Still, white Southerners had demonstrated a remarkable endurance for their cause. Half of the 900,000 Confederate soldiers had been killed or wounded, and ragged, hungry women and children had sacrificed throughout one of the bloodiest wars then known to history.

The end came with a rush. On February 1, 1865, Sherman's troops stormed out of Savannah into South Carolina, the "cradle of the Confederacy." In Virginia, Lee abandoned Petersburg on April 2, and Richmond fell on April 3. Grant pursued Lee until he surrendered on April 9, 1865, at Appomattox Court House, Virginia. Grant offered generous peace terms. He allowed Lee's men to return home and to keep their horses to help "put in a crop to carry themselves and their families through the next winter." With Lee gone, the remaining Confederate armies lost hope and gave up within two weeks. After four years, the war was over.

No one was more relieved than Lincoln, but his celebration was restrained. He told his cabinet that his postwar burdens would weigh almost as heavily as those of wartime. Seeking a distraction, Lincoln attended Ford's Theatre on the evening of Good Friday, April 14, 1865. John Wilkes Booth, an actor with southern sympathies, slipped into the president's box and shot Lincoln, who died the next morning. Vice President Andrew Johnson became president. The man who had led the nation through the war would not lead it during the postwar search for a just peace.

> **QUICK REVIEW**

Why were the siege of Vicksburg and the battle of Gettysburg critical turning points in the war?

CHAPTER LOCATOR | How did the war begin? | Why did each side expect to win? | How did each side fare in the early years of the war?

422 CHAPTER 15
THE CRUCIBLE OF WAR, 1861–1865

Kansas State Historical Society.

Conclusion: In what ways was the Civil War a "Second American Revolution"?

A TRANSFORMED NATION emerged from the crucible of war. Antebellum America was decentralized politically and loosely integrated economically. To bend the resources of the country to a Union victory, Congress enacted legislation that reshaped the nation's political and economic character. It created a transcontinental railroad and miles of telegraph lines to bind the West to the rest of the nation. The massive changes brought about by the war—the creation of a national government, a national economy, and a national spirit—led one historian to call the American Civil War the "Second American Revolution."

The Civil War also had a profound effect on individual lives. Men in uniform fought and suffered for what they passionately believed was right. The war disrupted families, leaving women at home with additional responsibilities while offering new opportunities to others for wartime work in factories, offices, and hospitals. It offered blacks new and more effective ways to resist slavery and agitate for equality.

The war devastated the South. Three-fourths of southern white men of military age served in the Confederate army, and at least half of them were captured, wounded, or killed or died of disease. The war destroyed two-fifths of the South's livestock, wrecked half of the farm machinery, and blackened dozens of cities and towns. The struggle also cost the North a heavy price: 360,000 lives. But rather than devastating the land, war stimulated the economy. The radical shift in power from the South to the North signaled a new direction in American development: the long decline of agriculture and the rise of industrial capitalism.

Most revolutionary of all, the war ended slavery. Nearly 200,000 black men dedicated their wartime service to its eradication. Because slavery was both a labor and a racial system, the institution was entangled in almost every aspect of southern life. Slavery's uprooting inevitably meant fundamental change. But the full meaning of abolition remained unclear in 1865 and the status of ex-slaves would be the principal task of reconstruction.

SO NOW YOU KNOW

By 1863, the war had evolved from one to preserve the Union to a war to preserve the Union *and* to end slavery. African Americans were able to participate by enlisting and fighting at a rate substantially higher than that of white men, playing a decisive role in the Union victory that ended slavery.

Why did the war for union become a fight for black freedom?	What problems did the Confederacy face at home?	How did the war affect the economy and politics of the North?	How did the Union finally win the war?	Conclusion: In what ways was the Civil War a "Second American Revolution"?

STEP 1

GETTING STARTED

Below are basic terms from this period in American history. Can you identify each term and explain why it matters? To do this exercise online or to download this chart, visit bedfordstmartins.com/roarkunderstanding.

TERM	WHO OR WHAT & WHEN	WHY IT MATTERS
Fort Sumter, p. 397		
battle of Bull Run (Manassas), p. 402		
George B. McClellan, p. 403		
Robert E. Lee, p. 405		
battle of Antietam, p. 405		
Ulysses S. Grant, p. 405		
King Cotton diplomacy, p. 406		
Emancipation Proclamation, p. 410		
New York City draft riots, p. 417		
siege of Vicksburg, p. 418		
battle of Gettysburg, p. 419		
Sherman's March to the Sea, p. 421		

STEP 2

MOVING BEYOND THE BASICS

The exercise below represents a more advanced understanding of the chapter material. Assess the strengths and weaknesses of the North and South at the outset of the Civil War. First, use the chart below to describe the two sides' strengths and weaknesses in four categories: population, industry, financial resources, and leadership. Then describe the initial war strategy of the North and South. When you are finished, see if you can make connections between each side's assets and its strategy. Why did the war take much longer than most people imagined at the outset? To do this exercise online or to download this chart, visit bedfordstmartins.com/roarkunderstanding.

Category	South	North
Population		
Industry		
Financial resources		
Leadership		
War strategy		

Now that you've reviewed various parts of the chapter, take a step back and try to see the big picture by answering these questions. Remember to use specific examples from the chapter in your answers. To do this exercise online, visit bedfordstmartins.com/roarkunderstanding.

THE EARLY YEARS OF THE WAR

▶ Why did the North, with all its advantages, fail to achieve a rapid victory over the South?

▶ Why did the South fail to attract international support for its cause?

THE HOME FRONT

▶ Why did Lincoln decide to issue the Emancipation Proclamation? How did Northerners respond to this decision?

▶ Why did conditions in the South deteriorate as the war went on? How did problems on the home front undermine the South's war effort?

UNION VICTORY

▶ What was Grant's strategy? How did it turn the tide of the war?

▶ Is it possible to identify a point at which Union victory became inevitable? Explain your reasoning.

LOOKING BACKWARD, LOOKING AHEAD

▶ Argue for or against the following statement: "The root cause of the Civil War was the failure of the architects of the Constitution to resolve the issue of slavery once and for all."

▶ What changes that occurred during the Civil War might have forecast what a northern victory would mean for the nation?

IN YOUR OWN WORDS

Imagine that you must explain chapter 15 to someone who hasn't read it. What would be the most important points to include and why?

16
RECONSTRUCTING A NATION

1863–1877

> This chapter explores the period known as Reconstruction, in which the nation struggled to define the defeated South's status within the Union and the meaning of freedom for ex-slaves. Despite the end of the Civil War, the nation entered one of its most violent eras, as victorious Northerners, defeated white Southerners, and newly freed African Americans battled to shape the postwar South.

> What were Lincoln's plans for wartime reconstruction?

> What vision did Andrew Johnson have for presidential reconstruction?

> How radical was congressional reconstruction?

> How was the battle over reconstruction fought in the South?

> Why did reconstruction collapse?

> Conclusion: What were the achievements and failures of reconstruction?

SAML. DOVE wishes to know of the whereabouts of his mother, Areno, his sisters Maria, Neziah, and Peggy, and his brother Edmond, who were owned by Geo. Dove, of Rockingham county, Shenandoah Valley, Va. Sold in Richmond, after which Saml. and Edmond were taken to Nashville, Tenn., by Joe Mick; Areno was left at the Eagle Tavern, Richmond
Respectfully yours,
SAML. DOVE.
Utica, New York, Aug. 5, 1865–3m
U. S. CHRISTIAN COMMISSION,
NASHVILLE, TENN., July 19, 1865.

DID YOU KNOW?

The priorities for newly freed African Americans were to locate family members, acquire land, and worship in their own churches.

Voting day, June 5, 1867. Black freedmen line up to vote in Washington, D.C.

> What were Lincoln's plans for wartime reconstruction?

Military Auction of Condemned Property, Beaufort, South Carolina, 1865

During the war, thousands of acres of land in the South came into federal hands as abandoned property or as a result of seizures because of nonpayment of taxes. The government authorized the sale of some of this land at public auction. This rare photograph shows expectant blacks (and a few whites) gathered in Beaufort, South Carolina, for a sale.
The Huntington Library, San Marino, California.

RECONSTRUCTION OF THE SOUTH did not wait for the end of war. As the odds of a northern victory increased, thinking about reunification quickened. Both President Abraham Lincoln, believing that reconstruction was an executive responsibility, and Congress, believing that reconstruction lay in its jurisdiction, developed plans. Fueling the argument about who had the authority to set the terms of reconstruction were significant differences about the terms themselves. In their eagerness to formulate a plan for political reunification, neither Lincoln nor Congress gave much attention to the South's land and labor problems. But as the war eroded slavery and traditional plantation agriculture, Yankee military commanders in the Union-occupied areas of the Confederacy had no choice but to oversee the emergence of a new labor system.

"To Bind Up the Nation's Wounds"

As early as 1863, Lincoln contemplated how "to bind up the nation's wounds" and achieve "a just, and a lasting peace." While compassion for the defeated enemy guided his thinking, his plan for reconstruction aimed primarily at shortening the war and ending slavery.

Lincoln's Proclamation of Amnesty and Reconstruction in December 1863 set out easy terms for the reintegration of Confederate states into the Union. Lincoln's plan did not require ex-rebels to extend social or political rights to ex-slaves, nor did it anticipate a program of long-term federal assistance to freedmen. Clearly, the president looked forward to the speedy, forgiving restoration of the broken Union.

CHAPTER LOCATOR | What were Lincoln's plans for wartime reconstruction?

Lincoln's Plan for Reconstruction

All property and political rights were to be restored to rebels willing to renounce secession and to accept the emancipation of slaves.

High-ranking Confederate military and political officers and a few other groups were to be excluded from this offer.

When 10 percent of a state's voting population had taken an oath of allegiance, the state could organize a new government.

CHRONOLOGY

1863
- President Lincoln issues Proclamation of Amnesty and Reconstruction.

1864
- Lincoln vetoes Wade-Davis bill imposing more severe restrictions on former Confederates.

1865
- General Sherman sets aside part of the coast south of Charleston for black settlement.
- Freedmen's Bureau is established and places 10,000 black families on half a million acres abandoned by planters.

Lincoln's plan enraged abolitionists such as Wendell Phillips of Boston, who charged that the president "makes the negro's freedom a mere sham." He "is willing that the negro should be free but seeks nothing else for him." Phillips and other northern radicals called instead for a thorough overhaul of southern society. Their ideas proved to be too drastic for most Republicans during the war years, but Congress agreed that Lincoln's plan was inadequate. It wanted greater assurances of white loyalty and greater guarantees of black rights.

In July 1864, Congressman Henry Winter Davis of Maryland and Senator Benjamin Wade of Ohio jointly sponsored a bill that demanded that at least half of the voters in a conquered rebel state take the oath of allegiance before reconstruction could begin. The Wade-Davis bill also banned all ex-Confederates from participating in the drafting of new state constitutions. Finally, the bill guaranteed the equality of freedmen before the law. When Lincoln refused to sign the bill and let it die, Wade and Davis charged the president with usurpation of power.

Undeterred, Lincoln continued to nurture the formation of loyal state governments under his own plan. Four states—Louisiana, Arkansas, Tennessee, and Virginia—fulfilled the president's requirements, but Congress refused to seat representatives from the "Lincoln states." In his last public address in April 1865, Lincoln defended his plan but for the first time expressed publicly his endorsement of suffrage for southern blacks, at least "the very intelligent, and . . . those who serve our cause as soldiers." The announcement demonstrated that Lincoln's thinking about reconstruction was still evolving. Four days later, he was dead.

Land and Labor

Of all the problems raised by the North's victory in the war, none proved more critical than the South's transition from slavery to free labor. As federal armies invaded and occupied the Confederacy, hundreds of thousands of slaves became free workers. In addition, Union armies controlled vast territories in the South where legal title to land had become unclear. The Confiscation Acts punished "traitors" by taking away their property. The question of what to do with federally occupied land and how to organize labor on it engaged former slaves, former slaveholders, Union military commanders, and federal government officials long before the war ended.

In the Mississippi valley, occupying federal troops announced a new labor code. It required slaveholders to sign contracts with ex-slaves and to pay wages. It also required black laborers to enter into contracts, work diligently, and remain subordinate and obedient. Military leaders clearly had no intention of promoting a social or economic revolution. Instead, they sought to restore plantation agriculture with wage labor.

| What vision did Andrew Johnson have for presidential reconstruction? | How radical was congressional reconstruction? | How was the battle over reconstruction fought in the South? | Why did reconstruction collapse? | Conclusion: What were the achievements and failures of reconstruction? |

The system pleased no one. Planters complained because the new system fell short of slavery. Without the right to whip, ex-masters argued, the new labor system did not have a chance. African Americans found the new regime too reminiscent of slavery to be called free labor. Its chief deficiency, they believed, was the failure to provide them with land of their own. "What's the use of being free if you don't own land enough to be buried in?" one man asked. Several wartime developments led freedmen to believe that the federal government planned to undergird black freedom with landownership.

In January 1865, General William Tecumseh Sherman set aside part of the coast south of Charleston for black settlement. By June 1865, some 40,000 freedmen sat on 400,000 acres of "Sherman land." In March 1865, Congress passed a bill establishing the Bureau of Refugees, Freedmen, and Abandoned Lands. The **Freedmen's Bureau**, as it was called, distributed food and clothing to destitute Southerners and eased the transition of blacks from slaves to free persons. Congress also authorized the agency to divide abandoned and confiscated land into 40-acre plots, to rent them to freedmen, and eventually to sell them "with such title as the United States can convey." By June 1865, the bureau had situated nearly 10,000 black families on half a million acres abandoned by fleeing planters. Other ex-slaves eagerly anticipated farms of their own.

Freedmen's Bureau

▶ Government organization created in March 1865 to distribute food and clothing to destitute Southerners and to ease the transition of blacks from slaves to free persons. Early efforts by the Freedmen's Bureau to distribute land to newly freed blacks were later overturned by President Johnson.

Harry Stephens and Family, 1866 Dressed in their Sunday best, this Virginia family sits proudly for a photograph. Many black families were not as fortunate as the Stephens family and spent years seeking missing family members. The Metropolitan Museum of Art, Gilman Collection, Purchase, The Horace W. Goldsmith Foundation Gift, 2005 (2005.100.277).

CHAPTER LOCATOR | What were Lincoln's plans for wartime reconstruction?

The African American Quest for Autonomy

Ex-slaves never had any doubt about what they wanted from freedom. They had only to contemplate what they had been denied as slaves. Slaves had to remain on their plantations; freedom allowed blacks to see what was on the other side of the hill. Slaves had to be at work in the fields by dawn; freedom permitted blacks to sleep through a sunrise. Freedmen also tested the etiquette of racial subordination. "Lizzie's maid passed me today when I was coming from church *without speaking to me*," huffed one plantation mistress.

To whites, emancipation looked like pure anarchy. Blacks, they said, had reverted to their natural condition: lazy, irresponsible, and wild. Actually, former slaves were experimenting with freedom, but they could not long afford to roam the countryside, neglect work, and casually provoke whites. Soon, most were back at work in whites' kitchens and fields.

But they continued to dream of land and economic independence. "The way we can best take care of ourselves is to have land," one former slave declared in 1865, "and turn it and till it by our own labor." Freedmen also wanted to learn to read and write. "I wishes the Childern all in School," one black veteran asserted. "It is beter for them then to be their Surveing a mistes [mistress]."

The restoration of broken families was another persistent black aspiration. Thousands of freedmen took to the roads in 1865 to look for kin who had been sold away or to free those who were being held illegally as slaves. A black soldier from Missouri wrote his daughters that he was coming for them. "I will have you if it cost me my life," he declared. "Your Miss Kitty said that I tried to steal you," he told them. "But I'll let her know that god never intended for a man to steal his own flesh and blood." And he swore that "if she meets me with ten thousand soldiers, she [will] meet her enemy."

Independent worship was another continuing aspiration. Some African Americans joined the newly established southern branches of all-black northern churches, such as the African Methodist Episcopal Church. Others formed black versions of the major southern denominations, Baptists and Methodists.

QUICK REVIEW

What were the goals of Lincoln's wartime plans for reconstruction? To what extent did these goals reflect the concerns of the newly freed slaves?

| What vision did Andrew Johnson have for presidential reconstruction? | How radical was congressional reconstruction? | How was the battle over reconstruction fought in the South? | Why did reconstruction collapse? | Conclusion: What were the achievements and failures of reconstruction? |

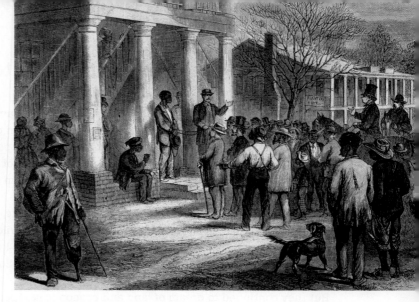

> # What vision did Andrew Johnson have for presidential reconstruction?

The Black Codes

Titled "Selling a Freeman to Pay His Fine at Monticello, Florida," this 1867 drawing from a northern magazine equates black codes with the reinstitution of slavery. The ascension of Andrew Johnson to the presidency emboldened many southern states to pass laws severely restricting blacks' freedom. Granger Collection.

WITH ABRAHAM LINCOLN'S death on April 15, 1865, Vice President Andrew Johnson of Tennessee became the new president. Congress had adjourned in March and would not reconvene until December. Thus, throughout the summer and fall, Johnson drew up and executed a plan of reconstruction without congressional advice.

Congress reconvened in December to find that, as far as the president and former Confederates were concerned, reconstruction was completed. Most Republicans, however, thought Johnson's puny demands of ex-rebels encouraged the rebirth of the Old South at the expense of black liberty. They proceeded to dismantle Johnson's program and substitute a program of their own.

Johnson's Program of Reconciliation

Andrew Johnson

▶ President of the United States from 1865 to 1869, Vice President Johnson became president after the assassination of Abraham Lincoln. Like Lincoln, Johnson sought the quick restoration of civil government in the South and pardoned most ex-Confederates. Johnson battled with Congress over the course of Reconstruction and was the first president in U.S. history to be impeached by the House of Representatives. He barely escaped removal from office by the Senate.

Born in 1808 in Raleigh, North Carolina, **Andrew Johnson** was the son of illiterate parents. Self-educated and ambitious, Johnson moved to Tennessee, where he built a career in politics championing the South's common white people and assailing its "illegitimate, swaggering, bastard, scrub aristocracy." The only senator from a Confederate state to remain loyal to the Union, Johnson held the planter class responsible for secession.

A Democrat all his life, Johnson occupied the White House only because the Republican Party in 1864 had needed a vice presidential candidate who would appeal to loyal, Union-supporting Democrats. Johnson vigorously defended states' rights (but not secession) and opposed Republican efforts to expand the power of the federal government. A steadfast supporter of slavery, Johnson grudgingly accepted emancipation more because he hated planters than because he sympathized with slaves. "Damn the negroes," he said. "I am fighting those traitorous aristocrats, their masters." The new president harbored unshakable racist convictions. Africans, Johnson said, were "inferior to the white man in point of intellect—better calculated in physical structure to undergo drudgery and hardship."

CHAPTER LOCATOR | What were Lincoln's plans for wartime reconstruction?

Like Lincoln, Johnson stressed the rapid restoration of civil government in the South. Like Lincoln, he promised to pardon most, but not all, ex-rebels. Johnson recognized the state governments created by Lincoln but set out his own requirements for restoring the other rebel states to the Union. All that the citizens of a state had to do was to renounce the right of secession, deny that the debts of the Confederacy were legal and binding, and ratify the Thirteenth Amendment, abolishing slavery, which became part of the Constitution in December 1865.

Johnson also returned to pardoned ex-Confederates all confiscated and abandoned land, even if it was in the hands of freedmen. Reformers were shocked. Instead of punishing planters as Republicans expected, his instructions canceled the promising beginnings made by General Sherman and the Freedmen's Bureau to settle blacks on land of their own. As one freedman observed, "Things was hurt by Mr. Lincoln getting killed."

White Southern Resistance and Black Codes

In the summer of 1865, delegates across the South gathered to draw up the new state constitutions required by Johnson's plan of reconstruction. Rather than accept Johnson's plan, delegates balked at even the president's mild requirements to renounce secession, disown their war debts, and ratify the Thirteenth Amendment. Despite this defiance, Johnson did nothing. White Southerners began to think that by standing up for themselves they could define the terms of reconstruction.

State governments across the South adopted a series of laws known as **black codes**, which made a travesty of black freedom. The codes sought to keep ex-slaves subordinate to whites by subjecting them to every sort of discrimination.

Black Codes

Several states made it illegal for blacks to own a gun.
Mississippi made insulting gestures and language by blacks a criminal offense.
The codes barred blacks from jury duty.
Not a single southern state granted any black the right to vote.

At the core of the black codes, however, lay the matter of labor and the desire to force freedmen back to the plantations. South Carolina attempted to limit blacks to either farmwork or domestic service by requiring them to pay annual taxes of $10 to $100 to work in any other occupation. Mississippi declared that blacks who did not possess written evidence of employment could be declared vagrants and be subject to involuntary plantation labor. Under so-called apprenticeship laws, courts bound thousands of black children—orphans and others whose parents they deemed unable to support them—to work for planter "guardians."

Johnson, a staunch defender of states' rights and white supremacy, refused to intervene. His stance was politically advantageous. A conservative Tennessee Democrat at the head of a northern Republican Party, he had begun to look southward for political allies. By pardoning powerful whites, by accepting governments even when they failed to satisfy his minimal demands, and by acquiescing in the black codes, he won useful southern friends.

In the fall elections of 1865, white Southerners dramatically expressed their mood. To represent them in Congress, they chose former Confederates, many of whom had

CHRONOLOGY

1865
- President Abraham Lincoln is shot; dies on April 15; is succeeded by Andrew Johnson.
- Johnson carries out rapid restoration of civil government in the South.
- Johnson returns confiscated and abandoned land to pardoned ex-Confederates.
- Southern states enact black codes.
- The Thirteenth Amendment, abolishing slavery, becomes part of Constitution.

1866
- Civil Rights Act nullifies black codes and extends civil rights to blacks.

black codes
▶ Laws passed by state governments in the South in 1865 that sought to keep ex-slaves subordinate to whites. At the core of the black codes lay the desire to force freedmen back to the plantations.

What vision did Andrew Johnson have for presidential reconstruction?

How radical was congressional reconstruction?

How was the battle over reconstruction fought in the South?

Why did reconstruction collapse?

Conclusion: What were the achievements and failures of reconstruction?

been high-ranking military and government officials in the Confederacy. As one Georgian remarked, "It looked as though Richmond had moved to Washington."

Expansion of Federal Authority and Black Rights

Southerners had assumed that what Andrew Johnson was willing to accept, Republicans would accept as well. But southern intransigence compelled even moderate Republicans to conclude that ex-rebels were still untrustworthy and dangerous. The black codes became a symbol of southern intentions to "restore all of slavery but its name." "We tell the white men of Mississippi," the *Chicago Tribune* roared, "that the men of the North will convert the State of Mississippi into a frog pond before they will allow such laws to disgrace one foot of the soil in which the bones of our soldiers sleep and over which the flag of freedom waves."

The moderate majority of the Republican Party did not champion black equality, the confiscation of plantations, or black voting, as did the radicals. But southern obstinacy had succeeded in forging temporary unity among Republican factions. In December 1865, Republicans refused to seat the southern representatives elected in the fall elections. Rather than accept Johnson's claim that the "work of restoration" was done, Congress challenged his executive power.

Republican senator Lyman Trumbull declared that the president's policy meant that ex-slaves would "be tyrannized over, abused, and virtually reenslaved without some legislation by the nation for [their] protection." Early in 1866, the moderates produced two bills that strengthened the federal shield. The first, the Freedmen's Bureau bill, prolonged the life of the agency established by the previous Congress. Arguing that the Constitution never contemplated a "system for the support of indigent persons," President Andrew Johnson vetoed the bill. Congress failed by a narrow margin to override the president's veto.

The moderates designed their second measure, the Civil Rights Act, to nullify the black codes by affirming African Americans' rights to "full and equal benefit of all laws and proceedings for the security of person and property as is enjoyed by white citizens." The act required the end of racial discrimination in state laws and represented an extraordinary expansion of black rights and federal authority. The president argued that the civil rights bill amounted to "unconstitutional invasion of states' rights" and vetoed it.

In April 1866, an incensed Republican Congress passed the civil rights bill again and overrode the presidential veto. In July, it passed another Freedmen's Bureau bill and overrode Johnson's veto. For the first time in American history, Congress had overridden presidential vetoes of major legislation. As a worried South Carolinian observed, Johnson had succeeded in uniting the Republicans and probably touched off "a fight this fall such as has never been seen."

> ## QUICK REVIEW

When the southern states passed the black codes, how did President Andrew Johnson respond? How did congressional Republicans respond?

CHAPTER LOCATOR | What were Lincoln's plans for wartime reconstruction?

434 CHAPTER 16 RECONSTRUCTING A NATION, 1863–1877

How radical was congressional reconstruction?

State Convention at Richmond, Virginia Between 1867 and 1869, every southern state except Tennessee held a convention to draft a new constitution. In Virginia, where blacks were more than 40 percent of the population, they made up about 20 percent of the convention. Richmond History Center.

BY THE SUMMER OF 1866, President Andrew Johnson and Congress were locked in a battle unprecedented in American history. Johnson made it clear that he would not budge on either constitutional issues or policy. Moderate Republicans responded by amending the Constitution. But the obstinacy of Johnson and white Southerners pushed Republican moderates ever closer to the radicals and to acceptance of additional federal intervention in the South. Congress also voted to impeach the president. In time, Congress debated whether to make voting rights color-blind, while women sought to make voting sex-blind as well.

The Fourteenth Amendment and Escalating Violence

In June 1866, Congress passed the **Fourteenth Amendment** to the Constitution, and two years later the states ratified it. The most important provisions of this complex amendment made all native-born or naturalized persons American citizens and prohibited states from abridging the "privileges and immunities" of citizens, depriving them of "life, liberty, or property without due process of law," and denying them "equal protection of the laws." By making blacks national citizens, the amendment provided a national guarantee of equality before the law. In essence, it protected blacks against violation by southern state governments.

Fourteenth Amendment
▶ Constitutional amendment ratified in 1868 that made all native-born or naturalized persons U.S. citizens and prohibited states from abridging the rights of national citizens. The amendment hoped to provide a guarantee of equality before the law for black citizens.

| What vision did Andrew Johnson have for presidential reconstruction? | **How radical was congressional reconstruction?** | How was the battle over reconstruction fought in the South? | Why did reconstruction collapse? | Conclusion: What were the achievements and failures of reconstruction? |

1866
- Congress approves Fourteenth Amendment, granting citizenship and equal rights to former slaves.
- Elizabeth Cady Stanton and Susan B. Anthony found the American Equal Rights Association to support woman suffrage.

1867
- Military Reconstruction Act initiates military occupation of the South and, with black suffrage and the disfranchisement of many ex-rebels, guarantees Republican governments in the South.

1868
- Impeachment trial of President Andrew Johnson.

1869
- Congress approves Fifteenth Amendment, making it illegal to deny voting rights on the basis of race.

The Fourteenth Amendment also dealt with voting rights. It gave Congress the right to reduce the congressional representation of states that withheld suffrage from some of its adult male population. In other words, white Southerners could either allow black men to vote or see their representation in Washington slashed.

The Fourteenth Amendment's suffrage provisions ignored the small band of women who had emerged from the war demanding "the ballot for the two disenfranchised classes, negroes and women." Founding the American Equal Rights Association in 1866, Susan B. Anthony and Elizabeth Cady Stanton lobbied for "a government by the people, and the whole people; for the people and the whole people." They felt betrayed when their old antislavery allies refused to work for their goals. "It was the Negro's hour," Frederick Douglass explained. Senator Charles Sumner suggested that woman suffrage could be "the great question of the future."

The Fourteenth Amendment provided for punishment of any state that excluded voters on the basis of race but not on the basis of sex. The amendment also introduced the word *male* into the Constitution when it referred to a citizen's right to vote. Stanton predicted that "if that word 'male' be inserted, it will take us a century at least to get it out."

Tennessee approved the Fourteenth Amendment in July, and Congress promptly welcomed the state's representatives and senators back. Had President Johnson counseled other southern states to ratify this relatively mild amendment, they might have listened. Instead, Johnson advised Southerners to reject the Fourteenth Amendment and to rely on him to trounce the Republicans in the fall congressional elections.

Johnson had decided to make the Fourteenth Amendment the overriding issue of the 1866 elections and to gather its white opponents into a new conservative party, the National Union Party. The president's strategy suffered a setback

Andrew Johnson Cartoon

Appearing in 1868 during President Andrew Johnson's impeachment trial, this cartoon includes captions that read: "This little boy would persist in handling books above his capacity" and "And this was the disastrous result."
The cartoonist's portrait of Johnson being crushed by the Constitution refers to the president's flouting of the Tenure of Office Act, which caused Republicans to vote for his impeachment.
Granger Collection.

THIS LITTLE BOY WOULD PERSIST IN HANDLING BOOKS ABOVE HIS CAPACITY.

AND THIS WAS THE DISASTROUS RESULT.

CHAPTER LOCATOR | What were Lincoln's plans for wartime reconstruction?

when whites in several southern cities went on rampages against blacks. The mob violence shocked Northerners and renewed skepticism about Johnson's claim that southern whites could be trusted. "Who doubts that the Freedmen's Bureau ought to be abolished forthwith," a New Yorker observed sarcastically, "and the blacks remitted to the paternal care of their old masters, who 'understand the nigger, you know, a great deal better than the Yankees can.'"

The 1866 elections resulted in an overwhelming Republican victory. Johnson had bet that Northerners would not support federal protection of black rights and that a racist backlash would blast the Republican Party. But the war was still fresh in northern minds, and as one Republican explained, southern whites "with all their intelligence were traitors, the blacks with all their ignorance were loyal."

Radical Reconstruction and Military Rule

When Johnson continued to urge Southerners to reject the Fourteenth Amendment, every southern state except Tennessee voted it down. "The last one of the sinful ten," thundered Representative James A. Garfield of Ohio, "has flung back into our teeth the magnanimous offer of a generous nation." After the South rejected the moderates' program, the radicals seized the initiative.

Each act of defiance by southern whites had boosted the standing of the radicals within the Republican Party. Radicals such as Massachusetts senator Charles Sumner and Pennsylvania representative Thaddeus Stevens did not speak with a single voice, but they united in demanding civil and political equality for ex-slaves. Southern states were "like clay in the hands of the potter," Stevens declared in January 1867, and he called on Congress to begin reconstruction all over again.

In March 1867, Congress overturned the Johnson state governments and initiated military rule of the South. The **Military Reconstruction Act** (and three subsequent acts) divided the ten unreconstructed Confederate states into five military districts. Congress placed a Union general in charge of each district and instructed him to "suppress insurrection, disorder, and violence" and to begin political reform. After the military had completed voter registration, which would include black men, voters in each state would elect delegates to conventions that would draw up new state constitutions. Each constitution would guarantee black suffrage. When the voters of each state had approved the constitution and the state legislature had ratified the Fourteenth Amendment, the state could submit its work to Congress. If Congress approved, the state's senators and representatives could be seated, and political reunification would be accomplished.

Radicals proclaimed the provision for black suffrage "a prodigious triumph," for it extended far beyond the limited suffrage provisions of the Fourteenth Amendment. When combined with the disfranchisement of thousands of ex-rebels, it promised to cripple any neo-Confederate resurgence and guarantee Republican state governments in the South.

Despite its bold suffrage provision, the Military Reconstruction Act of 1867 disappointed those who also advocated the confiscation and redistribution of southern plantations to ex-slaves. Thaddeus Stevens agreed with the freedman who said, "Give us our own land and we take care of ourselves, but without land, the old masters can hire us or starve us, as they please." But most Republicans

Reconstruction Military Districts, 1867

Military Reconstruction Act

▶ Congressional act of March 1867 that initiated military rule of the South. Congressional reconstruction divided the ten unreconstructed Confederate states into five military districts, each under the direction of a Union general. It also established the procedure by which unreconstructed states could reenter the Union.

| What vision did Andrew Johnson have for presidential reconstruction? | **How radical was congressional reconstruction?** | How was the battle over reconstruction fought in the South? | Why did reconstruction collapse? | Conclusion: What were the achievements and failures of reconstruction? |

believed they had provided blacks with what they needed: equal legal rights and the ballot. If blacks were to get land, they would have to gain it themselves.

Declaring that he would rather sever his right arm than sign such a formula for "anarchy and chaos," Andrew Johnson vetoed the Military Reconstruction Act, but Congress quickly overrode his veto. With the passage of the Reconstruction Acts of 1867, congressional reconstruction was virtually completed. Congress left whites owning most of the South's land but, in a departure that justified the term "radical reconstruction," had given black men the ballot.

Impeaching a President

Despite his defeats, Andrew Johnson had no intention of yielding control of reconstruction. In a dozen ways, he sabotaged Congress's will and encouraged southern whites to resist. He issued a flood of pardons, waged war against the Freedmen's Bureau, and replaced Union generals eager to enforce Congress's Reconstruction Acts with conservative men eager to defeat them. Johnson claimed that he was merely defending the "violated Constitution." At bottom, however, the president subverted congressional reconstruction to protect southern whites from what he considered the horrors of "Negro domination."

Radicals argued that Johnson's abuse of constitutional powers and his failure to fulfill constitutional obligations to enforce the law were impeachable offenses. But moderates disagreed, arguing that only actual violations of criminal statutes were impeachable offenses. As long as Johnson refrained from breaking the law, impeachment (the process of formal charges of wrongdoing against the president or other federal official) remained stalled.

Then in August 1867, Johnson suspended Secretary of War Edwin M. Stanton from office. As required by the Tenure of Office Act, which demanded the approval of the Senate for the removal of any government official who had been appointed with Senate approval, the president requested the Senate to consent to the dismissal. When the Senate balked, Johnson removed Stanton anyway. "Is the President crazy, or only drunk?" asked a dumbfounded Republican moderate. "I'm afraid his doings will make us all favor impeachment."

News of Johnson's open defiance of the law convinced every Republican in the House to vote for a resolution impeaching the president. Supreme Court chief justice Salmon Chase presided over the Senate trial, which lasted from March until May 1868. When the critical vote came, thirty-five senators voted guilty and nineteen not guilty. The impeachment forces fell one vote short of the two-thirds needed to convict.

After his trial, Johnson called a truce, and for the remaining ten months of his term, congressional reconstruction proceeded unhindered by presidential interference. Without interference from Johnson, Congress revisited the suffrage issue.

The Fifteenth Amendment and Women's Demands

In February 1869, Republicans passed the **Fifteenth Amendment** to the Constitution, which prohibited states from depriving any citizen of the right to vote

Fifteenth Amendment

▶ Constitutional amendment ratified in 1870 prohibiting states from depriving any citizen of the right to vote because of "race, color, or previous condition of servitude." The Reconstruction Acts of 1867 already required black suffrage in the South; the Fifteenth Amendment extended black suffrage nationwide. Woman suffrage advocates, in particular Susan B. Anthony and Elizabeth Cady Stanton, were disappointed with the Fifteenth Amendment's failure to extend voting rights to women.

CHAPTER LOCATOR | What were Lincoln's plans for wartime reconstruction?

because of "race, color, or previous condition of servitude." The Reconstruction Acts of 1867 already required black suffrage in the South; the Fifteenth Amendment extended black voting nationwide.

Some Republicans, however, found the final wording of the Fifteenth Amendment "lame and halting." Rather than absolutely guaranteeing the right to vote, the amendment merely prohibited exclusion on the grounds of race. The distinction would prove to be significant. In time, white Southerners would devise tests of literacy and property and other apparently nonracial measures that would effectively disfranchise blacks yet not violate the Fifteenth Amendment. But an amendment that fully guaranteed the right to vote courted defeat outside the South. Rising antiforeign sentiment—against the Chinese in California and European immigrants in the Northeast—caused states to resist giving up total control of suffrage requirements. In March 1870, after three-fourths of the states had ratified it, the Fifteenth Amendment became part of the Constitution. Republicans generally breathed a sigh of relief, confident that black suffrage was "the last great point that remained to be settled of the issues of the war."

Woman suffrage advocates, however, were sorely disappointed with the Fifteenth Amendment's failure to extend voting rights to women. Elizabeth Cady Stanton and Susan B. Anthony condemned the Republicans' "negro first" strategy and pointed out that women remained "the only class of citizens wholly unrepresented in the government." Stanton wondered aloud why ignorant black men should legislate for educated and cultured white women. The Fifteenth Amendment severed the early feminist movement from its abolitionist roots. Over the next several decades, feminists established an independent suffrage crusade that drew millions of women into political life.

Republicans took enough satisfaction in the Fifteenth Amendment to promptly scratch the "Negro question" from the agenda of national politics. Even that steadfast crusader for equality Wendell Phillips concluded that the black man now held "sufficient shield in his own hands. . . . Whatever he suffers will be largely now, and in future, his own fault." Northerners had no idea of the violent struggles that lay ahead.

QUICK REVIEW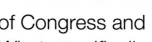

Why and how did the aims of Congress and the president diverge? What specifically were the issues over which they clashed?

| What vision did Andrew Johnson have for presidential reconstruction? | **How radical was congressional reconstruction?** | How was the battle over reconstruction fought in the South? | Why did reconstruction collapse? | Conclusion: What were the achievements and failures of reconstruction? |

How was the battle over reconstruction fought in the South?

Black Woman in Cotton Fields, Thomasville, Georgia

Few images of everyday black women during the Reconstruction era survive. This photograph was taken in 1895, but it nevertheless goes to the heart of the labor struggle after the Civil War. Before emancipation, black women worked in the fields; after emancipation, white landlords wanted them to continue working there. Freedom allowed some women to escape field labor, but not this Georgian, who probably worked to survive. Courtesy, Georgia Department of Archives and History, Atlanta, Georgia.

NORTHERNERS BELIEVED THEY HAD discharged their responsibilities with the Reconstruction Acts and the amendments to the Constitution, but Southerners knew that the battle had just begun. Black suffrage established the foundation for the rise of the Republican Party in the South. Gathering together outsiders and outcasts, southern Republicans won elections, wrote new state constitutions, and formed new state governments.

Challenging the established class for political control was dangerous business. Equally dangerous were the confrontations that took place on southern farms and plantations, where blacks sought to give economic meaning to their newly won legal and political equality. Freedom remained contested territory, and Southerners fought pitched battles with one another to determine the contours of their new world.

Freedmen, Yankees, and Yeomen

African Americans made up the majority of southern Republicans. After gaining voting rights in 1867, nearly all eligible black men registered to vote as Republicans. Southern blacks did not have identical political priorities, but they united in their desire for education and equal treatment before the law.

Northern whites who made the South their home after the war were a second element of the South's Republican Party. Conservative white Southerners called

CHAPTER LOCATOR | What were Lincoln's plans for wartime reconstruction?

them carpetbaggers, opportunistic men who put all their belongings in a single carpet-sided suitcase and headed south to "fatten on our misfortunes." But most Northerners who moved south were young men who looked upon the South as they did the West—as a promising place to make a living. Northerners in the southern Republican Party consistently supported programs that encouraged vigorous economic development along the lines of the northern free-labor model.

Southern whites made up the third element of the South's Republican Party. Approximately one out of four white Southerners voted Republican. The other three condemned the one who did as a traitor to his region and his race and called him a scalawag, a term for runty horses and low-down, good-for-nothing rascals. Yeoman farmers accounted for the majority of southern white Republicans. Some were Unionists who emerged from the war with bitter memories of Confederate persecution. Others were small farmers who wanted to end state governments' favoritism toward plantation owners. Yeomen supported initiatives for public schools and for expanding economic opportunity in the South.

The South's Republican Party, then, was made up of freedmen, Yankees, and yeomen—an improbable coalition. The mix of races, regions, and classes inevitably meant friction as each group maneuvered to define the party. But Reconstruction represents an extraordinary moment in American politics: Blacks and whites joined together in the Republican Party to pursue political change. Formally, of course, only men participated in politics—casting ballots and holding offices—but white and black women also played a part in the political struggle by joining in parades and rallies, attending stump speeches, and even campaigning.

Most whites in the South condemned southern Republicans as illegitimate and felt justified in doing whatever they could to stamp them out. Violence against blacks—the "white terror"—took brutal institutional form in 1866 with the formation in Tennessee of the **Ku Klux Klan**, a social club of Confederate veterans that quickly developed into a paramilitary organization supporting Democrats. The Klan went on a rampage of murder and mayhem to defeat Republicans and restore white supremacy. Rapid demobilization of the Union army after the war left only twenty thousand troops to patrol the entire South. Without effective military protection, southern Republicans had to take care of themselves.

Republican Rule

In the fall of 1867, southern states held elections for delegates to state constitutional conventions, as required by the Reconstruction Acts. About 40 percent of the white electorate stayed home because they had been disfranchised or because they had decided to boycott politics. Republicans won three-fourths of the seats. About 15 percent of the Republican delegates to the conventions were Northerners who had moved south, 25 percent were African Americans, and 60 percent were white Southerners. As a British visitor observed, the delegate elections reflected "the mighty revolution that had taken place in America."

The reconstruction constitutions introduced two broad categories of changes in the South: those that reduced aristocratic privilege and increased democratic equality and those that expanded the state's responsibility for the general welfare. In the first category, the constitutions adopted universal male suffrage, abolished property qualifications for holding office, and made more offices elective and fewer appointed. In the second category, they enacted prison reform; made

CHRONOLOGY

1866
– Ku Klux Klan is founded.

1867
– Southern African Americans gain voting rights under the Military Reconstruction Act.
– In elections for state constitutional convention delegates, Republicans win three-fourths of the seats.

1875
– One-half of South Carolina's and Mississippi's children, the majority of whom are black, are attending school.
– Sharecropping is the dominant labor system for rural southern blacks.

Ku Klux Klan

▶ A paramilitary organization formed in Tennessee in 1866 that supported Democrats. With too few Union troops in the South to control the region, the Klan went on a rampage of murder and mayhem to defeat Republicans and restore white supremacy. Legislative efforts by Congress to suppress violence in the South were undermined by failures of enforcement.

| What vision did Andrew Johnson have for presidential reconstruction? | How radical was congressional reconstruction? | **How was the battle over reconstruction fought in the South?** | Why did reconstruction collapse? | Conclusion: What were the achievements and failures of reconstruction? |

441

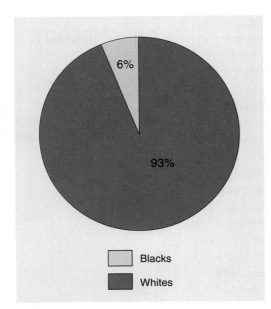

FIGURE 16.1 ■ Southern Congressional Delegations, 1865–1877
The statistics contradict the myth of black domination of congressional representation during Reconstruction.

the state responsible for caring for orphans, the insane, and the deaf and mute; and exempted debtors' homes from seizure.

To Democrats, however, these forward-looking state constitutions looked like wild revolution. Democrats were blind to the fact that no constitution confiscated and redistributed land, as virtually every former slave wished, or disfranchised ex-rebels wholesale, as most southern Unionists advocated. And they were convinced that the new constitutions initiated "Negro domination" in politics. In fact, although 80 percent of Republican voters were black men, only 6 percent of Southerners in Congress during Reconstruction were black (**Figure 16.1**). And no state legislature experienced "Negro rule," despite black majorities in the populations of some states.

Southern voters ratified the new constitutions and swept Republicans into power. When the former Confederate states ratified the Fourteenth Amendment, Congress readmitted them. Southern Republicans then turned to the staggering array of problems that faced them. The southern landscape and economy lay in ruins. Making matters worse, racial harassment and reactionary violence dogged Southerners who sought reform. It was in this context that Republicans struggled to reform and rebuild the region.

Activity focused on three areas—education, civil rights, and economic development. Every state inaugurated a system of public education. Before the Civil War, whites had deliberately kept slaves illiterate, and planter-dominated governments rarely spent tax money to educate the children of yeomen. By 1875, half of Mississippi's and South Carolina's eligible children (the majority of whom were black) were attending school. Although schools were underfunded, literacy rates rose sharply. Public schools were racially segregated, but education remained for many blacks a tangible, deeply satisfying benefit of freedom and Republican rule.

State legislatures also attacked racial discrimination and defended civil rights. Republicans especially resisted efforts to segregate blacks from whites in public transportation. Mississippi levied fines of up to $1,000 and three years in jail for railroads and steamboats that pushed blacks into "smoking cars" or to lower decks. A Mississippian complained: "Money cannot buy for a colored man or woman decent treatment and the comforts that white people claim and can obtain." But passing color-blind laws was one thing; enforcing them was another. Despite the laws, segregation—later called Jim Crow—developed at white insistence and became a feature of southern life long before the end of the Reconstruction era.

Republican governments also launched ambitious programs of economic development. They envisioned a South of diversified agriculture, roaring factories, and booming towns. State legislatures chartered scores of banks and industrial companies, appropriated funds to fix ruined levees and drain swamps, and went on a railroad-building binge. These efforts fell far short of solving the South's economic troubles, however. Republican spending to stimulate economic growth also meant rising taxes and enormous debt, which drained funds from schools and other programs.

The southern Republicans' record, then, was mixed. To their credit, the biracial party took up an ambitious agenda to change the South. Their agenda, however, faced difficult obstacles. Money was scarce, the Democrats continued

CHAPTER LOCATOR | What were Lincoln's plans for wartime reconstruction?

their harassment, and factionalism and corruption threatened the Republican Party from within. Despite shortcomings, however, the Republican Party made headway in its efforts to purge the South of aristocratic privilege and racist oppression. Republican governments had less success in overthrowing the long-established white oppression of black farm laborers in the rural South.

White Landlords, Black Sharecroppers

Ex-slaves who wished to escape slave labor and ex-masters who wanted to reinstitute old ways clashed repeatedly. Except for having to pay subsistence wages, planters had not been required to offer many concessions to emancipation. They continued to believe that African Americans would not work without coercion. Whites moved quickly to restore work regimes that were as close to those of slavery as possible.

Ex-slaves resisted every effort to turn back the clock. They argued that if any class could be described as "lazy," it was the planters, who, as one ex-slave noted, "lived in idleness all their lives on stolen labor." Land of their own would anchor their economic independence, they believed, and end planters' interference in their personal lives. They could then, for example, make their own decisions about whether women and children would labor in the fields. Indeed, within months after the war, perhaps one-third of black women abandoned field labor to work on chores in their own cabins just as poor white women did. Hundreds of thousands of black children enrolled in school. But without their own land, ex-slaves had little choice but to work on plantations.

Although forced to return to the planters' fields, freedmen resisted efforts to restore slavelike conditions. Instead of working for wages, a South Carolinian observed, "the negroes all seem disposed to rent land," which increased their independence from whites. Out of this tug-of-war between white landlords and black laborers emerged a new system of southern agriculture.

Sharecropping was a compromise that offered both ex-masters and ex-slaves something but satisfied neither. Under the new system, planters divided their cotton plantations into small farms that freedmen rented, paying with a share of each year's crop, usually half. Sharecropping gave blacks more freedom than did the system of wages and labor gangs and released them from the day-to-day supervision of whites. Black families abandoned the old slave quarters and scattered over plantations, building separate cabins for themselves on the patches of land they rented (**Map 16.1**). Still, most blacks remained dependent on white landlords, who had the power to expel them at the end of each growing season. For planters, sharecropping offered a way to resume agricultural production, but it did not restore the old slave plantation.

Sharecropping introduced a new figure—the country merchant—into the agricultural equation. Landlords supplied sharecroppers with land, mules, seeds, and tools, but blacks also needed credit to obtain essential food and clothing before they harvested their crops. Thousands of small crossroads stores sprang up to offer credit. Under an arrangement called a crop lien, a merchant would advance goods to a sharecropper in exchange for a lien, or legal claim, on the farmer's future crop. Some merchants charged exorbitant rates of interest, as much as 60 percent, on the goods they sold. At the end of the growing season, after the landlord had taken half of the farmer's crop for rent, the merchant took most of the

sharecropping
▶ System of southern agriculture that emerged in the decade following the Civil War. Under the system, planters divided their cotton plantations into small farms that freedmen rented, paying with a share of each year's crop. Sharecropping gave blacks more freedom than did the system of wages and labor gangs and released them from the day-to-day supervision of whites. White landowners, however, used a variety of tactics, particularly debt, to restrict the freedom of sharecroppers.

| What vision did Andrew Johnson have for presidential reconstruction? | How radical was congressional reconstruction? | **How was the battle over reconstruction fought in the South?** | Why did reconstruction collapse? | Conclusion: What were the achievements and failures of reconstruction? |

443

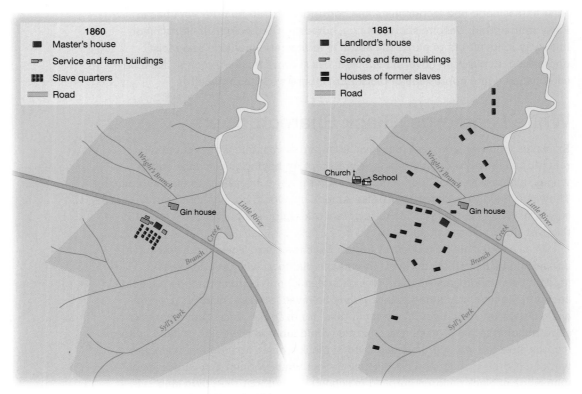

MAP 16.1 ■ A Southern Plantation in 1860 and 1881
These maps of the Barrow plantation in Georgia illustrate some of the ways in which ex-slaves expressed their freedom. Freedmen and freedwomen deserted the clustered living quarters behind the master's house, scattered over the plantation, built family cabins, and farmed rented land. The former Barrow slaves also worked together to build a school and a church.

> ▶ FOR MORE HELP ANALYZING THIS MAP, see the map activity for this chapter in the Online Study Guide at bedfordstmartins.com/roarkunderstanding.

rest. Sometimes, the farmer's debt to the merchant exceeded the income he received from his remaining half of the crop, and the farmer would have no choice but to borrow more from the merchant and begin the cycle all over again.

An experiment at first, sharecropping spread quickly and soon dominated the cotton South. Lien merchants forced tenants to plant cotton, which was easy to sell, instead of food crops. The result was excessive production of cotton and falling cotton prices, developments that cost thousands of small white farmers their land and pushed them into the ranks of sharecroppers. The new sharecropping system of agriculture took shape just as the political power of Republicans in the South began to buckle under Democratic pressure.

> **QUICK REVIEW**

How did politics and economics shape the lives of postwar blacks in the South?

CHAPTER LOCATOR | What were Lincoln's plans for wartime reconstruction?

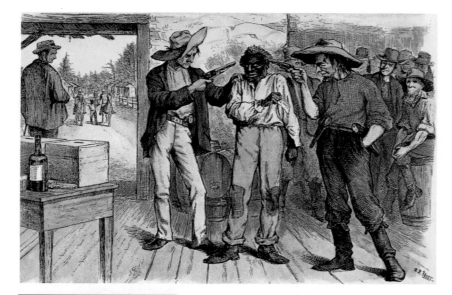

| "Of Course He Wants to Vote the Democratic Ticket" | This Republican cartoon from the October 21, 1876, issue of *Harper's Weekly* comments sarcastically on the possibility of honest elections in the South. The caption reads, "You're free as air, ain't you? Say you are or I'll blow yer black head off." Granger Collection. |

► FOR MORE HELP ANALYZING THIS IMAGE, see the visual activity for this chapter in the Online Study Guide at bedfordstmartins.com/roarkunderstanding.

Why did reconstruction collapse?

BY 1870, after a decade of war and reconstruction, Northerners wanted to put "the southern problem" behind them. While northern commitment to defend black freedom eroded, southern commitment to white supremacy intensified. Without northern protection, southern Republicans were no match for the Democrats' economic coercion, political corruption, and bloody violence. The election of 1876 both confirmed and completed the collapse of reconstruction.

Grant's Troubled Presidency

In 1868, the Republican nominee for president was Ulysses S. Grant. Hero of the Civil War and a supporter of congressional reconstruction, Grant was the obvious choice. His Democratic opponent, Horatio Seymour of New York, ran on a platform that blasted congressional reconstruction as "a flagrant usurpation of power . . . unconstitutional, revolutionary, and void." The Republicans answered by waving the bloody shirt—that is, they reminded voters that the Democrats were "the party of rebellion." Grant won a narrow 309,000-vote margin in the popular vote and a substantial victory (214 votes to 80) in the electoral college (**Map 16.2**).

The talents Grant had demonstrated on the battlefield— decisiveness, clarity, and resolution—were less obvious in the White House. He surrounded himself with friends and family

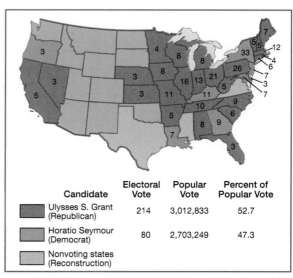

Candidate	Electoral Vote	Popular Vote	Percent of Popular Vote
Ulysses S. Grant (Republican)	214	3,012,833	52.7
Horatio Seymour (Democrat)	80	2,703,249	47.3
Nonvoting states (Reconstruction)			

MAP 16.2 ■ The Election of 1868

What vision did Andrew Johnson have for presidential reconstruction?	How radical was congressional reconstruction?	How was the battle over reconstruction fought in the South?	Why did reconstruction collapse?	Conclusion: What were the achievements and failures of reconstruction?

1868
- Republican Ulysses S. Grant is elected president.

1871
- Ku Klux Klan Act makes interference with voting rights a felony.

1872
- Liberal Party is formed; calls for end of government corruption and the end of reconstruction.
- President Grant is reelected.

1873
- Economic depression sets in for the remainder of the decade.
- In the *Slaughterhouse* cases, the U.S. Supreme Court rules that the Fourteenth Amendment protects only those rights that stem from the federal government.

1874
- Democrats win majority in House of Representatives.

1875
- Civil Rights Act outlaws racial discrimination in transportation, public accommodations, and juries.

1876
- In *United States v. Cruikshank*, the U.S. Supreme Court rules that the reconstruction amendments give Congress the power to legislate against discrimination by states but not by individuals.

1877
- Republican Rutherford B. Hayes assumes presidency; Reconstruction era ends.

Grant and Scandal

This anti-Grant cartoon by Thomas Nast, the nation's most celebrated political cartoonist, shows the president falling headfirst into the barrel of fraud and corruption that tainted his administration. Library of Congress.

▶ FOR MORE HELP ANALYZING THIS IMAGE, see the visual activity for this chapter in the Online Study Guide at bedfordstmartins.com/roarkunderstanding.

and made a string of dubious appointments that led to a series of damaging scandals. Charges of corruption tainted his vice president, Schuyler Colfax, and brought down two of his cabinet officers. Though never personally implicated in any scandal, Grant was seemingly blind to the rot that filled his administration.

In 1872, anti-Grant Republicans bolted and launched the Liberal Party. To clean up the graft and corruption, Liberals proposed the creation of a nonpartisan civil service commission that would oversee competitive examinations for appointment to government offices. Liberals also demanded that the federal government remove its troops from the South and restore "home rule" (southern white control). Democrats liked the Liberals' southern policy and endorsed the Liberal presidential candidate, Horace Greeley, the longtime editor of the *New York Tribune*. The nation, however, still felt enormous affection for the man who had saved the Union and reelected Grant with 56 percent of the popular vote.

Northern Resolve Withers

Although Grant genuinely wanted to see blacks' civil and political rights protected, he understood that most Northerners had grown weary of reconstruction

CHAPTER LOCATOR | What were Lincoln's plans for wartime reconstruction?

and were increasingly willing to let southern whites manage their own affairs. Citizens wanted to shift their attention to other issues, especially after the nation slipped into a devastating economic depression in 1873. More than eighteen thousand businesses collapsed, leaving more than a million workers on the streets. Northern businessmen wanted to invest in the South but believed that recurrent federal intrusion was itself a major cause of instability in the region. Republican leaders began to question the wisdom of their party's alliance with the South's lower classes—its small farmers and sharecroppers. One member of Grant's administration proposed allying with the "thinking and influential native southerners . . . the intelligent, well-to-do, and controlling class."

Congress, too, wanted to leave reconstruction behind, but southern Republicans made that difficult. When the South's Republicans begged for federal protection from Klan violence, Congress enacted three laws in 1870 and 1871 that were intended to break the back of white terrorism. The severest of the three, the Ku Klux Klan Act (1871), made interference with voting rights a felony. Federal marshals arrested thousands of Klansmen and came close to destroying the Klan, but they did not end all terrorism against blacks. Congress also passed the Civil Rights Act of 1875, which boldly outlawed racial discrimination in transportation, public accommodations, and juries. But federal authorities never enforced the law aggressively, and segregated facilities remained the rule throughout the South.

By the early 1870s, the Republican Party had lost its leading champions of African American rights to death or defeat at the polls. Other Republicans concluded that the quest for black equality was mistaken or hopelessly naive. In May 1872, Congress restored the right of officeholding to all but three hundred ex-rebels. Many Republicans had come to believe that traditional white leaders offered the best hope for honesty, order, and prosperity in the South.

Underlying the North's abandonment of reconstruction was unyielding racial prejudice. Northerners had learned to accept black freedom during the war, but deep-seated prejudice prevented many from accepting black equality. Even the actions they took on behalf of blacks often served partisan political advantage. Northerners generally supported Indiana senator Thomas A. Hendricks's harsh declaration that "this is a white man's Government, made by the white man for the white man."

The U.S. Supreme Court also did its part to undermine reconstruction. The Court issued a series of decisions that significantly weakened the federal government's ability to protect black Southerners. In the *Slaughterhouse* cases (1873), the Court distinguished between national and state citizenship and ruled that the Fourteenth Amendment protected only those rights that stemmed from the federal government, such as voting in federal elections and interstate travel. Since the Court decided that most rights derived from the states, it sharply curtailed the federal government's authority to defend black citizens. Even more devastating, the *United States v. Cruikshank* ruling (1876) said that the reconstruction amendments gave Congress the power to legislate against discrimination only by states, not by individuals. The "suppression of ordinary crime," such as assault, remained a state responsibility. The Supreme Court did not declare reconstruction unconstitutional but eroded its legal foundation.

The mood of the North found political expression in the election of 1874, when for the first time in eighteen years the Democrats gained control of the House of Representatives. As one Republican observed, the people had grown

| What vision did Andrew Johnson have for presidential reconstruction? | How radical was congressional reconstruction? | How was the battle over reconstruction fought in the South? | **Why did reconstruction collapse?** | Conclusion: What were the achievements and failures of reconstruction? |

tired of the "negro question, with all its complications, and the reconstruction of Southern States, with all its interminable embroilments." Reconstruction had come apart. Rather than defend reconstruction from its southern enemies, Northerners steadily backed away from the challenge. By the early 1870s, southern Republicans faced the forces of reaction largely on their own.

White Supremacy Triumphs

Republican governments in the South attracted more hatred than any other political regimes in American history. To most whites, Republican rule meant an intolerable reversal of what they saw as the natural racial hierarchy. The northern retreat from reconstruction permitted southern Democrats to set things right.

Taking the name Redeemers, they promised to replace "bayonet rule" (a few federal troops continued to be stationed in the South) with "home rule." They promised that honest, thrifty Democrats would supplant the corrupt and irresponsible tax-and-spend Republicans. Above all, Redeemers swore to save southern civilization from a descent into "African barbarism." As one man put it, "We must render this either a white man's government, or convert the land into a Negro man's cemetery."

Southern Democrats adopted a multipronged strategy to overthrow Republican governments. First, they sought to polarize the parties around color. They went about gathering all the South's white voters into the Democratic Party, leaving the Republicans to depend on blacks, who made up a minority of population in almost every southern state. To dislodge whites from the Republican Party, Democrats fanned the flames of racial prejudice. A South Carolina Democrat crowed that his party appealed to the "proud Caucasian race, whose sovereignty on earth God has proclaimed." Local newspapers published the names of whites who kept company with blacks, and neighbors ostracized offenders.

Democrats also exploited the severe economic plight of small white farmers by blaming it on Republican financial policy. Government spending soared during reconstruction, and small farmers saw their tax burden skyrocket. "This is tax time," a South Carolinian reported. "We are nearly all on our head about them. They are so high & so little money to pay with" that farmers were "selling every egg and chicken they can get." In 1871, Mississippi reported that one-seventh of the state's land—3.3 million acres—had been forfeited for nonpayment of taxes. The small farmers' economic distress had a racial dimension. Because few freedmen succeeded in acquiring land, they rarely paid taxes. In Georgia in 1874, blacks made up 45 percent of the population but paid only 2 percent of the taxes. From the perspective of a small white farmer, Republican rule meant that he was paying more taxes and paying them to aid blacks.

If racial pride, social isolation, and financial hardship proved insufficient to drive yeomen from the Republican Party, Democrats turned to terrorism. "Night riders" targeted white Republicans as well as blacks for murder and assassination. Whether white or black, a "dead Radical is very harmless," South Carolina Democratic leader Martin Gary told his followers.

But the primary victims of white violence were black Republicans. The object was to "kill out the leading men of the republican party," a black Republican from Florida declared. But violence targeted all black voters, not just leaders. And it escalated to unprecedented levels. In 1873, a clash between black militiamen and

CHAPTER LOCATOR | What were Lincoln's plans for wartime reconstruction?

whites in Louisiana killed two white men and an estimated seventy black men. The whites slaughtered half of the black men after they surrendered. Although the federal government indicted more than one hundred of the white men, local juries failed to convict even one.

Even before adopting the all-out white supremacist tactics of the 1870s, Democrats had taken control of the governments of Virginia, Tennessee, and North Carolina. The new campaign brought fresh gains. The Redeemers retook Georgia in 1871, Texas in 1873, and Arkansas and Alabama in 1874. As the state election in Mississippi approached in 1876, Governor Adelbert Ames appealed to Washington for federal troops to control Democratic violence, only to hear from the attorney general that the "whole public are tired of these annual autumnal outbreaks in the South." Abandoned, Mississippi Republicans succumbed to the Democratic onslaught in the fall elections. By 1877, only three Republican state governments survived in the South (**Map 16.3**).

An Election and a Compromise

The year 1876 witnessed one of the most tumultuous elections in American history. The election took place in November, but not until March 2 of the following year did the nation know who would be inaugurated president on March 4. The Democrats nominated New York's governor, Samuel J. Tilden, who immediately targeted the corruption of the Grant administration and the "despotism" of Republican reconstruction. The Republicans put forward Rutherford B. Hayes, governor of Ohio. Privately, Hayes considered "bayonet rule" a mistake but concluded that waving the bloody shirt remained the Republicans' best political strategy.

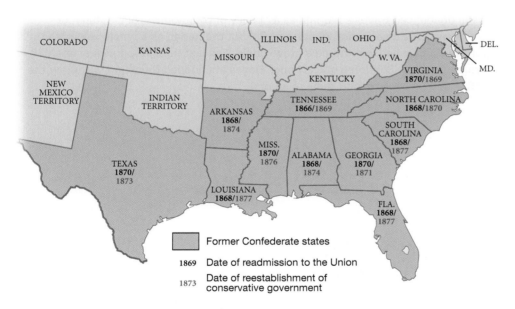

MAP 16.3 ■ The Reconstruction of the South
Myth has it that Republican rule of the former Confederacy was not only harsh but long. In most states, however, conservative southern whites stormed back into power in months or just a few years. By the election of 1876, Republican governments could be found in only three states, and they soon fell.

What vision did Andrew Johnson have for presidential reconstruction?	How radical was congressional reconstruction?	How was the battle over reconstruction fought in the South?	Why did reconstruction collapse?	Conclusion: What were the achievements and failures of reconstruction?

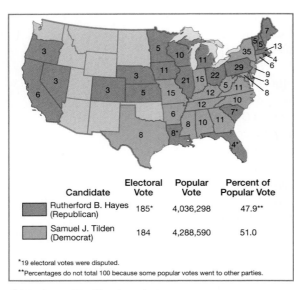

Candidate	Electoral Vote	Popular Vote	Percent of Popular Vote
Rutherford B. Hayes (Republican)	185*	4,036,298	47.9**
Samuel J. Tilden (Democrat)	184	4,288,590	51.0

*19 electoral votes were disputed.
**Percentages do not total 100 because some popular votes went to other parties.

MAP 16.4 ■ The Election of 1876

Compromise of 1877
▶ Political compromise that delivered the presidency to Rutherford B. Hayes. In exchange for a Democratic promise not to block Hayes's inauguration and to deal fairly with the freedmen, Hayes vowed to refrain from using the army to uphold the remaining Republican regimes in the South and to provide the South with substantial federal subsidies for internal improvements. The Compromise of 1877 effectively brought Reconstruction to an end.

On election day, Tilden tallied 4,288,590 votes to Hayes's 4,036,000. But in the all-important electoral college, Tilden fell one vote short of the majority required for victory. The electoral votes of three states—South Carolina, Louisiana, and Florida, the only remaining Republican governments in the South— remained in doubt because both Republicans and Democrats in those states claimed victory. To win, Tilden needed only one of the nineteen contested votes. Hayes had to have all of them.

Congress had to decide who had actually won the elections in the three southern states and thus who would be president. The Constitution provided no guidance for this situation. Moreover, Democrats controlled the House, and Republicans controlled the Senate. Congress created a special electoral commission to arbitrate the disputed returns. All of the commissioners voted their party affiliation, giving every state to the Republican Hayes and putting him over the top in electoral votes (**Map 16.4**).

Some outraged Democrats vowed to resist Hayes's victory. Rumors flew of an impending coup and renewed civil war. But the impasse was broken when negotiations behind the scenes resulted in an informal understanding known as the **Compromise of 1877**. In exchange for a Democratic promise not to block Hayes's inauguration and to deal fairly with the freedmen, Hayes vowed to refrain from using the army to uphold the remaining Republican regimes in the South and to provide the South with substantial federal subsidies for internal improvements.

Stubborn Tilden supporters bemoaned the "stolen election" and damned "His Fraudulency," Rutherford B. Hayes. Old-guard radicals such as William Lloyd Garrison denounced Hayes's bargain as a "policy of compromise, of credulity, of weakness, of subserviency, of surrender." But the nation as a whole celebrated, for the country had weathered a grave crisis. The last three Republican state governments in the South fell quickly once Hayes abandoned them and withdrew the U.S. Army. Reconstruction came to an end.

> **QUICK REVIEW**

How did the decline of northern support for reconstruction help southern Democrats "redeem" the South?

CHAPTER LOCATOR | What were Lincoln's plans for wartime reconstruction?

450 CHAPTER 16 RECONSTRUCTING A NATION, 1863–1877

The Granger Collection, New York.

Conclusion: What were the achievements and failures of reconstruction?

MOST WHITE SOUTHERNERS resisted the passage from slavery to free labor, from white racial despotism to equal justice, and from white political monopoly to biracial democracy. The old elite wanted as little change as possible, while African Americans and some whites were eager to exploit the revolutionary implications of emancipation.

The northern-dominated Republican Congress pushed the revolution along. Congress employed constitutional amendments to require ex-Confederates to accept legal equality and share political power with black men. Conservative southern whites fought ferociously to recover their power and privilege. When Democrats regained control of politics, whites used both state power and private violence to wipe out many of the gains of Reconstruction.

Yet Northern victory in the Civil War ensured that ex-slaves no longer faced the auction block and could send their children to school, worship in their own churches, and work independently on their own rented farms. Sharecropping, with all its hardships, provided more autonomy and economic welfare than bondage had.

The Civil War and emancipation set in motion the most profound upheaval in the nation's history. War destroyed the largest slave society in the New World and gave birth to a modern nation-state. Washington increased its role in national affairs, and the victorious North set the nation's compass toward the expansion of industrial capitalism and the final conquest of the West.

Despite massive changes, however, the Civil War remained only a "half accomplished" revolution. By not fulfilling the promises the nation seemed to hold out to black Americans at war's end, reconstruction represents a tragedy of enormous proportions. The failure to protect blacks and guarantee their rights had enduring consequences. It was the failure of the first reconstruction that made the modern civil rights movement necessary.

SAML. DOVE wishes to know of the whereabouts of his mother, Areno, his sisters Maria, Neziah, and Peggy, and his brother Edmond, who were owned by Geo. Dove, of Rockingham county, Shenandoah Valley, Va. Sold in Richmond, after which Saml. and Edmond were taken to Nashville, Tenn., by Joe Mick; Areno was left at the Eagle Tavern, Richmond
Respectfully yours,
SAML. DOVE.
Utica, New York, Aug. 5, 1865–3m

U. S. CHRISTIAN COMMISSION,
NASHVILLE, TENN., July 19, 1865.

SO NOW YOU KNOW

Even though newly freed African Americans had their own ideas of freedom—family, land, and independence—the politics of Reconstruction in both the North and South and the violent reaction of many white Southerners undermined these hopes. By the end of the era, political rights for most southern blacks were restricted, and economic independence was rare.

> CHAPTER 16 STUDY GUIDE

Online Study Guide
bedfordstmartins.com/roarkunderstanding

STEP 1 GETTING STARTED

Below are basic terms from this period in American history. Can you identify each term below and explain why it matters? To do this exercise online or to download this chart, visit bedfordstmartins.com/roarkunderstanding.

TERM	WHO OR WHAT & WHEN	WHY IT MATTERS
Freedmen's Bureau, p. 430		
Andrew Johnson, p. 432		
black codes, p. 433		
Fourteenth Amendment, p. 435		
Military Reconstruction Act, p. 437		
Fifteenth Amendment, p. 438		
Ku Klux Klan, p. 441		
sharecropping, p. 443		
Compromise of 1877, p. 450		

STEP 2 MOVING BEYOND THE BASICS

The exercise below represents a more advanced understanding of the chapter material. Indicate how each phase of reconstruction addressed the key issues involved. When assessing the achievements and failures of each plan, consider the unintended or indirect consequences. To do this exercise online or to download this chart, visit bedfordstmartins.com/roarkunderstanding.

Phase of reconstruction	Requirements for readmission	Role/rights of freedmen	Achievements	Failures
Wartime reconstruction (Lincoln)				
Presidential reconstruction (Johnson)				
Congressional reconstruction				

Now that you've reviewed various parts of the chapter, take a step back and try to see the big picture by answering these questions. Remember to use specific examples from the chapter in your answers. To do this exercise online, visit bedfordsmartins.com/roarkunderstanding.

PRESIDENTIAL AND CONGRESSIONAL RECONSTRUCTION

▶ What role did the black codes play in shaping the course of reconstruction?

▶ What steps did Congress take between 1865 and 1869 to assist ex-slaves in their lives as freedmen? How effective were these actions?

SOUTHERN RECONSTRUCTION IN ACTION

▶ How did white Southerners respond during Reconstruction? Consider both Democrats and Republicans in your response.

▶ How did southern African Americans attempt to shape their own lives during Reconstruction?

THE END OF RECONSTRUCTION

▶ How and why did the decline of northern support for Reconstruction help southern Democrats "redeem" the South?

▶ Why did white supremacy become the foundation of southern politics in the 1870s?

LOOKING BACKWARD, LOOKING AHEAD

▶ How did long-held racial views among whites, in both the South and the North, shape Reconstruction?

▶ What were the lasting accomplishments of Reconstruction? What were its most important failures?

IN YOUR OWN WORDS

Imagine that you must explain chapter 16 to someone who hasn't read it. What would be the most important points to include and why?

SPOT ARTIFACT CREDITS

INDEX

Federalists, 221, *241,* 244, 257, 266, 268, 302
   Alien and Sedition Acts and, 243
   election of 1796 and, 241–242
   election of 1800 and, 251
   as political party, 256
   ratification of Constitution and, *217*–219, 217 *(i),* 220
   after War of 1812, 261
Female academies, *264*–265
Females. *See* Feminists and feminism; Women
Female Society of Lynn, 282
Feme covert doctrine, *262*
Feminists and feminism, Fifteenth Amendment and, 439
Ferdinand (Spain), 36, 37, 38, 48
Fifteenth Amendment, **438**–439
"Fifty-four Forty or Fight," 323
Fillmore, Millard, 370, 376 *(m),* 379
Finances
   for Civil War, 401, 413
   credit and, 283
   during Revolution, 171, 183
Finney, Charles Grandison, 295–296
Fire, Native American uses of, 24
Fire-eaters (radical Southerners), 369, 386
First Bank of the United States, 233–234, 282
First Congress, 227, 234, 235
First Continental Congress (1774), **161**
Fishing and fishing industry
   common people and, 358
   in New England, 96, 115
   along Pacific Coast, 23
Fitzhugh, George, 342
Five Civilized Tribes, 405
Florida, 72, 309, 339, 450
   de Soto in, 42
   invasion by Andrew Jackson, 269–270
   Ponce de León in, 42
   secession of, 389, 390 *(m)*
Flour milling, in middle colonies, 122
Folsom points, **11,** 12
Food(s). *See also* Diet (food); Hunters and hunting
   Columbian exchange and, 39
   in Confederacy, 401
   in Great Basin region, 12
   Indian, 24, 57–58
   in Massachusetts, 87
   slave, 127
   in Virginia colony, 59
Foote, Henry S., 369
Force Bill (1833), 290
Ford's Theatre, 422
Foreign policy. *See also* Diplomacy; specific presidents
   Monroe Doctrine and, 269–270
Fort(s). *See also* specific forts
   British, 239
   in Ohio River region, 142–144, 144 *(m),* 237–238
   along Oregon Trail, 318 *(m)*
   in Seven Years' War, 146
Fort Wayne, Treaty of, 259
Forty-niners, 326
Founding Fathers. *See* Constitution (U.S.)
Fourier, Charles, 329

Fourteenth Amendment, **435**–436, 437
   ratification by southern states, 442
   women's voting rights and, 436
4th U.S. Colored Infantry, 411 *(i)*
Framers. *See* Constitution (U.S.)
France. *See also* French Revolution
   Britain and, 142–144, 143 *(m)*
   Caribbean islands and, 146 147 *(m)*
   colonies of, 106, 129
   cotton from South and, 400
   exploration by, 50
   fur trade and, 106
   Haiti and, 240
   military forts of, 142–144, 143 *(m)*
   Revolutionary War alliance with, 173, 186–187, 191, 191 *(i),* 193
   Seven Years' War and, 146, 147 *(m)*
   trans-Mississippi region and, 253
   XYZ Affair and, 242–243
Franchise. *See also* Voting and voting rights
   for women, 201 *(i)*
Franciscans, in California, 321
Franklin, Benjamin, **138,** 212
   Albany Plan of Union and, 145
   Enlightenment and, 132
   Great Awakening and, 133
   Poor Richard's Almanack of, 119 *(i),* 122
   Second Continental Congress and, 170
Fredericksburg, battle of (1862), 404
Free blacks, 332. *See also* African Americans
   during Civil War, 417
   in Continental army, 176
   elite, 355
   laws restricting, 354–355
   as slaveholders, 355
   in southern society, 354–355
   in states, 204, 205
   voting and, 203, 204, 267
   wealth of, 313
Freedmen, 427
   black codes and, 432 *(i),* 433, 434
   education and, 431, 442, 443
   labor by women, 440 *(i),* 443
   labor code and, 429–430
   land for, 430, 433, 437–438, 443
   on plantations, 443, 444 *(m)*
   during reconstruction, 448–449
   in Republican Party, 440
   search for families by, 430 *(i),* 431
   sharecropping by, 443–444
   taxes and, 433
   voting rights for, 426 *(i),* 438–439
Freedmen's Bureau, **430,** 433
Freedmen's Bureau bill
   of 1865, 430
   of 1866, 434
Freedom(s)
   for free blacks, 355
   for freedmen, 431
   religious, 93–94
   for slaves, 204–205, 408–409, 414
   of speech, 202, 228
   in states' bills of rights, 202
   for whites, 78, 333
"Freedom papers," 354 *(i)*
Free farmers, 68
Free labor
   immigrants and, 314–315
   during reconstruction, 429–430

   vs. slavery, 342, 378, 429–430
   woman's rights and, 331
Free-labor ideal, 312–*313,* 328, 333
Freeman, Elizabeth (Mum Bett), 204
Freeport Doctrine, 384
Free soil doctrine, 367
Free-Soil Party, 368, 370
Free-soil settlers, in Kansas, 380–381
Free speech, 417
   defense of slavery and, 360
Free states, 267, 322, 323, 361
Freewill Baptists, 263
Frémont, Jessie, 375 *(i),* 379
Frémont, John C., 321, 375 *(i),* 376 *(m),* 379, 409
French and Indian War. *See* Seven Years' War
French Empire, 135 *(m). See also* New France
French Revolution, 238–239, 240
Frobisher, Martin, 50
Frontier
   colonial, 134–135
   in Revolutionary War, 192
   Spanish, 135, 135 *(m)*
   violence along, 70
Fugitive Slave Act (1850), 370, 371–*372,* 391
Fugitive slave provision, of Northwest Ordinance, 211
Fugitive slaves
   in Civil War, 409, 414
   Compromise of 1850 and, 370, 371–372
   resistance by, 352
   Revolutionary War and, 164, 192
   underground railroad and, 332
Fuller, Margaret, 329
Fulton, Robert, 276 *(i),* 279
Furniture, 132 *(i)*
Fur trade, 100, 106, 134, 146, 237
   Indians and, 121

Gabriel (slave), 251
Gabriel's Rebellion (1800), 251–252
Gadsden, James, 373
Gadsden Purchase (1853), 373, 373 *(m)*
Gage, Thomas, 160–161, 162, 172
"Gag rule," in Congress, 300
Galloway, Joseph, 161
Gama, Vasco da, 34
Gambian culture, 124
Gangs, slave, 340, 350
Garfield, James A., 437
Garner family, escape from slavery, 371 *(i)*
Garnet, Henry Highland, 331
Garrison, William Lloyd, **297,** 298 *(i),* 369, 386, 450
Gary, Martin, 448
Gaspée (ship), 158
Gates, Horatio, 185, 189, 189 *(m)*
Gathering Corn in Virginia (Darley), 356 *(i)*
Gender and gender issues. *See also* Men; Women
   in Chesapeake region, 65
   in colonies, 155–156
   equality and, 263
   politics and, 229
   religion and, 263–264
   separate spheres, 293–295
   of slaves, 125
   in Spanish colonies, 45

General Court (Massachusetts), 92
General Historie of Virginia, A (Smith), 54 *(i)*
General welfare clause, in Constitution, 216, 234
Genoa, 32
Gentry, slaveholding, **128**
Geographic mobility, free labor and, 313
Geographic revolution, 38–40
George III (England), 148, 149, 169 *(i)*, 172, 181
Georgia, 199
    Cherokee removal and, 289
    Civil War in, 421
    power of planters in, 360
    Revolutionary War and, 188–189, 189 *(m)*, 190
    secession and, 389, 390 *(m)*
    Spanish exploration of, 42
German Americans, 314
Germany
    immigrants from, 118–119, 185, 314
    Revolutionary mercenaries (Hessians) from, 179
Gettysburg, battle of (1863), **419,** 419 *(m)*, 420, 420 *(m)*
Ghent, Treaty of (1814), 261, 270
Gilbert, Humphrey, 50
Girdling, in clearing fields, 62–63
Girls. *See* Women
Glaciers, 7, 9
Global markets, for southern cotton, 407 *(f)*
Glorieta Pass, battle at (1862), 405, 405 *(m)*
Glorious Revolution (England), 106
Godspeed (ship), 57
Gold
    in Colorado, 366
    from New World, 42, 45 *(f)*
Gold rush, in California, 326–327, 366
Goliad, massacre at (1836), 321
Gorgas, Josiah, 401
Government. *See also* Government (U.S.)
    of British colonies, 129
    colonial, 136
    Jefferson on, 253
    of Massachusetts, 87–89, 106
    in New England colonies, 105
    of New Netherland, 100
    of Pennsylvania, 102
    Puritan, 92–93
    republicanism and, 201–202
    state, during reconstruction, 441–442
    of Virginia, 61
    Woodland chiefdoms and, 17–18
Government (U.S.)
    under Articles of Confederation, 198–200
    branches of, 216
    Civil War and, 415–416
    Jackson and, 286
    Jefferson and, 253, 273
    land policy of, 309
    limits and checks on, 216
    stability in, 226–229
Governors, colonial, 136, 155
Gradual emancipation, 204–205, 211, 267
Grain
    in middle colonies, 122
    trade in, 230

Grant, Ulysses S., 405
    in Civil War, 405–406, 418, 419 *(m)*, 420–421, 422
    corruption and, 446, 446 *(i)*
    election of 1868 and, 445, 445 *(m)*
    election of 1872 and, 446
    presidency of, 445–446
    reconstruction and, 445, 446–447
Grasse (Comte de), 191
Graves, A. J. (Mrs.), 293
Graves, Thomas, 66 *(i)*
***Great Awakening, 132*–**133
    Second, 295–296
Great Basin
    cultures of, 12–13
    Native Americans of, 21
Great Britain. *See* England (Britain)
Great Compromise, 215
Great Lakes region, 280
    French in, 106
    Indians of, 21
Great Plains
    Indians of, 21, 23, 317–318, 318 *(m)*, 374
    in Louisiana Purchase, 253, 254 *(m)*
    Spanish in, 42
Great Salt Lake, 319
Great Tenochtitlan, The (Rivera), 2 *(i)*
Greeley, Horace, 401, 446
Greene, Nathanael, 189 *(m)*
Greenville, Treaty of (1795), 236 *(i)*, **238**
Grenville, George, 149–150, 149 *(i)*
Grimké sisters (Angelina and Sarah), 298
Griswold, Roger, 241 *(i)*
Guadalupe Hidalgo, Treaty of (1848), **325**–326
Guerrilla war
    during Civil War, 397, 405
    in Kansas, 381
    in Revolutionary War, 190
Gun industry, interchangeable parts and, 310
Gutenberg, Johannes, 33

Habeas corpus, Lincoln and, 397
Haiti, 240, 332
Haitian Revolution, 240, 251
Hakluyt, Richard, 57
Hale, John P., 376 *(m)*
Halfway Covenant, 97
Hamilton, Alexander, 213, 214, 219, ***230***
    economy and, 230, 232–234
    election of 1796 and, 242
    election of 1800 and, 251
    Federalist Papers and, 220
    as treasury secretary, 227
    Trumbull portrait of, 230 *(i)*
    Whiskey Rebellion and, 235
Hamilton, Fort, 237
Hammond, James H., 350, 367
Hancock, John, 114 *(i)*, 151
Hannastown, Pennsylvania, Indian attack on, 187 *(m)*
Hard money, 183, 232, 234, 301
Harmar, Josiah, 237
Harpers Ferry, Brown's raid on (1859), 386
Harper's Weekly, 445 *(i)*
Harrison, William Henry, 258, 259, 260, 300, 301, 322
Hartford Convention (1814), 261
Hartford Seminary, 264

Hayes, Rutherford B., election of 1876 and, 449–450
Headright, 64
Hemings, Sally, 250 *(i)*
Hendrick (Mohawk Indians), 144, 145 *(i)*
Hendricks, Thomas A., 447
Henry VIII (England), 84
Henry, Fort
    battle of (Civil War), 405
    in Revolution, 187 *(m)*
Henry the Navigator, Prince (Portugal), **34**
Henry, Patrick, 151, 158, 161, 213–214, 220
Henry Frank (steamboat), 338 *(i)*
Heresy
    Hutchinson and, 95
    Quakers and, 97
Hessians, 179
Hickory Clubs, 285
Hierarchies
    of Catholic Church, 85
    social and racial in New Spain, 45
Higginson, Thomas W., 411 *(i)*
Higher education
    in 1830s, 295
    by mid-1820s, 264–265
"Higher law" doctrine, of Seward, 388
Hill, Aaron (Mohawk Indians), 208
Hispaniola, Spanish settlement on, 40
History, archaeology and, 4–5
Hohokam culture, 16
Holidays, Puritan celebration of, 83, 91, 107
Holland, Separatists in, 87
Holmes, George F., 372
Holy experiment, of Penn, 101
Holy Roman Empire, 48
Home and Away: . . . (Krimmel), 265 *(i)*
Home front
    in Civil War, 412–414, 415–417
    in Revolutionary War, 180–183
Homespun cloth, 156
Homestead Act (1862), 416
Homo erectus, 6
Homo sapiens, 5, 6–7
Hone, Philip, 301
Honor, in South, 346–347
Hood, John B., 421
Hopewell culture, 18–19
Hopi Indians, 17
Horses, 12, 317
Horseshoe Bend, battle of (1814), 260
House of Burgesses, 61, 69, 70, 151
House of Commons, virtual representation in, 150
House of Representatives, 215, 219, 251, 270
Housing
    Anasazi, 17
    in Chesapeake region, 68 *(i)*
    in Hudson valley, 121
    for Indians, 24
    Iroquoian, 22
    on plantations, 347 *(f)*
    slave, 127, 336 *(i)*, 346, 347 *(f)*, 349 *(i)*
Houston, Sam, 321
Howe, William, 172, 179, 183, 184–185, 189
Hudson, Carrie, 349
Hudson, Henry, 99
Hudson River region, 279–280
    Revolution in, 177, 178 *(m)*, 179, 182 *(m)*, 184

West Indies
    Carolina and, 76–77
    French, 239
    sugar and slavery from, 74–76
West Point, 190
West Virginia, 398
Westward movement
    agriculture and, 309
    manifest destiny and, 316–317
    Northwest Ordinance and, 210
Wheat, 122, 230, 309
Wheatley, Phillis, 162 *(i),* **164**
Wheelock, Eleazar, 180 *(i)*
Whigs (Whig Party), **286,** 299, 302
    collapse of, 375–377
    election of 1840 and, 301
    election of 1848 and, 368–369, 369 *(m),*
        376 *(m)*
    election of 1852 and, 375, 376 *(m)*
    Mexican-American War and, 323
    National Republicans as, 285, 291
    panic of 1837 and, 301
Whiskey, taxation on, 252
Whiskey Rebellion (1794), 234–**235**
White, Hugh Lawson, 300
White, John, 48 *(i)*
White Eyes (Delaware Indians), 186
Whitefield, George, 133
White House, 258, 260
White male suffrage, 359
Whites
    in Chesapeake region, 77–78
    in New England, 117
    in northern and southern colonies, 338
    Plains Indians and, 318
    racism of, 121
    in South, 341 *(f),* 342, 357–358, 359–360
    in southern Democratic Party, 448–449
    in southern Republican Party, 441
White supremacy
    free blacks and, 332
    Johnson, Andrew, and, 433
    Ku Klux Klan and, 441
    North and, 341
    reconstruction and, 441, 448–449
    in South, 341, 448–449
"White terror," 441
Whitney, Eli, 230, 343
Wichita Indians, 317
Wilderness, battle of the (1864), 419 *(m),*
    420, 421
Wilkinson, Eliza, 181
Wilkinson, Jemima, 263
Willard, Emma Hart, 262 *(i),* 264
William III (of Orange, English king), 106
Williams, Roger, 93–**94**
Williamsburg, capture of, 190
Wilmot, David, 367, 391

Wilmot Proviso (1846), **367,** 369, 379
Winthrop, John, 88–89, 93, 95
Wisconsin, 309, 369
Wisconsin glaciation, 7
Witchcraft, New Salem trials and,
    98, 98 *(i)*
Wives. *See also* Married women
    feme covert and, 262
    of loyalists, 182
    republican, 228–229
    separate spheres and, 294
Woman's rights movement, 379
Woman suffrage, 201 *(i),* 331, 379
    Fifteenth Amendment and, 438, 439
    Fourteenth Amendment and, 436
Women. *See also* Feminists and feminism;
        Gender and gender issues
    in abolition movement, 298
    academies for, 264–265
    activism by, 329–331
    Adams, Abigail, and, 173
    in Chesapeake region, 65
    church governance and, 263–264
    in Civil War, 412 *(i),* 413, 416–417
    colonial protests by, 140 *(i)*
    education for, 228–229, 264–265
    exclusion from voting, 202–203
    Fourteenth Amendment and, 436
    French Revolution and, 238, 239 *(i)*
    in Great Awakening, 133
    Indian, 60, 254
    in Iroquoian society, 22
    labor unions and, 281
    law and, 262–263
    moral reform by, 297
    in New England, 89
    in nursing, 416–417
    patriotism of, 181
    on plantations, 346–347
    politics and, 257–258, 270, 288–289
    polygamy and, 319
    property and, 203, 347
    in public affairs, 155
    Puritan, 92
    as Quakers, 97
    reconstruction and, 436, 439, 440 *(i),*
        441, 443
    reform and, 295, 296, 297, 298
    in Republican Party, 379
    as republican wife and mother, 228–229
    Revolution and, 176, 181, 184
    rights for, 347
    Second Great Awakening and, 295, 296
    separate spheres doctrine and, 293–295
    as servants, 65, 66
    in slavery, 347, 350
    southern, 347–348, 360
    in Spanish colonies, 45

    strikes by, 281
    in teaching, 295, 313
    in textile industry, 280–281
    voting by, 203, 263, 436
    in westward movement, 318–319
    witchcraft accusations against,
        98, 98 *(i)*
    in workforce, 280–282
    yeomen, 358
Women's rights, 263–263. *See also*
        Feminists and feminism; Women
    abolition movement and, 298
    activists for, 329–331
    conventions for, 331
Woodland Indians, 17–19, 21, 23. *See also*
        Eastern Woodland Indians
Woodside, John A., 248 *(i)*
Woodville, Richard Caton, cartoon by,
    306 *(i)*
Worcester v. Georgia (1832), 289, 290
Workday, for slaves, 346, 351
Workers. *See also* Child labor; Factories;
        Labor; Labor unions; Strikes
    in textile industry, 280–281
    women as, 280–282, 440 *(i)*
Workforce. *See also* Labor; Workers
    factory workers in, 308
    women in, 280–282, 416
World Turn'd Upside Down, The
    (pamphlet), 92 *(i)*
Worth, William, 325 *(i)*
Writing
    archaeology, history, and, 5
    North American peoples and, 23
Wyandot Indians, 236 *(i)*
Wyoming, 323

XYZ Affair, 242–**243**

Yamasee Indians, 134
Yamasee War (1715), 134
Yeomen, 68, 356
    during Civil War, 413
    plantation belt, 356–357
    politics and, 360
    southern, 356 *(i)*
    southern Republican Party and, 441, 448
    taxation and, 448
    upcountry, 357
York, Duke of. *See* James I
Yorktown, battle of (1781), 188 *(i),* 189 *(m),*
    190 *(m),* **191**
Young, Brigham, 319
Young people, education and training
    of, 295

Zemis (Taino spirits), 36, 36 *(i)*
Zuñi Indians, 17, 42